P9-DZA-256

AFFIRMATIVE ACTION

AFFIRMATIVE ACTION

An Encyclopedia

Volume I: A–I

Edited by ***James A. Beckman***

Advisory Editors
Maria D. Beckman and Paulina X. Ruf

Greenwood Press
Westport, Connecticut • London

Library of Congress Cataloging-in-Publication Data

Affirmative action : an encyclopedia / edited by James A. Beckman.
p. cm.
Includes bibliographical references and index.
ISBN 1–57356–519–9 (set : alk. paper)—ISBN 0–313–33023–9 (vol. 1 : alk. paper)—ISBN 0–313–33024–7 (vol. 2 : alk. paper)
1. Affirmative action programs—United States—Encyclopedias. I. Beckman, James A.
HF5549.5.A34A426 2004
331.13'3'097303—dc22 2003064257

British Library Cataloguing in Publication Data is available.

Library of Congress Catalog Card Number: 2003064257
ISBN: 1–57356–519–9 (set)
0–313–33023–9 (vol. I)
0–313–33024–7 (vol. II)

First published in 2004

Greenwood Press, 88 Post Road West, Westport, CT 06881
An imprint of Greenwood Publishing Group, Inc.
www.greenwood.com

Printed in the United States of America

The paper used in this book complies with the Permanent Paper Standard issued by the National Information Standards Organization (Z39.48–1984).

10 9 8 7 6 5 4 3 2 1

This work is dedicated to my parents, Robert and Jean Beckman, who have been a great source of inspiration and strength to me all of my life. They taught me the value of education, scholarship, and hard work without having to forsake the simple joys of life. Sadly, my father passed away while the first draft of the book was being finalized in June 2003. While he never had the chance to see the book in print or to comment on the content, his work ethic in life was contagious, and so, in a sense, he has contributed to the worthy endeavor of this book by serving as a role model and a source of inspiration for me.

CONTENTS

LIST OF EDITORS AND CONTRIBUTORS

Editor

James A. Beckman, B.A., J.D., LL.M.
Assistant Professor, University of Tampa
Tampa, Florida

Advisory Editors

Maria D. Beckman, B.A., J.D.*
Practicing Attorney, Federal Government
Tampa, Florida

Paulina X. Ruf, B.A., M.A., M.D.A., Ph.D.
Assistant Professor, University of Tampa
Tampa, Florida

Contributors

Thomas A. Adamich, B.A., M.L.S.
Librarian, Ohio Public School System
Cuyahoga Falls, Ohio

Adalberto Aguirre Jr., B.A., M.A., Ph.D.
Professor, University of California at Riverside
Riverside, California

Mohammed B. Alam, B.A., M.A., M.Phil., Ph.D.
Professor, Miyazaki International College
Miyazaki, Japan

Gayle Avant, B.A., M.A., Ph.D.
Associate Professor, Baylor University
Waco, Texas

Maya Alexandra Beasley, B.A., M.A., Ph.D.
Postdoctorate Fellowship
Harvard University
Cambridge, Massachusetts

James A. Beckman, B.A., J.D., LL.M.
Assistant Professor, University of Tampa
Tampa, Florida

Maria D. Beckman, B.A., J.D.*
Practicing Attorney, Federal Government
Tampa, Florida

Mirza Asmer Beg, B.A., M.A., M.Phil., Ph.D.
Associate Professor, Aligarh Muslim University
Aligarh, India

Richard J. Bennett, B.S., J.D.
Practicing Attorney, Private Practice
Adjunct Faculty, John Carroll University
Cleveland, Ohio

Ann Marie Bissessar, B.A., LL.B., M.S., Ph.D.
Lecturer, University of the West Indies
St. Augustine, Trinidad

*The views expressed by these contributors are their own and do not necessarily reflect those of the federal government or of the particular federal agency with which the contributor is affiliated.

Sheila Bluhm, B.A., M.A., Ph.D.
Lecturer, University of Michigan
Ann Arbor, Michigan

Rachel Bowen, B.A., J.D., (Ph.D. candidate)
Georgetown University
Washington, D.C.

Scott S. Brenneman, B.A., J.D.*
Assistant Professor, U.S. Military Academy
West Point, New York

Susan F. Brinkley, B.A., M.A., Ph.D.
Associate Professor, University of Tampa
Tampa, Florida

F. Erik Brooks, B.A., M.S., M.P.A., M.Ed., Ph.D.
Assistant Professor, Georgia Southern University
Statesboro, Georgia

Christopher R. Capsambelis, B.S., M.A., Ph.D.
Chair, Criminology Department
Associate Professor, University of Tampa
Tampa, Florida

Pamela C. Corley, B.A., M.A., J.D., (Ph.D. candidate)
Georgia State University
Atlanta, Georgia

Jack A. Covarrubias, B.A., M.S.
University of Southern Mississippi
Long Beach, Mississippi

John W. Dietrich, B.A., M.A., Ph.D.
Assistant Professor, Bryant College
Smithfield, Rhode Island

Paulette Patterson Dilworth, B.A., M.A., Ph.D.
Assistant Professor, Indiana University
Bloomington, Indiana

Marc Dollinger, B.A., M.A., Ph.D.
Professor and Richard Goldman Chair in Jewish Studies, San Francisco State University
San Francisco, California

Gregory M. Duhl, B.A., J.D., LL.M.
Lecturer, Temple University
Philadelphia, Pennsylvania

Lisa A. Ennis, B.A., M.A., M.S.
Assistant Professor, Austin Peay State University
Clarksville, Tennessee

Abby L. Ferber, B.A., M.A., Ph.D.
Director of Women's Studies
Associate Professor, University of Colorado
Colorado Springs, Colorado

Christopher Flannery, B.A., M.A., Ph.D.
Chair, Department of History and Political Science
Professor, Azusa Pacific University
Azusa, California

Jayson J. Funke, B.A., M.A.
Wrentham, Massachusetts

Robert Don Gifford II, B.A., J.D.*
Practicing Attorney, Federal Government
Reno, Nevada

Denise O'Neil Green, B.A., M.P.A., Ph.D.
Assistant Professor, University of Illinois
Champaign, Illinois

Kyra R. Greene, B.A., M.A., (Ph.D. candidate)
Stanford University
Stanford, California

Paul M. Haridakis, B.A., J.D., Ph.D.
Assistant Professor, Kent State University
Kent, Ohio

Thomas J. Hickey, B.A., M.A., J.D., Ph.D.
Professor, University of Tampa
Tampa, Florida

Arthur M. Holst, B.S., M.P.A., Ph.D.
Government Affairs Manager, City of Philadelphia
Philadelphia, Pennsylvania

Paul M. Hughes, B.A., M.A., Ph.D.
Chair, Department of Humanities
Associate Professor, University of Michigan at Dearborn
Dearborn, Michigan

Eileen Husselbaugh, B.A., J.D.*
Practicing Attorney, Federal Government
Adjunct Faculty, University of Tampa
Tampa, Florida

Janis Judson, B.A., M.A., Ph.D.
Professor, Hood College
Frederick, Maryland

Jeffrey Kraus, B.A., M.A., M.Phil., Ph.D.
Professor, Wagner College
Staten Island, New York

Tom Lansford, B.A., M.A., Ph.D.
Assistant Professor, University of Southern Mississippi
Long Beach, Mississippi

Michael K. Lee, B.S., J.D.
Practicing Attorney, Private Practice
Southfield, Michigan

Sharon Meyers, B.A., (M.S. candidate)
University of Southern Mississippi
Long Beach, Mississippi

Carlton Morse, B.A.
Azusa, California

Rae W. Newstad, B.A., M.A., Ph.D.
Blanchard, Oklahoma

Paul Obiyo Mbanaso Njemanze, B.A., M.A., Ph.D.
Professor, University of Lagos
Yaba, Lagos, Nigeria

Betty Nyangoni, B.A., M.A., Ph.D.
Educational Consultant
Washington, D.C.

Kingsley Ufuoma Omoyibo, B.S., M.S., Ph.D.
Lecturer, University of Benin
Benin, Nigeria

Peter L. Platteborze, B.S., Ph.D.*
Major, U.S. Army
Frederick, Maryland

Michael D. Quigley, B.A., M.A., J.D., Ph.D.
Lecturer, California State University at Pomona
Pomona, California

Aimée Hobby Rhodes, B.A., J.D.*
Assistant Professor, U.S. Military Academy
West Point, New York

Sean Richey, B.A., M.A., Ph.D.
Adjunct Faculty, City University of New York
New York, New York

Naomi Robertson, B.A., B.S., M.P.A., Ph.D.
Assistant Professor, Macon State College
Macon, Georgia

Paulina X. Ruf, B.A., M.A., M.D.A., Ph.D.
Assistant Professor, University of Tampa
Tampa, Florida

Robert A. Russ, B.A., M.A., Ph.D.
Assistant Professor, Elon University
Elon, North Carolina

James P. Scanlan, B.A., J.D.
Practicing Attorney, Private Practice
Washington, D.C.

Mark J. Senediak, B.A., M.S.
Financial Risk Analyst
Mount Lebanon, Pennsylvania

Maria Jose Sotelo, B.A., M.A., Ph.D.
Professor, Universidad de Santiago de Compostela
A Caruna, Spain

Glenn L. Starks, B.S., M.S., Ph.D.*
Chief, Planning and Requirements, Defense Supply, U.S. Defense Department
Richmond, Virginia

Arthur K. Steinberg, B.A., J.D., Ph.D.
Professor, Catawba College
Salisbury, North Carolina

Nicole M. Stephens, B.A., M.A., Ph.D., Ed.S.
Assistant Professor, St. Louis University
St. Louis, Missouri

Mfanya D. Tryman, A.A., B.A., M.S., Ph.D.
Dean, College of Liberal Arts
Professor, Mississippi State University
Starkville, Mississippi

Ronnie B. Tucker Sr., B.A., M.A., Th.D., Ph.D.
Assistant Professor, Shippensburg University
Shippensburg, Pennsylvania

La Trice M. Washington, B.A., M.A., Ph.D.
Assistant Professor, Otterbein College
Westerville, Ohio

David L. Weeks, B.A., M.A., Ph.D.
Dean, College of Liberal Arts and Sciences
Professor, Azusa Pacific University
Azusa, California

LIST OF ENTRIES

GUIDE TO RELATED TOPICS

Affirmative Action–Related Laws

Alaska Native Claims Settlement Act
Busing
Civil Rights Act of 1866
Civil Rights Act of 1875
Civil Rights Act of 1957
Civil Rights Act of 1960
Civil Rights Act of 1964
Civil Rights Act of 1968
Civil Rights Act of 1991
Civil Rights Restoration Act of 1988
Civil Service Reform Act of 1978
Civil War (Reconstruction) Amendments and Civil Rights Acts
Equal Employment Opportunity Act of 1972
Equal Opportunity Act of 1995
Equal Pay Act of 1963
Fair Housing Amendments Act of 1988
GI Bill
Head Start
Housing and Urban Development Act of 1968
Immigration Act of 1965
National Labor Relations Act of 1935 (Wagner Act)
One Florida Initiative
Percentage Plans
Proposition 209
Public Works Employment Act of 1977
Rehabilitation Act of 1973
Title VI of the Civil Rights Act of 1964
Title VII of the Civil Rights Act of 1964
Title IX of the Education Amendments of 1972
Voting Rights Act of 1965
Washington Initiative 200

Alternatives to Traditional Affirmative Action

Affirmative Access
Affirmative Action, Arguments for
Affirmative Action, Criticisms of
Affirmative Action, Decline in Usage of
Affirmative Action, Myths and Misconceptions of
Class-Based Affirmative Action
Color-Blind Constitution
Economically Disadvantaged
Head Start
Majority-Group Resentment
Merit Selections
Meritocracy
One Florida Initiative
Percentage Plans
Performance-Based Selections
Proposition 209
Race-Neutral Criteria
Scapegoating/Displaced-Aggression Theories
Washington Initiative 200

Beneficiaries of Affirmative Action

African Americans
Alaskan Natives

Civil Rights Movement and Events

Constitutional Concepts and Events

Contracting and Affirmative Action

Adarand Constructors, Inc. v. Peña
City of Richmond v. J.A. Croson Co.
Contracting and Affirmative Action
Disadvantaged Business Enterprises
Executive Order 8802
Executive Order 10925
Executive Order 11246
Executive Order 13005
Fullilove v. Klutznick
Public Works Employment Act of 1977

Court Decisions and Cases

Adarand Constructors, Inc. v. Peña
Albemarle Paper Co. v. Moody
Baker v. Carr
Berea College v. Commonwealth of Kentucky
Bolling v. Sharpe
Bradwell v. State of Illinois
Brown v. Board of Education
City of Richmond v. J.A. Croson Co.
Civil Rights Cases
Coalition for Economic Equity v. Wilson
DeFunis v. Odegaard
Detroit Police Officers Association v. Young
Diaz v. Pan American World Airways
Dred Scott v. Sandford
Firefighters Local Union No. 1784 v. Stotts
Franks v. Bowman
Frontiero v. Richardson
Fullilove v. Klutznick
Gratz v. Bollinger and *Grutter v. Bollinger*
Griggs v. Duke Power Co.
Grove City College v. Bell
Hopwood v. Texas
Johnson v. Board of Regents of the University of Georgia
Johnson v. Transportation Agency, Santa Clara County
Knight v. Alabama
Korematsu v. United States
Lau v. Nichols
Local 28 of the Sheet Metal Workers' International Association v. EEOC
Local No. 93, International Association of Firefighters v. City of Cleveland
Lorance v. AT&T Technologies, Inc.
Lutheran Church–Missouri Synod v. FCC
Maryland Troopers Association v. Evans
Messer v. Meno
Metro Broadcasting, Inc. v. FCC
Minor v. Happersett
Mississippi University for Women v. Hogan
Morton v. Mancari
Patterson v. McLean Credit Union
Plessy v. Ferguson
Podberesky v. Kirwan
Price Waterhouse v. Hopkins
Red Lion Broadcasting Co. v. FCC
Regents of the University of California v. Bakke
Rice v. Cayetano
Roberts v. City of Boston
San Antonio School District v. Rodriguez
Shaw v. Reno
Sipuel v. Regents of the University of Oklahoma
Smith v. University of Washington Law School
Strauder v. West Virginia
Sweatt v. Painter
Taxman v. Piscataway Township Board of Education
United States v. Fordice
United States v. Louisiana
United States v. Paradise
United Steelworkers of America v. Weber
Wards Cove Packing Co. v. Atonio
Wygant v. Jackson Board of Education
Yick Wo v. Hopkins

Education and Affirmative Action

Affirmative Access
Affirmative Action Plan/Program
All Deliberate Speed
The Bell Curve
Berea College v. Commonwealth of Kentucky
Bethune, Mary Jane McLeod
Bolling v. Sharpe
Brown v. Board of Education
Busing
DeFunis v. Odegaard
Education and Affirmative Action
Executive Order 12900
Gates Millennium Scholars Program
GI Bill

Employment and Affirmative Action

Executive Orders

Gender-Based Affirmative Action and Women's Issues

Laidlaw, Harriet Burton
Minor v. Happersett
Mississippi University for Women v. Hogan
Mott, Lucretia Coffin
National Organization for Women
Nineteenth Amendment
Seneca Falls Convention
Sex and Gender
Sex Discrimination
Sexism
Stanton, Elizabeth Cady
Stereotypes, Gender
Stone, Lucy
Suffrage Movement
Women and the Workplace
Women's Education

Global Perspectives, Practices, and Laws Pertaining to Affirmative Action

African Charter on Human and People's Rights
American Convention on Human Rights
Apartheid
Australia and Affirmative Action
Brazil and Affirmative Action
Canada and Affirmative Action
China and Affirmative Action
Colonial Governments and Equality
Convention on the Elimination of All Forms of Discrimination against Women
Convention on the Elimination of All Forms of Racial Discrimination
Eurocentrism
European Court of Human Rights
European Human Rights Convention
European Union and Affirmative Action
Global Implementation of Affirmative Action Programs
Great Britain and Affirmative Action
India and Affirmative Action
Islamic-Based Nationality and Affirmative Action
Japan and Affirmative Action
Malaysia and Affirmative Action
South Africa and Affirmative Action
United Nations Commission on the Status of Women
United Nations Conferences on Women

Government Agencies/Departments/ Bureaus/Offices

Bureau of the Census
Bureau of Labor Statistics
Civil Service Commission
Department of Education
Department of Health and Human Services
Department of Housing and Urban Development
Department of Justice
Department of Labor
Economic Development Administration
Equal Employment Opportunity Commission
Federal Communications Commission
General Accounting Office
Glass Ceiling Commission
Office of Federal Contract Compliance Programs
President's Committee on Equal Employment Opportunity
Supreme Court and Affirmative Action
U.S. Commission on Civil Rights

Historical Persons

Abolitionists
Anthony, Susan Brownell
Bethune, Mary Jane McLeod
Brotherhood of Sleeping Car Porters
Bunche, Ralph J.
Carmichael, Stokely
Chisholm, Shirley
Clark, Kenneth Bancroft
Diggs, Charles Coles, Jr.
Douglass, Frederick
Du Bois, William Edward Burghardt
Eisenhower, Dwight David
Garvey, Marcus
Johnson, Lyndon Baines
Kennedy, John Fitzgerald
King, Martin Luther, Jr.
Malcolm X
Marshall, Thurgood

Mott, Lucretia Coffin
Moynihan, Daniel Patrick
Nixon, Richard Milhous
Powell, Adam Clayton, Jr.
Randolph, Asa Philip
Roosevelt, Eleanor
Roosevelt, Franklin Delano
Stanton, Elizabeth Cady
Stone, Harlan Fiske
Stone, Lucy
Truman, Harry
Washington, Booker T.

Housing and Land Issues

Alaska Native Claims Settlement Act
Busing
Civil Rights Act of 1866
Civil Rights Act of 1875
Civil Rights Act of 1968
Department of Housing and Urban Development
Environmental Racism
Fair Housing Amendments Act of 1988
Gentrification
Housing
Housing and Urban Development Act of 1968
Lending Practices and Affirmative Action
Zoning and Affirmative Action

Implementation Issues and Alternatives to Affirmative Action

Affirmative Access
Affirmative Action, Arguments for
Affirmative Action, Criticisms of
Affirmative Action, Decline in Usage of
Affirmative Action, Myths and Misconceptions of
Affirmative Action Plan/Program
Census Classifications, Ethnic and Racial
Class-Based Affirmative Action
Diversity
Diversity Management
Good-Old-Boy Factor
Majority-Group Resentment
Merit Selections
Narrowly Tailored Affirmative Action Plans
Percentage Plans
Performance-Based Selections
Quotas
Race-Neutral Criteria
Role Model Theory
Scapegoating/Displaced-Aggression Theories
Standardized Testing
Statistical Proof of Discrimination
Supreme Court and Affirmative Action

Legal Theories/Concepts

All Deliberate Speed
Benign Discrimination
Color-Blind Constitution
Compelling Governmental Interest
De Facto and De Jure Segregation
Disability Classifications under the Fifth and Fourteenth Amendments
Discrete and Insular Minority
Disparate Treatment and Disparate Impact
Equal Protection Clause
Intermediate Scrutiny
Invidious Discrimination
Manifest Imbalance Standard
Narrowly Tailored Affirmative Action Plans
Rational Basis Scrutiny
Reverse Discrimination
Strict Scrutiny
Suspect Classification

Media and Affirmative Action

Federal Communications Commission
First Amendment
Licensing and Affirmative Action
Lutheran Church–Missouri Synod v. FCC
Media and Affirmative Action
Metro Broadcasting, Inc. v. FCC
Red Lion Broadcasting Co. v. FCC

Military and Veterans

Executive Order 8802
GI Bill
Military and Affirmative Action
Powell, Colin

Organizations (Nongovernmental)

Political Leaders, Events, and Concepts

Presidents and Supreme Court Justices

Race-Based Programs, Concepts, and Miscellaneous Issues

Sociological Theories and Concepts

Writers, Scholars, and Activists

TIMELINE OF MAJOR EVENTS IMPACTING AFFIRMATIVE ACTION

See individual entries for an in-depth description of these events.

Major Historical Events Relating to Affirmative Action

1865

End of American Civil War.

Ratification of the Thirteenth Amendment, constitutionally abolishing the institution of slavery.

Freedmen's Bureau Act is passed by Congress; the Freedmen's Bureau is later described by Justice Thurgood Marshall as one of the country's earliest affirmative action programs.

1866

Civil Rights Act of 1866 enacted by Congress; act identifies certain basic civil rights that shall not be abridged on account of race.

1868

Ratification of the Fourteenth Amendment, which in part provides that states shall not deprive an individual of due process of law or the equal protection of the laws.

1870

Ratification of the Fifteenth Amendment, prohibiting states from depriving an individual of the right to vote on account of race or previous condition of involuntary servitude.

1875

Congress enacts the Civil Rights Act of 1875, which provides sweeping civil rights in the area of public accommodations; however, most of the act is held unconstitutional eight years later in the *Civil Rights Cases.*

1876

Reconstruction ends in the South; beginning of segregationist and discriminatory Jim Crow laws throughout the South.

1883

The Supreme Court decides the *Civil Rights Cases*, declaring the Civil Rights Act of 1875 unconstitutional and declaring that Congress lacks the authority to regulate private conduct under the Fourteenth Amendment; the *Civil Rights Cases* decision represents a colossal setback for civil rights in the South.

1896

The Supreme Court decides *Plessy v. Ferguson*, ratifying the state practice of "Jim Crow" and segregation and creating the separate-but-equal doctrine.

1920

Ratification of the Nineteenth Amendment, granting women the right to vote.

1935

The first usage of the term "affirmative action" is found in Section 10c of the National Labor Relations Act of 1935, which states that the National Labor Relations Board (in a case involving unfair labor practices) might "take such affirmative action, including reinstatement of employees with or without back pay."

1941

President Franklin Roosevelt issues Executive Order 8802, requiring nondiscrimination practices by defense contractors.

1945

Congress enacts the GI Bill, providing special benefits to veterans and arguably becoming the largest affirmative action program in U.S. history.

1954

The Supreme Court decides *Brown v. Board of Education*, holding "separate-but-equal" racial segregation in public schools to be a violation of the Fourteenth Amendment.

Major Current Events Relating to Affirmative Action

1961

President John Kennedy issues Executive Order 10925, making the first modern reference to "affirmative action" in federal government policy by mandating that federal contractors "take affirmative action" to ensure that no discrimination is employed against minorities.

1964

Congress enacts the Civil Rights Act of 1964, a sweeping piece of legislation that bars discrimination based upon race, color, sex, religion, or national origin in public accommodations, in employment, and in federally funded educational programs.

1965

President Lyndon B. Johnson gives his famous Howard University speech, in which he argues that civil rights laws alone are not adequate to remedy discrimination and inequality; Johnson uses the "chained-runner" metaphor during the speech.

President Johnson issues Executive Order 11246, expanding on President Kennedy's Executive Order 10925 and ordering "affirmative action" to ensure no discrimination by contractors and federal employees on account of race, creed, color, or national origin in the hiring and employment of minority employees; E.O. 11246 also requires contractors to document their compliance with the executive order.

Congress enacts the Voting Rights Act of 1965, which ensures that the rights of citizens to vote will not be denied or impaired because of racial or language discrimination.

1967

President Lyndon B. Johnson amends Executive Order 11246 to cover gender discrimination, as does Executive Order 11375.

1969

President Richard M. Nixon promotes race-conscious affirmative action in his Philadelphia Plan, the most forceful race-conscious/preferential program for minorities up to that time; the Philadelphia Plan calls for timetables and goals by which the construction industry is obligated to increase minority employment.

Executive Order 11478 is promulgated. Executive Order 11478 supersedes Executive Order 11246 in part and prohibits discrimination on the basis of race, color, religion, sex, or national origin (and is later amended to prohibit discrimination on the basis of handicap, age, sexual orientation, and status as a parent). The order requires most federal government employers to take affirmative action to ensure equal employment opportunities.

1972

Congress enacts the Equal Employment Opportunity Act, which amends and strengthens Title VII of the Civil Rights Act of 1964, which had made it illegal for employers to discriminate against any individual because of race, color, religion, sex, or national origin; the 1972 act expands the groups covered by Title VII and gives the Equal Employment Opportunity Commission (EEOC) new enforcement powers.

Congress enacts the Education Amendments (Title IX), which prohibit gender-based discrimination by public and private institutions receiving public funds.

1973

Congress enacts the Vocational Rehabilitation Act, which includes qualified individuals with disabilities in affirmative action requirements for federal contractors.

1974

The Supreme Court decides *DeFunis v. Odegaard*, the first Supreme Court case dealing with the constitutionality of affirmative action as the central issue in the case. The Court rules that a white student's challenge of "reverse discrimination" in a university affirmative action admission plan is moot (and not reviewable on the merits) because the student was subsequently admitted to the school. The Court will not take another case dealing with this topic until the seminal *Regents of the University of California v. Bakke* case in 1978.

Congress enacts the Vietnam Era Veterans' Readjustment Assistance Act, which includes veterans with disabilities and Vietnam veterans in the then-typical affirmative action requirements for federal contractors.

1975

The Supreme Court decides *Albemarle Paper Co. v. Moody*, stating that the goals of antidiscrimination laws are twofold, to bar "like discrimination in the future" and "eliminate the discriminatory effects of the past"; the goal of eliminating the discriminatory effects of the past becomes the chief compelling government interest for affirmative action plans.

1976

The Supreme Court decides *Franks v. Bowman*, in part holding that affirmative action may be appropriate to eliminate discriminatory effects of the past.

1978

The Supreme Court decides *Regents of the University of California v. Bakke*, a landmark affirmative action case that rejects fixed racial quotas in the educational context as unconstitutional while allowing for the use of race as one factor in admissions policies.

1979

The Supreme Court decides *United Steelworkers of America v. Weber*, holding that a voluntary affirmative action plan by a private employer is permissible under Title VII provided that a "manifest racial imbalance" exists in the job at issue, the job is historically one that was segregated by race, and the plan does not "unnecessarily trammel" the rights of nonminority employees and is temporary.

1980

The Supreme Court decides *Fullilove v. Klutznick*, allowing flexible modest quotas/set-asides (10 percent set-aside for minority contractors) in the federal contracting context for minority contractors in response to prior institutional discrimination.

1984

The Supreme Court decides *Firefighters Local Union No. 1784 v. Stotts*, holding that white employees with more seniority on the job cannot be laid off in lieu of newer minority employees on the job, regardless of the existence of affirmative action plans; that is, a bona fide seniority system is a legitimate and protected practice under Title VII of the 1964 Civil Rights Act.

1986

The Supreme Court decides *Wygant v. Jackson Board of Education*, declaring that affirmative action plans that lay off nonminority teachers on account of race are not legally permissible; the Court also rejects the "role model theory" and concern for diversity in the general population as legitimate justifications for imposing an affirmative action plan upon employees and holds that affirmative action cannot be lawfully used in the context of reduction-in-force layoffs where race is a factor.

The Supreme Court decides *Local 93, International Association of Firefighters v. City of Cleveland* and *Local 28 of the Sheet Metal Workers' International Association v. EEOC,* upholding in both cases court-ordered (i.e., not voluntary) racially conscious hiring and promotion affirmative action plans after past discrimination has been documented.

1987

The Supreme Court decides *Johnson v. Transportation Agency, Santa Clara County,* upholding a gender-based affirmative action plan and holding that a severe underrepresentation of women and minorities when compared to the qualified labor force is sufficient justification for maintaining a gender-conscious affirmative action plan, so long as the use of race and/or gender is only "one factor" in choosing candidates.

The Supreme Court decides *United States v. Paradise,* upholding a lower federal court's imposition of strict racial quotas in the employment hiring context as an appropriate remedial measure in response to four decades of overt and defiant racism by the State of Alabama Department of Public Safety.

1989

The Supreme Court decides *City of Richmond v. J.A. Croson Co.*, holding that the use of state/local racial quotas/set-asides (30 percent set-asides for minority contractors) in the contracting arena is impermissible; the *Croson* decision rejects a contracting set-aside scheme similar to the one the Court had approved in *Fullilove* in the 1980s; in *Croson,* the Court states for the first time that affirmative action is a "highly suspect tool," a decision that marks the beginning of the current era, where the Court views affirmative action with suspicion. Before *Croson,* the Supreme Court was generally considered to be supportive of affirmative action.

1990

The Supreme Court decides *Metro Broadcasting, Inc. v. FCC,* ultimately holding that the Federal Communications Commission's minority preference policies do not violate the Equal Protection Clause because they are consistent with legitimate congressional objectives of increasing program diversity.

President George H.W. Bush refuses to sign the Civil Rights Act of 1990, which Bush believes will inevitably lead to rigid racial quotas in affirmative action plans in employment.

1991

Congress enacts the Civil Rights Act of 1991, containing many of the same provisions as the failed Civil Rights Act of 1990; the 1991 measure contains many provisions meant to reverse Supreme Court decisions of 1988–1989, which were deemed too draconian, onerous, or unfavorable to the employee in the Title VII and affirmative action contexts.

1992

The U.S. Circuit Court of Appeals for the Fourth Circuit holds in *Podberesky v. Kirwin* that race-based scholarship programs do not satisfy a "compelling governmental interest" as is required for race-conscious plans under the Fourteenth Amendment unless there is a finding of a need for the program to remedy the present effects of past discrimination.

1995

The Supreme Court decides *Adarand Constructors, Inc. v. Peña,* holding that the use of federal race-based preferences in the contracting context is impermissible except in the most exceptional circumstances; the Court imposes the strict scrutiny standard on federal racial classifications, holding that use of a racial classification must be narrowly tailored to fulfill a "compelling governmental interest"; this decision explicitly overrules the *Metro Broadcasting* and *Fullilove* decisions to the extent that those decisions applied a less onerous test than strict scrutiny.

In a speech after the *Adarand* decision, President Bill Clinton states that affirmative action is still needed by society, but should be restructured to ensure that the plan does not reversely discriminate, a speech (and proposal) that becomes known as "Mend It, Don't End It"; on the same day as the speech, Clinton releases a White House memorandum that calls for the elimination of any affirmative action program that (1) uses fixed racial quotas; (2) creates preferences for the unqualified; (3) reversely discriminates; or (4) is not temporary in nature (i.e., no permanent programs).

1996

The Federal Fifth Circuit Court decides *Hopwood v. Texas,* rejecting the University of Texas's affirmative action program under the Fourteenth Amendment and rejecting Justice Lewis Powell's assertion in the *Bakke* case that diversity in higher education could be a compelling state interest; the *Hopwood* decision is the first of several important and conflicting federal circuit court cases on this subject, ultimately leading to Supreme Court review of the *Gratz v. Bollinger/Grutter v. Bollinger* cases in 2003.

1997

California's Proposition 209 goes into effect, essentially abolishing affirmative action in the state; Proposition 209 prohibits affirmative action (granting any preferential treatment to any individual or group based upon race, sex, color, or ethnicity) in the areas of public employment, contracting, or education.

In response to the *Hopwood* decision, Texas adopts its "10 Percent" percentage plan as a race-neutral alternative to affirmative action in higher education, requiring all public colleges and universities in the state to admit the top 10 percent of the graduating high-school classes in the state; Florida follows Texas's lead several years later, becoming the second state to adopt a percentage plan in lieu of affirmative action.

The U.S. Court of Appeals for the Ninth Circuit upholds the constitutionality of California Proposition 209 in *Coalition for Economic Equity v. Wilson*; the Supreme Court refuses review of the case.

A lawsuit is filed in federal district court in Michigan challenging the University of Michigan's admissions program as providing unjust preferences to minorities; this lawsuit culminates in 2003 in the landmark decisions by the Supreme Court on affirmative action in *Gratz v. Bollinger* and *Grutter v. Bollinger.*

1998

Washington State adopts Initiative 200, which, like Proposition 209 in California, abolishes affirmative action in the state.

2000

Florida adopts the educational component of Governor Jeb Bush's One Florida Plan, ending the use of affirmative action in the state.

A federal district court judge upholds the use of race as constitutional and as a permissible factor to consider in admissions at the University of Michigan in *Gratz v. Bollinger*; the case is appealed.

2001

A federal district court judge rejects an affirmative action plan used at the University of Michigan law school in *Grutter v. Bollinger*; the case is appealed.

2002

The federal Sixth Circuit in the University of Michigan law school case (*Grutter*) holds that the affirmative action program being used is unconstitutional; however, before the Sixth Circuit can issue an opinion in the undergraduate case (*Gratz*), the Supreme Court announces that it will consolidate and review both cases.

2003

The Supreme Court decides the *Gratz v. Bollinger* and *Grutter v. Bollinger* cases, heralded as the "Alamo for affirmative action" and as landmark cases even before the Court issues its decisions. In *Gratz*, the Court declares the University of Michigan undergraduate admissions process unconstitutional in violation of the Fourteenth Amendment because the plan uses race-conscious preferences that, according to the Court, make race the determining factor for many applicants and interfere with the individualized consideration of each applicant. In *Grutter*, the Court upholds the affirmative action plan utilized at the University of Michigan Law School, holding that the plan is narrowly tailored to achieve a compelling governmental interest because it does allow for individual consideration of each applicant. In so holding, the Court declares that diversity in higher education is a compelling government interest, adopting Justice Powell's diversity rationale announced twenty-five years earlier in *Regents of the University of California v. Bakke.* However, the majority opinion also states that affirmative action in higher education should no longer be needed in twenty-five years (i.e., 2028).

PREFACE

Affirmative action is one of the most divisive issues in the United States and has been a highly contentious issue in America since the late 1970s. The emotions surrounding this issue run deep and are never far from the surface in any debate on the topic. All one has to do is turn on the television to a channel airing a debate or discussion on the topic to see firsthand the display of emotions and raw nerves. It is understandable why the issue of affirmative action conjures up such emotions: it deals with one of the essential bedrock principles of the United States, equality of all men and women, and with concepts of fair treatment in our democracy. Regardless of one's position on affirmative action, the issue often boils down to notions of fairness and equality. The staunchest supporter of affirmative action argues that affirmative action programs are needed to ensure that all can pursue the American dream with equal opportunity. The supporter argues, in essence, that affirmative action is needed to ensure true equality for all individuals in society. The staunchest critic also often bases his or her opposition to affirmative action on notions of equality. The critic of affirmative action believes that the government is discriminating on account of race or gender, and that such a program reversely discriminates against another who arguably might have benefited from government action but for the affirmative action program. The national debate on affirmative action has produced a maze of scholarly literature, judicial cases, statutes, executive orders, regulations, studies, and popular writings on the subject.

Thus it was with much trepidation that we commenced this project three years ago. This encyclopedia is intended to provide an overview of current scholarship on topics related to affirmative action and impacting a diverse array of disciplines, such as law, political science, history, and sociology. To the utmost extent possible, these volumes are intended to be a dispassionate exploration of the subject of affirmative action. The encyclopedia takes neither a critical nor a supportive stance regarding the efficacy and desirability of affirmative action, but seeks instead to provide sufficient information for the reader to draw his or her own conclusions. The encyclopedia also offers a comprehensive examination of all major and a host of minor topics related to affirmative action, seeking always to clarify the knotty issues surrounding the concepts of affirmative action and equality in modern society. Contributing authors were drawn from many parts of the world, including India, Japan, Europe, Africa, and the Caribbean, as well as from a diverse array of disciplines and institutions of higher learning in the United States. Many entries were written by those responsible for practicing and implementing affirmative action outside the academic "ivory tower." Contributors from heterogeneous ethnic and racial backgrounds have brought a diversity of viewpoints to bear on this important societal issue. Recognizing that resolution of the often-factious debate on affirmative action is probably not possible, my hope is that the encyclopedia will serve as a reference/research aid for those struggling to make sense of the affirmative action debate, the history of race relations, and the myriad of subtopics and issues related to the debate. Put simply, the goal of the editors and contributors was to make this two-volume set the standard starting-point reference work on affirmative action.

This encyclopedia is meant to be an aid to those who desire to obtain a comprehensive cross-discipline reference (a road map, if you will) on affirmative action that adequately describes the plethora of historical, sociological, philosophical, legal, and economic issues pertaining to affirmative action. In the following pages, the reader can explore the theories of affirmative action, the politics and legality of affirmative action, how affirmative action is practiced, and the contentions of affirmative action. The reader can examine the arguments on both sides of this issue, the major and minor issues and subplots, which have been debated nearly everywhere in the United States over the past three and a half decades—in classrooms, newspapers, workplaces, union halls, taverns, legislative chambers, and the U.S. Supreme Court.

Intended for a wide range of users, including high-school and college students, the interested general public, and professionals in various fields who deal with issues of race, equality, and affirmative action, the encyclopedia offers almost 500 entries providing current, basic information on relevant concepts, events, individuals, organizations, statutes, court cases, movements, and ethnic groups. The volumes also contain a series of entries exploring issues of equality and affirmative action in other countries, such as Australia, Brazil, India, and South Africa. Many entries are illustrated, and the encyclopedia also provides a timeline of important events since 1865, a guide to related topics that will help users trace broad themes and concepts across a web of related entries, and two appendices reprinting the full text of the landmark affirmative action decisions handed down by the Supreme Court in June 2003.

Information can be accessed in various ways. The encyclopedia is arranged alphabetically. If a reader has a particular topic in mind, he or she can go directly to that entry in the work. At the end of the entry, a series of "*See also*" cross-references will allow the reader to quickly find related entries. Each entry also concludes with a bibliography of information resources, both print and electronic, that can serve as a starting point for further research. The detailed subject index is yet another way in which entries are cross-referenced. The index allows the reader to find topics, theories, persons, or events that are mentioned in the text, but that do not have their own separate entries. The index also allows the reader to locate every reference to a particular topic, theory, person, event, or other distinguishable concept that appears in the entire work. For example, if the reader wished to learn more about a particular president or Supreme Court justice, he or she could look up the name in the index and be directed to each entry and page number in which the person's name appears. Through these various aids, the reader will find a host of information on many interrelated topics.

My hope is that the reader will find this reference work to be of great value in determining his or her position on the important issue of affirmative action in today's society. This work was certainly a labor of love for many of the individuals involved in this project, and my fervent hope is that it will advance an understanding of the myriad of issues relating to affirmative action that transcends the raw emotions and helps promote a rational, erudite, and respectful debate of this important issue, regardless of the ultimate conclusions.

ACKNOWLEDGMENTS

This work would not have been possible without the guidance and support of several key individuals. First, several individuals at the Greenwood Press were essential to the ultimate publication of this work. Specifically, from the very earliest point in the process more than three years ago, Senior Acquisitions Editor Marie Ellen Larcada offered the essential support and guidance needed to get this project off the ground, as well as the inspiration required for initiating a project of this magnitude. Likewise, the expertise of Senior Development Editor John Wagner was indispensable in handling a myriad of logistical and administrative details, such as finalizing the illustrations to this work, substantively reviewing installment drafts of the work, and ensuring that all the paperwork was in the proper order. He also reviewed the draft manuscript and recommended key revisions and additions that greatly strengthened and improved the final edited version of this work. Larcada and Wagner were of invaluable assistance in ensuring the ultimate completion of this work. Additional thanks and appreciation should also be extended to countless other individuals at Greenwood who worked on, or reviewed, portions of this work, including the production editor, Agnes Priscsak.

I would also like to extend my thanks and gratitude to the University of Tampa for being supportive of this work. Many supplies, pieces of equipment, and reference works needed to complete this project were provided by the University of Tampa, specifically through the University of Tampa David Delo Research Grant. In addition to the institutional support, I would like to specifically note the encouragement and support of Dean Jeffrey Klepfer of the College of Liberal Arts and Sciences and of many members of the Government and World Affairs Department, who recognized the importance of this project and took this work into account when evaluating my workload as a departmental member these last several years. I would like to extend thanks to University of Tampa faculty member Paulina X. Ruf for her services as a major contributor to this work, as well as her review of many entries in her capacity as an advisory editor. Her research skills and knowledge in the areas of sociology, women's studies, and race relations were invaluable. Finally, I was also fortunate to have the assistance of a couple of University of Tampa students at several junctures of this work and would specifically like to thank Jessica Burns for her early work on this project.

Last and most important, I wish to acknowledge perhaps one of the most important people affiliated with this project, my wife, Maria D. Beckman. She is a civil rights and employment law expert, having practiced for years in the civil rights and employment law context in private practice in New York City and in federal government practice in Washington, D.C. As an advisory editor, she brought lucidity to much of the work during the editing process. Without her knowledge of employment law and civil rights issues generally, this work certainly would not have been possible. However, beyond this valuable service as an advisory editor and contributor, she offered me her unconditional love and support throughout the duration of this project. She listened patiently to my hours of discussions on largely arcane points relating to some entry in the work, did without my presence on countless evenings and weekends devoted to this project, and sacrificed much of her own free time these last three years for the betterment of this encyclopedia as well. For her love, support, encouragement, counsel, and companionship this last decade, I am forever grateful.

INTRODUCTION

Affirmative action is positive action to improve the participation of members of certain groups in various aspects of society, such as the workforce and higher education. The groups targeted by affirmative action are typically those groups defined by a personal characteristic, such as race or gender, on the basis of which the group's members have historically been subject to systematic or institutional discrimination. Affirmative action often involves providing special benefits or allocating special resources to improve the group's situation. Most often, affirmative action is used to refer to programs that consider the group's personal characteristic as a positive factor in determining whether an individual is entitled to the benefits of the program. For example, some affirmative action programs use race preferences or are race conscious because entitlement to the benefits of the program is based, at least in part, on whether an individual is a member of a minority racial group. However, not all affirmative action involves preferences. Some affirmative action programs do not consider the group characteristic (such as minority racial status or gender) in allocating benefits. Such programs aim to increase the participation of the targeted groups via other means, such as taking action to ensure that targeted group members are aware of the program's benefits, to ensure that group members can seek the benefits on equal terms with others, and to identify and eliminate discriminatory practices. In the modern era, the number of groups viewed as potential affirmative action beneficiaries has been expanding to include veterans of the U.S. armed forces and persons with disabilities. However, there is a continuing debate as to which groups (if any) should receive the benefits of affirmative action, particularly when the affirmative action program involves group-based preferences.

When preferences are used to provide benefits to these groups pursuant to an affirmative action program or plan, the governmental or private organization engages in what has been described as "benign discrimination" (or "positive discrimination," a term used by the European Union, Canada, and South Africa, among others). Benign discrimination is often distinguished from "invidious discrimination," which is discrimination intended to burden groups in society and is prohibited under various federal civil rights statutes and federal judicial decisions. "Benign discrimination" means that the government (or private organization) is indeed discriminating on the basis of skin color, gender, or other group characteristic; however, the discrimination is done with a benign purpose: to benefit persons instead of to burden them. Those not ultimately receiving benefits they believe they deserve or have earned because of their merit or other factors often claim that such "benign discrimination" is, in essence, not benign, but malignant as it relates to them, and is classified as "reverse discrimination."

Affirmative action has been one of the most controversial issues in the United States during the last several decades. Perhaps no issue in the modern American dialogue engenders such intense debate, controversy, and, sometimes, heated argument as the topic of affirmative action. The debate covers not only the proper scope and role of affirmative action programs, but also the question of whether or not such programs should exist at all under the U.S. Constitution. Thus affirmative action is debated not only from a political perspective, but also from the historical, sociological, moral, and constitutional/legal perspectives. The issue also encompasses conflicting concerns. For example, polls taken in 2002 suggested that a majority of Americans considered themselves concerned with equality and issues of fairness, even though approximately 70 to 80 percent of individuals polled were generally opposed to affirmative action that involved "preferences" or "quotas" and believed that such programs should be eliminated. A poll in the May 2, 2003, edition of the *Chronicle of Higher Education* similarly reported that 80 percent of the individuals (four of every five) polled stated that it was important for colleges and universities to adequately prepare minority students, while 64 percent of the same individuals stated that they opposed or strongly opposed the notion that colleges and universities should admit applicants who were statistically (i.e., on the basis of grade point averages and standardized test scores) less qualified to achieve diversity under affirmative action plans.

Such opposition, like many issues of affirmative action, appears to be divided along racial lines, with only 3 percent of the white individuals polled saying that they strongly support the use of racial preferences in higher education. Phrased another way, if pollsters are to be believed, white individuals statistically do not generally support affirmative action, while people of color generally do. The same *Chronicle of Higher Education* report indicated that only 7 percent of the white individuals polled strongly agreed with the notion that affirmative action programs in higher education benefited society as a whole. Conversely, 27 percent of black respondents and 22 percent of Hispanic respondents strongly agreed with the notion that affirmative action programs in higher education benefited society. In between these two groups, roughly 14 percent of the Asian Americans polled strongly agreed with the notion of affirmative action benefiting society as a whole.

While "affirmative action" is considered a modern term created in the 1960s, the history of the concept of affirmative action is older and more extensive than most people realize. This history can be traced back hundreds of years, depending on how broadly one defines the term "affirmative action." In *A History of Affirmative Action, 1619–2000* (2001), Philip Rubio argues that to fully understand all the issues of "affirmative action" in the United States today, one must trace its origins back to early slavery in the United States and the resulting relationship between whites and minority groups in America. Rubio thus begins his treatment of "affirmative action" with the landing of the first Africans at Jamestown in 1619. In describing the long lineage of affirmative action in America, Rubio writes as follows:

> More than any other controversy in the 1990s (with the possible exception of the one surrounding the criminal justice system), affirmative action sums up the story of the United States: the struggle for justice, equality, and self-determination and whether African Americans will or even should be able to enjoy chosen labor and increased life chances. It represents the history of white supremacy, privilege, and guilt versus black protest, militance, and demands for compensation and reparations; black reality against white denial; formal equality versus remedial preferential treatment; and the debate over integration, assimilation, segregation, and separation. The black-led struggle against discrimination has been the primary impetus for people of color, women, and other oppressed groups also to demand political and social equality. (Rubio 2001, 3)

Thurgood Marshall, the first African American to serve on the U.S. Supreme Court, took a similar approach to dating the genesis of affirmative action in America. Justice Marshall once commented that the Reconstruction (1865–1875) Amendments (Thirteenth, Fourteenth, and Fifteenth) to the U.S. Constitution, along with Reconstruction civil rights legislation such as the Freedmen's Bureau, were meant to provide benefits to the newly freed slaves in the South and thus constituted the first real affirmative action program in America. In fact, Marshall once stated in his separate opinion in the famous case *Regents of the University of California v. Bakke*, 438 U.S. 265 (1978), that the United States had "several affirmative action programs" during the middle to late 1800s.

Thus the concept of affirmative action dates back far beyond the modern period, and this encyclopedia, therefore, contains many references and entries dealing with the broader historical moorings of affirmative action. It would do the reader a great disservice to exclude entries on the historical context and merely focus on the last several decades of modern affirmative action usage. Echoes of the famous century-old debates between Booker T. Washington and W.E.B. Du Bois concerning how to improve the lot of racial minority groups in America and ensure equality can be heard in affirmative action debates today. It was this historical context in the antebellum period, the postbellum period, Reconstruction, and the segregationist era that ultimately gave birth first to antidiscrimination laws, such as the various civil rights acts, and then to modern affirmative action programs.

Yet despite the early history and forms of affirmative action in the United States dating back to the 1860s and 1870s, for some, the notion of affirmative action has its real genesis in the twentieth century, when the term "affirmative action" was first officially sanctioned by the federal government. The term first appears in the labor context as part of the National Labor Relations Act of 1935. This legislation specified that employers should use "affirmative action" to ensure that victims of discrimination (workers) were put back in the situation they had been in prior to the discrimination. However, the first official usage of the term "affirmative action" in conjunction with providing equal opportunities for racial minorities came in 1961, when President John F. Kennedy issued Executive Order 10925, which required federal contractors to take "affirmative action" in employing workers on a nondiscriminatory basis. Since 1961, various presidents have sought to expand or reduce the usage of affirmative action to include different beneficiaries or different topical areas.

Affirmative action programs were initially envisioned as temporary programs needed to provide a level playing field for minorities and other groups that had suffered historical discrimination. Once the field was leveled, or, to use another metaphor, once all runners in the race were able to fairly compete by starting from the same point and without being hobbled by previous discrimination, then the need for affirmative action would arguably be eviscerated. As most modern affirmative action programs are largely an extension of the antidiscrimination laws of the 1950s and 1960s, it would again be shortsighted not to include in the encyclopedia entries on antidiscrimination laws. When antidiscrimination laws alone proved to be only partially effective in breaking down the vestiges of inequality, segregation, racism, and sexism in the United States, affirmative action programs were advanced as a more aggressive and proactive alternative means to achieve equality. Some people subdivide affirmative action programs into "soft" or "weak" and "hard" or "strong" programs. For such individuals, soft affirmative action programs involve the enforcement of civil rights laws in an aggressive fashion, but nothing more, and such programs certainly do not use racial or gender preferences. Hard affirmative action programs involve the use of preferences to advance one group over another. Hence an understanding of these earlier antidiscrimination laws is relevant to the affirmative action debate, in part to gauge whether affirmative action is a necessary corollary and in part to understand the entire history of affirmative action.

From the relatively straightforward use of preferences or bonuses in contracting, education, and employment, affirmative action has grown to impact many other programs, such as busing, housing, lending, licensing, redistricting, and voting. Thus the idea of affirmative action today involves a plethora of different fields and government programs and practices, not just the traditional areas of education, employment, and contracting. Likewise, the group of beneficiaries of such programs has been expanding from African Americans to other minority groups, then to females, and more recently to people with disabilities and to U.S. veterans. Each group has its own reason(s) for considering itself a proper beneficiary of affirmative action programs, most typically that the group has been the victim of past systematic discrimination. Today, many advocate affirmative action based on socioeconomic factors, claiming that those who come from economically disadvantaged backgrounds should receive the benefit of such programs.

Interestingly, if one defines the concept of preferences in the broad sense, the United States has employed preferences in many different contexts beyond race or gender. Veterans receiving special benefits as a result of active-duty military service are an example of the government discriminating against one class of individuals (nonveterans) to the benefit of another class (veterans). Similarly, when colleges and universities offer a seat to an entering student due to his or her parents' attendance at that institution (i.e., legacy) or by virtue of one's athletic abilities, the school is employing a preference of a sort and is discriminating against one class of individuals (nonathlete or nonlegacy student) to the benefit of another. Supporters of affirmative action today, especially those who argue for the use of hard or strong racial preferences, point to the accepted use of preferences in other areas of society. In essence, the argument is that society has permitted and condoned the use of preferences for other groups for years, and allowing preferences for members of minority classes should be treated no differently now. Opponents of affirmative action argue that racial preferences are unique in that the constitutional equal protection guarantee, which forbids a state to deny a citizen the "equal protection of the laws" on account of race, was specifically intended to make race irrelevant in modern society. Thus, for opponents of affirmative action, veterans' preferences or a legacy preference are not analogous to racial preferences on constitutional grounds.

Starting with the seminal Supreme Court decision in *Regents of the University of California v. Bakke* (1978), courts entered the modern debate on the constitutionality of governmental affirmative action programs primarily by addressing challenges to such programs under the Equal Protection Clause of the Fourteenth Amendment (as it relates to state governments and actions) and the Due Process Clause of the Fifth Amendment (as it relates to actions taken by the federal government). The Equal Protection Clause, ratified in 1868 as part of the Fourteenth Amendment, specifies that no state shall deprive an individual of "the equal protection of the laws." The Due Process Clause of the Fifth Amendment specifies that a person shall not be deprived of his or her life, liberty, or property, without due process of law. The debate regarding the constitutionality of programs that favor one race over another also has its genesis in the Reconstruction Amendments, namely, the Thirteenth, Fourteenth, and Fifteenth Amendments. The Supreme Court began reviewing the constitutionality of such programs as early as 1883 in the *Civil Rights Cases,* 109 U.S. 3 (1883), a consolidated case dealing with the constitutionality of the sweeping Civil Rights Act of 1875. In this infamous case, the Supreme Court held most of the Civil Rights Act of 1875 to be unconstitutional. The Court further held that African Americans should no longer be, in the words of one justice, "the special favorites of the law." The Court also held in the *Civil Rights Cases* that America's several early "affirmative action programs" (in the words of Thurgood Marshall) for the benefit of African Americans were no longer needed. The decision in the case was clearly out of touch with the condition of African Americans in society, as the country was entering what has been described as the nadir of race relations and equality for minorities in the United States. Nonetheless, the Court concluded in 1883 that substantial equality had been achieved and progressive legislation was no longer needed. The 1883 case is also remembered today for the stinging rebuke contained in the dissent to the decision by Justice John Marshall Harlan, who asserted that African Americans and other minorities in the United States still needed affirmative assistance to achieve equality and opportunity.

Thus, starting with the *Civil Rights Cases,* the constitutionality of preferential programs has been an issue. Since the *Civil Rights Cases,* and continuing through the modern era in such cases as *Regents of the University of California v. Bakke, Adarand Constructors, Inc. v. Peña,* and *Gratz v. Bollinger* and *Grutter v. Bollinger,* the framework for analysis of the constitutionality of a race- or gender-based preference program on the state level has been the Fourteenth Amendment and, in particular, the Equal Protection Clause; on the federal level, the framework has been the Fifth Amendment Due Process Clause (which the Supreme Court has stated implies an equal protection clause applicable to the federal government). Each case has refined in some way our constitutional understanding of preferential programs under the Fourteenth or Fifth Amendments or has implied some type of limitation on when an affirmative action plan can be used. Therefore, many of the entries in the following pages concern the most important and influential affirmative action cases. Obtaining an understanding of the constitutionality of such programs is, of course, essential in the debate as to whether or not the country should continue to employ race- or gender-based affirmative action plans.

In the 1980s and 1990s, attacks against the use of affirmative action intensified. During the Reagan administration, the federal government was hostile to affirmative action and the aggressive promotion of civil rights issues. During the 1990s, several courts began to declare affirmative action to be illegal in different contexts. In the late 1990s and the first several years of the new century, several states, through statewide initiatives, began to pass state laws or referenda prohibiting the use of affirmative action plans to favor one race over another. The most notable state actions were California's Proposition 209, Washington Initiative 200, and the One Florida Plan Initiative.

The practice of affirmative action in the United States has international comparisons as well. Countries such as India, Canada, and Malaysia have long employed affirmative action programs, and regional affiliations such as the European Union have also practiced affirmative action. A host of other countries have also experimented with affirmative action in recent years, including Australia, Brazil, China, Japan, Great Britain, and South Africa. Additionally, as argued by Supreme Court justice Ruth Bader Ginsburg in a 1999 law review article, several treaties impose affirmative action obligations. Examination of these different international practices, often referred to as "positive discrimination" or "compensatory discrimination," as well as the international treaties that impose affirmative action obligations upon their signatories, may be helpful in analyzing the use of affirmative action in the United States. Therefore, entries describing international affirmative action practices are included in this work.

Today, countless questions abound from a variety of disciplines regarding affirmative action. In the legal discipline, a multitude of questions arise: Are affirmative action programs unconstitutional? Do they violate federal antidiscrimination statutes? Does the Fourteenth Amendment require color-blind or gender-blind behavior by the government, or can racial/gender preferences be employed under affirmative action programs? What are the legal barriers or mandates for affirmative action today? What legal requirements must be met for the proper use of affirmative action programs?

Sociological research, data, and theories are helpful in the debate, and such research and data generate countless other questions: Has equality been achieved? Has the goal of a "level playing field" been achieved? Does a "glass ceiling" exist for minorities and women in employment and education, and if so, are affirmative action programs the appropriate means to rectify the situation? What groups have been discriminated against? How broad or narrow should the remedy be to cure past discriminations? Do affirmative action plans or programs actually help or hurt the classes they are supposed to benefit? Do affirmative action programs create backlash, displaced aggression, and increased racial friction? Many of the entries in this work address these legal and sociological questions.

Likewise, in the realms of political science and history, questions abound as to whether the allocation of goods and resources of society is being handled properly through affirmative action programs. Modern affirmative action programs were deemed to be of a temporary nature, yet no end to such programs appears in sight. What is the final end date for such programs? Will there ever be an end date? How can society achieve the dream of Dr. Martin Luther King Jr. that individuals be judged upon the content of their character, as opposed to the color of their skin? Is affirmative action the appropriate means? Does it work? Should society rely on a less aggressive means of achieving true equality, such as relying on antidiscrimination laws alone, or is affirmative action not enough, and should society seek more aggressive remedial means such as reparations?

Thus, taken in its totality, the topic of affirmative action today involves a maze of historical events (some going back hundreds of years), scholarly literature and research, judicial cases, constitutional restrictions, statutes, executive orders, regulations, studies, and popular writings on the subject. The list of questions grows the more one reads and studies the issue of affirmative action in the United States. The increasing interrelatedness and connection of various issues from different disciplines, from historical events to sociological research, from legal restrictions to philosophical beliefs of justice, makes the field of affirmative action hard to completely comprehend. Yet knowledge of all of these different areas is essential in understanding and formulating conclusions on affirmative action. Harvard law professor Christopher Edley commented in 1998 that in discussing affirmative action, many individuals do not adequately prepare as they would for other topics and, through this lack of preparation, propagate misconceptions. According to Edley, in the area of affirmative action, "many [individuals] think that shooting from the hip should suffice. This is not rocket science; this is harder than rocket science" (Roach 1998, 26).

References

Roach, Ronald. 1998. "Panel Critiques Media Coverage of the Affirmative Action Story." *Black Issues in Higher Education* 15, no. 13:26–27.

Rubio, Philip F. 2001. *A History of Affirmative Action: 1619–2000.* Jackson: University Press of Mississippi.

Selinjo, Jeffrey. 2003. "What Americans Think about Higher Education." *Chronicle of Higher Education* May 2, 10–13.

AFFIRMATIVE ACTION

A

Abolitionists

The abolitionists were a group of reform-minded individuals (mostly Northerners) who formed a movement during the eighteenth and nineteenth centuries to end the enslavement of Africans in the United States. The abolitionist movement was one of the many causes leading up to the American Civil War. Entire sections of the country relied on the continuation of slavery for their economic prosperity and violently resisted the abolitionists' efforts. However, the abolitionists persisted, and their continued efforts resulted in the end of slavery in the United States in 1865. Once the Civil War began, abolitionists and Northern politicians debated and put forward many social programs meant to benefit the newly freed black slaves from the South. These social programs began during the Civil War and then carried over into Reconstruction. Supreme Court justice Thurgood Marshall and others have argued that the first true historical precedents to modern affirmative action are those programs that were formulated in the Civil War and the Reconstruction period by abolitionists and were intended to affirmatively improve the chances for equality and opportunity for the newly emerging black citizens. Such programs included such initiatives as the Freedmen's Bureau and new schools throughout the South for educating freed slaves. Thus the abolitionists could be rightly considered to be the original founders or framers of what society today refers to as affirmative action programs.

The origins of the abolitionists can be traced to the members of the Society of Friends, commonly known as the Quakers. They were appalled at the brutality of slavery and believed that all people, regardless of race, were equal in the eyes of God. Victory in the American Revolution forced many white Americans to reconsider the essence of liberty and universal natural rights. By 1804, all of the Northern states had either ended slavery or had provided for its gradual abolition. The early abolitionists were linked to the American Colonization Society, which sought to transport free blacks to West Africa and provide them their own country. However, by the 1820s this platform became anathema to the abolitionists because it did not endorse the abolition of slavery.

Illustration in *Harper's Weekly*, December 15, 1860, captioned the "expulsion of Negroes and abolitionists from Tremont Temple, Boston, Massachusetts, on December 3, 1860." Courtesy of Library of Congress.

During this time frame, the more radical abolitionists came to the forefront. In 1831, William Lloyd Garrison began publishing his weekly antislavery newspaper the *Liberator*. In the first issue, he clearly stated his intentions: "I do not wish to think, or speak, or write with moderation . . . I am in earnest—I will not equivocate—I will not excuse—I will not retreat a single inch—AND I WILL BE HEARD." Two years later, Garrison allied the Quakers, free blacks, evangelists, and the New England community to form the American Anti-Slavery Society (AASS). They sought immediate, uncompensated emancipation and equal rights for blacks. They initially focused their efforts on church members and clergymen, assuming that if their antislavery platform were conveyed from the pulpits, then the attitudes of whites would eventually change. The AASS grew, and by 1840 its auxiliary societies numbered 2,000 with a total membership around 200,000. While its immediate goals did not come to fruition, it did succeed in bringing the matter of slavery to the national forefront, which resulted in the split of all the major American Christian churches. However, these efforts also produced a maelstrom: in both the North and the South, angry white mobs opposed these changes. In 1837, abolitionist newspaper publisher Elijah P. Lovejoy was murdered in Illinois while trying to protect his printing press from such a mob.

After several tumultuous years, Garrison and others realized the necessity to change tactics. It seemed logical that unless the education of blacks was increased, white society would never accept them as equals. These actions heightened Northern white paranoia, causing many to suspect that manumission of blacks would threaten their economic survival by unleashing a flood of black migrants into the North that would compete for jobs. While the abolitionist movement was growing in the North, in the antebellum South the movement was completely disappearing. In fact, many Southern state legislatures outright banned any antislavery material.

In 1839, the Cuban slave ship *Amistad* was seized off Long Island. On board were African slaves who had killed the majority of the crew and sought to be returned home. Arguments persisted on what to do with the Africans. The abolitionists opposed extradition and raised money to defend them. The case reached the Supreme Court in 1841, and former president and abolitionist John Quincy Adams argued the defendants' case. The Court decided in favor of the Africans, and those still alive were returned to their homeland. Despite rallying behind the *Amistad* case, by the late 1830s the AASS had become internally divided. Two new groups emerged, the American and Foreign Anti-Slavery Society, which primarily fostered abolitionism in the church, and the Liberty Party, which nominated abolitionist candidates for public office. Also during this time, Frederick Douglass, a former slave and protégé of Garrison, was gaining national attention. He was to become one of the most powerful apostles of antislavery.

Despite America growing and spanning the entire continent, national exuberance turned sour when the country was confronted with several critical issues in the 1840s and 1850s. These events led to an irrevocable division between the North and the South. The question of the extension of slavery into new territories, not abolition itself, became the most foremost political issue. In 1848, the Liberty Party merged into the larger and more politically significant Free-Soil Party, which opposed the extension of slavery into new territory. Two years later, the Fugitive Slave Act was passed, which made it a crime to help slaves escape and made it easier for masters to reclaim escapees. This event reinvigorated the Underground Railroad, a collective name for a variety of regional semisecret networks run by abolitionists that helped runaway slaves escape into the North and Canada. It also fueled riots by abolitionists and aroused the anger of many Northern citizens who otherwise would have ignored the slavery issue. One such person was Harriet Beecher Stowe, who in response published *Uncle Tom's Cabin* in 1852. The book was a forceful indictment of slavery and became the premier antislavery novel of the antebellum period. It sold 300,000 copies in its first year, and an estimated 2 million Northerners embraced the antislavery cause because of her book. Many abolitionists became convinced that slavery could not be abolished peacefully, so when fighting broke out in the mid-1850s between proslavery and antislavery forces in Kansas, they helped arm the latter group. Fanatical white abolitionist John Brown, acting on this belief, led a biracial band in a raid on Harpers Ferry in October 1859, hoping to capture a federal arsenal and incite a slave rebellion. His subsequent capture, trial, and execution aroused great sympathy in the North, and he was viewed as a martyr by the abolitionists. Despite condemnation of the raid by Abraham Lincoln, the fact that it had occurred confirmed Southerners' worst fears.

These national issues strained and then shattered the nation's two-party system. From the turmoil emerged the newly formed Republican Party, an alliance of former Whigs, Northern Democrats, and the Free-Soilers. They opposed the expansion of slavery into the new territories but generally condoned the South's peculiar institution, primarily for economic reasons. Despite these moderate views on slavery, most abolitionists supported the election of the first Republican president, Abraham Lincoln, in 1860. Lincoln was opposed to the proslavery doctrine recently enshrined by the Supreme Court in the case of *Dred Scott v. Sandford*, 19 How. 393 (1857). The Court, led by Chief Justice Roger B. Taney, ruled that blacks were not included as U.S. citizens in either the Declaration of Independence or the Constitution. Effectively, blacks had no rights, and Dred Scott was no different than mere property.

Lincoln's election led to the secession of South Carolina from the Union in 1860 and shortly thereafter the first shots of the American Civil War. In 1862, Lincoln issued the Emancipation Proclamation, which decreed the abolition of slavery in areas not under Union army control. Abolitionists were disappointed in the semantics since about 1 million slaves in Union territory remained officially enslaved; however, the document placed the South's peculiar institution on the road to extinction. After the proclamation, abolitionists continued to pursue the freedom of slaves in the remaining slave states and to better the conditions of black Americans generally. From these principles the U.S. civil rights movement was eventually to take form. Frederick Douglass served as the unofficial liaison between the abolitionists and President Lincoln. He encouraged the president to allow blacks to fight for the Union and sought the adoption of constitutional amendments that guaranteed voting rights and other civil liberties for blacks. In 1865, Northern victory and continuing abolitionist agitation led to the ratification of the Thirteenth Amendment to the Constitution. This banned involuntary servitude throughout the country, freeing all of the remaining slaves. With that achievement, the American abolitionist movement came to an end.

Undoubtedly the abolitionist movement's greatest achievement was the destruction of human bondage as an acceptable institution and the liberation of millions of blacks from slavery. It also established equal rights principles that have outlasted postemancipation efforts by Southern gentry to create social stratification and provided a basis for more recent efforts countering racial segregation and supporting racial justice. It can be argued that the abolitionists invented an idea that a multiracial society could exist in which all Americans could enjoy equal rights and equal treatment before the law.

See also American Civil War; Civil War (Reconstruction) Amendments and Civil Rights Acts; Douglass, Frederick; *Dred Scott v. Sandford*; Freedmen's Bureau; Marshall, Thurgood; Slavery; Thirteenth Amendment.

FURTHER READING: Douglass, Frederick, 1968 (reprint), *Narrative of the Life of Frederick Douglass, an American Slave*, New York: Penguin Putnam; McPherson, James M., 1988, *Battle Cry of Freedom*, New York: Oxford University Press; Rubio, Philip F., 2001, *A History of Affirmative Action, 1619–2000*, Jackson: University Press of Mississippi; Stowe, Harriet B., 1981 (reprint), *Uncle Tom's Cabin*, New York: Bantam Books.

PETER L. PLATTEBORZE

Adarand Constructors, Inc. v. Peña, 515 U.S. 200 (1995)

It is difficult to overestimate the impact that the 1995 U.S. Supreme Court decision in *Adarand Constructors, Inc. v. Peña* has had on the affirmative action efforts of the federal government. It is one of the most important affirmative action cases the Supreme Court has ever decided. The case overturned two leading affirmative action cases and revolutionized the way the federal government thought about affirmative action. It substantially limited the circumstances in which the federal government can take race or ethnicity into account in order to achieve affirmative action aims without violating the U.S. Constitution's Fifth Amendment's guarantee of equal protection.

Before *Adarand*, the Court had held in *Metro Broadcasting, Inc. v. FCC*, 497 U.S. 547 (1990), that "benign" racial classifications—those classifications intended to benefit minority racial groups—mandated by Congress were subject to intermediate scrutiny constitutional review. Intermediate scrutiny review requires only that the governmental action be substantially related to the achievement of important governmental objectives. *Adarand* overruled *Metro Broadcasting* and held that *all* racial classifications used by the federal government, whether meant to assist or burden minority racial groups, were subject to strict scrutiny constitutional review. Strict scrutiny review requires that the governmental action must be narrowly tailored to fulfill a compelling governmental interest. Strict scrutiny review has often been considered to be "strict in theory, but fatal in fact." That is, strict scrutiny review is so strict that few, if any, governmental actions have been held to survive the review.

Justice Sandra Day O'Connor, the author of the Court's opinion in *Adarand*, emphasized that this maxim was not accurate. She strongly implied that governmental race-based measures necessary to remedy discriminatory practices and effects may be constitutional if they are narrowly tailored. The view that some governmental race-based measures might be constitutional in some circumstances (such as in affirmative action programs) was shared by seven justices, three in the majority and four in the dissent. Justice Antonin Scalia and Justice Clarence Thomas, however, wrote concurring opinions suggesting that remedial race-based measures in affirmative action programs cannot be constitutional under any circumstances. The appropriate breadth and correct meaning of the *Adarand* decision continue to be debated in the lower federal courts.

A brief review of constitutional equal protection principles will aid in understanding the Court's opinion in *Adarand*. Both the Fifth Amendment and the Fourteenth Amendment to the U.S. Constitution guarantee that persons will be treated equally under the law. This means that governments must treat similarly situated persons the same. The Fourteenth Amendment protects persons against unequal treatment by state and local governments, and the Fifth Amendment applies to federal government action. The Fourteenth Amendment's Equal Protection Clause states that no state shall "deny to any person within its jurisdiction the equal protection of the laws." This is roughly a prohibition of intentional discrimination by states and local governments.

The Fifth Amendment's equal protection guarantee is not as explicit. The Fifth Amendment's Due Process Clause reads: "No person shall . . . be deprived of life, liberty, or property, without due process of law." Initially, the U.S. Supreme Court held that because the Fifth Amendment lacked an explicit equal protection clause, it prohibited only discrimination that amounted to a denial of due process, that is irrational and thus arbitrary deprivation of life, liberty, or property. Accordingly, the Court held in *Hirabayashi v. United States*, 320 U.S. 81 (1943), that a curfew for persons of Japanese ancestry during World War II was constitutional because the restriction was rational. However, the Supreme Court later began to change its mind about racially discriminatory measures of the federal government. In subsequent cases, the Court held that the Constitution could not be interpreted to allow the federal government to discriminate against minority groups while it prohibited state governments from doing so. The Court held in *Bolling v. Sharpe*, 347 U.S. 497 (1954), that because states are prohibited by the Constitution from maintaining segregated schools, the federal government must also be prohibited from doing so by the Constitution (in District of Columbia schools). Later cases held that equal protection claims challenging actions of the federal government that discriminated against racial minorities under the Due Process Clause of the Fifth Amendment should be analyzed by the same standards as those by which the racially discriminatory measures of a state are analyzed when challenged under the Equal Protection Clause of the Fourteenth Amendment, for example, in *Weinberger v. Wiesenfeld*, 420 U.S. 636 (1975).

The first step in determining whether a governmental action violates constitutional equal protection guarantees is to identify which standard of review applies. The U.S. Supreme Court has established three standards of review: strict scrutiny, intermediate scrutiny, and rational basis scrutiny. Which standard applies depends on the kind of government action challenged.

The most onerous standard of review is strict scrutiny review. This standard applies when the government action challenged utilizes a "suspect classification." Courts have recognized that, historically, governments have treated groups of persons less favorably than others because of their minority race or ethnicity and that these groups had little hope of protecting themselves through the political process. Therefore, courts view any governmental action based on race or ethnicity as "suspect." When a government action is based on race or ethnicity, the action utilizes a "suspect classification" and is presumptively invalid unless the government can show that the measure is narrowly tailored to meet a compelling governmental interest.

The next most onerous standard of review is intermediate scrutiny review. This standard applies when the government action utilizes a "quasi-suspect classification." A government action uses a quasi-suspect classification when it makes distinctions based on factors that have been misused by governments in the past but are nevertheless relevant to some government decision-making. Distinctions based on gender are generally considered to be quasi-suspect classifications. These classifications are constitutional only if they are substantially related to important governmental interests.

The easiest standard of review to meet is rational basis review. This standard applies when the government action does not utilize either a suspect classification or a quasi-suspect classification. If the government can show that the action is rationally related to a legitimate governmental interest, it will be upheld. This standard of review has been applied by courts to governmental action based on age, disability, and veterans status.

Most of the Supreme Court's early equal protection cases addressed governmental measures that disadvantaged groups in society that had previously been subject to discrimination. Some argued that the rigorous review standard applicable to invidious racial classifications should not apply to governmental race-based action that benefited racial minority groups—characterized as "benign racial classifications"—such as affirmative action programs. This argument was rejected with respect to racial classifications of state and local governments in the Supreme Court's decision in *City of Richmond v. J.A. Croson Co.*, 488 U.S. 469 (1989). The Court held that the Fourteenth Amendment required strict scrutiny review of all racial classifications of state and local governments—even those designed to benefit minorities.

Nevertheless, some argued that where the federal government uses suspect racial classifications to benefit minority groups, the Fifth Amendment allows the federal government greater latitude, and these classifications should not be judged by the rigorous strict scrutiny review. The federal government, it was argued, had not had the same history of intentional race and gender discrimination and historically was seen as the protector of minority rights against localized oppression. Moreover, Congress, in particular, may actually have legitimate reasons to consider race and gender in making governmental decisions when it is exercising its power under Section 5 of the Fourteenth Amendment to enforce the equal protection guarantee against the states. In fact, in the only two U.S. Supreme Court cases that dealt with federal affirmative action programs before *Adarand* (*Fullilove v. Klutznick*, 448 U.S. 448 [1980], and *Metro Broadcasting Inc. v. FCC*, 497 U.S. 547 [1990]), the U.S. Supreme Court suggested that the federal government was owed greater deference when using race as a factor to benefit members of racial minority groups.

In *Fullilove*, the Court examined a congressionally mandated 10 percent set-aside for minority businesses in federal contracting. The majority of justices agreed that the set-aside should be upheld, but did not agree on why. Three justices decided that the set-aside as applied to state and local governments was constitutional because (1) its objective (to prevent traditional state practices from perpetuating past discrimination against minorities and to ensure equal opportunity to minority businesses to participate in federal grant programs) was within the power of Congress under Section 5 of the Fourteenth Amendment to enforce the Equal Protection Clause against the states) and (2) Congress's use of racial and ethnic criteria in determining which firms were entitled to the preference was a constitutionally permissible means for implementing the objective because it was limited and narrowly tailored to achieve the objective.

The opinion in *Fullilove* did not explicitly denote its standard of review as "strict" or "intermediate." It stated that racial or ethnic criteria, even when used in the remedial context, were subject to "close examination," but also noted that Congress was entitled to deference. However, one of the justices, writing separately, stated that this was basically the strict scrutiny test. Three other justices agreed that the set-aside was constitutional, but concluded that the appropriate review standard was whether the set-asides "serve important governmental interests and are substantially related to achievement of those objectives"—the traditional intermediate scrutiny standard. These justices applied the lower level of scrutiny because the set-aside was remedial and designed to benefit minorities instead of to disadvantage minorities. Finally, three justices concluded that the set-aside was properly subject to the same strict scrutiny review standard as state racial classifications even though it was remedial and established by Congress. These justices concluded that the set-aside failed the strict review standard.

In *Metro Broadcasting*, in a 5–4 majority opinion (Justices William Brennan, Byron White, Thurgood Marshall, Harry Blackmun, and John Paul Stevens), the Court reviewed two policies of the Federal Communications Commission (FCC) granting preferences to minorities in order to increase broadcasting diversity. The Court applied intermediate scrutiny review and held that the minority preferences did not violate the Fifth Amendment. The Court concluded that intermediate (not strict) scrutiny review was appropriate because the preferences benefited rather than disadvantaged minorities (even though their purpose was not remedial) and because Congress has more latitude to use benign racial classifications than do states. Four justices dissented (O'Connor, Chief Justice William Rehnquist, Scalia, and Anthony Kennedy) and would have applied strict scrutiny review to the race-based federal policies.

The *Adarand* decision is so significant and was such a bombshell because it overruled *Fullilove* and *Metro Broadcasting* to the extent that these decisions held that racial classifications of the federal government should be subject to any less than strict scrutiny review. The opinion significantly altered previous notions within the federal government (based on *Fullilove* and *Metro Broadcasting*) of how aggressively it could act to address this country's struggle with its history of past racial discrimination and the resulting segregation that still exists in many sectors of society. The U.S. Department of Justice issued two memorandums interpreting the *Adarand* decision and providing guidance to federal agencies concerning how the decision might affect their affirmative action efforts. These guidance documents stated that although the Court in the *Adarand* case was reviewing a federal contracting program, its holding was much broader and applied to federal employment, health, education, and other programs.

The facts of the *Adarand* case, at least as described by the Court, are relatively straightforward. The U.S. Department of Transportation awarded a prime contract for a highway construction project to Mountain Gravel and Construction Company. Mountain Gravel solicited subcontractor bids for the guardrail portion of the project. Although Adarand Constructors submitted the low bid, Mountain Gravel selected Gonzales Construction Company. It was undisputed that Mountain Gravel chose Gonzales because it was a minority-owned and controlled business, and a clause in the prime contract, required by federal law, allowed additional compensation to prime contractors who selected subcontractors that were "owned and controlled by socially and economically disadvantaged persons." Mountain Gravel affirmed that it would have selected Adarand if it were not for the extra payment it received for hiring Gonzales. According to the Court, federal law also required the rebuttable presumption that "socially and economically disadvantaged" persons included "Black Americans, Hispanic Americans, Native Americans, Asian Pacific Americans, and other minorities, or any other individual found to be disadvantaged."

It was this presumption that Adarand Constructors challenged through litigation as violating the equal protection guarantee of the Fifth Amendment. The Court characterized this rebuttable presumption and the way it was implemented as an explicit "racial classification." The subcontracting program and its presumption were required by the Small Business Act. The act established a goal for participation of "socially and economically disadvantaged" businesses across the government at 5 percent. The purpose of the subcontracting program, as described by Solicitor General Drew Days at oral argument, was "to ensure to the greatest extent possible that federal procurement programs do not compound the continuing effects of well documented discrimination but, rather, serve to offset these consequences."

The U.S. District Court for the District of Colorado upheld the race-based presumptions. On appeal, the U.S. Court of Appeals for the Tenth Circuit affirmed the district court's approval of the presumption after analyzing the presumptions under the intermediate scrutiny review standard that it believed was required by *Fullilove* and *Metro Broadcasting*. However, the U.S. Supreme Court vacated the Tenth Circuit Court's decision and remanded the case because it held that the Tenth Circuit should have analyzed the race-conscious subcontracting clause under the more onerous strict scrutiny review standard. The Supreme Court's position came in the form of a 5–4 opinion, with Justice O'Connor writing the majority opinion, joined by Chief Justice William Rehnquist and Justices Anthony Kennedy and Clarence Thomas. Justice Antonin Scalia joined most of the Court's opinion and wrote his own concurring opinion. Justices John Paul Stevens, Ruth Bader Ginsburg, David Souter, and Stephen Breyer dissented.

The majority opinion reviewed Supreme Court jurisprudence establishing the standards by which federal courts should review the actions of the federal government when challenged as unconstitutional under the Fifth Amendment. The Court stated that its prior cases established three principles of analysis for government action that restricts the civil or political rights of a person or group because of race: skepticism, consistency, and congruence. First, it held that courts must be skeptical of all governmental action based on race or ethnicity (so-called racial or ethnic classification). Next, the standard of review for racial classifications does not depend "on the race of those burdened or benefited by a particular classification." This is the principle of consistency. These two principles are incompatible with the position that racial classifications intended and designed to benefit minority groups need not be considered inherently suspect and, accordingly, subject to exacting judicial review. The Court reasoned that the constitutional equal protection guarantees protect all individuals and not just certain groups. It stated that evaluating benign racial classifications—a group classification—by a more lenient standard does not comport with the Court's long-standing principle that racial classifications must be subject to detailed judicial inquiry "to ensure that the *personal* right to equal protection of the laws has not been infringed." The Court stated: "[W]henever the government treats any person unequally because of his or her race, that person has suffered an injury that falls squarely within the language and spirit of the Constitution's guarantee of equal protection." Moreover, the Court noted that it would be difficult to determine when a racial classification was benign. Subjecting all racial classifications to strict scrutiny would allow the Court to determine whether the motive was actually beneficent or malevolent.

Finally, the Court recognized that an equal protection claim challenging federal action under the Fifth Amendment's Due Process Clause is analyzed in the same way as an equal protection claim challenging state and local action under the Equal Protection Clause of the Fourteenth Amendment. This is the principle of congruence, the Court's way of expressing its view that the Due Process Clause provides the same protection against federal discrimination as the Equal Protection Clause provides against state governmental discrimination.

The Court stated its holding as follows: "[W]e hold today that all racial classifications, imposed by whatever federal, state, or local governmental actor, must be analyzed by a court under strict scrutiny. In other words, such classifications are constitutional only if they are narrowly tailored measures that further compelling governmental interests." The Court further explained the importance of establishing this broad and explicit rule "because racial characteristics seldom provide a relevant basis for disparate treatment" and "classifications based on race are potentially so harmful to the entire body politic."

The Court explained its decision not to follow but to explicitly overturn the Court's only previous majority opinion concerning a federal affirmative action program in *Metro Broadcasting* by stating that the *Metro Broadcasting* decision "squarely rejected" the principle of congruence and "undermined" the principles of skepticism and consistency that had been established by the Court's early equal protection cases. In a part of Justice O'Connor's opinion that was not for the majority, she stated that the Court should not follow precedent when it "involves collision with a prior doctrine more embracing in its scope, intrinsically sounder, and verified by experience."

Justice O'Connor also emphasized her view that strict scrutiny review, contrary to popular belief, is not "strict in theory, but fatal in fact." She specifically noted that not all racial classifications are equally objectionable. She described the "fundamental purpose" of strict scrutiny review as allowing the Court to take "relevant differences" into account. Perhaps a racial classification that is well intentioned or is used by a government actor with a particularly special reason to take race into account would be more likely to pass strict scrutiny. She importantly stated: "The unhappy persistence of both the practice and the lingering effects of racial discrimination against minority groups in this country is an unfortunate reality, and government is not disqualified from acting in response to it." This statement suggests that Justice O'Connor and the justices who joined her opinion believe that remedying discrimination and its effects is a compelling governmental interest. The four dissenting justices appear to have agreed with Justice O'Connor on this point. O'Connor's statement gives affirmative action proponents hope that, at least when necessary to eliminate the consequences and effects of discrimination, racial classifications in affirmative action that are narrowly tailored may be upheld. On the other hand, it is important to note that Justice O'Connor's opinion in *Adarand* was for the Court "except inasmuch as it might be inconsistent with the views expressed in the concurrence of" Justice Scalia. Justice Scalia's opinion states: "In my view, government can never have a 'compelling interest' in discriminating on the basis of race in order to 'make up' for past discrimination in the opposite direction." Thus it is unclear how much binding authority Justice O'Connor's suggestion that remedying discrimination and its effects is a compelling governmental interest has. Justice Scalia's concurrence demonstrates that he would declare unconstitutional any race-based affirmative action measure with a remedial purpose.

The Court did not apply the strict scrutiny test to the challenged federal program and, consequently, did not declare the program unconstitutional. Instead, it vacated the circuit court's opinion that applied only intermediate scrutiny and remanded the case to the lower courts so that they could more closely examine the program. The Court also did not provide further guidance concerning what "strict scrutiny review"

> entailed except to suggest that two factors appropriate to determining whether the federal program was "narrowly tailored" are (1) whether race-neutral alternatives were considered before the racial-based preference was adopted and (2) whether the program is limited so that the race-based measure lasts no longer than necessary to fulfill any compelling interest demonstrated. It also left several other issues unaddressed, such as the following: What are the criteria for determining whether a measure is a racial classification? Are preferences that favor American Indians racial classifications that require strict scrutiny review? What about racial preferences in judicial orders? How much deference is Congress entitled to when it is exercising its power under Section Five of the Fourteenth Amendment? Is there room in the strict scrutiny analysis for such deference?

Justice Clarence Thomas also filed a concurring opinion in which he rejected any legal distinction between benign measures and invidious measures. In his words, "[T]here is no racial paternalism exception to the principle of equal protection." He stated that discrimination characterized as "benign" teaches that minorities are incapable of achieving equally without the help of racial preferences. According to Justice Thomas, persons who are disadvantaged by these preferences come to believe that they are victims of discrimination themselves and/or that they are superior to the beneficiaries of the preference. Thus "benign" preferences are actually "badges of inferiority" that do not benefit minorities. He also declared, "[T]here can be no doubt that racial paternalism and its unintended consequences can be as poisonous and pernicious as any other form of discrimination." Therefore, of the five justices in the majority, two (Scalia and probably Thomas), at most, indicated that they would adopt the position that remedial race-based affirmative action is unconstitutional. The other three justices joining the majority opinion and the four dissenting justices indicated that race-based affirmative action may be constitutional in some circumstances.

Justice John Paul Stevens filed a dissenting opinion that was joined by Justice Ruth Bader Ginsburg. He argued that measures adopted by a majority race to provide a benefit to certain members of a previously disadvantaged minority race notwithstanding its incidental burden on some members of the majority should not be treated as equally as objectionable under the Constitution as those measures adopted by a majority race to impose a special burden on members of a minority race. He explained:

> Invidious discrimination is an engine of oppression, subjugating a disfavored group to enhance or maintain the power of the majority. Remedial race-based preferences reflect the opposite impulse: a desire to foster equality in society. No sensible conception of the Government's constitutional obligation to "govern impartially," . . . should ignore this distinction.

Justice Stevens also stated that subjecting benign racial classifications to strict scrutiny for "consistency" leads to the "anomalous result" that intermediate scrutiny would be applied to benign gender classifications because intermediate scrutiny has been applied to invidious gender classifications. This means that it would be easier for governments to utilize gender preferences to remedy past discrimination than preferences for African Americans under the equal protection guarantees even though those guarantees were originally meant to end discrimination against African Americans. Justice Stevens also addressed the challenge that minority preferences are not really benign. Although he recognized the argument that granting racial preferences to minorities may be in some respects harmful because such preferences may create the perception that the beneficiaries are less able, he expressed the view that this potential harm is not as severe as the harm of "racial subordination" that such benign affirmative action measures are designed to remedy. Justice Stevens also addressed the argument that "benign" affirmative action race-based measures should be treated the same as "invidious" race-based measures because whether a measure is benignly or invidiously discriminatory is difficult or impossible to determine. He argued that the term "affirmative action" is well understood, and people understand the difference between good intentions and bad intentions. He argued that the difference between measures intended to benefit a minority race and those designed to burden a minority race is obvious. He pointed out that determining which measures are benignly discriminatory and which are invidiously discriminatory is no more difficult than distinguishing between those measures that are intentionally discriminatory and those that have a discriminatory effect—a distinction historically required in equal protection jurisprudence.

Justice Stevens also criticized the Court's conclusion that the race-based measures of Congress must be subject to the same rigorous review as those of a state. Justice Stevens argued that because Congress had been given the authority to enforce the Fourteenth Amendment's Equal Protection Clause against the states and because the acts of Congress reflect the will of the nation, courts should give congressional race-based action more deference by subjecting it to a less rigorous standard of review.

Finally, Justice Stevens criticized the Court's failure to follow *Metro Broadcasting* and *Fullilove.* Justice Stevens noted that the Court overruled *Metro Broadcasting* (upholding federal affiirmative action racial preference after intermediate scrutiny review) in large part because it was inconsistent with the Court's earlier holding in *City of Richmond v. J.A. Croson Co.* (even the benign affirmative action–type racial classifications of state and local governments must be subject to strict scrutiny review). Justice Stevens, however, pointed out that the *Croson* opinion dealt with the racial classification in a municipality's affirmative action plan and explicitly distinguished *Fullilove* (the case on which *Metro Broadcasting* was based) because *Fullilove* concerned a federal affirmative action program. In *Fullilove,* although the Court's opinion was a plurality opinion and it is unclear what standard of review was applied by a majority of justices, a majority of the justices upheld the federal affirmative action program. Justice Stevens argued that the rebuttable presumption that racial minorities are socially and economically disadvantaged in *Adarand* is "no more objectionable" than the 10 percent set-aside for minority businesses in *Fullilove.* He therefore concluded that if the federal set-aside was constitutional in *Fullilove,* the race-based presumption in *Adarand* should also be constitutional. Justice Stevens suggested that the Court's subjection of the presumption to strict scrutiny review may put this ultimate holding in doubt. Justice Stevens would have simply upheld the racial presumption.

Justice Souter filed a separate dissenting opinion joined by Justices Ginsburg and Breyer. This opinion expressed the view that the Court should not have reached the broad question of what standard of review should apply to Fifth Amendment equal protection claims, but instead should have upheld the subcontracting-clause presumption based on *Fullilove.* Justice Souter's opinion also expressed the view that "nothing in today's opinion implies any view of Congress' §5 power and the deference due its exercise that differs from the views expressed by the Fullilove plurality" and concluded that "today's decision should leave §5 exactly where it is as the source of an interest of the federal government sufficiently important to satisfy the corresponding requirement of the strict scrutiny test."

The last opinion in this case was Justice Ginsburg's dissent, joined by Justice Breyer. In this opinion, Justice Ginsburg stated that she would have left the subcontracting program undisturbed, but also emphasized the common ground expressed by a majority of the justices in the various opinions. She stressed that the Court does recognize "the persistence of racial inequality and a majority's acknowledgement of Congress' authority to act affirmatively, not only to end discrimination, but also to counteract discrimination's lingering effects," which effects, Justice Ginsburg stated, "are evident in our workplaces, markets, and neighborhoods." She concluded that "Congress surely can conclude that a carefully designed affirmative action program may help to realize, finally, the 'equal protection of the laws' the Fourteenth Amendment has promised since 1868." She also pointed out that the Court's opinion does not apply strict scrutiny to all racial classifications because it believes that all racial classifications are unconstitutional, but because it must carefully examine them to ensure that the uses of race are legitimate.

On remand from the U.S. Supreme Court, the U.S. District Court for the District of Colorado held that the race-based presumption of "social disadvantage" was not narrowly tailored since it included members of the preferred groups who were not "socially disadvantaged" while excluding members of other groups that were and thus violated the Fifth Amendment. The district court enjoined the U.S. Department of Transportation (DOT) from using the subcontractor clause and its presumption. The government appealed this ruling to the U.S. Court of Appeals for the Tenth Circuit. While the appeal was pending, the state certifying entity changed its certifying procedures by eliminating the presumption. Instead, it merely required all subcontractors to certify that their owners had experienced "social disadvantage based upon the effect of racial, ethnic, or gender discrimination." The state then certified Adarand as a disadvantaged business enterprise (DBE). The Tenth Circuit Court of Appeals dismissed the case as moot and vacated the district court ruling in favor of Adarand Constructors.

Adarand appealed the dismissal back to the U.S. Supreme Court in 1999. The Supreme Court held that the challenge to the race-based presumption was not moot despite Adarand's certification by the state as a DBE because the DOT could not show that the unconstitutional conduct (using the race-based presumption) "could not be reasonably expected to recur." The Court reasoned: (1) the DOT certification regulations had not been amended and retained the race-based presumption, (2) Adarand had been certified as a DBE under procedures that did not comport with these regulations, and (3) it was far from certain that Adarand's DBE certification would be accepted by the DOT for purposes of the subcontractor's clause. In 2000, the Court reversed the Tenth Circuit's decision and remanded the case for further proceedings.

On remand, the Tenth Circuit upheld the then-current version of the subcontracting program because it was narrowly tailored to serve the compelling interest "in not perpetuating the effects of racial discrimination in its own distribution of federal funds and in remedying the effects of past discrimination in government contracting." Once again, the U.S. Supreme Court agreed to review the Tenth Circuit's ruling. However, in 2001, the Court changed its mind and dismissed the writ of certiorari as "improvidently granted" because the Tenth Circuit had held that Adarand Constructors lacked standing to challenge the federal measure that it asked the Supreme Court to review, and Adarand had not challenged the standing ruling on appeal.

The issue of how broadly the *Adarand* decision should be applied in the context of affirmative action continues to be debated. The decision itself states that all racial classifications of the federal government must be subject to strict scrutiny review. The question arises: What is a "racial classification," the use of which would trigger strict scrutiny review? One might argue that only a preference to which one is explicitly entitled solely because of race (as in *Adarand*) is a "racial classification" and that "soft" affirmative action measures that consider race as only one of many factors are not racial classifications. On the other hand, perhaps the Supreme Court meant that any time race is used as a factor or is considered in a governmental decision, it has employed a racial classification requiring strict scrutiny review. In its memorandums providing advice to agencies in developing affirmative employment programs in the wake of the *Adarand* opinion, the U.S. Department of Justice has reached this conclusion. One memorandum states: "The scope of race-based employment decisions that are subject to *Adarand* applies to both the final judgment as to a particular decision, as well as to the various steps leading to that judgment. Race-based decision-making includes situations where race is one of several factors as well as those in which race is the only factor" (U.S. Department of Justice 1996, 6–7). This conclusion is supported by a recent Supreme Court opinion (*Grutter v. Bollinger*, discussed later) that applied strict scrutiny review to a law school admissions policy of considering race as only one positive factor.

Another question raised by *Adarand* is how it affects federal measures that provide special benefits to American Indians. The federal government has historically treated Native Americans differently than other Americans. When challenged under the Constitution, these programs have enjoyed much deference. Generally, rational basis scrutiny has been applied, and, accordingly, most measures have been upheld. For example, in *Morton v. Mancari*, 417 U.S. 535 (1974), the U.S. Supreme Court held that a congressional act requiring the Bureau of Indian Affairs (BIA) to grant hiring preferences to "Indians" was subject to rational basis scrutiny rather than strict scrutiny because the preference, as applied, was not racial, but political, being based on the special relationship between the federal government and Native American tribes. The Court stated: "The preference, as applied, is granted to Indians not as a discrete racial group, but, rather, as members of quasi-sovereign tribal entities whose lives and activities are governed by the BIA in a unique fashion." Nevertheless, one of the qualifications for the preference was having at least 25 percent Indian blood. The Court's decision in *Adarand* may restrict the latitude with which the federal government can fashion programs that benefit Native Americans whenever it uses a racial criterion or blood criterion in determining the applicability of preferences in such programs. Indeed, the race-based preference held to strict scrutiny review in the *Adarand* decision also applied to Native Americans.

Perhaps the most important issue left unclear by the *Adarand* decision is how much deference will be given to affirmative action programs established or approved by Congress. Although the majority opinion held that congressional affirmative action programs are subject to strict scrutiny review, it did not foreclose the possibility that within the context of strict scrutiny review, courts may still grant Congress deference. As noted earlier, Justice O'Connor stated in the Court's opinion that the fundamental purpose of strict scrutiny review is to take "relevant differences" into account. The fact that a race-based affirmative action program has the imprimatur of Congress may be one factor that is relevant in the analysis and may tip the scales of strict scrutiny review, usually heavily weighted against the challenged measure, in favor of the program. The likelihood that future litigants may have success in arguing that courts must give congressional racial classifications some degree of deference increased after the U.S. Supreme Court opinion in *Grutter v. Bollinger*, 123 S. Ct. 2325, 2003 U.S. LEXIS 4800 (2003). In its majority *Grutter* opinion (again written by Justice O'Connor), the Court addressed the issue of whether a state-operated law school was permitted to use race as a positive factor in selecting applicants for admission. The Court reiterated its *Adarand* holding that all governmental racial classifications, including the law school's use of race, must be subject to strict scrutiny review when challenged as violative of constitutional equal protection guarantees. Nevertheless, the Court deferred to the school's determination that it had a compelling governmental interest in using race in its admission process and to the method by which the school uses race. For example, the Court wrote: " '[G]ood faith' on the part of a university is 'presumed' absent 'a showing to the contrary.' " This degree of deference, which the Court states is justified on the basis of the First Amendment's interest in academic freedom, is uncommon in strict scrutiny jurisprudence. Traditional strict scrutiny review presumes that a race-based classification is invalid unless shown otherwise. In future cases, courts may determine that deference to congressional racial classifications is required in a particular case because of Congress's authority to enforce the Fourteenth Amendment's Equal Protection Clause, because Congress expresses the will of the nation, for some First Amendment–related reason, or for other reasons.

The *Adarand* decision addressed the appropriate constitutional review standard applicable to federal measures based on race and ethnicity. It does not directly apply to measures based on sex or disability. However, the principle of consistency espoused by the Court—that constitutional equal protection guarantees do not vary according to the race of the persons benefited or burdened by the measure—suggests the level of scrutiny applicable to gender and disability preferences in affirmative action programs. If the same standard of review traditionally held to apply to race-based measures that disadvantage minorities should be applied to race-based measures designed to benefit minorities, then the standard of review traditionally held to apply to sex-based and disability-based measures that disadvantage women and persons with disabilities should be applied to sex-based and disability-based measures designed to benefit these groups. Traditionally, intermediate scrutiny has been applied to sex-based governmental action. Disability classifications have been subject only to rational basis scrutiny. As noted by Justice

Stevens in his dissenting opinion, this means that the federal government can act more freely and more aggressively in affirmative action programs benefiting women and persons with disabilities than in affirmative action programs benefiting members of racial minority groups.

See also African Americans; Benign Discrimination; Blackmun, Harry Andrew; *Bolling v. Sharpe*; Brennan, William Joseph; *City of Richmond v. J.A. Croson Co.*; Compelling Governmental Interest; Contracting and Affirmative Action; Department of Justice; Disadvantaged Business Enterprises; Economically Disadvantaged; Equal Protection Clause; Fifth Amendment; Fourteenth Amendment; *Fullilove v. Klutznick*; Ginsburg, Ruth Bader; *Gratz v. Bollinger/ Grutter v. Bollinger*; Hispanic Americans; Indian; Intermediate Scrutiny Review; Invidious Discrimination; Kennedy, Anthony McLeod; Marshall, Thurgood; *Metro Broadcasting Inc. v. FCC*; *Mississippi University for Women v. Hogan*; *Morton v. Mancari*; Narrowly Tailored Affirmative Action Plans; Native Americans; O'Connor, Sandra Day; One Drop Rule; Paternalistic Race Relations Theory; Persons with Disabilities and Affirmative Action; Rational Basis Scrutiny; Rehnquist, William Hobbs; Scalia, Antonin; Stevens, John Paul; Strict Scrutiny; Suspect Classification; Thomas, Clarence; Veterans' Preferences; White, Byron Raymond.

FURTHER READING: Gee, Harvey, 2001, "From the Pre-*Bakke* Cases to the Post-*Adarand* Decisions: The Evolution of Supreme Court Decisions on Race and Remedies," *Georgetown Immigration Law Journal* 16:173–189; Jayne, Andrew C., 2002, "Constitutional Law: Affirmative Action in the Public Sector: The Admissibility of Post-Enactment Evidence of Discrimination to Provide a Compelling Governmental Interest," *Oklahoma Law Review* 55:121–152; Lee, Kathryn K., 1996, "Surviving Strict Scrutiny: Upholding Federal Affirmative Action after *Adarand Constructors, Inc. v. Peña*," *Buffalo Law Review* 44:929–961; Rubin, Peter J., 2000, "Reconnecting Doctrine and Purpose: A Comprehensive Approach to Strict Scrutiny after Adarand and Shaw," *University of Pennsylvania Law Review* 149:1–170; Spann, Girardeau A., 2000, *The Law of Affirmative Action: Twenty-five Years of Supreme Court Decisions on Race and Remedies*, New York: New York University Press; U.S. Department of Justice, 1996, "Post-*Adarand* Guidance on Affirmative Action in Federal Employment," Memorandum, February 29, U.S. Department of Justice, Office of the Associate Attorney General.

MARIA D. BECKMAN

Adverse Impact

See Disparate Treatment and Disparate Impact.

Affirmative Access

"Affirmative access" is a term coined by the then governor of Texas, George W. Bush, as an alleged fairer alternative to traditional notions of affirmative action. Upon his ascendancy to the presidency, President Bush continued to define his position as being against affirmative action, but for "affirmative access." During the second presidential debate in October 2000 between George Bush and Al Gore, Bush defined "affirmative access" as follows: "I support what I call affirmative access—not quotas or double standards, because those divide and balkanize, but access—a fair shot for everyone." Thus, in part, the term "affirmative access" is offered as a symbolic alternative to the notion of affirmative action. However, if affirmative access is simply meant to entail "a fair shot for everyone," then the term more appropriately represents normal antidiscrimination and equal protection laws, as opposed to truly affirmative efforts to compensate for past wrongs, which are traditionally thought to include affirmative action plans or programs.

For some (including President George W. Bush), the notion of "affirmative access" is synonymous with race-neutral percentage plans, where the top percentage of students in all state high schools are guaranteed admission to the state's public university system, regardless of race or ethnicity. In fact, President Bush has utilized the Texas percentage-plan approach as an example of what he means by "affirmative access." Percentage plans were popularly utilized in three major state systems (Texas, Florida, and California) at the end of 2002. The actual percentage of students guaranteed a slot in the state university system differs from state to state, ranging from 4 to 20 percent. The first state to adopt a percentage-plan approach was Texas. Texas's percentage-plan program was crafted in response to the Fifth Circuit Court of Appeals 1996 case *Hopwood v. Texas,* 78 F.3d 932 (5th Cir. 1996). In that case, the court found that the affirmative action plan being used by the University of Texas Law School was placing too great a reliance on race as a factor and was therefore in violation of the Fourteenth Amendment's Equal Protection Clause. After the decision, minority-student enrollment began to drop in Texas. In response to the need to somehow enroll a larger minority population, the 10 percent percentage plan was adopted.

According to Bush, the Texas plan would be the perfect example of affirmative access (as opposed to an affirmative action plan) because the plan does not look at the race of the applicant. However, due to de facto racial segregation in school districts, the policy has an obvious racial element, as predominantly minority-filled schools will be able to generate a majority of minority students in the top 10 percent of the class based upon simple demographics. During his governorship, George Bush promoted this legislation and signed the legislation after passage by the Texas state legislature. The end result was that minority enrollment increased in Texas universities and colleges after this 10 percent program was enacted. According to proponents, affirmative access programs like percentage plans have the advantage of facilitating minority college enrollment without having to use race or gender preferences.

However, criticisms of affirmative access, or percentage plans, have also been raised. Percentage plans do not allow the admissions departments to evaluate standardized testing, various difficulties the student might have had, and level of course work taken. Further, students in very competitive high schools face an undue burden in cracking the 90th percentile in the class. Third, notions of meritocracy and appraisals of the intangible qualities of the student are missing in this rigid system, including taking into account such things as life experiences or hardships. Finally, another critique is that these programs are based on the current condition of segregation of high schools. That is, for percentage plans to positively affect minority enrollment, de facto segregated high schools are needed. If high schools become more integrated, then it is likely that the ability of the percentage-plan policy to diversify the incoming freshman class would actually decrease.

See also Affirmative Action Plan/Program; Bush, George W.; De Facto and De Jure Segregation; Education and Affirmative Action; Equal Protection Clause; Harvard Model; *Hopwood v. Texas*; Percentage Plans.

FURTHER READING: Editorial, "Bush and Bakke: Is the Administration Pro–Affirmative Action?" 2002, *Pittsburgh Post-Gazette,* December 20, A24; Nagourney, Adam, 2003, "Bush and Affirmative Action: The Context: With His Eye on Two Political Prizes, the President Picks His Words Carefully," *New York Times,* January 16, A26; Selingo, Jeffrey, 2000, "George W. Bush's Mixed Records on Higher Education in Texas," *Chronicle of Higher Education,* June 23, A32; Smith-Winkelman, C., and F.J. Crosby, 1994, "Affirmative Action: Setting the Record Straight," *Social Justice Research,* 7:309–328; Strickland, Leif, 2003, "Affirmative Access: Making the Grade," *Newsweek,* January 27, 36; Thompson, J. Phillip and Sarah Tobias, 2000, "The Texas Ten Percent Plan," *American Behavioral Scientist* 43, no. 7 (April): 1121–1140.

SEAN RICHEY

Affirmative Action, Arguments for

Proponents of affirmative action programs and initiatives typically support affirmative action on the basis of theories of justice, democracy, social utility, and diversity. Based on the premise of compensatory justice, supporters argue that affirmative action serves as compensation to minorities and women for the nation's history of discriminatory laws and practices aimed at curbing or suppressing constitutional rights. The premise of democracy holds that the inclusion of minorities and women in educational and work settings that previously did not accept these groups fosters the development of a democratic view by minorities and nonminorities through the development of a group consciousness and ideal of inclusiveness. The social utility premise contends that affirmative action benefits society by creating minority role models that motivate other minorities to achieve, creating a more diverse society inclusive of all groups, and increases the pool of applicants for universities and jobs by eliminating the biases inherent in merit testing.

The argument for affirmative action based on the premise of compensatory justice owed to women and minorities is centered on the rights guaranteed to all citizens under the Constitution and on the Lockean theory of natural rights. Proponents of affirmative action argue that minorities have been denied their constitutional rights of liberty and justice for centuries through slavery, the denial of the right to vote, "separate-but-equal" systems of education, and the denial of such basic liberties as equal access to public facilities. Many of these practices were institutionalized through the full support and sanction of many individual state governments and the federal government in many instances. Due to this history of discrimination and oppression, women and minorities are owed special consideration in employment and university admissions as repayment for the hardships they have been forced to endure and the subordinate social, political, and economic status in which they have been placed.

Tied to the argument based on compensatory justice is evidence that women and minorities are still being socially and systematically denied equality, as evidenced in the extremely small representation of these groups as chief executives of Fortune 500 companies, as holders of political offices at all levels of government, and in the population of students at the nation's most prestigious colleges and universities. Women still earn lower salaries than their male counterparts in many occupations. Affirmative action has been the most successful means to increase the percentage of minorities in positions to which they previously had no access and thus bolster their professional, social, and financial positions. Lawsuits against Texaco, Denny's, and Avis have shown that blatant discrimination by large companies still exists against their minority workers and customers. Women and minorities have made tremendous progress in education and in the workplace over the past few decades as a result of affirmative action programs. Eliminating these programs would only retard further progress or, even worse, reverse the progress these groups have already made.

The argument for affirmative action based on the principle of democracy contends that a diverse population fosters a society desiring inclusiveness and equality for all citizens. Social and educational learning in classrooms is maximized when students from different backgrounds share their diverse thoughts and perceptions, while only a limited amount of learning can be achieved solely through textbooks, lectures, and discourse among students from the same or similar backgrounds. As universities strive to create diverse student bodies by offering special consideration and financial privileges to athletes and musicians, they should also be allowed to offer the same advantages to minorities and women to ensure a demographically diverse student body. The same holds true for businesses striving to create a diverse environment by employing workers from different universities and possessing various talents and skills.

The argument for affirmative action based on a utilitarian view holds that affirmative action benefits all of society, not just minorities and women. First, creating a system that produces women and minority doctors, teachers, and lawyers produces a group of specialists and leaders more aware and willing to serve the needs of those less fortunate in their communities. That is, it is argued that minority professionals are more apt to practice their profession in traditionally underrepresented and diverse communities, thereby further spreading the allocation of services throughout society. These leaders also serve as role models for members of their minority group, inspiring other individuals to achieve the same degree of success in a given field.

Second, affirmative action eradicates discrimination. It is argued that affirmative action is a more aggressive and needed continuation to the antidiscrimination laws. That is, while the antidiscrimination laws were a necessary start in the war to achieve equality, more proactive and aggressive programs like affirmative action are needed to achieve full integration and equality in society. Third, it is sometimes argued that affirmative action programs actually increase the quality of job applicants and performance on the job. With some affirmative action programs, the pool of applicants for job positions and admission slots is increased and is more inclusive and more competitive because employers and universities are required to increase the scope of applicants they consider for vacancies. Overall, it is argued, the consequence of affirmative action is a society more able to deal with an increasingly diverse national economy.

Proponents also point to the societal detriment that can result without affirmative action. By 2050, it is estimated that the majority of the U.S. population will be comprised of minorities. Unless minorities are offered special opportunities in education and job placement, the nation will be unable to meet the demands of a more diverse society in years to come. It is argued that universities that do not actively seek minority applicants will be unable to financially support their institutions, and companies will have extremely limited employee pools. Classrooms and the workplace must reflect the diversity existing in the general population. As the baby-boom generation places a strain on the Social Security system, the pool of workers supporting this system will have to include highly qualified and well-paid minorities to boost revenues to Social Security. Statistics also show that more educated people commit fewer crimes and are more aware of the benefits of nutrition and healthy lifestyles. If minorities continue to represent the largest population of prison inmates and the least healthy of the American population through a lack of education and job opportunities, the health, welfare, and justice systems will be unable to bear the resulting financial burden produced over the next century as a result of the increasing minority population.

Supporters of affirmative action use the U.S. military's success in implementing affirmative action policies and programs as a prime example of the program's capability to succeed if properly implemented. The military forces have aggressively recruited and sought out qualified officer candidates from minority pools, coupled with the enforcement of antidiscriminatory policies and integrative programs. These actions have increased the proportion of minorities in high-level positions, produced a military workforce that views discrimination as being more prevalent in society at large than in the military, and fostered a perception that opportunities are open to all personnel regardless of race and gender.

See also Affirmative Action, Criticisms of; Affirmative Action Plan/Program; Constitution, Civil Rights, and Equality; Discrimination; Education and Affirmative Action; Employment (Private) and Affirmative Action; Employment (Public) and Affirmative Action; Equal Protection Clause; Military and Affirmative Action; Minority Professionals and Affirmative Action; Role Model Theory.

FURTHER READING: Bergmann, Barbara R., 1996, *In Defense of Affirmative Action*, New York: Basic Books; Carter, Stephen L., 1991, *Reflections of an Affirmative Action Baby*, New York: Basic Books; Eastland, Terry, 1996, *Ending Affirmative Action: The Case for Colorblind Justice*, New York: Basic Books; Tomasson, Richard F., Faye J. Crosby, and Sharon D. Herzberger, 1996, *Affirmative Action: The Pros and Cons of Policy and Practice*, Washington, DC: American University Press.

GLENN L. STARKS

Affirmative Action, Criticisms of

Continued examinations of affirmative action policies have forced opponents and proponents alike to reexamine the nation's societal goals against individual freedoms. Since the policy's inception, affirmative action as a racial (or gender) preference measure has generated much debate in the arenas of education, contracting, and employment. Although proponents and opponents have debated the merits of affirmative action, the vast writings on affirmative action policies reflect several arguments that have remained consistent through time and throughout the debate. These arguments have revolved around three rationales: compensatory, corrective, and redistributive. The moral, color-blind, and diversity rationales, which overlap the aforementioned positions, have been central to the debate as well. These different theories (as discussed more fully in this entry) may be summarized as the following criticisms: first, affirmative action programs engage in reverse discrimination against whites; second, affirmative action programs unfairly utilize race (and sometimes gender) as a selection/promotion device when such decisions should be based upon merit and qualifications alone; third, affirmative action policies move the United States away from the goal of a "color-blind" Constitution and society; fourth, affirmative action programs stigmatize recipients of the programs and cause others to unfairly doubt the strength of the recipient's true merit and qualifications for the position in question; fifth, affirmative action programs create a condition of dependency and expectation among recipients of the program (and minority-group members as a whole); and finally, if affirmative action was needed, it was needed only as a temporary measure to achieve equality in the 1960s to the 1980s, and as substantial equality has been achieved, the program should be terminated.

The notion of *compensation* posits that damages should be awarded to victims who have been harmed or injured. Some affirmative action supporters have argued that because of past forms of discrimination, such as slavery, Jim Crow laws, and de facto segregation (as well as the continuation of these events as negatively impacting minorities in employment and education), minority-group members are entitled to compensation. That is, because of lingering negative impacts of these past events, compensation should be paid to make up for these past forms of discrimination. In the context of education and admissions, the idea of compensation has met much opposition. Because minorities have been discriminated against due to their particular group membership and not individual qualities, supporters have argued that compensation for group discrimination should also be in the form of group remedies. While supporters have suggested that affirmative action is needed to remedy past discrimination, opponents have argued against racial preferences for the following reasons: first, racial preferences penalize those, especially present-day white males, who have done nothing to warrant their reduction of equal opportunities (i.e., racial preferences reversely discriminate against whites); and second, racial preferences award benefits to members of preferred groups who may not deserve the benefit of preferential treatment.

Corrective arguments for affirmative action pertain to efforts aimed at righting present wrongs, as opposed to compensation for past injuries to a group. For example, if government agencies, private businesses, or educational institutions enforce policies that have a disparate impact on particular racial/ethnic groups, then such organizations should discontinue their discriminatory practices. That is, if an organization has instituted employment guidelines, rules, or regulations that have no bearing on the tasks one needs to perform on the job, and in turn, evidence suggests that these same rules act as barriers for women or minorities, then these barriers should be dismantled to prevent future discrimination that is systemic in nature. Hence this remedy focuses on outcomes and relies on the assumption that parity between groups is the target goal. Supporters of corrective measures have argued that traditionally, white males have received most, if not all, social benefits and rewards, including college admissions to prestigious institutions. In contrast, qualified minorities have received proportionately very few of these same rewards. Affirmative action practices expand the pool to qualified applicants while including more minorities. Opponents have rebutted this practice for two major reasons: (1) individuals should not be rewarded based on their inherent qualities, such as race or sex, but should be rewarded based on their individual talents and merit; and (2) affirmative action violates the principle that "the prime function of government is to remove artificial barriers to equal opportunity" (Swanson 1981, 256). Opponents have argued that by supporting the use of affirmative action polices, the government actually facilitates barriers to equal opportunity.

Contrary to corrective arguments that focus on present discriminatory practices or wrongs, redistributive arguments assume that "society is in some ways unjust, and the injustice is sufficient to warrant taking steps toward a more just situation" (Francis 1993, 30). If the underlying assumption is that society is unjust, and, as a result, there are those who have and those who do not have within society, an attempt is made to strike a balance. The redistributive rationale concedes that there are limited social rewards and benefits that, if distributed disproportionately, will perpetuate inequality. Injustices of this nature in many cases need a redistributive measure to rectify such an imbalance in society. Supporters of redistributive measures have argued that rewards have been historically withheld from minorities because of their race and ethnicity. Hence by considering race, a more equitable distribution of rewards is encouraged. The consideration of race reduces the disparities of rewards between whites and underrepresented groups. Opponents have argued that using race to enforce policies that aim to redistribute wealth, social goods, or equality is incorrect and undermines the principles of equity and justice. Government contracts, entrance to elite postsecondary institutions, and employment should be distributed as a result of the talents and abilities of the individuals seeking entrance, employment, or contracts.

Although these rationales are very prominent, the moral position is central to both opponents' and supporters' sense of justice. In many cases, supporters argue from a moral standpoint that affirmative action is the right policy approach to take. The basis of this moral stance is that past racial discrimination, which according to supporters has not been adequately addressed in this country, continues to foster racial discrimination. In many cases, the moral position is intertwined with other supportive rationales, such as corrective and compensatory ones. Opponents of affirmative action policies typically argue in response that regardless of this rationale in support of such programs, affirmative action is immoral, wrong, and unfair. It is a discriminatory policy being used to correct discrimination. Phrased another way, there is no such thing as good discrimination and bad discrimination, or benign discrimination and invidious discrimination, only discrimination. Once again, affirmative action is considered unfair and wrong because there are identifiable losers, namely, those who lose out on an opportunity due to the racial preference embedded in the policy. With identifiable winners and losers, the game analogy is applied and the rules are scrutinized. If race is a factor that can tip the balance, the identified losers may emerge with a sense of relative deprivation, frustration, and discontent with the rules and eventually conclude that the game and rules were unfair.

Opponents of affirmative action have argued that whether the intent is invidious or benign, discrimination is wrong and immoral. Color-blind advocates have proposed that instead of implementing a policy that essentially perpetuates discrimination, antidiscrimination laws should be aggressively enforced to eliminate all forms of racial discrimination. Although opponents have acknowledged that discrimination exists, they continue to reject the use of race-specific remedies. The argument is that institutions should not solicit information about race or implement policies that take into account the racial composition of those impacted by the policies. It is proposed that using color-blind remedies, such as class-based affirmative action, which deemphasizes race, might yield redistributive outcomes. Color-blind remedies shift the focus from racial injustice measures to needs-based or welfare measures, which do not address the discrimination experienced by those minority groups who fall within the income group of the middle class. The argument is that class-based affirmative action is more likely to redistribute awards to the most needy and deserving. Supporters of affirmative action have varied in their responses to class-based strategies; however, the prevailing counterargument is that avoiding race-specific remedies is not possible if society wishes to correct the legacy of racial discrimination in order to foster equal opportunity and racial equality.

Diversity arguments take into consideration the changing demographics of the country and recognize that all racial/ethnic and cultural groups should be included in the economic and educational enterprises of the country. Proponents have argued that diversity yields favorable outcomes for individuals, organizations, and society. Opponents have argued that diversity arguments are weak and are not compelling enough to hold up in a court of law. Others have argued that diversity goals raise the issue of racial quotas and minimize merit. Essentially, diversity arguments have been countered by the same age-old arguments used against compensatory, corrective, and redistributive rationales.

In the 1990s, proponents of affirmative action and the diversity rationale faced a groundswell of opposition that emerged from the courts, the popular press, public referenda, and federal and state legislatures. In essence, a conservative ideological convergence of various sectors of society—legislative, judicial, and the media—aided in the growing opposition to diversity and affirmative action measures, in particular. However, in spite of the increased affirmative action challenges that were launched against higher-education institutions during this period and the early 2000s, diversity arguments gained ground and became central to the legal defense of these institutions, thereby adding credibility to the diversity rationale. It has been argued in the courts that U.S. Supreme Court justice Lewis Powell's decision in *Regents of the University of California v. Bakke*, 438 U.S. 265 (1978), asserted that student diversity in the arena of higher education enhances the educational experiences of those students, and therefore the use of race in this instance benefits society. In the words of Justice Harry Blackmun in *Bakke*, "[I]n order to get beyond racism, we must first take account of race . . . [a]nd in order to treat some persons equally, we must treat them differently. We cannot—we dare not—let the Equal Protection Clause perpetuate racial supremacy."

Since the *Bakke* decision, educators, as well as college administrators, have felt intuitively that diversity positively contributes to the educational environment and enhances students' learning outcomes. Due to this assumption, many colleges and universities have voluntarily implemented affirmative action admissions policies to be more inclusive of underrepresented groups. Before clear evidence was available, it was argued that a diverse student population provided educational benefits for the learning environment. Others, however, disagreed with this assertion and argued that diversity compromises standards of excellence. With the advent of new diversity research produced for the University of Michigan cases (*Grutter v. Bollinger*, 123 S. Ct. 2325, 2003 U.S. LEXIS 4800 [2003], and *Gratz v. Bollinger*, 123

S. Ct. 2411, 2003 U.S. LEXIS 4801 [2003]), substantial evidence has shown that educational benefits result from maintaining a racially and ethnically diverse student body. Furthermore, students of a diverse student body are more likely to learn how to work with people from different cultural/racial and class backgrounds and, therefore, are more attractive to potential employers. Opponents have conceded that diversity yields desirable benefits; nevertheless, they argue that affirmative action is not the appropriate means by which to achieve a diverse student body or workforce. However, affirmative action in higher education will exist for some time to come, as the Supreme Court in *Gratz* and *Grutter* declared diversity in higher education a compelling governmental interest that may be addressed by narrowly tailored race-conscious affirmative action plans.

See also Affirmative Action, Arguments for; Color-Blind Constitution; Constitution, Civil Rights, and Equality; De Facto and De Jure Segregation; Discrimination; Education and Affirmative Action; Equal Protection Clause; Fourteenth Amendment; *Gratz v. Bollinger/Grutter v. Bollinger*; Jim Crow Laws; Meritocracy; Relative Deprivation Theory; *Regents of the University of California v. Bakke*; Reverse Discrimination; Slavery.

FURTHER READING: Edley, Christopher, Jr., 1996, *Not All Black and White: Affirmative Action, Race, and American Values*, New York: Hill and Wang; Francis, L.P., 1993, "In Defense of Affirmative Action," in *Affirmative Action and the University*, edited by S.M. Cahn, Philadelphia: Temple University Press; Swanson, Katheryn, 1981, *Affirmative Action and Preferential Admissions in Higher Education: An Annotated Bibliography*, Metuchen, NJ: Scarecrow Press.

DENISE O'NEIL GREEN

Affirmative Action, Decline in Usage of

Affirmative action, which arguably was in its heyday in the 1970s and early 1980s, has been under attack in the 1990s and early 2000s on both the state and federal levels. Unlike the ultimate demise of segregation through Supreme Court rulings, affirmative action programs have been severely curbed or completely eradicated in various state education systems due to efforts by interest and citizen groups. These groups have instigated policy changes by rallying public support, spearheading the passage of state ballot initiatives, and swaying the opinions of state leaders. The most prominent group has been the California-based Center for Individual Rights (CIR), led by Ward Connerly. After eliminating affirmative action in California by successfully gaining voter support for its referendum, it successfully targeted affirmative action policies and effected policy changes in Texas, Michigan, Alabama, Washington, and Florida. On the federal level, in the court system, there have been several key cases that have been described as seriously limiting the ability of institutions to employ affirmative action programs. In the decisions of *Grutter v. Bollinger*, 123 S. Ct. 2325, 2003 U.S. LEXIS 4800 (2003), and *Gratz v. Bollinger*, 123 S. Ct. 2411, 2003 U.S. LEXIS 4801 (2003), the Supreme Court indicated that it did not expect affirmative action to be needed or employed in the United States by the end of the next quarter century (i.e., 2028, or twenty-five years from the date of the *Gratz* and *Grutter* decisions).

On the state level, ironically, the CIR has utilized the same strategy employed by the National Association for the Advancement of Colored People (NAACP) during the era of segregation. It has gained public and political support by pointing to the basic violation of constitutional and civil rights and has sought out court cases highlighting these violations. The group has been providing legal backing to plaintiffs and has systematically moved from state to state with the same strategy. The overall objective has been a sweeping reform to eliminate the use of affirmative action programs in all higher-education institutions across the nation. After the passage of Proposition 209 to amend the California Constitution in November 1996, a measure that ended that state's use of affirmative action in its university system, the CIR backed the plaintiff in *Hopwood v. Texas*, 78 F.3d 932 (5th Cir. 1996) and then filed a lawsuit against the University of Michigan on behalf of two white students who had been denied admission at the undergraduate and law school levels in the *Gratz* and *Grutter* cases, respectively. Similarly, in 1997, the CIR filed a lawsuit on behalf of four Alabama students who were not white and not eligible for scholarship funds used by the predominantly black Alabama State University and Alabama A&M University to attract white students as the result of a federal judge's order that each institution spend up to $1 million a year for ten years in new state funding on scholarships open exclusively to white students. In 1998, a public referendum was adopted in the state of Washington, titled Washington Initiative 200, which, like Proposition 209 in California, eliminated the use of affirmative action in public employment, public education, or public contracting. In 1999, Ward Connerly announced that Florida would be the next state whose university system would be targeted, but before the attack was mounted, Governor Jeb Bush announced the implementation of his One Florida Initiative, which, among other things, eliminated affirmative action in the state university system.

The success of the efforts by the CIR and like organizations to end affirmative action admission programs in the aforementioned states, along with the decision in *Hopwood* and similar court cases, created a sort of domino effect across the nation and brought affirmative action to the forefront of public debate. To the disappointment of many college leaders around the country, voters in Washington approved a measure to bar their public universities from using racial and gender preferences to admit students, hire employees, or award contracts in 1998. In 1999, the University of Massachusetts at Amherst stopped giving an edge to minority students in admissions. In the same year, Oklahoma announced that it had eliminated set-asides for female and minority students in a state scholarship program, and John T. Casteen III, president of the University of Virginia, announced that he had ended the university's use of a scoring system that gave extra admissions points to black applicants.

In *Johnson v. Board of Regents of the University of Georgia*, 263 F.3d 1234 (11th Cir. 2001), the federal Eleventh Circuit Court ruled that the race-based admissions practices the University of Georgia used in 1999 were unconstitutional, and that the university had engaged in "naked racial balancing" that was not adequately justified by the "amorphous goal" of promoting diversity. Race was one of several factors the university used in weighing "borderline" applicants. In 2001, University of Wisconsin regent Frederic Mohs announced a campaign to end racial preferences in admissions, although as of 2003, he has been unsuccessful in his efforts and his term expires in 2004. Furthermore, University of Wisconsin President Katharine C. Lydall has promised to continue the usage of racial preferences.

One of the greatest concerns from the onset of efforts to end affirmative action in higher education was that it would lead to a reduction in the number of minorities attending some of the nation's top public universities. Immediately after the passage of many of the aforementioned initiatives, this did occur. In 1997, Texas A&M failed to offer admission to any black students. After the passage of Proposition 209 in California, the University of California (UC) at Berkeley announced in 1998 that the number of African American students admitted as part of the freshman class dropped by 66 percent from 1997, while the number of Latinos dropped 53 percent. At UCLA, the numbers reportedly fell by 43 and 33 percent, respectively. Another concern was the creation of two-tiered and segregated university systems where white students would comprise an even larger majority of the student populations at the larger and most prestigious institutions within state university systems, while minorities would increase the numbers at institutions in these systems that had less stringent admissions criteria and were thus deemed "less prestigious." While UC Berkeley and UCLA were reporting declines in minority admissions, UC Santa Cruz and UC Riverside reported increases in African American and Latino admittants, fueling fears that the University of California system would develop into a two-tiered and racially segregated system. A third concern was the appropriateness of the continued use of standardized scores as valid measures of potential academic achievement since these scores would perhaps be the only allowable criteria in screening applicants if preference was not given to more "nonacademic criteria."

In efforts to revamp their admissions programs, many universities are implementing supplemental admissions programs with a dual goal of being race neutral in their selection criteria but still geared to benefiting potential applicants in disadvantaged socioeconomic groups. In 2000, Governor Jeb Bush announced his One Florida Initiative, which would guarantee students who graduated in the top 20 percent of their class and completed a college preparatory curriculum admission into one of the ten state universities. In July 2001, the University of California approved a new admissions policy to be implemented in 2003 that will guarantee admission to California students who graduate in the top 12.5 percent of their high-school class. UC officials estimate that up to 36 percent of the students eligible under dual admissions would be black, Hispanic, or American Indian. Many proponents of affirmative action oppose these programs as being unable to guarantee that minorities are equally represented in admitted student populations. It will be some time before an analysis can be conducted to determine if these programs are successful in meeting their goals.

On the federal level, particularly in the area of federal employment, affirmative action has been limited under a series of Supreme Court cases too voluminous to delineate in this entry (they appear as separate entries elsewhere in this work). Title VII of the Civil Rights Act of 1964 prohibits discrimination in employment against persons based on their race, color, religion, sex, or national origin. It applies to employers, labor organizations, including unions, and employment agencies. According to the Supreme Court, affirmative action plans utilized in the employment context must mirror the purposes of Title VII and not unnecessarily trammel the interests of nonminority employees affected by the plan. Also, according to the Supreme Court, the use of race-conscious affirmative action plans is only justified to remedy prior discrimination in the workplace. Thus other rationales for affirmative action that often appear in literature and discussions in higher education, such as the role model theory or seeking improvement of diversity in society, are not legitimate justifications for implementing an affirmative action plan in employment. Utilizing an affirmative action plan in employment for any other reason than remedying prior discrimination would be a violation of Title VII and render the employer liable for discrimination against the affected nonminority workers.

Finally, the Supreme Court handed down its decision in *Adarand Constructors, Inc. v. Peña*, 515 U.S. 200 (1995), which held that any race-conscious affirmative action plan is subject to strict scrutiny by the courts. That is, even affirmative action–type programs that engage in benign discrimination are subject to the highest scrutiny by the courts. The Court in *Adarand* specified that "all racial classifications, whether overtly invidious or purportedly benign, were subject to strict scrutiny." As such, the Rehnquist Court has indicated its intent to view affirmative action programs with suspicion and subject such plans to the highest rigors of judicial scrutiny available.

See also Adarand Constructors, Inc. v. Peña; Center for Individual Rights; Civil Rights Act of 1964; Connerly, Ward; Education and Affirmative Action; Employment (Public) and Affirmative Action; *Gratz v. Bollinger/Grutter v. Bollinger*; *Hopwood v. Texas*; *Johnson v. Board of Regents of the University of Georgia*; One Florida Initiative; Proposition 209; Rehnquist, William Hobbs; Strict Scrutiny; Supreme Court and Affirmative Action; Title VII of the Civil Rights Act of 1964; Washington Initiative 200.

FURTHER READING: Chin, Gabriel J., ed., 1998, *Affirmative Action and the Constitution*, vol. 3, *Judicial Reaction to Affirmative Action, 1989–1997: Things Fall Apart*, New York and London: Garland Publishing; Hebel, Sarah, 2000, "Courting a Place in Legal History," *Chronicle of Higher Education*, November 24, A23.

GLENN L. STARKS

Affirmative Action, Myths and Misconceptions of

Very few terms in public life have the potential of elevating themselves from a technical issue to a moral argument. Affirmative action is one of those terms. Ever since Justice Lewis Powell's opinion in *Regents of the University of California v. Bakke*, 438 U.S. 265 (1978), wherein he stated that ethnic diversity might be one factor in determining university admissions, affirmative action has been portrayed in public life by some as a threat to merit and equality. The portrayal, however, of affirmative action in public life is often based on faulty myths.

One myth about affirmative action is that it is not necessary in public life. The argument is advanced that race no longer matters in American society because remedies, such as *Brown v. Board of Education*, 347 U.S. 483 (1954), removed social barriers to racial equality. As a result of *Brown*, racial minorities are no longer at a disadvantage in American society. Affirmative action would thus threaten color-blind policies implemented in American society as a result of *Brown*. A second myth about affirmative action is that diversity is an attractive feature in American society but not a necessary one. Affirmative action is portrayed as a catalyst for transforming a diverse society into a fragmented one. The argument is advanced that affirmative action converts diversity into a vehicle for promoting competing racial differences in American society. As a result, affirmative action is portrayed as a social policy for maintaining diversity in American society that has too many costs.

A third myth about affirmative action is that women and racial and ethnic minorities do not actually benefit from the program. The argument is advanced that affirmative action tarnishes the accomplishments of women and racial and ethnic minorities in American society. Women and racial and ethnic minorities, as a result, are victims rather than beneficiaries of affirmative action. A fourth myth about affirmative action is that it fails to reduce or eliminate the gap in resource shares, especially educational and occupational ones, between the white population and minorities. Specifically, the argument is advanced that the gap in resource shares between white males and women and ethnic and racial minorities will not be reduced or eliminated by affirmative action. This myth accepts the dominant position of white males in American society by arguing that the gap exists due to merit and achievement differentials. As a result, affirmative action cannot reduce or eliminate the gap because it would challenge existing systems of merit and achievement crucial to maintaining order, and not equality, in American society.

Finally, a fifth myth about affirmative action is that it results in preferential treatment for racial and ethnic minorities in American society. The argument is advanced that affirmative action can work to remove barriers for minorities in American society only if it implements processes that give minorities preferential treatment over white persons. Affirmative action is thus portrayed as a social program that harms American society by trying to promote diversity at the expense of white persons.

See also Affirmative Action, Arguments for; Affirmative Action, Criticisms of; *Brown v. Board of Education*; Education and Affirmative Action; Powell, Lewis Franklin, Jr.; *Regents of the University of California v. Bakke*; Reverse Discrimination.

FURTHER READING: Bollinger, Lee, 2002, "Seven Myths about Affirmative Action in Universities," *Willamette Law Review* 38:535–547; Delgado, Richard, 1998, "Hugo L. Black Lecture: Ten Arguments against Affirmative Action—How Valid?" *Alabama Law Review* 50 (Fall): 135–154; Plous, S., 1996, "Ten Myths about Affirmative Action," *Journal of Social Issues* 52: 25–32.

ADALBERTO AGUIRRE JR.

Affirmative Action Plan/Program

An affirmative action plan or program is a written plan or management program put forward traditionally in the workplace or at an educational institution in order to achieve equal opportunities for all individuals regardless of race, gender, disabilities, and other such criteria. Affirmative action plans, properly designed, are intended to ensure equal opportunity by promoting participation from groups that have been historically underrepresented or historically discriminated against. Thus affirmative action plans, while designed in theory to achieve equal opportunity, should not be viewed as plans designed to assure nondiscrimination or color-blind or gender-nonspecific management practices. Furthermore, an affirmative action plan can be implemented in a voluntary fashion by the institution, or such a plan can be ordered by a court as a remedy under Title VII of the Civil Rights Act of 1964 (in the employment context). The plan may cover a variety of issues, such as selection, recruitment, promotion and advancement opportunities, and training opportunities. As affirmative action plans involve discrimination based upon race or gender, such plans are subject to a myriad of laws dealing with discrimination, such as Title VI (discrimination in public educational institutions or in a federally funded educational program) and Title VII (discrimination in employment) of the Civil Rights Act of 1964, as well as a bevy of federal judicial decisions on the permissibility of such plans (e.g., *United Steelworkers of America v. Weber*, 443 U.S. 193 [1979]) and constitutional provisions (i.e., the Fourteenth Amendment's Equal Protection Clause and the Fifth Amendment's Due Process Clause).

While the length and scope of affirmative action plans obviously vary by institution, several general observations can be noted about these plans. First, based upon requirements imposed by the Supreme Court in a series of cases, the plan must be well written, designed, and narrowly tailored to achieve its goals of remedying past discrimination. The plan must also be specifically tailored to the experiences at the institution in question and specifically delineate the justification for such a plan, as well as the specific actions and requirements of the plan. The plan also must not "unnecessarily trammel" the rights of nonminority individuals. Phrased in the lexicon of Supreme Court jurisprudence, the plan (if it is a race-conscious plan) must be "narrowly tailored" to achieve "compelling governmental interests."

In the employment context, it is permissible to implement an affirmative action program in order to ensure that the institution in question is in compliance with Title VII. Additionally, affirmative action plans may be ordered by the courts as a remedy for prior institutional discrimination. However, the Supreme Court has warned that affirmative action programs must mirror the purposes and intent of Title VII. As such, in a series of decisions, the Supreme Court has indicated that the only permissible justification in the employment context for such plans is to remedy prior historical discrimination by the institution. Under Supreme Court jurisprudence and case law, it is impermissible to implement an affirmative action program under other justifications, such as a concern for general diversity in society (*City of Richmond v. J.A. Croson Co.*, 488 U.S. 469 [1989]) or to foster or promote minority role models (*Wygant v. Jackson Board of Education*, 476 U.S. 267 [1986]).

In the educational realm, courts have also required states to implement mandatory affirmative action programs as a means of remedying specific prior discrimination and violations of Title VI of the Civil Rights Act of 1964 at educational institutions (see, e.g., *United States v. Fordice*, 505 U.S. 717 [1992], and *United States v. Louisiana*, 9 F.3d 1159 [5th Cir. 1993]). However, the Court has made clear that the use of fixed mandatory racial quotas is impermissible under both Title VI and the Fourteenth Amendment's Equal Protection Clause (*Regents of the University of California v. Bakke*, 438 U.S. 265 [1978]). The Court has additionally held in *Grutter v. Bollinger*, 123 S. Ct. 2325, 2003 U.S. LEXIS 4800 (2003), that concerns for diversity may be a consideration in implementing affirmative action plans as part of the admissions process as long as such plans are narrowly tailored and only use race as one factor among many in making the selection decision.

See also City of Richmond v. J.A. Croson Co.; Civil Rights Act of 1964; Compelling Governmental Interest; Equal Protection Clause; Fifth Amendment; Fourteenth Amendment; *Gratz v. Bollinger/Grutter v. Bollinger*; Narrowly Tailored Affirmative Action Plans; *Regents of the University of California v. Bakke*; Role Model Theory; Title VI of the Civil Rights Act of 1944; Title VII of the Civil Rights Act of 1964; *United States v. Fordice*; *United States v. Louisiana*; *United Steelworkers of America v. Weber*; *Wygant v. Jackson Board of Education.*

FURTHER READING: Crosby, Faye J., and Cheryl VanDeVeer, eds., 2000, *Sex, Race, and Merit: Debating Affirmative Action in Education and Employment*, Ann Arbor: University of Michigan Press; Spann, Girardeau A., 2000, *The Law of Affirmative Action: Twenty-five Years of Supreme Court Decisions on Race and Remedies*, New York: New York University Press.

JAMES A. BECKMAN

African Americans

African American is a term used to describe a racial group in the United States that is usually the group recipient of affirmative action programs. In fact, an effort to improve the plight of African Americans in light of the specific historical treatment this group was subject to was one of the chief reasons for modern affirmative action programs. Most African Americans claim dominant ancestry from sub-Saharan Africa. Many also claim European, Native American, or other ancestry as well. Several names have been used at different times in history to refer to this group. During the nineteenth century, members of this minority group were known as Anglo-African. Since that time, members of this group have been known variously as negroes, Negroes, colored, blacks, Blacks, and Afro-Americans. At the dawn of the twenty-first century, African Americans were called American Blacks or Black Americans. Except for blacks, most of the earlier name designations are no longer preferred and are therefore seldom used.

Immigrants who came to the United States during the latter part of the twentieth century from Africa, the Caribbean, and, to a lesser extent, from elsewhere are also sometimes classified as African Americans. This is an imprecise designation because these groups often have traditions, cultures, and languages that are different from those of traditional African Americans. These differences are observed mostly in the second or third generations, when they tend to blend into the African American group.

The African American population numbered 35.1 million or 13 percent of the U.S. population in 1999: 55 percent live in the South, 19 percent live in the Northeast, 18 percent live in the Midwest, and 8 percent live in the West. There is a large concentration of African Americans in urban areas, especially in the Northeast and pockets of the Midwest.

Historically, the majority of African Americans were brought to North America and other parts of the Western Hemisphere, such as Latin America and the Caribbean. The earliest known arrival of Africans was at the shores of Jamestown, Virginia, in 1619. Most African Americans came between the 1700s and early 1800s. By 1860, 4 million African American slaves made up one-third of the total population of the southern states. About 500,000 free blacks lived throughout the

United States. In addition to slaves, Africans who came to America were early explorers, freed prisoners, and other free persons. They brought linguistic contributions, religious beliefs, styles of worship, and musical forms and rhythms to their new home.

Between 1910 and 1950, more than 5 million African Americans migrated to the North and other parts of the country. Many from the South went to urban areas, such as New York, Philadelphia, Chicago, and Detroit, seeking improved economic and social conditions. However, in many instances, racial and economic separation still existed for them in the North. In 1954, the U.S. Supreme Court handed down a landmark decision, *Brown v. Board of Education of Topeka*, 347 U.S. 483 (1954), which led to the dismantling of legal segregation in the field of public education. African Americans pushed for more gains and acceptance into mainstream American society through the civil rights movement. Drawing on the tenets of nonviolence from Mahatma Gandhi of India, Martin Luther King Jr. led the civil rights movement through nonviolent protests, including marches, sit-ins, and boycotts, to break down the barriers that continued to keep African Americans from participating fully in all phases of American life. Parallel and subsequent to the civil rights movement, some African Americans engaged in another movement called the Black Power movement.

Under pressure from the civil rights movement, the U.S. government sought to open up new opportunities for African Americans. During the 1960s, President John F. Kennedy's administration designed a plan to increase employment opportunities for minorities (African Americans comprised a large percentage of those defined as minorities), calling for "affirmative action" to help minorities. President Lyndon B. Johnson expanded the concept to require affirmative action to compensate for past racial discrimination through the passage of the 1964 Civil Rights Act and the issuance of Executive Order 11246.

In some ways, African Americans have made inroads into areas of American life that are unprecedented in the history of the nation. However, affirmative action, which propelled much change for African Americans, has come under scrutiny. Today it is under attack from some quarters, and as it was initially envisioned as only a temporary measure, its future is now uncertain.

See also Black Panther Party; *Brown v. Board of Education*; Civil Rights Act of 1964; Civil Rights Movement; Equal Protection Clause; Executive Order 11246; Fifteenth Amendment; Fourteenth Amendment; Johnson, Lyndon Baines; Kennedy, John Fitzgerald; King, Martin Luther, Jr.; Malcolm X; Segregation; Slavery; Thirteenth Amendment.

FURTHER READING: Corbin, Raymond, 1997, *1,999 Facts about Blacks: A Sourcebook of African-American Achievement*, 2nd ed., Lanham, MD: Madison Books; Gates, Henry Louis, Jr., and Cornel West, 2000, *The African-American Century: How Black Americans Have Shaped Our Country*, New York: Free Press; Kelley, Robin, and Earl Lewis, eds., 2000, *To Make Our World Anew: A History of African Americans*, Oxford: Oxford University Press.

BETTY NYANGONI

African Charter on Human and People's Rights

Adopted in Nairobi, Kenya, by the Assembly of Heads of State and Government of the Organization of African Unity (OAU) on June 27, 1981, and entering into force on October 21, 1986, the African Charter on Human and People's Rights is a wide-ranging statement of fundamental human rights on the part of the signatory nations of Africa. While not as aggressive as other international treaties (e.g., the Convention on the Elimination of All Forms of Discrimination against Women, the Convention on the Elimination of All Forms Racial Discrimination, and the European Economic Community Treaty of Rome) in promoting the usage of affirmative action to combat discrimination, the African Charter does seem to support the use of affirmative action programs to combat gender discrimination. For example, Article 18(3) specifies that all member states "shall ensure the elimination of every discrimination against women." However, to date, the countries of Africa have been largely unsuccessful in implementing its tenets. Many studies suggest that gender discrimination is still rampant throughout Africa.

The charter provides for a broad array of rights, including protection against discrimination on the grounds of race, ethnic group, color, sex, language, religion, political or any other opinion, national and social origin, fortune, birth, or other status (Article 2). Member states are required to issue periodic reports on their compliance with the charter (Article 62). As of May 2001, thirty of the fifty-three member states had submitted at least one such report.

The African Commission of Human and People's Rights (ACHPR), which consists "of eleven members chosen from amongst African personalities of the highest reputation" (Article 31), has the responsibility of ensuring the promotion and protection of human rights in Africa. The commission elects a chairman and vice chairman (Rule 17) from among its members. The secretary general of the OAU appoints the secretary of the commission (Article 41). The secretary is responsible for the commission's secretariat, which is headquartered in Banjul, the Gambia. The commission held its first session on November 2, 1987, in Addis Ababa, Ethiopia. Under the Rules of Procedure adopted on October 6, 1995, the commission holds two ordinary sessions a year, each of which lasts two weeks (Rule 2). In addition to hearing cases, the body often encourages interaction between the parties: "[I]t is not unusual that a legal representative attending a Commission session . . . will be asked to speak with government representatives before he or she speaks with the Commission" (Doebbler 2002, 228). However, one weakness of the commission is that it lacks enforcement power, and it "can only deal with a matter submitted to it after making sure that all local remedies, if they exist, have been exhausted" (Article 50). In the past, the commission has recommended that affirmative action be utilized in promoting the purposes of the African Charter.

The powers for the implementation of the commission's recommendations lie with the Assembly of Heads of State and Government of the OAU (Article 53). As one author has observed, the commission functions at the mercy of the member nations, which may not be inclined to punish the transgressions of offending states lest they be subject to similar action in the future. This may explain, in part, why affirmative action recommendations of the commission have not been enforced.

Efforts have been made to enhance the charter through the addition of protocols. In June 1997, the Assembly of Heads of State and Government of the OAU, "concerned that . . . women in Africa still continue to be victims of discrimination and harmful practices" (OAU 1997), added a protocol to the charter on the rights of women. The protocol stated that women had a right to emotional and physical security (Article 4), called for an end to violence against women (Article 5), and called on member states to prohibit harmful practices such as the mutilation of female genitalia (Article 6). The protocol also called for member nations to grant women full political, economic, and social rights. However, this protocol has yet to be ratified by the requisite number of member states to enter into force.

A second protocol concerning the rights and welfare of the child (OAU Doc. CAB/LEG/24.9/49 [1990]) affirms that children have the right to an education (Article 11) and to be protected "from all forms of economic exploitation" (Article 15) "and all forms of torture, inhuman or degrading treatment" (Article 16), and "that no child shall take a direct part in hostilities" (Article 22). This protocol came into force in November 1999.

In 1997, recognizing the limitations of the commission, the OAU adopted a protocol to the charter establishing an African Court on Human and People's Rights. The eleven members of the court, to be elected for six-year terms by two-thirds of the OAU member states, would have the power to issue advisory opinions and orders pursuant to the charter. This protocol has not yet been ratified by the required number of member states to be effective.

In July 2002, the member nations of the OAU, meeting in Durban, South Africa, established the African Union, patterned after the European Union. One of the organs of the new African Union is a Court of Justice, which will have jurisdiction over human rights issues. Human Rights Watch, an international nongovernmental organization (NGO), declared in July 2002 that "the African Union will only succeed if it replaces the culture of impunity with the culture of accountability" (Human Rights Watch Press Release, July 2002).

See also Convention on the Elimination of All Forms of Discrimination against Women; Convention on the Elimination of All Forms of Racial Discrimination; European Union and Affirmative Action.

FURTHER READING: Doebbler, Curtis Francis, 2002, "Reading the African Charter on Human and People's Rights," *Texas International Law Journal* 37 (winter): 227–230; Human Rights Watch Press Release, 2002, "African Union Should Spotlight Human Rights," July 10; Murray, Rachel, 2000, *The African Commission on Human and People's Rights and International Law,* Oxford and Portland, OR: Hart Publishing; Odinkalu, Chidi Anselm, 2001, "Analysis of Paralysis by Analysis? Implementing Economic, Social, and Cultural Rights under the African Charter on Human and People's Rights," *Human Rights Quarterly* 23, no. 2 (May): 327–343; Okere, B. Obinna, 1984, "The Protection of Human Rights in Africa and the African Charter on Human and People's Rights: A Comparative Analysis with the European and American Systems," *Human Rights Quarterly* 6, no. 2 (May): 141–159; Udogu, E. Ike, 2001, "Human Rights and Minorities in Africa: A Theoretical and Conceptual Overview," *Journal of Third World Studies* 18 (spring): 87–105; Organization of African Unity, 1997, Protocol to the African Charter on the Establishment of the African Court on Human and People's Rights, OAU/LEG/MIN/AFCHPR/PROT.1rev.2.; Welch, Claude E., 1993, "Human Rights and African Women: A Comparison of Protection under Two Major Treaties," *Human Rights Quarterly* 15, no. 3 (August): 549–574.

JEFFREY KRAUS

Afrocentrism

The controversial term "Afrocentrism" refers to a loose collection of modern pseudoscholarly teachings aimed at undermining the dominant Eurocentric perspective in the study of history, literature, and philosophy and promoting higher self-esteem among African Americans by teaching them their "true" history that hegemonic Western civilization has ignored or, worse, hidden or even "stolen." The claims of the more moderate Afrocentrists rest on three seemingly simple though actually quite complex assumptions: first, that the land of modern Egypt is part of the African continent; second, that the ancient Egyptians were "black"; and third, that there was much more contact between Egypt and ancient Greece and more influence from Egypt upon Greece than modern classical scholars acknowledge. Its most extreme proponents make such bizarre and outlandish claims as that the "culture" of Greece was "stolen" from Egypt (Africa), and that that theft kept Africans (African Americans) from knowing their role in the building of Western civilization.

The controversial Afrocentrism movement is indirectly related to affirmative action. Rather than seek integration and assimilation, the Afrocentrism movement places a premium on separateness and largely rejects the dominant Eurocentric perspective in many fields. Although many of the notions associated with Afrocentrism, especially the more extreme versions, have a long and convoluted history, it was only at the end of the twentieth century that it burst upon the consciousness of the broader American public and become a particularly heated skirmish in the larger 'culture wars.' It may appear that whatever the truth may be about the ancient civilizations in Egypt and Greece, and the influence of one upon the other, these are questions and investigations that belong to scholars and do not influence the policies and programs of affirmative action in college selection and employment actions. A closer look, though, reveals that all of these issues are wound in an intricate web of mutually influencing perspectives, desires, and conceptions of identity and culture and of rights and obligations. As a gesture toward building black self-esteem and black success in America, it seems ill founded to establish an alternative worldview emphasizing black separation from American culture, and one built upon the historically dubious notions of a glorious past black Egyptian civilization that comprises a "stolen legacy" of African Americans. Opponents of the Afrocentrism movement argue that the literature of Afrocentrism and the schools that indoctrinate students with this alternative worldview ill prepare them academically for competition in what is considered a "Eurocentrically" biased society. Additionally, critics of Afrocentrism argue that such theories perpetuate an image of black people as victims throughout history, and the more extreme Afrocentrists stir racial hatreds that promise to exacerbate the racial divisions within American society. Finally, in the affirmative action context, adherents of Afrocentrism are often quick to brand black critics of affirmative action (like Shelby Steele or Dinesh D'Souza) as Eurocentric, disloyal (to the black cause), racist, or "Uncle Toms."

Although many aspects that came to be called "Afrocentrism" date from much earlier in the twentieth century, the term itself was invented in 1976 by Molefi Kete Asante, a professor of African American studies at Temple University, who has given the most extensive and visible theoretical grounding for the tenets of Afrocentrism, which he prefers to call "Afrocentricity." In such works as *The Afrocentric Idea* (1987, revised 1998), *Afrocentricity* (1988), and *Kemet, Afrocentricity, and Knowledge* (1990), Asante's Afrocentric project questions and seeks to overturn the assumptions and dominance of Eurocentrism. Linking his own thinking to that of the Senegalese scholar Cheikh Anta Diop, Asante claims that "we can never understand Africa until we dare to link Africans to their classical past" (Asante 1998, xii). This program calls for a radically separatist agenda in education and, consequently, throughout American society as well. Interestingly, this separatist agenda goes against one of the modern stated goals of affirmative action, namely, to promote integration in society.

While Asante denies that Afrocentrism is simply a black version of Eurocentrism, his program appears to be immersed in many of the same racist assumptions about identity that shackled African Americans first in slavery and then in segregation and discrimination. More than any other assumption—explicit or implicit—driving the Afrocentric agenda is the conception, to some extent shared with the *négritude* movement and Pan-Africanists, that persons of African descent are essentially different from persons not of African descent: they have a different psychology; they have different modes of learning; they have different values; they have a different culture. Their political/social/cultural project should, therefore, in all aspects be oriented toward their African "home."

Divergence on this single fundamental principle has made even the more informed debates on the merits of Afrocentrism, or Afrocentricity, degenerate into insults, professional and personal attacks, and name-calling. White scholars who do not accept the basic premises of Afrocentric thinking may be considered not only Eurocentric, but racist, and black scholars must be "self-hating" supporters of Eurocentrism. Accusations of sloppy scholarship abound, as do ad hominem attacks and personal and professional insults. Black critics of the Afrocentric program, Asante claims, "are often so eager to support the Eurocentric foundation of their knowledge base that they disregard facts and run quickly to empty flourishes which have little meaning in the concrete realities of millions of African people" (Asante 2000, 77). Shelby Steele and Dinesh D'Souza are among those especially singled out for vilification on numerous occasions, and Kwame Anthony Appiah's "bitter, acrimonious articles" contrary to Afrocentrism, Asante believes, must originate in his "own identity crisis," which makes him a traitor and stems from his (Appiah's) choice "to speak and write as if he is white" (Asante 2000, 77–78).

In his much-praised, much-vilified *Losing the Race: Self-Sabotage in Black America* (2001), John McWhorter, a professor of linguistics at the University of California at Berkeley, denounces affirmative action in higher education and delivers a scathing critique of what he sees as a mentality of victimology, separatism, and anti-intellectualism pervading African American culture. The war against racism and discrimination, McWhorter believes, is being won, not lost, and to portray it otherwise is a self-defeating distortion of reality. Also self-defeating are the agents creating a mind-set of a black separatist culture of "middle-class black people who hold mainstream culture at arm's length and consider sociohistorical misfortunes as justification for lowered bars of evaluation" (McWhorter 2000, 75). A black culture that characterizes academic success as "acting white," he says, promotes academic mediocrity—or failure. For McWhorter, Afrocentric revisionism is part of the large picture of contemporary black "identity." In *Losing the Race,* McWhorter is not much concerned with Afrocentrism in itself, but as a symptom of a broader phenomenon of victimology and separatism in society. In fact, until recently, Afrocentrism has hardly registered on "mainstream," "Eurocentric" culture, although it has had a longer history as a quasi-underground alternative worldview among African Americans.

See also Assimilation Theory; D'Souza, Dinesh; Ethnocentrism; Eurocentrism; Historically Black Colleges and Universities; Integration; Racial Discrimination; Steele, Shelby; Uncle Tom.

FURTHER READING: Asante, Molefi Kete, 1988, *Afrocentricity*, Trenton, NJ: Africa World Press, 1988; Asante, Molefi Kete, 1998, *The Afrocentric Idea*, Philadelphia: Temple University Press; Asante, Molefi Kete, 2000, *The Painful Demise of Eurocentrism: An Afrocentric Response to Critics*, Trenton, NJ: Africa World Press; Bernal, Martin, 1991, *Black Athena: The Afroasiatic Roots of Classical Civilization*, vol. 2, *The Archaeological and Documentary Evidence*, New Brunswick, NJ: Rutgers University Press; Howe, Stephen, 1988, *Afrocentrism: Mythical Pasts and Imagined Homes*, New York: Verso; Lefkowitz, Mary, 1996, *Not Out of Africa: How Afrocentrism Became an Excuse to Teach Myth as History*, New York: Basic Books; McWhorter, John, 2001, *Losing the Race: Self-Sabotage in Black America*, New York: Perennial; Moses, Wilson J., 1994, "In Fairness to Afrocentrism," in *Alternatives to Afrocentrism*, edited by John J. Miller, Washington, DC: Center for the New American Community.

ROBERT A. RUSS

Alaska Native Claims Settlement Act

Passed in 1971, the Alaska Native Claims Settlement Act (ANCSA) is the most important piece of legislation affecting Native Alaskans and represents a unique experiment in the governance and fair treatment of indigenous people within the United States. The ANCSA represents affirmative legislation directed at improving the plight of Native Alaskans, who are also one of the beneficiaries of typical affirmative action programs or plans as well. The act settled the land claims of the Native Alaskans, provided some 44 million acres and nearly $1 billion to the Native Alaskans for the purposes of economic development, and created development corporations for each of more than 200 Native Alaskan villages as well as thirteen (now twelve) regional corporations. In 1996, the Supreme Court also determined that ANCSA extinguished tribal sovereignty in Alaska.

In exchange for extinguishing Native Alaskan claims to the territory of the entire state, Congress ordered the secretary of the interior to transfer title to some 44 million acres to the Native Alaskans. This land was to be transferred in two classes. The first class of land transfers would go to villages and would be entirely within a statutorily defined area near the village. The size of these transfers varied with the population of the village and was generally intended to allow Native Alaskan villages to continue traditional subsistence methods as well as more general economic development projects to be determined by the village corporation. The second class of transfers would go to the regional corporations. These transfers were much larger and were intended primarily for the purposes of economic development projects. All of the money was transferred to the regional corporations.

The development corporations created by the act represented a somewhat novel way of providing for tribal control of development. Each individual Native Alaskan living on the date when the act went into force was given 100 shares in his village corporation and another 100 shares in his regional corporation. These shares were inalienable and could only be transferred through inheritance. This restriction on alienation severely constrained the value of the shares to the individual shareholder, but helped to ensure continuing Native Alaskan control of economic development projects. While the boards of directors of these corporations were not required to be Native Alaskan—indeed, one finds that most regional corporation boards are mixed—the board could be controlled by a shareholder population that was entirely Native Alaskan. The thirteenth regional corporation was intended to aid and represent Native Alaskans residing permanently outside of Alaska as of 1971. This corporation was not awarded any land, but was given a proportional share of the monetary award. It was able to accomplish very little. Much of the money was distributed to shareholders in dividends, and the thirteenth regional corporation is no longer in operation.

The other twelve regional corporations continue to operate and have met with varied success. The most financially successful has been Cook Inlet Regional Corporation (CIRI), which petitioned Congress to allow it to trade some of its land allowances for properties the federal government had come to control through the savings and loan scandal. CIRI has since become a major radio network operator. Other regional corporations have developed coal mines, logging operations, ecotourism projects, and one of Alaska's largest staffing companies.

ANCSA is unique in two very important ways. The first is the sheer size of the settlement. No other Indian claims settlement approaches the amounts of land and money awarded to the Native Alaskans. This can be attributed to the timing of the claims. Native Alaskans began pressing their land claims, including filing—and winning—cases before the Indian Claims Commission in the 1950s and 1960s. During that same period, oil and gas exploration was suggesting that Alaska could hold substantial mineral wealth. After the sale of oil and gas leases to developers, both the state and the federal governments became very concerned that Native land claims could stymie the development of Alaska's valuable natural resources. Facing the loss of potentially billions of dollars' worth of oil and natural gas, the federal government was anxious to settle the land claims.

The second way in which ANCSA is unique is the corporate model of governance. All other federally recognized Native American communities in the United States are organized around governments on reservation lands. Alaskan Native corporations represented a political experiment in governance. In 1971, when the act was passed, there was widespread awareness of the problems involved with reservations. Poverty, poor education, lack of opportunity, and corruption among both tribal governments and the Bureau of Indian Affairs led many to the conclusion that reservations were an unacceptable alternative for the Native Alaskans. The corporate shareholder model of governance did provide a greater degree of self-governance, particularly regarding economic development issues, than was available for Native Americans on reservations. Since that time, however, Native American communities on reservations have been able to use their tribal sovereignty to their advantage in areas of political autonomy and economic development. When Native Alaskan villages tried to do this, they found that the corporate shareholder model did not provide for sovereignty.

In *Alaska v. Native Village of Venetie Tribal Government*, 522 U.S. 520 (1998), the Supreme Court determined that ANCSA extinguished tribal sovereignty in the sense that it exists in the forty-eight contiguous states. The case concerned an economic development tax enacted by the village government of the Native Village of Venetie, a remote village inaccessible by road in the interior of the state. The village government attempted to enforce this tax against a contractor who was building a new high school in the village. Because the contractor worked for the state government, the village ultimately attempted to enforce the tax against the state government. When the state government refused, the village sued in tribal court.

The state immediately initiated an action in state court, which the tribe immediately had removed to federal court on the question of whether or not principles of federal law regarding tribal sovereignty required that the case be heard in tribal court. Once the case was in federal court, the legal question began to coalesce around whether or not Native Alaskan villages occupy "Indian Country" and are therefore sovereign. If the village of Venetie occupied Indian Country, it could require the state of Alaska to appear in its tribal court and to pay its tax. If not, the state would win.

In 1998, the Supreme Court held in a unanimous decision that ANCSA precluded the possibility of Indian Country in Alaska. Its argument rested on the provisions of the act in which the claims to aboriginal title in the state of Alaska were extinguished. The village had argued that this provision referred only to the areas of the state that would leave Native control and not the 44 million acres that were owned and controlled by native corporations. The Supreme Court disagreed, however, and ruled that the extinguishment of aboriginal title applied to all of the land in Alaska. ANCSA provides fee-simple control of land, but not sovereignty.

See also Alaskan Natives; Native Americans.

FURTHER READING: Alaska Native Claims Settlement Act of 1971, 43 U.S.C. § 1601–1629f; *Alaska v. Native Village of Venetie Tribal Government*, 522 U.S. 520 (1998); Berger, Thomas R., 1988, *Village Journey: The Report of the Alaska Native Review Commission*, New York: Hill and Wang; Case, David S., 1984, *Alaska Natives and American Laws*, Fairbanks: University of Alaska Press; Pardes, Joan, 2000, "Nearly 30 Years Later: The Alaska Native Claims Settlement Act," *Alaska Business Monthly* 16, no. 9 (September): 86–89.

RACHEL BOWEN

Alaskan Natives

Alaskan Natives, also referred to as Native Alaskans, are the descendants of the indigenous populations of Alaska and are typically a type of minority group provided for in affirmative action programs and plans. Native Alaskans were 15.6 percent of the Alaskan population in the 2000 census. Modern laws governing Native Americans apply equally to Native Alaskans. However, Native Alaskans are also subject to several unique laws and agreements that set them apart from other Native American groups.

The primary groups that comprise the population of Native Alaskans are the Athapaskan Indians of the interior of the state and the Inupiaq and Yup'iq Eskimos of the Arctic Ocean and Bering Sea coasts, as well as the Aleut Indians of the Aleutian Islands and the Tlinget, Haida, and Tsimshian of the southeastern panhandle. Although communities vary greatly in the number of people who still speak native languages, each of these groups is distinguished by its own distinct language and customs. The Tlinget and Haida, for instance, are known for their large painted wooden totems and related art, while the Yup'iq and Inupiaq are known for masks and other artifacts made from whale or walrus bone and furs.

As compared with other Native American groups, Native Alaskans generally came into contact with Europeans quite late historically. Russia only began to colonize the territory for the fur trade in 1732 and even then was only able to maintain political control over a small area and only for a short time. By the time the United States purchased Alaska in 1867, the Russian colonists were in firm occupation of a single fort at New Archangel (Sitka). The first major influx of whites did not occur until the Klondike gold rush of 1897. Even today, outside of the oil areas and the south central portion of the state, which contains Anchorage, Native Alaskans have generally not experienced the land pressures that have driven many of the conflicts between Native Americans and their neighbors.

Nonetheless, there has been a long history of discrimination and differential treatment of Native Alaskans. Due to their concentration in the rural areas of the state and the relatively high proportion of the Alaskan Native population that maintains traditional cultural lifestyles and languages, they still remain a community apart. Their geographical concentration, however, has aided the development of significant political power for Native Alaskans. Native Alaskans are regularly represented in large numbers in the state legislature and constitute an important constituency in any statewide election.

The primary legal difference between Native Alaskans and other Native American communities is the issue of sovereignty. The U.S. Supreme Court ruled in *Alaska v. Native Village of Venetie Tribal Government*, 522 U.S. 520 (1998), that Native Alaskan tribal corporation lands do not qualify as "Indian Country." This determination means that Native Alaskan governments do not have the same sovereign rights that adhere to Native American reservations in the rest of the United States. However, Native Alaskans continue to qualify for federal programs, including hiring preferences, that are justified by Native American sovereignty. Nonetheless, many Native Alaskan villages are sufficiently geographically remote that they operate under a de facto sovereignty that can be more powerful than the legal sovereignty enjoyed by many reservations recognized as Indian Country.

There are several federal laws that apply only to Native Alaskans. The first chronologically was the Native Allotment Act, originally passed in 1906, and amended in 1956. This act is very similar to the General Allotment Act (Dawes Act) of 1887, which distributed tribal reservation lands to individual tribal members as alienable property. The Native Allotment Act gave each Native Alaskan the right to select and receive up to 160 acres of federally owned land (99 percent of land in Alaska at the time of statehood in 1959). While the Dawes Act is often criticized for reducing the amount of land held by Native Americans, and especially by tribes, the Native Allotment Act is generally credited with increasing the total amount of land controlled by Native Alaskans either directly or through development corporations. The Native Allotment Act continued in operation until it was repealed in 1971 by the Alaska Native Claims Settlement Act, before which there was a substantial drive to register allotments for individual Native Alaskans.

The most significant federal law is the Alaska Native Claims Settlement Act of

1971 (ANCSA). This law extinguished Native claims to the state of Alaska, thus allowing oil development to go forward, in exchange for a settlement of nearly $1 billion and 44 million acres. ANCSA created village and regional development corporations to which the land and money would be transferred. The corporations were entrusted with the development of these resources to meet the needs of the Native Alaskan population. Each Native Alaskan living and able to be identified as of the date the act was passed was given shares in one regional and one village corporation; these shares are only alienable through inheritance.

See also Alaska Native Claims Settlement Act; *Morton v. Mancari*; Native Americans.

FURTHER READING: *Alaska v. Native Village of Venetie Tribal Government*, 522 U.S. 520 (1998); Case, David S., 1984, *Alaska Natives and American Laws*, Fairbanks: University of Alaska Press; Mitchell, Donald Craig, 1997, *Sold American: The Story of Alaska Natives and Their Land, 1867–1959*, Hanover, NH: University Press of New England; Mitchell, Donald Craig, 2001, *Take My Land, Take My Life: The Story of Congress's Historic Settlement of Alaska Native Land Claims, 1960–1971*, Fairbanks: University of Alaska Press.

RACHEL BOWEN

Albemarle Paper Co. v. Moody, 422 U.S. 405 (1975)

Albemarle Paper Co. v. Moody was the U.S. Supreme Court case that held that employees who have been discriminated against by the practices of their employer should be awarded back pay unless denying such an award would not frustrate the purposes of Title VII of the Civil Rights Act of 1964. The Court also held that preemployment testing that has a disparate impact on protected groups may be allowed if the employer can demonstrate that the testing is job related, and the complaining party fails to show that there are equal tests, less discriminatory in nature, available to measure the ability to perform the job in question. Perhaps most important for future decisions, the Court sanctioned the use of voluntary preferences in a racially conscious manner (for temporary periods) to eliminate vestiges of racial discrimination and/or segregation, even if such temporary measures adversely affect white employees. The Court stated that it was requiring "employers and unions to self-examine and self-evaluate their employment practices and to endeavor to eliminate, so far as possible, the last vestiges of an unfortunate and ignominious page in this country's history." This language in the decision sanctioning the use of voluntary affirmative action plans became important to a future Supreme Court dealing with the permissibility of such voluntary plans in *United Steelworkers of America v. Weber*, 443 U.S. 193 (1979).

The suit was originally brought by a group of black employees at a paper company. In the mid-1960s, the paper plant segregated white and black workers into different "lines" or teams. The higher-paying and more skilled jobs went to the white workers. In 1968, the lines were integrated, and the plant went to a promotion system based on seniority. Since the white workers had been in the higher-paying job categories for longer periods of time, they continued to be promoted over their black counterparts. The black employees sued, claiming that the plant's actions violated Title VII of the Civil Rights Act of 1964. In addition to the seniority system, the employees also argued that the preemployment testing procedures for all applicants were discriminatory. They asked the court for injunctive relief. After five years of discovery, they amended their petition to include a request for back pay for those workers who would have been promoted had the system not been discriminatory.

The federal district court first hearing the case found that the seniority system was discriminatory. However, the court refused to put an end to the preemployment testing. Furthermore, the court stated that it would not award back pay to the employees because the employer had not acted in bad faith when it implemented the seniority system. The district court found that it was not the intent of the employer to discriminate. The employees then appealed the decision, and the federal appellate court reversed the ruling of the district court. It held that the preemployment testing should be enjoined because these tests are impermissible unless they are predictive of the employees' work habits or job skills. The court also found that back pay should be denied only for reasons that would not frustrate the purposes of the Civil Rights Act of 1964 to eradicate employment discrimination and make victims of such discrimination whole for their injuries.

On certiorari, the Supreme Court held that discriminatory employment tests are prohibited unless the employer can show that there is a "manifest relationship to the employment in question." In effect, the employees have the burden to prove the prima facie case of discrimination. To do this, the employees must prove that the tests select applicants in a racial pattern that is significantly different from that of the pool of applicants. Once this is accomplished, the employer has the opportunity to demonstrate a "manifest relationship to the employment" (i.e., that the testing measures an applicant's ability to do the job at hand). If it can show this relationship, the testing is valid, even though the effect is discriminatory. According to the Court, the burden then shifts back to the employee to demonstrate that the employer's argument is purely pretextual. One way to do this is for the employee to show that there are other tests available to evaluate the same criteria as the test at issue without the discriminatory effect that was originally in question. If the employees can demonstrate that the employer's argument is pretextual, the test is deemed illegal. The Court also relied heavily on the Equal Employment Opportunity Commission's employee selection guidelines as a way to ensure that employers do not engage in disparate impact in their hiring practices.

On the issue of back pay, the Court held that it is not an automatic remedy. It is within the discretion of the district court to grant it or deny it. However, the Court noted that the purpose of Title VII is to make amends to people who suffer from illegal discrimination practices. Therefore, according to the Court, once a finding of discrimination is made, back pay should be denied only for reasons that do not frustrate the purpose of the statute. If a district court refused to award back pay, the court must give specific reasons for its refusal. A lack of bad faith on the part of the employer is not an adequate reason to withhold back pay, because the statute is not only concerned with the motivation for the employer's action or practice, but also with the consequences of employment practices.

See also Civil Rights Act of 1964; Disparate Treatment and Disparate Impact; Employment (Private) and Affirmative Action; Employment (Public) and Affirmative Action; Equal Employment Opportunity Commission; *Griggs v. Duke Power*

Co.; Reverse Discrimination; Title VII of the Civil Rights Act of 1964; *United Steelworkers of America v. Weber.*

FURTHER READING: Rodwig, Susan Talley, 1980, "Note: Employment Discrimination—Plaintiff's Prima Facie Case and Defendant's Rebuttal in a Disparate Impact Case," *Tulane Law Review* 45:1187–1198; Royer, Christina M., 2000, "Note: *West v. Gibson*: Federal Employees Win the Battle, but Ultimately Lose the War for Compensatory Damages under Title VII," *Akron Law Review* 33:417–450.

AIMÉE HOBBY RHODES

All Deliberate Speed

"All deliberate speed" is a phrase used in the Supreme Court's decision in the desegregation case *Brown v. Board of Education (II)*, 349 U.S. 294 (1955). In *Brown II*, the Supreme Court ordered the lower federal courts to require "defendants to make a prompt and reasonable start toward full compliance" by ensuring that the "parties to these cases" were admitted "to public school on a racially nondiscriminatory bases with *all deliberate speed*" (italics added). The phrase was so ambiguous that it was interpreted in a variety of ways, especially by southern states. The concept relates to affirmative action today in that all deliberate speed in integration equated often to "no speed" in the school desegregation context. Thus affirmative action programs were increasingly relied on in the 1970s and 1980s at the university/college level as a means to rectify the past practices of discrimination and to recruit and select minority students into schools where minorities were historically underrepresented.

On May 17, 1954, in the case *Brown v. Board of Education (Brown I)*, 347 U.S. 483 (1954), the U.S. Supreme Court handed down a decision that revolutionized America's way of thinking about institutionalized racism. Since the 1940s, the National Association for the Advancement of Colored People (NAACP), through its Legal Defense Fund, had attempted to overturn the doctrine of separate but equal established in *Plessy v. Ferguson*, 163 U.S. 537 (1896). Led by Thurgood Marshall, who later became the first African American Supreme Court justice, the NAACP challenged the separate-but-equal doctrine by filing a class-action suit representing children in Topeka, Kansas, South Carolina, Virginia, and Delaware.

In *Brown I*, the Supreme Court declared in a unanimous decision that "separate but equal" had no place in public education, and that separate educational facilities were "inherently unequal." *Brown I* thus abolished separate educational facilities and, by inference, overturned separate but equal in all public facilities as established in *Plessy v. Ferguson.* However, the decision in *Brown (I)* was very broad and did not specify how separate educational facilities should be eradicated. The Court, therefore, decided that the parties to the case should appear during the Court's next term to determine the implementation of the decision in *Brown I.*

Following the Supreme Court's announcement of its decision in *Brown II*, it was expected that school districts would come up with desegregation plans. However, the phrase "all deliberate speed" was interpreted by southern segregationists to mean deliberately slow. School boards openly defied the Court's order and used various delay tactics and bureaucratic ploys to avoid compliance. Defiance became the rule, rather than the exception, especially in the Deep South. Violence sometimes ensued, as in 1957, when President Dwight Eisenhower had to dispatch federalized troops to Little Rock, Arkansas, to ensure the safety of the African American students who integrated Central High School. In 1959, Prince Edward County, Virginia, closed all of its public schools to prevent desegregation. Another reaction to desegregation was white flight. Many white parents sent their children to newly organized private schools, while former all-white schools became totally black.

Brown II was criticized on several grounds. The Court did not establish any definitive guidelines for desegregation; it allowed too much time for implementation; and its focus was more on compliance than on principle (Wasby, D'Amato, and Metrailer 1977, 123). According to Yale law professor Alexander Bickel, the phrase "all deliberate speed" also allowed other branches of government to get involved in the desegregation process (Wasby, D'Amato, and Metrailer 1977, 124). Furthermore, the year between *Brown I* and *Brown II* gave segregation opponents the opportunity to build coalitions.

Enforcement of the Supreme Court's decision was difficult and went through a lengthy litigation process. After many delays and failure to comply with the Court rulings, it eventually became apparent that southern states were using "all deliberate speed" to prolong segregation. In defiance, about 200 state segregation statutes were enacted. The school boards used many deliberative tactics under the pretense that they were acting within the Court's guidelines. They claimed that they were in the process of creating desegregation plans, many of which were worthless. Other tactics included integrating one grade at a time, or integrating the high school or grade school over a long period of time. Additionally, all types of elaborated selection and placement plans, designed to keep blacks out of all-white schools, were created. The state legislatures also enacted laws that penalized school boards for complying with *Brown I* and *II* or withheld their funding if they integrated schools.

The Supreme Court was becoming very impatient with the tactics and delays used by the state legislatures and school boards. In four separate cases in the early 1960s, the Court warned that the context in which it had decided *Brown II* had been altered and that there was too much deliberation. Finally, in an 8–0 decision in *Alexander v. Holmes County Board of Education*, 396 U.S. 19 (1969), the Supreme Court announced the death of the concept of "all deliberate speed," stating, "All deliberate speed for desegregation is no longer constitutionally permissible. . . . The obligation of every school district is to terminate dual school systems at once and to operate now and hereafter only unitary school systems." More than fifteen years after *Brown I* and more than fourteen years after *Brown II*, the concept of "all deliberate speed" was replaced with "at once."

See also Brown v. Board of Education; Busing; Eisenhower, Dwight David; Marshall, Thurgood; National Association for the Advancement of Colored People; *Plessy v. Ferguson*; Segregation.

FURTHER READING: Abraham, Henry J., and Barbara A. Perry, 1994, *Freedom and the Court: Civil Rights and Liberties in the United States*, 6th ed., New York: Oxford University Press; Hall, Kermit, William M. Wiecek, and Paul Finkelman, 1991, *American Legal History: Cases and*

Materials, New York: Oxford University Press; Wasby, Stephen L., Anthony A. D'Amato, and Rosemary Metrailer, 1977, *Desegregation from Brown to Alexander: An Exploration of Supreme Court Strategies* Carbondale: Southern Illinois University Press.

NAOMI ROBERTSON

Amalgamation

The term "amalgamation" refers to the elimination of differences through repeated intermarriage and interbreeding of different racial groups. Milton Gordon (1964) proposed three models of intergroup relations: assimilation, pluralism, and separatism. In the first model, Gordon described two types of assimilation, cultural and structural assimilation. Cultural assimilation takes place when two or more groups develop a common culture over time and increasingly see themselves as one group. However, the culture that develops tends to resemble more closely the culture of the dominant group. Structural assimilation is more complex. It occurs when two or more groups come to share the same social structure; that is, they share the same social institutions, organizations, and social networks. According to Gordon, when structural assimilation is complete, the various group members hold relatively equal positions in society. The most difficult type of structural assimilation is marital assimilation, which takes place when there is widespread intermarriage between the different racial and ethnic groups. When marital assimilation occurs and continues over time, the result is amalgamation. According to Gordon, amalgamation would bring about equality (or close to it) among societal members, rendering affirmative action policies and programs unnecessary.

Over the years, the percentage of white Americans who approve of interracial marriage has increased (from 4 percent in the late 1950s to 61 percent in 1991). This means, however, that almost 40 percent of whites (and about 25 percent of African Americans) do not approve of such marriages. Interestingly, this survey also found age to be a significant factor: the younger the person, the more likely he or she is to approve of interracial marriage (Gallup Organization, 1997). Although the number of interracial marriages remains relatively low, they have significantly increased since the 1960s. In 1997, there were eight times as many interracial marriages (1.26 million) as there were in 1960 (U.S. Bureau of the Census, 1998).

See also Assimilation Theory; Integration; Pluralism.

FURTHER READING: Gallup Organization, 1997, "Special Reports: Black/White Relations in the U.S," http://www.gallup.com/Special_Reports/black-white.htm; Gordon, Milton M., 1964, *Assimilation in American Life*, New York: Oxford University Press; Moran, Rachel F., 2001, *Interracial Intimacy: The Regulation of Race and Romance*, Chicago: University of Chicago Press; U.S. Bureau of the Census, 1998, "Interracial Married Couples, 1960 to Present," http://www.census.gov/population/socdemo/ms-la/tabms-3.txt.

PAULINA X. RUF

American Association for Affirmative Action

The American Association for Affirmative Action (AAAA) was founded in 1974 by a group of affirmative action officers working in higher-education institutions.

Today, the AAAA membership has grown to include professionals who manage affirmative action, equal opportunity, diversity, and other human relations programs in a variety of institutional and organizational settings. Members of the AAAA support the advancement of affirmative action, equal opportunity, and the elimination of discrimination on the basis of race, gender, ethnic background, or any other criterion that deprives people of opportunities to live and work. Membership in the AAAA is open to higher education, federal, state, and municipal governments, and public and private corporate entities. In 1999, the AAAA was named as an organization that is "making a difference" in higher education by the periodical *Black Issues in Higher Education.*

The primary purpose of the AAAA is to help members to be more successful and productive in their careers by promoting understanding and advocacy of affirmative action to enhance access and equality in employment, economic, and educational opportunities. Members of the AAAA seek to foster effective affirmative action and equal opportunity programs nationwide; establish and maintain ethical standards for affirmative action professionals; and actively serve as a liaison with federal, state, and local agencies involved with equal opportunity compliance in education and employment such as the Office for Civil Rights and the Equal Employment Opportunity Commission.

The AAAA national headquarters is located in Washington, D.C. The AAAA has a network of professionals working across the nation. Each of the ten regional directors is elected from the membership in the states and territories in the region and represents the region on the Board of Directors. The director is a member volunteer elected by the membership and serves a term of two years. Within each region, state coordinators are responsible for promoting the effectiveness of the association at the regional and state levels.

The organization's goals are realized through professional development activities designed to help equal employment opportunity/affirmative action (EEO/AA) practitioners be more successful and productive in their careers. The AAAA provides network opportunities with EEO/AA professionals for information, advice, and support. National and regional conferences bring together nationally acclaimed experts in EEO/AA practices, human resources, legal issues, and professional development. These programs provide a foundation in the basics for new EEO/AA staff or management and continuing education for seasoned professionals. Additionally, regional AAAA affiliates hold meetings and seminars that provide many opportunities for professional development, continuing education, and networking. A network made up of volunteer leadership actively communicates AAAA' positions on pending legislation and regulatory issues to Congress and governmental agencies. The AAAA Board of Directors, staff, and legislative committee monitor all congressional action that could affect equal opportunity, affirmative action, and diversity issues.

The AAAA publishes a newsletter, *AAAA News*, and a *Legislative Alert* bulletin covering developments in the field. Training institutes and certification in EEO/AA program management are held four times throughout the year. The training institutes offer seminars on EEO and affirmative action law, complaint processing, counseling and resolution, affirmative action plan development, workplace mediation methods, analyzing the Americans with Disabilities Act (ADA), harassment and sexual harassment, affirmative action and emerging concepts in diversity, and negotiation principles.

The AAAA Educational Foundation received its 501(c)(3) tax-exempt status on August 18, 1997, to pursue its mission to provide resources for research and development initiatives that promote and enhance access and equity in employment, economic, and educational opportunity. The foundation's current goals are to secure enough support for the AAAA Professional Development and Training Institute (PDTI) to become financially self-sufficient and eventually obtain university status, and to garner sponsorships for the AAAA annual conferences. A primary goal of the foundation is to serve as a source for funded research and studies on the impact and significance of affirmative action, equal opportunity, and social justice in the United States.

See also Affirmative Action Plan/Program; Department of Justice; Equal Employment Opportunity Commission; Persons with Disabilities and Affirmative Action.

FURTHER READING: American Association for Affirmative Action, 2003, web site: http://www.affirmativeaction.org; Richardson, Susan, 1997, "Equal Opportunity Officers Seek Ways to Defend against Attacks on Affirmative Action," *Black Issues in Higher Education* 14, no. 6 (May 15): 26–28.

PAULETTE PATTERSON DILWORTH

American Association of University Professors

The American Association of University Professors (AAUP) was formed in 1915 at Johns Hopkins University as a means to ensure academic freedom for faculty members after the 1900 firing of Edward Ross from Stanford University. Ross's firing came as a result of his views on immigrant labor and railroad monopolies, which were unpopular with Mrs. Leland Stanford, a benefactor of the school. AAUP polices and safeguards the practice of academic freedom and has also become involved in issues ranging from affirmative action to faculty salaries and benefits. The AAUP often censures a college or university that engages in discrimination or reverse discrimination. The AAUP often supports affirmative action in cases in the federal court system by filing amicus curiae (friend-of-the-court) briefs with the court. AAUP filed a brief in support of affirmative action in the seminal Supreme Court case *Regents of the University of California v. Bakke,* 438 U.S. 265 (1978). AAUP also filed a brief in support of affirmative action in the latest affirmative action cases to reach the Supreme Court, *Grutter v. Bollinger,* 123 S. Ct. 2325, 2003 U.S. LEXIS 4800 (2003), and *Gratz v. Bollinger,* 123 S. Ct. 2411, 2003 U.S. LEXIS 4801 (2003). According to an AAUP media release (February 13, 2003), the AAUP's "support for affirmative action stems from the well-documented educational benefits of racial diversity in higher education, and from the necessity of preserving educators' academic freedom to determine criteria for student admissions."

With more than 45,000 members at more than 500 campuses, the AAUP has made a continued effort to put affirmative action at the forefront of academic debate. Not only is AAUP concerned with the affirmative action issues related to faculty, librarians, and academic professionals, but also with issues related to students. The stated goal of the AAUP is to ensure that college and university environments are diverse with respect to race, gender, religion, and national origin. The AAUP also publishes its own magazine, *Academe*, which often carries articles covering affirmative action–related topics. On its web site, the AAUP offers an array of archived articles dealing with affirmative action in higher education.

The efforts of the AAUP are centered on cases involving student recruitment, admissions and financial aid, desegregation, federal programs at universities, faculty employment, and, finally, elementary and secondary education. The AAUP may assist in some of these cases directly or may supply amicus curiae briefs on behalf of its membership. The AAUP affords the academic community the assurance that it will speak on behalf of diversity, maintain academic due process and academic freedom, and offer debate on issues of discrimination.

See also Education and Affirmative Action; *Gratz v. Bollinger/Grutter v. Bollinger; Regents of the University of California v. Bakke.*

FURTHER READING: American Association of University Professors, web site: http://www.aaup.org.

SUSAN F. BRINKLEY

American Bar Association

The American Bar Association (ABA) is responsible for regulating the professional, educational, and administrative activities of the legal community, including law firms, law schools, federal and state courts, and other law-creating agencies. The ABA has been described as the nation's largest lawyers' interest group. The ABA is responsible for promoting the rule of law in the United States (and within the legal profession and the courts), but also acts as a very powerful lobbying organization. The ABA also publishes a wide array of information (in its printed journals and on its web site) on the topic of affirmative action. Historically, the ABA offered materials on the affirmative action debate, but did not take a position. However, in 1995, the ABA issued its first formal policy supporting affirmative action. Specifically, in 1995, the ABA endorsed "legal remedies and voluntary actions that take into account . . . race, national origin or gender to eliminate or prevent discrimination."

The ABA was founded on August 21, 1878, in Saratoga Springs, New York, by only 100 lawyers. At that time, lawyers were generally sole practitioners who had no national code of ethics; thus the thought was that the legal profession needed a national organization to serve as a forum for discussion of the increasingly complex issues involved in legal practice. The result was the ABA. Today, the ABA boasts approximately 400,000 members, roughly one-half of the practicing lawyers in the United States. Membership in the ABA is open to any lawyer who is licensed in one of the fifty state jurisdictions and in "good standing." Associate memberships are available for nonlawyers. The ABA lobbies on behalf of its members and the legal profession as a whole.

As a regulating and philosophical body for the legal profession, the ABA has several major goals. These include promoting the rule of law in the United States, spearheading efforts to improve the legal profession, the justice system, and laws in the United States, representing the legal profession's interests, providing benefits to its members, offering educational services, and so on. In regard to affirmative action, one of the ABA's chief goals is "to promote full and equal participation in the legal profession by minorities and women." Prior to 1995, the ABA did not take a position on affirmative action and merely offered its members information on the debate through its publications and meetings. However, in 1995, for the first time, the ABA went on record as being in favor of affirmative action in the United States. In the words of the first female president of the ABA, Roberta Cooper Ramo, "Affirmative action is about recognizing that we have had in this country a history of racism and sexism that is not going to be overcome just by wishing it away" (Jet 1995, 39). Hence since 1995, the ABA has positioned itself as a national advocacy organization for equal opportunity and support for affirmative action, both internally and externally.

See also Minority Professionals and Affirmative Action.

FURTHER READING: American Bar Association, web site: http://www.abanet.org; American Bar Association, 1979, *Centennial: A Century of Service,* Chicago: ABA; "American Bar Association Backs Affirmative Action," *Jet* 88, no. 16 (August 28): 39.

THOMAS A. ADAMICH

American Civil Liberties Union

The American Civil Liberties Union (ACLU) is a private, volunteer, nonprofit, and national organization of decentralized independent affiliates including staff administrators and staff and affiliate attorneys that supports and defends affirmative action programs on the basis that they are necessary to provide equality of political, economic, and social results to groups that had been denied equal political, economic, and social rights through historical undemocratic governmental action. The ACLU's stated mission is to fight against undemocratic governmental action by advocating the protection and expansion of civil rights and liberties in conjunction with the U.S. Constitution's Bill of Rights through courtroom advocacy, legislative lobbying, and community activism.

The ACLU was created on January 19, 1920, to fight against suffocating World War I–era government-imposed and Supreme Court–sanctioned restrictions on First Amendment freedom of speech. The federal government had passed wartime and peacetime laws including the Espionage Act (1917) and its amendments, called the Alien and Sedition Act (1918), to restrict freedoms of speech, assembly, and the press by prosecuting, jailing, and occasionally deporting anyone who spoke or acted against the government or its war effort. After the war, the federal government utilized similar restrictions against labor, civil rights, and other progressive movements to quash civil unrest. The ACLU challenged these and other laws designed to restrict individual freedoms through legislative lobbying, community direct action, and direct or amicus (friend-of-the-court) legal action on behalf of individual clients through its staff and affiliate attorneys.

Throughout its history, the ACLU has wavered between its core mission to protect individual and group means of democratic action provided by the Bill of Rights regardless of their ends and a support of progressive causes in the interest of "good" social outcomes. Thus, while the ACLU has provided legal assistance to very divergent and even antagonistic groups, including the National Association for the Advancement of Colored People (NAACP) in its fight against racial segregation and the Ku Klux Klan (KKK) in efforts to gather and speak, its national platform contains strong support for affirmative action based on its purported outcomes. This mission and policy quagmire and the ACLU's voluntary, independent, and diverse nature have often produced dramatic internal struggles, contradictions, splits, and defections into and out of the organization.

See also Bill of Rights; First Amendment; Ku Klux Klan; National Association for the Advancement of Colored People; Segregation.

FURTHER READING: American Civil Liberties Union, 2000, *ACLU Position Paper: Affirmative Action*, fall, http://www.aclu.org; Walker, Samuel, 1990, *In Defense of American Liberties: A History of the ACLU*, New York: Oxford University Press.

MARK J. SENEDIAK

American Civil Rights Institute

The American Civil Rights Institute (ACRI) is a national, nonprofit, civil rights organization dedicated to combating the use of affirmative action. The ACRI was founded by noted anti–affirmative action activist Ward Connerly, who formed the ACRI with the goal of "educating the public about the need to move beyond racial and gender preferences." The ACRI is located in Sacramento, California, and has had a major role in combating affirmative action in California, Texas, and Florida. The ACRI also has been critical in the implementation of California's Proposition 209, a state ballot initiative that ended the use of racial and gender preferences in higher education and contracting in California. The ACRI also assists organizations in other states in battling what the ACRI perceives as unfair affirmative action programs. The ACRI submitted an amicus curiae (friend-of-the-court) brief to the Supreme Court in the latest affirmative action cases to reach the high Court, *Grutter v. Bollinger*, 123 S. Ct. 2325, 2003 U.S. LEXIS 4800 (2003), and *Gratz v. Bollinger*, 123 S. Ct. 2411, 2003 U.S. LEXIS 4801 (2003). The ACRI recommended in its brief to the Court that the Court grant certiorari (i.e., review of the case) in the case and reject race-based affirmative action as being unconstitutional under the Fourteenth Amendment.

On its web site, the ACRI delineates its goals as threefold: "assisting organizations in other states with their efforts to educate the public about racial and gender preferences, assisting federal representatives with public education on the issue, and monitoring implementation and legal action on California's Proposition 209." The ACRI web site also contains an array of resources, links, and articles, all largely geared toward the abolition of affirmative action. The ACRI is also the parent organization and founder of the American Civil Rights Coalition, a subsidiary organization to the ACRI.

See also Connerly, Ward; Fourteenth Amendment; *Gratz v. Bollinger/Grutter v. Bollinger*; Proposition 209.

FURTHER READING: ACRI, web site: http://www.acri.org; Schmidt, Peter, 2003, "Behind the Fight over Race-Conscious Admissions: Advocacy Groups—Working Together—Helped Shape the Legal and Political Debate," *Chronicle of Higher Education*, April 4, A22.

JAMES A. BECKMAN

American Civil War

The American Civil War was a pivotal event in race relations in the United States. The Reconstruction legislative initiatives that would follow in the aftermath of the Civil War would serve as the historical precedent for modern affirmative action programs. In his separate opinion in *Regents of the University of California v. Bakke*, 438 U.S. 265 (1978), Thurgood Marshall argued that the United States implemented "several affirmative action programs" (for example, the Freedmen's Bureau) in 1865 and the subsequent years following the Civil War. During this period, many different types of legislation (largely formulated by Northern politicians and abolitionists during the Civil War) sought to make black citizens the "special favorite of the laws" (as described by a Supreme Court justice in the *Civil Rights Cases*, 109 U.S. 3 [1883]). The various pieces of Reconstruction legislation (which began during the Civil War) sought to protect newly freed black slaves and ensure some semblance of equality and opportunity for advancement. Thus Thurgood Marshall and others have argued that the first true antecedents to modern affirmative action are those programs that were formulated during the Civil War and Reconstruction that gave preferences and benefits exclusively to black citizens as a means of achieving equality. Therefore, a basic understanding of the American Civil War and prevailing race relations is helpful in fully understanding the history of affirmative action in America.

At the start of the Civil War in 1861, the majority of Northern whites had little consideration for blacks and found the continuation of slavery acceptable. Innate to the American conscience was a conviction of white superiority that dominated people's minds at the very moment when they were starting to take a puzzling and painful road that would lead to equality. Many hoped that the South's peculiar institution would continue so that free blacks would not flood to the North and take away jobs and farms. Even President Abraham Lincoln, the Great Emancipator, did not actively seek an end to slavery during the earlier years of his presidency (and before). Instead, he proposed a gradual emancipation of slaves with compensation to their owners and favored colonizing freed slaves to other parts of the world. He once told a Southern friend that there was only one difference between Northerners and Southerners: "We think slavery is wrong and ought to be restricted; you think it is right and ought to be extended. That's the only difference" (Catton, 6). The abolitionists who sought manumission of the blacks were a vocal minority and were considered radicals.

Slavery was not a simple institution. Approximately 4 million blacks were held in bondage, most of them as field hands. They had no liberties, and whatever they received in the way of basic human necessities depended entirely upon their owner's benevolence or neglect. The slavery system was representative of a paternalistic race relations system. The slaves, as a whole, were generally perceived as very peaceful and remained so quiet in the antebellum years throughout much of the South that many people in both sections of the country assumed that they were content with their lot. Free blacks in the North were not slaves, but were very definitely below second-class citizenry. They had few rights, practically no privileges, and no social standing. In general, they were limited to the poorest jobs, the lowest wages, and the worst housing. In some cases, it can be argued that

$100 REWARD!

RANAWAY

From the undersigned, living on Current River, about twelve miles above Doniphan, in Ripley County, Mo., on 2nd of March, 1860, A NEGRO MAN, about 30 years old, weighs about 160 pounds; high forehead, with a scar on it; had on brown pants and coat very much worn, and an old black wool hat; shoes size No. 11.

The above reward will be given to any person who may apprehend this said negro out of the State; and fifty dollars if apprehended in this State outside of Ripley county, or $25 if taken in Ripley county.

APOS TUCKER.

Advisement dated 1860 announcing a reward for the apprehension of a runaway slave. The enforcement of fugitive slave laws constituted a significant source of friction between Northern and Southern states leading up to the Civil War. Courtesy of Library of Congress.

with the exception of not having their personal freedom, some of the slaves in the South might have been better off than some of the free Northern blacks.

The issues of emancipation and military service were intertwined from the onset of the Civil War. News from Fort Sumter, South Carolina, set off a rush by free black men and many fugitive slaves to enlist in the U.S. military. They were turned away, however, because federal law barred Negroes from bearing arms for the U.S. Army, although blacks had served in previous wars. Further, Lincoln, in attempting to preserve the Union, believed that all states were still under the Constitution, which clearly stated that fugitive slaves should be returned to their masters. Eventually the administration and the army came to realize that the slave workforce was a linchpin in the Southern economy, and since slaves were considered property, the army could accept them as captured war material (i.e., contraband). This resulted in large numbers of ex-slaves becoming associated with the army, and the North had to set up large camps to accommodate them. These were typically overcrowded and poorly managed, and malnutrition and disease were very common. There were cases where after a few weeks in such camps, ex-slaves asked if they could be returned to their old masters. When Union generals issued proclamations that emancipated slaves in their respective military regions and permitted them to enlist, their superiors sternly revoked their orders. However, by mid-1862, with the increasing number of contrabands, the reduced number of volunteers, and the pressing personnel needs of the army, the government began reconsidering the ban.

That was an election year, and as they had done in every previous election involving the Republican Party, Northern Democrats exploited the race issue. They campaigned that the black Republican "party of fanaticism" intended to free "two or three million semi-savages" to "overrun the North and enter into competition with the white laboring masses" and mix with "their sons and daughters." With that sort of rhetoric from their leaders, it was not surprising that some white workingmen took their prejudices into the streets, and antiblack riots broke out in several cities. Some of the worst violence occurred in Cincinnati, where the replacement of striking Irish dockworkers by Negroes set off a wave of attacks on black neighborhoods. In Brooklyn, a mob of Irish Americans tried to burn down a tobacco factory where two dozen black women and children were working. Northern race relations soured the following year, with the worst riots recorded during the Civil War occurring in New York City. In response to the start of conscription, a mob destroyed the draft office, set fires, and lynched as many blacks as they could capture. In the course of a week of mob rule, about 1,000 were killed or wounded.

Despite the turmoil in the North, the Lincoln administration was making significant progress in black civil rights. In 1862, Lincoln issued the Emancipation Proclamation, which declared all slaves in areas rebelling against the United States to be free, effective January 1, 1863. While this executive wartime order officially left approximately 1 million slaves enslaved in Union territory, the proclamation led the way to utilizing black troops in the Union army. Recruitment swelled with the encouragement of such leaders as Frederick Douglass, who proclaimed that by becoming soldiers, blacks would ensure eventual citizenship.

In addition to the perils of war faced by all soldiers, blacks faced additional problems stemming from discriminatory practices within the U.S. military. Segregated units were formed with black enlisted men and until 1865 were commanded solely by white officers. Initially there was a two-tier pay scale. Blacks were paid $10 per month, from which $3 was automatically deducted for clothing, resulting in a net pay of $7. In contrast, white soldiers received $13 per month, from which no clothing allowance was drawn. Blacks were often provided inferior arms, supplies, and medical care. Further, they were usually relegated to garrison or, worse, fatigue duty to relieve white soldiers of hard work. They were often considered a sort of labor gang that could repair roads, dig trenches, and pull wagons out of swamps, but they were not really to be counted on as soldiers. One of the first battles these troops had to fight was for a chance to prove themselves in combat. Fortunately, some units did see combat service and often acquitted themselves well. An early example that occurred in July 1863 was memorably dramatized in the film *Glory*, in which the Fifty-Fourth Massachusetts Volunteer Colored Regiment lost two-thirds of its officers and half of its troops assaulting Fort Wagner, South Carolina.

As the Native Americans before them had learned, blacks had unique problems with a loss on the battlefield. The Confederate forces proved brutal in their treatment of Union prisoners of war and even more so to black soldiers. Most that were captured were either executed or sold as slaves. In perhaps the most heinous known example of abuse, in 1864 Confederates under General Nathan Bedford Forrest overtly murdered black Union soldiers captured at Fort Pillow, Tennessee.

Not until June 1864 did Congress grant equal pay to the U.S. Colored Troops and make the action retroactive. Soon thereafter, black soldiers began to receive the same rations, supplies, arms, and medical care as their white counterparts. Eventually the Union troops came to accept the need to end slavery in the undivided nation. This was best exemplified when Lincoln received almost 80 percent of the soldier vote during reelection on a platform that pledged a constitutional amendment to abolish slavery. Black soldiers were also grudgingly accepted within the ranks of the army. The typical attitude of most white soldiers can be reflected in that of Union general Godfrey Weitzel. In 1863, he had vigorously objected when he was placed in command of recently raised black regiments. He did not believe in black troops and said that he could not handle them and that he did not want them. Two years later, after Grant broke Lee's lines, compelling the Confederate army to retreat from their capital, General Weitzel led the first Union troops into Richmond. Apparently the general found that he could handle black troops after all, since more than half of them were black regiments. All told, by the end of the Civil War, approximately 179,000 black men served as soldiers (10 percent of the Union army), and another 19,000 served in the navy. Nearly 40,000 of these died during the war, 30,000 from infection or disease often attributed to substandard medical care.

In the final year of the Civil War, President Lincoln, Congress, and many Northern states began to enact legislation to dissolve the pattern of third-class citizenship for Northern Negroes. Examples included the admission of black witnesses to federal courts; repeal of a law that barred them from carrying mail; prohibition of segregation on streetcars in the District of Columbia; repeal of black laws in several Northern states that had imposed certain kinds of discrimination against Negroes or barred their entry into the state; and steps to submit referenda to the voters of several states to grant the ballot to blacks. Further, in 1864, blacks were first allowed in congressional galleries, and in 1865, they were admitted to White House functions.

Effectively, the Civil War had to result in the end of human bondage. A permanent alteration in the colored man's status would blossom out of the fact that blacks had played a crucial role in the Northern victory. Any man who had worn the country's uniform and faced death in its service could not ultimately be anything less than a full-fledged citizen, and it was not possible to make citizens out of some blacks without making citizens out of all. Thus, shortly after the conclusion of hostilities in 1865, the Thirteenth Amendment, which guaranteed all blacks their freedom, was ratified. Following the Civil War, during the Reconstruction period of 1865–1877, a series of proactive legislation was put forward on a variety of subjects to help and advance the cause of newly freed black citizens, including the Freedmen's Bureau, the Fourteenth and Fifteenth Amendments, the Civil Rights Acts of 1866, 1870, and 1875, the formation of new schools of learning for black students, laws against the Ku Klux Kan, and so on. While slavery was no longer a material issue, the full garnering of black civil rights would continue for many more generations.

See also Abolitionists; Civil Rights Act of 1866; Civil Rights Act of 1875; Civil War (Reconstruction) Amendments and Civil Rights Acts; Douglass, Frederick; Fifteenth Amendment; Fourteenth Amendment; Freedmen's Bureau; Ku Klux Klan; Marshall, Thurgood; Paternalistic Race Relations Theory; *Regents of the University of California v. Bakke*; Slavery; Thirteenth Amendment.

FURTHER READING: Catton, Bruce, 1960, *The Civil War*, New York: Fairfax Press; Catton, Bruce, 1981, *Reflections on the Civil War*, Garden City, NY: Doubleday; McPherson, James M., 1988, *Battle Cry of Freedom*, New York: Oxford University Press; McPherson, James M., 1997, *For Cause and Comrades: Why Men Fought in the Civil War*, New York: Oxford University Press; Rubio, Philip F., 2001, *A History of Affirmative Action, 1619–2000*, Jackson: University Press of Mississippi; Winnick, Jay, 2002, *April 1865: The Month That Saved America*, New York: HarperCollins.

PETER L. PLATTEBORZE

American Convention on Human Rights

The American Convention on Human Rights is the principal inter-American human rights treaty. Adopted by members of the Organization of American States

(OAS) and opened for signature on November 22, 1969, the treaty went into force when the requisite eleventh country ratified it on July 18, 1978. By the 1990s, twenty-five states, including every Spanish-speaking country in the hemisphere except Cuba, had ratified the convention. Notably, although the United States signed the treaty in 1977, it has not been ratified by the U.S. Senate. The convention includes a long list of guaranteed civil and political rights and formally establishes the Inter-American Commission on Human Rights and the Inter-American Court of Human Rights. Advocates argue that the convention supports the idea of affirmative action in its basic guarantees of equality and the right to equal protection, in specific guarantees of rights such as free movement and residence, and in the idea of a right to remedy injustices. The convention's impact has been limited by the U.S. refusal to ratify, by related questions of legal jurisdiction, and by the issue of protecting individual versus group rights.

In its enumeration of rights, the convention is patterned on the European Convention for the Protection of Human Rights and Fundamental Freedoms and on the United Nations International Covenant on Civil and Political Rights, but it goes beyond these documents on such issues as rights to humane treatment and to participation in government. Chapter VII of the convention formalizes the Inter-American Commission on Human Rights, which first began functioning in 1960. The commission is composed of seven members nominated from any OAS state, whether or not that state has ratified the convention. The commission primarily prepares country reports on human rights conditions and examines individual petitions. Chapter VIII of the convention establishes an independent Court of Human Rights to which ratifying states can optionally give binding jurisdiction. The court has not yet become a major force, since few states have granted the binding jurisdiction and the commission has not referred many cases to the court.

In general, some advocates of affirmative action fear that it is too often seen as a form of preferential treatment rather than a way of providing guaranteed equal rights to all citizens. They therefore feel that the convention and other human rights documents should be seen as key documents justifying affirmative action policies. For example, U.S. Supreme Court justice Ruth Bader Ginsburg has argued that under human rights documents, "the discrepancies in racial well-being in the United States . . . demand affirmative government action." Under Article I of the convention, states "undertake to respect the rights and freedoms recognized herein and to ensure to all persons subject to their jurisdiction the free and full exercise of those rights and freedoms without any discrimination for reasons of race, color, sex, language, religion, political or other opinion, national or social origin, economic status, birth, or any other social condition." This statement is much more sweeping and inclusive of more groups than most existing U.S. civil rights laws. Advocates also point to specific enumerated rights as justifying affirmative action in such areas as housing. The convention is, however, more limited in this regard than some other documents such as the United Nations Universal Declaration of Human Rights, because the convention focuses on civil and political rights and not on social and economic rights, such as rights to employment or education. Finally, the convention provides for legal action to remedy existing discrimination.

The impact of the convention on affirmative action policies is greatly limited by the lack of U.S. ratification. President Jimmy Carter signed the convention in

1977, and it was in part due to international lobbying that the convention received the necessary ratifications to go into effect. Carter submitted the convention to the Senate along with three other human rights treaties, but conservative Republican opposition and international events such as the Soviet invasion of Afghanistan prevented any Senate action. In 1991, the Bush administration revived efforts to ratify the treaties, but while the Senate did eventually support the United Nations International Covenant on Civil and Political Rights, on which parts of the convention are based, the American Convention remains unratified.

U.S. opposition stems in part from specific language on a right to life that could affect abortion cases and on limits for the death penalty. More significant are the constitutional objections that are raised against many human rights treaties. The U.S. Constitution is the highest law in the land, so the validity of treaty guarantees that go beyond constitutional guarantees is questionable. Also, the Constitution grants Congress the exclusive power to consider and create all laws, so treaties that would require the United States to change laws are problematic. Usually, the United States has avoided these constitutional issues by proposing reservations to human rights treaties, but so far this tactic has not led to convention ratification. Another difficulty in employing the convention in support of affirmative action is the question of group versus individual rights. In some countries, such as Canada, minority groups such as native populations have been granted extensive group rights, but in the United States, the legal system is primarily based on individual rights. The convention speaks of protecting "persons" from discrimination, but it is disputed whether this justifies special programs for entire groups and classes of citizens.

See also Bush, George Herbert Walker; Carter, James "Jimmy" Earl, Jr.; European Human Rights Convention; European Union and Affirmative Action; Ginsburg, Ruth Bader; Housing.

FURTHER READING: Cerna, Christina, 2000, "The United States and the American Convention on Human Rights," in *The United States and Human Rights: Looking Inward and Outward*, edited by David P. Forsythe, 94–109, Lincoln: University of Nebraska Press; Ginsburg, Ruth Bader, 2000, "A Considered Opinion: Affirmative Action as an International Human Rights Dialogue," *Human Rights: Journal of the Section of Individual Rights and Responsibilities* 27:3–4; Harris, David J., and Stephen Livingstone, 1998, *The Inter-American System of Human Rights*, Oxford: Clarendon Press; Kly, Y.N., 1995, "Human Rights, American National Minorities, and Affirmative Action," *Black Scholar* 25:61–68.

JOHN W. DIETRICH

American Indian

See Indian; Native Americans.

American Jewish Committee

The American Jewish Committee (AJC), formed in 1906 "to prevent the infraction of the civil and religious rights of the Jews, in any part of the world," developed from an elite-run German American Jewish organization into a broader and more representative body in the post–World War II years. It emphasized dialogue and education as the preferred means of resolving intergroup disputes and emerged in the early 1960s as a proponent of affirmative action programs. The American Jewish Committee joined almost every major national Jewish organization in its opposition to quota-based affirmative action programs in the late 1960s and 1970s. In 2002, the American Jewish Committee argued "that specific problems in the implementation of affirmative action need to be rectified," but still held that "affirmative action will remain necessary so long as discrimination continues to plague our society" (Dollinger 2000, 12).

Between 1906 and the end of World War II, the American Jewish Committee worked primarily for the protection of Jews abroad and within the United States. Until the congressional restriction acts of the 1920s all but eliminated Jewish immigration to the United States, the American Jewish Committee took a leading role in the acculturation of eastern European Jewish immigrants. During the Great Depression of the 1930s, the American Jewish Committee stepped up its focus on intergroup relations in an attempt to combat anti-Semitic discrimination.

In the postwar years, the American Jewish Committee joined other national Jewish organizations in support of the civil rights movement. When the U.S. Supreme Court handed down its famed decision in *Brown v. Board of Education* (Brown I), 347 U.S. 483 (1954), the AJC boasted, "Not only were we active, along with our organizations, in the filing of an amicus brief, but we contributed materially to the social theory upon which the desegregation decision was based" (Dollinger, 182). AJC leaders organized national educational campaigns, developed a curriculum for use in public schools, and enlisted the support of political leaders to help spread their message of tolerance and inclusion.

When the federal government first instituted affirmative action programs, the American Jewish Committee offered its full support, praising the practice of giving "special assistance to special categories of people on whom society has enforced hardship and injustice" (Dollinger, 204). Sympathetic to the sociological research undergirding Lyndon Johnson's approach to the Great Society, the American Jewish Committee recognized the pervasive effects of racism and pressed for government and private-sector programs to ameliorate social inequities. At a time when many white ethnics retreated from civil rights activism and opposed all forms of affirmative action, the AJC continued to back a strong federal civil rights agenda.

Growing opposition to liberal Democratic civil rights causes in the mid- to late 1960s exacted a toll on the organized Jewish community. The American Jewish Committee opposed the use of race-based quotas in affirmative action programs. In a 1970 position paper, the American Jewish Committee noted that it "continues to oppose the creation of a system of quotas for any group including the disadvantaged in education, employment or any other area of American life" (Dollinger, 207). It affirmed that "our society is capable of providing ample educational and employment opportunities for all its people thus eliminating the need for benefiting one group at the expense of another or resorting to shortcut and dangerous solutions like quotas" (Dollinger, 207). With this, the American Jewish Committee joined almost all national Jewish organizations in opposition to quotas. The use of quotas, it maintained, threatened to limit the upward mobility of American Jews whose social achievements far outpaced their proportional representation in the nation. The split between Jewish organizations such as the American Jewish Committee and some black activists on the quota issue weakened historic ties between the two communities and revealed fundamental differences in each group's experience of American life.

The American Jewish Committee's opposition to quota-based affirmative action programs crystallized in the case *DeFunis v. Odegaard,* 416 U.S. 312 (1974). Decided four years before the more famous case *Regents of the University of California v. Bakke,* 438 U.S. 265 (1978), *DeFunis* split the organized American Jewish community, with the American Jewish Committee embracing the plaintiff, a white male applicant to the University of Washington Law School with a 3.71 grade point average who was rejected from the same class that counted minority applicants with lower test scores and grade point averages.

Yet the American Jewish Committee's opposition to the University of Washington's affirmative action program proved qualified, at best. During a vote of the American Jewish Committee's national legal committee, eighteen members sided with DeFunis, three backed the University of Washington's position, and five thought it best to stay "out of it altogether." At the local Seattle chapter, members voted by a slim majority not to take any side at all. "Our Seattle people," an American Jewish Committee representative explained, "had mixed feelings about the relative equities of the case, as well as concern over possible adverse community relations consequences in the event of AJC involvement in it." "In the final analysis," he held, "individual merit, measured as accurately and objectively as humanly possible, must be the crucial determinant in educational as well as in employment opportunity, rather than artificially imposed proportional representation based on racial or ethnic extraction. As we have already learned through painful experience, a double-standard society will not work for very long" (Dollinger, 210). The *DeFunis* case ended without a ruling since the plaintiff, admitted to the law school while the case went to trial, had already started his third and final year by the time the U.S. Supreme Court agreed to hear it.

In the years since the *DeFunis* case, the American Jewish Committee has maintained its support of affirmative action programs and its opposition to quotas. It filed an amicus brief in the *Bakke* case, siding with the white plaintiff in a case that polarized the nation's liberal civil rights community. The American Jewish Committee joined the American Jewish Congress and the Anti-Defamation League in a controversial decision to oppose the quota-based affirmative action program at the University of California at Davis Medical School. Since the *Bakke* case, the American Jewish Committee's national organizational focus has moved into other directions as school vouchers, religious freedom, anti-Semitism in the United States and abroad, and concerns over terrorism have eclipsed the civil rights movement and affirmative action on the American Jewish Committee's public policy agenda.

See also American Jewish Congress; Anti-Defamation League; Anti-Semitism, Jews, and Affirmative Action; Census Classifications, Ethnic and Racial; Civil Rights Act of 1964; Civil Rights Movement; Color-Blind Constitution; *DeFunis v. Odegaard;* Equal Protection Clause; Johnson, Lyndon Baines; Quotas; Race-Based Affirmative Action; *Regents of the University of California v. Bakke*; Reverse Discrimination.

FURTHER READING: Cohen, Naomi W., 1972, *Not Free to Desist: The American Jewish Committee, 1906–1966,* Philadelphia: Jewish Publication Society; Dollinger, Marc, 2000, *Quest for Inclusion: Jews and Liberalism in Modern America,* Princeton, NJ: Princeton University Press;

Friedman, Murray, 1995, *What Went Wrong? The Creation and Collapse of the Black-Jewish Alliance*, New York: Free Press; Fuchs, Lawrence H., 1986, *When to Count by Race: Affirmative Action, Quotas, and Equal Opportunity*, New York: American Jewish Committee; Svonkin, Stuart, 1997, *Jews against Prejudice: American Jews and the Fight for Civil Liberties*, New York: Columbia University Press.

MARC DOLLINGER

American Jewish Congress

The American Jewish Congress, created in 1916, emerged in the post–World War II years as a leading national Jewish organizational voice for social justice, civil rights, and affirmative action. In 1945, it created a Commission on Law and Social Action, charged with directing the group's ambitious civil rights program. As early as 1958, the American Jewish Congress invited Dr. Martin Luther King Jr. to serve as the keynote speaker for its annual convention. When President Lyndon Johnson called for affirmative action programs as part of his Great Society reforms, the American Jewish Congress offered its full support. By 1972, the American Jewish Congress, along with most of the organized Jewish community, reevaluated its policy decisions when some called for quota-based affirmative action programs. The American Jewish Congress has remained committed to non-quota-based affirmative action programs in the contemporary period, filing an amicus brief against California's Proposition 209, a 1996 ballot initiative that sought to end affirmative action programs in the Golden State.

In the years prior to John F. Kennedy's 1961 use of the term "affirmative action" in federal policy, the American Jewish Congress fought for enactment of fair employment practices legislation, creation and enforcement of civil rights laws, and acknowledgment of racism as a threat to all Americans. American Jewish Congress leaders supported calls for racial equality in the South during the 1950s, harnessing the strength of its Commission on Law and Social Action to keep civil rights cases in the courts and in the public eye.

The American Jewish Congress offered its full and complete support for affirmative action programs in both the Kennedy and Johnson administrations. For American Jewish Congress officials, affirmative action emerged as the logical consequence of racial inequality and a necessary remedy to ensure equal opportunity for all Americans. At a time when many white ethnics bolted to the Republican Party as a sign of their opposition to a new civil rights agenda, Jewish supporters of the American Jewish Congress stayed within the Democratic fold and remained committed to affirmative action.

The American Jewish Congress continued its commitment to affirmative action when the civil rights movement moved north, challenging the nation's urban dwellers to acknowledge the effects of racism in their own backyard. In a May 1968 statement, the American Jewish Congress positioned itself in the forefront of white liberal civil rights groups when it asserted that "the white community as a whole does not yet understand that the urban crisis and the resulting growth in racial tensions, crime, and violence will continue until proper housing, schools, training, and jobs are available for all" (Dollinger 2000, 203). American Jewish Congress officials followed the statement with an ambitious social reform program committed to affirmative action programs as a necessary remedy for past historical injustices.

The American Jewish Congress's first opposition to affirmative action programs emerged when some called for the establishment of quotas. The advent of quotas recalled an earlier era in U.S. history when American Jews faced anti-Semitic restrictions from universities, employers, and residential communities that imposed strict limits on the number of Jews they would permit. The idea of imposing collectivist definitions of need scared a Jewish community whose liberal philosophy always stressed individual rights and meritocratic advance.

Despite the American Jewish Congress's reputation as the most progressive of the major national Jewish organizations, it urged its constituents to "unequivocally oppose all quotas, with no exceptions." David Petegorsky, the executive director of the American Jewish Congress, called the practice of restrictive admissions both "indefensible and anti-democratic." Naomi Levine, the executive director designate in 1972, lamented that "what started out as a vague concept of 'affirmative action' in a presidential executive order limited to federal contractors has now been by administrative rulings defined as a responsibility to overcome 'the underutilization of minority groups in the workforce through goals, percentage hiring, and timetables' whether prior discrimination has or has not been established and whether the employer is or is not a federal contractor" (Dollinger, 208). Levine did not oppose the use of hiring goals unless they degenerated into strict quotas, but she did fear that government policy makers would continue to lead affirmative action programs down the path to quotas, preferential treatment, and reverse discrimination.

As an alternative, Levine and the American Jewish Congress developed a detailed affirmative action plan of their own, meant to protect both the needs of discriminated-against minorities and the rights of the majority. Their plan included employment directives encouraging "(a) massive government manpower training programs; (b) intensified efforts to open unions and union training programs; (c) career ladders for training in skills and technical occupations; (d) vigorous enforcement of anti-discrimination laws; (e) the use of examination and other selection processes which are free of cultural bias, and which are job-related and of predictive validity; (f) intensive recruitment of qualified members of minority groups; and (g) the use of sensitivity and attitudinal tests and criteria for those jobs dealing largely with minority groups." Education directives "urged the expansion of (a) college open enrollment programs, with full funding, which broaden educational opportunities for all persons, including racial minorities; (b) remedial programs such as SEEK and college discovery; (c) vigorous recruitment efforts to find qualified minority group members, including special efforts to recruit in colleges and high schools attended predominantly by minority group members; (d) flexible admission criteria (not including quotas or percentage goals) that would include—in addition to objective standards—relevant factors such as community service and qualifications that would help identify potentially successful students from disadvantaged backgrounds; and (e) conditional admission programs that accept students with lower grades on the condition that they complete special appropriate preparatory work programs which the university must make available" (Dollinger, 283–284).

To safeguard the rights of worthy nonminority candidates, Levine suggested that "only applicants who meet the minimum and reasonable qualifications applicable to all as established by the employer involved be regarded as eligible." She urged employers not to create new employment positions for minority candidates "by discharging any person already employed" and asked that goals "be established only on the basis of a bona fide finding as to available qualified talent in the disadvantaged group within the relevant job market, and not on the basis of the proportion of disadvantaged group members to the population as a whole." To prevent hiring goals from becoming institutionalized, Levine wanted them to be "used only as a criterion for judgment of good faith efforts" and asked that they be "discontinued when past imbalance has been corrected." Since the mid-1970s, successful legal challenges to quota-based affirmative action programs have moved the issue to the background of the American Jewish Congress's public policy agenda.

See also African Americans; American Jewish Committee; Anti-Defamation League; Anti-Semitism, Jews, and Affirmative Action; Black-Jewish Alliance; Civil Rights Movement; Color-Blind Constitution; Johnson, Lyndon Baines; Kennedy, John Fitzgerald; King, Martin Luther, Jr.; Meritocracy; Proposition 209; Quotas; Race-Based Affirmative Action; Republican Party and Affirmative Action; Reverse Discrimination.

FURTHER READING: American Jewish Congress, 1964, *CLSA Reports,* New York: American Jewish Congress; Commission on Law and Social Action, 1977, *Discrimination, Segregation, and Affirmative Action: 20 Recent Civil Rights Decisions Affecting the Jewish Community,* New York: American Jewish Congress; Dollinger, Marc, 2000, *Quest for Inclusion: Jews and Liberalism in Modern America,* Princeton, NJ: Princeton University Press; Levine, Naomi, ed., 1972, *Affirmative Action, Preferential Treatment, and Quotas: Papers from the Plenary Session,* New York: American Jewish Congress; Svonkin, Stuart, 1997, *Jews against Prejudice: American Jews and the Fight for Civil Liberties,* New York: Columbia University Press.

MARC DOLLINGER

Americans for Democratic Action

Americans for Democratic Action (ADA) is a national political organization dedicated to promoting individual liberties and economic policies through lobbying, legislation, and social action. ADA has been an active political voice in the fight to promote affirmative action initiatives and pushes for affirmative action through political lobbying and grassroots efforts. ADA is a nonprofit organization with sixteen chapters throughout the United States and one in Mexico. It also has an affiliate for youth called Youth for Democratic Action (YDA). It operates a political action committee that contributes funds to ADA-endorsed political candidates. It also operates the ADA Education Fund, which sponsors research on domestic, foreign, economic, military, social, and environmental policy, publishes issue papers and special reports, holds conferences, and disseminates information to the public using print and electronic media.

Having started in 1941 as the Union for Democratic Action, the organization supported policies associated with liberal politics and Franklin Roosevelt's New Deal initiatives. It garnered little immediate success in finding a popular constituency, so it quickly altered its political platform. Still a supporter of liberal policies, the newly named Americans for Democratic Action (January 1947) had quietly transformed itself into an active promoter of popular anti-Communist sentiments. The promotion of liberal policies and anti-Communism brought the transformed organization increased popularity, if not the membership its founders sought. Some of its most famous founders and members include prominent social figures such as former first lady Eleanor Roosevelt, historian Arthur Schlesinger Jr., labor leader Walter Reuther, theologian Reinhold Niebuhr, labor activist David Dubinsky, economist John Kenneth Galbraith, and former vice president Hubert Humphrey. The ADA's membership has traditionally been white, college-educated, middle-class men, and despite its liberal intentions, it has had difficulty drawing members from minority and labor groups even though it has openly supported and worked closely with them.

Part of the ADA's difficulty in attracting a larger group of supporters lay in the controversy over the organization's purpose. According to the ADA, its mission has been to promote education, organization, and political action dedicated to individual liberty and building economic justice at home and abroad through democratic principles at local, state, and national levels, and yet remain an independent liberal organization. But when it came to the organization's role in achieving these goals, some members believed that the ADA should be solely an independent voice for liberal policies, claiming that anything more would compromise its independent status. Other members thought that the organization would be more effective in promoting change as a political pressure group. Ultimately this controversy caused the ADA to play both sides of the fence, and perhaps as a result it lost much of its effectiveness as either a political voice or a lobbying group. At the same time, the ADA appears to have compromised its independent status by its nearly continuous support for Democratic Party initiatives and its endorsement of many Democratic presidential candidates, from Henry Wallace and Harry Truman to John F. Kennedy and William Clinton. Yet the Democratic Party itself usually saw many of the ADA's initiatives as too radical if not outright socialist, ensuring that the party would never fully accept the ADA. Furthermore, the organization's close association with the Democrats alienated Republicans, which likely hindered its lobbying efforts.

Yet despite its long struggle for popularity, the ADA has managed to achieve many of its political goals, particularly during the height of its influence with the Kennedy and Johnson administrations. Two of the ADA's most influential leaders, John Kenneth Galbraith and Arthur Schlesinger Jr., both served in the Kennedy administration and used their positions to promote ADA initiatives and to try to influence the president's decisions and policies. With such close association with the administration, the ADA saw a good deal of progress on the civil liberty policies it supported. Yet its internal conflict over its role had an effect on its ability to achieve even further success. Even though the ADA openly supported and helped generate many of Kennedy's civil liberty initiatives, the organization also officially opposed the Kennedy-sponsored war in Vietnam and criticized many of the president's civil liberty and economic policies for not going far enough. The ADA's public opposition to the war also resulted in organizational turmoil as internal division about the issue split its members into war supporters and opponents.

Despite these problems and Kennedy's assassination, the ADA continued to work with the Johnson administration to promote civil rights issues. In 1964, President Johnson signed the Civil Rights Act. Over the next several decades, the ADA continued to oppose many issues like the Vietnam War, apartheid in South Africa, giant corporate mergers, privatization of public services such as Social Security and Medicare, deportation of U.S. jobs, and unfair foreign trade agreements. It has also supported a full spectrum of liberal policies, including the push to impeach Richard Nixon, the increase of the minimum wage, support for workers' rights, universal health-care coverage, the livable wage, women's rights, civil rights, and affirmative action.

The ADA has been an active political voice in the fight to promote affirmative action initiatives, ensure their implementation, and defend their exigency. In the 1990s, the ADA opposed California's Proposition 209, which nevertheless passed in 1996, eliminating the state's affirmative action programs. Currently, the ADA's most visible support for affirmative action is through political lobbying and grassroots initiatives. The ADA's statement of support for affirmative action (Resolution 102) includes the following recommendations: the ADA (1) calls upon the president to reaffirm, strengthen, and expand efforts to realize the goals of affirmative action; (2) calls upon the president to implement a policy of outreach to constituencies underrepresented in the awarding of government contracts, grants, and opportunities; (3) urges the president to ensure that the government of the United States is a model employer in its own agencies by (a) issuing an executive order giving the administrative law judges of the Equal Employment Opportunity Commission the authority of administrative law judges in the federal government so that they may rule on complaints of discrimination by federal employers without being overridden by the agency that is charged and (b) requiring all federal agencies to document outreach in job recruitment, promotions, housing, and educational programs; (4) urges the Congress of the United States to support programs to provide experiences of cultural diversity for Americans of all backgrounds; (5) calls upon the president and Congress to increase funding for adequate implementation of EEOC policies and decisions; (6) urges the Democratic Party to retain its support for and commitment to affirmative action and to reject efforts to ban such programs at the federal level; (7) urges members from both parties to recognize the importance of affirmative action in our nation's efforts toward equality of opportunity and to cast a vote in favor of continuance of the policy; and (8) urges concrete actions that will give credibility to assertions on the value of diversity and the need for communities, employers, educational institutions, and governments at all levels to reach out to, mentor, and include all ethnic groups and genders.

See also Civil Rights Act of 1964; Clinton, William Jefferson; Democratic Party and Affirmative Action; Johnson, Lyndon Baines; Kennedy, John Fitzgerald; Nixon, Richard Milhous; Proposition 209; Republican Party and Affirmative Action; Roosevelt, Eleanor; Roosevelt, Franklin Delano; Truman, Harry.

FURTHER READING: Americans for Democratic Action, web site: http://www.adaction.org; Gillon, Steven M., 1987, *Politics and Vision: The ADA and American Liberalism, 1947–1985*, New York: Oxford University Press.

JAYSON J. FUNKE

Americans United for Affirmative Action

Americans United for Affirmative Action (AUAA) is a national, nonprofit organization that is committed to educating the general public about the significance of maintaining affirmative action programs and equality of opportunity in education and employment in the United States. The organization is made up of people from various racial and ethnic backgrounds (e.g., African American, Hispanic, Latino, Caucasian, and Native American). AUAA was founded in part by Martin Luther King III, the eldest son of the slain civil rights leader Martin Luther King Jr. He founded the organization in response to the anti–affirmative action message articulated by Ward Connerly to eliminate affirmative action programs in education, hiring, promotions, and contracting. Americans United for Affirmative Action was also established as an instrument to counteract the advocacy efforts of proponents of Proposition 209 in California. Supporters of Proposition 209 advocated eradicating affirmative action policies and programs in employment and academic admissions in California's higher-education system. The passage of the anti–affirmative action initiative by California voters further prompted King to organize a coalition of civil rights organizations as a more comprehensive and cohesive means of educating the public and advocating in favor of affirmative action programs and policies.

AUAA embarked upon its national campaign to educate, raise awareness among, and mobilize minorities and civil rights advocates in a concerted effort to preserve affirmative action programs. The organization was founded on the premise of collective action. The primary purpose and goal of AUAA is to educate people to understand the need for affirmative action policies and programs to ensure that all people enjoy equal opportunity to succeed and thrive in the United States. Furthermore, AUAA attempts to combat what King III calls a "backlash against hard-won gains made during the civil rights movement of the 1960s." The fundamental core of the organization's operation is the idea that teamwork is crucial to diminishing myths associated with affirmative action and educating Americans about the practical nature of the policy, which affords every citizen the opportunity to maximize his or her potential regardless of race, ethnicity, sex, or disability. The coalition of civil rights organizations that promotes affirmative action programs seeks to utilize the wisdom acquired by older individuals and more experienced civil rights activists while capitalizing on the enthusiasm, energy, and exuberance of America's youth. The organization has assisted in diminishing the generation gap between aging and young proponents of civil rights and affirmative action programs. The organization once maintained a web site that contained a plethora of materials, but the web site was not updated and has been removed from the Internet.

See also African Americans; Connerly, Ward; Hispanic Americans; King, Martin Luther, Jr.; Native Americans; Proposition 209.

FURTHER READING: "Affirmative Action Effort Launched," 1997, *Washington Post*, January 20, A6; Associated Press State and Local Wire, 1999, "Martin Luther King, III to Attend Bill Signing," January 4; Hentoff, Nat, 1997, "A Different Sort of Affirmative Action," *Washington Post*, February 8, A21; Jordan, Frederick, 1997, "Powell Case Shows Need for Affirmative Action," *New York Times*, December 24, A16; "Martin Luther King, III, Looks Ahead as a

New President of SCLC," 1998, *Jet*, January 19, 4; "Remembering Martin Luther King, Jr.: King's Son Starts Group for Civil Rights," 1997, *Atlanta Journal and Constitution*, January 20, B6.

LA TRICE M. WASHINGTON

Americans with Disabilities Act

See Persons with Disabilities and Affirmative Action.

Anthony, Susan Brownell (1820–1906)

Susan B. Anthony, born long before the advent of modern affirmative action programs, was one of America's best-known leaders in the advocacy of women's rights and suffrage. She strongly advocated ratification of the Nineteenth Amendment, which is often called the Susan B. Anthony Amendment in her honor. Anthony not only called for the political equality of women, but also promoted economic equality and equal wages for women, something that, despite modern affirmative action and equal pay laws, still has not been achieved. In 1851, Anthony called for women to "have independent incomes" and be paid equally "with wages as men are" paid. Anthony's dedication to political and social reform earned her the nicknames "the Invincible" and "the Napoleon of the woman's rights movement."

Her radicalism for women's rights is still invoked today, occasionally in the affirmative action context. For example, one author in 1987 wrote, "Ms. Anthony . . . it was you who defined feminism as more than a struggle for mere political equality. You aimed at bettering all women's lives in all spheres. Although we have gained much, we have also fallen short of your goals. We must continue the fight in the coming decades until your dreams become reality" (McHugh, 15). Ken Burns, producer of a 1999 Public Television special on Anthony and Elizabeth Cady Stanton, has commented that Anthony and Stanton "are most responsible for the largest social transformation in American history, a transformation that, unlike Jefferson's narrow (white, propertied males) Declaration of Independence, affected a majority of American citizens and has provided the model for a host of other twentieth-century agitations" (Burns 1999, 98).

Anthony, raised in an activist Quaker family, became a leading advocate of women's rights and suffrage, abolition, temperance, and education reform over the course of many decades. She was born in Adams, Massachusetts. Anthony's entire family was active in reform, participating in abolition, temperance, and women's rights movements. Daniel and Lucy Read Anthony raised their eight children as Quakers, although Lucy Anthony, a Baptist, never officially joined the Quakers. As a Quaker, Susan grew up in an environment that treated women on a par with men. Quakers held that women were equal before God, and as equals, women were heard and held church offices.

Originally a farming family, the Anthonys moved to New York in 1826, where Daniel took over the management of a large cotton mill. Daniel Anthony was especially liberal and made sure his daughters received the best education possible and developed the ability to support themselves. Even though Daniel's cotton business was doing well, he allowed Susan to spend her summers teaching. In 1838, the Anthonys fell victim to the panic of 1837; they lost everything. Susan continued to teach until the family was back on its feet. After a few false starts, Daniel, with the help of his brother-in-law, purchased a new farm in Rochester, New York, and farmed until he went to work for New York Life Insurance Company.

In Rochester, a center of reform, the Anthonys met a number of influential people, including Frederick Douglass and William Lloyd Garrison. Shortly after the family moved to Rochester, Susan was offered a teaching position as the head of the female department at Canajoharie Academy. Soon, however, she became unhappy with her teaching position, which paid four times less than comparable male positions, and in 1849 she returned to Rochester to manage the family farm.

Elizabeth Cady Stanton, seated, and Susan B. Anthony, standing, in a portrait depicting the two women considered instrumental in the women's rights movement. Courtesy of Library of Congress.

Back home, Susan became increasingly active in both temperance and abolition. It was through her involvement with the Rochester Daughters of Temperance that she met Elizabeth Cady Stanton in 1851. Anthony and Stanton formed an immediate friendship, and in 1852 Anthony attended her first women's rights meeting. At first, Anthony and Stanton worked to support the Thirteenth Amendment, believing that women's suffrage would follow. They established the American Equal Rights Association in 1866 and launched a newspaper, the *Republican,* in 1868 with the motto "Men their rights, and nothing more; women, their rights, and nothing less."

In 1869, the suffragist movement split into two groups. The first was Anthony and Stanton's National Woman Suffrage Association, which worked toward a constitutional amendment. The second group, made up of people dissatisfied with Anthony and Stanton, formed the American Woman Suffrage Association under the leadership of Lucy Stone, which strove to provide women the right to vote on a state-by-state basis. The two groups eventually merged in 1890, forming the National American Woman Suffrage Association, with Stanton as president and Anthony as vice president. Anthony worked tirelessly for the suffrage movement until her retirement at age eighty. She attended her last suffrage meeting in 1906 and died that same year of heart failure; the Nineteenth Amendment was ratified fourteen years later.

See also Abolitionists; Gender-Based Affirmative Action; Mott, Lucretia Coffin; Nineteenth Amendment; Stanton, Elizabeth Cady; Stone, Lucy; Suffrage Movement; Thirteenth Amendment.

FURTHER READING: Burns, Ken, and Geoffrey C. Ward, 1999, *Not for Ourselves Alone: The Story of Elizabeth Cady Stanton and Susan B. Anthony,* New York: Knopf; Gurko, Miriam, 1974, *The Ladies of Seneca Falls: The Birth of the Woman's Rights Movement,* New York: Schocken Books;

James, Edward T., 1971, *Notable American Women, 1607–1950: A Biographical Dictionary*, Cambridge, MA.: Harvard University Press; McHugh, Clare, 1987, "Letter to the Past," *Scholastic Update* 119 (May 18): 12–15; Sherr, Lynn, 1995, *Failure Is Impossible: Susan B. Anthony in Her Own Words*, New York: Times Books.

LISA A. ENNIS

Anti-Defamation League

The Anti-Defamation League (ADL), formerly known as the Anti-Defamation League of B'nai B'rith, emerged in the wake of the infamous 1915 lynching of Atlanta Jewish merchant Leo Frank. Created by attorney Sigmund Livingston "to stop, by appeals to reason and conscience, and if necessary, by appeals to law, the defamation of the Jewish people . . . [and] to secure justice and fair treatment to all citizens alike," the Anti-Defamation League grew to become a leading national voice for civil rights in the 1950s. With the enactment of the first government-sponsored affirmative action programs in the 1960s, the ADL joined the American Jewish Committee and the American Jewish Congress as strong and vocal national Jewish proponents of the new civil rights legislation. The introduction of quota-based affirmative action programs qualified ADL support, leading the Jewish civil rights group to offer a friend-of-the-court brief supporting plaintiff Allan Bakke in his famed case against the University of California at Davis Medical School, *Regents of the University of California v. Bakke,* 438 U.S. 265 (1978). Since the *Bakke* case, the ADL has opposed quota-based programs and limited its support to affirmative action programs that, according to ADL head Abraham Foxman, "provide education and training to compete equally in a merit-based process" (Dollinger 2000, 12).

The ADL supported affirmative action programs from their inception. A 1966 ADL-commissioned study pressed for more aggressive civil rights legislation, concluding that "under present conditions, mere nondiscrimination is no longer enough. Today the United States confronts the much larger task of *reversing* the cumulative effects of generation upon generation of enforced disadvantage." ADL leaders believed that "in essence, affirmative action connotes adding qualified minority group members to other qualified applicants for college admission and employment" (Dollinger, 203–204). The ADL backed the aims of Lyndon Johnson's Great Society, embraced much of the sociological research that pointed to systemic racial discrimination, and supported affirmative action programs intended to increase opportunities for members of designated minority groups.

By 1970, the ADL joined with most other national Jewish organizations in its opposition to quota-based affirmative action programs. As affirmative action procedures developed, the ADL lamented that programs were "being distorted and turned with increasing rapidity into preferential treatment for some Americans on the basis of their race or sex." ADL leaders argued that restrictive quotas were "undemocratic" and violated "the American tradition that the individual stands on his own merits." The Jewish defense organization rejected the system that said that "a student's rights are governed and limited by the faith of his fathers and not by his talents." "The quota system," it concluded, "arbitrarily renders educational opportunity the privilege of the majority, and denies it to the minority—though all have contributed historically to make this country great." The aim of affirmative action," the ADL believed, "should be broad social progress in achieving racial equality, not the assignment of historical blame, and then the penalizing of specific individuals who happen to be members of the majority" (Dollinger, 207).

The ADL's opposition to quota-based programs reached the federal level when Marco DeFunis, a white candidate to the University of Washington Law School, filed suit charging that the university's affirmative action policies unfairly discriminated against him. Emerging some four years before the more famous *Bakke* case, *DeFunis v. Odegaard*, 416 U.S. 312 (1974), revealed deep-seated splits within organized American Jewry. The ADL, joined by the American Jewish Congress and the American Jewish Committee, sided with DeFunis in opposition to the law school's affirmative action policy. The Reform movement's Union of American Hebrew Congregations joined the National Council of Jewish Women in defense of the University of Washington.

In an amicus brief filed with the Jewish Labor Committee, the Union of Orthodox Jewish Congregations, and several branches of the Jewish Community Relations Council, the ADL argued that the University of Washington's affirmative action program "undercut the principle of equal opportunity for all Americans." The ADL and its cosponsoring organizations regarded "quotas as inconsistent with principles of equality and as harmful in the long run to all, including these groups" (Dollinger, 210).

In a separate brief to the U.S. Supreme Court, the ADL engaged Alexander M. Bickel of Yale University and Philip B. Kurland of the University of Chicago to record their support of DeFunis. "If the Constitution prohibits exclusion of blacks and other minorities on racial grounds," Bickel and Kurland explained, "it cannot permit the exclusion of whites on racial grounds. For it must be the exclusion on racial grounds which offends the Constitution, and not the particular skin color of the person excluded." The authors of the ADL brief reminded the Court that "for at least a generation the lesson of the great decisions of this Court and the lessons of contemporary history have been the same: discrimination on the basis of race is illegal, immoral, unconstitutional, inherently wrong and destructive of democratic society. Now this is to be unlearned and we are told that this is not a matter of fundamental principle but only a matter of whose ox is gored" (Dollinger, 211).

Bickel and Kurland held that "a state-imposed racial quota is a per se violation of the equal protection clause because it utilizes a factor for measurement that is necessarily irrelevant to any constitutionally acceptable legislative purpose." For the ADL, the Washington law school's admissions program operated as a racial quota system regardless of the university administration's claims to the contrary. "A quota is no less a quota," Bickel and Kurland explained, "because it is not labeled as such or because it is subject to annual adjustment." Bickel and Kurland concluded that "the use of the quota system—the segregation of two groups of applicants by race with admission for each group limited to its assigned numbers, makes it clear that this is not simply a case where race was used as one among many factors to determine legislation. Instead, the law school used race as the criterion for imposing entirely separate admissions procedures."

The ADL authors drew an all-important connection between Marco DeFunis and the American Jewish experience. "To the Jewish community," they explained, DeFunis symbolized "all those Jewish sons and daughters who until very recent times were barred from colleges and graduate schools, including and especially some of the most prestigious, because of overt or tacit restrictive quotas and 'gentleman's agreements' on Jewish admission-barriers that finally came tumbling down only after World War II and only after a sustained fight by the Jewish community in behalf of itself and other minorities similarly discriminated against." The American Jewish response to the DeFunis case did not signal, in the ADL's eyes, a sea change in its constituents' political persuasion. "Jews," Bickel and Kurland claimed, were "not asking for their group share of the 'action.' " Instead, they held, American Jews were "demanding what they have always asked: that each American be accepted or rejected on the basis of his or her individual achievement and worth, without regard to race, religion, ethnic origin, or sex." They asserted that "[t]he right to be free of discrimination based on group identity was an individual right (a position consistently upheld by the United States Supreme Court), a right that may not be denied even by the well-intentioned effort to render justice toward a disadvantaged group."

The ADL considered "the closing of a door in the face of a Marco DeFunis . . . no more justifiable, no less wrong, than the closing of a door in the face of a James Meredith." What the Jewish community claimed was "no more or less than was demanded of employers, employment agencies, and labor organizations in the landmark 1964 Civil Rights Act. That is, equal opportunity for all, without regard to race." The ADL held firm in its belief in strict nondiscrimination. "The evils attendant upon preferential treatment," it concluded, "the invidious new discrimination imposed on individuals because of the accidents of their birth; the consequent loss to society of those who might serve it best; the demand for proportional quotas and the inevitable group antagonisms that follow, the ethnic census and ethnic reporting, with their invasion of privacy and threat of discrimination (old style and new style)—far outweigh any temporary or even long-range social benefits it might help to achieve" (Dollinger, 212).

Since the *DeFunis* case, the ADL has maintained its opposition to quotas. In a 1995 position paper, ADL head Abraham H. Foxman wrote that his organization had "been profoundly troubled by the evolution in this nation's concept of 'affirmative action' from devices to help create a level playing field for historic victims of discrimination into a system of discriminatory group preferences." Foxman backed court decisions banning quota-based affirmative action programs and encouraged the courts "to move away from race-conscious remedies" and move "in the direction of assistance for the economically disadvantaged, regardless of race" (Dollinger, 212).

See also American Jewish Committee; American Jewish Congress; Anti-Semitism, Jews, and Affirmative Action; Census Classifications, Ethnic and Racial; Civil Rights Act of 1964; Civil Rights Movement; Color-Blind Constitution; *DeFunis v. Odegaard*; Equal Protection Clause; Johnson, Lyndon Baines; Quotas; Race-Based Affirmative Action; *Regents of the University of California v. Bakke*; Reverse Discrimination.

FURTHER READING: Dollinger, Marc, 2000, *Quest for Inclusion: Jews and Liberalism in Modern America*, Princeton, NJ: Princeton University Press; Friedman, Murray, 1995, *What Went Wrong? The Creation and Collapse of the Black-Jewish Alliance*, New York: Free Press; Grier, George W., 1966, *Equality and Beyond: Housing Segregation and the Goals of the Great Society*, Chicago: Quadrangle Books; Levine, Naomi, ed., 1972, *Affirmative Action, Preferential Treat-*

ment, and Quotas: Papers from the Plenary Session, New York: American Jewish Congress; Svonkin, Stuart, 1997, *Jews against Prejudice: American Jews and the Fight for Civil Liberties,* New York: Columbia University Press.

MARC DOLLINGER

Anti-Defamation League of B'nai B'rith

See Anti-Defamation League.

Antidiscrimination Four

See Regents of the University of California v. Bakke.

Anti-Semitism, Jews, and Affirmative Action

American Jews have been, and remain, the nation's most liberal white ethnic group, having supported modern affirmative action programs from their inception in the Kennedy administration. Jewish leaders empathized with the plight of African Americans, whose experience they paralleled to that of Jews historically limited by anti-Semitic discrimination. Public opinion polls revealed that American Jews supported affirmative action more than any other white ethnic group. Jewish support for affirmative action reached its limit when the advent of strict race-based quota programs raised fears of anti-Semitic discrimination. Recalling a history of anti-Semitism punctuated by the use of restrictive quotas against Jews in the 1920s, leaders of organized Jewry almost unanimously opposed the introduction of quotas as part of affirmative action programs in the 1960s and 1970s. Since the 1970s, most national Jewish leaders have limited their support of affirmative action programs to those that do not employ race-based quotas.

American Jewish fears of quota-based anti-Semitic discrimination began in the 1920s, when institutions of higher learning and many of the nation's leading businesses enacted strict quotas limiting Jewish mobility. Until the mid-1950s, the number of Jews enrolled in medical and law schools consistently followed university-imposed percentage targets more than they adhered to the merits of any individual applicant. After graduation, American Jews rarely earned positions as professors and almost never enjoyed the security of tenure. In 1947, President Harry Truman's Commission on Higher Education issued a report reiterating what American Jews had known for a generation, that "quota systems and policies of exclusion practiced by American institutions of higher learning had prevented young people of many religious and racial groups—but particularly Jews and Negroes—from obtaining higher education and professional training." The following year, after the conclusion of a ten-year study of Jewish acceptances and rejections at American graduate schools, Stephen S. Wise noted that "the enrollment of Jewish students between the years 1935 and 1946 in professional schools throughout the country declined sharply. In law, Jewish enrollment declined by 57%; in medicine, 20.1%, in business administration, 35.9%, in dentistry, 33%; in optometry, 53.3%, in pharmacy, 38.4%" (Dollinger 2000, 206). The results of a 1948 study commissioned by the state of New York, a 1949 Connecticut report, and a

1949 American Council on Education finding all confirmed anti-Jewish discrimination.

Most national Jewish leaders saw little difference between the earlier quota programs designed to restrict Jewish mobility and the 1960s version intended to benefit historically disadvantaged minorities. American Jews, by virtue of their rapid social mobility between the 1920s and 1960s, once again faced quota-based marginalization. Yet they also understood the necessity of instituting more aggressive civil rights measures. In Los Angeles, the chair of the Jewish Community Relations Council (JCRC) explained the awkward position of American Jews: "On the one hand, we are unequivocally opposed to quotas. The very word 'quota' evokes memories of the disabilities imposed on Jews for generations." Yet, the JCRC official asked, "how do we prevent an integrated neighborhood or school or housing project from going beyond the tipping point and becoming completely segregated if not by some kind of quota?" (Dollinger, 206).

Every major national Jewish organization made opposition to hiring quotas a priority. "We concluded shortly after the nightmare of the Holocaust," a Philadelphia JCRC member explained, "that Jewish security and the strength of the American democratic process were inextricably interwoven." Linking quota programs to medieval institutions that strictly limited mobility and cared little about merit, he warned that the "Jewish self-interest in the long run could not tolerate a society that permitted a caste system." The Jewish leader feared that "[t]he inevitable turbulence and strife resulting from the failure to end the caste system would in the course of time, as history has so painfully taught us, fall upon the Jewish head" (Dollinger, 206–207).

In a 1970 position paper, the American Jewish Committee noted that it "continues to oppose the creation of a system of quotas for any group including the disadvantaged in education, employment or any other area of American life." It affirmed that "our society is capable of providing ample educational and employment opportunities for all its people thus eliminating the need for benefiting one group at the expense of another or resorting to shortcut and dangerous solutions like quotas." The Anti-Defamation League countered that restrictive quotas were "undemocratic" and violated "the American tradition that the individual stands on his own merits." The Jewish defense organization rejected the system that said that "a student's rights are governed and limited by the faith of his fathers and not by his talents." "The quota system," it concluded, "arbitrarily renders educational opportunity the privilege of the majority, and denies it to the minority—though all have contributed historically to make this country great" (Dollinger, 207).

As affirmative action procedures developed, the Anti-Defamation League lamented that programs were "being distorted and turned with increasing rapidity into preferential treatment for some Americans on the basis of their race or sex." While the ADL acknowledged that "the intent is eradication of the all too pervasive reality of unequal opportunity for oppressed minorities," it concluded that "the means constitutes discrimination in reverse." The ADL supported a program that required "a company, government agency or university to add to its recruitment schedules colleges and universities at which substantial numbers of minority group students are to be found" and opposed plans that advocated an abandonment of "usual recruiting schedules." "The aim of affirmative action," it concluded, "should be broad social progress in achieving racial equality, not the assignment of historical blame, and then the penalizing of specific individuals who happen to be members of the majority" (Dollinger, 207).

The National Jewish Community Relations Advisory Council (NJCRAC), an umbrella organization comprising most major Jewish organizations, warned that affirmative action programs "often resulted in practices that are inconsistent with the principle of nondiscrimination and the goal of equal opportunity such programs are designed to achieve." It went on record as being opposed to "such practices, foremost among which is the use of quotas and proportional representation in hiring, upgrading and admission of minority groups" and viewed quotas "as inconsistent with principles of equality" and "harmful in the long run to all." While target goals "serve as a yardstick to measure good faith," a NJCRAC leader admonished, quotas constitute "a fixed, rigid requirement." He concluded that "making an idol out of meritocracy may blind us to other values" of import to a diverse and equitable society (Dollinger, 207).

One of the nation's Orthodox bodies, Agudath Israel, presented the most scathing critique of the quota system. "It is highly improper," Bernard Fryshman argued, "to permit remedial action or compensation for 'historical wrongs' when applied to an arbitrarily defined group." Fryshman noted that "the people who suffer are almost always young white males who themselves did no discriminating; they find doors shut to them simply because they are white males." The traditional Jewish leader criticized both "the distorted manner in which the affirmative action programs have been implemented" and what he termed "the almost mindless use of statistical data and the glib adoption of unsupported a priori assumptions." For the Orthodox leader, "Quotas, described by whatever euphemisms and hidden by whatever legal language and structures have no place in America." Fryshman based his opposition to quotas on his contempt for Great Society liberalism and its emphasis on communitarianism. "We reject the concept of group rights; even more so do we reject group guilt," he explained; "we cannot accept a situation in which a white male with no personal involvement in the discrimination of others should be required to suffer discrimination only because of the fact that he is white and is male." "We feel it is entirely improper," he concluded, "to correct historical wrongs of the past by assigning guilt and penalties to innocent individuals simply because of their race and sex" (Dollinger, 207–208).

Even the American Jewish Congress, known for its progressive political views and willingness to break with the more moderate Jewish organizations, urged its constituents to oppose all quotas. Quotas were labeled by David Petegorsky, the executive director of the American Jewish Congress, as "indefensible and antidemocratic." Similarly Naomi Levine, the executive director designate in 1972, complained that "what started out as a vague concept of 'affirmative action' in a presidential executive order limited to federal contractors has now been by administrative rulings defined as a responsibility to overcome 'the under-utilization of minority groups in the workforce through goals, percentage hiring, and timetables' whether prior discrimination has or has not been established and whether the employer is or is not a federal contractor." For Levine, the use of hiring goals was not objectionable unless they degenerated into strict quotas. Consequently, Levine and the American Jewish Congress developed a detailed affirmative action plan of their own as an alternative proposal to the concept of rigid quotas, meant both to protect the needs of discriminated minorities and the rights of the majority.

To safeguard the rights of worthy nonminority candidates, the American Jewish Congress proposal suggested that "only applicants who meet the minimum and reasonable qualifications applicable to all as established by the employer involved be regarded as eligible." Furthermore, Levine urged employers not to create new employment positions for minority candidates "by discharging any person already employed" and asked that goals "be established only on the basis of a bona fide finding as to available qualified talent in the disadvantaged group within the relevant job market, and not on the basis of the proportion of disadvantaged group members to the population as a whole." To prevent hiring goals from becoming institutionalized, the American Jewish Congress proposal also delineated that the goals and guidelines are to be "used only as a criterion for judgment of good faith efforts" and asked that they be "discontinued when past imbalance has been corrected."

Position papers and press releases issued by most national Jewish organizations in the years since quota-based programs first appeared continue to oppose this form of affirmative action. Contemporary Jewish leaders still consider quotas a threat to Jewish life and the principles of American democracy. With the exception of some Jewish leftist groups, the organized Jewish community has not wavered in its belief that quota-based affirmative action programs lead to anti-Semitic discrimination.

See also African Americans; American Jewish Committee; American Jewish Congress; Anti-Defamation League; Black-Jewish Alliance; Caste System; Color-Blind Constitution; Kennedy, John Fitzgerald; Legacy Admissions Policy; Meritocracy; Quotas; Race-Based Affirmative Action; Reverse Discrimination; Truman, Harry.

FURTHER READING: Commission on Law and Social Action, 1977, *Discrimination, Segregation, and Affirmative Action: 20 Recent Civil Rights Decisions Affecting the Jewish Community*, New York: American Jewish Congress; Dinnerstein, Leonard, 1994, *Anti-Semitism in America*, New York: Oxford University Press; Dollinger, Marc, 2000, *Quest for Inclusion: Jews and Liberalism in Modern America*, Princeton, NJ: Princeton University Press; Fuchs, Lawrence H., 1986, *When to Count by Race: Affirmative Action, Quotas, and Equal Opportunity*, New York: American Jewish Committee; Grier, George W., 1966, *Equality and Beyond: Housing Segregation and the Goals of the Great Society*, Chicago: Quadrangle Books; Levine, Naomi, ed., 1972, *Affirmative Action, Preferential Treatment, and Quotas: Papers from the Plenary Session*, New York: American Jewish Congress; Svonkin, Stuart, 1997, *Jews against Prejudice: American Jews and the Fight for Civil Liberties*, New York: Columbia University Press.

MARC DOLLINGER

Apartheid

Apartheid was the official policy of segregation pursued by the South African government from 1948 until 1991 and was roughly analogous to de jure segregation in the southern United States. The term means "separateness" in the Afrikaans language (the dominant language of South Africa's white population, who were descendants of the original Dutch settlers), and the policy legally established a regime of strict racial division between the minority white population (which governed South Africa until 1994) and the nonwhite majority. Apartheid covered all aspects of South African society. At their height, these laws determined where members of different racial groups could live, what jobs they could hold, and what kind of education they could obtain. While racial separation had been a tradition in South Africa, the National Party proposed apartheid as part of its 1948 election campaign and put its proposal into law after taking power.

The history of apartheid relates to affirmative action in the United States in an indirect fashion. Currently, as a means of remedying years of segregation in South Africa as a result of apartheid, the South African government employs what it calls "positive discrimination," which is akin to affirmative action plans in the United States. Justice Ruth Bader Ginsburg, in the oral arguments to the Supreme Court in *Grutter v. Bollinger,* 123 S. Ct. 2325, 2003 U.S. LEXIS 4800 (2003), and *Gratz v. Bollinger,* 123 S. Ct. 2411, 2003 U.S. LEXIS 4801 (2003), illustrated this connection when she asked the counsel for one of the plaintiffs in the case why the United States should not employ affirmative action to achieve diversity and to remedy prior discrimination when countries such as South Africa, which had a similar tradition (and some say worse) of segregation, do employ affirmative action as a means to achieve political equality and equality of opportunity between the races.

In the years before the introduction of apartheid, South Africa had already established a state based on the principle of white supremacy. In 1910, parliamentary membership was limited to whites. In 1911, the Mines and Works Act limited blacks to menial labor. Two years later, the Land Act was passed. Under this law, white settlers claimed 87 percent of South Africa's land, forcing blacks into so-called homelands. Blacks were not permitted to own property outside of the homelands. In response to these policies, the African National Congress (ANC) was formed in 1912 to challenge these policies.

The ANC and other opposition groups were largely ineffective. However, in the years immediately after World War II, black workers engaged in a number of violent strikes. In 1948, the Afrikaner-dominated National Party, capitalizing on the white hysteria caused by the black unrest, swept to power under the leadership of Dr. Daniel F. Malan, who promised to officially implement apartheid in order to repress black unrest. Malan's government then introduced a number of laws formalizing apartheid. Marriage between whites and nonwhites was prohibited, and the government sanctioned "whites-only" jobs. The Group Areas Act (1950) segregated communities and forced blacks to live on a small percentage of the country's land. The purpose of the act was to restore segregation in urban areas. As whites moved into new areas, blacks and coloreds were forced to relocate.

The Population Registration Act (1950) required all South Africans to register their race with the government. Under this law, South Africans were classified as being white, black (African, who made up about 75 percent of South Africa's population), or colored (mixed lineage), which included Indians and Asians. A government agency, the Department of Home Affairs, was given responsibility for classifying South Africans.

In 1951, the Bantu Authorities Act established a basis for government in the "Bantustands" (homelands). Under the policy of separate development pursued by the National Party, blacks were assigned to each of these homelands (which the government envisioned as eventually becoming sovereign independent states, leaving South Africa to the white minority). All political rights, including the right to vote, held by Africans would be limited to the homelands. Beginning in 1952, all blacks would be required to carry passbooks. These passbooks were internal passports that enabled the government to regulate and monitor the travel of blacks throughout the country.

In 1953, the last legislative pieces of apartheid were put in place. Parliament enacted the Separate Amenities Act. This law established separate public facilities for whites and nonwhites. The Public Safety Act and Criminal Law Amendment Act gave the government the power to declare states of emergency and increased the penalties for protesting against or supporting the repeal of a law. Under states of emergency, anyone could be detained by the police without a hearing for up to six months. In addition, those convicted under these laws could be sentenced to death, exile, or (as would be the case with Nelson Mandela in 1964) life imprisonment.

Over the next four decades, opposition to apartheid developed both inside and outside South Africa. In 1955, the ANC and other opposition groups adopted the Freedom Charter, which called for equal political rights for all races in South Africa. In 1960, when a number of blacks in Sharpeville refused to carry their passes, the government declared a state of emergency. Police killed 69 unarmed protesters and wounded another 187. The government also banned all opposition groups, including the ANC.

In 1961, South Africa declared itself a republic. Until that time, it had been an independent member of the British Commonwealth. However, criticism of apartheid by African and Asian member states of the Commonwealth prompted the National Party to formally break with the group of onetime British colonies. In the same year, three South African denominations of the Dutch Reformed Church left the World Council of Churches rather than renounce apartheid. In 1962, the South African government established the Transkei as the homeland for the Xhosa and granted it self-government. Nine additional homelands would be granted self-governing status, with four eventually being granted independence from South Africa. However, the lands set aside for the homelands were unsuitable for farming, and there were few other economic opportunities for the blacks living in the homelands. In 1963, the United Nations General Assembly suspended South Africa from participating in the General Assembly, leading to South Africa's recall of its ambassador. Eventually, many nations (including the United States) imposed economic sanctions on South Africa as part of an international effort to end apartheid.

In 1976, a student protest in the black township of Soweto against mandatory education in Afrikaans erupted. The government's eight-month-long crackdown resulted in 575 people being killed. The following year, Steven Biko, one of the most influential black student leaders in South Africa, died in police custody. Biko's death led to international condemnation of apartheid and the government's repressive policies. Around this time, the ANC had become a more effective opposition, establishing an underground network. In response, the government attempted to create a police state while ridding itself of responsibility for the homelands. In 1976, South Africa granted independence to Transkei. No other nation-state would recognize Transkei's independence (and that of other homelands, Ciskei, Bophuthatswana, and KwaZulu).

In 1983, white South African voters approved a new constitution that gave

Asians and coloreds (but not blacks) separate chambers in the South African Parliament. In 1986, the law that required blacks to carry passbooks was repealed, making it the first apartheid law to be overturned. In 1989, F.W. de Klerk was elected president of South Africa. Under de Klerk, the legal basis for apartheid began to unravel as the South African economy began to feel the effects of a worldwide economic and trade embargo. Shortly after his election, de Klerk announced that he supported repeal of the Separate Amenities Act, which was then repealed by the Parliament. In February 1990, de Klerk ended the ban on the ANC and ordered Nelson Mandela's release from prison. In January 1991, black students were permitted to enter previously all-white public schools. Later in the year, the Lands Act, the Group Areas Act, and the Population Registration Act were all repealed. The end of these laws led U.S. President George H.W. Bush to lift virtually all economic sanctions against South Africa.

In 1992, South African voters approved de Klerk's proposal for negotiations with the black majority to establish a majority-rule constitution in South Africa. In February 1993, the National Party government and the ANC reached an agreement on a transitional "government of national unity" in which both parties would be partners. Later in 1993, an agreement was reached on a new majority-rule constitution that provided rights (including the right to vote) to the black South African majority. Under the constitution, the ten self-governing black homelands were dissolved and restored to South Africa. In response to these developments, the United Nations and the United States lifted all remaining sanctions, and de Klerk and Mandela were awarded the Nobel Peace Prize "for their work for the peaceful termination of the apartheid regime, and for laying the foundations for a new democratic South Africa" (Norwegian Nobel Committee 1993).

In April 1994, the first election in which blacks were permitted to vote in South Africa took place. In May 1994, Nelson Mandela was inaugurated as South Africa's first black president. The new government established the South African Truth and Resolution Commission under the Promotion of National Unity and Reconciliation Act of 1995 to examine what had taken place during the apartheid era. Over a seven-year period (1995–2002), the commission examined a number of cases from the apartheid era. Among the revelations uncovered by the commission was that the South African government had considered developing a bacterium that would kill only blacks (BBC News 1998).

While legal apartheid has been dismantled and blacks have attained full political rights, the lesser economic and social position of blacks in South Africa, due to generations of white supremacy, is likely to persist for quite some time. Furthermore, efforts by South Africa to remedy the past incidents of discrimination by virtue of apartheid has led to "positive discrimination" programs, programs employing racial preferences to dole benefits and resources to beneficiaries, much like affirmative action programs in the United States.

See also Bush, George H.W.; De Facto and De Jure Segregation; Ginsburg, Ruth Bader; *Gratz v. Bollinger/Grutter v. Bollinger;* Segregation; South Africa and Affirmative Action.

FURTHER READING: Alden, Chris, 1996, *Apartheid's Last Stand: The Rise and Fall of the South African Security State*, New York: St. Martin's Press; Asmal, Kader, Louise Asmal, and Ronald Suresh Roberts, 1996, *Reconciliation through Truth: A Reckoning of Apartheid's Criminal Gover-*

nance, Bellville, South Africa: Mayibuye Books, University of Western Cape; Benson, Mary, 1989, *A Far Cry*, London: Viking; Dugard, John, Nicholas Haysom, and Gilbert Marcus, 1992, *The Last Years of Apartheid: Civil Liberties in South Africa*, New York: Ford Foundation; Kuperus, Tracy, 1999, *State, Civil Society, and Apartheid in South Africa: An Examination of Dutch Reformed Church–State Relations*, New York: St. Martin's Press; Lewis, Stephen R., 1990, *The Economics of Apartheid*, New York: Council on Foreign Relations Press; Maylam, Paul, 2001, *South Africa's Racial Past: The History and Historiography of Racism, Segregation, and Apartheid*, Aldershot: Ashgate; Parker, Peter, and Joyce Mokhesi-Parker, 1998, *In the Shadow of Sharpeville: Apartheid and Criminal Justice*, Basingstoke: Macmillan; Posel, Deborah, 1997, *The Making of Apartheid, 1948–1961: Conflict and Compromise*, New York: Oxford University Press; Robinson, Jennifer, 1996, *The Power of Apartheid: State, Power, and Space in South African Cities*, Oxford: Butterworth-Heinemann.

JEFFREY KRAUS

Articles of Confederation

The Articles of Confederation and Perpetual Union, which established the first central government of the United States of America as a league of thirteen sovereign and independent states and served as the precursor to the U.S. Constitution, did not grant individual rights. Instead, the Articles largely left that up to the discretion of state legislatures, except that they did require states to grant the same rights to "free inhabitants" residing in other states that they granted to their own residents. This requirement was not extended to paupers, vagabonds, fugitives from justice, and "un-free inhabitants," including slaves. Despite the claim once made by W.E.B. Du Bois that the Articles of Confederation did not distinguish between the white and black races, the Articles of Confederation contained several provisions that set up separate treatment for both black and white inhabitants of the nascent republic. The Articles of Confederation, along with the U.S. Constitution and the Declaration of Independence, are considered the primary founding documents of the new republic, a republic dedicated to the proposition that all men are created equal.

In the mid-1700s, the thirteen American colonies were torn by political conflict pitting Radicals against Conservatives and colony against colony. Radicals sought to overturn the existing economic and political order by taking over colonial legislatures controlled by wealthy Conservatives. Individual colonies argued over their borders, western claims, and intracolony trade, and when conflict seemed imminent, Great Britain intervened on the side of Conservative interests to stabilize the situation. However, in the 1770s, too much intervention in colonial affairs alienated the colonies from Great Britain. In 1775, with the colonies moving closer to declaring independence, Benjamin Franklin submitted the first draft of a plan for a confederation of the colonies independent of Great Britain to the Continental Congress. Conservatives seeking reconciliation with Great Britain pushed it and two other drafts aside until the summer of 1776, when the war and Radical pressure made a declaration of independence imminent. Radical leaders, though generally fearful of a strong central government, realized that they needed one to organize the war effort and to seek international recognition. Radicals and Revolutionary Conservatives, who finally understood that revolution was unstoppable, agreed that they needed to establish a confederated central government, but they disagreed on how powerful to make it. Conservatives, seeking protection from internal rebellions against the new nation, wanted to simply replace the Crown's rule with a strong central government modeled after that of Great Britain. Radicals, who had growing power over state legislatures, sought a weak central government based on natural law and state sovereignty.

In June 1776, John Dickinson, a Conservative from Pennsylvania, submitted the fourth draft of a plan for a confederation featuring a comparably strong central government. This draft was revised to become the Articles of Confederation. During deliberation on the draft, old colonial conflicts created bitter debate among the Congress over the comparable voting power of each state, the apportionment of state contributions to the common treasury, the settlement of "western" claim boundary disputes, and limitations on state sovereignty. On the subject of voting power, small colonies wanted each state to have one vote, while large colonies wanted to allocate voting power according to state size. In the end, each state was given one vote in a unicameral Congress. On the subject of apportionment of contributions to the common treasury, wealthy and sparsely populated colonies wanted contributions apportioned by state population, while poor and populous colonies wanted contributions apportioned by property wealth. While the Dickinson draft initially called for apportionment by population including slaves, the final Articles apportioned contribution by property wealth. On the subject of settlement of boundaries and "western" land claims, colonies with fixed or tentative boundaries or weak claims wanted the central government to resolve all disputes, while powerful colonies with large claims wanted the central government to be only the arbitrator of last resort. While the Dickinson draft initially placed the central government in charge of resolving all conflicts over borders and "western" lands, the final Articles made it only the arbitrator of last resort. On the subject of limitations on state sovereignty, Conservatives, as noted in Dickinson's draft, sought to limit state sovereignty to police powers and their present laws, rights, and customs as long as they did not interfere with the central government's implementation of the Articles of Confederation, but Radicals, who were taking control of state legislatures, amended the final Articles to assert each state's sovereignty and independence, limiting the central government's coercive powers to those enumerated in the Articles.

In the end, the Articles of Confederation created a league of thirteen independent and sovereign colonies bound together for mutual defense and international relations, but not a nation. Accordingly, the Articles of Confederation did not grant individual rights to all of the nation's inhabitants. Instead, each colony had a strict social class system that gave out political and civil rights to individuals according to their property holdings, gender, and race. The Articles only required that states not discriminate in favor of their own free residents against those residing in other states, but it excluded paupers, vagabonds, fugitives from justice, and "un-free inhabitants," including slaves, who were considered property, from this requirement. Thus each state retained its ability to distribute rights along class lines, but it had to treat free individuals of the same class residing in different states equally to those residing within the state. On the other hand, states could grant some rights to excluded inhabitants residing in their own territory and refuse those rights to excluded people visiting from other states. Slaves had no rights and were considered property by the Articles. This was made clear when during the debate on whether to count slaves in population calculations, delegates from colonies where slaves made up a large portion of the population contended that including slaves would be equivalent to counting horses. The point was further made when Thomas Lynch of South Carolina threatened to end the confederation if slaves' status as property was even debated.

After the Articles were ratified in 1781, many problems quickly surfaced that necessitated their replacement by the U.S. Constitution of 1787, which became effective in 1789 and created a strong federal government and a nation. The central government under the Articles was too weak to maintain order, counteract economic distress, foster growth, or handle a whole list of other national issues. It did not provide for an executive or grant Congress any coercive ability to enforce its laws. Congress could only request troops, but had no way to force a state to send them. Congress did not have the power to tax, and requests for funds were often not successful. Congress could only pass laws if nine of thirteen states voted for them, which was a supermajority that was hard to obtain. Congress lacked the ability to regulate interstate trade, leading to dangerous disputes between states. Also, Congress could not amend the Articles unless the changes were unanimous. The era of the Articles from 1781 to 1789 has been called "the critical period" because the confederation almost did not survive.

See also Bill of Rights; Civil War (Reconstruction) Amendments and Civil Rights Acts; Color-blind Constitution; Constitution, Civil Rights, and Equality; Declaration of Independence and Equality; Du Bois, William Edward Burghardt; Three-Fifths Compromise.

FURTHER READING: Jensen, Merrill, 1940, *The Articles of Confederation: An Interpretation of the Social-Constitutional History of the American Revolution, 1774–1781*, Madison: University of Wisconsin Press; Lynd, Staughton, 1967, *Class Conflict, Slavery, and the United States Constitution*, Indianapolis: Bobbs-Merrill; Rubio, Philip F., 2001, *A History of Affirmative Action, 1619–2000*, Jackson: University Press of Mississippi; Thompson, Kenneth W., ed., 1990, *The Political Theory of the Constitution*, Lanham, MD: University Press of America.

MARK J. SENEDIAK

Asian Americans

Asian Americans, described by some as the "model minorities," are a significant presence in the American population. The term "Asian American" usually refers to people of Japanese, Chinese, Taiwanese, Korean, Vietnamese, Cambodian, Thai, or Filipino descent. The group is rapidly expanding, and it is expected that they will number 20 million in the United States by 2020. As a minority group, Asian Americans are often included within affirmative action plans/programs. Historically, the group has been the subject of racism and xenophobia in the United States.

The first wave of immigration from Asia arrived in the United States between the 1850s and the 1930s. The second major wave of Asian immigration from Southeast Asia occurred in the 1970s as a result of the American involvement in Vietnam. Asian immigrants first arrived from China. They were largely ousted from their home country for political reasons. Immigrants from Korea, Japan, and the Philippines were also brought to work in sugar plantations of Hawaii. Immigrants from India, mainly Sikhs, came to America in search of jobs and economic prosperity.

This fast-growing group became a cause for concern in America. They were subjected to political, social, and economic discrimination, like many other minority groups in the United States. Some states enacted laws that were directed against them. Moreover, they were denied the rights of naturalization. The highly discriminatory Immigration Acts of 1917 and 1924 were passed to limit further migration to the United States. Driven into a corner, the Asian American community attempted to organize to ensure their survival. They formed their own political associations. Through these associations, the different Asian American groups also maintained their contacts with their countries of origin.

Active Asian American participation in electoral politics started in the first quarter of the twentieth century. Although it was difficult for them to gain acceptability, those who won elections were instrumental in highlighting the problems of Asian Americans and the discrimination to which they were subjected in daily society. Active participation in mass protest politics on the part of Asian Americans started in the 1950s and 1960s. Incidents of violence against people belonging to this group have led them to mobilize politically. Today, Asian Americans have excelled in all walks of life. Their children are well represented in elite schools and colleges. Several universities have now introduced courses in Asian American studies. Professionally, Asian Americans are also doing much better than other minority groups. Their presence in the political life of the country is slowly being felt, in part because of being included as beneficiaries in traditional affirmative action programs in the fields of education and employment.

While some affirmative action programs may exclude Asian Americans from the list of beneficiaries, studies reflect that such exclusion depends on the program. For example, one study reported in the *Chronicle of Higher Education* indicated that Asian Americans are generally included as beneficiaries to affirmative action plans in many of the selective undergraduate colleges. On the professional schooling level, "one in six medical schools and four of five law schools granted some sort of preference to Asian applicants" (Schmidt 2003, 24). Anecdotal information also abounds as to the continuing need of affirmative action for Asian Americans. For example, Karen Narasaki, the Executive Director of the National Asian Pacific American Legal Consortium, has commented that many Asian Americans like herself gained admittance to top schools and to professional occupations in part due to supportive affirmative action programs. Narasaki wrote in 1998:

> These days Asian-Americans are being cast as victims of affirmative action. Many White Americans have held us up as "model minorities, giving us status as honorary Whites. Most of us are not deceived—we know the sting of racism and xenophobia. In this time of rising intolerance, we cannot afford to remain silent. . . . Yale had instituted an affirmative-action program that gave me the chance to prove myself. . . . (Narasaki, 1997, 56)

Despite such comments supporting the need for affirmative action for Asian Americans, opponents often argue that affirmative action is not needed for Asian Americans because, as a group, the group fares quite well in admittance to higher education institutions and ascendancy into many professions. For example, in 1997, the University of Texas at Austin accepted 81 percent of its Asian applicants, without the use of any affirmative action program. Additionally, a poll conducted by the *Chronicle of Higher Education* in May 2003 suggested that Asian Americans are collectively ambivalent about affirmative action, and, as a group, are less supportive of affirmative action than African American or Hispanic groups.

See also Census Classifications, Ethnic and Racial; Model Minorities (Stereotyping Asian Americans); Xenophobia.

FURTHER READING: Chan, Sucheng, 1991, *Asian Americans: An Interpretive History*, Boston: Twayne; Fawcett, James T., and Benjamin V. Carino, eds., 1987, *Pacific Bridges: The New Immigration from Asia and the Pacific Islands*, New York: Centre for Migration Studies; Gutierrez, Gitanjali S., 2001, "Taking Account of Another Race: Reframing Asian-American Challenges to Race Conscious Admissions in Public Schools," *Cornell Law Review* 86 (September): 1283–1333; Narasaki, Karen, 1997, "I, Too, Am an Affirmative Action Baby," *Essence* 28, no. 6 (October): 56; Schmidt, Peter, 2003, "For Asians, Affirmative Action Cuts Both Ways," *Chronicle of Higher Education*, June 6, 24; Takagi, Dana Y., 1993, "Asian Americans and Racial Politics: A Postmodern Paradox," *Social Justice* 20, nos. 1–2 (spring–summer): 115–128.

MIRZA ASMER BEG

Assimilation Theory

The historical American approach to diversity was long based upon the theory of assimilation. Minority groups were expected to cast off their minority cultural identity and assimilate socially, economically, and politically into mainstream American society. Hence the assimilation theory connotes a process of absorption of persons or groups of differing ethnic heritage into the dominant culture of a society. Most typically, the individuals involved were immigrants or previously isolated minorities who, through contact and day-to-day living in the larger culture, eventually gave up most of their previous culture traits and assumed new societal traits to such a degree that eventually the individuals became indistinguishable from other members of the larger society. One purpose of affirmative action programs today is to promote and preserve uniqueness and diversity, a purpose arguably antithetical to the assimilation theory.

Total assimilation is rare and occurs only when the individuals at issue relocate and their families are broken up. The difficulty in achieving complete absorption is exemplified by the large presence of regional cultures in Europe despite centuries of conquest and war and multiple attempts to force assimilation. Total assimilation of one group into another is difficult because when two cultures come into contact, culture change takes place, ranging from cultural borrowings to acculturation (i.e., individual changes in beliefs, values, and practices) and syncretism (i.e., changes or modifications to religious beliefs or practices as a result of exposure to another cultural world). This iron law of human society hinges on the fact that culture is dynamic, adaptive, and resilient. One can only expect complete absorption in the case of a very small number of people who are not just demographically very insignificant, but effectively cut off from their ancestral homeland for a long period of time, thereby eliminating reinforcing or rejuvenating cultural influences. Additionally, there must be profound intergroup marriages to dissolve the cohesion of the alien group and effect its integration and absorption into the dominant culture.

In the U.S. context, the assimilation theory has been advanced in some circles to explain the historical approach to diversity. The historical assimilation of minority groups into mainstream society in the United States has been labeled Anglo-conformity. This white Anglo-Saxon Protestant (WASP) culture, as the ideological commitment of the colonists and the Founding Fathers, was claimed to have molded a fixed, homogeneous American culture, rooted in the English language and English political institutions and social patterns. Immigrants were expected to divest themselves of their cultures and imbibe WASP culture. Africans and other minority classes in the United States were subjected to a scheme of domination based upon this mind-set. The concept of Anglo-conformity should be distinguished from other forms of assimilation, such as the melting-pot theory or cultural pluralism. The concept of the "melting pot," expressed in the eighteenth century by the French writer J. Hector St. John de Crèvecoeur and popularized in the early twentieth century by the Jewish-English writer Israel Zangwill, asserts that all immigrants to America have contributed to "God's crucible, the great melting pot"—a homogeneous but constantly changing American culture. That is, under the melting-pot theory of assimilation, both the mainstream and immigrant/minority cultures change with exposures to each other. Finally, the concept of cultural pluralism, expressed in 1915 by the Jewish-American philosopher Horace Kallen, recognizes U.S. society as a "mixing bowl," "cultural mosaic," or "symphony of cultures" and states that all immigrants should absorb these aspects of a uniform culture—the English language and English political ideals and economic institutions—while retaining their cultural heritages.

See also Amalgamation; Diversity; Integration; Pluralism; Socialization Theory of Equality; WASP (White Anglo-Saxon Protestant).

FURTHER READING: Gordon, Irving, 1980, *American Studies: A Conceptual Approach*, New York: Amsco School Publications; Mattox, H.E., 1992, "The American Melting Pot: E Pluribus Unum," *Nigerian Journal of American Studies* 2 (July): 118–126; Novak, Michael, 1971, *The Rise of the Unmeltable Ethnics*, New York: Macmillan; Uya, Okon Edet, 1992, *African Diaspora and the Black Experience in the New World Slavery*, New York: Third Press; Young, Crawford, 1979, *The Politics of Cultural Pluralism*, Madison: University of Wisconsin Press.

PAUL OBIYO MBANASO NJEMANZE

Australia and Affirmative Action

Australia has lightly experimented in affirmative action programs for the benefit of women, people with disabilities, and the aboriginal population. By far, Australia's experimentation with affirmative action was most extensive in the area of gender-based affirmative action. However, Australia's practice of affirmative action appears quite weak when compared with the United States' practice. Australia experimented with gender-based affirmative action starting in 1986, but moved away from employing affirmative action after several years with the implementation of new legislation on the subject in 1999. The Equal Opportunity for Women in the Workplace Act of 1999 came into effect on January 1, 2000, renaming and updating the previous legislation in effect, the Affirmative Action or Equal Employment Opportunity for Women Act of 1986. The 1999 act requires that private-sector companies, community organizations, nongovernment schools, unions, group-training companies, and higher-education institutions with 100 or more people establish a workplace program to remove the barriers to women entering and advancing in their organizations. However, the new legislation noticeably curtailed the usage of affirmative action to achieve these goals.

When the original legislation was introduced into Parliament in 1986, the government maintained that legislation was needed to ensure that all large employers took seriously their obligations to their female employees. Hence the act required the promotion of equal opportunity for women in employment and the elimination of discrimination by employers against women in employment. All organizations with 100 or more employees were required to develop and implement affirmative action programs and annually report the progress of these programs. Organizations were required to provide numerical goals for the employment of women and specify a time period in which these goals would be achieved. In addition, the act established the Affirmative Action Agency, which was responsible for the administration of the act and reported to Parliament on its operations. The effectiveness of the act was reviewed in 1991–1992, and as a result, the act was amended to include coverage of nongovernment schools, community organizations, and group-training companies with 100 or more employees.

However, the Equal Opportunity for Women in the Workplace Act of 1999 moved away from the language of affirmative action toward that of equal employment opportunity. It reduced annual reporting requirements to biennial reports and provided employers with more flexibility in program implementation. However, employers are still required to present a quantitative workplace profile and action plans every two years. The Equal Opportunity for Women in the Workplace Act of 1999 does not require employers to set goals and targets; rather, they "need to demonstrate that they have 'intentionally' identified the issues for women and taken action to address them" (www.eeo.gov.au).

Australia has experimented in very limited fashion as it relates to people with disabilities and as it relates to the aboriginal population. In the area of disabilities, Australia enacted in 1992 the Disability Discrimination Act (DDA), which (similar to the Americans with Disabilities Act of 1990) strove to make unlawful discrimination on account of one's physical disabilities. The DDA is occasionally described as an affirmative action measure because the DDA "requires a degree of positive action on the part of others to make appropriate adjustments for a disabled person's specific requirements . . . [f]or example, to adjust the disabling aspects of a workplace in a bid to accommodate an individual's impairments." Furthermore, the DDA "also requires employers, service providers, and so on to take disability into account when considering disabled people for employment or in the provision of goods and services, so that substantive outcomes are more equitable" (Handley 2001, 518).

Finally, Australia has experimented in a very limited fashion with affirmative action for the aboriginal population, usually on the territorial (state) government level and often dealing land allocation and land rights. For example, under the 1975 territorial legislation entitled the Pitjantjatjara Land Rights Act of South Australia, "a large area of north-west South Australia was vested in the Pitjantjatjara people, who had unrestricted access to the land, while non-Pitjantjatjaras had to have special permission" to enter and/or use the land. The Australian legislation has sanctioned such preferential territorial legislation in favor of aboriginal tribes through passage of the Commonwealth Racial Discrimination Act of 1975. Section 8 of this act specifies that "special measures" utilized to benignly discriminate on account of race and to benefit aboriginal populations does not constitute unlawful discrimination. Furthermore, the courts in Australia have reviewed section 8 of the Commonwealth Racial Discrimination Act of 1975, and have held it to a valid law, thus in theory opening the way for further territorial legislation giving preferences to the aboriginal population.

See also Brazil and Affirmative Action; Canada and Affirmative Action; China and Affirmative Action; European Union and Affirmative Action; Global Implementation of Affirmative Action Programs; Great Britain and Affirmative Action; India and Affirmative Action; Japan and Affirmative Action; South Africa and Affirmative Action.

FURTHER READING: Affirmative Action Agency, 1990, *Taking Steps: Employers' Progress in Affirmative Action,* Canberra, Australia: AGPS; *Affirmative Action (Equal Employment Opportunity) Act (1986),* Canberra, Australia: Canberra Publishing Services; Australian Government, 2003, Equal Opportunity for Women in the Workplace Agency web site: http://www.eeo.gov/au; Braithwaite, V., 1992, *First Steps: Business Reactions to Implementing the Affirmative Action Act,* Report to the Affirmative Action Agency, Canberra, Australia: Research School of Social Sciences, ANU; Braithwaite, V., and J. Bush, 1998, "Affirmative Action in Australia: A Consensus-Based Dialogic Approach," *NWSA Journal* 10, no. 11:115–130; Burton, C., 1991, *The Promise and the Price: The Struggle for Equal Opportunity in Women's Employment,* North Sydney, Australia: Allen and Unwin; Handley, Peter, 2001, " 'Caught between a Rock and Hard Place': Anti-Discrimination Legislation in the Liberal State and the Fate of the Australian Disability Discrimination Act," *Australian Journal of Political Science* 36, no. 3 (November): 515–529; Hodges-Aeberhard, 1999, "Affirmative Action in Employment: Recent Court Approaches to a Difficult Concept," *International Labour Review* 138, no. 3 (autumn): 247–271; O'Connor, Julia, Ann Shola Orloff, and Sheila Shaver, 1999, *States, Markets, Families: Gender, Liberalism, and Social Policy in Australia, Canada, Great Britain, and the United States,* Cambridge: Cambridge University Press; Thornton, M., 1990, *The Liberal Promise: Anti-Discrimination Legislation in Australia,* Melbourne, Australia: Oxford University Press.

PAULINA X. RUF

B

Baker v. Carr, 369 U.S. 186 (1962)

In *Baker v. Carr*, the U.S. Supreme Court determined that federal courts had jurisdiction to resolve certain challenges to electoral districting and apportionment by the states. The Court went on to find that voters who alleged that their voting rights were impaired by arbitrary apportionment could state a justiciable claim under the Equal Protection Clause of the Fourteenth Amendment. The Court's decision in *Baker v. Carr* laid the foundation for the Court to articulate its principle of "one person, one vote" in *Wesberry v. Sanders*, 376 U.S. 1 (1964), and *Reynolds v. Sims*, 377 U.S. 533 (1964), and to open up the federal courts to lawsuits by minority voters whose voting rights were diluted. Over time, white voters were to capitalize on the Court's voting rights jurisprudence as well and bring their own challenges to states that practiced affirmative action in apportionment and developed race-conscious redistricting plans that benefited traditionally underrepresented minority groups.

Tennessee's 1901 Apportionment Act established a system whereby state General Assembly seats (thirty-three in the Senate and ninety nine in the lower house) were allocated in accordance with the 1900 federal census. All attempts by the legislature to reapportion itself after 1901 failed. By the time the Supreme Court heard the plaintiffs' challenge to the Tennessee act, districting in Tennessee reflected demographics that were more than sixty years old, resulting in the largest House district having nineteen times the population of the smallest House district.

The plaintiffs, urban voters residing in heavily populated districts, claimed that the Tennessee Apportionment Act was in violation of the Fourteenth Amendment's Equal Protection Clause and that it "arbitrarily and capriciously apportioned representatives in the Senate and House without reference . . . to any logical or reasonable formula whatever." The plaintiffs alleged that "because of the population changes since 1900 and the failure of the Legislature to reapportion itself since 1901," the apportionment statute diluted the worth of their votes and served as a barrier to their equal representation in the General Assembly. In claiming that the act violated the Equal Protection Clause, the plaintiffs contended that they were unable to change the apportionment mechanism through legislative action because the 1901 Tennessee statute prevented them from having an effective voice in the General Assembly. They asked the U.S. District Court for the Middle District of Tennessee to declare the act unconstitutional and to enjoin future elections in which representation was to be based on the apportionment in the 1901 act.

A three-judge panel of the district court acknowledged the plaintiffs' allegation of a constitutional violation but claimed that it was unable to correct it. The district court ruled that it lacked jurisdiction over the case because it did not fall within the jurisdiction of the federal courts stated in Article III of the U.S. Constitution. It also ruled that the case was not justiciable because it involved a political question: the distribution of political power for legislative purposes. The court based its justiciability finding on the separation-of-powers principle that courts are allowed to address only legal questions and not political ones. Because the district court found that the plaintiffs' complaint was not justiciable, the court also dismissed the complaint for failure to state a claim upon which relief could be granted.

In an opinion written by Justice William Brennan, the Supreme Court overturned the lower court's ruling, finding that the district court did in fact possess jurisdiction over the subject matter of the plaintiffs' claim and that the plaintiffs' stated claim was eligible for relief in federal court. The Supreme Court noted that Article III of the U.S. Constitution gives federal courts jurisdiction over any matter that "arises under" the Constitution, and the plaintiffs alleged that the 1901 Tennessee Apportionment Act deprived them of equal protection under the Fourteenth Amendment. In addressing the district court's second concern (that the plaintiffs failed to state a claim upon which relief could be granted), the Supreme Court ruled that the Equal Protection Clause of the Constitution offered the plaintiffs a cause of action and remedy—that is, voting equality. The Court did not reach the merits of the plaintiffs' complaint and, therefore, sent the case back to the district court for trial and, if appropriate, a determination as to the relief to which the plaintiffs were entitled.

The Court did, however, acknowledge the district court's concern over the nonjusticiability of a political question. For example, the Court noted that many questions involving foreign relations are political and, therefore, outside judicial purview; yet the fact that a suit seeks the protection of a political right such as voting does not necessarily mean that it presents a political question. The Supreme Court decided that the plaintiffs' suit was not limited to a political question because (*a*) the plaintiffs were asking whether the Tennessee statute was consistent with the U.S. Constitution, and (*b*) the plaintiffs were not asking the Court to make policy determinations for which there were no judicial standards. In its decision, the Court noted that "judicial standards under the Equal Protection Clause are well developed and familiar, and it has been open to courts since the enactment of the Fourteenth Amendment to determine, if on the particular facts . . . [an act of] . . . discrimination reflects no policy but simply arbitrary and capricious action."

The Court ruled as it did despite Justice Felix Frankfurter's and Justice John Marshall Harlan's dissents, in each of which the other joined. Justice Frankfurter wrote in his dissent that the plaintiffs had presented a political question that was not justiciable, and Justice Harlan found in his that there was nothing in the Equal Protection Clause that required states to apportion legislative districts so that each voter has roughly an equal voice in the political process.

Despite these dissents, the case resolved definitively that federal courts were empowered to consider whether state apportionment violated the Equal Protection Clause. By deciding that such equal protection challenges were not political questions, the Supreme Court created an important enforcement mechanism to prevent states from discriminating against minority voters, and ultimately, it became a mechanism by which white voters challenged state affirmative action in apportionment, specific redistricting that consciously benefited minority groups.

See also Brennan, William Joseph; Equal Protection Clause; Fourteenth Amendment; Voting Rights Act of 1965.

FURTHER READING: Balinski, Michael L., and H. Peyton Young, 1982, *Fair Representation: Meeting the Ideal of One Man, One Vote,* New Haven, CT: Yale University Press; Graham, Gene, 1972, *One Man, One Vote: Baker v. Carr and the American Levellers,* Boston: Atlantic Monthly Press/Little, Brown and Co.; Grofman, Bernard N., 1990, *Voting Rights, Voting Wrongs: The Legacy of Baker v. Carr,* New York: Priority Press Publications; Strauss, Larry, 1998, *One Man, One Vote,* Los Angeles: Holloway House.

GREGORY M. DUHL

Basically Qualified

See Quotas.

The Bell Curve

In 1994, the extremely controversial and incendiary book *The Bell Curve* by Richard Herrnstein and Charles Murray was published. The late Richard Herrnstein was a psychology professor at Harvard. Charles Murray, a political scientist, is an outspoken critic of affirmative action and social welfare programs. In Murray's previous books (*Losing Ground: American Social Policy, 1950–1980* [1984] and *In Pursuit of Happiness and Good Government* [1988]), he argued that African Americans are actually hurt by affirmative action because it makes them dependent on welfare and causes recipients to lose self-respect. In *The Bell Curve,* Herrnstein and Murray purported to explain differences in intelligence in the United States and related policy implications using quantitative analyses. Critics denounced the science used in *The Bell Curve* and condemned its authors as being unqualified to speak on issues of genetics or intelligence. Despite the fact that it has been highly criticized, the book is still occasionally cited in affirmative action literature, usually for the statistics reported therein (e.g., Kahlenberg 1996, 65–66).

The Bell Curve is based on six main assumptions. First, there is a general factor of cognitive ability along which people differ. Second, this general factor can be measured to some degree by standardized tests of academic aptitude, but is most accurately measured by IQ tests whose sole purpose is to do so. Third, IQ scores delineate intelligence. Fourth, IQ scores are significantly stable over the life course of the individual. Fifth, IQ tests, when administered correctly, are not biased against different racial, ethnic, or other social groups. Finally, cognitive ability is largely hereditary. The basic conclusions drawn from these assumptions are as follows. American society is increasingly becoming cognitively stratified; more intelligent Americans are selected for college and high-end occupations, while those less intelligent are left to blue-collar work or unemployment. Herrnstein and Murray assert that because the most intelligent employees are also the most capable, they make the most money and in turn can live in elite neighborhoods and attend separate institutions such as schools, churches, shopping areas, and so on, which in turn leads to a physical separation from the rest of society. Just as the most intelligent among society are necessarily the wealthiest, Herrnstein and Murray claim that poverty and its associated problems stem from the behaviors of those with lower cognitive ability. Thus, contrary to the more popular belief that socioeconomic status contributes to poverty, *The Bell Curve* argues that low IQ is the single greatest source. In particular, the authors contend that low intelligence increases the chances of doing poorly in school and attaining a higher education, which subsequently leads to higher pay. In addition, low IQ is associated with unemployment, divorce and illegitimate pregnancies, welfare dependency, crime, lack of civic responsibility, and poor parenting skills and their results. In essence, *The Bell Curve* takes a blatant blame-the-victim stance.

Perhaps the most controversial claim of *The Bell Curve* is that cognitive ability or intelligence is directly related to race. Herrnstein and Murray delineate a hierarchy in which East Asians fare the highest, while white Americans come in second, and African Americans rank a distant third. They maintain that these differences remain even when holding socioeconomic status constant and that the greatest differences appear, in fact, among those at the highest income levels.

The final portion of *The Bell Curve* is devoted to a discussion of public policies that might serve to remedy the lower cognitive abilities of certain social groups. Because the worst social problems are concentrated in a population that the authors argue has the lowest intelligence, public policies aimed at helping these communities should be designed to take into consideration their lower cognitive ability. Specifically, the authors recommend that mothers with low intelligence voluntarily give their children up for adoption to raise the IQs of their children. They explain that social programs such as Women, Infants, and Children (WIC) and Head Start have little if any impact on increasing intelligence and that this is the better solution. They also advocate that federal funds be transferred from programs aimed at helping the disadvantaged to programs aimed at helping the gifted. They explain that schools have been remedial and "dumbing-down" to accommodate the low cognitive abilities of certain children and that many children therefore miss the opportunity to develop to their potential. Similarly, the authors claim that affirmative action programs in higher education and the workplace have largely benefited those with lower IQs and that such workers are less productive, resulting in racial animosity. Instead, they advocate a color-blind affirmative action (class-based affirmative action) aimed at helping more intellectually qualified members of the disadvantaged populations.

The critique of *The Bell Curve* is founded on two basic arguments. The first is that the authors were unqualified to write a book about genetics and IQ. Charles Murray is a political scientist whose work has been concerned primarily with welfare and affirmative action. His career has been spent primarily at conservative think tanks advocating against social welfare policies. At the time of his death, shortly before the publication of *The Bell Curve*, Richard Herrnstein was the occupant of Harvard's oldest chair in psychology. The basis of much of his work was experimental, often relying on lab animals rather than human subjects, and was not focused on genetics. Although Herrnstein did publish several articles regarding intelligence, none of his peer-reviewed journal articles were related to this topic.

The second major objection to *The Bell Curve* is that many of the data used were invalid or unreliable and that the analyses of the data were unsound. Indeed, the book caused such an uproar that the American Psychological Association created a task force to review the work and its topic. One of the main conclusions reached by the task force was that many of the data used in the analyses were flawed. Indeed, some of the sources used were themselves considered invalid. For example, some of the data were derived from work produced at the Pioneer Fund, a neo-Nazi group whose founder campaigned to send African Americans back to Africa, and whose primary contemporary objective has been to support eugenic policies. In addition, researchers associated with the Human Genome Project argued that Herrnstein and Murray relied too heavily on an unfounded presupposition of the heritability of cognitive ability and maintained that genetics is a far more complex issue than the authors would have readers believe. One of the most often argued critiques was that *The Bell Curve* failed to substantiate the primary claim, that the number referred to as the general factor of intelligence captures a real mental phenomenon or that standardized tests, particularly IQ tests, are able to measure this factor well.

See also African Americans; Asian Americans; Class-Based Affirmative Action; Economically Disadvantaged; Eugenics; Head Start; Ideological Racism/Racist Ideology; Scientific Racism.

FURTHER READING: Dorfman, Donald D., 1995, "Soft Science with a Neoconservative Agenda," *Contemporary Psychology* 40, no. 5:418–421; Herrnstein, Richard J., and Charles Murray, 1994, *The Bell Curve: Intelligence and Class Structure in American Life*, New York: Free Press; Kahlenberg, Richard D., 1996, *The Remedy: Class, Race, and Affirmative Action*, New York: Basic Books.

MAYA ALEXANDRA BEASLEY

Bell, Derrick A., Jr. (1930–)

Derrick Bell, a law professor, is a nationally known advocate of affirmative action and reparations. Bell is also well known for his series of books that feature a fictional civil rights leader, Geneva Crenshaw. These books include *And We Are Not Saved, Faces at the Bottom of the Well, Gospel Choirs*, and *Afrolantica Legacies*. In addition, Derrick Bell published *Race, Racism, and America Law* (1973), now a standard law school text. Derrick Bell is a respected activist for the rights of blacks and other minorities and has spent his life on a "justice quest," pursuing the end of discrimination and suffering. In 1990, Bell received national attention when he went on a leave of absence to protest the failure of Harvard Law School to hire a tenured minority female professor. When he still had not returned two years later, Harvard refused to extend his leave of absence any further, and he lost his tenured Harvard Law School professorship in 1992. Along with Cornel West, Henry Louis

Gates Jr., and Toni Morrison, Bell signed a national advertisement in 1996 advocating the continuation of affirmative action in the United States.

Derrick Bell was born in Pittsburgh, Pennsylvania, on November 6, 1930. He received his B.A. from Duquesne University in 1952 and, after serving in the Korean War, earned a law degree from the University of Pittsburgh Law School in 1957. Bell started his legal career at the U.S. Department of Justice, where he was a staff attorney in the Civil Rights Division. The Justice Department felt that his membership in the National Association for the Advancement of Colored People (NAACP) represented a conflict of interest with his work in civil rights, and rather than resigning his membership, he resigned his position in the department in 1959. He was executive secretary to the Pittsburgh branch of the NAACP until 1960, when he was recruited by Thurgood Marshall to join the Legal Defense and Educational Fund of the NAACP. In 1971, Derrick Bell became the first black tenured professor at Harvard Law School, a position he gave up 1992 in protest of the university's lack of minority women faculty members, a struggle documented in his book *Confronting Authority: Reflections of an Ardent Protester* (1994). Currently, he is a full-time visiting professor of law at New York University's School of Law.

See also Department of Justice; Gates, Henry Louis, Jr.; Marshall, Thurgood; Morrison, Toni; National Association for the Advancement of Colored People; Reparations; West, Cornel.

FURTHER READING: Bell, Derrick, 1987, *And We Are Not Saved: The Elusive Quest for Racial Justice*, New York: Basic Books; "A Class Sends Message to Harvard Law School," 1990, *New York Times*, November 21, 11; Bell, Derrick, 1994, "The Freedom of Employment Act: Affirmative Reaction," *Nation* 258, no. 20 (May 23): 708–714; Bell, Derrick, 2002, *Ethical Ambition: Living a Life of Meaning and Worth*, New York: Bloomsbury; Taylor, Lynda Guydon, 2001, "Professor Says Civil Rights Changes Always in Favor of Whites," *Pittsburgh Post-Gazette*, May 20, W3.

PAULINA X. RUF

Benign Discrimination

The term "benign discrimination" denotes measures intended and designed to benefit individuals or groups by taking account of their protected group status (such as race, sex, or disability). Benign discrimination is distinguished from measures intended and designed to disadvantage or injure individuals or groups based on this group status, usually termed "invidious discrimination." Affirmative action programs that utilize preferences to benefit minorities and women have been characterized as "benign discrimination," particularly by defenders of such measures. It is generally accepted that such programs discriminate on the basis of race or sex. However, defenders argue that laws prohibiting race and sex discrimination prohibit only invidious discrimination and do not prohibit affirmative action–type benign discrimination because such measures may be necessary to eliminate the effects of invidious discrimination against these groups.

Characterization of affirmative action measures that use preferences as benign discrimination in order to defend them has met with varying degrees of success. One of the formidable challenges to this argument is that distinguishing between "benign discrimination" and "invidious discrimination" is not easy and, indeed, has led to results that proponents would find objectionable. Another formidable challenge is the claim that "benign" discrimination does not exist. Some argue that preferences that might be described as benign are actually harmful both to the persons who are not entitled to the preference and to the recipients of the preference.

Indeed, before affirmative action measures were characterized as "benign discrimination," the concept was used to defend measures that, in fact, limited or injured minorities, women, and persons with disabilities on the grounds that the measures were well intended to prevent harm to the subjects of the measures. For example, so-called state protective legislation excluded women from certain types of jobs in order to protect them from the hazards of the jobs. Courts struck down these laws, finding that while they might have been intended to benefit women, they were based on negative sex-based stereotypes about the capabilities of women and, in fact, injured women by limiting their opportunities. As another example, the U.S. Supreme Court rejected the argument that a prison should be able to segregate prison inmates by race, in part to protect the prisoners and the guards by preventing interracial violence.

On the other hand, courts have held that affirmative action measures of private (nongovernmental) entities that give preferences to minorities and women and that were intended and designed to eliminate demonstrated discrimination or its lingering effects do not violate antidiscrimination statutes, such as Title VII of the Civil Rights Act of 1964, because this goal was held to "mirror the purpose" of the antidiscrimination laws. In order to be legal, however, such measures, intended to benefit minorities and women, could not be too burdensome on whites or on males (*United Steelworkers of America v. Weber*, 443 U.S. 193 [1979], and *Johnson v. Transportation Agency, Santa Clara County*, 480 U.S. 616 [1987]).

The argument that "benignly discriminatory" affirmative action measures of governments are not illegal has not been as successful. In addition to being subject to many antidiscrimination statutes, state, local, and federal governmental actions are also subject to the Fifth Amendment (federal actions) and the Fourteenth Amendment (state and local actions) to the U.S. Constitution. The equal protection guarantees of these amendments prohibit governments from subjecting similarly situated persons to different treatment under law. Whether governments may treat groups differently on the basis of certain immutable personal characteristics such as race, gender, age, or disability depends, in part, on how closely the courts examine the purpose for the difference in treatment and the way in which the purpose is achieved. The term "benign discrimination" is often used in U.S. Supreme Court decisions in discussions concerning what "level of scrutiny" should be applied to affirmative action programs of the federal government and of state and local governments in order to ensure that they do not violate these equal protection guarantees. The more rigorous the level of scrutiny, the less likely it is that the measure under examination will be upheld as constitutional. Proponents of governmental affirmative action programs that utilize preferences for minorities and women argue that these measures, which would normally be subject to rigorous scrutiny by the courts because they use racial and gender-based classifications, should be subject to less rigorous scrutiny because they are "benign."

In *City of Richmond v. J.A. Croson Co.*, 488 U.S. 469 (1989), the U.S. Supreme

Court applied strict scrutiny review to Richmond's affirmative action program requiring prime contractors hired by the city to use at least 30 percent of the contract's proceeds to employ "minority business enterprises" as subcontractors. Measures survive strict scrutiny review only if they are narrowly tailored to achieve a compelling governmental interest. Strict scrutiny review has been frequently characterized as "strict in theory, but fatal in fact," because most measures examined under this standard have been held to be unconstitutional. In an attempt to avoid a similar fate, the city of Richmond argued that its affirmative action measures should not be subject to strict scrutiny review because they were benign measures intended to benefit minorities who had been the victims of invidious discrimination. The Court rejected this argument, stating, "Absent searching judicial inquiry into the justification for such race-based measures, there is simply no way of determining what classifications are 'benign' or 'remedial' and what classifications are in fact motivated by illegitimate notions of racial inferiority or simple racial politics." The Court also rejected the position that striking down benign racial classifications used by majority racial groups to benefit minority groups and to disadvantage themselves does not further one of the purposes of the Fourteenth Amendment Equal Protection Clause: to protect "discrete and insular minorities" from majoritarian prejudice. The Court concluded that this argument did not support a less rigorous standard in this case. The Court explained that blacks appeared to be a political majority in Richmond and held a majority on the city council that adopted the affirmative action program.

However, the U.S. Supreme Court, in its opinion in the case of *Metro Broadcasting, Inc. v. FCC*, 497 U.S. 547 (1990), was convinced that Congress—as opposed to states—should be able to use racial classifications in affirmative action programs with more freedom than it could employ other types of racial classifications because such racial classifications were benign. The Court explained that the benign racial classifications of the federal government as used in affirmative action programs do not violate constitutional equal protection guarantees if they "serve important governmental objectives within the power of Congress and are substantially related to achievement of those objectives." This standard is less rigorous and significantly easier to meet than the strict scrutiny standard usually applied to racial classifications. To address the issue of how a benign measure employed by Congress should be distinguished from an invidiously discriminatory measure, the Supreme Court expressed "confiden[ce] that an 'examination of the legislative scheme and its history' will separate benign measures from other types of racial classifications." The Court found that the Federal Communication Commission's order providing preferences to minority-owned firms in order to increase broadcasting diversity did not violate constitutional equal protection guarantees because it satisfied this relaxed review standard.

However, in 1995, the U.S. Supreme Court issued its decision in *Adarand Constructors, Inc. v. Peña*, 515 U.S. 200 (1995). At issue in *Adarand* was a federal program that required extra compensation to prime contractors for federal contracts who employed disadvantaged businesses as subcontractors and that presumed that minority-owned businesses were disadvantaged. Justice Sandra Day O'Connor, writing for a plurality of the Court, stated that measures that benignly discriminate and those that invidiously discriminate must both be subject to the same standard of review whether or not these measures are used by state governments or by the federal government. In the case of race-based measures, the correct standard was strict scrutiny review. Justice O'Connor explained that both benign and invidious measures must be exceedingly closely scrutinized because it would not always be clear when a measure is benign as opposed to invidious. Justice O'Connor also emphasized that the Constitution's equal protection guarantee demands that individuals be treated equally without regard to their race except for the most compelling reasons and that courts cannot ensure this guarantee without subjecting all racial classifications, whether assertedly benign or invidious, to the strictest judicial scrutiny. Justice Clarence Thomas, in a concurring opinion, rejected any legal distinction between benign and invidious measures because he believed that discrimination characterized as "benign" teaches that minorities are incapable of achieving equally without the help of racial preferences. Persons who are disadvantaged by these preferences come to believe that they are victims of discrimination themselves and/or that they are superior to the beneficiaries of the preference. Thus, according to Justice Thomas, "benign" preferences are actually "badges of inferiority" that do not benefit minorities.

Justice John Paul Stevens, in his dissenting opinion joined by Justice Ruth Bader Ginsburg, disagreed. He contended that benign race-based programs should not be subject to "strict scrutiny" review. Justice Stevens feared that such programs might no longer be possible because actions usually do not survive strict scrutiny review. Governments should have more flexibility in implementing programs that benefit racial minority groups that have historically been subject to discrimination when the purpose of such programs is to achieve equality. These affirmative action programs should not be viewed as equally suspect as government programs intended to oppress minority groups. Thus, Justice Stevens contended that it was not necessary to subject these programs to strict review. Justice Stevens recognized that governmental minority preferences may cause some harm by fostering a belief that beneficiaries are not as able as others. However, he contended that this potential harm is not as great as the lingering effects of racial subordination which preferential programs are designed to remedy. Justice Stevens rejected the contention that determining whether a preference is benignly discriminatory or invidiously discriminatory is difficult or impossible. He believed that courts are readily able to distinguish between good and bad intentions and that the term "affirmative action" is well understood in contemporary lexicon.

Justice O'Connor's opinion in *Adarand* specifically assured that subjecting race-based affirmative action programs to strict scrutiny review was not automatically the death knell for such programs. She stated that government is not disqualified from responding to the persistent practice and effects of invidious racial discrimination—even with race-based measures if necessary—as long as the measures are narrowly tailored. There is also some indication in Justice O'Connor's decision that the benign nature of a race-based measure would be a relevant factor in the strict scrutiny calculus militating in favor of the constitutionality of the measure. Justice O'Connor specifically noted that not all racial classifications are equally objectionable. She described the "fundamental purpose" of strict scrutiny review as allowing the Court to take "relevant differences" into account. Justice O'Connor repeated this sentiment in writing the Court's 2003 decision in *Grutter v. Bollinger*, 123 S. Ct. 2325, 2003 U.S. LEXIS 4800 (2003). In *Grutter*, the Court addressed the issue of whether a state-operated law school was permitted to use race as a positive factor in selecting applicants for admission. Justice O'Connor stated: "Not every decision influenced by race is equally objectionable and strict scrutiny is designed to provide a framework for carefully examining the importance and the sincerity of the reasons advanced by the governmental decisionmaker for the use of race in that particular context." Perhaps a racial classification that is well intentioned or is used by a government actor with a particularly special reason to take race into account would be more likely to pass scrutiny. Indeed, the Court upheld the affirmative action program in *Grutter*. However, in his dissenting opinion in *Grutter*, Chief Justice William Rehnquist argued that the majority applied a less strict standard to the affirmative action plan because it thought that race was being used "in good faith" even though this approach had been rejected by the Court. He quoted the Court's *Adarand* opinion that "[m]ore than good motives should be required when government seeks to allocate resources by way of an explicit racial classification system."

Governmental affirmative action programs that employ gender-based preferences have been subject to an intermediate level of scrutiny. Under intermediate scrutiny review, the measure must be substantially related to important governmental objectives. This is the same standard of review applied to invidious gender-based classifications. Although it is a heightened standard of review, it is less rigorous than strict scrutiny review. The U.S. Supreme Court's decision to apply the same standard of review under the Fifth and Fourteenth Amendment's equal protection guarantees to benignly discriminatory measures as to invidiously discriminatory measures leads to what some would call an anomalous result. As Justice Stevens noted in his *Adarand* dissent, governments can more easily and aggressively act to remedy gender-based discrimination than to remedy race-based discrimination even though the Constitution's equal protection guarantees were primarily intended to end discrimination against freed persons.

See also Adarand Constructors, Inc. v. Peña; City of Richmond v. J.A. Croson Co.; Civil Rights Act of 1964; Discrimination; Equal Protection Clause; Federal Communications Commission; Fifth Amendment; Fourteenth Amendment; Gender-Based Affirmative Action; Ginsburg, Ruth Bader; *Gratz v. Bollinger/Grutter v. Bollinger*; Intermediate Scrutiny Review; Invidious Discrimination; *Johnson v. Transportation Agency, Santa Clara County; Metro Broadcasting, Inc. v. FCC*; O'Connor, Sandra Day; Rational Basis Scrutiny; Reverse Discrimination; Strict Scrutiny; Stevens, John Paul; Supreme Court and Affirmative Action; Thomas, Clarence; Title VII of the Civil Rights Act of 1964; *United Steelworkers of America v. Weber*.

FURTHER READING: Bhagwat, Ashutosh, 2002, "Affirmative Action and Compelling Interests: Equal Protection at the Crossroads," *University of Pennsylvania Journal of Constitutional Law* 4 (January): 260–280; Bohrer, Robert A., 1981, "*Bakke, Weber*, and *Fullilove*: Benign Discrimination and Congressional Power to Enforce the Fourteenth Amendment," *Indiana Law Journal* 56:473–513; Rubenfield, Jed, 2002, "The Anti-Antidiscrimination Agenda," *Yale Law Journal* 111 (March): 1141–1178.

MARIA D. BECKMAN

Berea College v. Commonwealth of Kentucky, 211 U.S. 483 (1908)

Berea College v. Commonwealth of Kentucky was the first higher-education segregation case under the Fourteenth Amendment to be argued before the U.S. Supreme Court. The connection between affirmative action and the Berea College case is indirect. The case best relates to the history of race relations and segregation in the South, which leads to antidiscrimination laws and affirmative action cases. The majority opinion in the *Berea College* case today stands as an illustration of how pervasive the segregationist separate-but-equal doctrine was in the United States. The decision also meant that many states were free to pass racially exclusionary laws forbidding innocent and private associations in society. In the *Berea College* case, it meant that the state of Kentucky could penalize voluntary interracial association of students at private schools.

Berea College, a small private college, had had a long tradition of interracial education dating from before the American Civil War. Berea College had had both black and white students receiving instruction together since the college's inception in 1854. By 1904, it had 753 white students and 174 black students. The college was a private institution, receiving no state aid or assistance, and only persons who subscribed to the integrated educational setting were students. Then, approximately half a century after the school's founding, the Kentucky legislature enacted a statute, effective July 1904, prohibiting the maintenance of any "school, college or institution where persons of the white and Negro races are both received as pupils for instruction." The college refused to change its charter or student composition after the law's passage and was thereafter indicted, convicted, and fined $1,000.

The Supreme Court of Kentucky affirmed the conviction and the legality of the Kentucky statute. The court stated that any interracial associations were evil and unnatural and that any association "at all, under certain conditions, leads to the main evil, which is amalgamation." The court also stated that the college operated by virtue of a state charter, something the state could revoke or revise at will. Finally, the Kentucky court had no problem disregarding the Equal Protection Clause of the Fourteenth Amendment, holding that the law "applies equally to all citizens."

The case was then appealed to the U.S. Supreme Court on a writ of error. Before the Supreme Court, attorneys for Berea College argued that the state could not exercise its police power in a manner that violated the Thirteenth Amendment, the Fourteenth Amendment, and/or the Fifteenth Amendment to the U.S. Constitution. Furthermore, the attorneys for Berea College believed that the U.S. Constitution guaranteed absolute civil equality and emphasized that the state statute prohibited the freedom of choice in selecting a college in Kentucky. In essence, the attorneys for Berea College argued that attending the school was a voluntary private association, and the government did not have the right to regulate this purely private association. Furthermore, according to Berea College, if the government did attempt to enforce its segregationist statute, it would be a clear violation of the Equal Protection Clause of the Fourteenth Amendment.

However, much to the chagrin of the advocates of Berea College, the U.S. Supreme Court ultimately eschewed the constitutional issue and relied on the lower state court's ruling in the case. In a 7–2 decision, the U.S. Supreme Court upheld the state's right to create laws to regulate state-chartered private entities on the basis of race, for example, by mandating segregated railroad passenger cars and banning interracial marriages. In essence, the U.S. Supreme Court legitimized segregation in higher education through its decision in this case. In his dissent,

Justice John Marshall Harlan noted that the statute sought to prevent association between the races. He specifically stated, "I am of the opinion that in its essential parts, the statute is an arbitrary invasion of the rights of liberty and property guaranteed by the Fourteenth Amendment against hostile state action and is therefore void." The Commonwealth of Kentucky amended its Day Law in 1950 to remove the interracial educational barrier, and shortly thereafter black students began reenrolling at Berea College. In 2001, Berea College reported that approximately 17 percent of its matriculating freshman class was African American, which is significantly more than the 5–6 percent representation of African Americans in the general population in communities surrounding Berea College.

See also African Americans; Amalgamation; *Brown v. Board of Education*; Equal Protection Clause; Fifteenth Amendment; Fourteenth Amendment; *Plessy v. Ferguson; Roberts v. City of Boston*; Segregation; Thirteenth Amendment.

FURTHER READING: Abramson, Rudy, 1993, "From the Beginning Berea Nurtured Those Most in Need," *Smithsonian* 24, no. 9 (December): 92–101; Berea College, web site: http://www.berea.edu; Bullock, Henry, 1967, *Simple Justice*, Cambridge, MA: Harvard University Press; Kluger, Richard, 1977, *A History of Negro Education in the South*, New York: Vintage Books; Miller, Loren, 1972, *The United States Supreme Court and the Negro*, New York: Pantheon Books; Preer, Jean L., 1982, *Lawyers v. Educators: Black Colleges and Desegregation in Public Higher Education*, Westport, CT: Greenwood Press.

F. ERIK BROOKS

Bethune, Mary Jane McLeod (1875–1955)

Mary McLeod Bethune dedicated her life to working tirelessly for eradicating discrimination and increasing educational opportunities for African Americans. She was an educator, presidential advisor, public servant in the federal government, lecturer, newspaper columnist, and consultant. Indisputably, she became one of the most revered activists of her time. She has been described as "the most influential African-American woman in the twentieth century, whose legacy is found in the fields of education, government, politics, economics, social activism, and women's rights" (Franklin 1996, 13). Likewise, another author has commented that in the realm of education, "Mary McLeod Bethune in the twentieth century and probably in the entire history of blacks in America set a record of influence that no one has yet approached" (Berry 1982, 290). In an article she authored shortly before her death (published posthumously in August 1955 in *Ebony*) and titled "My Last Will and Testament," Bethune wrote that the struggle for equality was not over with the advent of the modern civil rights movement. Bethune wrote that "children must never lose their zeal for building a better world. They must not be discouraged from aspiring to greatness . . . nor must they forget that the masses of our people are still underprivileged, ill-housed, impoverished and victimized by discrimination. . . . [T]he Freedom Gates are half ajar. We must pry them fully open" (Ebony 1990, 133).

Bethune was born on July 10, 1875, to two former slaves, Patsy McIntosh McLeod and Samuel McLeod. Her birthplace was Mayesville, South Carolina, where her family lived on land they had purchased, called "the Homestead." She was the fifteenth of seventeen children. Bethune was fortunate to receive formal education at the Trinity Presbyterian Mission School in her hometown. At the age of ten or eleven, she graduated and, with a scholarship provided by a Detroit benefactor, entered Scotia Seminary, a Presbyterian school for African American women in Concord, North Carolina. It was there that Mary developed an interest in missionary work. Upon finishing in 1894, she matriculated at Moody Bible Institute in Chicago. Her goal was to serve as a missionary in Africa. That did not work out, so she ended up returning to teach in her hometown of Mayesville, as well as teaching in Sumter, South Carolina, and Savannah, Georgia.

While teaching at the Kendall Institute in Sumter, Mary married a fellow choir member, Albertus Bethune, and they had one son, who was born in 1899. After other teaching and social work jobs, she was persuaded to move with the family to Palatka, Florida. To help support the family, she sold life insurance. But the restless African American could not stifle the desire to do more not only for her family, but her people and society as a whole. She set as a goal to establish a school for African American girls, so she started a school for girls in Daytona Beach, Florida. In October 1904, the Daytona Educational and Industrial Training School opened with five students, who paid fifty cents a week for tuition. In 1923, the school became coeducational after merging with Cookman Institute of Jacksonville, Florida. It became known as Bethune-Cookman College by 1931. Today, the college occupies fifty-two acres with a 2,700-member student body. It is fully accredited and serves as a living memorial to the forward vision of Mary McLeod Bethune nearly a century after it was founded. She served as president of the college from 1904 to 1921 and in 1946–1947.

In 1912, Bethune joined the fight for women's suffrage and in fact became a member of the Equal Suffrage League. Even though she was a fervent supporter of voting rights for women, because of segregated conditions where she lived, she was barred from marching and publicly demonstrating for the cause. She established a literacy training program. This was bold and much needed, for this was the era in which African Americans were often subjected to literacy tests and poll taxes to deter them from voting. She was warned by the Ku Klux Klan to cease the literacy program, but Bethune was undeterred in light of the fact that this was in 1920, and the Nineteenth Amendment had recently been ratified. The next day after the Ku Klux Klan confronted her, Bethune led 100 African Americans to the polls to vote for the first time.

Once more the indomitable spirit of Mary McLeod Bethune continued to soar. As if these accomplishments were not enough, she plunged into a life of public service that would take her far beyond Daytona Beach and the state of Florida. Her marriage was over by this time. She became what was called at that time a "club woman." The clubs and groups that she joined were geared to pursuing equality in society on a national scale. In 1920, she was elected to the National Urban League's Executive Board. Later she served as president of the Southeastern Federation of Women's Clubs and president of the National Association of Colored Women. Also, she was president of the National Association of Teachers in Colored Schools, a leader of the Interracial Council of America, and vice president of the National Association for the Advancement of Colored People. The National Council of Negro Women tapped her to be its first president. As one of the founders, she eagerly accepted the challenge. With her leadership, the National Council of Negro Women became a strong voice for promoting equality and abolishing discrimination in the country. Today, the organization has 4.5 million members, thirty-four national affiliates, and more than 250 local sections. Its headquarters stands on Pennsylvania Avenue between the nation's Capitol and the White House in Washington, D.C.

It is widely acknowledged that Bethune's after discussions with President Woodrow Wilson's vice president, Thomas Riley Marshall, the National Red Cross desegregated. She worked in various capacities under Presidents Calvin Coolidge, Herbert Hoover, and Theodore Roosevelt. Further, she gained more acclaim as director of Negro affairs in the National Youth Administration from 1936 to 1944. As a consultant, she worked for the U.S. secretary of war in selecting the first female African American officer candidates in the Women's Army Auxiliary Corps. Perhaps Mary McLeod Bethune is best known for her work with Franklin D. Roosevelt as a member of the "kitchen cabinet," also known as his "black cabinet," This was an unofficial advisory group to the president. During this time, Eleanor Roosevelt and Mary McLeod Bethune became close. They worked together on social issues of the time. Often they appeared together in public. They were ardent advocates for the need to break down barriers of segregation.

From 1948 to 1955, Bethune wrote weekly newspaper columns for the *Chicago Defender*. Her columns were widely circulated. Standing as a tangible testimony to the myriad accomplishments of this trailblazer for equal rights are numerous prestigious awards. Some were the Spingarn Medal in 1935, the Frances Drexel Award for Distinguished Service in 1937, the Thomas Jefferson Award for Leadership in 1942, an honorary doctorate from Rollins College in 1945, the Medal of Honor and Merit from the Republic of Haiti in 1949, and the Star of Africa from the Republic of Liberia in 1952. A majestic statue of Mary McLeod Bethune is located in Lincoln Park in Washington, D.C. It is distinguished for being the first statue of a woman placed in a national public park. Also, a U.S. postage stamp commemorates her. On May 18, 1955, Mary Mcleod Bethune passed away, leaving an enduring legacy to the nation.

See also African Americans; Civil Rights Movement; Ku Klux Klan; National Association for the Advancement of Colored People; Nineteenth Amendment; Roosevelt, Eleanor; Roosevelt, Franklin Delano; Urban League.

FURTHER READING: Berry, Mary Frances, 1982, "Twentieth Century Black Women in Education," *Journal of Negro Education* 51, no. 3 (summer): 288–300; Bullock, Ralph, 1927, *Mary McLeod Bethune: In Spite of Handicaps*, New York: Books for Libraries Press; Ebony, 1990, "My Last Will and Testament," 46, no. 1:128–133 (orig. pub. August 1955); Franklin, V.P., 1996, "Biography, Race Vindication, and African-American Intellectuals: Introductory Essay," *Journal of Negro History* 81, nos. 1–4 (winter–autumn): 1–16; Holt, Rockham, 1964, *Mary McLeod Bethune: A Biography*, Garden City, NY: Doubleday; Metzer, Milton, 1987, *Mary McLeod Bethune: Voice of Hope*, New York: Viking Press; Sterne, Emma Gilders, 1957, *Mary McLeod Bethune*, New York: Alfred A. Knopf.

BETTY NYANGONI

Bigotry

Bigotry is a condition in which a person holds a creed or opinion in an obstinate and narrow-minded way and is inaccessible to all reason and logic in respect to that belief. Bigotry by definition is nonaccommodative, nonflexible, and irrational. It is a threat to democratic thinking. It also runs contrary to notions of pluralism, which is a doctrine of diversity, accommodation, and toleration. A distinguishing characteristic of bigotry is that it relies on stereotypes (oversimplified generalizations) about the group against which its prejudice is directed. Racism and sexism are modes of bigotry. Bigotry has proved extremely difficult to eradicate even when integration is enforced by law. Affirmative action programs seek to combat bigotry through the socialization theory of equality, which argues that by bringing different walks of life together and promoting diversity, bigotry will decrease.

A bigot tries to force his or her opinions and beliefs on others, is passionately aggressive, has a parochial worldview, and is totally inward looking. Any deviation from the tightly held opinions and beliefs is viewed as sacrilegious. The bigot assumes that all insider values are acceptable, right, and good; conversely, all outsider values are unacceptable. Indeed, a more pernicious feature of bigotry entails the belief that some groups, those of a certain color or hue, are inferior, and others of another color or hue are deemed superior. Lately, attention has also been drawn to the fact that bigotry may be a more consciously directed act and idea than previously assumed. Many parents, in fact, socialize their children to be bigots. Training in bigotry did not occur by chance. Children are guided in their training of bigotry by adults, mainly by their parents.

Bigotry practiced by the state is very dangerous. It forms the basis of theocratic and totalitarian state systems. Bigot states are highly intolerant and prejudiced against those religious beliefs and political opinions that are contrary to those accepted by the theocratic or totalitarian state. Liberal democratic states are so structured as to discourage all forms of bigotry, but it does rear its head continually and in different forms. Right-wing parties in several such states are typically bigoted. The xenophobic National Front in France led by Jean-Marie Le Pen is a case in point. It calls for an end to all immigration, using the slogan "France for the French."

However, bigotry is a more serious problem of third-world political systems. In these countries, which are characterized by poverty, illiteracy, and scarcity of resources, it becomes relatively easier for some form of bigotry to gain political ground and prosper by exploiting the gullible masses. One theory suggests that bigotry is nurtured in periods of social instability and crisis. Passions and frustrations engendered during such periods are theoretically deflected onto scapegoats, such as an available isolated minority.

See also Pluralism; Prejudice; Racial Discrimination; Scapegoating/Displaced-Aggression Theories; Stereotyping and Minority Classes; Xenophobia.

FURTHER READING: Macedo, Donaldo, and Lilia I. Bartolomé, 2000, *Dancing with Bigotry: Beyond the Politics of Tolerance*, New York: St. Martin's Press; Scarr, S., 1981, *Race, Social Class, and Individual Differences in I.Q.*, Hillsdale, NJ: Lawrence Erlbaum Associates.

MIRZA ASMER BEG

Bill of Rights

The Bill of Rights is the name given to the first ten amendments to the U.S. Constitution (or, substantively, the first eight amendments). The Bill of Rights is an integral part of the American Constitution today, yet after lengthy discussions, it was not included directly in the body of the Constitution. When the Founders added the first ten amendments to the Constitution primarily at the behest of many southern delegates to the Philadelphia Convention, they espoused concern for individual liberty, individual equality, autonomy, and self-reliance. That is, the overriding concern was that the populace be protected from a potentially tyrannical new central government and be allowed to be left to their own autonomy and individuality as they relate to fundamental areas such as speech, religion, sanctity of the home, and so on. The essential element of significance lay in the revolutionary and antifederalist concern to reserve the center of legal authority to the sovereign, the citizen. The fulcrum, the balancing act, meant equality for all citizens in every sphere of American life. Having experienced the colonial relationship, the Founders recognized the necessity of reserving the protection of equality to the people. As an example, the First Amendment of the Bill of Rights guarantees the freedoms essential to a republican-democratic society, namely, freedom of speech, religion, and assembly and the ability to petition the government.

The Bill of Rights relates to affirmative action in several important ways. First, many argue that social engineering programs such as affirmative action are antithetical to the original purposes of the Bill of Rights. That is, the Bill of Rights was meant to preserve self-reliance, individuality, and autonomy, not to be utilized as a means of engaging in paternalistic state action. Second, as the Supreme Court pointed out in *Barron v. Baltimore*, 32 U.S. 243 (1833), the Bill of Rights was only applicable (initially) as restrictions upon the federal government and not upon the individual state governments. Likewise, the Fourteenth Amendment, which contains the Equal Protection Clause that is central in affirmative action debates today, is not applicable to the federal government, but only to state governments. Hence to make equal protection requirements applicable to the federal government, the Supreme Court in *Bolling v. Sharpe*, 347 U.S. 497 (1954), interpreted the Fifth Amendment's Due Process Clause (applicable to the federal government only) as impliedly containing an equal protection requirement as well. Thus all federal affirmative action programs are analyzed under the Fifth Amendment Due Process Clause, while all state affirmative action programs are analyzed under the Fourteenth Amendment Equal Protection Clause. Finally, today, many of the provisions of the Bill of Rights have been held to be applicable to the state governments through the process of selective incorporation, whereby the Court selectively incorporates a provision of the Bill of Rights to be applicable to the states via the Due Process Clause of the Fourteenth Amendment.

Critics of affirmative action point out that the original purpose of the Bill of Rights is inconsistent with governmentally imposed affirmative action programs. It is the provisions of the Bill of Rights, some critics argue, that mark President Lyndon Johnson's well-meaning Executive Order 11246 of 1965 and other executive orders on the federal and state levels as contrary to the spirit of the Bill of Rights. While the supporters of affirmative action contend that a particular group of citizens is entitled to privileged legal considerations under the Due Process Clause of the Fifth Amendment (or under the Equal Protection Clause of the Fourteenth Amendment), other categories of Americans have found themselves arguably denied their constitutional rights, as well as the ability to be self-reliant, autonomous, and free from government paternalism. Critics of affirmative action therefore argue that governmental policies neglect the Founders' desire not to inject the law into the lives of Americans, and such a desire has been reversed by a policy of granting privileges to one targeted group to the detriment of the majority of the population. Critics point out that the constitutional rights contained in the Bill of Rights are all stated in the negative fashion. That is, the Bill of Rights is a listing of prohibitions on governmental action (almost procedural protections) and does not impose upon the government some obligation to affirmatively act to paternalistically promote rights. In the words of one author, the Bill of Rights

> commanded "Thou Shalt Not." They [the framers/drafters of the Bill of Rights] thereby avoided many dangers of ambiguity . . . the essential guarantees were procedural. They required equal treatment, not equal results. Equal opportunity meant freedom to demonstrate merit, not an entitlement to equal achievement. (Graham 2002, 24)

For example, the First Amendment protects freedom of religion by providing that the federal government shall not infringe on one's freedom of religion or favor one religion over another. State governments often have their own religious protections as part of their respective constitutions. Thus this limitation on government action, a prohibition against violating religious preferences, has refereed the religious tensions that pervade the United States. No particular group has been sanctioned with privileges; rather, all religious groups are protected by the Constitution. The Bill of Rights is replete with legal protections for the members of the multitude of religious observers throughout the United States.

Yet in the affirmative action context, supporters of affirmative action claim that the Bill of Rights, which normally is viewed as placing restrictions on the ability of a government to act, actually justifies or allows for affirmative action. Thus the legal philosophy espoused by affirmative action allows a petitioner to pursue a cause of action under the Bill of Rights without the same level of due process as would be the case in non–affirmative action cases. For example, in *Adarand Constructors, Inc. v. Peña*, 515 U.S. 200 (1995), the Supreme Court of the United States invoked the tough "strict scrutiny" standard in reviewing the constitutionality of federal affirmative action programs. The strict scrutiny standard is that standard of review utilized for cases involving any discrimination based upon race. Hence the Court was not making any distinction between benign discrimination or invidious racial discrimination in applying the strict scrutiny standard. Furthermore, consistent with the overarching purpose of the Bill of Rights, the Court specified that the government program at issue was not a legitimate form of governmental action absent a compelling state interest. Many advocates of affirmative action, not happy with the Supreme Court's decision in *Adarand*, criticized the decision as one that "critically undermines affirmative action." Critics of affirmative action argue that this is a hypocritical position; in effect, according to the critics, the supporter of affirmative action says that one may not be discriminated against in society, but that affirmative action and "fair" or benign discrimination should be allowed. Critics argue that the Supreme Court got it right in *Adarand*, and that federal governmental discrimination in a paternalistic fashion is not permitted under the Fifth Amendment unless a compelling governmental interest is put forward by the government. Otherwise, the government action is contrary to the application and spirit of the Bill of Rights.

See also Adarand Constructors, Inc. v. Peña; Benign Discrimination; *Bolling v. Sharpe*; Compelling Governmental Interest; Equal Protection Clause; Executive Order 11246; Fifth Amendment; First Amendment; Fourteenth Amendment; Invidious Discrimination; Paternalistic Race Relations Theory; Social Engineering; Strict Scrutiny.

FURTHER READING: Edley, Christopher, Jr., 1996, *Not All Black and White: Affirmative Action, Race, and American Values*, New York: Hill and Wang; Graham, Hugh Davis, 2002, *Collision Course: The Strange Convergence of Affirmative Action and Immigration Policy in America*, New York: Oxford University Press.

ARTHUR K. STEINBERG

Black Nationalism

Black Nationalism, which appeared on the U.S. firmament in the nineteenth century as a movement aimed at establishing political power for the economic, social, and political advancement of blacks, came to prominence primarily because of the harshness and oppression meted out to African Americans, both free and slaves. The Black Nationalism movement calls for the racial solidarity, self-determination, and self-reliance of African Americans. The Black Nationalism movement advocates the separate cultural, political, and social identity of black Americans and is opposed to integration and assimilation into one "American" culture. In fact, some adherents of the Black Nationalism movement prefer the term "Africans in America" rather than "African Americans" to describe their opposition to assimilation and integration. Ironically, while affirmative action programs were created in part to address some of the issues raised by the Black Nationalists, with the aim of erasing Black Nationalist aspirations and promoting a more racially harmoniously integrated society, the Black Nationalism movement calls for the black community to set itself apart from mainstream America and effectuate its own solutions.

Commenting on the rise of Black Nationalism, one work has noted:

> The Black Nationalist strain in American intellectual thought can be traced back to Martin Delany, a graduate of Harvard Medical School. In an age when black was considered anything but beautiful and the black race was held mentally and morally inferior to others, Delany preached racial pride. . . . Central to Delany's thought was the belief that blacks formed a nation within a nation: "a Broken Nation of four-and-a-half millions." (Dorn and Carrington 1991, 7)

This, Delany believed, was necessary since it would be in consonance with "the Welsh, Irish and Scotch in the British dominions . . . who still retain their native peculiarities of language, habits, and various other traits," and that "the claims of no people, according to established policy and usage, are respected by any nation, until they are presented in a national capacity."

To attain this objective of Black Nationalism in the nineteenth century, a settlement scheme was proposed for the eastern coast of Africa in 1852. Though the project was not funded, it laid the foundation for the National Emigration Convention's 1859 Niger Valley exploring party led by Delany. The American Colonization Movement, advocating the emigration of African Americans to such places as Liberia and Haiti, was also seen by some as a way to attain the goals of Black Nationalism.

After decades of near inaction, Martin Delany's old concept of "the broken nation" was revived in the 1960s when Robert Williams, a former leader of the National Association for the Advancement of Colored People in North Carolina, returned from exile in Africa to proclaim the Republic of New Africa. Arguing that community control of the decaying cities of the North was not enough on which to build a new nation, Williams claimed as the "National Territory of the Black Nation" the five southern states with the largest black populations (Alabama, Georgia, Louisiana, Mississippi, and South Carolina). While the attempt to actually create a black nation out of the Black Belt in the South never got much beyond the dedication of a parcel of land in Mississippi in 1971 as "the first African capital of the northern Western Hemisphere," the spirit of the Black Nationalism movement still lingers on in the political beliefs of some (Dorn and Carrington 1991, 14).

In the same vein, the Black Muslims, which doubled as a religious sect and a Black Nationalist group, sought to achieve black separation. "The Black Muslims demanded that, as long-overdue 'back wages', a considerable portion of the United States be turned over to them for the creation of a separate black state" (Gordon 1980, 119). Like the previous efforts to achieve black separation and nationhood, the Black Muslims did not see their dream come true. Black Nationalism, aimed at separation and foundation of an African American nation within the United States of America, increasingly lost its appeal because of political, social, and economic gains made by the African American community thanks to the civil rights movement and, in part, affirmative action programs that ushered in a new hope for integration and equality among the races.

See also African Americans; Assimilation Theory; Black Panther Party; Farrakhan, Louis; Garvey, Marcus; Integration; Malcolm X; National Association for the Advancement of Colored People; Reparations.

FURTHER READING: Dorn, Edwin, and Walter C. Carrington, 1991, *Africa in the Minds and Deeds of Black American Leaders*, Washington, DC: Joint Center for Political and Economic Studies; Franklin, John Hope, and Isidore Starr, 1967, *The Negro in Twentieth Century America: A Reader on the Struggle for Civil Rights*, New York: Vintage Books; Gordon, Irving L., 1980, *American Studies: A Conceptual Approach*, New York: Amsco School Publications; Hill, Adelaide Cromwell, and Martin Kilson, eds., 1969, *Apropos of Africa: Sentiments of Negro American Leaders on Africa from the 1800s to 1960s*, London: Frank Cass; Uya, Okon Edet, ed., *The Black Brotherhood: Afro-Americans and Africa*, Lexington, MA: D.C. Heath.

PAUL OBIYO MBANASO NJEMANZE

Black Panther Party

The Black Panther Party for Self-Defense (BPP), a black militant political organization, was officially launched on October 15, 1966, in Oakland, California, by Bobby Seale and Huey Newton. Newton became minister of defense, and Seale was named chairman. Led by Marxist principles, they advocated self-defense and the restructuring of American society. They urged political, social, and economic equality for all black Americans by drawing up a ten-point platform and program titled "What We Want, What We Believe." In essence, the plan advocated freedom for the black community, full employment, decent housing, exemption of black males from the military, a true education, an end to police brutality, and trial by jury of one's peers. In its ten-point plan, while not mentioning "affirmative action" by name, the BPP clearly supported preferential programs that would guarantee blacks full employment and housing. The BPP also clearly supported reparations, a more aggressive type of compensation, for the black community. As an illustration of the BPP's demand for compensation and reparations, the third point of the BPP's ten-point plan was stated as follows:

> We believe that this racist government has robbed us and now we are demanding the overdue debt of forty acres and two mules. Forty acres and two mules were promised 100 years ago as restitution for slave labor and mass murder of Black people. We will accept the payment in currency which will be distributed to our many communities. The American racist has taken part in the slaughter of our fifty million Black people. Therefore, we feel this is a modest demand that we make. (http://www.blackpanther.org/TenPoint.htm)

The BPP made similar demands in the areas of political autonomy (the first point of the plan), full employment (second point), housing (fourth point), education (fifth point), free health care for all black and oppressed people (sixth point), and "land, bread, housing, education, clothing, justice, peace and people's community control of modern technology" (tenth point). In 1999, Elaine Brown, ex-chairperson of the BPP, gave a speech advocating reparations and cash payments over affirmative action. Brown stated, "Where's our payback? Affirmative action? I'll take $20 million [in reparations] and never ask another question."

In its heyday, the BPP established chapters throughout the United States, in cities such as New York, Chicago, Hartford, Denver, and others. It advocated violence as a legitimate alternative to Dr. Martin Luther King's "peaceful, but passive resistance" movement. Its members even carried guns and conducted patrols of black communities to monitor police brutality. The BPP combined elements of socialism and Black Nationalism. Influenced by Malcolm X, it wanted blacks to unite, work together, and control their own economic and social destiny. The BPP co-opted white activists because members believed that if revolutionaries worked together, they could change the world. It eventually formed an alliance with the Student Nonviolent Coordinating Committee (SNCC), but the partnership did not last long because Stokely Carmichael, the leader of the SNCC and a proponent of Black Power, and other committee representatives did not want to work with whites. Carmichael believed that whites stood in the way of black autonomy and self-reliance. Carmichael was eventually ousted from the SNCC and later disassociated himself from the BPP.

Despite its radical and militant stance, the BPP initiated programs that served as models for social programs of the 1970s and 1980s. In 1968, it started the first free breakfast program for children in Oakland. This program was duplicated by other chapters throughout the country. In 1970, it initiated its Survival Program, which provided free health clinics, free sickle-cell-anemia screening, a free shoe program, escorts for the elderly, and free ambulance service. The Oakland Community Learning Center, a school for at-risk black children, was considered one of its most successful projects.

Throughout the 1960s, racial tension increased. There were a number of confrontations and shoot-outs with police and raids on BPP headquarters. Leaders of the BPP also ordered assassinations and murders of their own members if they were suspected of being Federal Bureau of Investigation (FBI) informants or disloyal to the BPP. The FBI blamed the Black Panthers for riots and other violence that erupted and instituted COINTELPRO (counterintelligence program) to disrupt the activities of black militant groups and weaken the organizations by planting informants and working through local police departments. A 1969 police raid in Chicago left two Panthers, Fred Hampton and Mark Clark, dead. By the end of the 1960s, it was believed that at least twenty-eight Panthers had been killed, and numerous others were either in jail or in exile to avoid prosecution.

When Newton was charged with the murder of an Oakland policeman in 1967, Eldridge Cleaver, a former convict, took over Newton's position in the organization. While Cleaver was in exile in Algiers, he and Newton split in 1970 over the direction the party should go. After a trip to China in 1971, Newton returned to the United States and announced that the BPP would recognize the equality of women. At Newton's request, Bobby Seale ran for mayor of Oakland and Elaine Brown, the deputy minister for information for the southern California chapter, ran for a council position. Although they did not win, they were successful in galvanizing the black community, and thousands registered to vote for the first time.

In 1974, Elaine Brown was named chairperson of the Panthers, the highest position ever held by a woman. Other women assumed leadership positions of the party and were instrumental in changing the party's direction and image. After dropping the "for self-defense" portion of its name, the BPP became even more politically active. It was instrumental in registering more than 90,000 black Democrats so they could vote in the 1977 Oakland mayoral election. The party membership was instrumental in electing Lionel Wilson the first black mayor of Oakland. The Oakland Learning Center, under the tutelage of Erika Huggins, received a commendation from the California legislature for setting the highest educational standard of any school in the state. However, the reputation of the BPP was marred by Newton when he returned to Oakland in 1977 after a three-year exile in Cuba.

By the early 1980s, the radical groups of the 1960s and 1970s were destroyed due to internal strife, murders, arrests, and imprisonments. Following Newton's murder in 1989, there was some interest in resurrecting aspects of the Panthers' program and the *Black Panther* newspaper. Although it was considered an extreme radical group, the Black Panther Party left a significant legacy. The BPP is a defunct organization today, although there have been several new organizations claiming to be the "New Black Panthers."

See also Black Nationalism; Carmichael, Stokely; Civil Rights Movement; King, Martin Luther, Jr.; Malcolm X; Marxist Theory and Affirmative Action; Reparations.

FURTHER READING: Brown, Elaine, 1992, *A Taste of Power: A Black Woman's Story*, New York: Pantheon Books; Cleaver, Eldridge, 1968, *Soul on Ice*, New York: Dell Publishing; Haskins, James, 1972, *Profiles in Black Power*, Garden City, NY: Doubleday; Pearson, Hugh, 1994, *The Shadow of the Panther: Huey Newton and the Price of Black Power in America*, Reading, MA:

Addison-Wesley; Seale, Bobby, 1970, *Seize the Time: The Story of the Black Panther Party and Huey P. Newton*, New York: Random House.

NAOMI ROBERTSON

Black-Jewish Alliance

The term "black-Jewish alliance" refers to the coming together of the African American and Jewish communities with the aim of fostering understanding and cooperation between members of the two communities in light of both groups' similar history of mistreatment and discrimination. The black-Jewish alliance has been a matter of great academic controversy. Critical to the debate are issues ranging from its very existence to its arguable collapse and revival. The establishment and operation of affirmative action within the United States have caused a chasm in the black-Jewish alliance's ranks. While many Jewish groups were supporters of affirmative action during the early years of the civil rights movement, most Jewish groups today are firm opponents of race-based affirmative action, to the extent the affirmative action plan or program is based on quotas.

It is a law of human society that common experience serves as a unifying force among disparate groups and populations. This law applied with great force to the Jewish and black communities. In the United States, both African Americans and Jews found themselves confronted historically by discrimination and oppression of great magnitude and, in some cases, by a common foe. For example, both groups were hated and oppressed by the Ku Klux Klan and the American Nazi Party. As regards African Americans, in slavery and in freedom, blacks were discriminated against and tremendously dehumanized by American mainstream society. African Americans were treated as outcasts, kept in "the depth below the depth," "last hired and first fired" in employment, compelled to flee scenes of persecution (causing massive migration and emigration), disenfranchised, terrorized, ghettoized in urban centers, stereotyped, and regarded as inferior beings. Social mobility was very difficult, while the road to equality was rough and tortuous.

Like African Americans, Jews in the United States also suffered discrimination, degrading treatment, and demeaning stereotyping by mainstream society. Commenting on the persecution of the Jews in the United States, one author noted as follows:

> The nativists were perturbed that many of the "new immigrants"—from Eastern Europe—were Jews. Agitators stressed that Jews observed strange and different customs; they labeled them as ambitious, greedy, and materialistic; they charged them with being wealthy international bankers conspiring to rule the world; and, with no logic or sense, charged them also with being impoverished radicals fomenting revolutions. In the 1890s, serious anti-Semitic demonstrations took place in several Northern towns and in the rural South. In the 1920s, anti-Semitism increased. Employers rejected qualified Jewish job applicants; colleges set quotas restricting the admission of Jewish students; social clubs and real estate agents practiced discrimination. In the rural South and Middle West, the Ku Klux Klan stressed anti-Semitism. (Gordon 1980, 22)

In light of the similar treatment of both groups, the black-Jewish alliance was forged during the civil rights movement of the 1950s and the 1960s. The cooperation that the two communities fostered in those grim days of struggle largely fizzled out with the end of the civil rights movement. Blame has been apportioned on both sides of the partnership. Today, the major groups representing African Americans and the groups representing Jews are split on the issue of affirmative action. Most Jewish groups today are firmly opposed to race-based affirmative action plans that employ preferences and view such plans as reverse discrimination. These groups are opposed to any quota-based system of allocating goods and resources and believe that such a quota-based system erodes merit and competency in the workforce or educational arena. Conversely, most major groups representing African Americans embrace affirmative action programs as necessary to overcome previous incidents of discriminatory treatment.

See also American Jewish Committee; American Jewish Congress; Anti-Defamation League; Anti-Semitism, Jews, and Affirmative Action; Civil Rights Movement.

FURTHER READING: Engerman, Stanley L., and Eugene D. Genovese, eds., 1975, *Race and Slavery in the Western Hemisphere: Quantitative Studies,* Princeton, NJ: Princeton University Press; Friedman, Murray, 1995, *What Went Wrong? The Creation and Collapse of the Black-Jewish Alliance,* New York: Free Press; Gordon, Irving L., 1980, *American Studies: A Conceptual Approach,* New York: Amsco School Publications.

PAUL OBIYO MBANASO NJEMANZE

Blackmun, Harry Andrew (1908–1999)

Harry Blackmun served as an associate justice of the U.S. Supreme Court from 1970 to 1994. Along with Justices William Brennan and Thurgood Marshall, Blackmun was one of the strongest supporters of affirmative action on the high court. As Georgetown University professor of law Girardeau Spann has noted, "The members of the liberal bloc" who always voted to uphold affirmative action "were Justices Brennan, Marshall, and Blackmun. Of the twenty-four votes cast by members of this initial liberal bloc in the nine constitutional affirmative action cases considered by a member of the bloc, all twenty-four votes were cast in favor of the affirmative action programs at issue" (Spann 2000, 160). In strongly supporting affirmative action, Blackmun embraced the idea of benign discrimination to improve the lot of historically disadvantaged groups and rejected the notion that the Fourteenth Amendment should be strictly construed in a "color-blind" fashion. In this regard, Blackmun famously remarked as part of his separate opinion in *Regents of the University of California v. Bakke,* 438 U.S. 265 (1978), that "in order to get beyond racism, we must first take account of race . . . [a]nd in order to treat some persons equally, we must treat them differently. We cannot—we dare not—let the Equal Protection Clause perpetuate racial supremacy."

Harry Blackmun was born on November 12, 1908, in Nashville, Illinois, although he grew up in St. Paul, Minnesota. Blackmun attended Harvard University, where he studied mathematics, and then went on to Harvard Law School to study law. After law school, Blackmun clerked with a judge on the U.S. Court of Appeals for the Eighth Circuit; in 1959, President Dwight Eisenhower nominated Blackmun to replace this judge when his seat on the Eighth Circuit came open.

In 1970, Blackmun was elevated to the U.S. Supreme Court by President Richard Nixon. Blackmun was actually Nixon's third choice to fill the vacant Supreme

Court seat after Nixon's first two nominees were rejected by the Senate during the confirmation process. Ironically, at the time, Blackmun was viewed as a conservative middle-of-the-road judge. During his first few years on the Court, Blackmun did consistently align himself with the Court's conservative wing. In fact, Blackmun was said to side so often with Chief Justice Warren Burger that the two were dubbed "the Minnesota Twins." In the 1980s, Blackmun began to align himself more frequently with the liberal bloc and with Justices Marshall and Brennan in particular.

In time, Blackmun proved to be one of the staunchest supporters of affirmative action ever to sit on the high court. He never failed to cast his vote in favor of the affirmative action plan at issue, regardless of the case or factual context. In the seminal case *Regents of the University of California v. Bakke,* Blackmun was one of the "antidiscrimination four," and he would have upheld as constitutional the affirmative action quota system employed by the University of California at Davis Medical School. His position in support of affirmative action is also apparent in the other major affirmative action cases that came before the Court during his tenure, including *Shaw v. Reno,* 509 U.S. 630 (1993); *Metro Broadcasting Inc. v. FCC,* 497 U.S. 547 (1990); *City of Richmond v. J. A. Croson Co.*, 488 U.S. 469 (1989); and *Wygant v. Jackson Board of Education,* 476 U.S. 267 (1986).

See also Brennan, William Joseph; Burger Court and Affirmative Action; *City of Richmond v. J.A. Croson Co.*; Color-Blind Constitution; Equal Protection Clause; Fourteenth Amendment; Marshall, Thurgood; *Metro Broadcasting, Inc. v. FCC*; Nixon, Richard Milhous; *Regents of the University of California v. Bakke; Shaw v. Reno; Wygant v. Jackson Board of Education.*

FURTHER READING: Hall, Kermit, ed., 1992, *The Oxford Companion to the Supreme Court of the United States,* New York: Oxford University Press; Spann, Girardeau A., 2000, *The Law of Affirmative Action: Twenty-five Years of Supreme Court Decisions on Race and Remedies,* New York: New York University Press.

JAMES A. BECKMAN

Bok, Derek

See The Shape of the River.

Bolick, Clint (1958–)

Clint Bolick is a frequent critic of traditional affirmative action programs and a prolific author. Bolick argues that most current affirmative action laws do not fairly or substantively improve the status of minorities and women. His many publications reflect a somewhat different view of civil rights and affirmative action than traditional proponents advocate. As a libertarian, Bolick argues against distributing opportunities by using race and gender. He believes that counting race ultimately harms or stigmatizes everyone, even those who are supposed to benefit from the practice. He supports the empowerment of the individual. Bolick has called for a needs-based affirmative action that is grounded upon whether one is socially or economically disadvantaged and not upon race or gender. He opposes Directive 15, adopted by the federal Office of Management and Budget (OMB) in 1977. Directive 15 instructed federal agencies to collect statistics identifying people within racial and ethnic categories.

Clint Bolick has authored many works pertaining to affirmative action, including *Transformation: The Promise and Politics of Empowerment* (1998); *Grassroots Tyranny: The Limits of Federalism* (1993); *Unfinished Business: A Civil Rights Strategy for America's Third Century* (1990); and *Changing Course: Civil Rights at the Crossroads* (1988). Bolick also cofounded the Institute for Justice in 1991 "to protect individual liberty and to challenge the regulatory welfare state." He has served as vice president and legislative director of this organization. The institute is located in Washington, D.C., and engages primarily in constitutional litigation to protect individual liberty and personal autonomy.

As an active attorney, Bolick is involved in legal cases around the nation, defending school choice programs, challenging barriers to entrepreneurship, and helping defend the California Civil Rights Initiative, Proposition 209. He defended Arizona's state income tax credit for private scholarship contributions and challenged regulatory barriers to start-up businesses in the inner city. He also occasionally writes editorials on affirmative action and is the author of the 1993 editorial that described Lani Guinier, President Bill Clinton's failed first choice for assistant attorney general, as the "quota queen" based upon her alleged position on affirmative action.

Bolick's academic background includes a bachelor of arts degree in political science and history from Drew University in 1979 and a juris doctorate from the University of California at Davis in 1982. His previous positions include serving as an attorney in the Civil Rights Division of the U.S. Department of Justice during the Reagan administration, as well as in the U.S. Equal Employment Opportunity Commission and the Mountain State Legal Foundation.

See also Clinton, William Jefferson; Department of Justice; Economically Disadvantaged; Guinier, Lani; Proposition 209.

FURTHER READING: Bolick, Clint, 1996, *The Affirmative Action Fraud: Can We Restore the American Civil Rights Vision?* Washington, DC: Cato Institute; Bolick, Clint, 1998, *Transformation: The Promise and Politics of Empowerment,* Oakland, CA: ICS Press; *Source Book 2000: A Calvert Directory of Mid-Atlantic Free Market Experts and Conservatives,* 2002, http://www.calvertinstitute.org/lab.

BETTY NYANGONI

Bolling v. Sharpe, 347 U.S. 497 (1954)

In *Bolling v. Sharpe,* school segregation in Washington, D.C., was declared unconstitutional under the Due Process Clause of the Fifth Amendment in a unanimous decision rendered by the Supreme Court on May 17, 1954. On the same day, the Court ruled in *Brown v. Board of Education,* 347 U.S. 483 (1954), that segregated education within the forty-eight states violated the Equal Protection Clause of the Fourteenth Amendment. *Bolling,* although a companion case to *Brown,* raised distinct constitutional issues that factor into subsequent affirmative action cases.

This case was filed on behalf of Spottswood Thomas Bolling Jr. and several other black children who had been denied the right to attend John Philip Sousa

Junior High School in the District of Columbia. The schoolchildren were represented by George E.C. Hayes, general counsel and professor at the Howard University School of Law, and James M. Nabrit Jr., another Howard law professor and prominent NAACP Legal Defense Fund advisor. The U.S. Court of Appeals for the District of Columbia Circuit had recently upheld the constitutionality of segregated schools in the District of Columbia in *Carr v. Corning*, 86 U.S. App. D.C. 173 (1950). *Bolling*, a challenge to that earlier ruling, was still pending before the court of appeals when the Supreme Court, desiring to rule on all pending segregation cases at the same time, took the unusual step of inviting the parties to file certiorari petitions in conjunction with four other segregation cases before it.

The *Bolling* case presented a unique challenge because the Fourteenth Amendment's Equal Protection Clause—the constitutional basis of the four cases arising out of Delaware, Kansas, South Carolina, and Virginia—was inapplicable in the District of Columbia. Thus *Bolling* raised a different constitutional question: whether the liberty protected by the Fifth Amendment's Due Process Clause provided equal protection to all citizens residing in the District of Columbia in such a way as to exclude segregated education. Hayes and Nabrit, in particular, argued before the Court that Bolling's educational rights were among the fundamental rights protected by the liberty provision of the Fifth Amendment's Due Process Clause. They also claimed that all race-based classifications merited the highest standard of review, strict scrutiny. The Court ultimately agreed on both counts.

In six short paragraphs, Chief Justice Earl Warren announced the Court's opinion. Speaking for a unanimous Court, Warren said that although the Equal Protection and Due Process Clauses are different, they are not mutually exclusive—both are related to "the American ideal of fairness." There are times that "discrimination may be so unjustifiable as to be violative of due process." Without a hint of irony, Warren cited the Japanese American cases of 1943–1944, in which Justice Hugo Black (in *Korematsu v. United States*, 323 U.S. 214 [1944]) wrote, "All legal restrictions which curtail the civil rights of a single racial group are immediately suspect. . . . Courts must subject them to the most rigid scrutiny. Pressing public necessity may sometimes justify the existence of such restrictions; racial antagonism never can." The necessity of strict judicial scrutiny for all race-based classifications was a point not made in *Brown*, but it had been vigorously argued by Nabrit throughout the *Bolling* controversy. After close scrutiny, the Court concluded that the segregated public schools in Washington, D.C., were the product of "racial antagonism," not "pressing public necessity."

Which civil right was infringed by segregation? Warren identified the liberty that is protected by the Fifth Amendment. Segregation "of Negro children of the District of Columbia," Warren concluded, "constitutes an arbitrary deprivation of their liberty in violation of the Due Process Clause." In other words, the liberty provision of the Due Process Clause provides equal protection in a fashion quite similar to, even if not identical with, the Equal Protection Clause of the Fourteenth Amendment. Warren was extending the Due Process Clause in new ways. To explain, he noted that having struck down segregation at the state level, "it would be unthinkable that the same constitution would impose a lesser duty on the Federal Government."

Bolling was rescheduled, along with *Brown*, on the Court's docket to resolve questions about implementation. On May 31, 1955, the Court directed the District Court of the District of Columbia to "enter such orders and decrees . . . as are necessary and proper to admit [all] to public schools on a racially nondiscriminatory basis," thus empowering a federal district court judge to be the final arbiter of a fair implementation of desegregation, *Brown v. Board of Education,* 349 U.S. 294, 301 (1955).

This case became important for future affirmative action cases that involved action of the federal government as opposed to state and private action. For example, the Court employed the equal protection component of the Fifth Amendment in cases involving the federal government such as *Fullilove v. Klutznick,* 448 U.S. 448 (1980). Moreover, in spite of objections of some justices, the Supreme Court has consistently employed strict scrutiny in cases involving racial classifications, *Adarand Constructors, Inc. v. Peña,* 515 U.S. 200 (1995). This approach, emphasized by those who see affirmative action as a form of reverse discrimination, has led the Court to strike down some affirmative action programs, even when they were adopted with benevolent intentions.

See also Adarand Constructors, Inc. v. Peña; All Deliberate Speed; *Brown v. Board of Education;* Equal Protection Clause; Fifth Amendment; Fourteenth Amendment; *Fullilove v. Klutznick;* National Association for the Advancement of Colored People; Strict Scrutiny; Warren Court and Affirmative Action.

FURTHER READING: Friedman, Leon, ed., 1969, *Argument: The Oral Argument before the Supreme Court in Brown v. Board of Education of Topeka, 1952–1955,* New York: Chelsea House; Kluger, Richard, 1976, *Simple Justice: The History of Brown v. Board of Education and Black America's Struggle for Equality,* New York: Alfred A. Knopf; Wasby, Stephen L., Anthony A. D'Amato, and Rosemary Metrailer, 1977, *Desegregation from Brown to Alexander: An Exploration of Supreme Court Strategies,* Carbondale: Southern Illinois University Press.

DAVID L. WEEKS

Bona Fide Occupational Qualifications

See Diaz v. Pan American World Airways.

Bowen, William G.

See The Shape of the River.

Bradwell v. State of Illinois, 83 U.S 130 (1873)

Bradwell v. State of Illinois was a U.S. Supreme Court decision that held that the Fourteenth Amendment Equal Protection and Privileges and Immunities Clauses did not protect a woman from a state government's decision to deprive women of the ability to hold a law license or practice law. The Supreme Court held that it was perfectly within the discretion and power of a sovereign state government to decide who should be able to practice law within the state as part of the state's residual police powers. The Supreme Court took a very literal and narrow reading of the Fourteenth Amendment in so holding in favor of the state of Illinois. Thus the *Bradwell* decision, dealing with gender and equality under the Fourteenth

Amendment, has been compared with other infamous Supreme Court decisions dealing with race issued during the same period, such as *Plessy v. Ferguson*, 163 U.S. 537 (1896), and the *Civil Rights Cases*, 109 U.S. 3 (1883). Today, the case is relevant in understanding the historical background to discrimination and the historical interpretation of the Fourteenth Amendment by the Supreme Court.

Myra Colby Bradwell was born on February 12, 1831, and grew up in a period when the American legal system was still largely impacted by the English common law. As part of this grafting, its provisions prescribed married women's rights. Despite her education, she was limited in her choice of profession; she became a schoolteacher after attending schools in Illinois and Wisconsin. Bradwell objected to the legal status of women in Illinois society, both single and married. Since her husband, James, was a member of the Illinois bar and eventually became a judge, a legal atmosphere pervaded her home. She studied the law under her husband's supervision and established the *Chicago Daily News* in October 1868. It became the most read legal journal in the Midwest and gained a wide acceptance in the legal profession. Given her legal status, her husband was required to petition the state for a special charter to allow her the right to contract as a female. She served as the newspaper's editor and business manager; she expanded the business to include the publication of other periodicals and printed and sold stationery and legal forms. Over a period of time, the *Chicago Daily News* became a vehicle for her muckraking functions with which to attack incompetent and dishonest judges and attorneys. Although her enterprise was destroyed by fire in 1871, she continued to fight for women's rights. She was instrumental in the passage of Illinois' Married Women's Property Act in 1861 and the Earning Act of 1869 that gave married women control of their earnings and property.

Possibly with a sense of hope arising from the aforementioned legislation, Bradwell stood for the Illinois bar in August 1869. A circuit judge and the state's attorney both declared her qualified and subsequently recommended her admission to the bar to the state supreme court. In October 1869, the clerk denied her petition because she was married and under legal disabilities that prevented her from entering into contracts. She responded that since she was allowed to own property, she was empowered to engage in contractual relations. Upon re-petition, the Illinois Supreme Court again denied her a license on February 5, 1870.

She then appealed to the U.S. Supreme Court. Her arguments included an interpretation of the Fourteenth Amendment's Privileges and Immunities Clause, as well as the Equal Protection Clause. In essence, Bradwell claimed that she was not being treated equally and fairly by the state of Illinois. The U.S. Supreme Court's arguments for denying Bradwell's petition were hoarish. A reading of the decision provides common-law justifications for denial, none of which were pertinent to a growing industrial society. For example, the brief contains a citation that the Illinois Constitution, as adopted, which made no reference to women attorneys. In fact, the Court diligently noted that women attorneys were unknown to the English courts and included references to the legal profession going back to the reign of James I. The rationalizations for denial given by the Court concluded with asserting that the Illinois legislature or Constitution had evidenced no expectations that the privilege to practice law should be, or would be, extended to women. The U.S. Supreme Court ruled that it was exclusively within Illinois's authority as a sovereign state to rule on whoever was admitted to the state bar. Therefore, according to the Court, the denial of Bradwell's petition was not a violation of the privileges and immunities of a citizen of the United States. The high court held that Illinois's action of denial was beyond the pale of the Fourteenth Amendment because she was a citizen of the state and also that under the police powers doctrine states had the authority to regulate the granting of law licenses.

The Supreme Court justices also relied on the "traditional" differences of the sexes to confirm the common-law dictum that a married woman merges into the body of her husband; consequently, she could not function independently, which made her incapable of performing the duties and adhering to the obligations that are within the realm of an attorney. The Court also adhered to the common-law doctrine that single women did not fall within the legal disabilities of married women since they did not merge into their husband and did not lose their individuality for contractual purposes.

The Court also offered several reasons for denying Bradwell's petition and appeal. The Court confirmed its adherence to the common law and the usages of Westminster Hall and, since the legislature had not legislated to the contrary, the Court decreed that it had not intended to act in derogation of the legislature's enactments. Since the legislature acted with reason, nature, and experience, its intent must be honored; the legislature established the terms for admission to support the efficient and proper administration of justice. The Court was mindful of the federalism doctrine; it had not delved into the realm of judicial interpretation and expansion of the Reconstruction Amendments, nor did it appreciate the use of the Fifth Amendment's Due Process Clause. The Court then pursued a course that would violate modern civil rights legislation today. The Court asserted that the right to practice law in the courts of the state of Illinois was not guaranteed by the federal Constitution since this right did not depend upon American citizenship.

Public awareness of Bradwell's case, along with the refusal of the Illinois state legislature to act favorably on other woman applicants for admission to the state bar, caused groups throughout the United States to organize to lobby state legislatures to reverse the prohibition. Finally, a bill was passed in March 1872, and Alta Hulett became the first woman in Illinois to be admitted to the bar. Bradwell prepared the petitions and other supporting documentation. Bradwell remained undaunted and pushed her contribution to the suffrage movement to the national level. Subsequent to her activities in organizing and speaking at a suffrage convention in 1869, the Illinois state governor appointed her an official representative for Illinois to several conventions, and she was active in the Chicago Bar Association. Her efforts illustrate a commitment to lifting any social restrictions imposed upon women. Her tireless efforts to raise the level of the legal profession contributed to the evolving social changes that led the Illinois state government to act. The Illinois Supreme Court ruled on its own initiative in 1890 to approve her original petition for admission to the Illinois state bar by a reversal of its narrow interpretation of the Privileges and Immunities Clause. The court's interpretation of the Fourteenth Amendment was now given a broader venue. On March 28, 1892, two years after her admission to the bar, she appeared before the U.S. Supreme Court.

See also Civil Rights Cases; Equal Protection Clause; Fourteenth Amendment; Gender Norms; *Minor v. Happersett*; *Plessy v. Ferguson*; Stereotypes, Gender.

FURTHER READING: Aynes, Richard L., 1999, "*Bradwell v. Illinois*: Chief Justice Chase's Dissent and the 'Sphere of Women's Work'," *Louisiana Law Review* 59 (winter): 521–541; *Bradwell v. State of Illinois*, 83 U.S 130 (1873).

ARTHUR K. STEINBERG

Brazil and Affirmative Action

At the same time that the United States questions the future of affirmative action, countries such as South Africa, India, Malaysia, and Brazil are developing and implementing affirmative action programs in an effort to deal with racial discrimination and inequities. After Nigeria, Brazil is the second-largest black nation in the world and the most populous nation in South America. Although Brazil has long boasted of being a racial democracy, research has shown that even though intergroup relations appear to be good, there are significant economic and social disparities between blacks and whites. For instance, blacks comprise almost half of the country's population, yet only 2.2 percent of college students are black. Also, more than two-thirds of Brazil's poor are black, and whites earn twice as much as blacks earn. The increased awareness of these racial inequities has led to a national movement calling for affirmative action to be implemented in the country. On May 13, 2002, sociologist and then President Fernando Henrique Cardoso of Brazil signed a decree instituting the National Program for Affirmative Action. The primary goal of this program is to foster the principles of diversity and pluralism in the recruitment of employees for the federal public administration and the provision of services to governmental agencies.

Many of the affirmative action measures in Brazil involve strict quotas. For instance, black actors are now guaranteed 25 percent of all television, movie, and theater roles; the Labor Ministry has reserved 20 percent of its job-training budget for programs to benefit blacks; about 40 percent of new hires at the Ministry of Social Security will be black; and the state universities in Rio de Janeiro are setting aside 40 percent of admissions for students of African descent. Similar racial quotas are expected at other state-operated universities around the country. Political parties are required to have at least 30 percent of their candidates be black. At least 20 percent of public servants are required to be black; this also applies to private enterprises with twenty or more employees. The main focus of affirmative action in Brazil is education, followed closely by government representation.

On March 21, 2003, current Brazilian president Luiz Inácio Lula da Silva announced the creation of a Special Secretariat for Devising Policies to Promote Racial Equality. This new secretariat, which is headed by Matilde Ribeiro, serves as an advisory body answering directly to President da Silva. Its goals are to promote equality and protect the rights of all people from ethnic and racial minority communities—especially members of the black community—who experience the consequences of discrimination. The new secretariat includes an Undersecretariat for Planning and Formulating Polices to Promote Racial Equality, an Undersecretariat for International Liaison, and an Undersecretariat to Develop Programs for Affirmative Action. Currently, the Lula administration is evaluating the National Program for Affirmative Action and preparing to reshape it in the near future.

See also Australia and Affirmative Action; Canada and Affirmative Action; China and Affirmative Action; European Union and Affirmative Action; Global Implementation of Affirmative Action Programs; Great Britain and Affirmative Action; India and Affirmative Action; Japan and Affirmative Action; Malaysia and Affirmative Action; South Africa and Affirmative Action.

FURTHER READING: Downie, Andrew, 2001, "Brazil Latest to Try Racial Preferences," *Christian Science Monitor*, August 7, 1; Gomes, Joaquim B. Barbosa, 2001, *Ação Afirmativa & Princípio Constitucional da Igualdade*, Rio de Janeiro: Renovar; Guillebeau, Christopher, 1999, "Affirmative Action in a Global Perspective: The Cases of South Africa and Brazil," *Sociological Spectrum* 19:443–465; Hall, Kevin G., 2002, "Brazil's-Blacks Get Affirmative Action 114 Years after Emancipation," Knight Ridder Tribune News Service, May 31; Jones, Patrice M., 2001, "Brazil Debates Affirmative Action: Many Lawmakers Push Racial Quotas," *Chicago Tribune*, December 27, 5; Pereira, Marcelo, 2003, "Brazil: New Racial Equality Minister Favors Affirmative Action," Global Information Network, May 10; Sowell, Thomas, 1990, *Preferential Policies: An International Perspective*, New York: William Morrow.

PAULINA X. RUF

Brennan, William Joseph (1906–1993)

William Joseph Brennan Jr. who served as a U.S. Supreme Court justice from 1956 to 1990, is best known in the affirmative action context today for his unwavering support of affirmative action during his longtime tenure on the Court. Brennan, along with Justices Thurgood Marshall and Harry Blackmun, comprised a three-justice bloc that always voted to uphold affirmative action plans when the constitutionality of such plans was called into question. Brennan voted to affirm affirmative action plans at issue in eight major affirmative action cases that come to the Court during his more than three decades on the Court: *Metro Broadcasting, Inc. v. FCC*, 497 U.S. 547 (1990); *City of Richmond v. J.A. Croson Co.*, 488 U.S. 469 (1989); *United States v. Paradise*, 480 U.S. 149 (1987); *United Steelworkers of America v. Weber*, 443 U.S. 193 (1979); *Wygant v. Jackson Board of Education*, 476 U.S. 267 (1986); *Fullilove v. Klutznick*, 448 U.S. 448 (1980); *Regents of the University of California v. Bakke*, 438 U.S. 265 (1978); and *United Jewish Organization v. Carey*, 430 U.S. 144 (1977). Of particular note, in *Regents of the University of California v. Bakke*, Brennan was one of the "antidiscrimination four" (Justices Brennan, Byron White, Marshall, and Blackmun). Brennan voted to uphold the affirmative action plan at issue in the case and to apply an intermediate and less rigid standard of scrutiny for racial classification plans that were instituted to cure the effects of past discrimination. Brennan also authored the majority opinion in *Metro Broadcasting, Inc. v. FCC*, in which the Court ultimately upheld two minority preference plans for the allocation of broadcast licenses to minority groups to ensure diversity that had been adopted by the Federal Communications Commission.

Brennan was born in Newark, New Jersey, on April 25, 1906. He attended the Wharton School of the University of Pennsylvania and Harvard Law School. After graduation from law school, Brennan spent much of his pre-Court legal career in private practice in New Jersey. He served in the army during World War II and, after the war, returned to private practice and served as a judge in the New Jersey state court system. Within three years, Brennan had ascended from the trial court level to the New Jersey Supreme Court.

In the fall of 1956, U.S. Supreme Court justice Sherman Minton announced that he planned to retire a month later. This sudden announcement forced President Dwight Eisenhower to ask Attorney General Herbert Brownell to help him search for Minton's replacement. President Eisenhower was quite particular in the specifics of the credentials that he wanted for Minton's replacement: "a very good Catholic, with judicial experience, no more than age sixty-two, and who was a conservative Democrat." Knowing that there had not been a Catholic on the high court since Justice Frank Murphy's death in 1949, Eisenhower wanted to prove that he believed that the U.S. Supreme Court should be nonpartisan.

More than likely, Brennan's name to fill the vacancy on the Court was submitted by subsequent Attorney General William P. Rogers, who succeeded Brownell. Rogers was impressed with Brennan after hearing him give a presentation on court reform a few months earlier. Brownell claimed to have closely examined Brennan's credentials and tenure of service on the New Jersey Supreme Court. If so, he defied President Eisenhower's instructions for Minton's replacement because Brennan was not a conservative Democrat, but on the contrary an openly liberal Democrat. Eisenhower would later remark that nominating Brennan and Earl Warren to the Supreme Court were two of his worst mistakes as president.

William Brennan was a strong supporter of civil rights, affirmative action programs, and a strong federal judiciary willing to protect individual rights. Some scholars have suggested that Brennan's greatest legacy was in the equal protection area. He was noted to be a vociferous supporter of gender equality and played a pivotal role in ensuring the constitutionality of affirmative action measures in several key cases. Brennan died in 1993 and is buried in Arlington National Cemetery.

See also Blackmun, Harry Andrew; *City of Richmond v. J.A. Croson Co.*; *Fullilove v. Klutznick*; Marshall, Thurgood; *Metro Broadcasting, Inc. v. FCC*; *Regents of the University of California v. Bakke*; *United States v. Paradise*; *United Steelworkers of America v. Weber*; *Wygant v. Jackson Board of Education.*

FURTHER READING: Eisler, Kim, 1993, *A Justice for All: William J. Brennan, Jr.: Decisions That Transformed America*, New York: Simon and Schuster; Goldman, Roger, and David Gallen, 1994, *Justice William J. Brennan, Jr.: Freedom First*, New York: Carroll and Graf; Irons, Peter, 1994, *Brennan vs. Rehnquist: The Battle for the Constitution*, New York: Alfred A. Knopf; Powe, Lucas, 2000, *The Warren Court and American Politics*, Cambridge, MA: Harvard University Press; Spann, Girardeau A. *The Law of Affirmative Action: Twenty-five Years of Supreme Court Decisions on Race and Remedies*, New York: New York University Press.

F. ERIK BROOKS

Breyer, Stephen Gerald (1938–)

Stephen Gerald Breyer was nominated by President Bill Clinton in 1994 to serve on the U.S. Supreme Court, replacing Justice Harry Blackmun, who had resigned from the Court. Breyer was easily confirmed by the Senate by an 87–9 vote on July 29, 1994, and has served as an associate justice on the Supreme Court since August 8, 1994. Breyer is considered to be strongly supportive of affirmative action. According to Georgetown University law professor Girardeau Spann, "In addition to Justice Stevens, the other three justices who make up the present Court's liberal bloc on affirmative action—Justices Souter, Ginsburg, and Breyer—have voted to uphold each affirmative action program that they considered in a constitutional case" (Spann 2000, 161).

Breyer was born into a middle-class family on August 15, 1938, in San Francisco and spent his early years in the San Francisco area. Breyer attended Stanford University, earning his undergraduate degree in 1959. He then attended Oxford University under a Marshall scholarship, earning another bachelor's degree in 1961 and graduating with the highest honors. When Breyer returned to the United States, he attended Harvard Law School, serving as articles editor on the law review. Upon his graduation from law school, he was selected to serve as a law clerk to Justice Arthur Goldberg, which Breyer did in 1964–1965. During his clerkship, Breyer worked on several important cases and is said to have written the first draft of the landmark right-to-privacy case *Griswold v. Connecticut*, 381 U.S. 479 (1965).

During the ensuing years between the end of the clerkship and 1981, Breyer taught law at Harvard University, as well as holding several positions as an attorney for the federal government during the same time period, including serving as an assistant special prosecutor for the Watergate Special Prosecution Force in 1973 and serving as a special counsel and chief counsel for the U.S. Senate Judiciary Committee in 1974–1975 and 1979–1980, respectively. In 1980, in the waning days of the Carter administration, he was nominated to serve as a federal judge on the U.S. Court of Appeals for the First Circuit. His confirmation easily passed the Senate, and he assumed the bench on the First Circuit on December 10, 1980. In 1990, Breyer became the chief judge in the First Circuit. During his time on the First Circuit Court of Appeals, Breyer earned the reputation of being pragmatic and analytic judge.

In 1994, President Clinton nominated Breyer to serve on the Supreme Court. Because he had a reputation as a pragmatic justice who was not ideologically bent on furthering the traditional liberal agenda, he had supporters from both sides of the Senate. On the Court, Breyer continues to be labeled as a moderate and pragmatic jurist, although he has voted consistently and uniformly in favor of affirmative action. In perhaps the three biggest affirmative action cases that he has reviewed on the high court, *Adarand Constructors, Inc. v. Peña*, 515 U.S. 200 (1995), *Grutter v. Bollinger*, 123 S. Ct. 2325, 2003 U.S. LEXIS 4800 (2003), and *Gratz v. Bollinger*, 123 S. Ct. 2411, 2003 U.S. LEXIS 4801 (2003), Breyer has come out as a firm supporter of affirmative action, as illustrated by his position in these cases. In Adarand, Breyer joined both Justice Ginsburg and Justice Souter's dissenting opinions. In essence, Breyer acknowledged the continuing existence of racism in society and that Congress should be allowed to legislate affirmative action plans (or give federal agencies the authority) to eradicate the last vestiges of racism in society. In *Gratz and Grutter*, Breyer supported the use of race in the admission decisions under affirmative action plans.

See also Adarand Constructors, Inc. v. Peña; Blackmun, Harry Andrew; Clinton, William Jefferson; Ginsburg, Ruth Bader; *Gratz v. Bollinger/Grutter v. Bollinger*; Souter, David; Stevens, John Paul.

FURTHER READING: Spann, Girardeau A., 2000, *The Law of Affirmative Action: Twenty-five Years of Supreme Court Decisions on Race and Remedies*, New York: New York University Press.

JAMES A. BECKMAN

Brooke, Edward W. (1919–)

Edward Brooke was a two-term black U.S. senator from the state of Massachusetts. He was first elected to this office in 1966, the first black to serve in the Senate since Reconstruction. Until the election of Carol Moseley Braun in 1992 (the first black woman), Brooke was the only black American in modern times to serve in the Senate. Brooke was also the only African American to be reelected to the Senate in modern times. The election of Brooke to the Senate was largely the result of a relatively liberal and overwhelmingly Democratic electorate in Massachusetts, a state whose population is only 4 percent black. During Brooke's tenure in the Senate, he was influential in many civil rights issues. Brooke was a leading Senate supporter of affirmative action, integration, and minority business development during his two terms. Finally, Brooke was instrumental in ensuring that the Civil Rights Act of 1968 be broadened to include housing discrimination as part of its scope.

Brooke was the son of black middle-class parents in Washington, D.C., where he attended public schools and graduated from Howard University. He served in the U.S. Army during World War II and rose to the rank of captain in an all-black segregated unit. He was awarded a Bronze Star for intelligence-related work. In his book *The Challenge of Change: Crisis in Our Two-Party System* (1966), Brooke wrote about the mixed messages many black soldiers received from the United States during time of war:

> Why are we fighting this war? It's supposed to be a war against Nazism—against racism and for democracy. Well, what about us? Why are black men fighting a white man's war? What's all this double-talk about democracy? They were not easy questions to answer. I tried to explain that the first task was to defeat the common enemy. And I asked them to bear with America's racial injustices until the war was won. But I knew that this was no more than a rationalization. ("Edward Brooke," http://www.africanpubs.com)

After the war he took up residency in Massachusetts, where he earned two law degrees (LL.B. and LL.M.) from Boston University Law School and served as an editor on the law review. After graduation, he became a practicing attorney. Although he encountered a significant degree of resistance in his own Republican Party, he was nominated for the post of state attorney general. Subsequently, he won the Republican primary and in 1962 became the first African American to be elected a state attorney general.

In 1966, Brooke was elected to the Senate. Brooke's demeanor while in the Senate and public eye was that of a soft-spoken, articulate, and intelligent senator who operated in a pragmatic manner. Although he was a member at the time of a fairly diminutive Republican minority, he was effective in a number of ways in achieving his goals. Brooke served as the ranking Republican on several committees and subcommittees that involved housing, urban affairs, and labor. Near the end of his career in the Senate, he also pushed for civil rights and social welfare legislation. While in the upper house, Brooke was also a champion of government-funded abortions, busing for school integration, and housing for the poor. In 1967, President Lyndon Johnson appointed Brooke to serve on the President's

Commission on Civil Disorders. The commission recommended that the federal government better protect blacks from harassment. At the behest of Senators Brooke and Walter Mondale, the commission also recommended that the problem of housing discrimination be addressed in federal legislation. This commission recommendation led to the Civil Rights Act of 1968 and the subsequent federal legislation on housing.

After Richard Nixon's election to the presidency in 1968, he chose nominees for the U.S. Supreme Court as part of his "southern strategy." This strategy included a "payback" to southern whites for their electoral support, which had helped him win the presidency over Hubert H. Humphrey, the Democratic nominee. This payback would be in the form of the selection of nominees to the Supreme Court who had racial segregation ties. Nixon's selections first of Clement F. Haynsworth and later of G. Harrold Carswell were met with strong opposition by Senator Brooke, who was the first senator to publicly oppose Haynesworth and clearly voiced his opposition to the president. Similarly, Brooke played a role in mobilizing the seventeen critical Republican votes against Carswell's nomination in the Senate. Nixon also failed to consult the only black member of the Republican Party on a number of policy-related issues. Partly as a result of this omission and partly in response to the pressures of civil rights groups and black militants, Brooke became an ardent opponent of Nixon's domestic civil rights policies and publicly resisted him on a number of issues. In 1971, Brooke, who had initially supported the Vietnam War, came out publicly in favor of the McGovern-Hatfield Amendment, which called for bringing American troops home from Vietnam.

Brooke was defeated for reelection in 1978 by liberal congressman Paul Tsongas, who was supported by Senator Teddy Kennedy. Factors in his defeat included a combination of a well-publicized divorce and a subsequent investigation, confirmed charges of lying with regard to his financial statement, and a well-financed and able opponent in Tsongas. After leaving the Senate, Brooke resumed a law practice.

When Ronald Reagan won the presidency in the 1980 election, Edward Brooke's name was among those of a number of black conservatives being considered for cabinet posts, but he was not selected. Brooke has received more than thirty honorary degrees and numerous civic awards and currently resides with his second wife, Anne Fleming, in Warrenton, Virginia.

See also Civil Rights Act of 1968; Congressional Black Caucus; Housing; Johnson, Lyndon Baines; Military and Affirmative Action; Nixon, Richard Milhous; Reagan, Ronald; Republican Party and Affirmative Action.

FURTHER READING: African American Publications, "Edward Brooke," www.africanpubs.com (accessed January 2004); Becker, John F., and Eugene E. Heaton Jr., 1967, "The Election of Senator Edward W. Brooke," *Public Opinion Quarterly* 31, no. 3 (Autumn): 346–358; Cross, Theodore, 1984, *The Black Power Imperative*, New York: Faulkner Books; Estell, Kenneth, ed., 1994, *African America: Portrait of a People*, Detroit: Visible Ink Press; Ploski, Harry A., and Ernest Kaiser, 1971, *The Negro Almanac*, 2nd ed., New York: Bellwether Company.

MFANYA D. TRYMAN

Brotherhood of Sleeping Car Porters

The Brotherhood of Sleeping Car Porters was the first union of predominantly African American workers to be granted a charter by the American Federation of Labor. The Brotherhood of Sleeping Car Porters, under the leadership of A. Philip Randolph, mobilized sufficient pressure through a threatened strike and protest march in Washington, D.C., to prompt President Franklin D. Roosevelt to issue Executive Order 8802, an antidiscrimination measure designed to open up the World War II economy to African Americans. Executive Order 8802 declared that "there shall be no discrimination in the employment of workers in defense industries or government because of race, creed, color, or national origin, and . . . it is the duty of employers and of labor organizations, in furtherance . . . of this order, to provide for the full and equitable participation of all workers in defense industries, without discrimination because of race, creed, color, or national origin." Thus the Brotherhood of Sleeping Car Porters was both a labor organization and an early civil rights organization.

By the beginning of World War I, the Pullman Company employed nearly 12,000 porters and was considered one of the most powerful businesses in the country at the time. The company had been founded in 1867 by George Pullman and had originally been named the Pullman Palace Car Company. Train travel was the preferred mode of travel for many people who had to go long distances. Company employees were called porters. They were expected to secure passengers' luggage and provide services that would assure supreme comfort to them. The porters were nattily attired in dark uniforms, starched shirts, perfectly arranged neckties, and shiny shoes. They were polite and always stood ready to do whatever was necessary to keep the passengers happy. In the years before the turn of the century, only black men were hired as porters. It was considered by many to be a coveted job for the upwardly mobile.

However, all was not well in the Pullman Company according to a young man, A. Philip Randolph. He publicly accused George Pullman of exploiting the porters and described their status as an extension of former slavery. He further charged that African Americans were not hired in the company's repair and erection shops and were explicitly barred from being conductors, so the hiring of black porters was not the altruistic act that the Pullman Corporation claimed. After federal control of the railroads ended in 1920, inequities within the company were exposed: long hours, low wages, and unfair company policies. The porters looked around for a leader to help change their work status, whom they found in Randolph. The Brotherhood of Sleeping Car Porters originated one summer night in 1925 when 500 porters met at the Elks Lodge on 129th Street in Harlem, New York. Thus began their vigorous pursuit of higher wages and shorter working hours for employees.

One leader who worked alongside A. Philip Randolph was Milton P. Webster, head of the Chicago division of the Brotherhood of Sleeping Car Porters. He captured the essence of what the Brotherhood was and would become when he stated that it was not just a union, but a civil rights movement fighting for fuller citizenship rights. The Ida B. Wells Club and the Northern District Association of Colored Women joined in to support the fledgling union. Women claimed a role in this new movement. In December 1927, Webster created a formal Citizens'

Committee of supporters that sponsored the Brotherhood of Sleeping Car Porters annual conferences. The group's magazine, called the *Messenger*, served as an effective tool. The yearly conferences educated the porters and the public about labor and civil rights issues. Initially, there was strong resistance to this new movement from within the African American community, especially among some ministers and the black press. Also, labor organizations such as the American Federation of Labor (AFL) were not supportive. President Franklin D. Roosevelt's New Deal legislation guaranteed workers the right to organize. The new policies required corporations to negotiate with workers through their unions. In 1935, for the first time, the mighty Pullman Company heeded the official mandate to negotiate with the porters. Then the challenge was to become recognized as a bona fide union with official union recognition. At the AFL convention in 1935 where Randolph argued the case for the Brotherhood of Sleeping Car Porters to become officially affiliated with the AFL, there was a divisire fight among the AFL members as to whether to organize by craft or industry. Those who chose the latter were expelled and later became the Congress of Industrial Organizations (CIO) (years later the two organizations reunited as the AFL-CIO in 1955).

The Brotherhood remained in the AFL, and in 1937 negotiations culminated in the first contract between a corporation and a black union. A. Philip Randolph and the Brotherhood gained recognition as trailblazers in the field of civil rights. Randolph, as head of the Brotherhood, focused his attention on black unemployment and the increasing number of defense jobs completed by contractors that did not hire blacks. He proposed a huge march on Washington to protest. Before this happened, President Roosevelt responded to the call from many quarters to issue an executive order banning discrimination within the government and among the defense industries that had government contracts. A Fair Employment Practices Committee was set up to implement the order. The march was not held. President Roosevelt's Executive Order 8802 was be a precursor to modern civil rights antidiscrimination legislation.

Randolph was also one of the leading and most vocal voices against segregation in the military. As a result of Randolph's lobbying on this front, on July 26, 1948, President Harry Truman signed Executive Order 9981 barring discrimination in the military. Randolph, along with his trusted aide Bayard Rustin, accomplished some successes in government, but the main focus on organized labor for which the Brotherhood had been founded remained elusive. He joined forces with many civil rights organizations of the time to change social, economic, and educational conditions of African Americans. A dignified, articulate, and skillful person, he was an acknowledged elder statesman of the civil rights movement. In 1957, Randolph was elected a vice president of the AFL-CIO. He and Rustin are credited with keeping the peace among the diverse civil rights organizations that came together for the historic March on Washington in 1963. After the march, Randolph joined Martin Luther King Jr. and other African American leaders in meeting with President John F. Kennedy. In less than a year, the Civil Rights Act of 1964 was signed.

One year before Randolph's death, the Brotherhood of Sleeping Car Porters merged with a larger union, the Brotherhood of Railway and Airline Clerks. Society had changed. The civil rights movement had evolved. Even the unions had shifted their stands on some issues. Randolph died at the age of ninety in 1979.

See also Civil Rights Act of 1964; Civil Rights Movement; Executive Order 8802; Kennedy, John Fitzgerald; King, Martin Luther, Jr.; Military and Affirmative Action; Randolph, Asa Philip; Roosevelt, Franklin Delano; Truman, Harry.

FURTHER READING: Brazeal, Brailsford, 1946, *The Brotherhood of Sleeping Car Porters*, New York: Harper and Row; Chateauvert, Melinda, 1997, *Marching Together: Women of the Brotherhood of Sleeping Car Porters*, New York: Walker and Co.; Harris, William H., 1991, *Keeping the Faith: A. Philip Randolph, Milton P. Webster, and the Brotherhood of Sleeping Car Porters, 1925–37*, Urbana: University of Illinois Press; Wilson, Joseph F., ed., 1969, *Tearing Down the Color Barriers*, New York: Columbia University Press.

BETTY NYANGONI

Brown v. Board of Education, 347 U.S. 483 (1954)

On May 17, 1954, *Brown v. Board of Education* became one of the most pivotal and groundbreaking decisions ever to be issued by the Supreme Court. The Court in *Brown* ruled that the practice of racial segregation in public schools pursuant to the separate-but-equal doctrine was constitutionally flawed under the Fourteenth Amendment's Equal Protection Clause. The *Brown* decision overturned the pernicious separate-but-equal doctrine that had been put forward a half century earlier in *Plessy v. Ferguson*, 163 U.S. 537 (1896), which stated that public facilities (railroad cars in the *Plessy* case) could be segregated along racial lines so long as separate, equal facilities were provided by the state for minorities. In *Brown*, the Court stated that separate facilities designated by race are inherently unequal and can never be equal under the Equal Protection Clause of the Fourteenth Amendment. The *Brown* decision has been described as igniting "a legal and social revolution in race relations and constitutionalism" (Hall 1993, 93). The decision would also be codified in Title VI of the Civil Rights Act of 1964.

While the *Brown* decision repudiated the separate-but-equal doctrine and began the long process of desegregating schools in the South, it is still cited today in affirmative action debates. For example, during the April 2003 oral arguments to the U.S. Supreme Court in *Grutter v. Bollinger*, 123 S. Ct. 2325, 2003 U.S. LEXIS 4800 (2003), and *Gratz v. Bollinger*, 123 S. Ct. 2411, 2003 U.S. LEXIS 4801 (2003), protesters in favor of affirmative action held a rally on the front steps of the Supreme Court, some holding signs that read, "Do Not Reverse *Brown v. Board of Education*." The apparent message of the signs was that if the Supreme Court restricted or eliminated affirmative action in higher education, the practical effects would be to reverse the *Brown v. Board of Education* decision, returning higher education to a de facto segregated, separate-but-equal system. While the message on the signs was obviously incorrect (the *Gratz* and *Grutter* cases had little to do with *Brown*), it illustrates how milestone landmark cases like *Brown* are still emotionally cited in affirmative action debates today.

The *Brown* case was part of a broader attack on the separate-but-equal doctrine. Starting in the 1930s, the National Association for the Advancement of Colored People (NAACP) and its Legal Defense and Educational Fund were the biggest forces behind the efforts to change the separate-but-equal doctrine of the *Plessy* decision. The strategy involved litigation at the state and federal levels, challenging the separate-but-equal doctrine throughout the South. The strategy involved first

Mrs. Nettie Hunt, sitting on the steps of the U.S. Supreme Court, holding a newspaper and explaining to her daughter Nikie the meaning of the Supreme Court's decision banning school segregation as unconstitutional. Courtesy of Library of Congress.

litigating separate-but-equal cases at the college and university level. The rationale was that there would be a greater likelihood of desegregation at the higher-education level than at grade schools and high schools. Thus the *Brown* case only came about after a series of cases involving higher education, such as *Missouri ex rel. Gaines v. Canada*, 305 U.S. 337 (1938), *Sweatt v. Painter*, 339 U.S. 629 (1950), *Sipuel v. Regents of the University of Oklahoma*, 332 U.S. 631 (1948), and *McLaurin v. Oklahoma State Board of Regents*, 339 U.S. 637 (1950).

Thurgood Marshall, who would eventually become the first black solicitor general and Supreme Court justice in U.S. history, helped to fight for desegregated schools in the *Brown* case. Marshall was the chief attorney in the case at the time. He was no stranger to civil rights and desegregation cases, having been fighting for the rights of black families and schools for years. Marshall had worked with Charles H. Houston, who was the legal counsel for the NAACP. Prior to *Brown*, Charles Houston, along with Thurgood Marshall and their team of attorneys and consultants, had concentrated on higher-education cases, hoping that good court decisions in the university cases would trickle down to fair and moral decisions for elementary and secondary institutions to become desegregated as well.

The *Brown* case was a collective group of five individual cases that came from five distinct lawsuits challenging segregated elementary schools in the states of Delaware, Virginia, Kansas, and South Carolina. The NAACP in 1949 decided to take on these cases and fought them in their state districts. During the trial, Marshall (among other NAACP lawyers) argued before the Supreme Court, with the first hearing being held on December 9, 1952. The case was then held over a term and reargued on December 8, 1953.

The most compelling arguments presented by the NAACP and lawyers working for the Legal Defense and Educational Fund came from evidence about both the inferior conditions of the segregated black schools in terms of resources and buildings and the psychological effects of segregated schools on black children, according to research given by a prominent social psychologist, Kenneth Clark. Clark conducted controversial research and interviews of black children (which were later incorporated by the Supreme Court in the *Brown* decision and cited in the controversial Footnote 11 to the decision) that established that black children had very low self-esteem by virtue of attending segregated schools. The lawyers in the case also stated that even if the conditions of the schools were equal to those of white schools, which in many cases they were not, and even if segregation did not cause psychological damage to black children, school segregation was illegal because "restrictions . . . based upon race . . . disregarded the equal protection clause written in the Fourteenth Amendment."

After the initial arguments in the case, it appeared as if the Court was divided. However, in 1953, Chief Justice Fred Vinson died and was replaced by Chief Justice Earl Warren, who was able to build a unanimous sentiment of the Court on the case. Warren was able to convince his brethren on the Court to issue a short opinion in *Brown* on the merits of the case and the issue of segregation (*Brown I*) and then issue a separate opinion at a later point dealing with enforcement of the decision (which became known as *Brown v. Board of Education II*, 349 U.S. 294 [1955], and imposed the obligation on states to desegregate with "all deliberate speed"). Ultimately, the decision of the Court in *Brown I* was a short opinion, devoid of technical legal reasoning and citations and brimming with moral certainty. According to many scholars, the opinion avoided the harder legal questions, such as the original intent of the Fourteenth Amendment (a question that the parties had been asked to specifically address in the second oral arguments to the Court in 1953).

After nearly fifty years, theorists, lawyers, practitioners, educators, parents, and historians question if *Brown* was worth the fight in light of the existence of de facto segregation today. Although state-sponsored segregation in schools was declared unconstitutional in *Brown*, some allege that schools today, particularly in urban and suburban centers, are becoming more separate than ever before in terms of racial and ethnic lines. As a result, some advocate more aggressive, affirmative means of achieving integration in schools, such as changes to housing or forced busing of children to schools outside their own neighborhoods.

See also All Deliberate Speed; Busing; Civil Rights Act of 1964; Clark, Kenneth Bancroft; De Facto and De Jure Segregation; Education and Affirmative Action; Equal Protection Clause; Fourteenth Amendment; Marshall, Thurgood; National Association for the Advancement of Colored People; *Plessy v. Ferguson;* Segregation; *Sipuel v. Regents of the University of Oklahoma; Sweatt v. Painter*, Title VI of the Civil Rights Act of 1964; Warren Court and Affirmative Action.

FURTHER READING: Hall, Kermit, ed., 1992, *The Oxford Companion to the Supreme Court of the United States*, New York: Oxford University Press; Irons, Peter, 1999, *A People's History of the Supreme Court*, New York: Viking Press; Wilkinson, J. Harvie, III, 1979, *From Brown to Bakke: The Supreme Court and School Integration, 1954–1978*, New York: Oxford University Press.

NICOLE M. STEPHENS

Bunche, Ralph J. (1904–1971)

A revered figure in the annals of African American history, Ralph Johnson Bunche broke down many barriers of discrimination against African Americans in education and international relations. Bunche was the first African American to win the Nobel Peace Prize in 1950 for his role in brokering a peace agreement between the Arabs and Israelis, and he helped convince Arab nations to recognize the new state of Israel. Long before the advent of modern affirmative action programs, he was also instrumental in the struggle to improve race relations in the United States and, through his prolific writings, called for proactive and aggressive social programs to benefit the entire African American community. Bunche once remarked that "no Negro American can be free from the disabilities of race in this country until the lowliest Negro in Mississippi is no longer disadvantaged because of his race" (Maxwell 2000, 15A).

Ralph Bunche was born in Detroit, Michigan, on August 7, 1904. The family moved to Albuquerque, New Mexico, and then to Los Angeles. He finished Jefferson High School as class valedictorian and earned a sports scholarship to UCLA, at that time called the University of California, Southern Branch. In 1907, he completed his undergraduate degree in political science. He finished Phi Beta Kappa and first in his class. As valedictorian, he gave the commencement address. His speech contained topics that formed Bunche's approach to the great challenges of his career.

After winning a tuition-free scholarship to Harvard and assistance from African American women of the Friday Morning Club of Los Angeles, Bunche left for Harvard University to pursue a master's degree in government. He met several persons with whom he formed friendships that lasted past the Harvard years. William Hastie, who became the first black federal judge, and Robert Weaver, an economist who was active in President Franklin Roosevelt's New Deal and was secretary of housing and urban development under President Lyndon Johnson, were two of those he met there.

Bunche left Harvard University in 1928 to go to Howard University in Washington, D.C. His responsibility was to expand the political science department at Howard. Along with John Davis and A. Philip Randolph, he founded the National Negro Congress. This was Bunche's first major organizing effort to bring more social and political equality between blacks and whites. The objective of the National Negro Congress was to provide the basis for a broad coalition of blacks and whites, trade unions, and religious, civic, and fraternal groups. It was established to formulate a comprehensive program for social, political, and economic change. From there he occasionally took leave to complete his doctoral work at Harvard. Initially, he wanted to study race relations in the United States, but his professors steered him toward colonialism in Africa.

All through this period of his life, he was a prolific writer on issues related to equality for African Americans in the United States. Perhaps the most memorable published works of this period in Bunche's life were contributions to the research efforts of *An American Dilemma: The Negro Problem and Modern Democracy*, a comprehensive study of blacks in the United States that was commissioned by the Carnegie Corporation of New York and led by Gunnar Myrdal, the Swedish social economist. While other African American intellectuals such as Doxey Wilkerson, Sterling

Brown, E. Franklin Frazier, Kenneth Clark, and Alain Locke served on the research team, it was Bunche who was closest to Myrdal. This study was the largest and broadest investigation into race relations in the United States. Heretofore, research had mostly avoided promoting change in public policy or social reform. Even the New Deal had focused mostly on economic changes. Bunche made it clear that this landmark study would break new ground when he wrote: "We feel that a frank appraisal of the position of the Negro minority in the United States at this time will constitute a striking document, one that should be helpful to the Negro in his struggle for equality." The U.S. Supreme Court would cite this landmark study in a footnote in its famous desegregation decision in *Brown v. Board of Education*, 347 U.S. 483 (1954).

Bunche spent much of his career prolifically writing on the need for legislation giving assistance to African Americans to reverse the effects of discrimination. For example, in an article titled "A Critique of New Deal Social Planning As It Affects Negroes" that appeared in the January 1936 issue of the *Journal of Negro Education*, Bunche argued that the New Deal legislation was of little help to African Americans and that greater focus should be given to the plight of African Americans and raising their wages:

> [F]or the Negro population, the New Deal means the same thing, but more of it. Striking at no fundamental social conditions, the New Deal at best can only fix the disadvantages, the differentials, the discriminations, under which the Negro population has labored all along. . . . [T]herefore, the first efforts of the NRA should have been directed toward assuring Negro workers that real wage which would make possible for them a decent standard of living. (Bunche 1936, 62)

In another article titled "The Programs of Organizations Devoted to the Improvement of the Status of the American Negro," which appeared in the July 1939 issue of the *Journal of Negro Education*, Bunche called for organizations that would ensure the economic equity of wages for black workers.

During World War II, Ralph Bunche was friendly with First Lady Eleanor Roosevelt, lobbying her to use her influence to push for a more fair and just war and society and especially to provide jobs in the new war industry. He worked as a senior social science analyst in the Office of Strategic Services (OSS), from which the Central Intelligence Agency grew. There he handled issues regarding African Americans serving abroad in the armed services, discrimination against black drivers in the local Capital Transit Company of Washington, D.C., and the need for blacks in the whole war effort.

After being transferred to the State Department, he worked on plans for postwar Africa. Emerging from this experience was a series of events that put him on the international stage in a way that no African American had previously attained. Bunche represented the United States at the Dumbarton Oaks Convention and the San Francisco Conference on International Organization, which culminated in the creation of the United Nations. Bunche worked tirelessly in crafting language for the charter that committed the international community to the advancement of dependent peoples and the decolonization of developing countries. As a U.S. representative to the first session of the United Nations, he vigorously advocated for a yearly progress report on the status of decolonization. This was not a popular position, but he persisted and won. He served as a negotiator on several occasions in Europe, Africa, and the Middle East. For these peacekeeping efforts he was awarded the Nobel Peace Prize in 1950. Modestly he insisted that peacekeeping was simply part of his job at the United Nations.

After fighting accusations of being a Communist, he was exonerated by a congressional investigation board. By 1954, Dag Hammanskjöld, secretary general of the United Nations, had brought in Bunche as undersecretary general. This was an unprecedented achievement for an American, and certainly for an African American, at the time. Throughout the 1950s, Bunche continued to serve in the United Nations, most often as the troubleshooter to colonial areas. The U.S. Medal of Freedom, the highest honor for a civilian, was bestowed on him. Ironically, at the same time he was serving as one of the highest-ranking officials in the United Nations, he experienced racism and discrimination at home. In Washington, D.C., Bunche had trouble renting or buying property in the still segregated neighborhoods. The racism and segregation were so bad in Washington that Bunche once declined the position of assistant secretary of state, in part because there was "too much Jim Crow in Washington for me."

By the 1960s, Bunche was turning more attention to domestic affairs. In the beginning, the black protest movement was a middle-class movement to secure black constitutional rights through court action and legislation. In midstream, it shifted to include more than the middle class, with emphasis on direct action. He took great interest in the civil rights movement. He supported integration and decried racial separation, once stating that "segregation and democracy are incompatible." He participated in the 1963 March on Washington. On December 9, 1971, Ralph Bunche died at age sixty-seven after a lifetime of being a trailblazer in the pursuit of equality in the United States and abroad. His image was placed on a twenty-cent postage stamp in 1982.

See also African Americans; *Brown v. Board of Education*; Civil Rights Movement; Clark, Kenneth Bancroft; Integration; Randolph, Asa Philip; Roosevelt, Eleanor; Roosevelt, Franklin Delano; Segregation.

FURTHER READING: Bunche, Ralph, 1936, "A Critique of New Deal Social Planning As It Affects Negroes," *Journal of Negro Education* 5, no. 1 (January): 59–65; Bunche, Ralph, 1939, "The Programs of Organizations Devoted to the Improvement of the Status of the American Negro," *Journal of Negro Education* 8, no. 3 (July): 539–550; Bunche, Ralph, 1941, "The Negro in the Political Life of the United States," *Journal of Negro Education* 10, no. 3 (July): 567–584; Mann, Peggy, 1975, *Ralph Bunche: UN Peacemaker*, New York: Coward, McCann and Geoghegan; Maxwell, Bill, 2000, "Honored Diplomat Felt Racism at Home," *St. Petersburg Times*, July 19, 15A; Rivlin, Benjamin, ed., 1990, *Ralph Bunche: The Man and His Times*, New York: Holmes and Meier; Urquhart, Brian, 1993, *Ralph Bunche: An American Odyssey*, New York: W.W. Norton.

BETTY NYANGONI

Bureau of Labor Statistics

The U.S. Bureau of Labor Statistics (BLS) is the federal government agency within the Department of Labor that uses raw data collected by the U.S. Bureau of the Census to objectively segment, calculate, and publish labor and business statistics. These statistics include racial, color, and gender segmentations utilized by government, business, and the general public in the creation and evaluation of social and economic programs and policies, including affirmative action policies. Important statistical categories include employment, unemployment, inflation, consumer spending, wages, earnings, benefits, productivity, safety, health, occupations, demographics, industries, business costs, and international trade.

The modern BLS traces its roots back to 1869, when the political influence of organized labor resulted in the establishment of the first bureau of labor statistics to collect and calculate labor statistics in the state of Massachusetts. While initially a labor advocate, the bureau became an objective and well-respected statistical organization under Carroll Wright, who was named bureau head in 1873. In 1884, President Chester A. Arthur created the Bureau of Labor (BOL) within the Department of the Interior to gather data on working people. Carroll Wright was named its first commissioner. While it was not clear if the new bureau would be impartial or an advocate of labor when it was created, Wright made it impartial and successful as a governmental agency. The BOL became independent and increased its size and responsibilities in 1888 by conducting the 1890 national population census. In 1903, Wright resigned when the BOL became a part of the newly established cabinet-level Department of Commerce and Labor. Wright believed that the BOL was under the control of big business and had lost its independence. In 1913, under pressure from labor unions, a cabinet-level Department of Labor (DOL) was created to advocate the causes of laborers. The DOL included the old BOL, which became the modern BLS, tasked with the sole responsibility of calculating objective labor statistics, which remains its role today.

See also Bureau of the Census; Census Classifications, Ethnic and Racial; Department of Housing and Urban Development; Department of Labor; Equal Employment Opportunity Commission.

FURTHER READING: Cutrona, Cheryl, 1988, *Know Your Government: The Department of Labor*, New York: Chelsea House; Halacy, Dan, 1980, *Census: 190 Years of Counting America*, New York: Elsevier/Nelson Books; Wainwright, Jon S., 2000, *Racial Discrimination and Minority Business Enterprise: Evidence from the 1990 Census*, New York: Garland Publishing.

MARK J. SENEDIAK

Bureau of the Census

The U.S. Bureau of the Census is the federal agency within the U.S. Department of Commerce responsible for collecting raw demographic and economic data on the U.S. population. These data are used to meet constitutional data requirements and to assist government, business, and the general public in the creation and evaluation of social and economic programs and policies that are heavily dependent on these data, including affirmative action policies.

Before 1790, individual colonies conducted censuses or counting of their populations on an ad hoc basis. Article I, Section 2, of the U.S. Constitution required that starting in 1790 and continuing every ten years thereafter, the population of the country would be counted to determine apportionment of direct taxes and congressional representation for each state. Successive presidents and Congresses have continually added new types of data and increased the detail level of the data to be collected for additional purposes. From 1790 until 1902, Congress created temporary organizations every ten years to conduct and publish each census.

The Bureau of the Census was created in 1902 as the permanent governmental agency charged with creating, cataloging, and storing collected data. Currently, it collects demographic, economic, and geographic data on population, transportation, housing, agriculture, irrigation, drainage, government, and business through a diverse selection of survey instruments. The American Community Survey, the American Housing Survey, the Current Population Survey, the Residential Finance Survey, the Women- and Minority-Owned Business Survey, the Characteristics of Business Owners Survey, and the Public Use Microdata Samples are the primary data resources utilized for affirmative action policy research, legislation, and enforcement.

See also Bureau of Labor Statistics; Census Classifications, Ethnic and Racial; Department of Housing and Urban Development; Equal Employment Opportunity Commission.

FURTHER READING: Halacy, Dan, 1980, *Census: 190 Years of Counting America*, New York: Elsevier/Nelson Books; Wainwright, Jon S., 2000, *Racial Discrimination and Minority Business Enterprise: Evidence from the 1990 Census*, New York: Garland Publishing.

MARK J. SENEDIAK

Burger Court and Affirmative Action

The tenure of Warren E. Burger as chief justice of the U.S. Supreme Court, 1969 to 1986 (the Burger Court), saw race-conscious affirmative action programs both advocated and attacked with increasing vehemence and frequency. A survey of the Supreme Court's pertinent decisions during these years reveals a Court sharply divided in approach, opinion, and rationale; nevertheless, certain trends are identifiable. The Burger Court broadened the scope and impact of affirmative action by expressly permitting race-conscious remedies to counter effects of past discrimination, by expanding the definition of beneficiaries, and by endorsing racial distinctions and preferences to promote minority interests. The justices subjected private, state, and local practices and regulations to heightened scrutiny, but deferred to Congress when reviewing federal affirmative action legislation. Eight representative cases, discussed here, illustrate these trends.

Challenges to racial preference in higher-education admissions policy began to appear in the nation's courts early in the 1970s. In 1974, the Burger Court refused to rule on the first such case before it, dismissing the complaint by a vote of 5–4 on grounds of mootness in *DeFunis v. Odegaard*, 416 U.S. 312 (1974). At the trial court level, Marco DeFunis Jr. claimed that his denial of admission to the University of Washington School of Law constituted discrimination because he was not a member of the minority groups given special preference. The trial court ruled in his favor and ordered his admission. During the appeals process, DeFunis attended law school and was in his final term when the Supreme Court agreed to consider his certiorari petition. A majority of the justices, in a per curiam opinion, concluded that the case was moot because DeFunis, nearing graduation, would not be subject to the university's admissions policies again (his case was not "capable of repetition"). A judgment by the Court at that point could neither "compel nor prevent" DeFunis's desired outcome, and since the case had not been filed as a class action, a majority of justices determined that no other deliberation was appropriate: "[W]e conclude that the Court cannot, consistently with the limitations of Art. III of the Constitution, consider the substantive constitutional issues tendered by the parties."

Justice William O. Douglas, writing separately in dissent, condemned racial preferences on constitutional grounds, interpreting the Fourteenth Amendment to prohibit all but "racially neutral" criteria. He acknowledged, however, that in certain instances cultural biases in admissions procedures might require examination. Justices William Brennan, Byron White, and Thurgood Marshall, also dissenting, accused the Court of evading responsibility by refusing to "decide the merits of the very important constitutional questions" presented in *DeFunis*, questions certain to reappear in another guise, and soon.

Four years later, they did so in *Regents of the University of California v. Bakke*, 438 U.S. 265 (1978), arguably the Court's most famous affirmative action case. Again at issue was racial preference in higher-education admissions policies, specifically those of the University of California at Davis Medical School, adopted to ensure enrollment of 16 minority applicants ("Blacks, Chicanos, Asians, and American Indians") in an entering class of 100. Allan Bakke, denied admission under "general standards," challenged the university's racial policies that admitted minority applicants having grade point averages and Medical College Admission Test (MCAT) and benchmark scores "significantly lower" than his own. The case would be decided by the Court's interpretation of Title VI of the Civil Rights Act of 1964, which provides that "[n]o person in the United States shall, on the ground of race, color, or national origin, be excluded from participation in, be denied the benefits of, or be subjected to discrimination under any program or activity receiving Federal financial assistance."

In California state court, Bakke sued the university on the grounds that the special race-conscious policies (1) had injured him personally; (2) contravened the California Constitution; (3) violated Title VI of the Civil Rights Act of 1964; and (4) violated the Equal Protection Clause of the Fourteenth Amendment of the U.S. Constitution. The trial court agreed with the last three arguments, 2 to 4 but not with the first, that Bakke had been personally injured by the policies. He had not, in their view, satisfactorily shown that he would have been admitted to the program "but for" the race-conscious standards. On appeal, the California Supreme Court reversed this latter holding, arguing that Bakke was not required to prove injury, but did not address either the statutory or state constitutional issues. Ruling only that the school's admission policies violated the Equal Protection Clause of the Fourteenth Amendment, the court ordered Bakke's admission. The case moved to the U.S. Supreme Court in 1978.

There the justices were divided, not only on the standard of review appropriate to the case, but even on what question or questions they were being asked to resolve. Although the case turned on the vote of Justice Lewis Powell, who rendered the judgment, his analysis of the issues failed to attract a majority of his colleagues. Chief Justice Burger and Justices Potter Stewart, William Rehnquist, and John Paul Stevens argued that the medical school's affirmative action program violated Title VI; therefore, they did not proceed to the constitutional issue. They joined Powell in affirming Bakke's court-ordered enrollment.

Justices Brennan, White, Marshall, and Harry Blackmun determined that the Davis program violated neither the Fourteenth Amendment nor Title VI. They joined Justice Powell, in separate opinions, in reversing that part of the California Supreme Court's ruling that prohibited consideration of race in programs receiving federal funding. They argued that Title VI banned only such racial discrimination as was unlawful under the Fourteenth Amendment, and, further, that that amendment did not ban all racial classifications. Powell's assertion that "race or ethnic background may be deemed a 'plus' in a particular applicant's file" appeared to allow admissions committees to classify applicants by race and to grant preference to minority applicants to achieve diversity "goals"—although not "clear, strict racial quotas"—provided the selections did not unlawfully burden nonminority individuals.

Powell reached his conclusions in *Bakke* using strict scrutiny, wherein governmental practices or statutes that restrict "fundamental rights" or contain "suspect classifications" are permissible only when they are narrowly tailored to promote a compelling governmental interest. Brennan, however, argued that race-conscious affirmative action programs should be subject to a lowered level of scrutiny. A government objective, he asserted, need only be "important" and the means to attain it "substantially related" to the goal. In Brennan's judgment, the medical school's policies under review passed constitutional muster. *Bakke* was the first of a trilogy of important Carter-era cases in which the Court gave splintered support for race-conscious measures designed to promote minority interests. In the two other cases, the justices wrestled with key constitutional and statutory issues.

Race-conscious affirmative action components of contracts and other employment agreements came before the Burger Court with some frequency beginning in the late 1970s. In *United Steelworkers of America v. Weber*, 443 U.S. 193 (1979), the Court examined Title VII of the Civil Rights Act of 1964, which bans discrimination in employment, specifically analyzing section 703(j) of Title VII: "Nothing contained in this title shall be interpreted to require any employer, employment agency, labor organization, or joint labor-management committee subject to this title to grant preferential treatment" to anyone due to "race, color, religion, sex, or national origin."

In 1974, the United Steelworkers of America and Kaiser Aluminum Chemical Corporation incorporated an affirmative action plan into their master collective-bargaining agreement. To redress Kaiser's marked employee racial imbalance, 50 percent of in-plant training openings were reserved for black applicants until the percentage of minority workers in each of fifteen Kaiser plants equaled the percentage of the local adult minority population. A white employee brought a class-action suit in federal district court charging discrimination under Title VII of the Civil Rights Act of 1964.

By a vote of 5–2, the Court held that the language of section 703(j) of Title VII did not expressly forbid race-conscious affirmative action programs voluntarily undertaken by private employers or negotiated in employer-union bargaining, independent of state intervention, for the purpose of attaining racial balancing. Justice Brennan announced the opinion, joined by Justices Stewart, White, Marshall, and Blackmun. In the opinion, Brennan offered an interpretation of the legislative intent of the law. Congress, he wrote, alive to past discrimination, nowhere had recorded an intention to prohibit private race-conscious affirmative action plans. The statute's specific language refused only to require such programs; it left open the possibility of permitting them.

Justices Powell and Stevens did not participate in the ruling, but Chief Justice Burger, joining Justice Rehnquist, vigorously dissented. The legislative history of Title VII expressed its writer's intentions in language so clear that "no one should doubt its meaning": the language "forecloses the reading which the Court gives the statute today." The chief justice continued, "I suspect there is some truth to [the] adage . . . that hard cases make bad law," for hard cases "always tempt judges to exceed the limits of their authority, as the Court does today by totally rewriting a crucial part of Title VII to reach a 'desirable' result." No agreement was reached on the appropriate judicial standard of review for affirmative action cases, and a majority decision regarding racial preferences still eluded the Court.

Fullilove v. Klutznick, 448 U.S. 448 (1980), was another case that, although decided by a 6–3 vote, failed to yield a majority opinion. The Burger Court in *Fullilove* upheld a federal minority business enterprise (MBE) provision or "set-aside program" of the Public Works Employment Act of 1977 that required that, absent administrative waiver, at least 10 percent of federal grant monies for local public works projects must be expended on contracts with businesses controlled by minority owners ("Negroes, Spanish-speaking, Orientals, Indians, Eskimos, and Aleuts").

A group of contractors and subcontractors filed suit in federal district court seeking declaratory and injunctive relief. They alleged that the MBE requirement caused economic damage and violated, on its face, the Equal Protection Clause of the Fourteenth Amendment and the equal protection component of the Due Process Clause of the Fifth Amendment. Both the district court and the Court of Appeals for the Second Circuit upheld the validity of the MBE requirement.

Chief Justice Burger announced the plurality opinion, joined by Justices White and Powell. Showing "appropriate deference" to the federal legislature, he argued that "in no organ of government [does] there repose a more comprehensive remedial power" than in the U.S. Congress. Critics erred, he charged, in contending that Congress could formulate only "color-blind" remedies. Race-conscious programs, such as the one under scrutiny, could be "independently justified" by the regulatory power of Congress under Section 5 of the Fourteenth Amendment, the Commerce Clause (Article I, Section 8, Clause 3), and its spending power under Article I, Section 8, Clause 1. In fact, Burger argued, the Commerce Clause alone would suffice: Congress had a "rational basis" for concluding that accepted contracting practices "could perpetuate the prevailing impaired access by minority businesses to public contracting opportunities," thereby adversely affecting interstate commerce. This emphasis on congressional power permitted Burger to bypass mention of any equal protection standard of review.

Eschewing strict scrutiny in favor of the lesser level of scrutiny he supported in *Bakke*, Justice Marshall, joined by Justices Brennan and Blackmun, concurred with the judgment: "[T]he racial classifications employed in the set-aside provision are substantially related to the achievement of the important and congressionally articulated goal of remedying the present effects of past racial discrimination." Justice Stewart, joined by Justice Rehnquist, dissented in strong terms. Equal protection "absolutely prohibits invidious discrimination"; if a law is unconstitutional, they argued, "it is no less unconstitutional just because it is a product of [Congress]." Justice Stevens also dissented, calling the set-aside a "somewhat perverse form of reparation." He characterized the Public Works Employment Act of

1977 as a "slapdash statute" that unlawfully "creates monopoly privileges" for a class of persons "defined solely by race."

Issues still debatable after *Fullilove* included the extent to which federal affirmative action programs might be restricted or, conversely, encouraged by judicial reading of the equal protection component of the Fifth Amendment of the U.S. Constitution. If some racial classifications were allowed, how should the inclusiveness of a proposed classification be evaluated? Additionally, it was unclear how far Congress's interpretation of its own powers under the Fourteenth Amendment might justify future expansion of racial preferences via legislation. Also unresolved was the extent of judges' power under Title VII in private cases. *Weber* had given great latitude to the parties of voluntary agreements, but how far could judges go in forcing involuntary agreements on unwilling parties? How far could state and local institutions stretch the Equal Protection Clause when enacting public programs? No single theory or standard of judicial review had attracted more than three votes in *Fullilove,* limiting its reliability in future cases. It was plain, however, that the Court would examine federal affirmative action legislation with far more deference than state, local, or private policies inspired.

Another statutory dispute, *Firefighters Local Union No. 1784 v. Stotts,* 467 U.S. 561 (1984), revolved around attempts to force racial balance within the Memphis, Tennessee, firefighters union by means of a Title VII consent decree and subsequent court injunction. Black firefighters had sued the city under Title VII, forcing it to accept a consent decree by which the city agreed to hire and promote firefighters in a nondiscriminatory manner while not admitting to past intentional discrimination. When the city was later forced by budgetary constraints to begin laying off firefighters, it followed the "last hired, first fired" seniority rule. A lower court, noting the city's hitherto inadequate hiring and promotion of black firefighters, issued a preliminary injunction modifying in part the consent decree and ordering the city to lay off white firefighters and retain newly hired black firefighters so that layoffs would not effect a resegregation of the force. The union challenged the injunction as a contravention of the previously negotiated seniority clause of its current contract with the city.

If the city of Memphis had voluntarily adopted racial balancing policies, the case would have entailed both constitutional and statutory complications, forcing the Court to consider (1) whether public-sector employers could initiate affirmative action plans such as the voluntary initiative permitted in *Weber* and (2) whether such plans would violate the Equal Protection Clause of the Fourteenth Amendment. As Justice White's written opinion reveals, however, the majority of justices in *Stotts* took care to avoid these issues. Important in this judgment was the fact that the city of Memphis had neither admitted to nor been found guilty of intentional racial discrimination. The Court could therefore confine its ruling to confirmation of precedent (*International Brotherhood of Teamsters v. United States,* 431 U.S. 324 (1977): a legally binding seniority clause, absent a demonstrated discriminatory intent, will be held valid (*Stotts,* 578).

Three more employment cases argued in 1986 presented the Burger Court with additional opportunities to formulate a majority opinion on both the constitutional and the statutory aspects of affirmative action. The first of these was *Wygant v. Jackson Board of Education,* 476 U.S. 267 (1986). In *Wygant,* the Supreme Court by a 5–4 vote overturned decisions by a federal district court and court of appeals.

These lower courts had endorsed the Jackson school board's "proportional layoff agreement," which formed part of the teachers' union collective-bargaining agreement with the board. According to this contract, should layoffs become necessary, the board would adhere to the criterion of seniority "except that at no time will there be a greater percentage of minority personnel laid off than the current percentage of minority personnel employed at the time of the layoff." White teachers who, despite their seniority, had been laid off sued the board.

The majority of the Supreme Court agreed that the board's action was unconstitutional, although standards of review varied among the justices. Justice Powell wrote the plurality opinion, joined by Chief Justice Burger and Justice Rehnquist and, in part, by Justice Sandra Day O'Connor. Powell applied strict scrutiny to the racial classification, demanding that such a practice be "narrowly tailored to promote a compelling government interest." For Powell, the alleged justification for proportional layoffs—supplying "minority role models" to remedy "past societal discrimination" (*Wygant*, 275–276)—was insufficient to meet the standard of a compelling interest because the school board, as a public employer, had not proved prior discrimination. However, Powell saw no need to request such evidence, for even if proof had been presented, the layoff plan failed to satisfy his definition of a "narrowly tailored" solution. He distinguished the "diffuse" burden imposed by racial hiring goals from the too-intrusive burden imposed by actual job losses due to racially proportional layoffs: he could approve the former, but would disallow the latter.

In her concurrence, Justice O'Connor argued that public employers could implement racial affirmative action programs to balance their workforces if those programs did not "disproportionately burden" nonminority workers. Justice White, writing separately in concurrence with the plurality judgment, did not appeal to any prior Supreme Court decision or recognized standard of review. He did find, however, that removing nonminority workers from their jobs to produce racial balancing violated the Equal Protection Clause.

In their dissent, Justices Marshall, Brennan, and Blackmun found race-based remedies valid and constitutional if they proved only "substantially related" to "important governmental goals," a considerably lower standard of scrutiny than that demanded in Powell's opinion. They approved the board's provision of minority role models as adequate justification for the proportional layoff plan and argued that the case be remanded and the lower court be required to "develop a factual record" of past discrimination by the Jackson school board. Writing separately and joined by no other justices, Justice Stevens also dissented, but on different grounds. He argued against a set standard of review and for case-by-case determinations in affirmative action decisions; the key issue was whether or not a specific program served societal interests. In his view, the school board's actions did so.

Two other decisions, handed down on the same day in 1986, dramatically broadened the role of the courts in encouraging and even mandating the use of racial preference in hiring and promotion. In a 6–3 judgment in *Local No. 93, International Association of Firefighters v. City of Cleveland*, 478 U.S. 501 (1986), the Burger Court let stand a racial preference plan whose beneficiaries were not limited to identified victims of past discrimination. Furthermore, the Court determined that whether or not section 706(g) of Title VII of the Civil Rights Act of

1964 "precludes a court from imposing certain forms of race-conscious relief after trial," consent decrees were exempt from restriction.

The question arose after the Vanguards, an organization of black and Hispanic firefighters in Cleveland, Ohio, filed a class action in federal district court charging the city with discrimination in "hiring, assigning and promoting firefighters" in violation of Title VII of the Civil Rights Act of 1964. The court agreed and adopted a consent decree prescribing an integration plan; among other requirements, this plan set aside a specified proportion of promotions for minority members. The immediate effect was the promotion of every minority applicant in the subsequent promotion cycle, and a challenge ensued. The Court of Appeals affirmed the lower court's action, and the case moved to the Supreme Court, where the fact that the city of Cleveland had had to defend itself in previous race discrimination suits was duly noted.

Announcing the majority opinion, Justice Brennan dismissed the claim that section 706(g) of Title VII was "concerned with voluntary agreements [made] by employers or unions." In his words, the only issue to be resolved was "whether Section 706(g) barred the district court from approving the consent decree. We hold that it did not." The Court's decision in *Local No. 93 v. Cleveland* left unanswered the constitutional question of whether the equal protection provision of the Fifth Amendment might itself bar the federal courts from enforcing all or part of similar decrees.

Dissenting, Justice White found that the decree required unlawful "leapfrogging [of] minorities over senior and better qualified whites," a practice already declared impermissible under Title VII in *Firefighters v. Stotts.* With Chief Justice Burger joining, Justice Rehnquist further questioned the majority's citing of precedent with regard to consent decrees. The majority had in fact claimed to rely on *Stotts* and on *Railway Employees v. Wright,* 364 U.S. 642 (1961), but Rehnquist found their use misleading. The majority, he wrote, had "implicitly repudiate[d]" language in these two most relevant cases, turning instead "to cases that simply do not speak to the question presently before us" to wrench from their language some support for its definition of "consent decree." Rehnquist also faulted the majority for having misinterpreted the present decree as "voluntary": "the decree entered by the District Court in this case was a consent decree only between [the] Vanguards . . . and the City; the petitioner union, representing the majority of firefighters, never consented to the decree at all."

Local 28 of the Sheet Metal Workers' International Association v. EEOC, 478 U.S. 421 (1986), more solidly established the Burger Court's influence on behalf of affirmative action. For the first time, the Court approved a court order in a Title VII private discrimination suit that extended benefits to individuals who were not victims of discrimination. The case came to the high court after more than a decade of contention. In 1975, the United States (replaced as petitioner by the Equal Employment Opportunity Commission [EEOC] in the course of litigation) had first brought an action in federal district court against Local 28 under Title VII of the Civil Rights Act of 1964, charging discrimination against blacks and Hispanics. The court, finding the union guilty of long-standing racially discriminatory practices, mandated remedies, including a 29 percent "minority membership goal." In subsequent contempt judgments, the court imposed a $150,000 fine and other monetary penalties on the union and appointed an administrator to oversee collection and disbursement of the resulting fund to recruit, educate, and otherwise assist potential minority apprentices and members. The union's appeal failed, and the challenge was argued before the Burger Court in 1986.

Writing in part for a plurality and in part for a five-justice majority, Justice Brennan affirmed the district court's authority to order and enforce racial preferences in recruitment, selection, and training of union members, including the setting of "goals" or quotas to implement the order; beneficiaries of the programs need not be identifiable victims of past discrimination. Brennan claimed both statutory and constitutional authority for the decision, under Title VII and the Equal Protection Clause of the Fourteenth Amendment, respectively. A majority of the justices applied strict scrutiny to the district court's holdings and found both the minority membership percentage and the fund "necessary" to redress past egregious discrimination, a "compelling interest," according to Justice Powell's concurrence. Neither Brennan nor Powell admitted that their conclusions in the case were tantamount to validating racial quotas and forced racial balancing in the workplace, but Justice O'Connor, dissenting, argued that in ordering both the minority membership "goal" and the fund arrangements, the lower court had mandated racial quotas, in contravention of the clear language of the 1964 Civil Rights Act.

The Burger Court was the first to confront the issue of affirmative action. Revealing deep fractures along both ideological and practical lines, the Court's decisions nevertheless inexorably expanded the scope and potency of race-conscious programs, usually without the support of the Court's namesake. Liberal Justices Brennan, Marshall, and Blackmun endorsed affirmative action in every instance. Justice Rehnquist as consistently opposed it, as did Chief Justice Burger, with one exception. In the early years, Justice Stevens steadfastly argued against affirmative action while Justice White advocated it; as time passed, these two switched positions.

Virtually every Court decision on affirmative action was closely decided, by either a 6–3 or, more often, 5–4 margin. Rarely did a majority agree on both a decision and a rationale. Most decisions were announced as plurality opinions, accompanied by numerous and divergent concurrences and dissents. Except in the first case, *DeFunis*, declared moot in a per curiam decision, no fewer than four separate opinions followed each argument, with as many as six justices contributing written opinions on a single case, *Bakke*. Fragile coalitions and profound disagreements among the justices mirrored social uncertainties about race-conscious affirmative action and together guaranteed that the issue would continue to trouble both the new Rehnquist Court and society as a whole.

See also Blackmun, Harry Andrew; Brennan, William Joseph; Carter, "Jimmy" James Earl, Jr.; Civil Rights Act of 1964; Color-Blind Constitution; Compelling Governmental Interest; *DeFunis v. Odegaard*; Diversity; Equal Protection Clause; Fifth Amendment; *Firefighters Local Union No. 1784 v. Stotts*; Fourteenth Amendment; *Fullilove v. Klutznick*; *Local 28 of the Sheet Metal Workers' International Association v. EEOC; Local No. 93, International Association of Firefighters v. City of Cleveland*; Marshall, Thurgood; Narrowly Tailored Affirmative Action Plans; O'Connor, Sandra Day; Powell, Lewis Franklin, Jr.; Public Works Employment Act of 1977; Quotas; Race-Neutral Criteria; Rational Basis Scrutiny; *Regents of the University of California v. Bakke*; Rehnquist, William Hobbs; Reparations; Role Model Theory;

Stevens, John Paul; Strict Scrutiny; Supreme Court and Affirmative Action; Suspect Classification; Title VI of the Civil Rights Act of 1964; Title VII of the Civil Rights Act of 1964; *United Steelworkers of America v. Weber*; Warren Court and Affirmative Action; White, Byron Raymond; *Wygant v. Jackson Board of Education*.

FURTHER READING: Belz, Herman, 1991, *Equality Transformed: A Quarter-Century of Affirmative Action*, New Brunswick, NJ: Social Philosophy and Policy Center and Transaction Publishers; Halpern, Stephen C., and Charles M. Lamb, eds., 1991, *The Burger Court: Political and Judicial Profiles*, Urbana: University of Illinois Press; Schwartz, Herman, 1987, "The 1986 and 1987 Affirmative Action Cases: It's All Over but the Shouting," *Michigan Law Review* 86: 524–576; Spann, Girardeau A., 2000, *The Law of Affirmative Action: Twenty-five Years of Supreme Court Decisions on Race and Remedies*, New York: New York University Press.

RAE W. NEWSTAD and DAVID L. WEEKS

Burger, Warren

See Burger Court and Affirmative Action.

Bush, George Herbert Walker (1924–)

George H.W. Bush, the forty-first president of the United States and father of the forty-third president of the United States, left an ambiguous record on affirmative action. President Bush stated that he was supportive of affirmative action, but in practice he rejected all but the narrowest types of affirmative action plans. In a 1988 speech to a convention of the National Association for the Advancement of Colored People (NAACP), Bush commented "I've always supported affirmative action, and I always will" (Freeman 1992, 4B). When Bush signed the Civil Rights Act of 1991, he stated that "I say again today that I support affirmative action" (Rosenthal 1991, A1). At other times in his presidency, Bush spoke of his distaste for programs that reversely discriminate or utilize quotas or preferences. Yet while rallying against quotas, he supported minority business enterprise incentives and set-asides. As illustrative of this position, the Republican Party platform in 1988, the year he ran as the Republican nominee for president, appeared to endorse affirmative action for minority businesses when it stated, "We will increase, strengthen, and reinvigorate minority business development efforts." In the area of affirmative action and education, Bush once obliquely remarked that "you need to be a little careful when you see nothing wrong with that kind of preference or affirmative action" that allows admittance of thousands of students under an affirmative action plan and would be "damaging to our constitutional process." However, he also supported scholarships available to minorities only and was a supporter of causes like the United Negro College Fund. In a press conference in December 1990, Bush stated that his "own view has been all along—in my own life and everything else—committed to this concept of minority scholarships. . . . I am for affirmative action, and I am for trying to help the groups that have been the most disadvantaged, through scholarships. And that's what I think has been resolved in the Department of Education at least in the foreseeable future, and I hope it stands."

While not overtly declaring war on affirmative action in employment, the Bush

White House silently supported and assisted a white teacher (Sharon Taxman) in her claims of reverse discrimination against a local school board's affirmative action plan in *Taxman v. Piscataway Township Board of Education*, 91 F.3d 1547 (3rd Cir. 1996), *cert. granted*, 117 S. Ct. 2506 (1997), *cert. dismissed*, 118 S. Ct. 595 (1997). By the end of the 1990s, the *Taxman v. Piscataway* case would become one of the major points of discussion in the field of affirmative action. Bush also vetoed the Civil Rights Bill of 1990 over the issue of affirmative action and quotas. While the bill contained language expressly prohibiting the use of quotas in hiring and promotion, Bush believed that it would lead to such practices and vetoed it on that account. The proposed 1990 Civil Rights Act was meant largely to overturn a series of interpretative decisions by the Supreme Court under Title VII. Ironically, many of the provisions of the proposed bill were signed into law by Bush when he signed the Civil Rights Act of 1991.

However, perhaps the most emblematic feature of his ambiguous record on affirmative action can be found in his appointments of two justices to the U.S. Supreme Court: Clarence Thomas in 1991, who would become one of the most conservative justices on the high court on the issue of affirmative action, advocating abolishment of affirmative action and not voting to uphold affirmative action in any case before him on the Court, and David Souter in 1990, who is one of the justices in the liberal bloc on affirmative action and has voted to uphold affirmative action, in each case on the issue he has heard. The justices have served as polar opposites on the issue of affirmative action, much like the two sides of George Bush when dealing with the topic of affirmative action.

Bush was born into the prominent and wealthy family of Prescott Sheldon Bush and Dorothy Walker Bush. Prescott Bush was a successful banker and a U.S. senator from Connecticut, while Dorothy Bush came from a wealthy family from St. Louis, Missouri. Bush grew up in Connecticut and attended high school at the socially exclusive Phillips Academy in Andover, Massachusetts. After graduating from high school, Bush joined the navy and distinguished himself as a pilot flying multiple combat missions (he was even shot down once by the Japanese), earning the Distinguished Flying Cross for his service. Upon his return home following the end of the war, Bush attended Yale University, graduating in 1948.

When Bush graduated from Yale, he moved to Texas and worked in the oil industry. After an unsuccessful run for the U.S. Senate in 1964, he was able to win an election in 1966 in a primarily Republican district for a seat in the U.S. House of Representatives. After four years, he gave up his seat in the House of Representatives to again run for the Senate, and he again lost (this time to Democrat Lloyd Bentsen, who in 1988, as the Democratic nominee for vice president along with Michael Dukakis, lost to the Bush ticket in the race for president). However, after his loss to Bentsen, Richard Nixon selected Bush to serve as the U.S. ambassador to the United Nations (1971–1972). During the ensuing years, he held a variety of important and nationally prominent positions, including chairman of the Republican National Committee, U.S. representative to China, director of the Central Intelligence Agency, and vice president of the United States for two terms under President Ronald Reagan.

In 1988, Bush assumed the presidency after defeating the Democratic candidate, Michael Dukakis, in a campaign that was characterized as negative. One particularly negative advertisement blamed Dukakis for a heinous crime commit-

President George W. Bush and his father, former president George H. Bush, arrive on the South Lawn of the White House Sunday, June 3, 2001, to watch a T-ball game. © AP/Wide World Photos.

ted by a black prisoner, Willie Horton, after he had been released from prison in Massachusetts. Critics argued that the ad was inaccurate in terms of Dukakis's actual involvement in Horton's case and played upon the racial fears of white America. Yet at the same time, Bush attempted to reach out to black groups such as the NAACP and promised not to continue the racially insensitive polices that were followed during the Reagan administration.

As president, Bush is best known for his accomplishments in the foreign affairs arena, and not domestic issues. Most notably, Bush brought together and led, under United Nations auspices, a multinational military force that evicted Saddam Hussein's invading Iraqi army from Kuwait during the Persian Gulf War (1991–1992). Bush also sent U.S. troops into Panama in 1989 to topple and arrest Manuel Noriega. Also, on the international front, Bush presided over the United States as the former Soviet Union disintegrated and the Berlin Wall came down. However, Bush was accused of not caring about domestic issues and a suffering economy, an issue that ultimately resulted in his defeat at the hands of challenger William Jefferson Clinton in 1992.

After leaving the White House, Bush, along with his wife Barbara, left Washington, D.C., probably not imagining that they would be intimately involved again with the White House eight years later. In 2000, their son, George W. Bush, already a two-term governor of Texas, was elected president of the United States, making them only the second father-son team to both hold the presidency. The first father-son team was John Adams and John Quincy Adams. In addition to their son George W. Bush, there are several other prominent members of the Bush family, including Jeb Bush, the governor of Florida who eliminated affirmative action in higher education in that state.

See also Bush, George W.; Civil Rights Act of 1991; Clinton, William Jefferson; Contracting and Affirmative Action; Department of Education; Disadvantaged Business Enterprises; National Association for the Advancement of Colored People; One Florida Initiative; Quotas; Reagan, Ronald; Republican Party and Affirmative Action; Reverse Discrimination; Souter, David Hackett; *Taxman v. Piscataway Township Board of Education*; Thomas, Clarence; Title VII of the Civil Rights Act of 1964.

FURTHER READING: Bush, George H., 1987, *Looking Forward: An Autobiography*, Garden City, NY: Doubleday; "Civil Rights Veto President Plays Obstructionist Role," 1990, *Post-Standard*, October 26, A14; "Equal Opportunity Needs Action, Not Platitudes," 1989 *Post-Standard*, August 11, A14; Freeman, Gregory, 1992, "Bush Still Wrong on Civil Rights," *St.*

Louis Post-Dispatch, August 23, 4B; Hess, David, 1988, "Bush Tells NAACP Convention He Backs Affirmative Action," *Record*, July 13, A8; Kinsley, Michael, 1991, "Race Unconscious," *New Republic*, December 16, 4–6; Kurkjian, Stephen, 1989, "Activists Rap Bush Refusal to Redress Rights Rulings," *Boston Globe*, July 1, 1A.

JAMES A. BECKMAN

Bush, George W. (1946–)

George W. Bush, the forty-third president of the United States, is the son of George Herbert Walker Bush, the forty-first president. In 2000, George W. Bush won one of the closest presidential elections in U.S. history and was the first president since 1888 to win the election despite losing the popular vote. Bush, who labels his policies as "compassionate conservatism," is an outspoken critic of traditional affirmative action programs and has called for "affirmative access" as opposed to affirmative action. In one of his debates with Al Gore in the fall of 2000, he was asked to define his position on this issue. Bush commented that "affirmative action is a term that means many things to many people. I support what I call 'affirmative access'—not quotas or double standards, because those divide and balkanize, but access—a fair shot for everyone." On January 15, 2003, Bush gave a nationally aired speech declaring his opposition to the affirmative action plans utilized by the University of Michigan in *Grutter v. Bollinger*, 123 S. Ct. 2325, 2003 U.S. LEXIS 4800 (2003), and *Gratz v. Bollinger*, 123 S. Ct. 2411, 2003 U.S. LEXIS 4801 (2003), declaring such affirmative action usage to be "divisive, unfair and impossible to square with the Constitution." Bush has also nominated conservative judges to the federal judiciary who appear to be generally opposed to affirmative action.

Bush was born on July 6, 1946, in New Haven, Connecticut, into a politically prominent family. He attended Yale University, graduating with a bachelor of arts in 1968. His critics on the issue of affirmative action have alleged that Bush benefited from affirmative action, because he allegedly gained entrance to Yale as a result of his father's attendance at Yale, a practice known as a legacy. He served a stint in the Texas Air National Guard from 1968 to 1973 and earned a master of business administration from Harvard University in 1975. In the late 1970s, Bush moved to Texas, where he worked in the oil industry. Bush tried his hand at politics, losing a race for Congress in 1978. He continued to work in the oil industry until the mid-1980s and in 1989, as part of a group of investors, bought the Texas Rangers baseball team. He served as managing director of the baseball team until his election as governor of Texas in 1994.

As governor, Bush set several records. First, upon his victory over incumbent opponent Ann Richards, Bush was the first individual to be elected as a governor whose father had served as president. Second, when Bush won reelection in 1998, he became the first Texas governor to win a second consecutive four-year term. Finally, Bush and his father became only the second father-son combination to both hold the presidency; the first combination being John Adams (1797–1801) and John Quincy Adams (1825–1829).

As governor of Texas (1995–2000), Bush oversaw the dismantling of the use of affirmative action in higher education after the decision of the Fifth Circuit Court of Appeals' in *Hopwood v. Texas*, 78 F.3d 932 (5th Cir.1996) and the state's subsequent adoption of its race-neutral percentage plan. As governor, Bush was proud of his non-race-conscious admissions program for higher education. In the presidential debates of 2000, Bush stated that "I signed legislation in Texas requiring the top 10 percent of graduates from Texas high schools be automatically accepted in any public university in Texas. As a result of this policy, minority enrollment in Texas universities is at an all-time high." Bush also claimed to have improved minority/disadvantaged business enterprises in Texas by eliminating race-based set-asides. Bush claimed that "in Texas, my race-neutral outreach efforts at improving minority contracting have resulted in a 47 percent increase in state contracts going to women-owned businesses, a 58 percent increase in state contracts going to Hispanic-owned businesses, and a 78 percent increase in state contracts going to African-American businesses." Bush described his plan as one that strips "bureaucratic regulations, such as high permitting and licensing fees, which disproportionately hurt minority-owned businesses." Bush has also proposed giving companies awards for subcontracting or partnering with disadvantaged business enterprises.

After his close election victory over Vice President Al Gore, Bush remained quiet on the issue of affirmative action. However, in 2002–2003, he clearly announced his opposition to affirmative action. In his 2002 State of the Union address, Bush called for race-neutral programs like those he sponsored in Texas, and not affirmative action. He also encouraged other alternatives to affirmative action. Second, in January 2003, he went on record as opposing the University of Michigan's affirmative action program. Bush commented that he

> strongly supports diversity of all kinds, including racial diversity in higher education, but the method used by the University of Michigan to achieve this important goal is fundamentally flawed. At their core the Michigan policies amount to a quota system that unfairly rewards or penalizes prospective students based solely on their race. (AP Press 2003)

Furthermore, during oral arguments in the *Gratz and Grutter* cases in April 2003, Bush's solicitor general, Theodore Olson, strongly argued to the Supreme Court that affirmative action programs in higher education are incompatible with the purpose of the Fourteenth Amendment.

Bush also promoted and signed the "No Child Left Behind" law that promotes "excellence" in education, primarily through testing and the potential of denying federal funds to school districts with low test scores. He characterized this program as a solution to the affirmative action dilemma because it will universally increase educational opportunities for all Americans regardless of race. His critics charged that teachers will merely "teach the test" by focusing on having the students get higher scores at the expense of learning the material. Other critics argue that reliance on standardized testing is unfair and culturally biased.

Outside of the affirmative action area, Bush's biggest accomplishments as president are promoting and ensuring a nationwide tax cut and presiding over a grief-stricken country in the aftermath of the terrorist attacks on September 11, 2001. In the foreign affairs arena, Bush also orchestrated the military's destruction of much of the Al Qaeda terrorist network in Afghanistan and toppling the Taliban. In 2003, Bush advocated overthrowing Saddam Hussein of Iraq to rid the country of weapons of mass destruction, a position that subsequently led to the military invasion of Iraq, primarily by British and American troops. The invasion then led to the apprehension of Saddam husein, the creation of a provisional government under U.S. and UN auspice, and the movement towards returning sovereignty to the Iraqi people.

See also Affirmative Access; Bush, George Herbert Walker; Contracting and Affirmative Action; Fourteenth Amendment; *Gratz v. Bollinger/Grutter v. Bollinger*; *Hopwood v. Texas*; Percentage Plans.

FURTHER READING: AP Press State & Local Wire, 2003, "Text of President Bush's Remarks," January 15; "Bush and Bakke: Is the Administration Pro–Affirmative Action?" 2002, *Pittsburgh Post-Gazette*, December 20, A24; Goldstein, Amy, 2003, "Bush Joins Admissions Case Fight," *Washington Post*, January 16; Nagourney, Adam, 2003, "Bush and Affirmative Action: The Context: With His Eye on Two Political Prizes, the President Picks His Words Carefully," *New York Times*, January 16, A26; Selingo, Jeffrey, 2000, "George W. Bush's Mixed Records on Higher Education in Texas," *Chronicle of Higher Education*, June 23, A32; Smith-Winkelman, C., and F.J. Crosby, 1994, "Affirmative Action: Setting the Record Straight," *Social Justice Research* 7:309–328; Strickland, Leif, 2003, "Affirmative Access: Making the Grade," *Newsweek*, January 27, 36; Tobias, Sarah, and J. Phillip Thompson, "The Texas Ten Percent Plan," *American Behavioral Scientist* 43, no. 7 (April): 1121–1140.

SEAN RICHEY

Busing

An affirmative technique often utilized by the federal courts to desegregate schools by redrawing school lines and transporting children outside of their neighborhoods, busing was initiated in the late 1960s and early 1970s primarily to eliminate segregation and to integrate school systems that had been historically resistant to racial integration following *Brown v. Board of Education*, 347 U.S. 483 (1954). The practice of busing is an example of trying to achieve equality through more aggressive, affirmative means. While not an affirmative action program in terms of awarding preferences or bonuses, it is roughly analogous to what affirmative action programs attempt to achieve, namely, equality in education and opportunity by more aggressive proactive means. Also, like affirmative action, busing often focuses on race, taking minority students from the inner city and busing them to wealthier white suburbs (and vice versa). Finally, the children from wealthier suburbs are arguably adversely discriminated against by being forced to be bused to a school in an economically depressed area. Thus there are similarities between busing and affirmative action.

In the Supreme Court's *Brown v. Board of Education* decisions, *Brown I*, 347 U.S. 483 (1954), and *Brown II*, 349 U.S. 294 (1955), the Court declared that "separate schools are inherently unequal" and that schools had to be desegregated "with all deliberate speed," respectively. These decisions led to two decades of racial strife, frustration, boycotts, and busing. Southern states moved deliberately slowly toward achieving desegregation, and northern schools took little or no action at all. During argument in *Brown I*, the National Association for the Advancement of Colored People (NAACP) did not emphasize local control or as "close to the neighborhood" as racially and ethnically possible (Cruse 1987, 38). At that time, the NAACP believed that neighborhood schools were the product of segregation, and that court-enforced busing was the only way for blacks to achieve a quality education.

Although school desegregation began as a southern issue based on de jure segregation (by law), it eventually involved school districts throughout the entire United States, where the issue was de facto segregation (housing patterns or economic situations). The issue of school segregation in the North was complex. The Court found that many of the districts were discriminating by intentionally siting new schools and drawing school boundaries to exclude certain students and by using portable classrooms at overcrowded black schools.

By 1969, only about 30 percent of the African American students attended previously all-white schools, while the remainder of the African American students still attended all-black schools. Faced with pressure from the NAACP, southern federal judges finally offered their support to desegregate schools. The test case was *Swann v. Charlotte-Mecklenburg Board of Education,* 402 U.S. 1 (1971), which raised the question of whether or not the *Brown* decisions required "color-blind" assignment of students, and whether or not the practice of "busing" was constitutional. In a unanimous decision, the Supreme Court upheld a lower federal court's decision not only to bus students to achieve desegregation, but also to mandate the use of racial quotas, grouping of schools, and gerrymandering of attendance zones (Abraham and Perry 1994, 352–353). In its decision, the Court made a distinction between de jure segregation and de facto (by housing patterns or economic situation) segregation, normally found in northern school districts. However, the Court did not order the elimination of all-black schools or require racial balance. Although the *Swann* case was a landmark decision, many issues or problems were not answered.

When the federal courts began attacking the issue of segregation in the North, they obscured the distinction between de facto and de jure segregation. Officials of northern school districts thought that their school districts were immune to interference by the courts because segregation of schools was caused by housing patterns, unlike the dual school systems in the South based on race. The Justice Department found that compared to the school leaders in the North, southern school leaders displayed a better quality of leadership and were more receptive to integrating their schools in the long run.

One of the first desegregation cases occurring outside of the South to reach the Supreme Court was *Keyes v. School District #1, Denver, Colorado,* 413 U.S. 189 (1971). This case involved a pattern of de facto segregation. In a surprising 7–1 decision, the Court maintained a distinction between de jure and de facto segregation. Although there were no state or local statutes supporting school segregation in Colorado, the school district nevertheless practiced segregation by manipulating attendance zones and school sites and by supporting neighborhood schools. "The Court held that it was not necessary to demonstrate total segregation or a dual school system to find impermissible discrimination, but if there were pockets of segregation within a district, whether due to custom, laws, or zoning, that would be cause for applying judicial interdiction on the entire district" (Abraham and Perry 1994, 353).

Busing became a hot issue during the 1970s. Although the *Swann* and *Keyes* cases involved a single school district, several cases were presented to the Court that involved interdistrict busing between predominantly all-black central cities and predominantly all-white suburban school districts. One landmark case concerning interdistrict busing in the city of Detroit and its suburbs was *Milliken v.*

Students being transported to school via public buses. Courtesy of Library of Congress.

Bradley, 418 U.S. 717 (1971). This case involved the cross-county busing of 3,000 Detroit-area children. In a 5–4 decision, the Court declared that whatever the situation in Detroit was, the school district in the suburbs had not been accused of unlawful segregation. In essence, the Court was saying that it would not support cross-county busing unless it could be proven that intentional segregation in one district led to segregation in another district. In other cases that reached the Supreme Court, some of the lower court orders mandating interdistrict busing (Wilmington, Delaware, and Louisville, Kentucky, and respective suburbs) were upheld while others (Atlanta, Georgia, and its suburbs) were struck down.

One of the most explosive and televised cases involving busing occurred in the city of Boston. Led by the residents of a primarily white ethnic South Boston neighborhood, the residents defied the busing order of the local U.S. district court. Consequently, District Judge W. Arthur Garrity Jr. stripped the Boston School Committee, a popularly elected body, of most of its powers and placed the Boston schools under federal receivership. Richard Kahlenberg, in his book titled *The Remedy: Class, Race, and Affirmative Action*, has argued that the Boston incident illustrates how affirmative action programs need to be broader than just race based and should be based on eliminating differences in class. Kahlenberg states that

> school desegregation in Boston was a failure not only in execution—resulting in dramatic white flight—but more important, a failure to recognize the salience of class over race. Even if one could execute busing within the city of Boston without a hitch—desegregate the white working class and blacks perfectly, no strife, no white flight—one would still face the fact that the whites and blacks being bused simply do not have the same life chances as the whites (and occasional blacks) in the good suburban schools. (Kahlenberg 1996, 206)

Opposition to forced busing is not necessarily an indication that someone is a racist. Both black and white parents opposed forced busing, preferring that their children attend so-called neighborhood schools. Busing was not an acceptable means for improving the quality of education in predominantly black schools. In a Gallup Poll conducted in November 1974, it was found that 68 percent of the public opposed busing to achieve so-called racial balance.

Although Congress attempted on several occasions to pass legislation amending or striking down busing practices and orders, none passed. However, several riders were attached to appropriation bills prohibiting the use of federal funds to require the busing of any student to a school except the one nearest the student's home.

See also African Americans; All Deliberate Speed; *Brown v. Board of Education*; De Facto and De Jure Segregation; Department of Justice; Economically Disadvantaged; Housing; National Association for the Advancement of Colored People; Quotas; Segregation.

FURTHER READING: Abraham, Henry J., and Barbara A. Perry, 1994, *Freedom and the Court: Civil Rights and Liberties in the United States*, 6th ed., New York: Oxford University Press; Cruse, Harold, 1987, *Plural but Equal: Blacks & Minorities in America's Plural Society*, New York: Quill; Kahlenberg, Richard D., 1996, *The Remedy: Class, Race, and Affirmative Action*, New York: Basic Books; Miller, Andrew, 1974, "20 Years on Road to Integration," *Kansas City Star*, December 15, 14; Miller, Loren, 1966, *The Petitioners: The Story of the United States and the Negro*, New York: Pantheon Books.

NAOMI ROBERTSON

By Any Means Necessary

See Coalition to Defend Affirmative Action, Integration, and Fight for Equality by Any Means Necessary.

C

California Civil Rights Initiative

See Proposition 209.

Canada and Affirmative Action

The principle of affirmative action has been alive in Canada for several decades. For instance, as early as 1962, there was concern over the lack of representation of French Canadians in public service. At this time, the Royal Commission concluded that French Canadians were not receiving adequate service from government officials, and thus steps should be taken to increase their representation at all governmental levels. In addition, the commission recommended, and instituted in 1971, special French-language units within the civil service, with the assumption that these units would increase upward mobility for French Canadians in the civil service. During the 1970s, the Public Service Commission was increasingly focused on the ideals of affirmative action, and in a 1978 report, merit was one of five criteria concerning recruitment and promotion.

On March 1, 1978, the Canadian Human Rights Act received royal approval. Section 16 of the act gave affirmative action the force of law. Section 16(1) states, "It is not a discriminatory practice for a person to adopt or carry out a special program, plan or arrangement designed to prevent disadvantages that are likely to be suffered by, or to eliminate or reduce disadvantages that are suffered by, any group of individuals when those disadvantages would be based on or related to the prohibited grounds of discrimination, by improving opportunities respecting goods, services, facilities, accommodation or employment in relation to that group." The act also established the Canadian Human Rights Commission (section 21), which "may at any time (a) make general recommendations concerning desirable objectives for special programs, plans or arrangements referred to in subsection (1); and (b) on application, give such advice and assistance with respect to the adoption or carrying out of a special program, plan or arrangement referred to in subsection (1) as will serve to aid in the achievement of the objectives the program, plan or arrangement was designed to achieve" (quoted in Roberts 1982, 169). The act also banned individual acts of discrimination in employment as well as discriminatory employment policies and practices (sections 7 and 10). These are based on ten grounds: age, sex, religion, marital status, family status, national or ethnic origin, color, race, pardoned conviction, and disability. Further, the act required "equal pay for work of equal value" (pay equity).

In 1983, the Canadian government appointed Judge Rosalie Silberman Abella to evaluate the most efficient, effective, and equitable means of promoting employment opportunities, eliminating discrimination, and helping individuals equitably compete for employment opportunities. Judge Abella made numerous recommendations, including that all federally regulated employers be required to implement "employment equity" (the term "affirmative action" was not used to avoid the negative reactions associated with the term). Soon after the publication of the Abella report, Parliament asked the Standing Committee on Justice and Legal Affairs to report on the equality rights provisions in the Canadian Constitution. The Standing Committee recommended the legislation of employment equity at the federal level. As a result of the Abella Royal Commission Report and the Standing Committee's recommendation, Parliament passed the Employment Equity Act in June 1986.

The Employment Equity Act of 1986 requires the implementation of positive policies and practices to ensure that women, aboriginal peoples, persons with disabilities, and members of visible minorities "achieve a degree of representation in the various positions of employment with the employer that is at least proportionate to their representation (I) in the workforce; or (ii) in those segments of the workforce that are identifiable by qualification, eligibility or geography and from which the employer may reasonably be expected to draw or promote employees" (section 4). The act covers organizations under federal jurisdiction with 100 or more employees. Private works in the Yukon and Northwest Territories and government departments are exempt (the Canadian government has a separate employment equity program for its own employees under section 3 of the act).

On October 24, 1996, the revised Employment Equity Act came into effect (it was enacted in 1995). Its purpose is to achieve equality in the workplace by requiring employers to identify and eliminate barriers to the employment of members of the four designated groups (women, aboriginal peoples, persons with disabilities, and members of visible minorities). The act applied to the federal public service, federal Crown corporations, and federally regulated organizations with 100 or more employees. Also, the Canadian Human Rights Commission (established under the Canadian Human Rights Act of 1986 and responsible for administering the Federal Contractors Program for Employment Equity) requires employers who do business with the Canadian government to achieve and maintain a fair and representative workforce. Companies that employ 100 or more people and that obtain goods and services contracts valued at $200,000 or more are required to evaluate their workforce and review their employment policies and strategies to develop and implement an employment equity plan. Organizations are also required to report annually on the status of people from the four designated groups.

Although the main thrust of the 1986 act is alive in the 1996 act, the Canadian Parliament made several important changes to the law. It made the Human Rights

Commission the monitoring agency and bestowed upon it the authority to conduct audits of employers under federal jurisdiction and take the necessary steps to make sure that they are complying with the act's requirements. Notably, for the first time, obligations under the act were extended to the federal public service.

See also Australia and Affirmative Action; Brazil and Affirmative Action; China and Affirmative Action; European Union and Affirmative Action; Global Implementation of Affirmative Action Programs; Great Britain and Affirmative Action; India and Affirmative Action; Japan and Affirmative Action; Malaysia and Affirmative Action; South Africa and Affirmative Action.

FURTHER READING: Abella, R.S., 1984, *Equality in Employment: A Royal Commission Report*, Ottawa: Supply and Services Canada; Abella, R.S., 1984, *Equality in Employment: A Royal Commission Report General Summary*, Ottawa: Supply and Services Canada; Benimadhu, P., and R. Wright, 1992, *Implementing Employment Equity: A Canadian Experience*, Ottawa: Conference Board of Canada; Block, W.E., and M.A. Walker, eds., 1982, *Discrimination, Affirmative Action, and Equal Opportunity: An Economic and Social Perspective*, Vancouver: Fraser Institute; Boyer, P., 1985, *Equality for All: Report of the Parliamentary Committee on Equality Rights*, Ottawa: Queen's Printer for Canada; Jain, Harish C., 1990, "Affirmative Action/Employment Equity Programs in Canada: Issues and Policies," *Labor Law Journal* 41, no. 8 (August): 487–492; Raskin, Carl, 1994, "Employment Equity for the Disabled in Canada," *International Labour Review* 133, no. 1:75–88; Roberts, Lance W., 1982, "Understanding Affirmative Action," in *Discrimination, Affirmative Action, and Equal Opportunity: An Economic and Social Perspective*, edited by W.E. Block and M.A. Walker, Vancouver: Fraser Institute.

PAULINA X. RUF

Carmichael, Stokely (1941–1998)

Stokely Carmichael was an African American activist, leader, and militant who became famous for the cry "Black Power" and the theory of institutional racism. Carmichael was opposed to pacific methods of integration and assimilation into white society, programs such as affirmative action, and believed that eventually the capitalistic system of the United States would be overthrown by militant revolution. The famous cry, along with the symbol of the raised clenched fist, became the slogan and rallying point for the group later known as the Black Panther Party. As part of his institutional racism theory, Carmichael also believed that white people could never truly understand the "black experience," a unique reality and existence that cannot be fathomed by those who are not black. Carmichael has been criticized for his myopic and sexist views of women, especially in conjunction with his infamous 1964 statement that "the only place for women in the SNCC is prone."

Stokely Carmichael was born on June 29, 1941, in Port of Spain, Trinidad. In 1978, he changed his name to Kwame Ture. After receiving a segregated education at a British boys' school, Carmichael moved to Harlem, where he experienced a different lifestyle than he was accustomed to in Trinidad. In Trinidad, his parents were considered to be successful people, but in Harlem they were nothing more than average struggling African American citizens.

Carmichael graduated from high school during a period of social and political change in the United States. The civil rights movement was active, and, during this era, African Americans were engaging in lunch-counter sit-ins in segregated cafes and restaurants throughout the South. At first, Carmichael viewed this as a meaningless waste of time. However, upon seeing the plight of African Americans, he became engaged in sit-in demonstrations, including those demonstrations organized by the Congress of Racial Equality (CORE). Carmichael enrolled at Howard University in Washington, D.C., and became a part of the organization called the Freedom Riders. It was during a freedom ride sponsored by CORE that Carmichael personally experienced the violent mob behavior exerted against the activists. He was arrested along with others and jailed in Mississippi, where he spent fifty-three days.

After graduating from Howard University, Carmichael became an organizer for the Student Nonviolent Coordinating Committee (SNCC), better known as "Snick." He organized a task force in Lowndes County, Alabama, and increased the number of African American registered voters. This was of importance because in Lowndes County, African Americans outnumbered whites but had no share in the political power. The symbol for this group was a black panther leaping with a snarl. It was this symbol, along with Carmichael's cry of "Black Power," that became associated with the Black Panther organization. The slogan "Black Power" was used as a means of encouraging African American sharecroppers. Black power included political, economic, and legal power. It was Carmichael's hope that through black power, African Americans would gain control of the institutions of their communities and control of the land and stop the exploitation of nonwhite people around the world.

In 1966, Carmichael accepted the chairmanship of SNCC, calling for "black power." However, he resigned in 1967 and, because of his political views regarding Pan-Africanism, SNCC expelled him in 1968. After his resignation, he joined the Black Panther Party and organized more than two dozen chapters across the nation. In 1969, Carmichael went into self-exile in Africa. After his exile, Carmichael only briefly returned to the United States. He died of cancer on November 15, 1998, holding to his militant revolutionary notions to the end.

See also African Americans; Assimilation Theory; Black Nationalism; Black Panther Party; Civil Rights Movement; Congress of Racial Equality; Freedom Riders; Integration.

FURTHER READING: Barker, Paul, 1999, "All Things to All Accusers," *New Statesman* 129, no. 4429 (March 26): 25–28; Miller, Mike, 1998, "Kwame Ture: Memories," *Social Policy* 29, no. 2 (winter): 31–32; Wilkerson, Isabel, 1998, "Soul Survivor: From Stokely Carmichael to Kwame Ture, Still Ready for the Revolution," *Essence* 29, no. 1 (May): 108–116.

RONNIE B. TUCKER SR.

Carter, James "Jimmy" Earl, Jr. (1924–)

James "Jimmy" Earl Carter Jr., born on October 1, 1924, in the Black Belt of southwest Georgia, became Georgia's seventy-sixth governor and the thirty-ninth president of the United States. In the affirmative action context, Carter is best known for the creation of the Office of Federal Contract Compliance Programs (OFCCP) during his administration (which centralized all federal affirmative action agencies into one agency under the Department of Labor) and his administration's strong support of affirmative action in *Regents of the University of California v. Bakke*, 438 U.S. 265 (1978). While Carter's administration is generally viewed as friendly to affirmative action programs, Carter backed the use of "flexible affirmative action programs using goals" over inflexible or rigid racial or gender quotas (Kotlowski 2001, 124). From the humble surroundings of Plains, Georgia, Carter served with distinction in the navy and became a champion of peace and human rights. Although his presidency was marked by a number of failures and his record in affirmative action is sometimes labeled as inconclusive, he has proven himself to be a man of morals and courage.

Carter's parents raised all four of their children, Ruth, Gloria, Jimmy, and William Alton (Billy), to be independent and resourceful. His father, James Earl Carter Sr., was a successful farmer and businessman, and his mother, Lillian Gordy Carter, was a registered nurse. Carter's parents were far from typical. Earl Carter was the head of the household, but Lillian enjoyed a great deal of latitude and freedoms that her peers did not. As the only medical professional nearby, Lillian often served as caretaker for the area's white and black populations as well as holding a job at the Wise Sanitarium. Her salary allowed her to hire workers to look after the house and children. The financial success of Earl and Lillian ensured that the family always ate well even during the depression. Often Earl Carter would anonymously help out his neighbors if he heard they were in need. He also provided Lillian with medical supplies for patients unable to pay. The generosity and frugalness of Earl and Lillian left a strong impression on young Jimmy.

Young Jimmy demonstrated his business prowess early in life. Before he even started school, he was raising, boiling, and selling peanuts in town, and along with his cousins, he sold hotdogs and hamburgers on Saturdays. When he was nine, Jimmy bought five bales of cotton for the low price of five cents a pound. He stored the cotton until the price rose and then sold it for a considerable profit. Using that money, Jimmy bought five small dwellings occupied by poor black tenants who then paid him rent. Jimmy attended the Plains public school system, where he did well. From an early age, Carter wanted to attend the U.S. Naval Academy. During grade school, he sent for the entrance requirements. Unfortunately, Carter's local congressman had already recommended someone in 1940, so Carter enrolled in Georgia Southwestern College. In 1942, Carter was granted an appointment to Annapolis, but he would first need to complete a few science courses not offered at Georgia Southwestern. On the navy's recommendation, Carter enrolled at Georgia Tech, where he spent three terms and was in the top 10 percent of his class. Carter endured the trials of the Naval Academy and graduated with a bachelor of science degree in 1946.

In the summer of 1945, Carter met Rosalyn Smith, and the couple began to exchange letters. They married on July 7, 1946, in Plains and settled into life in the navy. Carter spent two years on surface ships and then applied for and received one of the few positions in the submarine service. The six-month-long training was a good experience for both. Carter's hours were relatively regular, and all the families of the men in training were housed together, providing an instant social group. Carter did well in the submarine service, rising to the rank of lieutenant senior grade. In 1952, Carter was accepted into Admiral Hyman Rickover's nuclear submarine program. Carter was assigned to the U.S. Atomic Energy Department,

Division of Reactor Development, in Schenectady, New York. The Carter family, now including three sons, John William, born in 1947, James Earl III, born in 1950, and Donnel Jeffrey, born in 1952, moved to New York. Carter excelled in the submarine service and under Rickover. In early 1953, however, Carter learned that his father was seriously ill.

Carter resigned his navy commission and returned home to take over the family farm and business; both Admiral Rickover and Rosalyn were disappointed. The year 1953 proved to be a turning point for Jimmy and Rosalyn. The 1953 drought meant that most of the farmers Earl Carter lent money to could not repay Jimmy. The Carters had to scrounge and borrow to keep the business afloat. Unable to hire help, Jimmy asked Rosalyn to come help in the office one day. Before long she was keeping the books, managing the office, and enjoying herself for the first time since they moved back to Georgia. Soon business was good again, and Carter began to involve himself in the community.

Among his many community involvements were serving as chairman of the county school board, president of the Georgia Planning Association, and as a volunteer at the hospital authority and the library. He refused, however, to serve on the local White Citizens' Council. Always striving, Carter was elected to the Georgia Senate in 1962. He ran for governor in 1966 and lost, but won the governorship in 1971. As governor, Carter was innovative and progressive. He opened Georgia's government to women and African Americans, reorganized the 300 state agencies into 22 superagencies, and required that they justify their budget every year. He initiated the "sunshine law" that opened state government meetings to the public. He also established a formidable record for environmental programs and a tough anticrime stance. The Carters also had another child: Amy Lynn Carter was born in 1967.

In 1974, Carter announced his candidacy for president and won the nomination in 1976 on the first ballot. As a candidate, Carter used his outsider image and his lack of national experience as an asset. Carter and his running mate, Walter Mondale, led in the public opinion polls. The election itself, however, was close: Carter received 297 electoral votes and Gerald Ford won 240. Once Carter was in office, however, his outsider image and method of dealing with Congress turned into a disability.

Carter's domestic policies revolved around the three pressing problems of unemployment, inflation, and energy. When he took office, the unemployment rate was 7 percent and the inflation rate was 6.8 percent. During his presidency, both rates rose. The energy crisis exacerbated both problems. During 1979, the overthrow of the shah in Iran caused a severe shortage of oil. Prices had begun to rise in 1973 with the Arab oil embargo and had steadily increased. In 1977, Carter submitted a comprehensive energy bill designed to lessen American dependence on foreign oil, but support for the bill was lacking. By 1979, it was too late for anything but conservation and rationing. Carter was blamed for the soaring gasoline prices.

Carter also created the Office of Federal Contract Compliance Programs (OFCCP), which centralized all federal affirmative action agencies into one agency under the Department of Labor. Early in his presidency, Carter confronted an affirmative action problem when Allan Bakke, a thirty-seven-year-old white former marine, filed suit against the University of California Board of Regents. Bakke

President Jimmy Carter shaking hands with Reverend Martin Luther King Sr. in 1976. Courtesy of Library of Congress.

argued that his rights were violated when the University of California at Davis Medical School admitted several less qualified minority applicants according to an affirmative action plan that reserved sixteen places for disadvantaged students. The California Supreme Court agreed with Bakke, and the Board of Regents appealed to the U.S. Supreme Court. The Justice Department's brief strongly endorsed affirmative action (at the behest of Carter), despite some in the solicitor general's office who wished to take a different approach in the case.

Carter also emphasized the appointment of minorities and women in his administration and placed more African Americans into federal offices than all previous presidents. Notably, he appointed the prominent African American activist Eleanor Holmes Norton chairperson of the Equal Employment Opportunity Commission (EEOC). Carter also promised to increase significantly the number of minorities and females nominated to the federal judiciary. Ironically, however, Carter was one of the few presidents not afforded the chance to nominate a Supreme Court justice. Despite his record on federal appointments, Carter was often criticized for failing to take a highly visible stand in support of affirmative action and civil rights in his speeches and policy statements.

In the area of foreign policy, Carter fared a bit better. Consistent with Richard Nixon and Gerald Ford, Carter continued to pursue diplomatic solutions to problems, improve relations with the Soviet Union, develop strategic arms reduction plans, and strengthen U.S. relations with China. What made Carter's foreign policy different was his emphasis on human rights. Carter's policy held nations accountable for their treatment of their citizens. While this policy provided important support for people in Eastern Europe, in some cases it weakened governments, leaving them prone to revolution.

Carter also successfully negotiated a new Panama Canal treaty, facilitated the Camp David Accords between Egypt and Israel, and signed the SALT II treaty with the Soviet Union. However, the defining event of Carter's presidency was the Iran hostage crisis. On November 4, 1979, thousands of Iranian students stormed the American Embassy in Tehran, taking sixty-six Americans prisoner. Carter did not want to use military force, although he would have had plenty of support for a military response, for fear that any military action would further endanger the lives of the hostages. Instead, he relied on economic sanctions. The Soviet invasion of Afghanistan further complicated an already tense situation. Carter immediately ordered sanctions against the Soviet Union, which included a ban on the sale of grains and technology. He also withdrew U.S. participation from the Olympic Games since they were in Moscow.

As the election approached, Carter worked to secure the release of the hostages. When talks broke down, he finally decided to use military force. A rescue attempt failed miserably and took the lives of eight servicemen. The main reasons for the failure were mechanical troubles and weather, but Carter took blame as commander in chief. The hostages were not released until the day Ronald Reagan was sworn in as president; they were held captive for 444 days.

Carter returned to Plains with the lowest approval rating recorded for any president. In 1982, Carter became University Distinguished Professor at Emory University in Atlanta, Georgia. With Emory University, Carter also founded the Carter Center. Under Carter's leadership, the Carter Center works toward resolving conflict, promoting democracy and human rights, and preventing disease. The Carter Center, dedicated in 1986, includes a library and museum.

Carter also serves as an ambassador for peace for the United States. He has traveled to a variety of countries at the request of the government to use his negotiating skills. Carter has also dedicated a tremendous amount of time and energy to charitable organizations. One of his best-known activities is his involvement as a volunteer and on the Board of Directors for Habitat for Humanity, a nonprofit organization that helps build homes for the underprivileged in the United States and abroad. Other than the Carter Center, Habitat for Humanity is the only organization allowed to use the Carters' names for fundraising. A devout Christian, Carter also teaches Sunday school in Plains. In 2002, Carter was awarded the Nobel Peace Prize.

Carter is also the author of fifteen books: *Why Not the Best?* (1975, 1996), *A Government as Good as Its People* (1977, 1996), *Keeping Faith: Memoirs of a President* (1982, 1995), *Negotiation: The Alternative to Hostility* (1984), *The Blood of Abraham* (1985, 1993), *Everything to Gain: Making the Most of the Rest of Your Life* (1987, 1995), *An Outdoor Journal* (1988, 1994), *Turning Point: A Candidate, a State, and a Nation Come of Age* (1992), *Talking Peace: A Vision for the Next Generation* (1993, 1995), *Always a Reckoning* (1995), *The Little Baby Snoogle-Fleejer* (1995), *Living Faith* (1996), *Sources of Strength: Meditations on Scripture for Daily Living* (1997), *The Virtues of Aging* (1998), and *An Hour before Daylight: Memories of a Rural Boyhood* (2001).

See also Department of Labor; Equal Employment Opportunity Commission; Norton, Eleanor Holmes; Office of Federal Contract Compliance Programs; *Regents of the University of California v. Bakke*; Quotas.

FURTHER READING: Bourne, Peter G., 1997, *Jimmy Carter: A Comprehensive Biography from Plains to Postpresidency*, New York: Scribner's; Carter Center, 2000, "Jimmy Carter," http://www.cartercenter.org; Jordan, Hamilton, 1982, *Crisis: The Last Year of the Carter Presidency*, New York: Putnam; Kotlowski, Dean J., 2001, *Nixon's Civil Rights: Politics, Principle, and Policy*, Cambridge, MA: Harvard University Press; Morris, Kenneth Earl, 1996, *Jimmy Carter, American Moralist*, Athens: University of Georgia Press; Smith, Gaddis, 1986, *Morality, Reason, and Power: American Diplomacy in the Carter Years*, New York: Hill and Wang.

LISA A. ENNIS

Carter, Stephen L. (1954–)

Stephen L. Carter, author and law professor, has been nationally known as an outspoken critic of affirmative action since the publication of his 1991 book *Reflections of an Affirmative Action Baby*. Carter advocates that affirmative action be either outright eliminated or restructured to assist economically disadvantaged individuals through a class-based affirmative action approach as opposed to a race-conscious approach. Carter has also argued that affirmative action is demeaning to African Americans and perpetuates the stereotype that African Americans are not able to compete with whites and win based upon their own merits. In this vein, Carter believes that "the durable and demeaning stereotype of black people as unable to compete with white ones is reinforced by advocates of certain forms of affirmative action" (Carter, 50). In the educational context, Carter has proposed an affirmative action pyramid solution whereby limited affirmative action would be utilized at the undergraduate level, a lesser amount at the graduate level, and no preferences after that in society.

Carter attended Stanford University, graduating with honors in 1976. He then attended Yale Law School, stating in a self-deprecating manner in the first passage in his *Reflections of an Affirmative Action Baby*, "I got into law school because I am black" (Carter, 11). Carter later became one of Yale's youngest tenured professors and also Yale's first black law professor. Carter reportedly did not like to be described as the law school's first black professor, stating, "I felt oppressed by this vision of tenure as an extension of affirmative action" (Carter, 56). Carter is currently the William Nelson Cromwell Professor of Law at Yale and is the author of many articles and several books, including *The Culture of Disbelief: How American Law and Politics Trivialize Religious Devotion* (1993), The *Confirmation Mess: Cleaning Up the Federal Appointments Process* (1994), and *Integrity* (1996).

See also Affirmative Action, Arguments for; Affirmative Action, Criticims of; African Americans; Meritocracy.

FURTHER READING: Carter, Stephen L., 1991, *Reflections of an Affirmative Action Baby*, New York: Basic Books; Megalli, Mark, 1995, "The High Priests of the Black Academic Right," *Journal of Blacks in Higher Education*, autumn, 71–77.

JAMES A. BECKMAN

Caste System

The term "caste system" has been used to describe the effects of gender and racial discrimination in the United States. Barbara Bergmann, for example, has

People picketing in 1963 outside an Atlanta restaurant that displays a sign against integration of races. Courtesy of Library of Congress.

stated that the purpose of affirmative action is to "dismantle the two caste systems" in the United States, "one based on race and another based on gender" (Bergmann 1996, 107). Castes are a special form of social class structure that tend to be present in every society. Castes differ from other forms of social classes, however, in that they have emerged into social consciousness to the point that custom and law enforce their rigid and permanent separation from one another.

For the sociologist Max Weber, a caste system is the outcome of the conjunction between status group and ethnic community. Also, the operation of a caste system places limits upon one's social/economic mobility. That is, one's placement within a caste limits one's choices of education and occupation in life, regardless of talents, merits, and abilities. Sociologist John Ogbu, in his work *Minority Education and Caste,* argues that membership in a caste has a debilitating result on one's ambitions (and, therefore, one's subsequent societal position) within the larger societal context. While every society could be said to have a caste system, India's caste system is arguably the modern world's best example of a true caste system.

See also Discrimination; India and Affirmative Action; Meritocracy; Segregation; Weber, Max.

FURTHER READING: Bergmann, Barbara R., 1996, *In Defense of Affirmative Action,* New York: Basic Books; Dumont, L., 1980, *Homo Hierarchicus: The Caste System and Its Implications,* translated by Mark Sanisbury, Louis Dumont, and Basia Gulati, Chicago: University of Chicago Press; Ogbu, John U., 1978, *Minority Education and Caste,* New York: Academic Press; Zinkin, Taya, 1962, *Caste Today,* London and New York: Oxford University Press.

MIRZA ASMER BEG

Census Classifications, Ethnic and Racial

Affirmative action and other government and social programs rely upon census definitions of race and ethnic groups. These definitions have been subject to debate and much change throughout the history of the census and reinforce confusion over the classification of race and ethnicity. For example, in 1920, Hindus, a religious group, were classified as a racial category. In 1930, Mexican, a nationality, was classified as a racial category, but then dropped due to the protests of the Mexican government. Until 1970, Mexican was included as a part of the white racial category, but in 1970 it was declared a separate ethnic category. As census history demonstrates, racial and ethnic classifications are social and political designations. These designations often have great impact on the distribution of government benefits and preferences through programs such as affirmative action.

Since the first census count in 1790, a question about race has been included. The initial purpose was to determine the numbers of slaves, Native Americans, and free whites in the colonies. Questions regarding ethnicity or national origin have been included on the majority of the census counts, but especially around times of large-scale immigration. Historically, these counts have been used for political purposes and have been tied to struggles over power and rights. Since the civil rights movement and resultant court decisions, census data on race and ethnicity have served a new purpose: to help dismantle inequality. The information is used in the implementation of court decisions, affirmative action cases and programs, civil rights compliance, voting access and districting, the allocation of resources, and so on.

The Office of Management and Budget (OMB) Statistical Policy Directive 15 mandates the standardization of government classifications of race and ethnicity for the purpose of consistency. The categories provided by OMB Directive 15 are used not only by the census, but by public schools, the Social Security Administration, public health offices, and other government agencies. This directive mandates the minimal racial and ethnic categories to be used in the census.

Census categories of race and ethnicity represent legal classifications for use in public policy programs and thus significantly shape the way we define our own racial and ethnic identity, as well as that of others. Institutions also use these classifications, further demonstrating that these classifications are not without consequence. Official classifications shape institutional arrangements. Sociologists argue that changing racial classifications reflect broader shifts in our political, social, demographic, and cultural context and tell society much about its predominant beliefs and ideologies of race.

The number and definition of racial classifications in the census have changed tremendously over time. A number of trends are evident in these changing classifications: race has been reduced to skin color; there has been a clear obsession with racial purity and the enforcement of boundaries between racial groups; and finally, over time, a variety of ethnic groups have been combined and collapsed into a smaller number of racial groups. One constant pattern that can be identified is the repeated use of white, black, American Indian, Chinese, and Japanese classifications.

Prior to 1850, white census enumerators were expected to use their own judgment in determining the race of respondents. Beginning in 1850, formal definitions of race were provided. In 1850, the first specification of racially mixed nonwhites, corresponding to the growing consciousness of the alleged danger posed by such mixtures, was introduced, and by 1890 the categories of "mulatto" ($3/8$ to $5/8$ black), "quadroon" ($1/4$ black) and "octoroon" ($1/8$ or less black) appeared. It was very difficult for census enumerators to place people into these categories. Because of the obsession with racial mixing at the time, these various classifications were developed to measure the extent of mixing occurring and to protect white racial purity. At the same time, the Chinese and Japanese were listed as distinct racial groups, despite their tiny numbers, reflecting the concern with immigration from these countries, increasing anti-Chinese and anti-Japanese sentiment, and more restrictive immigration law.

By 1930, the various definitions of black Americans were abandoned as the one-drop rule was increasingly accepted. The one-drop rule defined anyone with just a drop of black blood as black. For white Americans, this rule was essential to maintain segregation and white supremacy: clear definitions of who was and was not black were necessary. For black Americans, on the other hand, this rule contributed to greater unity and sense of identity in dealing with increasing racism and inequality.

Census classifications have always attempted to make the categories mutually exclusive: individuals could only be placed into one category, which, some argue, reflects a concern with mixing. In 1910, an "Other" category was created to deal with those who could not be classified into existing categories. Between 1980 and 1990, the number of people choosing to mark "Other" increased dramatically, and as a result of the growing multiracial movement, which argued that individuals of mixed ancestry should not be forced to choose only one designation, individuals were allowed to mark more than one category in the 2000 census. Nearly 7 million people chose to do so.

Historically, census classifications of race and ethnicity have been a powerful tool reinforcing inequality. Today, there is some debate over whether to continue to use such classifications. While some commentators argue for the abolition of racial classifications, others argue that racial classifications can be a useful tool for tracking and responding to inequality. Power, privilege, and resources are still allocated based upon race, and racial discrimination and hatred are still common. Thus, while race is a social classification, it is real in people's lives and has a real effect on determining life chances.

See also African Americans; Bureau of the Census; Glazer, Nathan; Immigration Act of 1965; Multiracialism; Native Americans; One-Drop Rule; Racial Privacy Initiative.

FURTHER READING: Ferrante, Joan, and Prince Browne Jr., 2001, *The Social Construction of Race and Ethnicity in the United States*, 2d ed., Upper Saddle River, NJ: Prentice Hall; Lee, Sharon M., 1993, "Racial Classification in the US Census, 1890–1990," *Ethnic and Racial Studies* 16, no. 1 (January): 75–94.

ABBY L. FERBER

Center for Equal Opportunity

The Center for Equal Opportunity is a nonprofit Washington, D.C.–based public policy research organization that was founded in 1995 by Linda Chavez, a former Reagan appointee and current president of the organization. The center is exclusively devoted to the promotion of color-blind equal opportunity and racial harmony. The center focuses on three particular areas: racial preferences, immigration and assimilation, and multicultural education. The Center for Equal Opportunity fervently opposes affirmative action and seeks to block the expansion of what it refers to as "racial preferences" and to prevent their implementation in employment, education, and voting.

The center maintains a web site that provides a plethora of on-line resources pertaining to the center's struggle to eliminate affirmative action on the state and federal levels. The organization strongly rejects affirmative action initiatives and programs, as illustrated by the amicus curiae (friend-of-the-court) brief filed by the center on behalf of the plaintiffs in the University of Michigan's affirmative action program cases *Grutter v. Bollinger*, 123 S. Ct. 2325, 2003 U.S. LEXIS 4800 (2003), and *Gratz v. Bollinger*, 123 S. Ct. 2411, 2003 U.S. LEXIS 4801 (2003).

See also Chavez, Linda; *Gratz v. Bollinger/Grutter v. Bollinger*; Reagan, Ronald.

FURTHER READINGS: Center for Equal Opportunity, web site: www.ceousa.org; Schmidt, Peter, 2003, "Behind the Fight over Race-Conscious Admissions: Advocacy Groups—Working Together—Helped Shape the Legal and Political Debate," *Chronicle of Higher Education*, April 4, A22.

PAULINA X. RUF

Center for Individual Rights

The Center for Individual Rights (CIR) is a conservative public interest law firm based in Washington, D.C., that is extremely critical of affirmative action and has waged an organized litigation campaign to eliminate affirmative action from American society. The periodical *Black Issues in Higher Education* in a 1997 article labeled the CIR as "mischief makers" and "the men behind all those anti–affirmative action lawsuits." The CIR has represented white female plaintiffs in a series of affirmative action cases alleging that affirmative action reversely discriminates against innocent (and qualified) nonminorities. The CIR has handled several of the most significant affirmative action cases in recent years, such as *Hopwood v. Texas*, 78 F.3d 932 (5th Cir. 1996), *Smith v. University of Washington Law School*, 233 F.3d 1188 (9th Cir. 2000), and *Gratz/Grutter v. Bollinger*, 288 F.3d 732 (6th Cir. 2002). The CIR was also responsible for the legal defense of California's Proposition 209 in *Coalition for Economic Equity v. Wilson*, 110 F.3d 1431 (9th Cir. 1997). The CIR also presented the plaintiffs' case to the high court in the landmark Supreme Court cases *Grutter v. Bollinger*, 123 S. Ct. 2325, 2003 U.S. LEXIS 4800 (2003), and *Gratz v. Bollinger*, 123 S. Ct. 2411, 2003 U.S. LEXIS 4801 (2003). Finally, the CIR utilizes the courthouse to effectuate social change (i.e., the abolition of affirmative action), a strategy that has earned the CIR comparisons with the National Association for the Advancement of Colored People (NAACP) and the American Civil Liberties Union (ACLU) and with the NAACP and ACLU's litigation approach in combating racial segregation and discrimination.

The CIR was founded in 1989 and, from the onset, focused on a small breadth of subject-matter cases; however, the CIR was dedicated to free speech and civil rights cases from the beginning. While the CIR started "small" in 1989, with several staff members and an operating budget of $200,000 (received from conservative donations), today it has a $1.3-million annual budget, along with a staff composed of nine to ten members. The CIR takes cases involving alleged violations of civil rights, even if the plaintiff cannot afford the lawsuit. Jennifer Gratz, the named plaintiff in the *Gratz/Grutter* case, said that she initially contemplated suing over her rejection from the University of Michigan, but was depressed that she could not afford the litigation. Gratz commented that "it really wasn't serious then. I knew we [Jennifer and her parents] didn't have the resources." However, the CIR took the case, which several years later would become what some have labeled as the most significant affirmative action case to reach the Supreme Court in the last quarter century.

See also American Civil Liberties Union; *Coalition for Economic Equity v. Wilson*; *Gratz v. Bollinger/Grutter v. Bollinger*; *Hopwood v. Texas*; National Association for the Advancement of Colored People; Proposition 209; *Smith v. University of Washington Law School.*

FURTHER READING: CIR, web site: http://www.cir-usa.org; Diaz, Idris M., 1997, "Mischief Makers: The Men behind All Those Anti–Affirmative Action Lawsuits," *Black Issues in Higher Education*, December 25, 15–23; Moore, W. John, 1997, "The Influence Game: A Little Group Makes Big Law," *National Journal*, November 15, 23; Schmidt, Peter, 2003, "Behind the Fight over Race-Conscious Admissions: Advocacy Groups—Working Together—Helped Shape the Legal and Political Debate," *Chronicle of Higher Education*, April 4, A22; Segal, David, 1998, "D.C. Public Interest Law Firm Puts Affirmative Action on Trial," *Washington Post*, February 20, A-1.

JAMES A. BECKMAN

Chained-Runner Metaphor

See Level Playing Field.

Chavez, Linda (1947–)

Linda Chavez is arguably the best-known female Hispanic voice on issues of race and education policy. She opposes and has long criticized race-based affirmative action and believes that the elimination of discrimination and racism can only be achieved in the United States through the elimination of race-conscious programs like affirmative action. Chavez believes that affirmative action programs have veered from their original purpose and now only constitute outright preferences based upon skin color or gender. She is the founder of the conservative Center for Equal Opportunity, which also opposes affirmative action. Chavez is a self-described former liberal and current neoconservative.

Since the late 1970s, Chavez has been an outspoken opponent of bilingual education and race-based affirmative action programs. She acquired a national audience as the editor of the *American Educator*, a publication of the American Federation of Teachers, a labor union composed of teachers and others involved in education services. She served as the director of the U.S. Commission on Civil Rights from 1983 to 1985 in the Reagan administration and has been described as the highest-ranking woman in the Reagan administration when she served as director of public liaison in 1985. She also served as the U.S. expert on the United Nations Subcommission on Human Rights from 1992 to 1996.

Chavez gained widespread attention in 2001 when then President-Elect George W. Bush nominated her for the position of secretary of labor. She withdrew her name from nomination after seven days of intense media scrutiny of a decade-past employment relationship with an illegal Guatemalan immigrant to whom Chavez had provided a room in her home. Chavez and the woman denied that their relationship was an employment relationship, both proposing that Chavez was providing assistance to a person in need. Civil rights groups and many labor unions opposed Chavez's nomination as secretary of labor because of her opposition to affirmative action. Her opposition to affirmative action was deemed relevant because the Department of Labor administers the largest affirmative action program in the nation. Labor unions also criticized her for opposing minimum-wage laws.

Chavez formed her opinions about affirmative action and bilingual education based on her experiences at the University of Colorado at Boulder and the University of California at Los Angeles. She opposes affirmative action programs because she observed that these programs ignored the skill gaps that exist between many disadvantaged minorities and the majority of white, middle-class students entering colleges and universities. She believes that by doing this, the programs reinforce, rather than undermine, stereotypes about racial minorities. In addition, she argues that the programs have negative impacts on the beneficiaries as well. Chavez argues that affirmative action programs encourage beneficiaries to engage in self-pity and often indoctrinate students into a liberal political stance that focuses on viewing the majority with hostility. In addition, she argues that bilingual education programs actually create isolation since she feels that many of the students can never be integrated into the English-speaking mainstream.

Chavez was a candidate for U.S. senator from Maryland in 1986. She has held a number of appointed positions, including two positions in the Reagan administration, first as the director of the U.S. Commission on Civil Rights and subsequently as the director of the White House public liaison office. In 1992, she was appointed to the United Nations Subcommission on the Prevention of Discrimination and the Protection of Minorities. She is the president of the Center for Equal Opportunity, which she founded in 1995. Chavez was also president of an organization called US English, which supported a constitutional amendment making English the official language of the United States. The publication of Chavez's first book, *Out of the Barrio: Toward a New Politics of Hispanic Assimilation*, was supported by the Manhattan Institute. Chavez is also the author of *An Unlikely Conservative: The Transformation of an Ex-Liberal*, as well as hundreds of articles for newspapers and magazines. She also has appeared as a regular guest on a variety of news programs, such as *CNN*, *The McLaughlin Group*, and others.

See also Bush, George W.; Center for Equal Opportunity; Department of Labor; Hispanic Americans; Race-Based Affirmative Action; Reagan, Ronald; U.S. Commission on Civil Rights.

FURTHER READING: Chavez, Linda, 1991, *Out of the Barrio: Toward a New Politics of Hispanic Assimilation*, New York: Basic Books; Chavez, Linda, 2002, *An Unlikely Conservative: The Transformation of an Ex-Liberal*, New York: Basic Books.

KYRA R. GREENE

Chicanismo

The term "Chicanismo" has its roots in a Chicano worldview. A Chicano is a person who self-identifies with a worldview that challenges and opposes the Anglo-American treatment of Mexican Americans as a subordinate people in U.S. society. As such, the term "Chicano" is pregnant with political meaning. By challenging the treatment of Chicanos in U.S. society, Chicanos promote a collective identity nested in a shared experience of being excluded, exploited, and discriminated. The Chicano weltanschauung is thus a bundled set of perceptions and experiences that oppose the imposition of Anglo-American reality on Chicano life.

Chicanismo refers to pride in promoting a Chicano worldview along moral and spiritual paths. Chicanismo enables Chicanos to know that their dignity resides in a commitment to show Anglo-American society that its discriminatory practices and prejudicial attitudes toward Chicanos are morally wrong. Chicanismo teaches Chicanos to have pride in a life experience that gives them voice in an Anglo-American society that seeks to silence them. Chicanismo is a capsule of the Chicano's soul—the Chicano's quest for spiritual expression in society. More important, it is a spiritual quest that binds the intuitive and subjective life experiences of Chicanos with each other. Chicanismo thus links Chicanos with each other spiritually and ideologically.

The philosophy of Chicanismo spearheaded the Chicano protest movements of the 1960s and 1970s. The expression of Chicanismo reached a noticeable level in U.S. society during the "brownouts" in Los Angeles schools in 1968. In 1968, Chicano students in Los Angeles high schools carried out large-scale demonstrations to protest the firing of a popular Chicano teacher, Sal Castro, and the lack of adequate classrooms and school facilities for Chicano students. Chicano students vowed not to return to the classroom until the Los Angeles school district hired more Chicano teachers, implemented a Chicano studies component into the curriculum, upgraded classrooms and school facilities for Chicano students, and increased the availability of library resources on Chicanos. The boycott of Los Angeles schools by Chicano students in 1968, which resulted in improvements in the curriculum and the hiring of more Mexican-American teachers, illustrates the value of Chicanismo as a form of agency for Chicanos.

See also Hispanic Americans.

FURTHER READING: Burciaga, José Antonio, 1993, *Drink Cultura: Chicanismo,* Santa Barbara, CA: Capra Press; Carranza, Elihu, 1978, *Chicanismo: Philosophical Fragments,* Dubuque, IA: Kendall/Hunt; Garcia, Ignacio M., 1997, *Chicanismo: The Forging of a Militant Ethos among Mexican Americans,* Tucson: University of Arizona Press.

ADALBERTO AGUIRRE JR.

China and Affirmative Action

China, referred to as the People's Republic of China (PRC), is the fourth-largest country in land size and the largest in population. It is an ethnically diverse country and has implemented an aggressive affirmative action program (referred to as "positive discrimination") as a means to achieve stability among the various ethnicities present within the PRC. China employs a broad affirmative action plan that gives preferences to minorities in government hiring and promotions, university admissions, and financing and taxation of businesses, as well as family planning (relaxed population control). China is said to have a progressive affirmative action program not out of any sense of democracy or concern for individual equality, but rather as a means to maintain stability among the minority groups. China is said also to be especially concerned about keeping minority groups happy, as it is reported that minorities occupy approximately 60 percent of the entire landmass of China and consist of more than 150 million minority-group members. It would be correct to say that China operates the most extensive affirmative action program in the world, with the most affirmative action beneficiaries anywhere in the world. It is ironic that one of the largest adherents to affirmative action is also said to have an overall poor record on human rights.

The population of China is roughly 1.3 billion, approximately 20 percent of the entire world population. The country is amazingly diverse, with fifty-six different nationalities, thus making it a multiethnic state. The country is comprised of twenty-two provinces, five autonomous regions, and three centrally administered municipalities. The autonomous regions are the areas of the country that have the highest amount of minority groups. The dominant majority is the Han Chinese, who constitute 91 to 92 percent of the total population. While a majority group that comprises 92 percent of the population may seem like a large amount, one must take into account the extraordinary size of the population. Minority groups, constituting 8 to 9 percent of the population, have more than 150 million members, larger than the population of many countries. Thus affirmative action programs in place directly affect more than 150 million minority individuals. Furthermore, the number of people seeking minority status is growing yearly.

The landmass of China is slightly smaller than the landmass of the United States and is fourth in total size after Canada, the United States, and Russia. The geography of China is relevant to affirmative action programs, as many have suggested that China has a liberal affirmative action program to placate minority groups who hold a majority of the land in China and control an abundance of natural resources. While Han Chinese constitute 91 to 92 percent of the population, they occupy only about 40 percent of the total landmass of China. Minority groups, which constitute only 8 to 9 percent of the population, occupy roughly 60 percent of the landmass of China. Additionally, many of the areas near borders are occupied by minority members. This is significant because many of these lands are considered valuable for their natural resources, such as timber and oil. Thus China appears to employ affirmative action as a crisis management tool.

The Constitution of China defines the PRC as "a socialist state under the people's democratic dictatorship led by the working class and based on an alliance of workers and peasants." However, in terms of governmental structure, the PRC is a Communist Party–run state. The Communist Party is the dominant actor and dictates the policy direction and agenda of the country. Furthermore, Communist Party membership in China has been very exclusive historically, constituting only 5 percent of the total population. One of the ironies, therefore, is that in a country that expansively utilizes affirmative action, with minority members receiving preferences in employment (hiring and promotion), university admissions, and family planning, these preferential programs do not translate into true political control of the country.

While the Communist Party (and in particular the Politburo and to a greater extent its standing committee and its chairman) hold the reins of real power in China, the constitution vests formal state authority in a hierarchical set of "people's congresses." The "highest organ of state power" (in the words of the constitution) is vested in the National People's Congress, which meets only once a year for a two-week period. As one moves down the hierarchical ladder, there are a series of congresses, ending at the bottom with local rural township congresses. While congresses at the bottom of the ladder have gained the air of democratic institutions, and the congresses have an array of institutional powers at each of the levels, the whole system remains dominated by the Communist Party. Also, while China has a system of provinces and autonomous regions that are run to some degree by minority nationalities, the PRC is in essence a unitary system in which all regional governments are subordinate to the National People's Congress and, more important, the Chinese Communist Party.

Interestingly, the Constitution of China states that all nationalities in the People's Republic of China are equal and that discrimination against or oppression of any nationality within China is prohibited. However, recent evidence suggests that the Han Chinese majority group still strongly holds racial stereotypes of the minority nationalities. The numerous affirmative action programs have not yet eradicated these strongly held views. Many Han Chinese are also opposed to the affirmative action programs already in place and resent the use of minority preferences.

Finally, it should be noted that despite constitutional and legal provisions that purport to give the people a full array of civil rights and protections, China is still infamous for its human rights abuses. For example, in 1989, the United Nations Subcommission on the Prevention of Discrimination and the Protection of Minorities placed China on a list of countries accused of seriously violating the human rights of their citizens. Investigations by nongovernmental organizations, such as the International League for Human Rights and Amnesty International, have also found China to be an violator of human rights. Movements for democratic participation in the government have been summarily crushed on several occasions. Minorities have been subjected to repression, and their members have been subjected to prolonged detention without charge or trial.

See also India and Affirmative Action; Japan and Affirmative Action; Riots, Economically and Racially Motivated.

FURTHER READING: Faison, Seth, 1999, "Uncivil Rights: Are Tibetans 'Citizens' of China?" *New York Times*, August 31, A4; Krieger, Joel, ed., 1993, *The Oxford Companion to Politics of the World*, 128–136, New York: Oxford University Press; Sautman, Barry, 1996, "The Impact of Affirmative Action on Han-Minority Relations in the PRC: The Case of Xinjiang," paper presented at Association for Asian Studies (AAS) 1996 Annual Meeting, Honolulu, HI (abstract, http://www.aasianst.org/absts/1996/intro.htm); Singer, Rena, 1997, "China Also Debates Affirmative Action," *Philadelphia Inquirer*, August 20, A1; Wang, James C.F., 1995, *Contemporary Chinese Politics: An Introduction*, 5th ed., Englewood Cliffs, NJ: Prentice Hall.

JAMES A. BECKMAN

Chisholm, Shirley (1924–)

Shirley Chisholm, a politician, civil right activist, feminist, and educator, was the first African American woman elected to Congress. Chisholm was also the first black and the first woman to seek a presidential nomination. She is a strong supporter of racial and gender equality and affirmative action. In 1999, the *Journal of Blacks in Higher Education* conducted a survey listing the most important African Americans of the twentieth century. In this study, Chisholm was ranked third of all African American elected officials who made the greatest contributions to American society in the twentieth century (Barbara Jordan and Adam Clayton Powell were ranked first and second, respectively). Shirley Chisholm and Barbara Jordan were the most prominent African American and female leaders in the U.S. Congress in the twentieth century.

Shirley Anita St. Hill Chisholm was born in Brooklyn, New York, on November 30, 1924, to Charles and Ruby St. Hill. She received her early childhood education in Barbados, where she and her two younger sisters lived with their grandmother. Graduating from a Brooklyn high school with a high academic average, she received several scholarships, including ones to Vassar and Oberlin. However, due to financial difficulties, Chisholm enrolled in Brooklyn College, majoring in psychology and minoring in Spanish. She later earned a master of arts degree from Columbia University, where she met her husband, Conrad Chisholm.

The idea of a political career was planted in Chisholm by her political science professor. However, her decision to really make a difference came when she heard a white man speak at Brooklyn College. In essence, the man said that black people will always have to be led by whites. This angered Chisholm so much that she vowed to prove that she could become a leader. She was one of the founders of the Unity Democratic Club, whose goal was to defeat and replace the Seventeenth Assembly District political machine. When the Unity Democratic Club's nominee for assemblyman was appointed to the bench, Chisholm ran for the seat and won by a very small margin. She served in the New York State Assembly for four years.

After a Supreme Court–ordered redistricting of New York, a new primarily black congressional district was created. Chisholm was chosen by a citizens' committee to run for the seat. She beat James Farmer, the former national chairman of the Congress of Racial Equality, by a landslide. She represented the Twelfth Congressional District of Brooklyn for seven terms, from 1968 to 1982. She was also the first black to make a bid for the Democratic nomination for president in 1972. She entered primaries in twelve states and won 151 first-ballot votes at the Democratic Convention. However, she did not receive the endorsement of the Congressional Black Caucus.

In Congress, Chisholm became very powerful. She was considered something of a maverick, often voting against her party. She was one of the first female black leaders to speak against racism and to support reproductive and abortion rights. Further, she was the founder of the National Political Congress of Black Women. Chisholm said that she felt more discriminated against because of her gender than because of her color. While introducing the Equal Rights Amendment on the floor of the House of Representatives on May 21, 1969, she stated, "As a black person, I am no stranger to race prejudice. But the truth is that in the political world I have been oftener discriminated against because I am a woman than because I am black."

Chisholm has received more than 100 honorary doctorate degrees and numerous citations and proclamations. She has written two books, *Unbought and Unbossed* and *The Good Fight.* President Bill Clinton nominated her to serve as the U.S. ambassador to Jamaica; however, she declined due to deteriorating eyesight. Chisholm currently resides in Florida.

See also Clinton, William Jefferson; Congress of Racial Equality; Congressional

Black Caucus; Equal Rights Amendment; Gendered Racism; Jordan, Barbara Charline; Powell, Adam Clayton, Jr.

FURTHER READING: Chisholm, Shirley, 1970, *Unbought and Unbossed,* Boston: Houghton Mifflin; Smith, Jessie Carney, ed., 1992, *Notable Black American Women,* 185–189, Detroit: Gale Research.

NAOMI ROBERTSON

Chronicle of Higher Education

The *Chronicle of Higher Education* is a weekly news and information publication that covers a range of topics directly and indirectly connected to higher education. Over the years, it has covered prominent court cases, federal and state actions, and national perspectives as they relate to affirmative action policies. Under the section "Issues in Depth," the *Chronicle of Higher Education* has compiled a collection of articles, documents, and data that pertain to affirmative action in college admissions and are available to researchers in determining the efficacy of affirmative action programs in higher education. The *Chronicle of Higher Education* also reports on colleges and universities that are censured by the American Association of University Professors for discrimination and violations of academic freedom. As such, the *Chronicle of Higher Education* remains a central source for those researching affirmative action issues and keeping on top of how race and gender issues impact higher education.

See also American Association of University Professors; Discrimination; Education and Affirmative Action; Historically Black Colleges and Universities.

FURTHER READING: *Chronicle of Higher Education,* web site: http://chronicle.com.

DENISE O'NEIL GREEN

Citizens' Commission on Civil Rights

The Citizens' Commission on Civil Rights (CCCR) was founded in 1982 as a response to what its founders believed was the Reagan administration's lack of commitment to the civil rights policies pursued by the federal government since the mid-1960s. Their goal was to revitalize the civil rights agenda at the national level. Among other things, the commission monitors and studies the issue of affirmative action. The CCCR also monitors civil rights enforcement, examines important policy issues affecting equality of opportunity, and publishes reports on major issues of concern. These reports have dealt with strengthening fair-housing laws, barriers to voter registration, equal employment and affirmative action, and reviews of civil rights policies of the Reagan, Bush, and Clinton administrations.

The commission was established with equal numbers of Republicans and Democrats who had held positions in the federal government during the previous two decades. They believed that the U.S. Commission on Civil Rights, the federal agency established by the Civil Rights Act of 1957 to monitor enforcement, foster public understanding of civil rights, and recommend new policies, had abdicated this responsibility. The original chair of the CCCR was Arthur Flemming, secretary of the Department of Health, Education, and Welfare (now the Department of Education and the Department of Health and Human Services) during the Eisenhower administration (1958–1961), who had chaired the U.S. Commission on Civil Rights between 1972 and 1981. Flemming had been forced out as chair of the federal agency because of his disagreement with the Reagan administration on civil rights policy.

See also Bush, George Herbert Walker; Civil Rights Act of 1957; Clinton, William Jefferson; Democratic Party and Affirmative Action; Department of Education; Eisenhower, Dwight David; Reagan, Ronald; Republican Party and Affirmative Action; U.S. Commission on Civil Rights.

FURTHER READING: Citizens' Commission on Civil Rights, web site: http://www.cccr.org; Citizens' Commission on Civil Rights, 1999, Report, *The Test of Our Progress: The Clinton Record on Civil Rights*, CCCR web site; Citizens' Commission on Civil Rights, 1999, Report, *Title I in Midstream: The Fights to Improve Schools for Poor Kids*, CCCR web site; Citizens' Commission on Civil Rights, 2002, Report, *Rights at Risk: Equality in an Age of Terrorism*, CCCR web site; Citizens' Commission on Civil Rights, 2002, Report, *Title I in California: Will the State Pass the Test?* CCCR web site.

JEFFREY KRAUS

Citizens' Initiative on Race and Ethnicity

The Citizens' Initiative on Race and Ethnicity (CIRE) is a nonprofit organization founded on the mission of examining the issue of race in America and providing "realistic recommendations on how race relations can be improved." The CIRE is composed of twelve members, most of whom are also known for their strongly critical views on affirmative action: Clint Bolick, Elaine Chao, Linda Chavez, Ward Connerly, Tamar Jacoby, Barbara Ledeen, T.J. Rogers, Shelby Steele, Abigail and Stephan Thernstrom, Robert Woodson, and C. Robert Zelnick. The CIRE has a web site that delineates the research focus of CIRE as including "education, economic opportunity, crime, social welfare programs, and legal actions."

See also Bolick, Clint; Chavez, Linda; Steele, Shelby; Thernstrom, Stephan, and Thernstrom, Abigail.

FURTHER READING: CIRE, web site: http://www.cire.org/.

JAMES A. BECKMAN

City of Richmond v. J.A. Croson Co., 488 U.S. 469 (1989)

In *City of Richmond v. J.A. Croson Co.*, the U.S. Supreme Court found that states, counties, and municipalities could institute affirmative action policies to remedy identified acts of discrimination, but not to address prior "societal discrimination." In rejecting the city of Richmond's minority set-aside plan for city contractors, the Court disapproved of the city's use of rigid racial quotas to remedy amorphous claims of past discrimination. The *Croson* case remains one of the most important affirmative action cases that the Court has handed down in the last several decades.

The city of Richmond had adopted the Minority Business Utilization Plan (MBUP), requiring contractors who were given prime construction contracts by the city to award at least 30 percent of the dollar amount of their contracts to minority business enterprises (MBEs), defined as any business with at least 51 percent ownership and control by African American, Spanish-speaking, Oriental, Indian, Eskimo, or Aleut citizens. The city described the plan as a remedial action for past years of discrimination within the local, state, and national construction industries. However, there was no direct evidence that the city itself had ever discriminated on the basis of race in allocating contracts or that its contractors had discriminated against minority subcontractors. The only specific evidence introduced by the city to show a need for such a plan was statistical evidence that the percentage of construction contracts awarded to minority businesses by the city (0.67 percent) was lower than the city's overall minority population (50 percent).

Opponents of the plan argued that the disparity between the city's minority population and the percentage of contracts awarded to minority businesses was an insufficient indicator of discrimination in the construction industry, in part, because the disparity did not account for the relatively small number of minority contractors in Richmond who were available to bid on city contracts. They also questioned whether there were enough minority businesses in the Richmond area to satisfy the 30 percent requirement.

The city of Richmond rejected J. A. Croson Company's sole bid for a city contract because the company did not commit to awarding 30 percent of the contract's dollars to MBEs. The company sought a waiver of the plan's requirement because it felt that there was no qualified MBE to which the company could subcontract the required amount. The city denied the request for a waiver, and Croson subsequently brought suit against the city of Richmond in federal court, claiming that the city's affirmative action plan, on its face and as applied to Croson, was unconstitutional under the Fourteenth Amendment's Equal Protection Clause. The U.S. District Court for the Eastern District of Virginia gave its complete support to the plan and thus denied Croson's claim, as did the U.S. Court of Appeals for the Fourth Circuit in its first opinion.

Upon remand from the U.S. Supreme Court, the Fourth Circuit, in its second opinion, sided with Croson. The Fourth Circuit ruled that under "strict scrutiny," the Richmond plan failed to pass constitutional muster. The appellate court found that (*a*) the plan was not justified by a "compelling governmental interest," since the record revealed no prior discrimination on the part of the city in awarding contracts, and (*b*) the 30 percent requirement "was not narrowly tailored to accomplish a remedial purpose."

The U.S. Supreme Court affirmed the decision of the Fourth Circuit, with Justice Sandra Day O'Connor delivering an opinion, parts of which served as the majority opinion. The majority first noted that because the city of Richmond lacked evidence of prior discrimination in the construction industry, the city did not have a compelling interest in the MBUP. While the Court acknowledged the "sorry" history of private and public discrimination in America, resulting in a lack of opportunities for black entrepreneurs, it felt that the country's historical record failed to justify a racial quota for the awarding of public contracts. Accordingly, without a compelling interest, the Richmond plan could not withstand strict scrutiny under the Equal Protection Clause.

The Court distinguished this case from *Fullilove v. Klutznick*, 448 U.S. 448

(1980), in which the Court held that the U.S. Congress has broad legislative authority under Section 5 of the Fourteenth Amendment to remedy past societal and governmental discrimination. Here the Court found that a municipality of a state, whose authority is limited by the Fourteenth Amendment, cannot use past societal discrimination as a justification for an affirmative action plan. In addition, Congress's finding of nationwide discrimination in the construction industry could not be used without evidence to show that such discrimination had existed in Richmond.

The Court also noted that the Richmond plan was not narrowly tailored to ameliorate whatever past discrimination had existed—the second obstacle to having the city plan withstand strict scrutiny. The city alleged past discrimination against African Americans, which, as the Court noted, did not justify the inclusion of other minority groups in the Richmond plan.

So even though the racial classifications adopted by the city of Richmond were remedial, the Court chose to apply "strict scrutiny." As Justice O'Connor stated, strict scrutiny enabled the courts to "smoke out illegitimate uses of race by assuring that the legislative body is pursuing a goal important enough to warrant use of a highly suspect tool." She went on to say that the Court should be especially sensitive to racial classifications because they entail a "danger of stigmatic harm." Justice O'Connor wrote that unless such classifications are used exclusively to address identified acts of discrimination, governments risk reinforcing stereotypes of inferiority, with certain racial groups depending on "special protection" to achieve success. While acknowledging that identified acts of discrimination in a jurisdiction could justify affirmative action, the Court, in effect, greatly limited the circumstances in which state entities could adopt affirmative action policies.

In his dissenting opinion, joined by Justice William Brennan and Justice Harry Blackman, Justice Thurgood Marshall disagreed with these limitations. He believed that unlike invidious and discriminatory classifications, benign racial classifications intended to "further remedial goals" did not warrant strict scrutiny under the Equal Protection Clause. Justice Marshall took the view that affirmative action only needed to be substantially related to important governmental objectives, which he called "intermediate scrutiny." He found that the city of Richmond had two important interests in enacting the MBUP: (*a*) remedying the effects of past discrimination (proven through much of the same evidence that the majority rejected) and (*b*) not utilizing city funds to perpetuate the effects of past discrimination. Justice Marshall found the Richmond plan substantially related to these interests because (*a*) it had a limited duration, (*b*) it applied prospectively and not to vested contract rights, (*c*) it had a waiver provision, and (*d*) it had minimal impact on innocent third parties because public contracting accounted for only 3 percent of all contracting dollars in the city.

See also Blackmun, Harry Andrew; Brennan, William Joseph; Compelling Governmental Interest; Disadvantaged Business Enterprises; Disparate Treatment and Disparate Impact; Equal Protection Clause; Fourteenth Amendment; *Fullilove v. Klutznick*; Intermediate Scrutiny Review; Invidious Discrimination; Marshall, Thurgood; Narrowly Tailored Affirmative Action Plans; O'Connor, Sandra Day; Statistical Proof of Discrimination; Strict Scrutiny; Supreme Court and Affirmative Action.

FURTHER READING: Drake, W. Avon, and Robert D. Holsworth, 1996, *Affirmative Action and the Stalled Quest for Black Progress,* Urbana: University of Illinois Press; Eastland, Terry, 1996, *Ending Affirmative Action: The Case for Colorblind Justice,* New York: Basic Books; Horne, Gerald, 1992, *Reversing Discrimination: The Case for Affirmative Action,* New York: International Press; La Noue, George R., 1997, "The Impact of Croson on Equal Protection Law and Policy," *Albany Law Review* 61: 1–41.

GREGORY M. DUHL

Civil Rights Act of 1866

The Civil Rights Act of 1866 was the first civil rights bill passed by the U.S. Congress following the Civil War. This was the first congressional effort to enact legislation regarding the issue of racial equality in the United States and was passed by Congress pursuant to the enforcement authorization clause of the Thirteenth Amendment, which was itself ratified a year earlier in 1865. The act would also become the foundation for several of the key provisions of the Fourteenth Amendment, which was ratified within two years of the adoption of the 1866 Act. This first civil rights act following the Civil War became a milestone in both civil rights and American constitutional law history. In his concurring opinion in *Regents of the University of California v. Bakke,* 438 U.S. 265 (1978), Justice Thurgood Marshall described this act (and the others of the era) as America's first attempt at affirmative action.

The primary author of the Civil Rights Act of 1866 was Senator Lyman Trumbull, who was a moderate Republican serving as the chair of the Senate Judiciary Committee. The Civil Rights Act of 1866 was the result of extensive compromising designed to advance Reconstruction efforts. The Civil Rights Act reflected the viewpoint of Radical Republicans in the area of fundamental rights. The objective of the act was to enforce the Thirteenth Amendment to the U.S. Constitution and to provide that all citizens, particularly African Americans, were to enjoy full and equal protection of all laws. The Civil Rights Act of 1866 was promulgated, in part, as a response to statutory black codes passed by some states that attempted to deprive African Americans of equal rights under the law.

President Andrew Johnson vetoed the Civil Rights Act of 1866 when it first passed Congress, believing that it was unconstitutional. However, Congress overwhelmingly overrode the presidential veto. Subsequent concerns over the legitimacy of the measure led to efforts to convert the major provisions of the Civil Rights Act into a new constitutional amendment (the Fourteenth Amendment) to ensure that the provisions would remain inviolate from subsequent acts of Congress or interpretation by the Supreme Court that the 1866 act was unconstitutional.

The Civil Rights Act of 1866 accomplished several things. First, it defined citizenship and stated: "That all persons born in the United States and not subject to any foreign power, excluding Indians not taxed, are hereby declared to be citizens of the United States." Thus the act's definition of national citizenship superseded the definition put forth by the Supreme Court in *Dred Scott v. Sandford,* 60 U.S. (19 How.) 393 (1857), which held in part that African Americans could never be citizens under the Constitution. The Civil Rights Act of 1866 also provided that all citizens were to enjoy full and equal protection of all laws and

Illustration in *Harper's Weekly*, May 12, 1866, covering the popular excitement of the Civil Rights Act of 1866. The illustration is captioned the "celebration of the abolition of slavery in the District of Columbia by the colored people, in Washington, April 19, 1866." Courtesy of Library of Congress.

procedures for the protection of persons and property and would be subject to like punishment without regard to race, color, or former slave status. The legislative objective of the Civil Rights Act of 1866 was to implement the Thirteenth Amendment, revoke portions of the *Dred Scott v. Sandford* decision dealing with the issue of African American citizenship, and dismantle the black codes that were in place throughout much of the South by this time.

The subject matter of the Civil Rights Act of 1866 was similar to that of sections of the Freedmen's Bureau Act. The Freedmen's Bureau Act was sectional in its application, whereas the Civil Rights Act was national in its application. A key point of discussion regarding the Civil Rights Act was its impact, if any, on Article IV of the U.S. Constitution relating to the Privileges and Immunities Clause. The consensus in 1866 was that the Civil Rights Act extended nationally based on notions of federalism and thus went beyond individual state-to-state enforcement.

Section 1 of the act granted all persons the same rights as white persons to make and enforce contracts, sue, be parties, give evidence, inherit, purchase, lease, sell, hold, and convey real and personal property, and enjoy the full and equal benefits of all laws and proceedings for the security of person and property. This provision of the 1866 act remains enforceable today, and these provisions have been incorporated under sections 1981 and 1982 of Title 42 of the U.S. Code. These sections have been utilized by litigants in the legal system in the continued quest for equality. This was seen in *Jones v. Alfred H. Mayer Co.* (1968), which focused on the issue of fair housing as related to the criteria established in section 1982. The Court in this case began setting the precedent for establishing the intent of the act as it related to racial discrimination in the sale or rental of public or private property. Significantly, the Court found that section 1982 eliminated all discrimination in the sale, leasing, or rental of private property.

Interpretation of section 1981 of the Civil Rights Act of 1866 was a key issue in three modern Supreme Court cases: *Johnson v. Railway Express Agency*, 421 U.S. 454 (1975), *Patterson v. McLean Credit Union*, 491 U.S. 164 (1989), and *General Building Contractors Assn. v. Pennsylvania*, 458 U.S. 375 (1982). In *Johnson*, the Court held that like section 1982, section 1981 also prohibited discrimination by private parties as well as by public entities. In *Patterson*, the issue before the Court was whether or not the act included protection against racial harassment on the job. According to the Court, section 1981 protected persons from race-based employment discrimination when one was applying for a job, such as a refusal to enter into an employment contract with someone on account of race, and where an offer to make a contract was made only on discriminatory terms. The Court held that section 1981 did not provide protection against racial discrimination once the person was on the job. At that point, other laws would apply to the situation, such as Title VII of the Civil Rights Act of 1964. In sum, the Court held that section 1981 provided protection only for entering into a contract and not for the fulfillment of the terms of a contract. In *General Building*, the Court held that section 1981 protected employees only against intentional racial discrimination, not against neutral practices that have a disparate impact because of race.

Section 2 of the Civil Rights Act of 1866 provided criminal penalties for the deprivation of any rights guaranteed by section 1 of the act. Also, in section 3 of the act, Congress gave federal courts the authority to remove from state to federal courts cases brought by individuals being denied their civil rights, cases involving federal officers as defendants, and those cases concerning privileges extended by the Freedmen's Bureau and rights guaranteed by habeas corpus statutes. The provisions of the Civil Rights Act of 1866 granted federal judges the authority to appoint special commissioners for the purpose of enforcing the guarantees of the act. The act also permitted judges to use the army or state militia under the command of the president to serve as enforcement officers. Under the auspices of the 1866 act, the appellate jurisdiction of the Supreme Court was expanded to include legal issues arising from the act. These provisions were important to give individuals an effective judicial forum to air their grievances, especially in light of the fact that many individual state courts at that time refused to respect equal rights for minority groups.

The Civil Rights Act of 1866 was designed to protect the economic and political rights of African American citizens. The parameters of the act limited protections only to areas of racial discrimination and did not include provisions for granting suffrage or other civil rights to African Americans. Because of the widespread opposition to African American suffrage, the Civil Rights Act of 1866 became the means for protecting African American civil rights against state and private interference. The act also did not provide statutory protection against discrimination in public accommodations. While the Civil Rights Act included provisions designed to give greater legal protections to African Americans, unfortunately the act did very little if anything to deter race riots, white terror, and intimidation and instead may have further instigated white violence and terror. Congress later passed the Fourteenth Amendment to the U.S. Constitution to supplement the provisions of the Civil Rights Act of 1866 and make those provisions of the act inviolate to subsequent acts of Congress or rulings by the Supreme Court.

See also Abolitionists; African Americans; American Civil War; Civil Rights Act of 1964; Civil War (Reconstruction) Amendments and Civil Rights Acts; *Dred Scott v. Sandford*; Fourteenth Amendment; Freedmen's Bureau; Housing; Marshall, Thurgood; *Patterson v. McLean Credit Union*; *Regents of the University of California v. Bakke*; Thirteenth Amendment; Title VII of the Civil Rights Act of 1964.

FURTHER READING: Kyrig, David, ed., 2000, *Unintended Consequences of Constitutional Amendment*, Athens: University of Georgia Press; Maltz, Earl M., 1990, *Civil Rights, the Constitution, and Congress, 1863–1869*, Lawrence: University Press of Kansas.

RONNIE B. TUCKER SR.

Civil Rights Act of 1875

The Civil Rights Act of 1875, "An Act to Protect All Citizens in Their Civil and Legal Rights," was the last of four acts passed by Congress between 1866 and 1875 that were designed to protect the rights of blacks. Signed into law on March 1, 1875, the Civil Rights Act of 1875 (also called the Second Civil Rights Act) represented the last effort by Congress to pass such an act for more than fifty years. The Civil Rights Act of 1875, along with the other three civil rights acts passed between 1866 and 1875, are often described as America's first efforts at an affirmative action program to remedy racial inequalities in the United States. While most of the Civil Rights Act of 1875 was ultimately declared unconstitutional by the U.S. Supreme Court in the *Civil Rights Cases* (1883), many of the provisions reappeared three-fourths of a century later in the Civil Rights Act of 1964.

The Thirteenth Amendment to the Constitution, ratified in 1865, declared that "neither slavery nor involuntary servitude . . . shall exist within the United States," thus ending chattel slavery. Although most southern whites accepted the demise of slavery, they did not accept blacks as equals. Many questions remained concerning their civil and legal status. President Andrew Johnson, a southerner and an avowed racist, who succeeded Lincoln upon his death, allowed former Confederates to participate in the reconstruction of the South. As a result, the new governments repassed their antebellum black codes or initiated new postbellum Jim Crow laws, both of which forced blacks into a state of quasi-slavery or serfdom. These codes severely limited black access to the same rights and liberties that whites enjoyed. To counter the black codes, Congress passed the Civil Rights Act of 1866 over President Johnson's veto. However, Johnson's refusal to help blacks and his policies that encouraged white resistance led to a life of poverty, disenfranchisement, and segregation for blacks.

In 1868, the Fourteenth Amendment made "all persons born or naturalized in the United States . . . citizens of the United States and of the States wherein they reside." It further stated, "No state shall abridge the privileges or immunities of citizens" and also guaranteed "due process" and "equal protection of the laws." The Fifteenth Amendment, ratified in 1870, guaranteed black males that the right to vote would not be denied on account of race or previous condition of servitude.

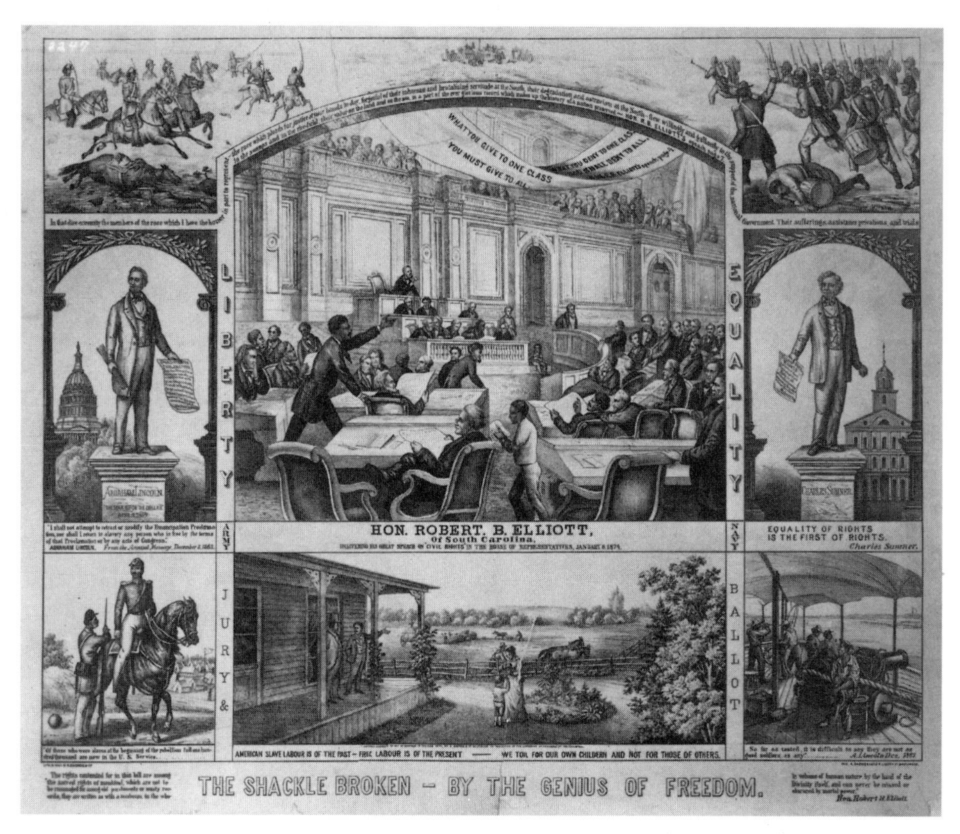

Lithograph from 1874 entitled "The Shackle Broken—by the Genius of Freedom," depicting South Carolina representative Robert B. Elliott's famous speech in favor of the Civil Rights Act during debates in the House of Representatives. The central image of the lithograph shows Congressman Elliott speaking from the floor of the House of Representatives. Hanging from the ceiling is a banner with a quotation from his speech: "What you give to one class you must give to all. What you deny to one class you shall deny to all." Other scenes depicted in the lithograph include Abraham Lincoln, Charles Sumner, and African American troops during the Civil War. Courtesy of Library of Congress.

At least as far as the law books were concerned, the Civil Rights Act of 1875, along with the Civil Rights Act of 1866, the Fourteenth and Fifteenth Amendments, and various other legislation, guaranteed blacks equal protection before the law and put them on an equal footing with whites in regard to courts, contracts, owning property, and access to public conveyances and inns. This notion of equality of the law is reflected in section 1 of the Civil Rights Act of 1875, which stated that "all persons within the jurisdiction of the United States shall be entitled to the full and equal enjoyment of the accommodations, advantages, facilities, and privileges of inns, public conveyances on land or water, theaters, and other places of public amusement; . . . applicable alike to citizens of every race and color, regardless of any previous condition of servitude."

However, most scholars assert that equality in the law and equality in fact were two different realities in the postbellum South (and indeed the country as a whole). Unfortunately, the passage of the various civil rights statutes and the Civil War Amendments (Thirteenth, Fourteenth, and Fifteenth) did not solve the race relations problems. Additionally, starting in 1875, the Supreme Court significantly undermined the acts and the Civil War Amendments through a series of decisions. As the power of the Supreme Court grew after the Civil War (and after the debacle of the decision of the Court in *Dred Scott v. Sandford* before the Civil War), it became obvious that it would again be asked to resolve the race relations issues. In 1883, the Court declared most of the Civil Rights Act of 1875 unconstitutional in the *Civil Rights Cases*, 109 U.S. 3 (1883).

Even before the Supreme Court's decision in the *Civil Rights Cases*, the act was not often enforced and had little practical effect on the lives of blacks. Yet the *Civil Rights Cases* consisted of five prosecutions and civil cases from California, Missouri, New York, Kansas, and Tennessee for denying blacks access to public accommodations and facilities under the Civil Rights Act of 1875. Some have described these prosecutions as politically driven to create a test case on the constitutionality of the 1875 act. Blacks were denied access to hotels, railroad cars, and theaters, and the owners of these establishments were prosecuted for violating the terms of the 1875 act. Speaking on behalf of the Court, Justice Joseph Bradley found the Civil Rights Act of 1875 unconstitutional because the Fourteenth Amendment prohibited state actions against discrimination, not actions of private institutions. Therefore, private owners of inns, railroads, theaters, and similar facilities could discriminate against blacks. Bradley believed that antidiscrimination laws should be under the purview of state governments, not the national government. Bradley also unbelievably stated that as of 1883, blacks were equal in America and should no longer be "the special favorites of the law."

Justice John Marshall Harlan, a former slave owner, dissented, claiming that the Court's interpretation rested upon narrow and artificial grounds, and encouraged a broad interpretation of the Thirteenth and Fourteenth Amendments. In his dissent, Harlan stated that discrimination in public accommodations amounted to state action because roads and highways were "established by the authority of these States." Additionally, Harlan argued,

> The difficulty has been to compel a recognition of the legal right of the black race to take the rank of citizens, and to secure the enjoyment of privileges belonging, under the law, to them. . . . To-day, it is the colored race which is denied, by corporations and individuals wielding public authority, rights fundamental in their freedom and citizenship.

It was not until the Civil Rights Act of 1964 that discrimination in public places of accommodations, such as hotels, restaurants, and public transportation, was again outlawed as a matter of federal law.

See also Civil Rights Act of 1866; Civil Rights Act of 1964; *Civil Rights Cases*; Civil War (Reconstruction) Amendments and Civil Rights Acts; *Dred Scott v. Sandford*; Fifteenth Amendment; Fourteenth Amendment; Jim Crow Laws; Segregation; Thirteenth Amendment.

FURTHER READING: The Civil Rights Act of March 1, 1875, U.S. Statutes at Large, vol. 18, 335–336; Hall, Kermit L., William M. Wiecek, and Paul Finkelman, 1991, *American Legal History: Cases and Materials*, New York: Oxford University Press; Wasby, Stephen L., Anthony A. D'Amato, and Rosemary Metrailer, 1977, *Desegregation from Brown to Alexander*, Carbondale: Southern Illinois University Press.

NAOMI ROBERTSON

Civil Rights Act of 1957

The Civil Rights Act of 1957 was the first major piece of civil rights legislation since Congress passed the Civil Rights Act of 1875. The Civil Rights Act of 1957 originally spanned four parts. Part I provided for the creation of a bipartisan U.S. Commission on Civil Rights for the purpose of studying discrimination and recommending remedial legislation to Congress. Part II provided for transforming the Justice Department's Civil Rights Section, which had been established by executive order, into a Civil Rights Division that would be headed by an assistant attorney general. Part III gave the attorney general the power to secure court injunctions in civil rights cases and provided that such cases be removed to the federal district courts, where civil rights supporters believed that they would be able to obtain legal relief that would end civil rights violations against African Americans in the South. Part IV increased the power of the Justice Department to seek injunctions against actual or threatened interference with the right to vote in federal primary and general elections.

In March 1956, Attorney General Herbert Brownell submitted a draft four-part civil rights bill to President Dwight Eisenhower's cabinet. Initially, Eisenhower endorsed only the first two points of Brownell's proposal. By October 1956, in the midst of his reelection campaign against Democrat Adlai Stevenson, Eisenhower declared his support for all four parts of the bill. In his 1957 State of the Union message, he urged Congress to enact all four provisions.

First introduced by Senate Majority Leader Lyndon B. Johnson (Democrat of Texas), it was the first civil rights law enacted by Congress since the Civil Rights Act of 1875. The law created the authority for establishing a civil rights office at the Department of Justice, the U.S. Commission on Civil Rights, and advisory committees to the U.S. Commission on Civil Rights in each of the states and the District of Columbia. It passed despite a filibuster led by Senator Strom Thurmond (Democrat of South Carolina, who switched to the Republican Party in 1964), during which he spoke for a Senate record of twenty-four hours and eighteen minutes. Senator Johnson was concerned with garnering the support of his colleagues. On one hand, he wanted the support of southerners, who had successfully blocked civil rights legislation for more than eighty years. On the other hand, Johnson was planning to run for the presidency in 1960, and he wished to make himself politically acceptable to liberals and northerners. As a result, the bill was watered down by the elimination of part III (which would be adopted in 1964) so as not to alienate and anger southern Democrats, leaving in place the "Jim Crow" laws that mandated segregation in the South.

On December 9, 1957, Attorney General Herbert Brownell issued the order establishing the Civil Rights Division, headed by an assistant attorney general. The division was given responsibility for the enforcement of all federal laws affecting civil rights, investigating complaints of civil rights violations, coordinating the enforcement of civil rights throughout the Justice Department, and consulting with and assisting other federal agencies in civil rights enforcement. Initially the division had fewer than ten lawyers, who focused on investigating civil rights violations in the South. In 2002, the division had more than 350 lawyers.

The Commission on Civil Rights, created in the executive branch, was empowered to investigate allegations of deprivation of an American citizen's right to vote and to appraise laws and policies of the federal government with respect to equal protection of the law and to submit a report to the president and to the Congress within two years. The law provided for a six-member commission to be appointed by the president with the consent of the Senate. Not more than three of the members at any one time could be of the same political party. In addition, the president was empowered to appoint a staff director, also with the consent of the Senate. The advisory committees were established pursuant to section 105c of the Civil Rights Act of 1957. Their functions are to advise the commission of all relevant information concerning their states on matters within the commission's jurisdiction.

Civil rights advocates were divided by the legislation. Ralph Bunche saw the bill as a sham and stated that he would have preferred that Congress had not passed any bill rather than the 1957 act. Bayard Rustin of the Congress of Racial Equality (CORE) believed that the bill was important because of the symbolism—the first civil rights bill since 1875.

See also Bunche, Ralph J.; Civil Rights Act of 1875; Congress of Racial Equality; Department of Justice; Eisenhower, Dwight David; Jim Crow Laws; Johnson, Lyndon Baines; U.S. Commission on Civil Rights.

FURTHER READING: Caro, Robert A., 2002, *Master of the Senate*, New York: Alfred A. Knopf; Jackson, Donald W., and James W. Riddlesperger Jr., 1993, "The Eisenhower Administration and the 1957 Civil Rights Act," in *Reexamining the Eisenhower Presidency*, edited by Shirley Anne Warshaw, Westport, CT: Greenwood Press; King, James D., and James W. Riddlesperger Jr., 1995, "Presidential Leadership Style and Civil Rights Legislation: The Civil Rights Act of 1957 and the Voting Rights Act of 1965," in *Presidential Leadership and Civil Rights Policy*, edited by James W. Riddlesperger Jr. and Donald W. Jackson, Westport, CT: Greenwood Press; Wexler, Sanford, 1993, *The Civil Rights Movement: An Eyewitness History*, New York: Facts on File.

JEFFREY KRAUS

Civil Rights Act of 1960

The Civil Rights Act of 1960 was passed during a time of increasing social and racial turmoil as the civil rights movement gained momentum, and in the shadow of *Brown v. Board of Education*, 347 U.S. 483 (1954), in which the U.S. Supreme Court ruled that separate public schools for whites and blacks were inherently unequal, and the 1957 Civil Rights Act. The 1957 act created the Civil Rights Division within the Department of Justice and empowered the attorney general to file lawsuits against states and local governments that engaged in racially discriminatory practices prohibited by the Constitution, specifically with regard to the Fifteenth Amendment, which guarantees that American citizens are not to be deprived of the right to vote on account of race. The 1957 act also created the Civil Rights Commission to serve as a watchdog agency and monitor civil rights violations and progress in the areas of housing, voting, and education.

Essentially a voting rights law, the 1960 Civil Rights Act was considered by many to be the first significant congressional legislation allowing for the actual enforcement of civil rights in eighty-five years, dating back to the Civil Rights Act of 1875. The legislation gave the attorney general authority to send federal officials to areas and states where blacks alleged that they were denied the right to vote or to register to vote. These officials would have the duty of examining voter registration rolls and actually supervising elections to ensure that blacks were not denied their registration and voting privileges. The legislation also authorized courts to register voters in areas where there was systemic racial discrimination. A punitive measure included in the act provided for stiff fines and prison terms for violations of voting rights and the interstate transportation of explosives and explosive devices. While the courts were mandated to appoint referees to handle difficult franchise cases, this turned out to be a slow and cumbersome process since it continued to rely upon litigation to provide a solution for chronic racial discrimination.

On May 16, 1960, the Supreme Court broadened the power of the Justice Department by ruling that states could be sued as defendants in voting rights cases. As a result, the Justice Department asked for an additional $100,000 in funds from Congress to strengthen its attack on voter disenfranchisement. In addition, new appointments were made in the voting rights area along with internal reorganization to make the department more effective. Consequently, six new voting rights suits were filed based upon the requests for records from twenty-three counties in southern states.

But even with aggressive measures, a number of official restrictions remained in place on the Justice Department as it waged war on voter disenfranchisement against blacks. These included a department-wide oversight committee responsible for initiating any new suits, an unnecessary test beyond the required preponderance of the evidence that meant evidence beyond a reasonable doubt, the underutilization of federal referees, who were used on only two occasions that resulted in the registration of only 100 more blacks, and the refusal to file any suits in the state of Mississippi, which displayed some of the most egregious examples of voter disenfranchisement. This refusal was in deference to the segregationist-oriented but very powerful Senator James O. Eastland of Mississippi, who chaired the Senate Judiciary Committee.

The 1960 Civil Rights Act still had loopholes in it that allowed white registrars and southern officials to thwart the potential of black voters in the electoral arena. Enforcement of the right to vote through judicial means still had limited value without a stronger federal law to enforce it. The Kennedy and Johnson administrations were confronted with this issue. Literacy tests, poll taxes, and other racially discriminatory measures indigenous to the South remained in place. Nevertheless, there were indications shortly after its passage that the 1960 Civil Rights Act would be effective in adding more blacks to voter registration rolls and increasing their voting in the electoral arena. In 1961, in a case in Macon County, Alabama, the Department of Justice successfully got an injunction to stop voter discrimination. Federal judge Frank M. Johnson of Alabama ruled in favor of the Justice Department and blacks after examining voter registration rolls that showed excessive voter discrimination. The judge ordered county officials to stop discriminatory measures and quicken their work schedule, enroll qualified voters, and report to him on a systematic basis. As a result, voter registration surged and more than doubled in a short time period, increasing to 2,500.

The 1960 Civil Rights Act, like its predecessor, the 1957 Civil Rights Act, had weaknesses. Nevertheless, perhaps its greatest significance lay in establishing an important precedent in the revitalized intervention efforts of the federal government in the battle against racial discrimination in the South. It would take additional civil rights legislation to completely erase the vestiges of voter discrimination.

See also Brown v. Board of Education; Civil Rights Act of 1875; Civil Rights Act of 1957; Civil Rights Act of 1964; Department of Justice; Fifteenth Amendment; Johnson, Lyndon Baines; Kennedy, John Fitzgerald; U.S. Commission on Civil Rights; Voting Rights Act of 1965.

FURTHER READING: Ivers, Greg, 2002, *American Constitutional Law: Power and Politics*, Boston: Houghton Mifflin; Lawson, Steven F., 1997, *Running for Freedom*, New York: McGraw-Hill; Lichtman, Allan, 1969, "The Federal Assault against Voting Discrimination in the Deep South, 1957–1967," *Journal of Negro History* 54, no. 4:346–367.

MFANYA D. TRYMAN

Civil Rights Act of 1964

The Civil Rights Act of 1964 was the most sweeping civil rights legislation passed by the U.S. Congress since Reconstruction. Congress had previously exercised its constitutional authority under the Equal Protection Clause of the Fourteenth Amendment to prohibit discrimination by state entities. In using its Commerce Clause power to pass the 1964 act, Congress extended the mandate of nondiscrimination to nonstate entities, including public establishments (Title II), programs receiving federal funding (Title VI), and employers (Title VII).

However, women were left unprotected from sex discrimination in education because Title VI only prohibited discrimination on the basis of race, color, and national origin. Consequently, as part of the Education Amendments of 1972, Congress passed Title IX, which prohibits sex discrimination in schools, including discrimination on the basis of marital status or pregnancy. Further, courts were skeptical of enforcing Title VII to protect women because Congress had added "sex" discrimination to its scope right before passage, leaving little legislative history to its inclusion. Not until the late 1980s and 1990s did the U.S. Supreme Court give Title VII enough teeth to protect women from sexual harassment in employment. While Titles VI, VII, and IX have provided historically disadvantaged groups a potent sword to be used to combat discrimination, the same titles have served as a shield for critics of affirmative action to wield in opposing benign racial and gender classifications.

The fight for racial equality that culminated in the passage of the 1964 act dated back at least 100 years. Segregation remained intact in the southern states even after the Civil War, with African Americans restricted to using facilities that were specifically set aside for them. Southern state legislatures passed black codes in an effort to restrict the freed slaves, prohibiting them from practicing certain professions, carrying guns in public, sitting on juries, and testifying against white persons. Since the majority of African Americans in the South were denied access to even the most basic education, state governments established literacy requirements to deny African Americans access to the voting booths.

Congress outlawed the black codes in 1866 when it passed the first of several nineteenth-century civil rights acts. In 1875, Congress approved a potentially sweeping civil rights law providing, in part: "That all persons within the jurisdiction

Civil rights march on Washington, D.C., in 1963, calling for equal rights, integrated schools, decent housing, and an end to racial biasness and discrimination. Courtesy of Library of Congress.

of the United States shall be entitled to the full and equal enjoyment of the accommodations, advantages, facilities, and privileges of inns, public conveyances on land or water, theaters, and other places of public amusement." The language seems clear enough, but the U.S. Supreme Court decided in the *Civil Rights Cases*, 109 U.S. 3 (1883), that Congress only had the authority under the Fourteenth Amendment to prohibit discrimination by the states. Business owners successfully defended the black code and Jim Crow practices by arguing that their firms were not part of any state and, therefore, were exempt from the 1875 act. The Supreme Court ruled that since no state agency participated in most black code and Jim Crow practices of business owners, no constitutional violations had occurred.

In response to the large numbers of lynchings, beatings, and murders of black Americans by white Americans, the U.S. Supreme Court left the responsibility for punishing offenders in the hands of state courts. In southern states, it was nearly impossible to get African Americans appointed to juries, which often consisted of friends and acquaintances of white defendants. Even when found guilty, these white defendants received the lightest possible sentences. The fear of being lynched, beaten, or assassinated kept African Americans in a state of psychological slavery. Thus by keeping punitive power in state courts and by protecting the racist actions of privately held businesses, the Supreme Court gutted the Civil Rights Act of 1875.

Race riots made headlines, but peaceful sit-ins and marches were rarely reported until 1955, when Rosa Parks spontaneously violated a Montgomery, Alabama, city law requiring blacks to give up their bus seats to whites when ordered to do so by the driver. To protest her arrest, the local chapter of the National Association for the Advancement of Colored People (NAACP), led by a young Baptist minister named Dr. Martin Luther King, organized a boycott of the city's bus system. The successful campaign to overturn the law made King a visible leader in the effort to end racial segregation and inequality in the United States.

Congress used many procedural strategies to make sure that any civil rights legislation passed in the 1950s had little impact. In 1957, U.S. representatives from several southern states willingly accepted a fairly strong civil rights bill in the House, knowing full well that it would be filibustered by their fellow southerners in the Senate. As originally written, part III of the 1957 bill gave the U.S. attorney general the power to file civil rights cases, which would have saved African Americans the frustration of having to challenge racist southern laws in racist southern courts. As expected, southern senators filibustered, and part III was removed at the behest of Senator Richard Russell of Georgia, who complained that the attorney general should not be granted so much power.

However, civil rights supporters did enjoy a major victory in Little Rock, Arkansas, in September 1957. In an effort to comply with the U.S. Supreme Court ruling in *Brown v. Board of Education*, 347 U.S. 483 (1954), the Little Rock School Board allowed nine African American students to enroll in an all-white high school. Arkansas governor Orval Faubus, arguing that civil unrest would undoubtedly occur if the nine students entered the school, ordered the Arkansas National Guard to block their entry. President Dwight Eisenhower used his power as commander in chief of the armed forces to replace the National Guard units with U.S. Army regulars whose orders were to ensure that integration proceeded as planned. These remarkable events resulted in one year of integration; Governor Faubus eventually ordered the closing of certain Little Rock schools to keep the school system segregated.

During the Eisenhower administration, one more attempt was made to pass a civil rights bill that would give the attorney general the power to file suits challenging segregationist laws. The 1960 bill included the same part III language that had been dropped in 1957; once again, southern senators initiated a filibuster, and once again supporters could not gain enough votes for a filibuster-ending cloture. Without part III, the Civil Rights Act of 1960 was very weak.

As a candidate for president, John F. Kennedy vowed to end racial segregation, but once in office, he did little on the civil rights front and proposed no civil rights legislation. His inactivity motivated King and other civil rights advocates to organize a broad range of demonstrations and peaceful acts of civil disobedience in southern states. In 1963, Birmingham, Alabama, became the focus of protest, with local police commissioner Eugene "Bull" Connor using violence against King and several dozen demonstrators who were calling for integrated public accommodations. The American people were exposed to graphic images on television and in newspapers of law enforcement using dogs and fire hoses against civil rights protesters. Kennedy had no choice but to respond.

Recognizing the growing potential for more extreme violence, Kennedy pushed Congress to pass a new civil rights bill. With memories of the 1960 defeat still fresh in their minds, senators and representatives from northern states took a cautious approach to getting what they wanted. Their tactic was to be purposefully conservative, making southern Republicans look bad if they failed to support the legislation. In response, southern Republicans felt compelled to introduce more progressive measures, including part III provisions that they had previously rejected, to ensure another filibuster resulting in the bill's failure. Each party tried to outmaneuver the other, essentially trying to force its opponents to make strategic mistakes that would cause them to lose face. By the time Kennedy was assassinated, the bill had yet to come up for a full vote in the House.

Kennedy's successor, Lyndon Johnson, made passage of the Civil Rights Act one of his top priorities, and a bill was passed and signed into law within the first six months of his administration. Using his extensive experience in the ways of Congress, Johnson was successful in pushing through a law that banned discrimination based on race, color, or national origin in public accommodations (Title II), programs receiving federal assistance (Title VI), and employment (Title VII), and that also banned discrimination on the basis of sex in employment (Title VII). In addition, Congress enacted stronger prohibitions against discrimination in voting (Title I) but refused to prohibit literacy tests, mandated desegregation in public facilities (Title III) and in public education (Title IV), and strengthened the investigative authority of the Civil Rights Commission (Title V).

With the enactment of Title VII, the Civil Rights Act of 1964 took a major step toward giving minority Americans opportunities to compete for jobs that had never before been open to them. To enforce Title VII, Congress also created the Equal Employment Opportunity Commission (EEOC) and staffed it with lawyers who had the power to file antidiscrimination lawsuits. Additionally, Title VII gave aggrieved employees and job applicants a private right of action, with the right to sue an employer in federal court after exhausting their administrative remedies. In the Equal Employment Opportunity Act of 1972, Congress extended Title VII to cover federal employment and public and private educational institutions and to give the EEOC the right to file suit in federal court against an employer.

Federal sexual harassment and gender discrimination law evolved out of the Civil Rights Act of 1964 as amended by Title IX of the Education Amendments of 1972 and the Civil Rights Act of 1991. Title IX arose out of the civil rights and feminist movements of the 1960s and early 1970s and prohibited educational institutions receiving federal funds from discriminating on the basis of gender in educational programs or activities. While the express statutory mechanism for enforcing Title IX was administrative (the federal agencies distributing educational funds were empowered to enforce Title IX), the U.S. Supreme Court held in *Cannon v. University of Chicago,* 441 U.S. 677 (1979), that an individual harassed or discriminated against on the basis of gender in an educational institution had a private right of action against the institution in federal court.

However, in the two decades after the passage of the 1964 act, federal courts were reluctant to find sexual harassment unlawful in the workplace under Title VII, in part because there was little legislative history to Congress's last-minute decision to prohibit gender discrimination in Title VII. In *Meritor Savings Bank v. Vinson,* 477 U.S. 57 (1986), the U.S. Supreme Court found both quid pro quo (illegal acts in which victims are forced to submit sexually to others' demands or else face negative consequences) and hostile work environment (a workplace where sexual language and behavior create a perceived impediment to an individual fulfilling his/her professional responsibilities) unlawful under Title VII. Since that time, victims of sexual harassment in workplaces of fifteen or more employees have had a private right of action in federal court against alleged harassers.

In the Civil Rights Act of 1991, Congress amended Title VII to give aggrieved parties the right to a jury trial and to both compensatory (for physical and emotional injuries) and punitive damages in the case of intentional discrimination or harassment. Additionally, Congress found that a plaintiff who proves a discriminatory motivation for an employment decision has a right to injunctive relief and attorneys' fees and costs, even if the employer would have made the same employment decision without the discriminatory motivation.

However, another legacy of the civil rights and feminist movements is affirmative action. Federal, state, and local governments, educational institutions, and employers began to extend preferences to historically disadvantaged minority groups and women. While proponents of affirmative action defended such preferences as consistent with the mission of the Civil Rights Act of 1964, critics thought that the nondiscrimination mandate of the 1964 act should apply to all racial classifications.

For example, in *Regents of the University of California v. Bakke,* 438 U.S. 265 (1978), the U.S. Supreme Court was confronted with the legality of the admissions policy of the University of California at Davis Medical School, in which the school set aside a certain percentage of seats in the entering class for minorities. A plurality of the Court, joined in judgment by Justice Lewis Powell, struck down the plan, finding that Title VI of the Civil Rights Act prohibited "race-conscious" admissions policies.

Title VII expressly states that employers do not have to give preference to historically disadvantaged groups and minorities to be in compliance with the 1964 act. While opponents of affirmative action argued that Title VII prohibited affirmative action in private employment, the U.S. Supreme Court, in *United Steelworkers of America v. Weber,* 443 U.S. 193 (1979), upheld Kaiser Chemical Corporation's affirmative action plan giving 50 percent of all skilled jobs to African Americans until the percentage of blacks employed at the company reflected the percentage of blacks in the general population. The Court held that not all "race-conscious" affirmative action plans are illegal, finding that a private employer can use affirmative action both to break down patterns of discrimination and to make opportunities available to African Americans in occupations that had not previously been open to them. However, in *Firefighters Local Union No. 1784 v. Stotts,* 467 U.S. 561 (1984), the Court was more skeptical of an affirmative action plan protecting black firefighters with less seniority than white firefighters from layoffs, striking down the plan because the plaintiffs did not prove that the policy was benefiting actual victims of past discrimination.

Last, the regulations passed under Title IX of the Education Amendments of 1972 specifically authorize educational institutions receiving federal funding to adopt programs and policies to overcome specific practices of past discrimination in admissions and employment. Recently, universities have begun to cut men's sports program as a sort of affirmative action to comply with the mandate of Title IX requiring gender equity between men's and women's sports.

See also African Americans; Benign Discrimination; *Brown v. Board of Education;* Civil Rights Act of 1875; Civil Rights Act of 1957; Civil Rights Act of 1960; Civil Rights Act of 1991; *Civil Rights Cases*; Civil War (Reconstruction) Amendments and Civil Rights Acts; Eisenhower, Dwight David; Employment (Private) and Affirmative Action; Employment (Public) and Affirmative Action; Equal Employment Opportunity Act of 1972; Equal Employment Opportunity Commission; Equal Protection Clause; *Firefighters Local Union No. 1784 v. Stotts*; Fourteenth Amendment; Jim Crow Laws; Johnson, Lyndon Baines; Jury Selection and Affirmative

Action; Kennedy, John Fitzgerald; King, Martin Luther, Jr.; National Association for the Advancement of Colored People; Powell, Lewis Franklin, Jr.; *Regents of the University of California v. Bakke*; Riots, Economically and Racially Motivated; Segregation; State Action Doctrine; Title VI of the Civil Rights Act of 1964; Title VII of the Civil Rights Act of 1964; Title IX of the Education Amendments of 1972; *United Steelworkers of America v. Weber.*

FURTHER READING: Chan, Anja, 1994, *Women and Sexual Harassment: A Guide to the Legal Protections of Title VII and the Hostile Environment Claim,* Binghamton, NY: Haworth Press; Grofman, Bernard, ed., 2000, *Legacies of the 1964 Civil Rights Act,* Charlottesville: University Press of Virginia; Halpern, Stephen C., 1995, *On the Limits of the Law: The Ironic Legacy of Title VI of the 1964 Civil Rights Act,* Baltimore: Johns Hopkins University Press; Loevy, Robert D., ed., 1997, *The Civil Rights Act of 1964: The Passage of the Law That Ended Racial Segregation,* Albany: State University of New York Press; Williams, Juan, 1988, *Eyes on the Prize: America's Civil Rights Years, 1954–1965,* New York: Penguin Press.

GREGORY M. DUHL

Civil Rights Act of 1968

The Civil Rights Act of 1968 deals with fair housing and is also known as Title VIII of the Fair Housing Act or simply the Fair Housing Act. The act, contained in Public Law 90–284, prohibits discrimination in the sale or rental of housing and the acquisition of financial loans based on race, color, religion, sex, or national origin. The act also contains provisions for the administration of all federal programs and activities relating to housing and urban development that are meant to protect people from discrimination in leasing or purchasing property. The Ninetieth Congress passed the act, and President Lyndon Baines Johnson, the thirty-sixth president of the United States, signed the bill into law on April 11, 1968.

The Civil Rights Act of 1968 makes it unlawful for anyone to interfere with, intimidate, or attempt to injure another individual due to his or her "race, color, religion, sex or disability, marital status or national origin" in the renting, selling, and purchasing of a home. The 1968 law also makes it unlawful to print and publish statements or advertisements that denote preferences on behalf of the seller or renter as they relate to the race, color, religion, sex, or national origin of the prospective renter or purchaser.

Senator Edward Kennedy, a prominent civil rights activist, in an article titled "Fair Housing—The Battle Goes On," noted that the passage of the Fair Housing Act of 1968 was indicative of Congress's attempt to secure a more tangible equal opportunity for persons of color, women, and individuals of religious backgrounds different from that of the majority population. Kennedy maintained that creating and implementing the Fair Housing Act was extremely difficult to achieve when compared to the Civil Rights Act of 1964 and the Voting Rights Act of 1965. He contended that housing policy was a "tough nut to crack" because the issue simply "hit too close to home" for many Americans.

President Lyndon Johnson called on Congress to pass a fair housing bill in 1966 and 1967. Unfortunately, during that two-year period, southern legislators who opposed fair-housing legislation outnumbered those who supported the president's public policy request. Thus southern legislators successfully blocked fair-housing legislation in 1966 and 1967. Clarence M. Mitchell Jr., then the director of the Washington Chapter of the National Association for the Advancement of Colored People (NAACP) and an active participant in the Leadership Conference on Civil Rights, strategically lobbied and utilized his political savvy in getting the legislation passed by Congress. Mitchell heavily appealed to Senator Walter Mondale, a Democrat from Minnesota, and Senator Edward Brooke, a Republican from Massachusetts. Mitchell negotiated with Mondale and Brooke and encouraged them to offer a bipartisan amendment on fair housing.

The passage of the proposed fair-housing law was so enormously controversial that there was a filibuster in the Senate to block the bill. While the Senate engaged in a filibuster to defeat the proposed fair-housing law, President Johnson established the National Advisory Commission on Civil Disorders to study and report on the urban riots of the 1960s. The commission was chaired by Otto Kerner, who had formerly served as governor of Illinois. The National Advisory Commission on Civil Disorders was assembled for the purpose of investigating ways in which municipal governing institutions could decrease and alleviate depressed urban living conditions. The Advisory Commission investigated twenty cities throughout the United States that experienced disturbances and riots in 1967. The commission released its report on March 1, 1968, and concluded in its report that the United States was moving toward "two separate societies, one Black and one White, separate and unequal." The report also detailed problems associated with residential segregation and the formation of racial slums as an underlying factor of social unrest in the United States in the mid- and late 1960s. The report also made a connection between racial segregation in housing and segregation in schools.

On March 4, 1968, three days after the findings of the Kerner Commission were made public, the Senate broke its filibuster against the fair-housing legislation. The controversy and debate over fair-housing legislation represented only the eighth time in America's history that a filibuster was ended. On April 4, 1968, the Reverend Dr. Martin Luther King Jr. was assassinated. Riots broke out in black urban neighborhoods across the country. On April 10, 1968, with the country still in a state of mourning and crisis, the House passed the Senate version of the Civil Rights Act of 1968 by a vote of 250–172.

The Civil Rights Act of 1968 stipulates that individuals having experienced housing discrimination in leasing or renting, purchasing, or financing a purchase of a home of their choice are instructed to report infractions of the law to the U.S. Department of Housing and Urban Development. Upon investigating the discrimination claim, the U.S. Department of Housing and Urban Development will determine the validity of the claim. The agency informs the individual making the claim, and an administrative hearing is scheduled within 120 days. Violations of the fair-housing law are enforced through civil litigation in federal and state courts by either the U.S. attorney general or the U.S. secretary of housing and urban development. According to the U.S. Department of Housing and Urban Development, those who are found to have violated the law may receive penalties from approximately $10,000 for a first offense to $50,000 for subsequent violations of the law. Additionally, courts have the discretion to award additional punitive and actual damages to the plaintiff. The U.S. Department of Housing and Urban Development files and litigates the claim on behalf of the person who initiated the claim.

The Civil Rights Act of 1968 is significant in that it represented the first attempt by the U.S. government to remove residential housing obstacles erected solely on the basis of the race or ethnic background of a prospective lessee, tenant, or buyer in securing property. The act was heavily opposed prior to increased incidences of urban riots, which threatened the stability and order of American society. The Kerner Report, commissioned by President Johnson, gave credence to the seriousness and detrimental effects of housing discrimination in the United States. The report also identified additional ramifications that posed potential long-term threats to the development of the country. The Kerner Report of the National Advisory Commission on Civil Disorders, coupled with the assassination of Martin Luther King Jr. and urban unrest, created a sense of urgency in enacting and implementing a federal housing policy that would protect the rights of blacks who wished to lease or purchase in nonblack neighborhoods. Because the 1968 act prohibited discrimination in housing based on race, color, or national origin, it set a precedent in public policy under which groups historically discriminated against in the United States could seek political redress. The act would be amended in 1974 to protect against gender based discrimination. In 1988, a significant amendment to the act was passed, and discrimination based on disability or family status was precluded. Thus the Civil Rights Act of 1968 is significant to all Americans because it helped eventually secure fair housing and equal opportunity for all persons despite their race, color, national origin, religion, sex, familial or marital status, or disability.

See also Civil Rights Act of 1964; Department of Housing and Urban Development; Fair Housing Amendments Act of 1988; Housing; Housing and Urban Development Act of 1968; Johnson, Lyndon Baines; Kerner Commission; King, Martin Luther, Jr.; National Association for the Advancement of Colored People; Riots, Economically and Racially Motivated; Voting Rights Act of 1965.

FURTHER READING: Civil Rights Act of 1968, Public Law 90-284, 42 U.S.C. §§ 3601–3639; Hahn, Harlan, 1970, "Civic Responses to Riots: A Reappraisal of the Kerner Commission Data," *Public Opinion Quarterly* 34, no. 1 (spring): 101–107; *Jones v. Alfred H. Mayer Co.*, 392 U.S. 409 (1968); Kennedy, Edward M., 1999, "Fair Housing—The Battle Goes On," *Cityscape: A Journal of Policy Development* 4, no. 3:19–20; U.S. Department of Housing and Urban Development, 2002, "Fair Housing—It's Your Right," www.hud.gov/offices/fheo/FHLaws/yourrights.cfm; U.S. National Advisory Commission, 1968, *Report of the National Advisory Commission on Civil Disorders*, Washington, DC: U.S. Government Printing Office; Yeater, Rosalind, 2002, "Historical Look at Fair Housing in America," www.metrokc.gov/dias/ocre/history.htm.

LA TRICE M. WASHINGTON

Civil Rights Act of 1991

The Civil Rights Act of 1991 amended federal laws against employment discrimination and was designed to strengthen the protections and prohibitions against discrimination in the workplace, as well as to respond to the 1989 Supreme Court decision in *Wards Cove Packing Co. v. Atonio*, 490 U.S. 642 (1989). President George

H. Bush signed the act into law on November 21, 1991. This act significantly altered two federal antidiscrimination laws, the Civil Rights Act of 1964 and the Rehabilitation Act of 1973. In total, the laws amended by the act included, in major or minor part, the Civil Rights Act of 1964, section 1981 of the Civil Rights Act of 1866, the Americans with Disabilities Act of 1990, the Age Discrimination in Employment Act of 1967, the Attorney's Fees Awards Act of 1976, and the Rehabilitation Act of 1973. The act also reversed, in whole or in part, several U.S. Supreme Court decisions handed down in 1989 and 1991 that arguably were unfavorable to the rights of persons protected by these laws. The act also provided additional protections to employees and provided some additional remedies. Finally, the act provided further rules and protections for employees in the implementation of affirmative action programs under Title VII of the Civil Rights Act of 1964.

While the full scope of the changes to civil rights legislation is beyond the scope of this entry, several provisions of importance should be noted. Specifically, the act includes modifications of pre-1991 law pertaining to damages available to the plaintiff, availability of jury trials in some cases, burden-of-proof rules in discrimination cases, Title VII protection of U.S. citizens working abroad, compensation for expert-witness and attorney fees in meritorious cases, changes to the "business necessity" doctrine, posthiring discrimination rules, statutes of limitations for suits challenging seniority systems, mixed-motive cases, and the "race norming" of test scores.

In terms of damages available to the plaintiff, the act expanded rules for potential compensation and damages under Title VII of the Civil Rights Act of 1964. The act authorized compensatory damages (i.e., damages that compensate the plaintiff for injuries suffered) and punitive damages (i.e., damages that punish the wrongdoer) in cases of intentional discrimination, provided the plaintiff cannot recover damages under section 1981. However, Title VII does not authorize punitive damages against government entities. Such damages are in addition to relief previously available under Title VII (back pay, reinstatement, and other appropriate equitable relief). The act also placed a cap on compensatory damages (for future pecuniary losses and nonpecuniary losses) and punitive damages available depending on the size of the employer (i.e., the number of employees). The act also provided for the possibility of jury trials for the first time in Title VII cases by providing that a plaintiff seeking compensatory and punitive damages can demand a jury trial in Title VII cases. Thus the right of jury trial under Title VII is only available in those cases seeking compensatory or punitive damages. Prior to the act, juries were not available in Title VII cases.

The act also significantly reinstated the shifting burden-of-proof requirements in disparate impact cases established by the Supreme Court in *Griggs v. Duke Power Co.*, 401 U.S. 424 (1971), that were modified by the Court in *Wards Cove Packing Co. v. Atonio* (1989). The *Wards Cove* decision required that plaintiffs alleging that an employment practice had a disparate impact on a protected group(s) demonstrate that the challenged practice or action caused a manifest racial or gender statistical imbalance in the workforce. Where a plaintiff demonstrated this manifest imbalance, the Court allowed the employer to rebut the demonstration by providing a legitimate business justification for the practice or action. Before *Wards Cove*, the Supreme Court had held in the 1971 case of *Griggs v. Duke Power*

Co. that to rebut the demonstration of a statistical imbalance, the employer had to demonstrate that the practice or action was required by "business necessity," a much more difficult task. The 1991 act revived the pre–*Wards Cove* rule that a practice or action that results in a disparate impact on a protected class(es) violates the act unless the employer can prove that it is justified by business necessity.

The act permitted section 1981 race and national origin discrimination suits to be filed directly in federal court without exhausting Equal Employment Opportunity Commission (EEOC) procedures. It provided further that such suits may be tried before a jury, and that unlimited compensatory and punitive damages can be sought if the claim involves intentional discrimination. The act also reversed the Supreme Court's holding in *Patterson v. McLean Credit Union,* 491 U.S. 164 (1989), which held that section 1981 barred racial discrimination in hiring and (at times) promotion, but not in posthiring employer actions (e.g., harassment). Section 101(b) of the 1991 act specifically provided that the section 1981 prohibition against discrimination in the making and enforcing of contracts "includes the making, performance, modification, and termination of contracts, and the enjoyment of all benefits, privileges, terms, and conditions of the contractual relationship." Section 1981 does not apply to the federal government.

The act provided that Title VII protection would extend to U.S. citizens working abroad for U.S. companies. This provision reversed, in part, *EEOC v. Arabian American Oil Co.*, 111 S. Ct. 1227 (1991), in which the Supreme Court held that Title VII did not apply extraterritorially to protect such employees. The act also responded to the Supreme Court's ruling in *Martin v. Wilks,* 490 U.S. 755 (1989). In *Martin v. Wilks,* the Supreme Court ruled that white workers could challenge race-conscious promotion decisions alleged to be required by a consent decree, even though the workers were not parties. Section 108 of the 1991 act responded to this decision by providing that consent decrees could not be challenged by (*a*) persons who had actual notice of the order/judgment and a reasonable opportunity to be heard prior to the order/judgment and (*b*) those who had a reasonable opportunity to object to the order/judgment, or "whose interests were adequately represented by another person who had previously challenged the judgment or order on the same legal grounds and with a similar factual situation, unless there has been an intervening change in law or fact."

Expert-witness fees, attorney fees, and statute-of-limitations rules were also changed by the act. First, regarding expert-witness and attorney fees, the act specifically provided that attorney fees could be recovered in a suit seeking damages for intentional discrimination. It also permitted prevailing plaintiffs to recover expert-witness fees. Second, regarding the statute of limitations, in *Lorance v. AT&T Technologies, Inc.* 490 U.S. 900 (1989), the Supreme Court indicated that the statute of limitations on a complaint based on an allegedly discriminatory seniority system began to run when the system was adopted. The 1991 act changed this interpretation of the statute-of-limitations period of Title VII. Specifically, the act permitted employees to challenge a seniority system (e.g., vacation, tiered wage scales) when it affects them (e.g., when application of the system injures them or when they become subject to it). Thus the statute-of-limitations period does not necessarily begin when the system is adopted. The act also amended the Age Discrimination in Employment Act by requiring that a suit be filed within ninety days of the receipt of notice of the EEOC's determination on the charge.

In mixed-motive cases (where there are both a legitimate business reason and an illegal discriminatory reason for the employment action), the act again reversed in part a 1989 Supreme Court case. In mixed-motive cases, the act provided that intentional discrimination is unlawful even if the employer can show that the same action would have occurred despite the discriminatory motive. However, the act imposed limits on remedies. This reversed, in part, *Price Waterhouse v. Hopkins*, 490 U.S. 228 (1989), which held that liability under Title VII could be avoided if the employer showed that the employer would have taken the same action for legitimate business reasons. Finally, in what is sometimes described as "race norming" of employment tests, the act prohibited adjusting scores on employment tests (e.g., cutoff scores or changing results) on the basis of race, color, religion, sex, or national origin (section 106).

See also Bush, George Herbert Walker; Civil Rights Act of 1866; Civil Rights Act of 1964; Disparate Treatment and Disparate Impact; Equal Employment Opportunity Commission; Employment (Private) and Affirmative Action; Employment (Public) and Affirmative Action; *Griggs v. Duke Power Co.*; *Lorance v. AT&T Technologies, Inc.*; Manifest Imbalance Standard; *Patterson v. McLean Credit Union; Price Waterhouse v. Hopkins*; Title VII of the Civil Rights Act of 1964; *Wards Cove Packing Co. v. Atonio.*

FURTHER READING: Davidson, Michael, 1992, "The Civil Rights Act of 1991," *Army Law* March: 3; Lindemann, Barbara, and Paul Grossman, 1996, *Employment Discrimination Law*, 3d ed., vols. 1 and 2, Chicago: American Bar Association; Munro, Don, 1995, "The Continuing Evolution of Affirmative Action under Title VII: New Directions after the Civil Rights Act of 1991," *Virginia Law Review* 81 (March): 565.

PAUL M. HARIDAKIS and RICHARD J. BENNETT

Civil Rights Cases, 109 U.S. 3 (1883)

On October 15, 1883, the Supreme Court declared sections 1 and 2 of the Civil Rights Act of 1875 unconstitutional and void in a ruling known as the *Civil Rights Cases.* Justice Joseph P. Bradley, speaking for an 8–1 majority, concluded that Congress lacked authority under either the Thirteenth Amendment or the Fourteenth Amendment to pass the Civil Rights Act. This decision was a monumental setback for early civil rights legislation and for racial equality in America.

The ruling was precipitated by four federal criminal indictments and one private suit in which a plaintiff sought damages under provisions of the Civil Rights Act of 1875. Congress passed this act to combat forced racial segregation under Jim Crow laws. Under section 1 of the act, all citizens of the United States, regardless of any previous condition of servitude, were guaranteed the right to "full and equal enjoyment of accommodations . . . of inns, public conveyances on land or water, theaters, and other places of public amusement." Section 2 imposed penalties on violators and gave victims of racial discrimination the right to file suit in federal court. In passing the civil rights legislation, Congress had cited its authority under the recently adopted Thirteenth and Fourteenth Amendments, which authorized Congress to enforce the provisions of each amendment "by appropriate legislation."

Although the Republican-dominated Supreme Court that heard the *Civil Rights*

Cases was generally sympathetic to the nationalizing effects of the Civil War Amendments, it was reluctant to tamper with some aspects of traditional federalism. Justice Bradley, the Grant appointee who wrote the Court's majority opinion, was a good example of this reluctance. Although hesitant to nationalize race relations, this learned man from humble origins harbored nationalistic views. For example, fearing state invasion of property rights, he dissented when the Court initially limited the scope of the Fourteenth Amendment by a 5–4 ruling in the famous *Slaughterhouse Cases*, 83 U.S. (16 Wall.) 36 (1873), that it only protected federal privileges and immunities. As a result of *Slaughterhouse*, the protection of most civil rights and liberties resided in the hands of the states, and their failure to provide such protection strengthened the demand for civil rights legislation like the Civil Rights Act of 1875. The specific failures that gave rise to the *Civil Rights Cases* surfaced in the states of New York, Kansas, Missouri, California, and Tennessee.

In ruling on the Civil Rights Act of 1875, however, the Supreme Court held that the act exceeded Congress's legislative power under the Fourteenth Amendment by usurping the authority to govern individuals that belonged properly to the states. Also, the Court held that the Thirteenth Amendment's abolition of slavery did not include the right to equal accommodation because such rights did not constitute "badges" of slavery or support the institution of slavery as commonly understood. The Court's opinion addressed only Congress's authority to pass the act and sidestepped the larger question of whether equal enjoyment of public accommodations is itself a constitutional right.

The majority interpreted the Fourteenth Amendment to limit only "State action." "Individual invasion of individual rights," they contended, "is not the subject-matter of the amendment." When states abridged privileges and immunities, deprived a person of life, liberty, or property without due process of law, or denied equal protection of the laws, Congress was empowered to enact remedial legislation, addressing the shortcomings of state action. Thus congressional power under the Fourteenth Amendment was reactive, not direct, must respond to a state action, and could not regulate individual state citizens. Congress was not empowered to pass general laws that supplanted the power granted to states by the Tenth Amendment to pass laws governing "the conduct of individuals in society towards each other." In brief, Congress could redress "adverse State legislation," but not "private wrongs," as the act sought to do.

The majority also examined the authority of Congress under the Thirteenth Amendment's abolition of slavery. While, Congress might pass direct legislation to prevent the institution of slavery under this amendment, the Court held that the denial of equal accommodation because of race imposed no "badge" of slavery and was thus outside the scope of the Thirteenth Amendment. The Thirteenth Amendment protected only "fundamental rights which appertain to the essence of citizenship, and the enjoyment or deprivation of which constitutes the essential distinction between freedom and slavery." It did not extend to individual relations between citizens such as those proscribed by the Civil Rights Act of 1875.

Thus, in the Court's view, the Civil Rights Act of 1875 was incompatible with the precise intention of the Thirteenth and Fourteenth Amendments. While the Thirteenth Amendment prohibited slavery, it was not intended to right all wrongs. The Fourteenth Amendment existed to ensure that citizens enjoyed equal protection of the laws, but only by protecting against state laws. The Court asserted that even if equal accommodations were rights under the Fourteenth Amendment, Congress's authority to protect them was limited to corrective legislation in response to adverse state legislation. Individuals must look to state law for redress in the face of private discrimination. The Civil Rights Act of 1875 unconstitutionally circumvented state law by regulating private wrongs, and in the Court's opinion, was not supported by the Thirteenth or Fourteenth Amendments.

In the case's single and somewhat prophetic dissent, Justice John Marshall Harlan voiced support for the Civil Rights Act under his alternative interpretation of the Thirteenth and Fourteenth Amendments. Appealing to precedent, Harlan, a southern aristocrat and former slave owner, pointed to the Court's upholding of the Fugitive Slave Law of 1793 in *Prigg v. Commonwealth of Pennsylvania,* 16 Pet. 539 (1842), and the Fugitive Slave Law of 1850 in *Ableman v. Booth,* 21 How. 506 (1859), in which the majority affirmed Congress's authority to compel individuals within the states to assist in retrieving fugitive slaves, regardless of state law. Justice Harlan later asserted that the framers of the Thirteenth Amendment gave Congress similar authority to uproot the institution of slavery by any legislation it deemed appropriate so that it need not rely on hostile state governments to protect civil liberties, and to allow for the eradication of all "badges" of slavery, including unequal accommodation. Furthermore, in *Munn v. State of Illinois,* 94 U.S. 113 (1877), the Court ruled that "property does become clothed with a public interest when used in a manner to make it of public consequence and affect the community at large" (*Munn,* 126). Thus, Harlan concluded, in his dissenting opinion in the *Civil Rights Cases* that corporations and individuals "in the exercise of quasi public employment," such as railroad workers or innkeepers, had a duty to enforce the universal freedom declared in the Thirteenth Amendment and were bound to respect the provisions of the act.

Harlan further noted that the Fourteenth Amendment was the "first instance in our history of the investiture of Congress with affirmative power, by legislation, to enforce an express prohibition upon the States." This was necessary, he argued, because the Fourteenth Amendment sought to secure freedom from race discrimination as a national right. Thus the duty to enforce it belonged to the national government rather than the states. Therefore, the majority's conclusions that (1) Congress could not act except in response to state law under the Fourteenth Amendment, and (2) that Congress could not regulate the relationship between citizens under the Thirteenth Amendment, were unauthorized both by the language of the amendments and by the precedent established in *Prigg* and *Ableman.* Whereas, in the past, Congress had been permitted to enforce the constitutional right of slavery with strict laws operating upon individuals, the current interpretation of the Fourteenth Amendment would paradoxically deny Congress the power to enforce, by similar legislation, the essential rights of citizenship. Finally, Justice Harlan noted the majority's failure to consider the applicability of the Interstate Commerce Clause of Article 1 of the Constitution in the current case. In his mind, the Court, as it had done in past cases, could have upheld the Civil Rights Act under Congress's Commerce Clause power despite the act's silence on the provision.

The precedent established by this case was affirmed thirteen years later in *Plessy v. Ferguson,* 163 U.S. 537 (1896), in which the Court upheld a Louisiana law that mandated racially segregated railroad transportation. Speaking for the majority, Justice Henry B. Brown restated the Court's belief that racial discrimination in public accommodations constituted no "badge" of slavery in violation of the Thirteenth Amendment. Again in dissent, Justice Harlan reaffirmed his belief articulated in this case that such discrimination violated both the Thirteenth and Fourteenth Amendments.

This decision severely limited the federal government's power to protect civil rights and discouraged Congress from enacting any further civil rights legislation until 1957. Although laws against discrimination later proliferated, the *Civil Rights Cases* have never been formally reversed. States eventually outlawed racial discrimination, even though the federal government was unable to force them to do so under the Fourteenth Amendment. Moreover, Congress found an effective weapon in the Interstate Commerce Clause. Using that clause, Congress enacted Title II of the Civil Rights Act of 1964 to outlaw discrimination in public accommodations. The Court upheld that law in *Heart of Atlanta Motel v. United States*, 379 U.S. 241 (1964), and *Katzenbach v. McClung*, 379 U.S. 294 (1964). Because of these developments, most federal affirmative action statutes regulating private conduct are based on the Interstate Commerce Clause rather than the Fourteenth Amendment.

See also Civil Rights Act of 1875; Civil Rights Act of 1964; Civil War (Reconstruction) Amendments and Civil Rights Acts; Federalism; Fourteenth Amendment; Jim Crow Laws; *Plessy v. Ferguson*; Slavery; State Action Doctrine; Thirteenth Amendment.

FURTHER READING: Engelman Lado, Marianne L., 1995, "African-American Legal Perspectives on the 1883 *Civil Rights Cases*," *Chicago-Kent Law Review* 70:1123–1195; Lurie, Jonathan, 2001, "Civil Rights or Last Rites?" in *Historic U.S. Court Cases: An Encyclopedia*, 2d ed., edited by John W. Johnson, New York: Routledge; McPherson, James M., 1965, "Abolitionists and the Civil Rights Act of 1875," *Journal of American History* 52:493–510; Westin, Alan F., 1962, "The Case of the Prejudiced Doorkeeper," in *Quarrels That Have Shaped the Constitution*, edited by John Garraty, New York: Harper and Row; Wyatt-Brown, Bertram, 1965, "The Civil Rights Act of 1875," *Western Political Quarterly* 18:763–775.

CARLTON MORSE and DAVID L. WEEKS

Civil Rights Movement

In the most proper sense, the civil rights movement refers to the political, legal, and social movement that took place throughout the United States in the 1950s and 1960s in the effort to end segregation and unequal treatment of blacks. In the broader sense, the civil rights movement can be described as an organizational, group, and personal struggle for the empowerment of the oppressed sections of the U.S. population, notably African Americans and women. The civil rights movement is considered to be one of the monumental chapters or epochs in U.S. history, finally fulfilling the Jeffersonian declaration "that all men are created equal" and "that they are endowed by their Creator with certain unalienable rights; that among these rights are life, liberty, and the pursuit of happiness." This democratic document, the Declaration of Independence, which formed the creed of the American Revolution, was also to serve as the ideological basis of the civil rights movement.

As will be discussed more fully later, while the civil rights movement achieved monumental victories, such as the Civil Rights Act of 1964, the Voting Rights Act of 1965, and *Brown v. Board of Education,* 347 U.S. 483 (1954), many in society also viewed the civil rights movement as not achieving full and true equality in society. The notion was that more aggressive measures were needed to augment the existing antidiscrimination laws that were ushered in during the civil rights movement. Thus the idea of affirmative action programs is both a natural development and a continuation of the struggle through other means. That is, affirmative action helps to right the historic wrongs that the civil rights movement set out to address, and to expunge from the U.S. body politic and, indeed, the fabric of society historic injustice and racial discrimination. The women's rights movement was an offspring of the civil rights movement.

The heritage and history of the civil rights movement can be traced back to the earliest days of the Republic, when a segment of men and women in society clamored for equal rights for minorities and women. The U.S. landscape was marked with enormous civil rights struggles at both individual and group levels for more than 200 years. The leaders of the civil rights movement in America certainly had inspiration from the early leaders in this area. For example, as far back as 1787, Abigail Adams wrote to her husband, John Adams, in Philadelphia, at the Constitutional Convention, calling for gender equality and asking that the "code of laws" for the new nation "be more generous" to ladies by not putting "unlimited power in the hands of husbands." She warned that they would not hold themselves "bound to obey the laws in which we have no voice or representation." Likewise, the work of the abolitionists was essential in the goal of eventual racial equality in the United States. Thus the lives and work of men and women such as John P. Hale, Benjamin Wade, Charles Sumner, Salmon Chase, Harriet Beecher Stowe, William Lloyd Garrison, and others are worthy of mention. Additionally, the suffrage movement of the early twentieth century was a source of inspiration for the modern civil rights movement. The leading women suffragettes and their male supporters also paved the way for the modern movement, individuals like Susan B. Anthony, Lucretia Mott, Elizabeth Cady Stanton, Lucy Stone, James Mott, Henry Stanton, Henry Blackwell, Frederick Douglass, Wendell Phillips, and Horace Greeley.

The modern civil rights movement is normally dated from the seminal case *Brown v. Board of Education.* The *Brown* decision is considered by many to be the watershed event in the modern civil rights movement because the ruling, which ordered desegregation in public schools, marked the beginning of the movement as a mass and well-coordinated effort. It was from this point that individual and isolated group civil rights protests and agitation were galvanized into a movement cutting across gender and racial lines. The principal organizations in the vanguard of the civil rights movement were the National Association for the Advancement of Colored People (NAACP), the National Urban League, and the Southern Christian Leadership Conference (SCLC).

The NAACP, the Urban League, and the SCLC formed a common front in the fight for equality. The NAACP, a biracial group founded in 1909, worked to put an end to extrajudicial killings (lynchings), promoted school integration, and advocated laws for fair practices in employment and housing. Through the use of publicity, lobbying, and legal action in the early to mid-1900s, the NAACP, led by its executive secretary, Roy Wilkins, slowly chiselled away at the pernicious doctrine of segregation. The NAACP was chiefly responsible for the victory in the *Brown* case. The Urban League, also a biracial group founded in 1910, endeavored to better facilities for blacks in health, housing, employment, and recreation. The SCLC, founded in 1957, opposed discrimination in the use of public facilities, in employment, and in voting.

The leading spirit and first president of the SCLC, and one of the fathers of the civil rights movement, was the Reverend Martin Luther King. King, who was inspired by Henry David Thoreau's essay "Civil Disobedience" and Mahatma Gandhi's use of passive resistance against British rule in India, adopted the practice of nonviolent resistance and protest, a theme that would largely embody the civil rights movement. King led peaceful, nonviolent demonstrations against racial injustice. In 1964, King was awarded the Nobel Peace Prize in recognition of his efforts in the promotion of nonviolence. However, it should be noted that there were other splinter organizations within the civil rights movement that did not adopt King's peaceful nonviolent resistance approach and did not adhere to King's goal of integration, including groups such as Elijah Muhammad's Black Muslims, Malcolm X's Black Muslims splinter group, and the Black Panthers.

The series of events that culminated in the enactment of the Civil Rights Act of 1964 began when Rosa Parks said her firm and profoundly significant "No" in 1955 in Montgomery, Alabama, in response to a bus driver's order to give up her seat to a white rider. She was arrested and charged with violation of a city ordinance. In the wake of her arrest, the local chapter of the NAACP, assisted by ministers and other prominent blacks, organized a boycott of the city's buses that lasted for more than one year and ended only when the Supreme Court affirmed a lower court ruling that segregation on the buses was unconstitutional. Next in the progression of the civil rights movement was the crisis at Central High School in Little Rock, Arkansas, in 1957. The battle at Central High School was over integration of the school and specifically in respect to the attendance of nine blacks, including Elizabeth Eckford, who was taunted by a hostile crowd on her way to the school. The opposition from Arkansas governor Orval Faubus compelled President Dwight Eisenhower to send in federal troops to escort the blacks to school. As harassment continued all year, schools were closed for the next year, waiting for the working out of a new plan.

In 1960, black students formed the Student Nonviolent Coordinating Committee (SNCC) and engaged in sit-ins in Nashville, Tennessee. Violence, arrests, jailing of individuals, and the bombing of a black lawyer's house ensued. Presidential candidate John F. Kennedy put aside advice not to inflame white southern voters and gave public support to the sit-ins. Also, in 1961, James Farmer, director of the Congress of Racial Equality (CORE), left Washington in two buses in May with some freedom riders, planning to challenge segregation practices along the way to New Orleans, Louisiana. They were attacked in Rock Hill in South Carolina and Anniston in Alabama and jailed without violence in Jackson, Mississippi for breaking state segregation laws.

In 1963, demonstrations again led to confrontation. There was a bloody riot in Mississippi over the admission of James Meredith to the state university, occasioning two deaths. In Jackson, Mississippi, in June 1963, the NAACP's Medgar Wiley Evers was shot in the back and murdered on his doorstep. The killer, Byron de

Several rows of civil rights activists, many holding hands, march down Chicago's Balboa Drive in 1965 to protest school segregation. Courtesy of Library of Congress.

La Beckwith, would not be finally successfully prosecuted and convicted until February 5, 1994. In Birmingham, Alabama, Martin Luther King's SCLC intensified the pressure with protests in which marchers, including King himself, were often put in jail. Police under the leadership of Eugene "Bull" Connor chased protesters with dogs and knocked down scores of demonstrators with water pumped through hoses. More than 900 children were hauled into prison in school buses for defying local laws.

The March on Washington in 1963 as well as the assassination of President John F. Kennedy prepared the final stage for the enactment of the 1964 Civil Rights Act. Between *Brown* and the eventual Civil Rights Act of 1964, there were some modest successes in terms of federal legislation, namely, the Civil Rights Acts of 1957 and 1960. The Civil Rights Act of 1957 created the Civil Rights Division of the Justice Department and vested federal prosecutors with the authority to obtain court injunctions against those who interfered with the right to vote. The act also created the U.S. Commission on Civil Rights, vested with the authority to investigate discriminatory conditions and to recommend measures to correct discrimination. The Civil Rights Act of 1960 expanded civil rights enforcement in the South a bit more by enabling federal judges to appoint referees to hear complaints from individuals claiming that they were denied the right to vote or denied the right to register to vote by state officials.

As helpful as the Civil Rights Acts of 1957 and 1960 were to the civil rights movement, the Civil Rights Act of 1964 marked a turning point because of how expansive and sweeping its provisions were in regard to racial equality. The 1964 law importantly prohibited racial discrimination in all schools or other educational programs receiving public funding, prohibited discrimination in employment, and also prohibited discriminatory practices in public facilities and accommodations. Additionally, following swiftly on the heels of the Civil Rights Act of 1964 was the Voting Rights Act of 1965, which removed all literacy tests and other qualification tests. These landmark civil rights laws are a shining example of the success of the civil rights movement. However, in 1968, Martin Luther King was murdered in Memphis, Tennessee, where he went to lead a protest march for striking sanitation workers. For many, the civil rights movement ended with King's death.

As the maxim goes, no epoch in history shall be considered closed as long as historians live, and every interpretation is subject to reinterpretation in the light of new evidence. In view of this maxim, it is pertinent to briefly analyze the legacy of the civil rights movement. The movement certainly accomplished great things, but many suggest that it fell short of achieving true equality, hence the need for aggressive social programs like affirmative action. For example, one author writes that blacks are discontented despite the advances of the civil rights movement:

> Despite some improvement in their conditions, many blacks remain discontented. They assert that not enough is being done to dispel white-majority racial prejudice: blacks are frustrated by white ethnocentrism, or the emotional attitude that whites are superior to black people; blacks are also frustrated by white xenophobia or the fear of black people as strange and different. Blacks also complain that communities are making slow progress in integrating schools and enrolling black voters. . . . Proportionately fewer black than white students gain high school and college education. . . . Blacks are concentrated in low-wage occupations. A disproportionately large number of blacks work as unskilled laborers and service workers. . . . Blacks suffer twice the unemployment rate of white workers. . . . Many blacks are confined to slum areas and have no access to decent housing in better neighborhoods. . . . Blacks have on average a life expectancy of 64 years as compared to 71 years for whites. (Gordon 1980, 120)

These feelings translate into a belief that the government ought to do more to rectify these problems, such as the implementation of affirmative action programs.

However, opponents of affirmative action often argue that the use of racial preferences in modern affirmative action programs is antithetical to the goal of the civil rights movement, namely, achieving a color-blind society. Opponents claim that race-conscious programs reversely discriminate and violate the same civil rights laws (e.g., Title VII of the Civil Rights Act of 1964) that many struggled so long and hard to achieve. This is the American dilemma: how to recover lost ground for those who were long denied the American dream and maintain equality and race neutrality by the same stroke; how to implement an affirmative action–type program without engendering a feeling of being discriminated against whites and of being condescended to and treated as inferior in minorities and women; indeed, how to strike a balance between merit and concession; and how to ensure the maintenance of "certain unalienable rights; that among these are life, liberty and the pursuit of happiness"—the very noble principles upon which the nation was founded on July 4, 1776.

See also Abolitionists; Anthony, Susan Brownell; Articles of Confederation; Black Panther Party; *Brown v. Board of Education*; Civil Rights Act of 1957; Civil Rights Act of 1960; Civil Rights Act of 1964; Color-Blind Constitution; Congress of Racial

Equality; Constitution, Civil Rights, and Equality; Declaration of Independence and Equality; Douglass, Frederick; Eisenhower, Dwight David; Ethnocentrism; Farmer, James; Kennedy, John Fitzgerald; King, Martin Luther, Jr.; Mott, Lucretia Coffin; National Association for the Advancement of Colored People; Southern Christian Leadership Conference; Stanton, Elizabeth Cady; Stone, Lucy; Title VII of the Civil Rights Act of 1964; Urban League; Voting Rights Act of 1965; White Supremacy; Xenophobia.

FURTHER READING: Chafe, William H., 1987, "Women and American Society," in *Making America: The Society and Culture of the United States*, edited by Luther S. Luedtke, 258–269, Washington, DC: U.S. Information Agency; Frazier, Thomas R., ed. 1970, *Afro-American History: Primary Sources*, New York: Harcourt, Brace and World; Gordon, Irving L., 1980, *American Studies: A Conceptual Approach*, New York: Amsco School Publications; Hall, Jacquelyn David, 2001, "Mobilizing Memory: Broadening Our View of the Civil-Rights Movement," *Chronicle of Higher Education*, July 27, B7–B11; Sitkoff, Harvard, 1981, *The Struggle for Black Equality, 1954–1980*, New York: Hill and Wang.

PAUL OBIYO MBANASO NJEMANZE

Civil Rights Restoration Act of 1988

The Civil Rights Restoration Act of 1988 was enacted by Congress over President Ronald Reagan's veto to negate the U.S. Supreme Court's ruling in *Grove City College v. Bell*, 465 U.S. 555 (1984). In that case, the Supreme Court held that educational institutions receiving federal financial assistance were required to abide by federal civil rights statutes (Title IX of the Education Amendments of 1972, Title IV of the Civil Rights Act of 1964, section 504 of the Rehabilitation Act of 1973, and the Age Discrimination Act of 1964) only in those programs for which they directly received federal funds.

In *Grove City*, the Supreme Court held that where the federal assistance consisted of Basic Education Opportunity Grants (now known as Pell Grants), only the school's financial aid program, not the entire institution, was to be subject to the federal antidiscrimination statutes. Programs that did not receive federal funds were free to discriminate, substantially narrowing the scope of enforcement of federal antidiscrimination statutes and Title IX specifically. During the Nixon (1969–1974), Ford (1974–1977), and Carter (1977–1981) administrations, the U.S. Department of Education (and its predecessor, the Department of Health, Education, and Welfare) had interpreted the statutes to require "institution-wide" compliance.

The Court's decision had a significant impact on colleges and universities, notably because of Title IX of the Education Amendments of 1972, which prohibited sex discrimination in educational institutions that received federal funds. Title IX had been the catalyst for the introduction of interscholastic and intercollegiate athletics for female students. Since these programs did not directly receive aid, the *Grove City* decision essentially ended Title IX's application to athletics. As a result of the *Grove City* decision, the Department of Education closed or narrowed 800 pending discrimination cases.

The bill that became the Civil Rights Restoration Act was first introduced by Senator Edward M. Kennedy of Massachusetts in 1985. However, the bill languished until the Democrats regained control of the U.S. Senate in the 1986 elections. The Civil Rights Restoration Act (introduced as S. 557 in 1987 by fifty-eight senators) negated *Grove City* by requiring that the statutes be applied to entire institutions (including state and local governments) if any part of those organizations received federal assistance.

As Leon Friedman noted in 2001, the legislative history of the statute stated that "certain aspects of recent decisions and opinions of the Supreme Court have unduly narrowed or cast doubt upon" a number of civil rights laws, and that "legislative action is necessary to restore the prior consistent and long-standing executive branch interpretations" of those laws. President Reagan vetoed this legislation because he believed that it interfered with the free exercise of religion. The legislation's supporters argued that religious institutions would continue to be free to operate without federal interference as long as they did not accept federal funding. Rather, the legislation, they contended, would ensure that federal funds would not be used to subsidize discrimination.

The law mandates that federal aid recipients, subrecipients, and contractors prevent discrimination and ensure nondiscrimination in all of their activities, whether those activities receive federal funds or not. This effort to prevent discrimination must address the program's impacts, access, benefits, participation, treatment, services, contracting opportunities, training opportunities, investigation of complaints, allocation of funds, and the prioritization of projects.

The most significant effect of the legislation has been in higher education, specifically intercollegiate athletics. In 1971–1972, women comprised 15 percent of college athletes; in 1997–1998, women accounted for 40 percent of the student-athletes in Division I (scholarship-granting) athletic programs.

See also Carter, James "Jimmy" Earl, Jr.; Civil Rights Act of 1964; Department of Education; Ford, Gerald Rudolph; *Grove City College v. Bell*; Nixon, Richard Milhous; Reagan, Ronald; Rehabilitation Act of 1973; Title IX of the Education Amendments of 1972.

FURTHER READING: Bryjak, George J., 2000, "The Ongoing Controversy over Title IX," *USA Today Magazine*, July, 62–64; Friedman, Leon, 2001, "Overruling the Court," *American Prospect* 12, no. 15 (August 27): 12–15; Marcus, Ruth, 1988, "Veto Override Turned Reagan's Court Victory into Major Loss," *Washington Post*, March 24, A4; Schultz, Jon S., 1989, *Legislative History and Analysis of the Civil Rights Restoration Act*, Littleton, CO: F.B. Rothman.

JEFFREY KRAUS

Civil Service Commission

The Civil Service Commission was created by the Pendleton Act in 1883 in an effort to aid reforms among the federal workforce. The commission was intended to be bipartisan and was tasked with overseeing the introduction of the merit system among government workers. The Civil Service Commission was also the principal agent for implementing affirmative action programs of various types involving the federal workforce over the years.

The 1883 Pendleton Act was designed to lessen the "spoils system" in government hiring and instead promote the establishment of a professional civil service. These goals were to be accomplished through the creation of entrance exams and promotion based on merit. The Civil Service Commission was created to oversee the implementation of the merit system and to serve as an advisory board to the president on the remaining patronage issues. The commission was responsible for overseeing entrance exams and providing lists of qualified applicants to agencies. Initially the commission was composed of three members and included such prominent politicians as future president Theodore Roosevelt (who served from 1889 to 1895).

Although the ultimate goals of the Civil Service Commission were neutrality in hiring practices and efficiency, employment preferences were accepted as a central component of the civil service. For instance, when the commission was created, there were existing preferences for hiring Civil War veterans. These preferences were institutionalized through the addition of points for veteran status on entrance exams. The commission oversaw the 1923 Classification Act that organized and created grades for all federal employees. The dramatic expansion of the federal workforce during the 1930s and World War II prompted increased political pressure on the administration of Franklin D. Roosevelt to expand civil service opportunities for African Americans. Roosevelt issued an executive order that banned discrimination by defense contractors in their federal hiring practices, but compliance was uneven even after the creation of the Fair Employment Practices Committee under the auspices of the Civil Service Commission.

The role of the Civil Service Commission in overseeing affirmative action programs expanded dramatically following President John F. Kennedy's Executive Order 10925 on affirmative action. Programs were further expanded under the Johnson and Nixon administrations to include other minority groups and women. As the scope of affirmative action programs was enlarged, the Civil Service Commission became the final arbiter for complaints and cases involving discrimination. In an effort to further reform the civil service, the 1978 Civil Service Reform Act abolished the Civil Service Commission and replaced it with two separate organizations: the Office of Personnel Management (OPM) and the Merit Systems Protection Board (MSPB). The reform came in response to criticisms that the Civil Service Commission acted too slowly and with inflexibility. The two new agencies divided responsibility for personnel decisions from merit considerations. The reform also created another agency, the Federal Labor Relations Authority, to deal with grievances over collective bargaining or other labor issues.

See also Civil Service Reform Act of 1978; Executive Order 10925; Johnson, Lyndon Baines; Kennedy, John Fitzgerald; Meritocracy; Nixon, Richard Milhous; Roosevelt, Franklin Delano; Veterans' Preferences.

FURTHER READING: Hoogenboom, Ari A., 1982, *Outlawing the Spoils: A History of the Civil Service Reform Movement, 1865–1883*, Westport, CT: Greenwood Press; Ingraham, Patricia Wallace, 1995, *The Foundation of Merit: Public Service in American Democracy*, Baltimore: Johns Hopkins University Press; Van Riper, Paul P., 1976, *History of the United States Civil Service*, Westport, CT: Greenwood Press.

TOM LANSFORD

Civil Service Reform Act of 1978

The Civil Service Reform Act of 1978, passed under President Jimmy Carter, established the most sweeping reforms in the federal civil service system since the Pendleton Act of 1883, which had previously created the long-standing Civil Service Commission. From 1883 until 1978, the Civil Service Commission was responsible for federal workforce selection issues and the implementation of various federal affirmative action programs. Under Title III of the Civil Service Reform Act of 1978, each federal agency was required to implement special recruitment programs to eliminate the underrepresentation of minorities and women in the federal workforce. The 1978 Civil Service Reform Act abolished the Civil Service Commission and replaced it with two separate organizations: the Office of Personnel Management (OPM) and the Merit Systems Protection Board (MSPB). Furthermore, the Equal Employment Opportunity Commission (EEOC) and the OPM were given responsibilities with respect to federal recruitment and affirmative action programs.

The purpose of the act was to "provide the people of the United States with a competent, honest, and productive federal workforce reflective of the nation's diversity, and to improve the quality of public service." Federal employees were guaranteed protection from agency reprisal when disclosing prohibited personnel practices and the use of unsound management practices. The act stipulated that "any employee who has authority to take, direct others to take, recommend or approve any personnel action" shall not discriminate "on the basis of race, color, religion, sex, or national origin" as prohibited under the Civil Rights Act of 1964. Discrimination is also forbidden on the basis of age, handicap, and marital status.

The act provided that it is the responsibility of the General Accounting Office to "conduct audits and reviews to assure compliance." The Merit Systems Protection Board, established by the act, hears and adjudicates cases and conducts special studies relating to the civil service. The act also established the Federal Labor Relations Authority (FLRA) as an independent agency to set and administer policies relating to federal labor-management relations and to resolve disputes. Prior to the passage of the civil service reform, labor relations in federal government employment were governed by presidential executive orders rather than by statute, which meant that policies and programs could be modified at the president's discretion and federal employees had no statutory protection of their right to join or organize labor unions.

See also Carter, James "Jimmy" Earl, Jr.; Civil Rights Act of 1964; Civil Service Commission; Discrimination; Employment (Public) and Affirmative Action; Equal Employment Opportunity Commission; General Accounting Office.

FURTHER READING: Ingraham, Patricia W., and Carolyn Ban, eds., 1984, *Legislating Bureaucratic Change: The Civil Service Reform Act of 1978*, Albany: State University of New York Press; Pfiffner, James P., and Douglas A. Brook, eds., 2000, *The Future of Merit: Twenty Years after the Civil Service Reform Act*, Washington, DC: Woodrow Wilson Center Press.

GLENN L. STARKS

Civil War

See American Civil War.

Civil War (Reconstruction) Amendments and Civil Rights Acts

Described by Thurgood Marshall as America's first affirmative action program, the Civil War/Reconstruction Amendments to the U.S. Constitution and the congressional civil rights enforcement statutes that followed in the wake of these amendments attempted to achieve legal equality among the races on a scale unparalleled in U.S. history. In the aftermath of the American Civil War in the middle to late nineteenth century, the Republican-led Congress endeavored to pass a series of constitutional amendments and civil rights acts that would abolish the institution of slavery and provide the legal framework by which to integrate the newly freed persons into American society. The Thirteenth Amendment abolished slavery, the Fourteenth Amendment provided citizenship to the freedmen and equal protection under the law, and the Fifteenth Amendment was designed to ensure voting rights. These amendments and various civil rights statutes initially failed to accomplish their objectives because of strong opposition from southern whites and the unwillingness of subsequent presidents and Congresses to provide enforcement mechanisms. As a result, patterns of racism and discrimination developed that perpetuated social and political inequality. Future efforts to redress these problems resulted in additional legislation and the development of affirmative action programs in the late twentieth century.

At the end of the Civil War, Republicans controlled Congress and most state governments. President Abraham Lincoln developed a relatively lenient reconstruction plan to reintegrate the Confederate states into the Union. However, following his assassination, Radical Republicans used their party's control of the federal and state governments to develop a more severe plan, mainly in an attempt to wrest control of the southern states away from the Democratic Party. The Radical Republicans were led by Senator Charles Sumner of Massachusetts, who was determined to bring about racial equality. Unfortunately, many of Sumner's more lofty goals were not supported by his fellow Radical Republicans, many of whom were mainly interested in punishing the Confederate states. Consequently, most of the Republican efforts were based more on political considerations than on any broad strategy to ensure full social integration. As a result, proposals for land redistribution or other economic aid for the newly freed persons only resulted in very limited programs, such as the Freedmen's Bureau.

The main obstacle for economic and political integration came from the former Confederate states: Following the Civil War, these states passed a series of laws, the black codes, that were designed to prevent African Americans from gaining full economic, social, or political equality. For instance, none of the former Confederate states passed legislation that would allow the newly freed persons the right to vote. Other restrictions included prohibitions on African Americans owning or possessing firearms. In addition, state and local governments in the South did little to protect the lives or property of African Americans from white supremacist groups such as the Ku Klux Klan. Congressional Republicans asserted that although the Thirteenth Amendment, ratified on December 6, 1865, had outlawed slavery in the United States, the black codes were an effort to force African Americans to remain a servile class.

Efforts to integrate African Americans were further undermined by the contentious relationship between President Andrew Johnson and Congress. Johnson's reconstruction plan was considered to be too moderate by the Radical Republicans. Meanwhile, the president liberally used his veto power in an effort to prevent the implementation of many of Congress's policies, including the 1866 veto of the bill to renew the Freedmen's Bureau. The congressional elections of 1866 gave the Radical Republicans control of the legislature with a veto-proof majority in both houses. Tensions between Congress and the president ultimately resulted in Johnson's impeachment in 1868, and the Senate came only one vote short of removing him from office. Nonetheless, from 1866 onward, the Radical Republicans were able to enact any legislation they chose.

This combination of impediments to equality created a two-track legislative process for the national government. Republicans were able to secure ratification of the three Civil War Amendments, but the formal implementation of the amendments required additional legislation, namely, the various civil rights acts that followed the ratification of the three Civil War/Reconstruction Amendments.

The first civil rights act was passed in March 1866. The measure was the precursor of the Fourteenth Amendment. It extended full citizenship to anyone born in the United States and called for full equality before the law for all citizens. The law also directed the president to use the nation's armed forces to enforce the act. Finally, the 1866 law provided that no person or individual acting under color of state action or authority should deprive any person of his or her rights guaranteed by law, a provision that is codified today at 42 U.S.C. § 1981. Johnson vetoed the legislation because he contended that it was unconstitutional. However, Congress overwhelmingly overrode the president's veto. Concerns over the legitimacy of the measure led to efforts to convert the major provisions of the first civil rights act into a constitutional amendment to ensure that the provisions would remain inviolate from subsequent acts of Congress or a declaration of the Supreme Court that the 1866 act was unconstitutional.

The measure that became the Fourteenth Amendment was initially known as the Omnibus Amendment. The amendment was ratified on July 9, 1868. Its main provisions extended citizenship to all people born or "naturalized" in the United States and guaranteed the equal protection of the law for all citizens. As such, it stated that all citizens were to be granted the same "privileges and immunities" and "due process." To ensure that Johnson did not show favoritism to former Confederates and that these same persons would not regain political power, the amendment also removed the pardon power of the president and forbade former Confederates from holding political or judicial office at the state or national level. The amendment further declared that if any state endeavored to prevent African Americans from voting, its congressional representation would be reduced in proportion to the number of citizens denied the ability to vote. The amendment precluded any payment of debts incurred by the Confederacy and any compensation for former slave owners because of the emancipation of slaves. Finally, the measure included the unusual step of vesting the enforcement power of the amendment in Congress instead of in the executive branch (another feature designed to prevent Johnson from diminishing the impact of the amendment).

In spite of Republican control of Congress and the state legislatures in the South, the presidential election of 1868 proved closer than most expected. Former Union general Ulysses S. Grant won the election by only 300,000 votes. Many Republicans considered the unexpected strength of the Democratic candidate, Horatio Seymour of New York, proof of the continuing disenfranchisement of African Americans in the South. To ensure voting rights, the Republicans initiated the Fifteenth Amendment, which was ratified on February 3, 1870. The amendment forbade discrimination in the voting context on account of race. That is, the Fifteenth Amendment prohibited states from depriving individuals of the right to vote on account of race or previous condition of servitude. For the former Confederate states to rejoin the Union, they had to ratify the Fourteenth and Fifteenth Amendments.

To ensure state compliance with the Fourteenth and Fifteenth Amendments, Congress passed a succession of civil rights bills designed to bolster the amendments. On May 31, 1870, Congress passed the Enforcement Act. This legislation provided specific criminal penalties for those who endeavored to prevent people from voting because of race. However, both northern and southern states began to enact legislation that effectively disenfranchised African Americans without using race as a criterion. The most common type of law was the poll tax, which imposed a fee before citizens could register to vote. Because of economic constraints faced by the newly freed persons, the poll tax proved to be one of the most widespread ways to circumvent the Fifteenth Amendment among both northern and southern states. Another example of this type of legislative impediment was the literacy test, which required applicants who were registering to vote to demonstrate their ability to read and write. Literacy tests took advantage of prohibitions against educating slaves and the fact that county voter registrars (who administered the tests) were almost universally white.

Groups such as the Ku Klux Klan (KKK) used violence and the threat of force to deprive African Americans of their Fourteenth Amendment rights to equal protection of the laws. Founded by former Confederate soldiers, the KKK was responsible for widespread lynching and less severe forms of intimidation against both former slaves and officials of the Reconstruction governments. The actions of the group prompted Congress to pass the 1872 Civil Rights Act, which was commonly known as the Anti–Ku Klux Klan Act. Under the terms of the new law, actions that were designed to deprive individuals of their rights or prevent equal protection were elevated to the status of federal crimes with specific penalties.

The Anti–Ku Klux Klan Act was followed by the most ambitious of the post–Civil War civil rights acts. Commonly known as the Second Civil Rights Act, the statute was enacted on March 1, 1875. The law forbade discrimination in public accommodations such as hotels or theaters. However, in the aftermath of the legislation came a series of Supreme Court decisions that essentially nullified all or most of the key elements of the civil rights acts and Fourteenth Amendment. For instance, in the *Slaughterhouse Cases*, 83 U.S. (16 Wall.) 36 (1873), the Supreme Court adopted a very narrow view of the Fourteenth Amendment that held that the federal government was not obligated to protect the privileges and immunities of the citizens of a state from actions by that state. More significantly, in the *Civil Rights Cases*, 109 U.S. 3 (1883), the Supreme Court rejected the 1875 Civil Rights Act and asserted that the Fourteenth Amendment was limited to official acts by a state government and could not be extended to include discriminatory acts by private citizens. In the end, the most substantial challenge to the intent of the amendments and legislation came in 1896 with the Supreme Court decision in *Plessy v. Ferguson*, 163 U.S. 537 (1896). This decision accepted that the doctrine of separate but equal was not in conflict with the Fourteenth Amendment's guarantee of equal protection. This provided the legal foundation for state-sponsored racial segregation throughout the country. The rise of segregation was facilitated by a new wave of discriminatory laws, known as the Jim Crow laws, that further eroded the efforts to develop legal and constitutional protections envisioned by the framers of the Civil War Amendments and acts.

See also Abolitionists; American Civil War; Civil Rights Act of 1866; Civil Rights Act of 1875; *Civil Rights Cases*; Equal Protection Clause; Fifteenth Amendment; Fourteenth Amendment; Freedmen's Bureau; Jim Crow Laws; Ku Klux Klan; Marshall, Thurgood; *Plessy v. Ferguson*; Segregation; Thirteenth Amendment.

FURTHER READING: Belz, Herman, 1976, *A New Birth of Freedom: The Republican Party and Freedmen's Rights, 1861 to 1866*, Westport, CT: Greenwood Press; Berger, Raoul, 1989, *The Fourteenth Amendment and the Bill of Rights*, Norman: University of Oklahoma Press; Curtis, Michael Kent, 1986, *No State Shall Abridge: The Fourteenth Amendment and the Bill of Rights*, Durham, NC: Duke University Press; Irons, Peter, 1999, *A People's History of the Supreme Court*, New York: Viking Press; Miller, Loren, 1966, *The Petitioners: The Story of the Supreme Court of the United States and the Negro*, New York: Pantheon Books; Woodward, C. Vann, 1957, *The Strange Career of Jim Crow*, New York: Oxford University Press.

TOM LANSFORD

Clark, Kenneth Bancroft (1914–)

Kenneth Bancroft Clark was an African American professor of psychology, an author, a social activist, and an entrepreneur whose work on the detrimental effects of racial segregation on blacks was important to the civil rights movement. His research on the detrimental effects of segregation on black schoolchildren was an important focal point in the ruling in *Brown v. Board of Education*, 347 U.S. 483 (1954), which ended racial segregation in public schools.

Clark was born on July 14, 1914, in the Panama Canal Zone, and at the age of five he and his mother moved to New York City. He earned a B.A. and an M.S. from Howard University and eventually graduated from Columbia University with a Ph.D. in experimental psychology, the first African American to earn that field's degree. At Columbia, Clark worked closely with Gunnar Myrdal, whose important book *An American Dilemma* (1944) examined the psychological effects of racial segregation. Clark went on to become the first permanent African American faculty member at the City University of New York (CUNY). During his years at CUNY, he published several books, including *Prejudice and Your Child* (1963), *Dark Ghetto: Dilemmas of Social Power* (1965), *The Negro American* (coauthored with Talcott Parsons, 1966), *Crisis in Urban Education* (1971), *A Possible Reality* (1972), *Pathos of Power* (1974), and *The American Revolution: Democratic Politics and Popular Education* (1974). In 1946, Clark helped found the Northside Center for Child Development in Harlem, in 1962, Harlem Youth Opportunities Unlimited, which was an outgrowth of Northside, and the Metropolitan Applied Research Center. He also helped establish Washington, D.C.,'s Joint Center for Political Studies, the only black think tank in existence at the time. In addition, Clark was a member of the New York State Board of Regents from 1966 to 1986 and was president of the American Psychological Association for a year, again the first African American to hold such a title. He was honored with journalism's Sidney Hillman Award for his book *Dark Ghetto*, earned the Spingarn Medal in 1961 from the National Association for the Advancement of Colored People (NAACP), and was awarded the Kurt Lewin Memorial Award in 1966 from the Society for Psychological Study of Social

Issues. Clark was also granted eight honorary degrees by various colleges and universities. After retiring from CUNY as professor emeritus, he formed the Kenneth B. Clark and Associates consulting firm, which specialized in affirmative action and race relations.

Clark testified at three of the four *Brown v. Board of Education* hearings on behalf of the NAACP. He presented to the Court his psychological study that demonstrated segregation's detrimental effects on the intellectual development of black children. In his study, Clark presented groups of black elementary-school children with two identical dolls, except that one was white and the other black. He then asked the children related questions that prompted them to identify, for example, which doll they liked best or would most like to play with; which doll looked like a white child; which doll looked like a colored child; which doll looked like a black child; which doll looked like them; which doll looked like the nice child; and which doll looked like the bad child. The test's results demonstrated that the majority of children identified the black doll in a negative fashion. Clark argued on the basis of these data that black children accepted negative stereotypes about their own racial group. Lawyers for the plaintiff then used the results as proof that segregation had contributed to feelings of racial inferiority and that as a result of these feelings children were less motivated to learn. Clark's testimony set off a heated debate over the validity of the study. Opponents claimed that the study and its conclusion were too vague and refused to view it as a professional scientific study. Lawyers on the plaintiff's side recognized the study's weakness, but still felt that it carried an important message that might help them earn a favorable ruling.

They were right. Clark's testimony was cited in a footnote in the ruling, and Chief Justice Earl Warren paraphrased Clark's findings when he stated that segregation "has a tendency to [retard] the educational and mental development of Negro children and to deprive them of some of the benefits they would receive in a racial[ly] integrated school system" (Cushman 1992, 368).

See also Brown v. Board of Education; Segregation; Warren Court and Affirmative Action.

FURTHER READING: Balfour, Lawrie, 2002, "Kenneth Bancroft Clark," http://www.africana.com; Beggs, Gordon, 1995, "Novel Expert Evidence in Federal Civil Rights Litigation," *American University Law Review* 45:2–75; Cushman, Robert F., 1992, *Leading Constitutional Decisions*, 18th ed., Englewood Cliffs, NJ: Prentice Hall.

JAYSON J. FUNKE

Class Identification

The study of class identification is based on Karl Marx's work, particularly on his concept of class consciousness. Marx was interested in identifying the conditions under which exploited people would become class conscious and rebel against those who exploited them. In Western societies, where people are less likely to take revolutionary paths, the study of class identification focuses on people's ability to place themselves within a class system and on identifying the meaning behind this placement, particularly as it reflects on individuals' lifestyles and life chances. Members of the upper class in the United States appear to be class conscious in that they are aware of one another and protective of their common interests. They are also less likely to support governmental attempts such as affirmative action policies and programs to address social problems such as occupational segregation.

Richard Centers (1949) was the first to measure class identification. Since then, studies have consistently shown that generally people have little difficulty placing themselves into a social class, and most place themselves either in the middle or the working class. Interestingly, in the United States, people seem to be unwilling to place themselves at either the top or the bottom of the class system (i.e., upper and lower classes). In addition, researchers have found a high correlation between occupation (i.e., mental versus manual labor) and the social class with which people identify. For instance, people who have blue-collar jobs (e.g., factory workers) usually place themselves in the working class, while those holding white-collar jobs (e.g., bank tellers) place themselves in the middle class. Also, differences by race and ethnicity have been observed: African Americans and Latinos are more likely to place themselves in the working class and whites in the middle class.

It appears that the significance of class identification lies in the social inequalities it reflects. People from different social classes have different lifestyles, which in turn affect their life chances. It was Max Weber who suggested that people with similar lifestyles tend to discriminate against others who are different. More recently, research has shown that people strongly prefer social contact with others within their own social class. These preferences can be observed in segregated neighborhoods around the country as well as in the workplaces of many Americans. Further, these preferences help explain, at least in part, the lack of representation of minority-group members in a variety of occupations, or occupational segregation. This type of segregation may stem from several factors, the most significant of which are rooted in racial/ethnic, gender, and social class differences.

See also African Americans; Class-Based Affirmative Action; Economically Disadvantaged; Hispanic Americans; Marxist Theory and Affirmative Action; Segregation; Weber, Max.

FURTHER READING: Centers, Richard, 1949, *The Psychology of Social Classes: A Study of Class Consciousness*, Princeton, NJ: Princeton University Press; Domhoff, G. William, 1990, *The Power Elite and the State: How Policy Is Made in America*, New York: Aldine de Gruyter; Dye, Thomas R., 1990, *Who's Running America? The Bush Era*, 5th ed., Englewood Cliffs, NJ: Prentice Hall; Heaton, Tim, 1987, "Objective Status and Class Consciousness," *Social Science Quarterly* 68 (September): 611–620; Jackman, Mary R., and Robert W. Jackman, 1983, *Class Awareness in the United States*, Berkeley: University of California Press; Robinson, Robert V., and Jonathan Kelley, 1979, "Class as Conceived by Marx and Dahrendorf: Effects on Income Inequality, Class Consciousness, and Class Conflict in the United States and Great Britain," *American Sociological Review* 44:38–58.

PAULINA X. RUF

Class-Based Affirmative Action

Is there an alternative to Justice Lewis Powell's opinion in *Regents of the University of California v. Bakke*, 438 U.S. 265 (1978), that ethnic diversity can be a factor in determining university admissions to have a diverse student body? One alternative to affirmative action measures based on race or gender to promote diversity is an approach called class-based or race-neutral affirmative action. The arguments for promoting class-based affirmative action are based on three underlying beliefs: first, race- or gender-based affirmative action fails because it subverts standards for merit and achievement in society; second, class-based affirmative action serves the "most deserving" members of society; and third, reliance on race-based affirmative action (and the practice of benign discrimination) discriminates against whites and therefore runs afoul of the Equal Protection Clause of the Fourteenth Amendment, whereby states are commanded to ensure that no citizen is deprived of the equal protection of the laws on account of race.

Class-based affirmative action is portrayed as a vehicle for improving the opportunities of the most disadvantaged in society by redistributing opportunity rather than expanding it. Specifically, the goal of class-based affirmative action is to recognize the talents of the disadvantaged despite the obstacles they face in developing and demonstrating their talents. How does it work? One must first assume that economic disadvantage limits the expression of talent by those persons located near the bottom of the social class structure. That is, a poor person will encounter more obstacles in his or her expression of talent than a middle-class person.

Second, one must assume that statistical measures, such as a standardized test, are reliable indicators of talent. Because economic disadvantage is closely linked with educational opportunity, persons located near the bottom of the social class structure are more likely to attend disadvantaged schools. That is, poor persons are more likely to attend schools lacking the educational resources necessary for increasing their chances of attaining a high score on standardized tests.

Given the preceding assumptions, consider the following scenario: Person A is considered to be economically disadvantaged. Person B is considered to be economically advantaged. Person B attains a higher score than person A on a standardized test used for college admission. According to the argument for class-based affirmative action, person A reflects more potential talent than person B, in light of the assumption that economic advantages correlate to higher test scores. Consequently, person A becomes a likely candidate for class-based affirmative action in order to level the economic playing field.

Critics of class-based affirmative action argue that focusing only on economic disadvantage is likely to benefit white persons more than minorities because there are numerically more white people than minorities in American society who can be classified as economically disadvantaged. As such, college campuses may become heterogeneous on the basis of social class at the cost of racial and ethnic diversity.

Supporters of class-based affirmative action argue that it increases the chances that economically disadvantaged minorities will be admitted to college. They also claim that race-based affirmative action results in economically advantaged minorities attending college. Focusing on economic disadvantage increases the chances that economically disadvantaged minority persons will benefit more than economically advantaged minority persons.

Finally, a generalized version of class-based affirmative action for college admissions has been implemented at the state level. California and Florida, for example, have implemented programs that guarantee admission to the state's public colleges and universities to students graduating at the top of their graduating class:

the top 4 percent in California for admission to the University of California and the top 20 percent in Florida for admission to the state's colleges and universities. Supporters of class-based affirmative action argue that these programs guarantee that talented minority students attending economically disadvantaged schools will attend college. Therefore, they argue that college campuses will be both racially and economically diverse.

See also Benign Discrimination; Economically Disadvantaged; Equal Protection Clause; Fourteenth Amendment; Gender-Based Affirmative Action; Meritocracy; Percentage Plans; Performance-Based Selections; Powell, Lewis Franklin, Jr.; Race-Based Affirmative Action; Race-Neutral Criteria; *Regents of the University of California v. Bakke*; Standardized Testing.

FURTHER READING: Bankston, Carl L., III, 2000, "Caste or Class? Race, Socioeconomic Status, and Educational Disadvantage," *National Journal of Sociology* 12, no. 2:57–88; Gray, W. Robert, 2001, *The Four Faces of Affirmative Action: Fundamental Answers and Actions*, Westport, CT: Greenwood Press; Kahlenberg, Richard D., 1996, *The Remedy: Class, Race, and Affirmative Action*. New York: Basic Books.

ADALBERTO AGUIRRE JR.

Clinton, William Jefferson (1946–)

William Jefferson Clinton, the forty-second president of the United States, served two terms in office. Clinton was the first Democratic president since Franklin D. Roosevelt to win a second term and the first since Harry S. Truman to lose control of the House of Representatives. After twelve years of Republican control of the White House, Clinton's election as president was grounded in high expectations for important federal policy changes. Clinton stood firm on certain traditional liberal goals, including reduced military expenditures, gun controls, legalized abortion, affirmative action programs, national health insurance, and gay rights. Clinton's record on affirmative action and equal opportunity programs received mixed support. He produced the first balanced budget in thirty years, ended a sixty-year federal entitlement to welfare, and memorably declared that "the era of big government is over." But he also won billions of dollars in increased funding for education, launched a major new federal effort to provide health care for uninsured children, and significantly enlarged government support for the working poor. In 1995, Clinton ordered a review of the government's affirmative action programs that concluded that affirmative action was still effective and necessary, despite the need for some reforms. He summarized his position on affirmative action with the slogan "Mend It, Don't End It." He expressed his strong opposition to the California Civil Rights Initiative/Proposition 209 and other efforts to "turn back the clock" on affirmative action. He also nominated two justices to the Supreme Court who would form part of the liberal bloc on the Court as it relates to affirmative action, Ruth Bader Ginsburg and Stephen Breyer.

During his first term as president, Clinton's actions indicated that he supported equal educational opportunity for students by making it possible for student loans to be more accessible through the Student Loan Reform Act. The HOPE Scholarship plan is a program in which students are provided with scholarships with tax credits if their performance is above average. Clinton also worked to expand the federal work-study program. Clinton supported school uniforms, signed the Goals 2000 bill that encouraged states to develop academic standards for public education, and expanded the Head Start program. Although Clinton supported giving parents a choice in public schools for their children's education, he opposed proposals to provide vouchers for private or parochial school education. Clinton viewed the Department of Education as essential to the functioning of the federal government and strongly opposed plans to eliminate the agency.

Clinton's support of women's rights was mixed. He supported the right of a woman to choose to have an abortion. During his presidency, he overturned the so-called gag rule that prohibited federally funded clinics from giving women advice about abortion, supported Medicaid funding of abortions for poor women, and signed the Freedom of Access to Clinic Entrances Act, which tries to prevent blockades of abortion clinics. He continually fought against the political opposition concerned with making sure that women do not have a voice in making decisions about their own bodies. During his term, he signed the Violence against Women Act, which was set up to fund such programs as rape prevention and battered women's shelters.

After the Supreme Court's negative opinion on affirmative action in *Adarand Constructors, Inc. v. Peña,* 515 U.S. 200 (1995), the Clinton administration thought it necessary to respond. Thus on July 9, 1995, Clinton delivered a major speech in defense of affirmative action programs at the National Archives in Washington, D.C. The speech, titled "Mend It, Don't End It," was delivered as a call to the American public to strongly consider the positive need for affirmative action programs. The speech distinguished Clinton's defense of affirmative action as an effort to "restore economic opportunity and solve social problems." In this speech, Clinton reminded the audience that the phrase "affirmative action" was "conceived during the Eisenhower administration, [and] was first used officially in President Kennedy's Executive Order 10925 of March 1961." Clinton used the opportunity to trace the history of affirmative action and ended the speech by stating that affirmative action is a way "to give the people the tools they need to make the most of their own lives, to give families and communities the tools they need to solve their own problems." While Clinton stated that "affirmative action has not always been perfect" and "should not go on forever," he also believed that affirmative action was needed and should be "reaffirmed." This major event also resulted in a report titled *Review of Federal Affirmative Action Programs: Report to the President,* which contained a comprehensive review of affirmative action in all major areas, including the military, contracting, employment, and education. The report, which is occasionally referred to as the Clinton Report on Affirmative Action, was completed under the leadership of Harvard law professor Christopher Edley, who is a nationally known supporter of affirmative action.

In 1997, Clinton raised hopes that he would be the first president since Lyndon Johnson to do something about racial conflict in the United States by appointing a race panel. On June 16, 1997, Clinton issued a challenge to everyone throughout the country to participate in discussions on race and ethnic relations. He said that ending affirmative action was a mistake, and he cited the drop in enrollment of African American students at the University of California as an example of that and other mistakes being made at institutions throughout the country. He also had a nationally reported confrontation with Abigail Thern-

Former president Bill Clinton is greeted on stage by Jesse Jackson at the annual convention of the Rainbow/PUSH Coalition on June 24, 2003, in Chicago, Illinois. In his speech, Clinton claimed that affirmative action would be needed for years to come to counteract the negative impact of the Bush administration on racial equality in America. © Getty Images/NewsCom.

strom in Akron, Ohio, on the issue of affirmative action. After Clinton opened the dialogue on race and affirmative action, conversations began in legislatures, at universities, in churches, and in communities. However, Clinton's inability or capacity to put any political muscle behind the panel's proposals doomed its work to be ineffective. Clinton also withdrew his support of Lani Guinier as his nominee to head the Justice Department's Civil Rights Division and of Jocelyn Elders as surgeon general after they received backlash from conservative Republicans. Clinton appointed blacks to several high administration positions and increased funding for AIDS prevention, minority businesses, education, and African relief.

As part of a plan to celebrate the millennium in 2000, Clinton called for a national initiative to end racial discrimination. He could point to the lowest unemployment rate in modern times, the lowest inflation rate in thirty years, the highest homeownership in the country's history, dropping crime rates in many places, and reduced welfare rolls. He proposed the first balanced budget in decades and achieved a budget surplus. After the failure in his second year of a huge program of health-care reform, Clinton shifted emphasis, declaring that "the era of big government is over." He sought legislation to upgrade education, to protect jobs of parents who must care for sick children, to restrict handgun sales, and to strengthen environmental rules.

In 1998, as a result of issues surrounding personal indiscretions with a young female White House intern, Clinton was the second U.S. president to be impeached by the House of Representatives. He was tried in the Senate and found not guilty of the charges brought against him. He apologized to the nation for his actions and continued to have unprecedented popular approval ratings for his job as president. In the world, he successfully dispatched peacekeeping forces to war-torn Bosnia and bombed Iraq when Saddam Hussein stopped United Nations inspections for evidence of nuclear, chemical, and biological weapons. He became a global proponent for an expanded NATO, more open international trade, and a worldwide campaign against drug trafficking. He drew huge crowds when he traveled through South America, Europe, Russia, Africa, and China advocating U.S.-style freedom. Clinton achieved these successes despite unrelenting personal attacks from the right wing of the Republican Party, the loss of Congress to the Republicans for the first time in forty years, and a humiliating but unsuccessful impeachment trial by the U.S. Senate. He fashioned himself as a "New Democrat" and has frequently been referred to as the "Comeback Kid."

Constrained by a hostile Congress for most of his term, Clinton indeed left behind few legislative achievements comparable to those of Lyndon B. Johnson or Franklin D. Roosevelt. Yet at the end of his tenure, Clinton left an unmistakable imprint on both parties. The Democratic primaries in 2000 testified to his success at shifting his own party's center of gravity: Challenger Bill Bradley, running a campaign largely on the argument that Clinton and Vice President Al Gore had abandoned too much of the party's liberal heritage, failed to win a single primary. Without Clinton's success at neutralizing the Gingrich revolution, it would be hard to envision a market in the GOP for George W. Bush's "compassionate conservatism," which moderated the party's hostility toward government and consciously echoed Clintonesque themes such as balancing opportunity and responsibility. Part of the difficulty in assessing Clinton's political and policy legacy is that there appeared to be distinct Clinton presidencies. In his chaotic first two years, he was the Clinton of mixed signals, with centrist achievements such as deficit reduction overshadowed by movement to the left on issues such as health care and gays in the military. From 1995 through mid-1997 came the Clinton of triangulation: the disciplined centrist who signed welfare reform and balanced-budget measures—under intense pressure from Republicans—and limited his new initiatives.

In his final years, there emerged a third Clinton: a more partisan president, bonded again to his party by the ordeal of impeachment and cautiously inching back toward a more expansive view of government's role and proposing expensive new initiatives such as a prescription drug benefit under Medicare. Yet through all these personalities, an identifiable policy pattern emerged that could be called Clintonism. At the core was his belief that he could blend liberal and conservative ideas previously considered incompatible. In part, his motive was to find a politically unassailable balance between left and right. But Clinton supporters argue that on issues such as welfare, crime, education, and urban policy, his goal was also to find new means to old ends—to craft an approach that accepted many conservative critiques of traditional liberal policies, but did not abandon the paramount liberal goal of expanding opportunity.

The 2000 campaign exposed the limits of Clinton's political success. Bush effectively portrayed Gore's long list of expensive new proposals as a return to "big government" and economic globalism. Clinton attempted to move the Democratic Party from its resistance to free trade. In 1993, with broad support from congressional Republicans, he overcame intense resistance from organized labor to win congressional approval of the North American Free Trade Agreement (NAFTA) with Mexico and Canada. His effort to expand NAFTA further into South America and to build a similar free-trade zone in Asia foundered during his second term when congressional Democrats refused to support the expedited trade-negotiating authority he needed to pursue these goals. These failures were partly offset by passage of legislation bringing China into the World Trade Organization by granting it permanent status as a preferred U.S. trading partner. Partly by necessity, partly by design, Clinton tried to change the way Washington pursued its goals. Rather than launching big new federal programs, he almost always argued that because the information age rewards decentralization, the federal government should advance its priorities indirectly through means such as tax credits and grants to states. This conceptual shift had two principal elements. One was a policy that might be called "flywheel federalism." Many of Clinton's most ambitious domestic initiatives followed the same example. He identified a promising policy trend that had emerged in a few states and tried to encourage other states to duplicate the pattern. In effect, he used the federal government as a flywheel, offering states generous grants if they would pursue emerging innovations such as community policing and charter schools. The second element consisted of policies meant to empower individuals or local institutions to solve problems. This instinct animated initiatives as diverse as the V chip (which gives parents more capacity to block television programming that they consider inappropriate for their children) and the replacement of conventional job-training programs with vouchers that workers could use to pick their own course of instruction. This approach may have reached its fullest expression in an area that critics accused Clinton of ignoring: urban policy. The left complained that Clinton never proposed major infusions of federal aid to struggling cities. In indirect ways, however, Clinton encouraged a significant increase in private investment in urban areas.

Through such means as toughening enforcement of the Community Reinvestment Act, which requires banks to lend in low-income neighborhoods, and requiring Fannie Mae and Freddie Mac (the giant federal mortgage-financing agencies) to subsidize more mortgages for low-income borrowers, his administration nurtured a historic boom in homeownership among minority and low-income families. Federal data show that from 1993 to 1999, the number of mortgages to black and Latino borrowers increased at three times the rate of increase of mortgages to whites; the numbers of African American and Latino homeowners have each increased by about 1 million since 1994, reaching historic highs in each case. Many urban neighborhoods remain troubled, but combined with the welfare reforms that have put families back to work and a reduction in crime, these gains have allowed many working poor communities to begin luring back shops and stores and recovering social stability.

In the political arena, Clinton left behind a complex legacy composed of contradictory trends. On the one hand, even his staunchest critics credit him with resuscitating his party's capacity to compete for the White House. In the three elections of the 1980s, the Democratic presidential nominees averaged just 58 electoral votes, less than 11 percent of the total electoral votes at stake. That was the smallest share of the available electoral votes that the Democrats had won in any three consecutive elections since the formation of the modern party system with Andrew Jackson in 1828. The Republican dominance was so pronounced and seemingly irreversible that political scientists spoke of a GOP hold on the electoral college. In his two elections, Clinton shattered that hold, averaging 375 electoral votes. With Ross Perot twice splintering the vote, Clinton never won an absolute majority of the popular vote, but his 49 percent showing in 1996 significantly improved on the party's 43 percent average over the previous seven elections.

Clinton held the party's traditional base, generating big margins among African Americans, union members, and single women, but his centrist message expanded the base. He became the first Democrat since Lyndon Johnson to carry a plurality of independents. He moved the Democrats up the income ladder, strengthening the party's performance among upper-middle-class voters, especially in 1996. Although Clinton did not improve the party's weak showing among white men, he made substantial gains among white women, especially the minivan- and SUV-driving married suburban women immortalized in 1996 as "soccer moms." These gains allowed Clinton to erase the GOP advantage in the electoral college by recapturing most of the key suburban counties outside of the South.

As both party leader and president, Clinton compiled significant achievements, but his time was also defined by missed opportunities, whether in the failure to provide universal health care or the inability to cement a true Democratic political realignment. Even amid the longest economic boom in U.S. history, he left the White House with Republicans in control of the presidency and Congress for the first time in nearly half a century. Clinton's imperfections complicated his talents. He changed the country, his party, and the debate between the parties. He presided over an economy that spread more benefits more broadly than any expansion since the 1960s. After Clinton's departure from the White House, he remains an important figure in a collective national consciousness.

See also Adarand Constructors, Inc. v. Peña; Breyer, Stephen Gerald; Bush, George W.; Democratic Party and Affirmative Action; Department of Justice; Executive Order 10925; Ginsburg, Ruth Bader; Guinier, Lani; Johnson, Lyndon Baines; Kennedy, John Fitzgerald; Lending Practices and Affirmative Action; Proposition 209; Roosevelt, Franklin Delano; Thernstrom, Stephan, and Thernstrom, Abigail; Truman, Harry.

FURTHER READING: Burns, J.M., and G.J. Sorenson, 1999, *Dead Center: Clinton-Gore Leadership and the Perils of Moderation*, New York: Scribner; Denton, R.E., and R.L. Holloway, eds., 1996, *The Clinton Presidency: Images, Issues, and Communication Strategies*, Westport, CT: Praeger; Edley, Christopher, Jr., 1996, *Not All Black and White: Affirmative Action, Race, and American Values*, New York: Hill and Wang; Renshon, S.A., 1996, *High Hopes: The Clinton Presidency and the Politics of Ambition*, New York: New York University Press; Yu, Corrine M. and William L. Taylor, eds., 1999, Report, *The Test of Our Progress: The Clinton Record on Civil Rights*, Washington, DC: Citizens Commission on Civil Rights.

PAULETTE PATTERSON DILWORTH

Coalition for Economic Equity v. Wilson, 110 F.3d 1431 (9th Cir. 1997)

Coalition for Economic Equity v. Wilson is the federal case dealing with the constitutionality of California's Proposition 209. In the case, the U.S. Court of Appeals for the Ninth Circuit held that Proposition 209 was not unconstitutional. Proposition 209, the California Civil Rights Initiative, was approved by a majority (54 percent) of California voters in the November 5, 1996, election. Proposition 209 bans discrimination or preferential treatment on the basis of race, sex, color, ethnicity, or national origin in public employment, education, and contracting. In essence, Proposition 209 does away with affirmative action on the state level in California.

On November 6, 1996, the Coalition for Economic Equity filed a complaint in the U.S. District Court for the Northern District of California. The Coalition for Economic Equity was a coalition of racial and ethnic minorities, women, and minority-owned business enterprises. The coalition alleged that Proposition 209 violated the Equal Protection Clause of the Fourteenth Amendment of the U.S.

Constitution by erecting barriers to the adoption of legislation by state and local governments in California that fashioned constitutionally permissible race- and gender-conscious programs to redress discrimination in the areas of public education, employment, and contracting.

On November 27, 1996, U.S. district court judge Thelton E. Henderson of San Francisco issued a temporary restraining order enjoining the governor and the attorney general from enforcing and implementing Proposition 209. On December 23, 1996, Judge Henderson issued a preliminary injunction against Proposition 209 that was designed to block enforcement of the proposition until the court determined whether the proposition violated the U.S. Constitution. In issuing the preliminary injunction, Judge Henderson also granted a motion that designated Governor Pete Wilson and Attorney General Dan Lungren to represent the class of defendants—all state officials and local government entities bound by Proposition 209.

The defendants appealed the lower court's issuance of the preliminary injunction to the U.S. Court of Appeals for the Ninth Circuit. On April 8, 1997, a three-judge panel of the Ninth Circuit overturned the lower court's preliminary injunction and ruled unanimously that Proposition 209 did not violate the U.S. Constitution. The panel stated in its ruling, "With no likelihood of success on the merits of their equal protection or preemption claims, plaintiffs are not entitled to a preliminary injunction" (*Coalition for Economic Equity v. Wilson*, 110 F.3d 1431 [9th Cir. 1997]).

On April 23, 1997, the Coalition for Economic Equity appealed the Ninth Circuit panel's decision by filing a petition for rehearing and suggestion for rehearing before an en banc panel of the Ninth Circuit Court of Appeals. On August 21, 1997, the full Ninth Circuit denied the coalition's request for a rehearing and/or rehearing en banc. On August 26, 1997, the Ninth Circuit denied the coalition's request for a stay of issuance pending the filing and determination of a petition for certiorari with the U.S. Supreme Court. On August 28, 1997, the federal district court's preliminary injunction against the proposition was lifted, and Proposition 209 became the law in California as a result of a mandate the Ninth Circuit Court of Appeals had issued on August 26, 1997.

On August 29, 1997, the coalition filed a petition for writ of certiorari with the U.S. Supreme Court (*Coalition for Economic Equity v. Wilson*, U.S. Docket No. 97-369, 66 U.S.L.W. 3171 [1997]) and sought an immediate stay. On November 2, 1997, the U.S. Supreme Court announced that it would not hear the coalition's challenge to Proposition 209 (*Coalition for Economic Equity v. Wilson, cert. denied*, 522 U.S. 963 [1997]).

See also Center for Individual Rights; Connerly, Ward; Contracting and Affirmative Action; Disadvantaged Business Enterprises; Discrimination; Employment (Private) and Affirmative Action; Employment (Public) and Affirmative Action; Equal Protection Clause; Fourteenth Amendment; Gender-Based Affirmative Action; Proposition 209; Race-Based Affirmative Action.

FURTHER READING: Capata, Juliana, 1998, "California Proposition 209 Does Not Impose Unconstitutional Burdens: *Coalition for Economic Equity v. Wilson*," *Boston College Law Review* 39:476–489; Vikram, David Amar, 1998, "Recent Cases: The Equal Protection Challenge to Proposition 209," *Asian Law Journal* 5:323–328.

ADALBERTO AGUIRRE JR.

Coalition to Defend Affirmative Action, Integration, and Fight for Equality by Any Means Necessary

The Coalition to Defend Affirmative Action, Integration, and Fight for Equality by Any Means Necessary (BAMN) was founded in July 1995 in Berkeley, California, in response to opposition to affirmative action in the University of California system. The main purpose of the coalition is to organize "the struggle against the resegregation of higher education." BAMN includes more than 1,000 student members from more than thirty-five colleges and universities and forty-five high schools around the United States. The coalition is an active youth-led civil rights organization that has effectively organized the struggle against anti–affirmative action efforts around the country. The coalition forced the University of California Regents to unanimously vote to reverse the ban on affirmative action practices in the University of California system in 2001.

BAMN is one of three student groups that filed friend-of-the-court briefs in two lawsuits challenging the University of Michigan's affirmative action program (*Grutter v. Bollinger*, 123 S. Ct. 2325, [2003] U.S. LEXIS 4800 [2003], and *Gratz v. Bollinger*, 123 S. Ct. 2411, 2003 U.S. LEXIS 4801 [2003]). On April 1, 2003, the day of oral arguments at the Supreme Court for the Michigan cases, BAMN organized a march on Washington, D.C., to defend affirmative action and to "save *Brown v. Board of Education*." BAMN protesters stood on the front steps of the Supreme Court, some holding signs that read "Do Not Reverse *Brown v. Board of Education*." BAMN also organized an emergency press conference and rally in defense of affirmative action and integration that was held at the University of Michigan Union the day the U.S. Supreme Court announced its decisions in the two University of Michigan affirmative action cases.

See also Brown v. Board of Education; Gratz v. Bollinger/Grutter v. Bollinger.

FURTHER READING: Johnson, Carmen, 2003, "Supporters at U. Michigan Maintain Faith in Admissions Policy," *Michigan Daily via U-Wire*, January 17; Schmidt, Peter, 2003, "Hundreds of Groups Back U. of Michigan on Affirmative Action," *Chronicle of Higher Education*, February 28, 24; Stern, Teresa, 2003, "Affirmative Action on Trial," *Ms* 13, no. 1 (spring): 68–70.

PAULINA X. RUF

Colonial America

See Race in Colonial America.

Colonial Governments and Equality

Colonial government by the imperial powers was essentially the government and administration of subject peoples who were deemed to be underdeveloped, inferior, or primitive by reference to criteria set in the imperial countries. It was essentially a system of superiority and subordination. It was accordingly a system of government for the unequal.

It should be recalled that during the early twentieth century, colonial administration became a large-scale undertaking by the British, French, Dutch, German, Spanish, and Portuguese. By July 1914, for instance, more than half the land surface of the earth and a good third of the global population were under colonial rule (Ansprenger, 1989, 13). However, the guidelines of colonial policy differed from one nation to another and from one imperial power to the other. In the British colonies, for example, a distinction was made according to the formalities of acquisition between Crown colonies and protectorates, to which were added the Sudan as an Anglo-Egyptian condominium, the leased territories on the Chinese coast, and the dominions. On the other hand, France viewed Algeria as part of the Republic of France and distinguished between the old colonies and the new colonies. The objectives of the colonizers, irrespective of their nationalities, however, were similar: they wanted to open up vast new areas for mass white settlement and for trade and the extraction of raw materials. Colonization therefore was a process that brought territories and people under new and more stringent forms of control.

All colonies were regarded as a source of wealth for the colonizing power, whether that wealth was from the extraction of precious metals, the supply of agricultural products, or access to trade. Thus the pattern of colonization depended on the commodity that was available. It also depended on other factors, including the geography and the climate of the country. In some places, for example, mountains and forests presented effective barriers to penetration and conquest; as a result, rights of trade and control had to be secured through treaties with local chiefs. Also, the suitability of the climate for Europeans was a critical issue when deciding whether or not that colony should be considered as "settler territory." Another consideration that influenced the pattern of colonization was the numbers and state of organization of the indigenous population. Beckford (1972, 35) observed, for instance, that in the highland regions of America and in parts of Asia, Europeans found societies that were highly politically organized. In these societies, the customary organization was used to form units of government through which the metropolitan powers exerted control.

Essentially, the income generated from these colonies served to promote industrialization and development in the metropolitan countries rather than in the colonies themselves. Economists argued that this economic system, or what some defined as a plantation model, was a system that promoted the interests of the imperial countries. They also suggested that the colonial territories were placed in a position of not only economic dependency but political dependency as well. Internally, political authority and control were centralized in the hands of the planters or settlers, and to a large extent the policies that were implemented were in keeping with the needs of these groups rather than being framed to meet the demands of the local population. Indeed, in the case of the West Indian colonies in 1939, the level of poverty was extremely high, and there was a lack of proper infrastructure and other facilities, including health care. Yet during this period, expatriate officers who were resident in the islands were generally considered well-off; their children were educated at private institutions, and private rooms were reserved for them at the public hospitals. Also, in these colonies and in a number of other countries, including Africa and India, there was not only a rigid stratification system where color and class lines were tautly drawn, but the local population was denied even some of what can be considered basic privileges. For example, public toilets were reserved for whites, eating places and bars had "white only" signs, and even in public transportation, a local or black person had to give up his or her seat to a white person if no other seat was available. In employment, local public officers were often bypassed for promotional opportunities since, as a memorandum from a former colonial secretary indicated, such persons "were not of pure European descent." The basic feature of colonial government, then, was that it was rooted in the political and economic dominance of one country over another; it was stratified on racial lines and was based on the conception of the moral and cultural superiority of Europeans over the dominated races. Essentially, colonial governments did not aim at an administrative system that was based on equity or neutrality. The system fostered inequity between and among groups and, some writers have argued, created societies with deep-seated psychological dependence on the outside world.

See also Eurocentrism; Global Implementation of Affirmative Action Programs; Paternalistic Race Relations Theory; Plantation System; Racial and Ethnic Stratification; White Supremacy.

FURTHER READING: Ansprenger, Franz, 1989, *The Dissolution of the Colonial Empires*, London: Routledge; Beckford, George L., 1972, *Persistent Poverty*, New York: Oxford University Press; Bissessar, Ann Marie, 2000, *Colonial Administration, Structural Adjustment, and New Public Management: The Agony of Reform*, St. Augustine, Trinidad, West Indies: School of Continuing Studies; Confidential Dispatches to Secretary of State, 1924–1925, St. Augustine, Trinidad: Archives, Trinidad; Knaplund, Paul, 1942, *The British Empire, 1815–1939*, London: Lowe and Brydone Printers; La Guerre, John Gaffar, 1999, *Politics, Society, and Culture in the Commonwealth Caribbean*, St. Augustine, Trinidad: School of Continuing Studies; *Principles and Methods of Colonial Administration*, 1950, Colston Papers, vol. 3, London: Butterworths.

ANN MARIE BISSESSAR

Color Consciousness

A decision, policy, or attitude is color conscious when it uses skin color as a criterion to determine treatment or outcome. Some affirmative action policies are color-conscious opportunity-rationing devices that group individuals on the basis of their skin color, prescribe minimum acceptable levels of economic, social, or political outcomes that protected groups must achieve, and authorize court-enforced remedial action to help these groups meet these requirements.

Historically, individuals have been segmented and treated differently by color-conscious governments, institutions, and individuals. Multi-generational slavery, black codes, Jim Crow laws, school segregation, real-estate redlining, racially restrictive land covenants, discriminatory employment contracts, and hiring quotas have involuntarily grouped individuals on the basis of their skin color and applied practices differently to each group, resulting in disparate treatment and life chances and de facto segregation. Until recently, most color-conscious practices were utilized by Caucasians to disadvantage, disenfranchise, and otherwise oppress color minorities for the benefit of the Caucasian majority population. These practices made economic, social, and life aspirations more difficult to obtain by minorities. These difficulties remain evident in today's social and economic landscape because color minorities hold a smaller proportion of economic, educational, and community resources than their proportion of the population would forecast under color-blind and random-success circumstances.

Currently, color-conscious governmental and institutional affirmative action policies providing preferential treatment to minority groups include credit assistance, hiring quotas, contract set-asides, and racially conscious electoral redistricting. These policies have an expressed intent to "improve" society or to eliminate the debilitating effects of historical antiminority color-conscious practices and any such practices that may still exist.

See also Color-Blind Constitution; De Facto and De Jure Segregation; Discrimination; Jim Crow Laws; Merit Selections; Performance-Based Selections; Race-Neutral Criteria; Segregation; Slavery.

FURTHER READING: Appiah, K. Anthony, and Amy Gutmann, 1996, *Color Conscious: The Political Morality of Race*, Princeton, NJ: Princeton University Press; Deloria, Vine, Jr., 1994, "Identity and Culture," in *From Different Shores: Perspectives on Race and Ethnicity*, edited by Ronald Takaki, New York: Oxford University Press; McDonald, Laughlin, and John A. Powell, 1993, *The Rights of Racial Minorities: The Basic ACLU Guide to Racial Minority Rights*, Carbondale: Southern Illinois University Press.

MARK J. SENEDIAK

Color-Blind Constitution

The phrase "color-blind constitution" comes from Supreme Court justice John Marshall Harlan's lone dissent in the Supreme Court case of *Plessy v. Ferguson*, 163 U.S. 537 (1896), the case that upheld separate-but-equal laws as constitutional under the Fourteenth Amendment. In Justice Harlan's dissent, he penned one of the famous quotes of Supreme Court history, that "our constitution is color-blind, and neither knows nor tolerates classes among citizens," and that in regard to civil rights, "all citizens are equal before the law." From his dissent, the notion or doctrine of a "color-blind" constitution emerged. Ironically, despite the fact that Justice Harlan penned these words in dissent against the pernicious doctrine of legal segregation, opponents of affirmative action have in recent years utilized his notion of a "color-blind" constitution as a weapon against affirmative action and remedial race and gender programs meant to cure past discrimination.

In theory, a color-blind constitution would revoke or prohibit any law or governmental practice or action that differentiates between people based on race, color, or ethnicity, including any race-, color-, or ethnicity-based affirmative action. However, the U.S. Constitution, the Bill of Rights, and all subsequent amendments to the Constitution do not include any provisions to explicitly make the Constitution color blind. In fact, from the Constitutional Convention of 1787 through the ratification of the Fourteenth Amendment in 1868, the Constitution was anything but color blind in application. Native Americans and African Americans were treated differently under the Constitution and Supreme Court interpretation of the document. From 1865 to the mid-1960s, judicial interpretation of the Constitution and its amendments came close to reaching that declaration before backing away from it in the late 1960s. If the U.S. Constitution were color blind, affirmative action laws or practices that provide preferences to any person on account of race, color, or ethnicity for any purpose would be unconstitutional and revoked.

Despite the Civil War/Reconstruction Amendments, many southern states after the Civil War enacted laws to deny former slaves basic civil rights such as the right to contract and hold property. In response, the Radical Republican consensus during Reconstruction was to amend the Constitution to expressly outlaw these laws, which were known as the black codes, before the rebellious states were allowed to rejoin the Union. Proponents of a color-blind constitution such as Wendell Phillips, who was a publisher of the antislavery *National Anti-slavery Standard* and onetime president of the American Anti-slavery Society, began to push for a constitutional amendment to make the Constitution truly color blind. After several revisions, abolitionist and U.S. Congressman Robert Dale Owen proposed an amendment to make any law in any state that discriminated between any individuals in any way on the basis of race, color, or previous condition of servitude unconstitutional. Grassroots opponents of this amendment, who feared that it would grant immediate black voting rights and allow interracial marriage, used election-year political pressure on the committee considering the amendment to change it. The rewritten amendment, which became the Fourteenth Amendment, granted equal constitutional protection instead of color blindness. It and the Fifteenth Amendment, which provides that no person shall be deprived of the right to vote on account of race, color, or previous condition of servitude, remain the basis for all subsequent claims that the Constitution should be interpreted to be color blind. Since neither amendment made the Constitution explicitly color blind, they left the U.S. Supreme Court with the responsibility of determining which laws would be considered unconstitutional according to the equal protection provision.

Since the adoption of the Fourteenth Amendment, the Supreme Court has dealt with this responsibility through a series of interpretations of the legal doctrine of separate but equal. Initially, this doctrine was interpreted to justify segregation up to and including the 1896 decision in the case *Plessy v. Ferguson* by proclaiming that separate could be equal. After *Plessy*, the Supreme Court began slowly to change this interpretation and to move toward an interpretation that would allow separate to be considered equal only if the law or practice in question was explicitly meant to fulfill a "good" governmental purpose at the highest level of judicial scrutiny or occurred in time of national crisis. This was the reason that the Supreme Court affirmed the constitutionality of Japanese internment camps in the case of *Korematsu v. United States*, 323 U.S. 214 (1944), during World War II.

During the early 1960s, several Supreme Court justices advocated a color-blind interpretation of the Constitution, but no case was ever decided and no judicial rule was ever established to that effect. Regardless, many people, including members of Congress, believed that the decision in *Brown v. Board of Education*, 347 U.S. 483 (1954), had in fact established a color-blind interpretation of the Constitution even though the justices went out of their way to declare that they based their decision on reversing the separate-but-equal doctrine. The Court had based its decision on the belief that separate educational facilities were inherently unequal because of the psychological damage that they caused to minority students. However, congressional misinterpretation of this decision and growing social unrest generated by the civil rights movement moved Congress to pass the Civil Rights Act of 1964, which explicitly prohibits discrimination by race, color, or ethnicity in a color-blind fashion. Nevertheless, Title VII of the Civil Rights Act has been interpreted to allow employers the ability to consider race, color, and ethnicity in pursuit of a valid affirmative action program.

Because passage of the 1964 Civil Rights Act has not eradicated segregation, the growth of economic and social outcome disparity, and social unrest, the federal government has replaced many of its color-blind provisions with color-conscious affirmative action laws that purport to end de facto segregation and ameliorate the negative effects of historical disparate governmental treatment of minorities. The Supreme Court has confirmed the constitutionality of most of these laws when they meet the strict scrutiny requirements necessary to allow disparate treatment (i.e., when they are narrowly tailored to achieve a compelling governmental interest).

See also Articles of Confederation; Bill of Rights; *Brown v. Board of Education*; Civil Rights Act of 1964; Civil War (Reconstruction) Amendments and Civil Rights Acts; Constitution, Civil Rights, and Equality; De Facto and De Jure Segregation; Declaration of Independence and Equality; Equal Protection Clause; Fifteenth Amendment; Fourteenth Amendment; Japanese Internment and World War II; Jim Crow Laws; *Korematsu v. United States*; *Plessy v. Ferguson*; Segregation; Strict Scrutiny; Title VII of the Civil Rights Act of 1964.

FURTHER READING: Irons, Peter, 1999, *A People's History of the Supreme Court*, New York: Viking Press; Kull, Andrew, 1992, *The Color-Blind Constitution*, Cambridge, MA: Harvard University Press; O'Connor, Karen, and Larry J. Sabato, 1993, *American Government: Roots and Reform*, New York: Macmillan; Schroder, Oliver, Jr., and David T. Smith, eds., 1965, *De Facto Segregation and Civil Rights*, Buffalo, NY: William S. Hein and Co.

MARK J. SENEDIAK

A Common Destiny: Blacks and American Society

A study on racism in America concluded in 1989, *A Common Destiny: Blacks and American Society* became an important report on racism and affirmative action. The report, the result of four years of intensive research and work by a panel of experts from a variety of disciplines, concluded that attitudes of racism still exist in the United States, especially in the areas of housing and personal private relationships, and that the goal of a color-blind society has not been met. While true equality, integration, and a color-blind society have not been achieved, the report also commented favorably on the effect of affirmative action programs in improving the lot of African Americans in the workforce. In regard to Executive Order 11246 (requiring contractors to take affirmative action in the employment of minorities and to set up goals and timetables for achieving better integration in the workforce), the report concluded that the executive order has resulted in "generally" positive results (National Research Council 1989, 317, 319). In regard to affirmative action remedies imposed by the courts for racial discrimination under Title VII of the Civil Rights Act of 1964, the report concluded that the effect of such affirmative action remedies upon minorities in the workforce was "tremendous" and that such programs "have had wide-reaching effects on blacks' relative position in the labor market" (National Research Council 1989, 317, 319).

A Common Destiny was the result of four years of intensive study by a field of experts under the auspices of the National Research Council and studied a variety of fields impacted by race relations, including employment, economics, education, criminal justice, governance/politics, health, crime, and so on. The study covered roughly five decades in U.S. history since the 1940s. In 1989, C. Vann Woodward, author and expert on segregation, Jim Crow laws, and race relations in the United States generally, stated, "If Gunnar Myrdal's *American Dilemma* (1944) and the *Kerner Report* (1968) were landmarks in the history of the Second Reconstruction, a new book titled *A Common Destiny: Blacks in American Society* (1989) may earn comparable status in time" (Woodward 1989, 38–39).

See also Civil Rights Act of 1964; Executive Order 11246; Kerner Commission; Title VII of the Civil Rights Act of 1964.

FURTHER READING: Miller, Russell L., 1990, "A Common Destiny: Blacks and American Society (Book Review)," *JAMA: The Journal of the American Medical Association* 263, no. 6 (February 9): 892–893; National Research Council, 1989, *A Common Destiny: Blacks and American Society*, edited by Jaynes Gerald David and Robin M. Williams Jr. on behalf of the Committee on the Status of Black Americans, Commission on Behavioral and Social Sciences and Education, National Research Council, Washington, DC: National Academy Press; Woodward, C. Vann, 1989, "The Crisis of Caste: From Segregation to 'Hypersegregation,' " *New Republic* 201, no. 19 (November 6): 38–42.

JAMES A. BECKMAN

Compelling Governmental Interest

When governmental racial classifications (including most affirmative action plans) are challenged on constitutional grounds, courts follow a standard of "strict scrutiny" in analyzing them. Given this country's history of discrimination and racial stereotyping, today's courts are especially suspicious of any law or mandate that uses race as its primary basis of classification. Even affirmative action plans intended to aid members of historically victimized racial groups conflict with the legal goal of color blindness. Thus the U.S. Supreme Court has ruled that racially based classifications should be adopted only in situations where there exists a "compelling governmental interest," and the classification is narrowly tailored to achieve that interest.

Currently, in the employment context, the only acceptable governmental justification for racial classifications that the U.S. Supreme Court has recognized is remedying past discrimination. In the context of affirmative action, a compelling governmental interest is the government's interest in ameliorating or, if possible, eliminating the clearly identified effects of past practices of discrimination. For such a remedial purpose to qualify as a compelling governmental interest, the racial designation must respond to specific identified acts of prior discrimination. However, in 2003, the Supreme Court allowed the use of race-conscious programs in the educational context to promote diversity in higher education (so long as race is utilized as one of many factors), which the Court also held to be a compelling governmental interest (*Grutter v. Bollinger*, 123 S. Ct. 2325, 2003 U.S. LEXIS 4800 [2003]).

The U.S. Supreme Court has rejected the governmental interest of remedying the "societal discrimination" that results from racial bias and stereotypes as too amorphous to be compelling. Such was the case in *City of Richmond v. J.A. Croson*

Co., 488 U.S. 469 (1989). In *Croson*, the Court rejected the city of Richmond's minority set-aside plan for municipal contractors because the city presented only general evidence of past discrimination in the local, state, and national construction industries. The Court found that without specific findings of past discrimination, the city could not know what injury it was seeking to remedy. Thus the Court rejected the city's stated remedial purpose, finding that it was not a compelling governmental interest.

Justice Lewis Powell made a similar finding in *Regents of the University of California v. Bakke*, 438 U.S. 265 (1978). Justice Powell analyzed generally whether the use of racial classifications in education could meet the compelling governmental interest requirement and found that state desegregation plans often did. In short, he ruled that if a state's laws had previously hurt a group of individuals, then "the legal rights of the victims must be vindicated." However, the Court said that the affirmative action plan under review, in which the University of California at Davis Medical School set aside a set number of positions in each class for minorities, failed the compelling governmental interest test. Justice Powell noted that unlike desegregation measures, there was no evidence of specific discriminatory actions by California universities, and, therefore, any racial imbalance that did exist in that area was because of societal discrimination. Without "judicial, legislative, or administrative findings of constitutional or statutory violations" leading to specific acts of discrimination that the state was trying to remedy, the state, according to Justice Powell, did not have a compelling interest in its affirmative action admissions program. However, in the landmark 2003 *Grutter* case, the Court reaffirmed Justice Powell's diversity rationale and reaffirmed diversity in higher education as a compelling governmental interest in the education context. In so doing, the Supreme Court upheld the University of Michigan Law School's affirmative action plan (*Grutter* case) and endorsed affirmative action plans that utilize race as one factor or ingredient (among many) in the overall evaluation of candidates.

Further, the Supreme Court has found that the government does not have a compelling interest in any affirmative action program establishing rigid quotas. In *Bakke*, five justices rejected the California admissions plan, in part because the plan set aside a specific number of spots for minority applicants. Justice Powell noted in his *Bakke* opinion that quotas equated to preferring individuals in one group solely on the basis of race, which was "facially invalid" because no government had a compelling interest in such a plan. Similarly, in the landmark case of *Gratz v. Bollinger*, 123 S. Ct. 2411, 2003 U.S. LEXIS 4801 (2003), a companion case to *Grutter*, the Court warned that fixed racial quotas and mechanized formulas (which have the effect of operating as a quota) would not be tolerated. In the *Gratz* decision, the Court struck down the University of Michigan undergraduate admissions affirmative plan that gave extra points for race alone. The plan struck down by the Court had awarded African American, Hispanic, and Native American applicants an automatic 20 points on a 150-point undergraduate admissions scale. This, the Court held, was akin to racial quotas, which violate the Fourteenth Amendment's Equal Protection Clause, as well as Title VI of the Civil Rights Act of 1964, which prohibits racial discrimination in educational institutions that are recipients of federal funds. The Court in *Croson* similarly rejected the city of Richmond's plan requiring prime city contractors to allocate 30 percent of contract dollars to minority-owned businesses as nothing more than a quota that could not further any compelling interest.

The U.S. Supreme Court has rejected a governmental interest in "fostering minority role models" as a compelling basis for an affirmative action plan. In *Wygant v. Jackson Board of Education*, 476 U.S. 267 (1986), the Court struck down a school board's teacher layoff policy that favored the retention of minority teachers over nonminority teachers, even if the nonminority teachers had greater seniority. The school board argued to the Court that it had an interest in retaining minority teachers to provide role models for students. The Court found that interest not constitutionally permissible because it had "no logical stopping point."

Even though lower courts generally reject nonremedial justifications for affirmative action plans such as providing role models or creating racially balanced workplaces, some lower courts are beginning to classify as compelling a nonremedial purpose in using racial classifications to further the operational needs of law-enforcement bodies. However, the courts in these cases have still required the introduction of evidence showing that the nonremedial purpose is legitimate and not discriminatory in and of itself, as racial profiling can often be, and, therefore, is acceptable as a "compelling governmental interest."

See also City of Richmond v. J.A. Croson Co.; Discrimination; *Gratz v. Bollinger/ Grutter v. Bollinger*; Narrowly Tailored Affirmative Action Plans; Powell, Lewis Franklin, Jr.; Quotas; *Regents of the University of California v. Bakke*; Role Model Theory; Stereotyping and Minority Classes; Strict Scrutiny; *Wygant v. Jackson Board of Education.*

FURTHER READING: Anderson, Elizabeth, 2002, "Integration, Affirmative Action, and Strict Scrutiny," *New York University Law Review* 77, no. 5:1195–1271; Chang, Mitchell J., Daria Witt, and James Jones, eds., 2003, *Compelling Interest: Examining the Evidence on Racial Dynamics in Colleges and Universities*, Stanford, CA: Stanford University Press.

GREGORY M. DUHL

Congress of Racial Equality

The Congress of Racial Equality (CORE) was founded in 1942 as the Committee of Racial Equality by a group of students in Chicago, Illinois. Many founding members had previously been affiliated with the Fellowship of Reconciliation (FOR), a pacifist group with roots in the civil disobedience traditions of Henry David Thoreau and Mahatma Gandhi. CORE was committed to the nonviolent elimination of racial segregation in the United States. Its earliest activities included organizing protests against racial segregation in public accommodations in the North. CORE was initially interracially codirected by George Houser (white) and James Farmer (black). Farmer became CORE's first national director in 1943.

With expansion of CORE's activities came internal debate over local control and national leadership, retention of its interracialist commitment, and the viability of nonhierarchical organizational structures. In the early 1960s, CORE expanded its operation to the South and became recognized as a prominent national civil rights organization noted for pioneering such nonviolent direct action strategies as sit-ins, jail-ins, and bus trips aimed at desegregating southern buses and bus stations (i.e., so-called freedom rides). By 1963, CORE began to shift its focus to segregation in the North and West, and its ideology and tactics began to change as new, predominantly black members began advocating more militant means to equality and freedom. In 1966, CORE endorsed the term "Black Power," and by 1967 the term "multiracial" had disappeared from its constitution. In 1968, Roy Innis replaced Farmer as the national director and soon thereafter denied active membership to whites. Innis also began advocating black separatism, for example, by promoting separate schools rather than desegregation in the South. By the 1990s, CORE chapters engaged in little direct action. Today, CORE is officially classified as a philanthropic human rights organization with a unique nongovernmental organization (NGO) consultative status at the United Nations.

The official CORE web site describes its chief aims as to "establish, in practice, the inalienable right for all people to determine their own destiny . . . the right to govern themselves," and "to bring about equality" by exposing and combating discrimination in the public and private sectors of society. Although interested in the protection of the civil rights of all citizens, CORE is primarily concerned with the civil rights and welfare of members of the black community and, more recently, with African American empowerment in business and government. CORE's involvement in the legal debate over gun control and the associated constitutional provision to keep and bear arms is also instructive of what some have regarded as a conservative turn in its political orientation. Like many groups, CORE views crime as the scourge of the black community, but it also views past and current gun-control legislation as part of the legacy of racism in the United States, arguing that gun-control legislation has been based in part on the old prejudice that the lower classes and minorities are not to be trusted with firearms. The practical effect of this discriminatory attitude is the denial of the right to bear arms for those citizens arguably most in need of adequate self-defense against criminal activity.

CORE's relation to affirmative action is complex and paradoxical. Though its activities as one of the earliest civil rights groups aimed at establishing "colorblind" laws and governmental policies predate affirmative action policies designed to help eliminate racial and gender discrimination, there can be no doubt that CORE's early activities helped set the long-term agenda for the struggle for social equality and justice in the United States, an agenda that includes affirmative action. Indeed, some of the leading social theorists and politicians influenced by CORE's earliest work thought that merely ending discriminatory laws and social policies was insufficient and took the next step to conceptualize and implement affirmative action as a further tool for combating racial and gender inequalities in American society. In 1961, President John F. Kennedy invoked the phrase "affirmative action" when he ordered federal contractors to "take affirmative action" to ensure that job applicants and employees were treated "without regard to race, creed, color, or national origin." This was followed in 1964 by the Civil Rights Act, of which Title VII specifically banned discrimination in employment and laid the groundwork for the ensuing development of affirmative action. The Equal Employment Opportunity Commission (EEOC), also created by the Civil Rights Act of 1964, became a key enforcement agency for affirmative action. Thus CORE, in concert with other leading civil rights groups, in the late 1950s and early 1960s helped set the foundation for affirmative action.

In its most recent official statements, however, CORE leaders argue that affirmative action has had an overall deleterious effect on race relations, and CORE has taken a stance of active opposition to what it regards as the immoral racial- and gender-preference programs of affirmative action. CORE's commitment to strict equality may nevertheless be compatible with its opposition to affirmative action, insofar as affirmative action policies are themselves viewed as mechanisms of discrimination, which is antithetical to CORE's guiding philosophy of equality. CORE's contemporary anti–affirmative action stance is consistent with the recent abolition of all affirmative action programs in California and with the general political assault on affirmative action waged since the late 1980s. It remains to be seen in the years ahead how CORE will react to newly created plans to establish diversity on college campuses and in the workplace that have arisen as a response to recently eliminated affirmative action schemes.

See also Affirmative Action, Criticisms of; African Americans; Civil Rights Act of 1964; Civil Rights Movement; Color-Blind Constitution; Diversity; Equal Employment Opportunity Commission; Farmer, James; Freedom Riders; Kennedy, John Fitzgerald; Multiracialism; Title VII of the Civil Rights Act of 1964.

FURTHER READING: Africana.com, 1999–2000, "Congress of Racial Equality or CORE," http://www.Africana.com; Congress of Racial Equality, web site: http://www.core-online.org; Custer, Kristine, 1999, "Interracial Communities and Civil Rights Activism in Lawrence, Kansas, 1945–1948," *Historian* 61, no. 4:783–786; Meier, August, and Elliott Rudwick, 1973, *CORE: A Study in the Civil Rights Movement, 1942–1968*, New York: Oxford University Press; Meier, August, and Elliott Rudwick, 2000, *Congress of Racial Equality Papers, 1959–1976*, Frederick, MO: University Publications of America; Rosen, Sumner M., 1999, "James Farmer, 1920–1999," *Social Policy* 30:47–48; Salmond, John A., 1997, *My Mind Set on Freedom: A History of the Civil Rights Movement, 1954–1968*, Chicago: Ivan R. Dee.

PAUL M. HUGHES

Congressional Black Caucus

The growth of the Congressional Black Caucus (CBC) has been partly a result of the Voting Rights Act of 1965, which changed the racial composition of Congress from only nine members in 1969 to more than four times that number by 1992. The beginning of the CBC can be traced to 1969 as an informal body that had no recognizable or legitimate status in Congress as a whole. Because of its small size, it did not represent a significant voting bloc. But this fledgling group, even during its early years, was able to articulate in an effective manner the concerns and issues that primarily affected black Americans and the need for policy initiatives, such as affirmative action, to address those concerns. In 1971, a group of 13 black legislators formally established the CBC. They initially confronted President Richard Nixon with a number of issues that they felt he had ignored. This confrontation brought some degree of recognition as well, as witnessed by President Gerald Ford, who invited the CBC to the White House once he took office.

The years from 1969 to 1971 can be considered the mobilizing years for the CBC. At this point, the organization was still in a developmental stage as it sought its own role and identity in Congress. It performed a number of functions, including serving as an investigatory arm and dispensing information on the status of blacks. But it was the confrontation with Nixon that put the organization on the political map. Because Nixon chose to ignore the CBC, members boycotted his State of the Union speech in 1971, creating some degree of embarrassment for the president. Two months later, the president decided to meet with the CBC, but promised little and did even less based upon sixty-one policy recommendations that the group presented to the chief executive. In addition to the national recognition that they achieved, anti-Nixon sentiment among the members assisted the organization in becoming a unified entity with a common focus upon the needs and concerns of blacks in the United States.

In 1974, Congressman Charles Rangel of New York replaced Louis Stokes of Ohio as chairman of the CBC. The CBC began to shift its emphasis from national politics and forums to specific legislative functions and politics. The new emphasis allowed the CBC to utilize the resources members had along with their expertise to address and push for legislation that affected blacks. Nevertheless, one of the biggest obstacles facing the CBC at this time was developing a positive relationship with President Ford, who had not previously shown any sympathy to black social and political issues as a congressman from Michigan. While the Republican president initially decided to meet with the all-Democrat and all-black CBC, it was obvious that his background and priorities would be quite different from their priorities. Two events served as portents of the division between the different political actors. First, the pardon of former president Nixon, who had almost been impeached and removed from office by the House and Senate for his involvement in Watergate, was ominous. Many felt that the pardon was the result of a deal and/or that the former president was "above the law." Two, President Ford spoke out forcefully and publicly against forced busing to achieve racial integration, although the U.S. Supreme Court had ruled previously that busing could be used as a tool for the racial integration of public schools.

With the election of Jimmy Carter of Georgia as president in 1976, the CBC had reason to feel that the strained relationship with Ford would be overcome with a fellow Democrat in the White House. But Carter, who had spoken in many black churches during his campaign, was essentially a conservative Democrat. Aside from the appointments of blacks Andrew Young as U.S. ambassador to the United Nations and Patricia Harris as secretary of housing and urban development, Carter did little to take the initiative on policy issues of concern to the CBC. His support and lobbying efforts were forthcoming, however, with the Humphrey-Hawkins full–employment bill, which was designed to reduce unemployment to less than 5 percent. While the bill passed in a watered-down version as the result of conservative opposition and several amendments, it did provide an opportunity for the CBC and Carter to cooperate on a major policy issue.

During the next two presidential terms, Ronald Reagan occupied the White House. Like Carter and Ford, he initially met with the CBC not long after his first election in 1980, but refused to meet with them after the first meeting. Several policy issues exacerbated the division between the president and the CBC. These included differences over civil rights (which the president felt were no longer a concern, because American society had overcome discrimination), foreign policy toward South Africa (Reagan sympathized with the oppressive white minority), and economic policies. The CBC was successful in assisting in the passage of the Anti-Apartheid Act of 1986 against South Africa over the veto of Reagan. It was also successful in coalescing with the various interest groups in Congress in overriding Reagan's veto of the Civil Rights Restoration Act of 1988, which was intended to supersede the Supreme Court's decision in *Grove City College v. Bell*, 465 U.S. 555 (1984), that limited the power of the federal government in antidiscrimination efforts with institutions that were recipients of money from the federal government. Although the CBC was successful in some instances, the Reagan administration changed the social and political climate, and there was less sympathy for issues related to people of color and the poor.

In 1988, the senior George Bush was elected president in a campaign that was racially divisive and in which race was openly used to appeal to fears and stereotypes of a segment of the white electorate. Bush used a mug shot of a black male who had raped a white woman while on parole to suggest that Michael Dukakis, his Democratic opponent, was "soft on crime." Bush agreed to a regular schedule of meetings with the CBC, but the opposing players did not see eye to eye on various policy issues. Two of these issues addressed political appointments of black conservatives to head the Civil Rights Division of the Justice Department and to serve on the Supreme Court. In both instances, the CBC was divided in the defeat of William Lucas for the former post and the success of Clarence Thomas in being appointed to the Court. In the latter instance, the only Republican member of the CBC at the time, Gary Franks, cast the lone vote from the CBC for Thomas.

Bill Clinton's election as president in 1992 marked a return of Democrats to the White House after twelve years of Republican rule, but the relationship of the CBC with the Clinton administration was not significantly improved over that with the GOP presidents. Clinton did appoint four blacks to cabinet-level positions in his administration, more than any president prior to him, in an attempt to make this body "look like America." But aside from the fact that Clinton was a Democrat, like almost all of the CBC members, they found little common ground in most of the major policy initiatives overall. Clinton did defend affirmative action against attacks by the GOP, but he succumbed to pressure from the right wing of his party and from the GOP and withdrew the nomination of Lani Guinier, a black female college professor, as a candidate for the position of assistant attorney general for civil rights. Guinier was painted by her opponents as an extremist, demanding preferential treatment for blacks and other people of color in her scholarly writings related to cumulative voting. As a result, Clinton withdrew her nomination amid the protests of the CBC and other civil rights and women's groups. Against the wishes of the CBC, Clinton also supported a welfare reform bill and federal crime legislation that contained a number of punitive measures that had a disproportionate impact upon people of color. In foreign policy, Clinton followed the policy of his predecessor, George Bush, in returning Haitian refugees who had fled the island nation to the shores of Florida. However, because of pressure from the CBC as well as other human rights organizations, the Clinton administration reversed itself and successfully supported an end to military rule and the tyranny that resulted in the refugee problem. The military stepped down from power, and democracy took root with the election of the popular Jean-Bertrand Aristide as president.

Clinton realized that while he overwhelmingly received the black vote in the 1992 and 1996 presidential elections, the CBC and black voters had no other options than the Republican Party, which was considered antipathetic to the needs of the black electorate. Clinton was also cognizant of the fact that the political center of the electorate had moved to the right, and that he was still on safe ground in courting that component of the electorate.

Beginning in 1969, the CBC has grown from a mere nine members during that year to 38 in 2004. With this growth has come added influence as members have gained experience and seniority that positioned them for powerful seats in various committees. In this regard, the CBC has become an important component of Congress. The body has gained additional independence from its fundraising ability, designed to fund staff positions and other expenses after the Republican majority decided in 1995 to cut money for CBC staff and funding for other activities. The CBC also maintains policy and research articles on affirmative action on its Web page.

See also Apartheid; Bush, George Herbert Walker; Busing; Carter, James "Jimmy" Earl, Jr.; Civil Rights Restoration Act of 1988; Clinton, William Jefferson; Democratic Party and Affirmative Action; Ford, Gerald Rudolph; *Grove City College v. Bell*; Guinier, Lani; Integration; Nixon, Richard Milhous; Rangel, Charles; Reagan, Ronald; Republican Party and Affirmative Action; South Africa and Affirmative Action; Stereotyping and Minority Classes; Thomas, Clarence.

FURTHER READING: Barker, Lucius J., Mack H. Jones, and Katherine Tate, 1999, *African Americans and the American Political System*, 4th ed., Upper Saddle River, NJ: Prentice Hall; Barker, Lucius J., and Jesse J. McCorry Jr., 1976, *Black Americans and the Political System*, Cambridge, MA: Winthrop Publishers; Johnson, James B., 1996, "Focus and Style Representational Roles of Congressional Black and Hispanic Caucus Members," *Journal of Black Studies* 26, no. 3:245–273; Miller, Jake C., 1979, "Black Legislators and African-American Relations, 1970–1975," *Journal of Black Studies* 10, no. 2:245–261; Whitby, Kenny J., 2000, *The Color of Representation: Congressional Behavior and Black Interests*, Ann Arbor: University of Michigan Press.

MFANYA D. TRYMAN

Connerly, Ward (1939–)

Ward Connerly, former chairman of the American Civil Rights Institute (ACRI) and founder of the Center for Individual Rights and member of the University of California Board of Regents, is currently one of the most notable and outspoken opponents of affirmative action in the United States. As a member of the University of California Board of Regents, Connerly led the Board of Regents in 1995 in rejecting the use of racial preferences in admissions and also spearheaded ending the use of preferences for employment and contracting throughout California. In the educational realm, Connerly strongly argues that universities should base their admissions decisions on allegedly objective criteria such as grade point averages and standardized test scores, rather than giving what he believes to be unfair preferences to some students based on their race or sex. After dismantling the use of racial preferences in the University of California system, Connerly accepted the chairmanship of the ACRI in late 1995. At that time, the ACRI was struggling. However, under his leadership, the ACRI spearheaded the passage of Proposition 209 in 1996 that ended the use of affirmative action in California's public university admissions policies, as well as barring the use of racial preferences in state employment and state contracting. The more formal name for Proposition 209, the California Civil Rights Initiative, borrows its name from the organization that spearheaded the campaign. Since 1996, Connerly has been targeting affirmative action and attempting affirmative action policy changes in Texas, Michigan, Alabama, and Florida. Connerly and the ACRI have utilized two tactics to gain support to end affirmative action programs. First, they have sought to gain voter support by spearheading the inclusion of referenda on the ballots of state elections. Second, they have organized and provided legal backing to student plaintiffs in affirmative action court cases.

In his autobiography, titled *Creating Equal: My Fight against Race Preferences*, Connerly stated that he did not accept a position on the University of California Board of Regents in 1993 with the intention to challenge the use of racial preferences. However, according to Connerly, once he was on the board, he came to see the use of racial preferences as identical to old-fashioned racial discrimination. Connerly also claimed that the use of racial preferences at the University of California resulted in less qualified students being admitted, while other deserving students were denied admission based solely on skin color. His views on racial preferences as being akin to racial discrimination are illustrated in his comments pertaining to Proposition 209 in his book:

> Proposition 209 was anathema to the Clintonites precisely because it unmasked affirmative action for what it had become over the last quarter century—not a "subtle plus" that imperceptibly affirmed black ambition, but a regime of systematic race preferences that put the government back in the same discrimination business that it had been in in 1954, when Thurgood Marshall, then lead attorney in *Brown vs. Board of Education*, wrote, "Distinctions by race are so evil, so arbitrary and insidious that a state bound to defend the equal protection of the laws must not allow them in any public sphere." (Connerly 2000, 320)

Connerly was appointed to the University of California Board of Regents by California governor Pete Wilson in 1993 and has served on the board since that time. His term on the board expires on March 1, 2005. As an appointed member of the board, he continues to focus the attention of the nation on the use of a race-based system of preferences in its admissions policy. Connerly has become a controversial figure to many proponents of affirmative action, and many people have criticized him for being untrue to his race (Connerly is African American) and have even called him an "Uncle Tom" for his position on the use of racial preferences. He is chief executive officer of Connerly and Associates, a Sacramento land-use consulting firm he founded in 1973. He has also received numerous awards for his efforts to end affirmative action programs, including the Patrick Henry Award (1995) from the Center for the Study of Popular Culture and Individual Rights Foundation, the Thomas Jefferson Award (1998) from the Council for National Policy, and the Ronald Reagan Award (1998) from the California Republican Party. He has been profiled on such prominent media channels as *60 Minutes*, the *New York Times*, *The News Hour with Jim Lehrer*, *Dateline*, and *Meet the Press*. He also is the author of countless articles and columns on affirmative action in the United States.

Ward Connerly was born on June 15, 1939, in Leesville, Louisiana. Connerly was raised by his grandmother and claims that he was poor throughout much of his childhood. He first attended American River Junior College and later Sacramento State College, serving as student body president at both institutions. He was the first in his family to graduate from college, earning a bachelor of arts degree in political science (with honors) from Sacramento State in 1962. After graduation, he worked throughout the 1960s as a government employee of the state of California, working on housing, redevelopment, and urban affairs issues. Then legislator Pete Wilson hired Connerly in 1969 as the chief consultant on urban affairs for a California State Assembly committee. In 1973, he left government employment and began his own business firm, which specialized in urban consultation and land use. In 1993, Governor Pete Wilson appointed Connerly to the University of California Board of Regents.

See also African Americans; American Civil Rights Institute; *Brown v. Board of Education*; Center for Individual Rights; Education and Affirmative Action; Marshall, Thurgood; One Florida Initiative; Proposition 209; Standardized Testing; Uncle Tom; Washington Initiative 200.

FURTHER READING: American Enterprise Institute for Public Policy Research, 2003, "Ward Connerly," *American Enterprise* 14, no. 13 (April–May): 18–21; Connerly, Ward, 2000, *Creating Equal: My Fight against Race Preferences*, San Francisco: Encounter Books; Connerly, Ward, 2001, "Losing the Soul of the GOP: Republicans Make Rotten Peace with Racial Preferences," *National Review* 53, no. 19 (October 1): 42–45; Pooley, Eric, 1997, "Fairness or Folly? Ward Connerly Brings His Campaign against Affirmative Action to a Wider Stage Just as Clinton Rolls Out a New Set of Race Initiatives," *Time* 149, no. 25 (June 23): 32–37; Zelnick, Bob, 1996, *Backfire: A Reporter's Look at Affirmative Action*, Washington, DC: Regnery Publishing.

GLENN L. STARKS

Constitution, Civil Rights, and Equality

The U.S. Constitution, the Declaration of Independence, and the Articles of Confederation are considered the primary founding documents of the new republic, a republic dedicated to the Jeffersonian proposition that all men are created equal. The Constitution was a far-reaching and revolutionary document in many areas, such as creating a democracy and representative form of government and enshrining a bill of rights for the people. Yet despite these great advances in political thought at the time, the plight of minorities and women was largely ignored in formulating the new republic. It would not be until ratification of the Civil War (Reconstruction) Amendments that the Constitution offered minimal levels of protection of civil liberties and rights for minorities in the United States. Today the Constitution and its various provisions (especially the Fifth and Fourteenth Amendments) play a crucial role in the affirmative action debate.

The framers of the American Constitution initially were not as concerned with civil liberties and civil rights for the common American as they were with the despotism of the king of England, who they felt continued to abuse the individual rights of elites in the thirteen colonies. The men commonly called the Founding Fathers accused the king of England of being a despot who trampled upon the rights of colonists and treated them as if they were slaves. This was made clear in the Declaration of Independence, in which they accused the king of imposing tyranny over the colonies. Their charges included mock trials, forgoing judicial proceedings with the accused, the lack of voting rights, the imposition of troops in colonial homes, transporting large armies to wreak death and destruction upon colonists, and a host of other grievances related to civil rights. The language of the independence document is full of references to "inhumanity," "barbarism," and related terms referencing the cruelty of the king.

Yet the authors of the document could not see the hypocrisy and contradictions between their own plight and the manner in which blacks were treated as slaves with no rights whatsoever under nascent American law. George Washington, Thomas Jefferson, and a number of others who signed the Declaration of Independence and later the Constitution were slave owners who failed to extend the most basic notions of humanity to what was considered chattel property. Nevertheless, they vehemently complained to the king of England regarding what they considered to be their inhumane treatment. In fact, when the Constitution was drafted, the inhumanity of which they accused the king was already "carved in stone" regarding the treatment and status of slaves, and a number of concessions were made to southern slave owners to bring them into the budding union.

While some northern framers of the Constitution (e.g., Benjamin Franklin and John Adams) were opposed in principle to enshrining the institution of slavery in the Constitution, the northern framers basically compromised with the southern framers on the issue of slavery to bring the southern states into the new union (earning the Constitutional Convention the appellation of the "Great Compromise of 1789"). Thus, while the words "slave" or "slavery" never appeared in the Constitution (and would not appear until ratification of the Thirteenth Amendment in 1865), the Constitution did contain several clauses euphemistically dealing with the institution of slavery. These included the infamous "Three-Fifths Compromise" clause and the compromise over the abolishment of the international slave trade, in which it was agreed that the importation of slaves from Africa would extend only until 1808. Since blacks were considered property without any rights, the new Constitution also specified that runaway slaves had to be returned to their owner through the process of extradition. Hence the document left untouched the practice of slavery in the various states. This prompted Thomas Jefferson to once remark that the issue of slavery lay undisturbed and coiled up like a serpent under the table at the Constitutional Convention, left to grow and become more menacing to the Republic with each passing year.

In 1857, the constitutional permissibility of slavery was tested at the highest court level, the U.S. Supreme Court, in the case of *Dred Scott v. Sandford*, 19 How. 393 (1857). Dred Scott, a slave, had been taken to a free state. Scott sued for his freedom, maintaining that since he was in a free state rather than a slave state, he was a free man. The Court ruled otherwise, and Scott was returned to the slave state from which he had come and remained a slave. In essence, the Court declared that the institution of slavery was valid under the Constitution, and Congress had no right to pass legislation to the contrary. With the Emancipation Proclamation by President Abraham Lincoln in 1863, and the ratification of the Thirteenth Amendment in 1865, blacks received their freedom, if not civil rights. The ratification of the Fourteenth and Fifteenth Amendments in 1868 and 1870, respectively, did much to enshrine civil rights protections for blacks in the Constitution. Additionally, with the passage of the Civil Rights Acts of 1866 and 1875, blacks obtained civil rights and access to public accommodations, though both would be of an ephemeral nature. The Supreme Court narrowly construed the Constitution and dismantled much of the Reconstruction civil rights acts through such cases as the *Civil Rights Cases*, 109 U.S. 3 (1883). After this, there would not be another significant civil rights act passed until 1957, some eighty-two years later.

In the meantime, after the turn of the twentieth century, the Supreme Court slowly began to chip away at efforts intended to deny civil rights for blacks in *Guinn v. United States*, 238 U.S. 347 (1915), which nullified grandfather clauses, and *Smith v. Allwright*, 321 U.S. 649 (1944), which did away with the white primary. White women, through the efforts of female leaders like Susan B. Anthony and the suffrage movement, gained the right to vote with the passage of the Nineteenth Amendment to the Constitution in 1920. The major legislation passed by Congress to ensure civil rights for blacks and black women came with the passage of the 1964 Civil Rights Act and the Voting Rights Act of 1965, which, taken together, among other things, eliminated literacy tests, attacked discrimination through a number of provisions, and removed the final barriers in the quest for the ballot and the right to vote. Under Title VII of the 1964 Civil Rights Act, antidiscrimination laws would eventually spawn affirmative action programs.

From the ratification of the Civil War (Reconstruction) Amendments to the 1960s, the concept of civil rights became associated, if not synonymous, with blacks more than with any other people of color or women in their struggle for full freedom, justice, and equality in the United States. Ironically, white women had more civil rights related to voting and holding office during the colonial period than after the American Revolution for independence. While the Constitution meant a brighter day for those protesting the treatment of the colonists by England, it would be viewed as a curse upon a significant segment of humanity that had neither civil rights nor human rights. Yet today, the struggle for civil rights under the Constitution has benefited many Americans, not just blacks, and it has created greater diversity in society and the workplace. The struggle has lasted more than 200 years and continues today as gays and lesbians, people with disabilities, and other classes make new claims regarding civil rights.

See also Articles of Confederation; Bill of Rights; Civil Rights Act of 1866; Civil Rights Act of 1875; Civil Rights Act of 1957; Civil Rights Act of 1964; *Civil Rights Cases*; Civil War (Reconstruction) Amendments and Civil Rights Acts; Declaration of Independence and Equality; *Dred Scott v. Sandford*; Fifth Amendment; Fourteenth Amendment; Nineteenth Amendment; Race in Colonial America; Slavery; Slavery and the Founding Fathers; Suffrage Movement; Thirteenth Amendment; Three-Fifths Compromise; Voting Rights Act of 1965.

FURTHER READING: Berman, Larry, and Bruce Allen Murphy, 1999, *Approaching Democracy*, 2d ed., Upper Saddle River, NJ: Prentice Hall; Hayes, Floyd W., 2000, *A Turbulent Voyage*, 3d ed., San Diego: Collegiate Press; Kaczorowski, Robert J., 1987, "To Begin the Nation Anew: Congress, Citizenship, and Civil Rights after the Civil War," *American Historical Review* 92, no. 1 (supplement to 92): 45–68.

MFANYA D. TRYMAN

Contract Theory

See Social Contract.

Contracting and Affirmative Action

Government contracting, education, and employment are the three areas in which affirmative action has been most utilized in the last several decades. Of these three areas, contracting was the first field in which notions of modern affirmative action were applied. In 1961, President John F. Kennedy issued his famous Executive Order 10925, which included the first official modern use of the term "affirmative action," ordering federal contractors to "take affirmative action" in ensuring no discrimination within the contractor's organization. In 1965, President Lyndon Johnson issued Executive Order 11246, which superseded Kennedy's Executive Order 10925 and again mandated that contractors take affirmative action to ensure that all employees and subcontractors were treated without regard to their race, creed, color, gender (added to Johnson's executive order in 1967), or national origin. President Richard Nixon also employed affirmative action in the contracting setting, most notably with his Philadelphia Plan, which for the first time required that contractors employ race-based preferences for the benefit of minorities (and not just "affirmative action" to ensure that nondiscrimination was the norm in the contractor's dealings with its employees or subcontractors). Toward the end of his presidency, through executive order, Nixon also expanded the coverage to include not just minorities, but also veterans and people with disabilities. Furthermore, in the years since these seminal executive orders, Congress, and state and local governments as well, have created set-asides for certain beneficiaries found to be underrepresented in contracting work in awarding government contracts.

Thus today, affirmative action impacts the contracting field in two chief ways: first, it requires that government contractors employ affirmative action in promoting certain groups (minority groups, veterans, persons with disabilities, and so on) within the contractor's organization or in the contractor's dealings with subcontractors; and second, certain government contracts may be awarded specially to disadvantaged business enterprises in certain areas.

However, to fully understand contracting and affirmative action, it is helpful to trace the history of the usage of affirmative action in contracting. As mentioned earlier, Kennedy's Executive Order 10925 forbade any contractors with the federal government to discriminate against their employees and mandated that "the contractor will take affirmative action to ensure that applicants are employed, and that employees are treated during employment, without regard to their race, creed, color, or national origin." This actually was not the first antidiscrimination executive order, as President Franklin Roosevelt had mandated nondiscrimination by defense contractors as early as 1941 through his Executive Order 8802. In fact, a nondiscrimination clause has been required in all government contracts since that time. However, President Kennedy's executive order is considered important as the starting point for discussions of affirmative action in general federal contracting because Kennedy first used the term "affirmative action" within the body of the order. Nevertheless, several years later, in 1965, President Johnson issued Executive Order 11246, which superseded Kennedy's Executive Order 10925 and remains today one of the essential federal rules imposing affirmative action obligations upon contractors doing business with the federal government ("federal contractors").

Prior to the 1970s, the notion of modern affirmative action was an amorphous one and was applied mostly in the contracting setting pursuant to Kennedy's Executive Order 10925 and, subsequently, Johnson's Executive Order 11246. It is interesting to note that Kennedy and Johnson's executive orders used the term "affirmative action" in the negative sense, to take affirmative action to ensure that there was no special treatment on account of race. For example, under Kennedy's Executive Order 10925, contractors were not permitted to discriminate and were required to take "affirmative action" in ensuring that considerations of race, color, or national origin did not enter the decision to hire minorities. The same is true of Johnson's Executive Order 11246, which also prohibited employment discrimination based on race, color, religion, or national origin by executive branch agencies and federal contractors and subcontractors. Thus it would be correct to describe the Kennedy and Johnson executive orders as race neutral in application.

However, during the Nixon administration, affirmative action took on color-conscious characteristics for the first time. Specifically, the Philadelphia Plan, part of Nixon's broader "southern strategy" (to win southern voters while dividing the labor and civil rights groups), imposed a race-conscious preferential affirmative action plan for the construction industry. Specifically, the Philadelphia Plan mandated that those contractors bidding for federal government business must meet the government-determined numerical amount of minority workers in the firm. Thus a business wishing to bid on and win a government contract had to establish that it had an explicit number or quota of minority workers in its organization to be successful in the bidding process. For this reason, the Philadelphia Plan has been described as the first federal use of "racial quotas" and the "greatest irony of all in the story of affirmative action" (Skrentny 1996, 177), as these affirmative race-conscious rules were initiated during the conservative presidency of Richard M. Nixon.

Today, there are three chief mandates imposing affirmative action obligations upon federal contractors: Johnson's Executive Order 11246 (as amended), the Rehabilitation Act of 1973, and the Vietnam Era Veterans' Readjustment Assistance Act (the Veterans Act) of 1974. Executive Order 11246, as amended, mandates affirmative action for the benefit of minorities and women. The Rehabilitation Act requires contractors to utilize affirmative action for people with disabilities. Last, the Veterans Act, as amended, requires affirmative action for veterans of the Vietnam War, veterans of other specified military operations, veterans who are disabled, or veterans who are "recently discharged" from active duty.

Holders of federal government contracts (i.e., those contractors who hold a governmental contract that exceeds $10,000) are not only required to adhere to and follow all workplace and employment antidiscrimination statutes that are applicable to businesses (e.g., Title VII of the Civil Rights Act of 1964), but must also follow several laws that mandate that the contractor utilize affirmative action in its dealings with its employees and subcontractors. Under current federal law, there are two tiers or levels of affirmative action obligations, depending largely upon the value of the federal government contracts. The first level, known as the "basic threshold," covers the following contractors: first, any contractor who has a single government contract that exceeds $10,000; second, any contractor with multiple contracts, the aggregate of which exceeds $10,000 during any twelve-month period; third, anyone holding a government bill of lading in any amount; and fourth, any financial institution serving as a depository of federal funds regardless of the amount. The second threshold level or tier, known as the "AAP threshold," applies to any nonconstruction contractor that has at least fifty employees and holds a federal contract that exceeds $50,000. Also, financial institutions that serve as depositories for federal funds, and holders of government bills of lading, meet the higher AAP threshold level if they employ fifty employees or more.

For the basic threshold level, contractors agree not to discriminate unlawfully and to take affirmative action to ensure equal employment opportunities within the contractor's business. Such affirmative action measures may include such things as recruiting minority members or offering special training programs. For the heightened AAP threshold, contractors must agree not to discriminate and to practice affirmative action (like those contractors subject to the basic threshold level), but must also develop and implement an affirmative action plan that sets forth specifically how the contractor will achieve equality for members of all minority groups, as well as for women. The affirmative action plan must be annually updated and must be provided to the Department of Labor, Office of Federal Contract Compliance Programs (OFCCP), if requested. The affirmative action plan is not a simple document and is subject to audit and inspection by the OFCCP. The plan must include a narrative section delineating affirmative action implementation strategies, as well as sections concerning the statistical "workforce analysis." Because of the comprehensiveness of the required plan, it has been described as "potentially . . . a liability document for an employer. It may create liability for a contractor in OFCCP proceedings (if the contractor did not comply with the regulations) as well as in private discrimination and other employment litigation (if the contractor failed to fulfill its AAP commitments)" (Lindemann and Grossman 1997, 1095). Additionally, special contract rules apply to businesses that hold "federally assisted construction contracts." Those businesses that hold construction contracts are required not to discriminate, to adopt a written affirmative action plan, to post notices regarding equal opportunity and nondiscrimination laws, and to provide OFFCP access for purposes of an OFFCP investigation or audit.

While these special affirmative action obligations are applicable only to businesses that hold government contracts, they significantly impact the American economy and workforce. It has been reported that "these [affirmative action requirements for contractors] cover an estimated $184 billion in federal contracts, pursuant to which approximately 27 million individuals—roughly one fourth of the national workforce—are employed" (Lindemann and Grossman 1997, 1081–1082). The Department of Labor is vested with ensuring compliance with all of the specific affirmative action rules. The secretary of labor has delegated this compliance responsibility to the OFCCP, which is chiefly responsible for administering and enforcing the various rules through reporting procedures, auditing, investigations, and other measures.

A second major aspect of contracting and affirmative action has to do with set-aside programs for disadvantaged business enterprises (DBEs) (formerly often referred to as minority business enterprises) at the federal, state, or local level. Under programs such as these, disadvantaged businesses may be reserved a percentage of certain types of contracts within the state. On the federal level, the 8(a) Business Development Program administered by the Small Business Administration (SBA) oversees such programs. Under federal law, to become a certified participant in the 8(a) program, a business must be at least 51 percent owned by a person who is economically and socially disadvantaged. Members of minority groups, including African Americans, Asian Americans, Hispanic Americans, and Native Americans, are presumed to be socially disadvantaged, although this is a rebuttable presumption. A non-minority-owned business must prove that it has an objective distinctive feature not common to non–socially disadvantaged society and that it has been socially disadvantaged within the United States because of that feature. Then a business owner must prove that his or her social disadvantage has made him or her economically disadvantaged by restricting his or her access to capital or credit resources. Once a business is certified, it is able to receive technical and financial assistance to improve its ability to supply services to government, and contract set-asides, bid preferences, and subcontractor compensation clauses are included in contract bid packages to increase the demand for DBE services. Finally, it should also be noted that government set-aside contracts based exclusively upon racial considerations (i.e., minority-owned business set-asides) have been viewed with suspicion and disfavored by the Supreme Court during recent years and in notable and famous cases such as *City of Richmond v. J.A. Croson Co.*, 488 U.S. 469 (1989), and *Adarand Constructors, Inc. v. Peña*, 515 U.S. 200 (1995).

See also Adarand Constructors, Inc. v. Peña; Affirmative Action Plan/Program; African Americans; Asian Americans; *City of Richmond v. J.A. Croson Co.*; Department of Labor; Disadvantaged Business Enterprises; Economically Disadvantaged; Employment (Public) and Affirmative Action; Executive Order 8802; Executive Order 10925; Executive Order 11246; Hispanic Americans; Johnson, Lyndon Baines; Kennedy, John Fitzgerald; Native Americans; Nixon, Richard Milhous; Persons with Disabilities and Affirmative Action; Quotas; Rehabilitation Act of 1973; Roosevelt, Franklin Delano; Title VII of the Civil Rights Act of 1964; Veterans' Preferences; Vietnam Era Veterans' Readjustment Assistance Act of 1974.

FURTHER READING: Canady, Charles T., and Robert C. Scott, 1998, "Should Washington End All Preferences in Hiring and Contracting?" *Insight on the News* 14, no. 15 (April 27): 24–28; Lindemann, Barbara, and Paul Grossman, 1996, *Employment Discrimination Law*, 3d ed., vol. 1, Washington, DC: Bureau of National Affairs; Millenson, Debra A., 1999, "Whither Affirmative Action: The Future of Executive Order 11246," *University of Memphis Law Review* 29 (spring/summer): 679–737; Skrentny, John David, 1996, *The Ironies of Affirmative Action*, Chicago: University of Chicago Press.

JAMES A. BECKMAN

Convention on the Elimination of All Forms of Discrimination against Women

Described as an international bill of rights for women, the Convention on the Elimination of All Forms of Discrimination against Women (CEDAW) was adopted by the United Nations General Assembly in 1979. The convention both defines discrimination against women and establishes an agenda for national action by signatory states to end discrimination against women. The CEDAW calls on nations to reduce barriers against women in employment, education, health care, finance, and other areas. The convention also explicitly supports affirmative action as a permissible temporary measure to achieve gender equality. For example, in the educational realm, the CEDAW calls for nations to "take all appropriate measures" to ensure equal educational opportunities. Once gender equality has been established, the convention mandates that affirmative action measures be abandoned. Furthermore, the CEDAW specifies that affirmative measures taken to eliminate gender discrimination "should not be deemed gender discrimination" for purposes of antidiscrimination laws. As of December 10, 2003, 175 states had become parties to the convention, which first went into force on September 3, 1981. On July 30, 2002, the U.S. Senate Foreign Relations Committee approved U.S. ratification of the CEDAW. As of January 2004, the full Senate has not debated or otherwise taken action on the CEDAW. The United States is the only industrialized country that has yet to ratify the convention.

Equal rights for men and women were one of the tenets of the Universal Declaration of Human Rights and were echoed in the Preamble to the Charter of the United Nations. This alone was enough to obligate all states to strive toward the goal of gender equality and to establish a Commission on the Status of Women as a subsidiary of the Human Rights Commission. Between 1949 and 1959, the commission elaborated several conventions designed to define specific rights of women. CEDAW was born of the desire to produce a comprehensive convention that would define all of the rights of women for the increasingly complex and sophisticated United Nations system. CEDAW was originally produced as a nonbinding declaration in 1967. Work soon began on a binding agreement, and CEDAW was finally adopted in 1979.

CEDAW was intended to be a convention that compelled states to action. Consequently, states that accept the convention commit themselves to pursuing specific policies to end discrimination against women. These actions can take a variety of forms, but common steps include incorporating equality for women and men into national laws and repealing laws that discriminate against women. The United Nations also seeks to have states attempt to eliminate discrimination against women by all social actors, including private enterprises. In furtherance of these goals, signatory states are also encouraged to establish special tribunals or other public institutions to police discrimination against women.

The human rights protections contained in CEDAW are quite broad. Discrimination against women is defined as "any distinction, exclusion or restriction made on the basis of sex which has the effect or purpose of impairing or nullifying the recognition, enjoyment or exercise by women irrespective of their marital status, on a basis of equality of men and women, of human rights and fundamental freedoms in the political, economic, social, cultural, civil or any other field" (CEDAW, Article 1).

Article 4 of the convention explicitly supports affirmative action as a temporary measure intended to create de facto equality between men and women. Such affirmative action is declared not to be discrimination for the purposes of the convention. Furthermore, it is declared that any affirmative action must be done without creating separate standards for men and women. Once de facto equality has been effectively accomplished, affirmative action programs are to be abandoned. This provision is distinct from the provisions requiring signatory states to take concrete steps to eliminate discriminatory laws or to take measures designed to foster the full development of women in cultural, political, economic, and social fields.

CEDAW is unique among international human rights treaties both in the specific protections it provides and its approach to culture and tradition. CEDAW is the only convention to explicitly protect reproductive rights of women. Although prior treaties have affirmed the rights of individuals to change or retain their nationality, CEDAW is the only one that specifically affirms that right for women and their children. CEDAW is also unique in its specific targeting of culture and tradition as forces that shape gender roles and family relations and may thereby encourage discrimination.

Indeed, in regard to changing cultural attitudes, CEDAW contains extensive obligations for states to change social attitudes toward women. States are obligated, for instance, to eliminate all gender biases and stereotypes about gender roles and appropriate subjects and levels of education for women and men. States are also obligated to ensure the protection of women in rural areas by creating cooperative organizations for rural women and providing education. The convention also prohibits child engagement or marriage, mandates that women and men have the same rights during marriage and responsibilities regarding parental duties, and provides that both spouses have an equal right to choose their married name.

Like many other international human rights treaties, the primary enforcement mechanism for CEDAW is reporting. Signatory states are obligated to produce a report on their compliance with its provisions every four years. There is some evidence that indicates that this reporting requirement has helped to shape the agenda of national policy and has facilitated the adoption of programs to fight discrimination against women.

The convention establishes a Committee on the Elimination of Discrimination against Women that will review these reports and monitor compliance and progress of signatory states. This committee is composed of twenty-three experts nominated by the signatory states themselves. This committee may also make suggestions and recommendations to states through the Economic and Social Council regarding progress in meeting the goals of the convention. The committee is somewhat constrained in its monitoring activities by the convention's stipulation that the committee would not normally meet for more than two weeks per year. As a consequence, the committee has developed a procedure of dialogue with state officials through written correspondence based on the states' periodic reporting.

As of the June 18, 2002, ratification by Bahrain, CEDAW had 90 signatories and 170 ratifications. The United States has signed the convention, but has not yet ratified it. Therefore, the United States is not bound by the provisions of the convention. Consequently, the United States participates in neither the committee nor the mandatory reporting. Numerous American human rights and women's rights organizations have encouraged the Senate to ratify CEDAW, but that has not yet happened.

See also Convention on the Elimination of All Forms of Racial Discrimination; United Nations Commission on the Status of Women.

FURTHER READING: Cohn, Marjorie, 2002, "Affirmative Action and the Equality Principle in Human Rights Treaties: United States' Violation of Its International Obligations," *Virginia*

Journal of International Law 43 (fall): 249–274; Ginsburg, Ruth Bader, and Deborah Jones Merritt, 1999, "Affirmative Action: An International Human Rights Dialogue," *Cardozo Law Review* 21 (October): 253–282; Halberstam, Malvina, "United States Ratification of the Convention on the Elimination of All Forms of Discrimination against Women," *George Washington Journal of International Law and Economics* 31: 49–77; Hoq, Laboni Amena, 2001, "The Women's Convention and Its Optional Protocol: Empowering Women to Claim Their Internationally Protected Rights," *Columbia Human Rights Law Review* 32 (summer): 677–726; O'Neill, Terry, and Janice Shaw Crouse, 2002, "Should the U.S. Senate Ratify the CEDAW Treaty?" *Insight on the News* 18, no. 34 (September 16): 40–44.

RACHEL BOWEN

Convention on the Elimination of All Forms of Racial Discrimination

Adopted by the United Nations General Assembly in 1965 and brought into full force in 1969, the Convention on the Elimination of All Forms of Racial Discrimination (CERD) is a human rights treaty under the United Nations system that encourages the use of affirmative action to remedy racial injustice. The convention commits its state parties to take affirmative steps to remedy racial discrimination and to report to the United Nations regarding progress in that regard. The CERD, in its preamble, specifies that member countries to the treaty should strive to "adopt all necessary measures for speedily eliminating racial discrimination in all its forms and manifestations." Furthermore, the CERD specifies, in Article 1, that affirmative measures taken to eliminate racial discrimination "should not be deemed racial discrimination" (e.g., reverse discrimination) for purposes of antidiscrimination laws. Finally, the CERD specifies that any affirmative measures taken shall only be temporary in nature. The convention entered into force for the United States on November 20, 1994; however, the United States entered into several reservations and understandings qualifying its obligations under the CERD when the Senate ratified it in 1994. Specifically, the Senate stipulated that the treaty is non-self-executing (i.e., subsequent legislation is required to implement any obligations contained within the treaty on the national level) and that the United States need not implement any obligation that is found to be inconsistent with the U.S. Constitution. As of November 2, 2003, there were 169 countries who were parties to this treaty.

The term "racial discrimination" in the CERD is defined broadly to include "any distinction, exclusion, restriction or preference based on race, colour, descent, or national or ethnic origin which has the purpose or effect of nullifying or impairing the recognition, enjoyment or exercise, on an equal footing, of human rights and fundamental freedoms in the political, economic, social, cultural or any other field of public life" (CERD, Article 1). Persons of all races are guaranteed the panoply of civil, political, and social rights contained in other United Nations conventions. States are further charged with assuring these rights to their subjects. Article 2 of the CERD mandates that "state parties shall, when circumstances so warrant, take, in the social, economic, cultural and other fields, special and concrete measures to ensure the adequate development and protection of certain racial groups." Further, Article 4 requires state parties to "adopt immediate and positive measures designed to eradicate . . . discrimination."

The state parties to CERD agree to undertake several measures to eliminate discrimination and promote understanding between races. These measures include legal reforms such as eliminating any explicitly discriminatory laws and refraining from engaging in any state-sponsored discrimination. State parties also agree to endeavor to eliminate discrimination by private groups and to encourage the development of integrationist multiracial unions. Several specific actions and policies are targeted by the convention. Apartheid and legal racial segregation are both explicitly condemned in Article 3. The convention also goes on to condemn a variety of cultural and intellectual expressions of racial discrimination, including propaganda and incitements to racial violence. States are exhorted to criminalize all such expressions. State actors are prohibited from engaging in them.

In 1993, the Office of the High Commissioner for Human Rights issued a general recommendation on implementation of CERD that implicitly approved of affirmative action. The high commissioner's recommendation indicates that a difference of treatment will not necessarily be considered discrimination. Rather, the Committee on the Elimination of Racial Discrimination will examine the intent of the difference. If the intent of the differential treatment is in furtherance of the convention's purposes, then the difference will not be considered discrimination under the convention. Only if the intent of the difference is directed against the convention will the difference be considered discrimination.

In 1999, the Office of the High Commissioner for Human Rights issued a general recommendation exhorting states to be sure to include all racial, ethnic, or national groups and all indigenous peoples present within the state in their periodic reporting. The high commissioner indicated that there have been problems with states frequently reporting on the situation and status of some racial, national, ethnic, or indigenous groups while disregarding others. The high commissioner further raised a concern that many states do not regularly collect data on the racial, ethnic, national, or indigenous identity of their populations. By failing to maintain these data, states may be inadvertently violating the rights of these persons.

As is the case with many human rights conventions, the primary enforcement mechanism contained in CERD is reporting. State parties are obligated to provide reports to the Committee on the Elimination of Racial Discrimination within one year of ratification of the convention and every two years after the initial report. These reports are intended to contain updates on the legislative, judicial, administrative, or other measures that states have adopted and that give effect to the provisions of the convention. These biennial reports have produced some controversy because states are criticized by their subjects as well as international actors for the failures reported and especially for the failures not reported. The convention provides for party states to make complaints to the committee regarding failures of other states if they are so moved. The variety of implementation recommendations issued by the high commissioner attests to the frequency of these complaints. The United States issued its initial report in September 2000 during the Clinton administration, five years after the United States first ratified the CERD. Interestingly, in the report, the United States took the position that "affirmative action plays an essential role in ensuring that economic and educational benefits are offered equally to all people in the United States, and that those programs can be developed in a way that is fair to all."

The convention established the Committee on the Elimination of Racial Discrimination, which consists of eighteen experts nominated by the state parties. The committee reviews the reports of state parties and additional complaints with the aim of monitoring compliance of state parties with the terms of the convention. The committee reports annually to the General Assembly on the progress of the convention. In the case of state party complaints, the committee is also authorized to establish a conciliation commission to investigate and resolve disputes between nations regarding implementation of the convention.

The Committee on the Elimination of Racial Discrimination was the first such committee created within the United Nations system to monitor compliance with a single convention. The General Assembly decided to create the committee as a part of the convention because it felt that without this enforcement mechanism, the convention would be ineffective. In the years following the adoption of the CERD and the creation of the committee, the United Nations has created five other treaty bodies. These committees monitor the rights of women, torture, the rights of the child, economic, social, and cultural rights, and human rights.

See also Census Classifications, Ethnic and Racial; Clinton, William Jefferson; Convention on the Elimination of All Forms of Discrimination against Women; Discrimination; Reverse Discrimination; Segregation.

FURTHER READING: Cohn, Marjorie, 2002, "Affirmative Action and the Equality Principle in Human Rights Treaties: United States' Violation of Its International Obligations," *Virginia Journal of International Law* 43 (fall): 249–274; Ginsburg, Ruth Bader, and Deborah Jones Merritt, 1999, "Affirmative Action: An International Human Rights Dialogue," *Cardozo Law Review* 21 (October): 253–282.

RACHEL BOWEN

Criminal Justice System and Affirmative Action

The American criminal justice system has historically been characterized as a white male series of institutions encompassing the areas of law enforcement, the courts, and corrections. As such, police, correctional systems, and to a lesser extent the courts have been slow to embrace women and people of color within their ranks. Much attention has been given in the professional literature to the discrimination that occurs against offenders in the subcomponents of the criminal justice system, while little attention has been focused upon the employees of those same systems. Affirmative action is therefore a useful tool to consider as a remedy in both contexts, as it is the lack of diversity within the criminal justice system that leads to racial discrimination against offenders. In a 2001 report, Human Rights Watch criticized the first international report submitted by the United States to the Committee on the Elimination of Racial Discrimination because the report inadequately considered racial discrimination within the criminal justice system of the United States. Likewise, in another report critical of the U.S. report to the Committee on the Elimination of Racial Discrimination, the Meiklejohn Civil Liberties Institute chronicled pervasive racial discrimination in the criminal justice system and alleged that minorities are disproportionately arrested, harassed, and prosecuted and are sentenced to harsher punishments than white individuals. Proponents of affirmative action argue that affirmative action is the best means to cure these problems of racial discrimination in the criminal justice system.

All societies have had some individuals whose job it was to maintain order and protect citizens. In some ancient societies, these were formal positions, with the main focus being to protect the ruler. Other ancient societies, such as the Greeks, relied upon informal mechanisms by which the family of the victim would be responsible for apprehending wrongdoers and bringing them before the authorities. During the Middle Ages, a feudal system developed in which kings began to assume the responsibility of order maintenance and the rule of law. The American experience with law enforcement can be traced back to the English system in which sheriffs were appointed based upon an organization of tithings. The rise of the professional police force is the result of the Thames Police Act of 1800, through which the Thames River in London and adjacent lands were protected from thieves. In 1829, the London Metropolitan Police Department was formed as the first professional police force and the one upon which American law enforcement is based.

As some cities in America became more populated and the amount of crime was on the rise, the need for organized police to act as safeguards for the citizenry became more important. With increasing populations and immigration rates, more police departments were formed throughout America during the nineteenth century. During the twentieth century, the trend continued with clear demarcations between local, state, and federal law-enforcement agencies. One characteristic of nearly every law-enforcement agency regardless of its jurisdiction until quite recently was the fact that the members of the forces were primarily white males. Part of the reason for the overwhelming representation of white males among law enforcement was recruiting practices that in effect discriminated against minorities and women.

During the 1960s and 1970s, the federal government, in response to charges of minority underrepresentation in law enforcement, authorized several commissions to study the problem and offer solutions. The 1967 President's Commission on Law Enforcement and Administration of Justice concluded that police departments across the country must hire and actively promote minority officers to help relationships with minority communities they were charged with protecting. About the same time, the National Advisory Commission on Criminal Justice Standards and Goals concluded that job discrimination existed in the field of law enforcement and offered a system of standards to which law-enforcement agencies must adhere to deal with discrimination. Some of these standards included the active recruitment of women and minorities. As a result of these studies and commissions and the civil rights climate in America, two pieces of legislation were passed by Congress to address these and similar issues. The Civil Rights Act of 1964, Title VII, and the Equal Employment Opportunity Act of 1972 provided vehicles by which lawsuits and affirmative action programs could be implemented.

As a result of this legislation, some departments made efforts to remedy past discrimination. Several reasons have been cited for the failure in those departments that did not succeed. First, departments did not recruit widely enough to secure a pool of candidates who were best suited for law enforcement. Second, minorities often did not meet the minimum educational requirements for positions in law enforcement. Finally, in the black community at least, law enforcement as a career was not thought of in a positive light. Thus police departments around the United States had to work very hard to ensure that their individual departments reflected the community they were sworn to protect and serve. Slowly, police administrators began to realize that a diverse police force can better serve the community than a police force that is overwhelmingly white. Even today, large metropolitan areas whose populations are largely black and Hispanic still have forces that are predominantly made up of white male officers. Recruitment of women in law enforcement has lagged behind recruitment of minority officers in most locations, where today women make up about 10 percent of the nation's police officers.

The courts have been a little more successful in reflecting the gender and racial makeup of America than has law enforcement. The courts include judges, prosecutors, and defense attorneys, and the primary reason why the courts have been fundamentally male and white is the historically discriminatory admission policies of law schools. If a school systematically excluded women or people of color, it is no wonder that diversity does not exist on the benches in courtrooms and in prosecuting cases or defending clients. It was not until the middle of the twentieth century that the majority of law schools in America actively admitted women and people of color, often because they were required to do so by law. For example, within the federal judiciary, the first woman appointed to the federal bench was Florence Allen in 1934 by President Franklin Roosevelt. The first black, William Hastie, was appointed in 1949 by President Harry Truman.

Prosecution and public defender offices are often avenues for new attorneys just graduating from law school to enter the profession. As more women and minorities were admitted to law schools and successfully graduating, more were seeking employment in either prosecution or public defender offices. Thus as more minorities were graduating from law school, the diversity of the prosecutors and the defense attorneys changed. Today, it is not unusual for some large prosecution and public defender offices to have nearly as many women as men, and they are beginning to support minority applicants in great numbers.

The final area that has been slow to reflect diversity in the workplace is corrections. Much like law enforcement, this profession has historically been dominated by white males, largely because corrections work was not seen as "appropriate" for women. Part of the reason women have been slow to enter the ranks of correctional employees is the lack of female prisoners housed within the United States. Not until the war on drugs, beginning in the late 1970s and continuing today, has the number of women incarcerated been large enough to warrant a significant number of female correctional officers. The traditional view was that women should not work in institutions for males because of the privacy issues and the fact that correctional facilities were very dangerous places. Thus few women worked in all-male prisons until the 1970s. There were a few exceptions to this, including the first female correctional administrator in the United States, Mary Weed, who in 1793 was named principal keeper of the Walnut Street Jail in Philadelphia, Pennsylvania. Other early women in corrections were Clara Barton, who served as superintendent of the Massachusetts Reformatory Prison for Women in 1882, and Eliza Farnham, who was head matron at New York's Sing Sing Prison between 1844 and 1848. These are certainly exceptions to the general rule precluding women from service as correctional officers. Today, fewer than 10 percent of the wardens and superintendents of American prisons are women.

It has been difficult for women to move up the ranks in state and federal correctional agencies. Typically there are certain jobs that are seen as steppingstones for advancement within these systems. These jobs have systematically excluded women either because of where they are located or because of the privacy issues revolving around the inmates housed where these jobs are located. Some cases have been filed by women that challenge the lack of advancement because they were excluded from "male-only" jobs that are required for promotion. One such case is *Hardin v. Stynchcomb*, 691 F.2d 1364 (11th Cir. 1982), in which a female deputy brought a class-action lawsuit claiming that she was discriminated against in the promotion process based upon her sex. Relying upon Title VII of the Civil Rights Act of 1964, she was able to establish the arbitrary practice of having some positions reserved only for male deputies, thus blocking her chances for advancement.

Clearly the criminal justice system is still dominated by white males. While this is slowly beginning to change, there is still a long way to go in terms of representation by minorities and women in these occupations consistent with the at-large percentage of these groups in society. It clearly makes sense for law-enforcement agencies to represent the community they patrol both in gender and in race. A department that "looks like" the community will be more effective in dealing with that community. Likewise, the courts should also function more effectively if they have more women and minorities in positions of power within the system. Finally, correctional facilities need to reflect the makeup of the inmate population. With more than 2 million prisoners in America and many of them being people of color, departments of corrections need to actively recruit qualified minorities to ensure that staff-inmate problems are not made worse because employees are all white males.

See also Civil Rights Act of 1964; Convention on the Elimination of All Forms of Racial Discrimination; Equal Employment Opportunity Act of 1972; Jury Selection and Affirmative Action; Minority Professionals and Affirmative Action; Racial Profiling; Roosevelt, Franklin Delano; Title VII of the Civil Rights Act of 1964; Truman, Harry.

FURTHER READING: Butler, Paul, 1997, "Affirmative Action: Diversity of Opinions: Affirmative Action and the Criminal Law," *University of Colorado Law Review* 68 (fall): 841–888; CivilRights.Org, 2003, Report, "Justice on Trial: Racial Disparities in the American Criminal Justice System"; Fukurai, Hiroshi, 1997, "A Quota Jury: Affirmative Action in Jury Selection," *Journal of Criminal Justice* 25:477–502; Highsmith, Gary, 1996, *Black Skin, White Justice: Race Matters in the Criminal Justice System*, Yale–New Haven Teachers Institute, http://www.yale.edu/ynhti/curriculum/units/1996/1/96.01.10.x.html; U.S. Commission on Civil Rights, 2000, Report, *Revisiting Who Is Guarding the Guardians? A Report on Police Practices and Civil Rights in America*, Washington, DC: U.S. Government Printing Office.

SUSAN F. BRINKLEY

Critical Race Theory

Critical race theory became noticeable in the mid-1970s when scholars of color realized that the civil rights movement of the 1960s had stalled and that there was a need for alternative and critical explanations for the continuing presence of racism in American society. While critical race theory has its origins in critical legal studies (CLS), critical race theory criticizes CLS for its emphasis on class and economic structure, but not on race, in its writings. Critical race theory is an intellectual movement that embraces critical legal scholars, especially scholars of color, who portray legal culture as subjective and biased toward people of color. For example, in the affirmative action context, critical race theorists have criticized the notion of objectively selecting individuals based upon merit. Richard Delgado, a critical race theory adherent, has argued that "merit sounds like white people's affirmative action. . . . A way of keeping their own deficiencies neatly hidden while assuring that only people like them get in." Critical race theory regards the law as an instrument of white supremacy that maintains and promotes the oppression and exploitation of people of color in American society. Critical race theory advocates a "race consciousness" that challenges the construction and representation of race in society and in the legal system. By challenging oppressive racial structures in society, critical race theory calls for change in social structure and institutional processes that subordinate people of color.

In the affirmative action context, many of the underlying premises or arguments in favor of, or against, affirmative action are challenged by critical race theorists as being biased against people of color. The notion of merit, or the possibility of meritocracy, is attacked as being flawed in how society defines merit, arguably focusing on irrelevant factors or factors of little overall importance, like performance on standardized test scores. Other traditional underlying arguments in favor of affirmative action are also challenged. For example, Richard Delgado has argued that insisting on affirmative action to promote diversity is wrong. Delgado claims that the focus on diversity as the chief justification for affirmative action suggests that minorities are used to benefit majority (white) students by contributing to their diversity and educational experience, while not focusing on the needs of minority candidates (which would be the true justification for affirmative action). Delgado also challenges the role model argument in favor of affirmative action, arguing that the underlying assumption of the role model theory is that minorities are expected to assimilate into white culture and then pass these lessons along to younger individuals of the same minority group.

Critical race theory is grounded in several themes. One theme is the emphasis on context as a tool for unraveling the racial injustice experienced by people of color in American society. Understanding the context of racial injustice that defines the lived experience of people of color in American society is a foundation for questioning the privileges conferred on white society by the law. A second theme focuses on interest-convergence theory. According to interest-convergence theory, white society promotes change or reform in the law for people of color only if it promotes and protects white interests. A third theme is that racism is normal in American society because it is the product of social forces and institutional processes that treat race as a discriminating dimension necessary to the maintenance of order in society. A fourth theme is a critique of liberalism. Critical race theory argues against liberal claims that the law is neutral, objective, and color blind.

A fifth theme, and perhaps the most noticeable, in critical race theory is an emphasis on the experiential knowledge of people of color and their communities in its study of society and its legal culture. Critical race theory uses narrative, usually in the form of stories or first-person accounts, to show how people of color experience racism in American society. The use of stories, parables, or family histories allows critical race theorists to give voice to people of color and their communities. The purpose in giving voice to people of color and their communities is to eliminate racial inequality and oppression. On the one hand, having voice empowers people of color to view their social reality as meaningful in a society that seeks to marginalize their presence. On the other hand, having voice enables people of color to engage in political practice that seeks the elimination of racism.

See also Civil Rights Movement; Diversity Management; Ideological Racism/Racist Ideology; Meritocracy; Role Model Theory; White Supremacy.

FURTHER READING: Aguirre, Adalberto, 2000, "Academic Storytelling: A Critical Race Theory Story of Affirmative Action," *Sociological Perspectives* 43, no. 2 (summer): 319–326; Crenshaw, Kimberle, Neil Gotanda, Gary Peller, and Kendall Thomas, eds., 1995, *Critical Race Theory: The Key Writings That Formed the Movement,* New York: New Press; Delgado, Richard, 1987, "The Ethereal Scholar: Does Critical Legal Studies Have What Minorities Want?" *Harvard Critical Legal Studies Law Review* 22:301–323; Delgado, Richard, ed., 1995, *Critical Race Theory: The Cutting Edge,* Philadelphia: Temple University Press; Matsuda, Mari J., Charles R. Lawrence, Richard Delgado, and Kimberle Crenshaw, 1993, *Words That Wound: Critical Race Theory, Assaultive Speech, and the First Amendment,* Boulder, CO: Westview Press; Nan, Carolos J., 1994, "Adding Salt to the Wound: Affirmative Action and Critical Race Theory," *Law and Inequality: A Journal of Theory and Practice* 12:553–572; Trucios-Haynes, Enid, 2001, "Why Race Matters: LatCrit Theory and Latina/o Racial Identity," *La Raza Law Journal* 12:1–42.

ADALBERTO AGUIRRE JR.

D

Darwinism

Darwinism refers to the scientific theories of Charles Robert Darwin (1809–1882), and largely those theories contained in his 1859 book *On the Origin of Species by Means of Natural Selection.* While Charles Darwin wrote in the scientific realm, his theories on evolution were misapplied to the social science, political, and economic realms. His theories that were applied in these non-science fields became known as "social Darwinism" and were simplified (and often incorrect) versions of his scientific theories. For example, some supporters of Darwin's theory of evolution simplified its biological principles of natural selection to merely "survival of the fittest." This "social Darwinism" theory served as the stimulus to individual and racial progress as a "scientific" justification for racism. Under the cloak of science, many critics of social programs to benefit one group over another call such programs unneeded paternalism and a violation of Darwin's theories applied in the economic setting, particularly the concept of "survival of the fittest." In the economic and labor setting, some like Herbert Spencer have argued that advancement should be based upon survival of the fittest and those who are not able to compete and advance should simply be left behind. Furthermore, *On the Origin of Species* impacted society (and the nonscientific fields) by implying that a kind of truth could be attained through science. Renowned evolutionist Stephen Jay Gould wrote that following its publication, "subsequent arguments for slavery, colonialism, racial differences, class structures and sex roles would go forth primarily under the banner of science" (Gould, 72).

Charles Robert Darwin launched a revolution in Western civilization with the 1859 publication of his book *On the Origin of Species by Means of Natural Selection; or, The Preservation of Favored Races in the Struggle for Life.* It immediately sold out, and Darwin wrote five more editions in his lifetime. Victorian society heavily attacked the work because it did not support the depiction of creation given in the Book of Genesis. Darwin's novel argument for evolution focused on the innovative concept of natural selection and how it worked automatically. He purposely avoided applying "natural selection" to human societies; however, others did not. The nineteenth-century English philosopher Herbert Spencer fathered the theories of social Darwinism. These now generally discredited theories were an attempt to legitimize social inequality and explain social class and processes by appealing to popular misunderstandings of Darwin's evolution theory.

In 1831, the British Empire authorized Darwin to sail around the world aboard the survey ship H.M.S. *Beagle* to observe and record different types of flora and fauna. During the five-year expedition, Darwin's observations forced him to question the then-current belief in the special creation of each species. After returning, Darwin used finches collected from the Galapagos Islands to investigate why it was that slightly different species inhabited each island. He noted that the bills of the various species were adapted for particular diets. Some had shorter ones useful for cracking seeds, while others had long, sharp beaks useful for prying insects out of their hiding places. He thought it improbable that each of the fourteen species had been individually created on each island. Further, finches observed on the mainland were clearly related. Based on ideas of inheritance and divergence, Darwin illustrated that the isolation provided by the Galapagos Islands permitted the finches to diverge from a common ancestor while adapting themselves to the local conditions on each island. Thus the division into new species could occur by ongoing variation, selection, and inheritance in isolation. In essence, his novel theory of evolution can be distilled into that statement that organisms better suited to their environment gain some survival advantage and pass this genetically transmitted advantage to their offspring.

In assessing the contributions of Darwin's work, it should be noted that the key role in heredity of the nucleus, chromosomes, and DNA had not been demonstrated. Furthermore, the theory of evolution was developed before the publication of Mendel's work on inheritance. More recent studies have drawn closely together the fields of evolution, genetics, and molecular biology, and modern molecular evidence has impressively boosted the theory of evolution. Examples appear to exist in today's human population. The inherited disease of sickle-cell anemia is caused by a single base mutation in one hemoglobin gene and appears with a high frequency in African populations, often upwards of 40 percent. While these individuals may have clinical problems, the mutation appears to provide a profound survival advantage against the most lethal form of malaria in Africa. Another example involves a selective short deletion within the CCR5 gene in European populations. This genetic alteration may have provided a survival advantage against the black plagues that scoured the countryside centuries ago. These examples reemphasize Darwin's theory that as the environment changes, individuals with new characteristics will do better, live longer, and produce more offspring until, eventually, the population will look very different from its original version.

Many countries, especially the British Empire, used the misapplied concepts of social Darwinism to help justify their cause of imperialism. American businessmen of the time warmly embraced these theories to keep the working class suppressed. Many people, from Karl Marx to Adolf Hitler, have also employed social Darwinism in their arguments. From this, the twentieth-century eugenics movement was spawned and unfortunately put into practice. It sought to "improve" human genetic stock, much as farmers do in agriculture, by promoting the perfection of the human race by removing its "undesirables" while multiplying its "desirables"—

in short, by encouraging the procreation of the social Darwinian fit and discouraging that of the unfit.

Despite the negative social implications associated with Darwin and his theory of evolution, it was a remarkable scientific landmark. The philosopher Daniel Dennett wrote, "If I were to give an award for the single best idea anyone has ever had, I'd give it to Darwin, ahead of Newton and Einstein and everyone else." It has been said that no book, other than the Bible, has had a greater effect on society than Darwin's *On the Origin of Species* (Dennett 1995, 21).

See also Eugenics; Marxist Theory and Affirmative Action; Racial Discrimination; Scientific Racism; Split-Labor-Market Theory.

FURTHER READING: Darwin, Charles R., 1964, *On the Origin of Species*, Cambridge, MA: Harvard University Press; Dennett, Daniel, 1995, *Darwin's Dangerous Idea*, New York: Simon & Schuster; Gould, Stephen J., 1981, *The Mismeasure of Man*, New York: W.W. Norton; Stryer, Lubert, 1988, *Biochemistry*, San Francisco: W.H. Freeman.

PETER L. PLATTEBORZE

De Facto and De Jure Segregation

De facto segregation is a social phenomenon in which individuals of different races, colors, or ethnicity live, work, and are educated separately with or without the existence of laws or formal policies prescribing this separation. While de facto segregation has been perpetuated on both ethnic and racial bases, its ethnic form (which was prominent during the late-nineteenth-century mass immigrations of central, eastern, and southern Europeans), has faded away, while its racial form remains. De jure segregation refers to the same pattern of separating individuals by race or ethnicity, except that such segregation is maintained by the authorization and sanctioning of the law.

Historically, individuals seeking to maintain ethnic and cultural purity have segregated themselves from members of other ethnic groups that they deem incompatible, inferior, or harmful. Initially, racial segregation was accomplished directly through segregation by law, that is, de jure segregation. De jure segregation forcibly separated individuals on the basis of race or color, reducing their interaction and establishing rigid social and geographic settlement patterns. These patterns persisted after de jure segregation laws were ruled to be unconstitutional under the Fourteenth Amendment by the Supreme Court in the 1954 case *Brown v. Board of Education*, 347 U.S. 483 (1954). The effects of decades of de jure segregation and new informal methods of segregation perpetuated by its advocates have kept de facto segregation in place. Segregated geographic housing patterns have been perpetuated through public housing siting, deed restriction, exclusionary zoning, realtor and lender practices, and, increasingly, economic disparity, and local governments have gerrymandered service boundaries to create segregated school districts and municipalities. Gradually, courts have ruled that many of these practices are unconstitutional as well, but economic disparity and renewed choices by both majority and minority ethnic groups to live in ethnically nondiverse locations have remained and drive de facto segregation today.

See also Apartheid; *Brown v. Board of Education*; Caste System; Civil Rights Act of 1964; Color Consciousness; Color-Blind Constitution; Fifteenth Amendment; Fourteenth Amendment; Jim Crow Laws; Segregation.

FURTHER READING: Higham, John, 1955, "Strangers in the Land: Nativism and Nationalism," in *From Different Shores: Perspectives on Race and Ethnicity in America*, edited by Ronald Takaki, New York: Oxford University Press; McDonald, Laughlin, and John A. Powell, 1993, *The Rights of Racial Minorities: The Basic ACLU Guide to Racial Minority Rights*, Carbondale: Southern Illinois University Press; Schroder, Oliver, Jr., and David T. Smith, eds., 1965, *De Facto Segregation and Civil Rights*, Buffalo, NY: William S. Hein and Co.

MARK J. SENEDIAK

Declaration of Independence and Equality

The Declaration of Independence, adopted by the Continental Congress on July 4, 1776, contains the authoritative expression of the idea of equality in the American political tradition: "All men are created equal." The most famous passage of the Declaration is a summation of the principled foundations and purposes of American government:

> We hold these truths to be self-evident, that all men are created equal, that they are endowed by their Creator with certain unalienable Rights, that among these are Life, Liberty and the pursuit of Happiness.—That to secure these rights, Governments are instituted among Men, deriving their just powers from the consent of the governed,—That whenever any Form of Government becomes destructive of these ends, it is the Right of the People to alter or to abolish it, and to institute new Government.

The self-evident truth "that all men are created equal" is the most fundamental and far-reaching principle affirmed in the Declaration. This is the central idea of the American political experiment from which all other ideas radiate. It is a philosophical idea about human nature, the natural relation of each human being to all others, and the place of all human beings in the natural or created universe.

The revolutionary and founding generation of Americans expressed this idea of human equality in a variety of ways. The language of the Declaration of Independence is "that all men are created equal." To express the same idea, the Virginia Declaration of Rights (June 12, 1776) stated that "all men are by nature equally free and independent" (Kurland and Lerner 1987, 6–7). The Declaration of the Rights of the Inhabitants of the Commonwealth of Massachusetts (March 2, 1780) stated that "all men are born free and equal" (Kurland and Lerner 1987, 11).

All of these phrases are different ways of expressing a doctrine about the "state all men are naturally in," which the American colonists had learned in large part from the English philosopher John Locke. Locke had written, less than a century before the Declaration of Independence, that all men are naturally in

> a *state of perfect freedom* to order their actions and dispose of their possessions and persons as they think fit, within the bounds of the law of nature, without asking leave or depending upon the will of any other man.
>
> A *state* also *of equality*, wherein all the power and jurisdiction is reciprocal, no one having more than another: there being nothing more evident than that creatures of the same species and rank promiscuously born to all the same advantages of nature, and the use of the same faculties, should also be equal one amongst another without subordination or subjection, unless the Lord and Master of them all, should by any manifest declaration of his will set oneabove another, and confer on him by an evi-

> dent and clear appointment an undoubted right to dominion and sovereignty. (Locke, 8)

To say that all men are by nature equal is to say that human beings are not naturally subordinated one to another. No man is by nature the master or the slave of another. As Thomas Jefferson stated in his last extant letter, written just a week before he died: "The mass of mankind has not been born with saddles on their backs, nor a favored few booted and spurred, ready to ride them legitimately, by the grace of God." Human beings, then, are naturally free as they are naturally equal. It is from natural human equality and freedom that the Founders derived the idea that government could justly be founded only on consent. Because human beings are not naturally subordinated to one another (they are equal and free), their consent must be obtained before any human being may rightfully exercise authority over them. They have a natural right to consent to any government that is to be placed over them.

Government among free and equal men is formed, the American Founders would say, by "social compact." In the words of the Massachusetts Constitution of 1780: "The body-politic is formed by a voluntary association of individuals: It is a social compact, by which the whole people covenants with each citizen, and each citizen with the whole people" (Kurland and Lerner 1987, 11). The American body politic is a social compact in which each equal citizen is pledged to the defense of all and all equally to the defense of each for the sake of the ends proclaimed in the American Declaration of Independence and elaborated in the U.S. Constitution.

Because they are equal and free by nature, human beings may not rightfully consent to just any government—to a form of tyranny, for example. In the idea of natural human equality and freedom is the recognition of human rationality and of the limits of human rationality. As Locke wrote, "We are *born free,* as we are born rational" (Locke, 34). Because human beings are by nature rational beings, one man may not rightly rule over another as he may rightly rule over a nonrational being (like a dog or a horse). But also, because no man is all-knowing or all-good—that is, because human reason is limited and fallible and subject to human passions—one human being may never rightly subject himself to the unrestrained will or unlimited power of another. This is what James Madison meant when he wrote that "government . . . [is] the greatest of all reflections on human nature":

> If men were angels, no government would be necessary. If angels were to govern men, neither external nor internal controuls on government would be necessary. In framing a government which is to be administered by men over men, the great difficulty lies in this: You must first enable the government to controul the governed; and in the next place, oblige it to controul itself. (Hamilton, 290)

Human nature or human equality—the fact that human beings are neither angels nor mindless brutes—is the idea that gives rise to the idea of constitutional or limited government. This is a political constitution that conforms to the natural constitution of man. Because human beings are fallible and because their reasons are sometimes subject to their passions, human government must be subject to law. Human beings would only reasonably consent to be ruled by laws made by another if that other agreed to be bound by the same laws.

In the words of Abraham Lincoln, a nation "dedicated to the proposition that all men are created equal" will—if circumstances permit—be under a "government of the people, by the people, for the people." In other words, the principle of equality gives rise most naturally to a democratic or republican form of government. James Madison expressed this idea best in number 39 of *The Federalist Papers*, where he considered whether the government proposed under the new constitution would be "strictly republican." "It is evident," he wrote,

> that no other form would be reconcilable with the genius of the people of America; with the fundamental principles of the Revolution; or with that honorable determination which animates every votary of freedom, to rest all our political experiments on the capacity of mankind for self-government. (Hamilton, 208)

Majorities govern by right in a democracy because they are the logical or natural political expression of human equality, of the equal right of the people to govern themselves. But the principle of equality does not lead to unqualified deference to majorities. Precisely because of human equality, minority rights are inseparable from majority rule. The same human equality that justifies majority rule sanctifies minority rights. Any majority that oppressively denies to the minority the exercise of equal rights has forfeited its claim to govern. Majority tyranny is as illegitimate as any other tyranny in the light of the principle of equality.

See also Articles of Confederation; Bill of Rights; Civil War (Reconstruction) Amendments and Civil Rights Acts; Constitution, Civil Rights, and Equality; Social Contract.

FURTHER READING: Hamilton, Alexander, et al., *The Federalist Papers*, 1999, edited by Clinton Rossiter with introduction and notes by Charles R. Kesler, New York: New American Library; Jefferson, Thomas, June 24, 1826, "To Roger C. Weightman," in *Writings*, 1984, edited by Merrill D. Peterson, New York: Literary Classics of the U.S.; Kurland, Phillip B., and Ralph Lerner, eds., 1987, *The Founders' Constitution*, vol. 1, Chicago: University of Chicago Press; Lincoln, Abraham, November 19, 1863, "The Gettysburg Address" in *The Collected Works of Abraham Lincoln*, 1953, edited by Roy P. Basler, New Brunswick, NJ: Rutgers University Press; Locke, John, 1690, *The Second Treatise of Government* in *Two Treatises of Government*, 1980, edited by C. B. Macpherson, Indianapolis, IN: Hackett Publishing Company.

CHRISTOPHER FLANNERY

Declaration of Sentiments

The Declaration of Sentiments was a document drafted by participants of the Women's Rights Convention at Seneca Falls, New York, in 1848 and proclaiming and demanding the political and economic rights of American women. The emphasis of the document is equality: women are entitled to the same rights as men. Women should be entitled to vote, as well as pursue careers in any and all trades or professions open to men, especially medicine, law, and the ministry. The document further insists that a married woman is entitled to a civil standing equal to that of a husband. Furthermore, it declares that all women are entitled to try to acquire property and, if they do acquire it, are entitled to control and personally benefit from this property in the same manner that men are entitled.

Modeled on the Declaration of Independence (DI), the Declaration of Sentiments (DS) begins by asserting that "mankind" is entitled to an explanation for the actions the delegates of the Women's Rights Convention intend to take to secure their rights as women. There are some important distinctions, however, between the two documents. The first paragraph of the DI begins, "When . . . it becomes necessary for one people to dissolve the political bands" and ends with "should declare the causes which impel them to . . . separation." The DS begins, however, "When . . . it becomes necessary for one portion of the family of man to assume among the people of the earth a position different from that which they have hitherto occupied." The drafters of the DS refer to the family as that of "man"; the general intention and "sentiment" of the document remains clear, however: to assert and demand a standing for women equal to that of men, including an equal standing within the bonds of marriage. Still, the DS promotes the idea of bonds rather than the idea of dissolution that characterizes the DI. The DS features the metaphor of the family, and the emphasis is not on independence, strictly speaking, but on civil equality and personal freedom with respect to the rights of both women and men.

The second part of the DS follows the content and structure of the DI even more closely, but with two important changes. First, the phrase "all men are created equal" that appears prominently in the DI has been expanded: "all men and women" are created equal in the DS. Second, whereas the intent of the DI is to abolish an unresponsive government, the intent of the DS is "refuse allegiance" to a male-dominated government until it recognizes the equality of women. The emphasis is on passive resistance to the abuses of the system rather than a complete rejection of the system itself. Aside from these differences in the two documents, however, the DS articulates with virtually identical language the same basic civic theory expressed in the DI: a theory founded on the ideas of natural rights—liberty and equality—as well as the Lockean idea of social contract.

Next, the DS lists the "injuries and usurpations" that American men have inflicted on women, much as the DI lists the injuries the king of Great Britain had inflicted on the colonies. First and foremost of the injuries the DS lists is the denial of the right to vote. Although single women could own property, which was taxed, these women had no voice in deciding, for example, how the taxes were spent: that is, taxation without representation. For married women, the problem was even more acute. Married women could not own property at all, or at least had no control over it. Neither married nor unmarried women could enjoy "profitable employments"—such as in medicine or law—and they received "scanty remuneration" for whatever modest work they could find. A college education was denied them. They were excluded from any position of leadership in the church. Finally, in that a woman was expected to defer to her husband on spiritual questions, she was denied the freedom of conscience, which placed the destiny of her soul in jeopardy.

The list of injuries is followed by a series of resolutions, most of which mirror the list of injuries. Essentially, the resolutions reaffirm the natural equality of women and demand that the structure of civil society reflect this fact. The first few of these resolutions all relate to the importance of suffrage. One hundred people signed the DS, even though some of the delegates to the Women's Rights Convention were reluctant initially to insist on the right to vote. This resolution was adopted finally, however, primarily due to the efforts of Elizabeth Cady Stanton and Jane Hunt, two of the five drafters of the DS. (The other three drafters were Mary Ann McClintock, Lucretia Mott, and Martha C. Wright.)

The DS borrows copiously and quite consciously from the DI, both in form and substance. Stanton and her coauthors were influenced undoubtedly by other sources and traditions, such as the work of Karl Marx and Friedrich Engels as well as the utopian and socialist ideas of American transcendentalism. Finally, however, the ideology of the DS is not essentially communistic or socialist. Arguably, the "sentiments" of the document are no more inconsistent with a capitalist model of production and distribution than are the sentiments of the DI. That the DS does frame the demand for equality within the metaphor of the family suggests, perhaps, a more intimate, cooperative model of social relations. The ideology of the DS does not preclude the idea of competition, however. Arguably, the women who drafted and signed this document simply wanted an equal opportunity to compete. Perhaps they were demanding no more than a level playing field or, even more pointedly, the same starting place in the "race" of life. Like the DI, the DS stresses the ideas of liberty and equality far more than fraternity, the metaphor of family in this latter document notwithstanding.

As might be expected, the DS was roundly belittled both in the American press and in the pulpit, and it had no immediate impact on the political or economic order. It is considered today, however, a seminal document in the history of the women's movement in America and in the history of American culture generally. It is reprinted in most anthologies of American literature and culture.

See also Declaration of Independence and Equality; Marxist Theory and Affirmative Action; Mott, Lucretia Coffin; Seneca Falls Convention; Social Contract; Stanton, Elizabeth Cady; Suffrage Movement.

FURTHER READING: Henry, David, 1997, "Garrison at Philadelphia: The 'Declaration of Sentiments' as Instrumental Rhetoric," in *Rhetoric and Political Culture in Nineteenth-Century America*, edited by Thomas Benson, East Lansing: Michigan State University Press; Lowell, Melissa, 1993, *Breaking the Ice*, New York: Bantam Books; Monfredo, Miriam, 1992, *Seneca Falls Inheritance*, New York: St. Martin's Press; Offen, Karen, 1999, "Women and the Question of 'Universal' Suffrage in 1848: A Transatlantic Comparison of Suffragist Rhetoric," *NWSA Journal* 11, no. 1:150–177; Swain, Gwenyth, 1996, *The Path to Seneca Falls: A Story about Elizabeth Cady Stanton*, Madison: Turtleback Books; Watson, Martha, 1997, "The Dynamics of Intertextuality: Re-reading the Declaration of Independence," in *Rhetoric and Political Culture in Nineteenth-Century America*, edited by Thomas Benson, East Lansing: Michigan State University Press; Young, Louise, 1976, "Women's Place in American Politics: The Historical Perspective," *Journal of Politics* 38, no. 3:295–335.

MICHAEL D. QUIGLEY

DeFunis v. Odegaard, 416 U.S. 312 (1974)

DeFunis v. Odegaard presented the U.S. Supreme Court with its first case concerning the constitutionality of affirmative action and the issue of "reverse discrimination" within the context of higher education. Ultimately, however, the Court did not address the issue of special admissions plans and reverse discrimination in the *DeFunis* case; rather, it dismissed the case on mootness grounds. As a result, the Court left in place the legality of special admissions programs for colleges and universities based on race. The legal question of whether special preferential race-based admission policies violated the Equal Protection Clause of the Fourteenth Amendment was not resolved during the 1974 term of the Court. The issue of whether affirmative action constitutes reverse discrimination and therefore violates the Equal Protection Clause of the Fourteenth Amendment, and whether affirmative action violates the Civil Rights Act of 1964, particularly Title VI, would confront the Court four years later in *Regents of the University of California v. Bakke*, 438 U.S. 265 (1978).

In the *DeFunis* case, Marco DeFunis argued that the admissions policy of the University of Washington Law School was racially discriminatory in violation of the Equal Protection Clause of the Fourteenth Amendment and that it invidiously discriminated against him solely on account of his race. He had been previously rejected from the law school, although his test scores and college grades were adequate to gain admittance if he had been a black, Filipino, Chicano, or Native American applicant. The admissions procedures contained an optional question regarding the ethnicity of the applicant. Applicants were asked to list their dominant ethnic group as either "black, Chicano, American Indian, or Filipino," the groups that were given preference in the minority admissions program. It was the answer to this optional question that determined the sole basis for admissions in the minority program. In the year that DeFunis was rejected for admission into the law school, most of the minority applicants had admission scores below the cutoff level. Furthermore, during the subsequent legal proceedings, the school's officials admitted that any minority applicant with DeFunis's test scores and grades would have been admitted. It was this procedure that DeFunis alleged denied him equal protection under the Fourteenth Amendment and thus constituted reverse discrimination.

The trial court agreed with DeFunis's claim and granted the requested relief. Consequently, DeFunis entered law school in the fall of 1971. However, on appeal, the Washington State Supreme Court, in a 7–2 decision, reversed the trial court decision and ruled that the admissions policy was not in violation of the Constitution. By the time of the Washington Supreme Court's decision, DeFunis was in his second year of law school. At this point, DeFunis petitioned the U.S. Supreme Court for a writ of certiorari, requesting that the Court review the lower court ruling. The request for review was granted by the Court. As a result of the stay that often accompanies the U.S. Supreme Court's decision to review a case, DeFunis was able to remain in law school, and the school promised that DeFunis could stay in school regardless of the ultimate outcome of the case.

On certiorari review, the U.S. Supreme Court vacated the Washington Supreme Court's judgment and remanded the case for proceedings deemed appropriate by the latter court. Since DeFunis was in his final year of law school, the Supreme Court considered another legal issue as taking priority over the issue of whether the affirmative action plan was a violation of the Fourteenth Amendment, namely, that of mootness. The U.S. Supreme Court, in a 5–4 decision, decided to vacate and remand the case as moot because DeFunis was no longer being injured by the allegedly discriminatory admissions practice of the University of Washington. Based on the legal doctrine of mootness, which stems from the language of Article III of the Constitution that requires a "case or controversy" for the Court to have jurisdiction, the Court ruled that there no longer existed a "live case" or "controversy," as DeFunis had already been admitted and had nearly finished his law school studies. Regardless of the action taken by the Supreme Court on the merits of the case, DeFunis would be entitled to complete the quarter and receive his degree if he fulfilled all requirements. Therefore, according to the Court, in the parlance of Article III, there was no longer a real live case or controversy, and, therefore, the Court lacked jurisdiction to continue with the case. It was also noted by the Court that DeFunis had not sought a class-action suit, and therefore, once he was admitted to the law school, there no longer existed a controversy establishing an "adverse legal" relationship, or other individuals within the class whose academic career might still be effected by the case. Thus the case was ultimately dismissed on neutral procedural jurisdictional grounds.

However, Justice William O. Douglas disagreed with the majority's procedural disposition of the case and wrote a lengthy dissenting opinion in which he argued that the Court should have upheld DeFunis's case on the merits. Douglas stated that "the Equal Protection Clause did not require that law schools employ an admission formula based solely upon testing results and undergraduate grades, nor did it prohibit evaluation of an applicant's prior achievement in light of the barriers that he had overcome." However, the key according to Justice Douglas was that each application must be considered on its individual merits in a racially neutral manner. Justice Douglas was certain that racial quotas or preferences alone should never be the sole factor, saying that "we have never held administrative convenience to justify racial discrimination."

Justice Douglas further explained that a university's admissions policy employing racial classification to favor certain minority groups was subject to strict scrutiny under the Equal Protection Clause of the Fourteenth Amendment. It was his position that in view of the differences in cultural backgrounds and the inadequacies of testing procedures for determining qualifications for admission to school, the law school in the instant action had acted properly in processing applications by students of color separately from other applications. It was the view of Justice Douglas that the record was insufficient to justify the conclusion that DeFunis had been excluded because of his race. Justice Douglas concluded that the case should be remanded for a new trial to consider whether Marco DeFunis had been invidiously discriminated against.

Justices Douglas, William Brennan, Byron White, and Thurgood Marshall wrote an additional dissent. Their argument focused on the fact that *DeFunis v. Odegaard* presented an important constitutional question and therefore could not be dismissed as moot. In support of their argument, the four justices set forth an interesting query: "What would have happened if DeFunis had experienced an unexpected event—such as illness, economic necessity, or academic failure—that prevented him from graduating at the end of the current school term?" In such a case, DeFunis would once again have had to apply to the law school under the allegedly unlawful admissions policy.

See also Brennan, William Joseph; Civil Rights Act of 1964; Color-Blind Constitution; Equal Protection Clause; Fourteenth Amendment; Marshall, Thurgood; *Regents of the University of California v. Bakke*; Reverse Discrimination; Strict Scrutiny; Title VI of the Civil Rights Act of 1964; White, Byron Raymond.

FURTHER READING: Beckwith, Francis J., and Todd E. Jones, eds., 1997, *Affirmative Action: Social Justice or Reverse Discrimination?* Amherst, NY: Prometheus Books; Bell, Derrick, 1992, *Race, Racism, and American Law*, Boston: Little, Brown and Company; Farber, Daniel A., William N. Eskridge Jr., and Philip P. Frickey, 1993, *Constitutional Law: Themes for the Constitution's Third Century*, St. Paul, MN: West Publishing Company; Spann, Girardeau A., 2000, *The Law of Affirmative Action: Twenty-five Years of Supreme Court Decisions on Race and Remedies*, New York: New York University Press; Tucker, Ronnie B., 2000, *Affirmative Action, the Supreme Court, and Political Power in the Old Confederacy*, Lanham, MD: University Press of America.

RONNIE B. TUCKER SR.

Democratic Party and Affirmative Action

The Democratic Party of the United States was founded in 1792 by Thomas Jefferson, third president of the United States and author of the Declaration of Independence, the document that put forth the Jeffersonian declaration that "all men are created equal." In 1800, the party, then known as the Democratic-Republican Party, won the presidency for the first time with the election of Jefferson. The Jeffersonian Democratic Party was founded on the principles of equality and in opposition to what was perceived as the elitism of the Federalist Party. Since the United States has never had a labor party or anything similar, the Democratic Party has historically represented the needs of the American working class. At the turn of the twentieth century, the Democratic Party welcomed millions of new American immigrants, thereby creating a voting base of diverse individuals who were not well represented by the probusiness agenda of the Republican Party, which had been founded in the 1850s on the basis of opposition to expansion of slavery into U.S. territories.

In 1912, Woodrow Wilson was elected the first Democratic president of the twentieth century. Wilson continued the Democratic tradition of creating stable and long-lasting social programs that benefited the underrepresented and exploited groups in society. Wilson passed the first labor and child-welfare laws in American history. During the Great Depression in the 1930s, Democratic President Franklin Roosevelt implemented additional social programs, such as the Civilian Conservation Corps and Social Security. After President John F. Kennedy was assassinated in 1963, President Lyndon Johnson pushed through the Civil Rights Act of 1964 and the Voting Rights Act of 1965 as well as affirmative action. The Civil Rights Act of 1964 was a landmark piece of legislation that prohibited "employment discrimination by large employers (over 15 employees), whether or not they have government contracts." The signing of the Civil Rights Act of 1964 was a final addition to John F. Kennedy's Executive Order 10925, which had instructed federal contractors to take affirmative action to ensure that applicants are treated equally without regard to race, color, religion, sex, or national origin.

In a speech at Howard University on June 4, 1965, President Johnson argued for the necessity of social programs that benefited minority members of the American public, mainly African Americans. Johnson saw the Civil Rights Act as giving "20 million Negroes the same chance as every other American to learn and grow, to work and share in society, to develop their abilities—physical, mental and spiritual, and to pursue their individual happiness." President Johnson believed that the implementation of affirmative action was justified because "Negro poverty is not white poverty. Many of its causes and many of its cures are the same. But there are differences—deep corrosive, obstinate differences—radiating painful roots into the community, and into the family, and the nature of the individual." Johnson emphasized that the differences between the African American population and the rest of America's citizens were not racial, but the result of a long history of oppression, prejudice, and brutality. Johnson argued that African Americans "just can not do it alone."

> You do not take a person who, for years, has been hobbled by chains and liberate him, bring him up to the starting line of a race and then say, 'you are free to compete with all the others,' and still justly believe that you have been completely fair. Thus it is not enough just to open the gates of opportunity. All our citizens must have the ability to walk through those gates. . . . We seek not just . . . equality as a right and a theory but equality as a fact and equality as a result.

Since the implementation of affirmative action by Johnson, every American president, Republican or Democrat, has supported it in his own way. According to John David Skrentny, professor of sociology at the University of Pennsylvania, Richard Nixon, a Republican, supported affirmative action in an attempt to drive a wedge between the Democrats' "blue-collar" union vote and southern African American vote. In Skrentny's book *The Ironies of Affirmative Action: Politics, Culture, and Justice in America*, he shows that even though Nixon did not directly support affirmative action policies, he needed either the blue-collar union vote or the southern African American vote, so he supported affirmative action toward the blue-collar unions, forcing the Democratic Party to take a stance on it as well. At their 1972 convention, the Democrats countered the Republican platform by establishing "quota-like mechanisms" to further enforce affirmative action policies.

In 1978, affirmative action quotas were ruled unlawful by the Supreme Court, despite President Jimmy Carter's urging (through the solicitor general's office) that the Court uphold race-based preferences. This decision came after the case *Regents of the University of California v. Bakke*, 438 U.S. 265 (1978), was finalized. The Court found that Bakke had been denied admission to the University of California at Davis Medical School because the school had admitted minority members instead of Bakke to fill its quota of 16 out of 100 seats reserved for "disadvantaged minority students." Even though the Court ruled quotas to be unlawful, it upheld that race may be used as a factor in choosing a diverse student body.

Although the Democratic Party did not hold the presidency during the 1980s, the party's platform continued to support affirmative action, both for minority members of society and for women. Elected in 1992, Bill Clinton was the first Democratic president in more than ten years; he officially reaffirmed the Democratic platform in support of affirmative action. Clinton reassessed all affirmative action programs in 1995 and announced after the review that his policy was "Mend it, don't end it."

The Democratic Party continues to support affirmative action, even among its own members. This is evident by the party's charter and bylaws from the 2000 presidential campaign. Article 8, Section 2, states that "discrimination in the conduct of Democratic Party affairs on the basis of sex, race, age (if of voting age), color, creed, national origin, religion, economic status, sexual orientation, ethnic identity or physical disability is prohibited, to the end that the Democratic Party at all levels shall be an open party." Section 3 goes on to state that the Democratic Party "shall adopt and implement an affirmative action program which provides for representation as nearly as practicable of the aforementioned groups, as indicated by their presence in the Democratic electorate."

See also Civil Rights Act of 1964; Clinton, William Jefferson; Executive Order 10925; Johnson, Lyndon Baines; Kennedy, John Fitzgerald; McGovern Commission; Nixon, Richard Milhous; *Regents of the University of California v. Bakke*; Republican Party and Affirmative Action; Voting Rights Act of 1965.

FURTHER READING: Democratic Party, 2002, web site: http://www.democrats.org; Democratic Party, 2002, "The Charter and Bylaws of the Democratic Party of the United States," January 19, http://www.democrats.org; DNC Services Corporation, 2002, "DNC: History of the Democratic Party," http://www.democrats.org/about/history.html; "The History of Affirmative Action Policies," 2002, *In Motion Magazine*, July 7, http://www.inmotion magazine.com/aahist.html; Nationalist Movement, 2000, "Petition to Abolish Affirmative Action," http://www.nationalist.org/docs/petitions/2000/affirmative.html; Plous, S., 1996, "Ten Myths about Affirmative Action," *Journal of Social Issues* 52, no. 4 (winter): 25–31; *Public Papers of the Presidents of the United States: Lyndon B. Johnson, 1965*, 1966, vol. 2, entry 301, 635–636, Washington, DC: Government Printing Office; Skrentny, John David, 1996, *The Ironies of Affirmative Action*, Chicago: University of Chicago Press.

ARTHUR M. HOLST

Department of Defense

See Military and Affirmative Action.

Department of Education

The Department of Education is a cabinet-level department charged with overseeing education issues in the United States. There are four major functions of the Department of Education: (1) to enforce federal statutes prohibiting discrimination in programs and activities receiving federal funds and to ensure equal access to education; (2) to identify major issues and problems in education and to focus attention on these problems; (3) to collect data and oversee research on America's schools and to disseminate this information to the public; and (4) to establish policies relating to financial aid for education, to administer distribution of these funds, and to monitor their use. The Department of Education also disseminates statistical information about legislation, programs, projects, and studies relating to education. The Department of Education has evolved into a formidable force in policy and policy making in all facets of education. The department's influence is undeniable on both the kindergarten through twelfth-grade levels and higher-education levels.

The genesis of the Department of Education began in 1867. President Andrew Johnson signed the enabling legislation to create the non-cabinet-level department; however, the department lasted for only one year. The early demise of the department was due to a fear that it would overstep its bounds and exercise too much control over local schools. Even in its early days, the Department of Education collected various statistics about the nation's schools.

During the 1950s, the winds of political and social change helped fuel a call for more public aid for education. In 1953, the Department of Health, Education, and Welfare (HEW) became the tenth cabinet department, and the Office of Education was a part of this department. Within HEW, there were several major divisions, including the Office of Education, the Public Health Services, Social Security, Welfare, and the Food and Drug Administration. In the 1960s, President Lyndon Johnson's "War on Poverty" helped pave the way for improvements in education for the poor. In the following decade, many educational efforts were focused on helping racial minorities, individuals with disabilities, and women. In 1979, Congress passed Public Law 96–88, the Department of Education Organization Act. This legislation created the Department of Education.

In 1980, the Department of Education became a new cabinet post, and HEW became known as the Department of Health and Human Services. Shirley Hufstedler was selected by President Jimmy Carter to become the first secretary of education and had only about six months to get the new department up and running. Hufstedler quickly assembled an agenda that focused on strengthening the political workings of federal and state relations in education. With the presidential election defeat of Jimmy Carter in 1981, new president Ronald Reagan replaced Shirley Hufstedler with Terrel H. Bell as secretary of education. Reagan's policies toward education were consistent with the decentralization of public education. Reagan believed in providing more state control over education. Bell was charged with dismantling the Department of Education. However, by the conclusion of Bell's tenure, it was decided that the department would remain a part of the president's cabinet. The succession of secretaries after Bell includes William Bennett, Lauro Cavazos, Lamar Alexander, and Richard Riley. In 2001, Rod Paige became the first African American to be named secretary of education.

All of the Department of Education's agencies and programs have their headquarters and operations in Washington, D.C. The Department of Education's organizational structure consists of many offices, and each office fulfills some part of the department's mission. The Office of the Secretary forms goals and represents the department in various functions. The Office of the Deputy Secretary is responsible for internal management of the department and works with the secretary to achieve policy goals. The Office of the Secretary also oversees programs and external relations. The Office of the Under Secretary provides advice about policy to the secretary and is also responsible for the Budget Office and the Office of Policy and Planning. The Office of the Chief Financial Officer oversees the department's financial matters and coordinates contracts and grants.

The Office of the Inspector General investigates agency programs and operations to prevent waste, fraud, and abuse. The Office of the General Counsel provides the department with legal services. The Office of Postsecondary Education provides financial assistance and leadership to students in postsecondary education. This department also assists institutions of higher education in developing appropriate housing, facilities, and instructional programs. The Office of Rehabilitative Services promotes and provides federal funding to improve education for disabled children and adults. The Office of Bilingual Education and Minority Languages Affairs oversees various programs to help students speak English proficiently. The Office of Vocational and Adult Education helps provide funding for programs to teach citizens basic skills for employment. The Office of Civil Rights enforces laws prohibiting discrimination in the different educational instructional programs that receive federal funds. This office also assists schools to achieve voluntary compliance with civil rights laws. The Office of Educational Research and Improvement oversees research funding, demonstrates methods to improve education, and provides statistical information about the status of education. The Office of Legislative Affairs serves as the liaison between Congress and the department and also coordinates legislative activities. The Office of Intergovernmental and Interagency Affairs serves as the intermediary to intergovernmental, international, and community groups. The Office of Human Resources and Administration provides the department with administrative, personnel, technology, and other support services.

See also Carter, James "Jimmy" Earl, Jr.; Department of Health and Human Services; Johnson, Lyndon Baines; Reagan, Ronald.

FURTHER READING: Department of Education, web site: http://www.ed.gov; Office of the Federal Register, National Archives and Records Administration, 1997, *The United States Government Manual,* Washington, DC: U.S. Government Printing Office.

F. ERIK BROOKS

Department of Health and Human Services

The Department of Health and Human Services (DHHS) is the executive branch of government most involved with the basic human concerns of the population. Its programs affect nearly all citizens, especially those who are least able to help themselves. Many of the DHHS–supervised programs are outreach-type programs that specifically target minority classes in an affirmative or proactive manner. The DHHS secretary is appointed by the president and is currently responsible for administering more than 300 programs in the fields of health care and social services. Some highlights include medical and social science research, Medicare, Medicaid, Head Start, substance-abuse treatment and prevention, services for older Americans, and comprehensive services for Native Americans. DHHS works closely with state, local, and tribal governments, and many DHHS-funded services are provided by these agencies or via private-sector grantees. In fact, DHHS is the largest grant-making agency in the federal government, providing around 60,000 grants annually. As such, the DHHS is involved with federal governmental programs that give benefits and resources to people based upon recognized preferences.

The department began as the Federal Security Agency in 1939 and became the Department of Health, Education, and Welfare in 1953. Both agencies administered programs in education in addition to health and social services. Largely due to the department's unwieldy size, in 1979 educational matters were transferred to a new and separate Department of Education. Shortly thereafter the remainder of the Department of Health, Education, and Welfare was renamed the Department of Health and Human Services. In 2002, DHHS employed 65,100 persons and had a budget of $460 billion.

The department is organized into twelve major divisions, nine agencies of which are public health divisions. These include the Food and Drug Administration, the National Institutes of Health, the Centers for Disease Control, the Substance Abuse and Mental Health Services Administration, the Administration on Aging, the Health Resources and Services Administration, the Indian Health Administration, the Agency for Toxic Substances and Disease Registry, and the Agency for Health Care Policy and Research.

The Administration on Aging administers a program of grants for state and local programs that serve older Americans. It is the lead agency in DHHS on all issues related to aging. In 2001, it began an adult immunization coverage for adults sixty-five years of age or older with a particular focus on African American and Hispanic communities. The Centers for Medicare and Medicaid operates programs that serve more than one-fifth of all U.S. residents. The Medicare program is the nation's largest health insurer, processing more than 900 million claims per year.

The Indian Health Administration makes available and accessible comprehensive, culturally acceptable personal and public health services to American Indian and Alaskan Native members of federally recognized tribes. The Health Resources and Services Administration has had a long-standing concern with the diverse health needs of rural minority populations. It administers a special grant initiative for AIDS education and prevention among rural minority youth who are not exposed to existing education campaigns.

The National Institutes of Health (NIH) is the federal focal point for medical and behavioral research. Its Office of Minority Health provides advice on public health issues affecting American Indians and Alaskan Natives, Asian Americans, Native Hawaiians and Other Pacific Islanders, blacks/African Americans, and Hispanics/Latinos. Its mission is to significantly improve the health of racial and ethnic populations via the development of effective health policies and programs that help eliminate disparities.

Despite notable progress in the overall health of the nation due to a greater focus on preventive medicine and dynamic new advances in medical technology, there are continuing disparities in the burden of illness and death experienced by American minorities as compared to the U.S. population as a whole. A closer look at some of the health challenges minority communities currently face reveals significant disparities in heart disease, diabetes, and HIV. Heart disease is the leading cause of death for all racial and ethnic groups in the United States. In 1999, death rates from cardiovascular disease were 30 percent higher among African American adults than among white adults. Rates for diabetes were even higher, 70 percent higher among African Americans and nearly 100 percent higher among Hispanics than among whites. Further, American Indians and Alaskan Natives are more than twice as likely relative to the total population to develop diabetes. In 2000, African Americans and Hispanics accounted for 75 percent of all adult HIV/AIDS cases, although they comprise only 25 percent of the U.S. population. African Americans and Hispanics also make up 81 percent of all pediatric AIDS cases.

Aware of these critical issues, NIH recently created a new component, the National Center on Minority Health and Health Disparities, which is designed to continue exploring and identifying cross-cutting strategies to eliminate these health disparities. In 2002, a strategic plan was developed that included broadening the scientific research and data on minority-related health disparities, heightening public awareness of the minority challenges, creating partnerships to mobilize the larger community and stakeholders, developing and enforcing policies, laws, and regulations to support minority needs, and ensuring access to essential health and human services. Many of these plans are currently being implemented. For example, funding for the HIV/AIDS initiative, a program designed to reduce the disproportionate impact of the disease in minority communities, has more than doubled since it was first developed in 1999.

The DHHS also has programs that promote the sound development of children from lower-income families. Examples include the Vaccines for Children Program, which provides free immunizations, and Head Start. The latter is a comprehensive child development program that serves children from birth to age five, pregnant women, and their families. It seeks to increase school readiness of young children by providing a range of individualized services in the areas of education and early childhood development, medical, dental, and mental health, nutrition, and parental involvement.

Title VI of the Civil Rights Act of 1964 prohibits discrimination on the grounds of race, color, or national origin in programs and activities that receive federal assistance. The DHHS Office of Civil Rights (OCR) ensures that Americans have equal access to participate in and receive DHHS services without facing unlawful discrimination. These include Medicaid, Medicare, and all other DHHS-funded programs. By providing for the equitable treatment of beneficiaries nationwide, OCR helps DHHS carry out its overall mission of improving the health and well-being of Americans.

In January 2002, DHHS released the report *Trends in Racial and Ethnic-Specific Rates for the Health Status Indicators: United States, 1990–1998.* The report revealed "significant improvements in the health of racial and ethnic minorities, but also indicated that important disparities in health persist among different populations." These promising results illustrate the positive impact DHHS programs have had on the social welfare of the nation. Providing there is continued federal support, DHHS will continue to improve minority welfare and address minority health issues until parity is ultimately achieved.

See also African Americans; Alaskan Natives; Civil Rights Act of 1964; Head Start; Hispanic Americans; Native Americans; Native Hawaiians; Title VI of the Civil Rights Act of 1964.

FURTHER READING: Department of Health and Human Services, web site: http://www.dhhs.gov; National Center for Health Statistics, web site: http://www.cdc.gov/nchs.

PETER L. PLATTEBORZE

Department of Housing and Urban Development

The U.S. Department of Housing and Urban Development (HUD) was created in 1965 to oversee federal housing and community development programs to support the home-construction and lending industries and to provide community planning services, a political voice for urban dwellers and minorities, and decent, affordable housing for the poor. HUD provides direct housing assistance to the poor through public housing developments, section 8 rent and rehabilitation subsidies, housing vouchers in replacement of section 8 financing, HOPE financing, assistance for the homeless, lead-paint-abatement programs, and research and development of new programs as needed. HUD represents and supports the interest of minorities and the physically challenged by ensuring the participation of small and disadvantaged business enterprises in HUD projects and by enforcing the 1968 Civil Rights Act through investigation of housing discrimination complaints and prosecution of its violators through the assistant secretary of fair housing and equal opportunity (FHEO).

Direct federal involvement in urban problems and housing policy began as part of Franklin Delano Roosevelt's New Deal effort to alleviate the disastrous economic effects of the Great Depression on the U.S. economy. While blight, poor housing, and homelessness had long been an overlooked problem in America's poor urban areas, damage to the construction and finance industries, which were hit hard when tens of thousands of unemployed homeowners defaulted on their mortgages, collapsing real-estate markets and halting new construction, caused the federal government to act. Federal housing policy designed to support these industries began with the establishment of the Home Owners' Loan Corporation (HOLC) in 1933. HOLC stemmed the flow of foreclosures, saving millions of families from eviction, and stabilized the finance industry by refinancing the short-term, high-interest mortgages of distressed homeowners with long-term, low–interest mortgages. This work continues today through the Federal National Mortgage Association (FNMA), which is a private corporation under HUD guidance that buys and sells mortgages from financial institutions, providing capital to the mortgage market. In 1934, the National Housing Act created the Federal Housing Administration (FHA) to support home builders, home buyers, and the finance industry by guaranteeing the repayment of mortgage loans to allow for low down payments, riskier originations, and more new construction. This work continues through HUD's Government National Mortgage Association (GNMA), which was created by the Housing and Urban Development Act of 1968 in conjunction with the departure of FNMA to absorb some of its governmental functionality when it became a private, nonprofit corporation.

In 1942 and 1947, the wartime National Housing Agency and its permanent replacement the Housing and Home Finance Agency (HHFA) were created to coordinate and increase the efficiency of these programs. In 1965, after years of resistance, Public Law 80-174 elevated the HHFA to become the cabinet-level Department of Housing and Urban Development. Robert C. Weaver was HUD's first secretary and the first African American cabinet member. In addition to retaining HHFA's responsibility for administration of federal housing programs, the new department was designated to provide for and to represent the interests of urban dwellers and minorities by providing financial and planning assistance to aid local community development, by expanding housing opportunities for the poor, and by ensuring equal opportunity in housing for minorities and the physically disabled. Financial and planning assistance was first provided through programs such as the short-lived Model Cities Program of the late 1960s, which allowed citizen participation for the first time, in stark contrast with earlier urban renewal, slum-clearing programs. These programs are continued today through Enterprise Zones, Urban Development Action Grants (UDAG), and Community Development Block Grants (CDBG), which replaced many previous community development programs providing less funding, local control, and HUD oversight over federal funds.

See also Civil Rights Act of 1968; Disadvantaged Business Enterprises; Fair Housing Amendments Act of 1988; Housing; Housing and Urban Development Act of 1968.

FURTHER READING: Bernotas, Bob, 1991, *Know Your Government: The Department of Housing and Urban Development*, New York: Chelsea House; McFarland, M. Carter, 1978, *Federal Government and Urban Problems: HUD: Successes, Failures, and the Fate of Our Cities*, Boulder, CO: Westview Press; U.S. Department of Housing and Urban Development Library Staff, 2000, "Library Resources for Understanding the Department of Housing and Urban Development," November, HUD web site: http://www.hud.gov/about/libraryresources.cfm.

MARK J. SENEDIAK

Department of Justice

Of particular interest in the study of affirmative action is the Civil Rights Division of the U.S. Department of Justice (DOJ). The Civil Rights Division was formed in 1957 as part of the Civil Rights Act of 1957. The Civil Rights Division of the DOJ has the responsibility to enforce all federal statutes prohibiting discrimination on the basis of race, sex, handicap, religion, or national origin. While the overall DOJ has the responsibility to enforce all laws passed by Congress, the Civil Rights Division focuses upon discrimination issues.

The role of the Civil Rights Division of the DOJ has grown steadily over the years since its inception. Today the division is responsible for enforcing laws that prohibit discrimination in any area from education and employment to voting and public accommodations. The division is also charged with the prosecution of violators of a number of statutes that are designed to prohibit discrimination based upon race, sex, handicap, religion, or national origin. Unlike other governmental agencies that have offices all over the country, the Civil Rights Division of the DOJ is located in Washington, D.C., and when investigations and prosecutions are warranted, employees travel to the area of the violation.

Examples of issues handled by the division include voting rights and the enforcement of the National Voter Registration Act of 1993, conditions of institutional confinement, law-enforcement misconduct, access to reproductive health, protection for prospective home buyers in lending practices, housing discrimination, employment discrimination, equal access to education, and rights of the disabled. A criminal division prosecutes violators of any of the laws on these issues. The criminal section investigates about 3,000 cases annually, the majority of which revolve around allegations of official misconduct. Once the criminal section has acted, the case may find its way to the Civil Rights Division's Appellate Section, charged with handling cases at the circuit court of appeals level and at the U.S. Supreme Court with the assistance of the Solicitor General's Office. This section also supplies amicus curiae briefs on behalf of cases that may affect the application of the law as it impacts the Civil Rights Division of the DOJ. Finally, it is the role of the Justice Department and the Division of Civil Rights to ensure that all Americans are treated fairly and justly under the laws of the United States.

See also Civil Rights Act of 1957.

FURTHER READING: U.S. Department of Justice, web site: http://www.usdoj.gov.

SUSAN F. BRINKLEY

Department of Labor

The U.S. Department of Labor (DOL), an agency of the U.S. federal government, is responsible for regulating the employment activities of the general workforce, government agencies, and government-contracted private corporations, with primary emphasis on activities related to federal government organizations and functions. Operating under the auspices of the legislative branch, the DOL enforces more than 180 federal statutes, including legislation related directly or indirectly to affirmative action initiatives. Encompassing a wide range of employment issues (wages, health and safety, employment rights, workers' compensation, and statistical analysis), the DOL is divided into numerous divisions with corresponding offices and units.

Most federal government–related affirmative action enforcement is conducted by the DOL's Employee Standards Administration (ESA) division and its Office of Federal Contract Compliance Programs (OFCCP). The OFCCP was originally formed in 1965 as a component of President Lyndon Johnson's Great Society initiative as the Office of Federal Contract Compliance. When OFCCP was consolidated into the ESA division in 1971, it assumed the de facto responsibility for government contract compliance and assumed control officially of all contract compliance functions in 1979 (when contract compliance activities from other federal government agencies were consolidated into the DOL). OFCCP's primary responsibilities are to administer, regulate, and enforce three main equal employment opportunity (EEO) statutes: Executive Order 11246, section 503 of the Rehabilitation Act of 1973, and the affirmative action sections of the Vietnam Era Veterans' Readjustment Assistance Act of 1974. Other related statutes in which the OFCCP acts as a regulatory body are Title I of the Americans with Disabilities Act (ADA), the Immigration Reform and Control Act, and the Family and Medical Leave Act.

See also Executive Order 11246; Glass Ceiling Commission; Office of Federal Contract Compliance Programs; Persons with Disabilities and Affirmative Action; Rehabilitation Act of 1973; Veterans' Preferences; Vietnam Era Veterans' Readjustment Assistance Act of 1974.

FURTHER READING: Department of Labor, web site: http://www.dol.gov.

THOMAS A. ADAMICH

Deracialization

The term "deracialization" refers to the dismantling of the remaining vestiges of societal racism or apartheid (as the case may be) through antidiscrimination laws or more proactive approaches, such as affirmative action, to ultimately achieve the actualization of the promise of political and social freedoms for all individuals in society. The theory of deracialization helps promote the notion of equal opportunity under conditions of lingering inequality and grinding poverty that persist during periods of active and institutional racism. Phrased differently, deracialization is a social and political strategy or attempt intended to address the exhibition and presumption of a particular skin color as a normative feature in multiracial societies. For instance, in the late eighteenth and nineteenth centuries in America, whiteness was exhibited and presumed as a normative feature in the society. It carried with it the term "superiority" and benefits over other multiracial groups. The goal of deracialization is to achieve a truly color-blind society.

The concept of deracialization also involves an active collaboration of both active and passive groups and individuals, institutions and organizations, writers and scholars, and political and social rights activists to eliminate invidious discrimination in society. In times of colonial struggles, the term "deracialization" meant a replacement of white rulers with blacks on the African continent. In other words, the inheritors of the postcolonial states saw the reformation of the state through the prism of power transfer from white to black, connoted by the term "deracialization." Thus, as it relates to colonial struggles, the term was meant to encompass the notion that the reins of government should be placed directly into the hands of indigenous people and that the government should strive to ensure nondomination, nondiscrimination, more stability, and unitedness of all the people for positive development. Thus deracialization is applied in many contexts. It is conceptualized as a process to resolve even global injustices among the comity of nations socially, politically, and economically. For instance, global economic policies and the campaign of globalization are believed to be fraught with racial biases in favor of the North or the West as against the South or developing nations. The cry for justice and equity to ensure a level playing field for all nations is hinged on deracialized global economic, political, and social policies.

Historical racism and the perpetuation of racial imagery exposed the changing paradigms of race consciousness and antiracist opposition. This was emphatically manifested in the color line, which laid the background and fundamentals of racial terms for nineteenth- and twentieth-century American legal, social, and political discussions. The work and writings of many individuals in the middle to late twentieth century laid the basis for the advocates of deracialization of the complex American society. The twentieth century encountered deracialization as a political strategy adopted by black candidates in America for the conduct of political campaigns in which racial issues and themes are minimized, thereby appealing to more white voters. The idea is to reduce the dangerous tension or dividing consequences of race by avoiding plain statements on race-specific issues while at the same time emphasizing those issues that cut across racial boundaries. Thus deracialization is also an effective tool of mobilization by public officers in multiracial societies.

See also Apartheid; Color-Blind Constitution; Institutional Discrimination; Racial Discrimination; Segregation; White Supremacy.

FURTHER READING: Casey, Thomas M., 1995, "The Contextual Effects of Race on White Voters Behaviour: The 1989 New York City Mayoral Election," *Journal of Politics* 57:221–228; Liu, Paul, 2001, "Seeking a Qualified Black Candidate," paper presented at the 2001 American Political Science Association annual meeting, August 29–September 2, San Francisco, CA, 2–5; Lockard, Joseph Franklin, 2000, "Writing Race in Nineteenth Century American

Literature," Ph.D. thesis, University of California at Berkeley; Mahmood, Mamdani, 1996, *Citizen and Subject: Contemporary Africa and the Legacy of the Late Colonialism*, Princeton, NJ: Princeton University Press.

KINGSLEY UFUOMA OMOYIBO

Detroit Police Officers Association v. Young, 989 F.2d 225 (6th Cir. 1993)

The case *Detroit Police Officers Association v. Young* is one of the significant employment affirmative action cases handed down at the federal court of appeals level and illustrates how protracted litigation can be over affirmative action plans. The case also deals with the utilization of affirmative action programs to make the criminal justice system less discriminatory in practice. Additionally, the decision illustrates how closely the justifications for affirmative action plans are scrutinized by the courts, and how issues of disparate impact and treatment are weighed by the courts. *Detroit Police Officers Association v. Young* was heard in the U.S. Court of Appeals for the Sixth Circuit on three separate occasions between 1979 and 1993 following the findings of the District Court for the Eastern District of Michigan in 1978.

The origin of this litigation dates back to 1968 when the Detroit Police Department began to take measures to remedy the effects of past discrimination in its police force by initiating a major recruitment effort to encourage blacks and other minorities to join the force. At the time, the total black component of the department was between 4 and 5 percent, with even less representation in positions with rank. The department made several adjustments to assist minority candidates to negotiate the selection process. The department also made adjustments to ensure that the selection procedure reflected the skills needed to perform a police officer's job. First, the department replaced the entry-level examination that was essentially an IQ test that did not properly measure the skills required of a police officer and was considered by many to be culturally biased. Second, adjustments were made in the initial screening of applicants to attract more minority candidates. Finally, a new "promotional model" for promotion from patrolman to sergeant that would be free of bias was established. Between 1968 and 1973, the department adopted several different tests for promotion, including contracting with the University of Chicago to develop a test, but failed to produce an examination that did not have an adverse impact on black candidates. As a result, the department decided to abandon its previous policy of selecting officers for promotion to sergeant in strict numerical order from the eligibility list and adopt a 50/50 ratio of minority to nonminority candidates for staffing at all levels. This policy led to an increase in the number of black officers promoted to sergeant at the expense of white officers who stood higher on the eligibility list. The Detroit Police Officers Association filed suit in the U.S. District Court for the Eastern District of Michigan, claiming that the promotion policy discriminated against the white officers.

The district court agreed with the Detroit Police Officers Association on several issues. First, the court ruled that the affirmative action plan of the department did discriminate against white officers in the promotional process, offended the Equal Protection Clause of the Fourteenth Amendment, and violated Titles VI and VII of the Civil Rights Act of 1964. Second, the court rejected the defense contention that prior racial discrimination warranted affirmative action for either the selection or the promotional process used by the department. Third, the court found no reason to believe, as the defense asserted, that the department was in jeopardy of losing Law Enforcement Assistance Administration (LEAA) grants because of its discriminatory employment practices. Finally, the court found "no factual basis" for the defendant's claim that the operational needs of the department required employment and promotion of greater numbers of blacks to improve police service to the Detroit community.

The decision by the district court was reversed on appeal by the U.S. Circuit Court of Appeals for the Sixth Circuit. With regard to the issue of prior discrimination in the selection and promotion of officers in the Detroit Police Department, the appellate court ruled that statistical evidence of racially disparate impact of employment practices did exist. The court pointed to evidence that from 1944 to 1968, the number of whites appointed far outdistanced the number of blacks appointed, and between 1968 and 1975, when the city took proactive measures to increase the pool of black appointees, the disparity between white and black appointees was still significant. The fact that the city determined that it might have been guilty of social discrimination in the past and attempted to correct the situation should have been given more consideration than the district court gave it, according to the appellate court. Based on the statistical evidence of disparate impact and the history of discriminatory treatment, the court believed that the lower court erred in requiring the city to prove specific acts of discrimination and produce individual victims of these discriminatory acts.

The appeals court also questioned the district court's dismissal of the testimony of high-ranking police officers that a more representative black presence on the department was required to better reflect the makeup of the community it served. The appellate court pointed to the numerous studies conducted by national commissions that have recommended the recruitment of additional numbers of minority officers as a means of improving community support and law-enforcement effectiveness. Finally, the court agreed with the department's adoption of the 50/50 promotional ratio as a reasonable response, although it pointed out that the district court did not adequately address the issue.

In 1987, the court of appeals again heard arguments regarding this issue when white patrolmen challenged the preference given to black patrolmen in the promotional process. Previously, when this court had remanded the case back to the district court, the district court had granted summary judgment in favor of the city's affirmative action plan to reach the 50/50 promotional ratio of black to white sergeants. The issue before the appeals court was whether the termination point of the plan was reasonable. The appeals court agreed that relitigation of the issue of the city's past discrimination should be barred, but disagreed with the lower court's determination that judicial review of the reasonableness of the remedy should also be barred and reversed the district court's grant of summary judgment.

In 1993, for the third time since 1968, the Detroit Police Officers Association again argued on behalf of white patrolmen who contended that they had been discriminated against by reason of race in the promotional process. The plaintiffs testified that the goal sought by the 50/50 promotional plan had been attained and, in actuality, white males represented the minority in the police department. This assertion was based on the fact that the ratio of black to white sergeants was virtually identical, higher-ranking levels reflected more blacks than whites, and only 42 percent of the entire department was white. As a result, the court of appeals ruled in favor of the plaintiffs and held that the city's plan for promotion to sergeant based on a 50/50 black/white ratio must be ended.

See also Affirmative Action Plan/Program; Civil Rights Act of 1964; Criminal Justice System and Affirmative Action; Disparate Treatment and Disparate Impact; Preferences; Title VI of the Civil Rights Act of 1964; Title VII of the Civil Rights Act of 1964.

FURTHER READING: Love, Nancy, 1982, "*Comment, Detroit Police Officers Association v. Young*: The Operational Needs Justification for Affirmative Action in the Context of Public Employment," *Black Law Journal* 7:200.

CHRISTOPHER R. CAPSAMBELIS

Diaz v. Pan American World Airways, 442 F.2d 385 (5th Cir. 1971), *cert. denied*, 404 U.S. 950 (1971)

Diaz v. Pan American World Airways is the U.S. Court of Appeals for the Fifth Circuit case that set forth the current test utilized by the courts under Title VII when determining whether gender can ever qualify as a "bona fide occupational qualification" (BFOQ), thereby meriting discrimination in favor of females over males (or vice versa) by virtue of gender alone. Section 703(e) of Title VII of the Civil Rights Act of 1964 states that it is unlawful for an employer to hire based solely on sex unless sex is a "bona fide occupational qualification reasonably necessary to the normal operation of that particular business or enterprise." In *Diaz*, the Fifth Circuit put forward the "essence-of-the-business test," which specified that BFOQ discrimination is valid only if the employer must discriminate between genders to ensure that the job can be performed. Phrased another way, if a male or female employee could perform the job in question, or carry out the functions of the business, then an employer may not discriminate in favor of women (or men) by virtue of their gender. In interpreting section 703, the court held that sex discrimination is only valid when the essence of the business operation would be undermined by not hiring members of one sex exclusively. Furthermore, under section 703, there is no BFOQ defense available for race-based employment decisions. Hence the only other means for an employer to lawfully discriminate on the basis of gender or race under Title VII would be pursuant to a bona fide affirmative action plan. Finally, the *Diaz* case is an illustration of the fact that Title VII permits reverse-discrimination lawsuits.

The plaintiff, a male individual named Celio Diaz, sued Pan American World Airways when the company refused to interview him for a job as a flight attendant. Diaz was rejected as an applicant solely because the airline hired only female attendants. Diaz filed a claim with the Equal Employment Opportunity Commission (EEOC). The EEOC found probable cause of discrimination but could not resolve the claim, so the plaintiff filed suit with the district court. At the district court, the airline claimed that being a woman was a "bona fide occupational qualification" for the job. It argued that throughout the history of the company, only women had served as flight attendants. The passengers overwhelmingly preferred to be served by women, and women were better at "providing reassurance to anxious passengers, giving courteous personalized service and, in general, making flights as pleasurable as possible." The district court agreed, stating that the policy was not unlawful. Diaz appealed to the Court of Appeals for the Fifth Circuit.

The Fifth Circuit applied section 703(e) of Title VII to the case and held that the primary purpose of Title VII was to provide equal access to the job market for men and women alike. It went on to adopt the guideline issued by the EEOC that states that a bona fide occupational qualification as to sex should be narrowly interpreted. The court stated that sex discrimination is only valid when "the essence of the business operation would be undermined by not hiring members of one sex exclusively." The business of the airline is to transport passengers from one location to another, not to courteously serve them. Thus, according to the Fifth Circuit, the airline's operation would not be undermined by a male flight attendant. The Fifth Circuit's ruling became known as the "business essence test" and is still utilized today as the leading test for determining BFOQ cases.

The Supreme Court subsequently reversed the district court's ruling and affirmed the Fifth Circuit by saying that the claims made by the airline were merely "tangential" to its business, not its reason for being in business. Customer preference cannot justify sex discrimination. It can only be taken into consideration when it is based on a company's inability to perform its primary function. The Court even went on to state that the preferences of the passengers are the very prejudices the Civil Rights Act was meant to overcome.

See also Civil Rights Act of 1964; Equal Employment Opportunity Commission; Equal Employment Opportunity Commission's Affirmative Employment Management Directives; Title VII of the Civil Rights Act of 1964.

FURTHER READING: Bryant, William R., 1998, "Justifiable Discrimination: The Need for a Statutory Bona Fide Occupational Qualification Defense for Race Discrimination," *Georgia Law Review* 33 (fall): 211–242; Whalen, Charles, and Barbara Whalen, 1985, *The Longest Debate: A Legislative History of the 1964 Civil Rights Act*, Cabin John, MD: Seven Locks Press.

AIMÉE HOBBY RHODES

Diggs, Charles Coles, Jr. (1922–1998)

As one of a handful of African Americans serving in the U.S. Congress in the late 1950s and 1960s, Charles Diggs was in a unique and strategic position to lead the effort in addressing issues relating to African Americans and their quest for equality. Although he represented Michigan's Thirteenth District, which included Detroit, he commanded a national platform to speak on behalf of the wider African American community. Diggs served twenty-six years in the House of Representatives and is best remembered for founding the Congressional Black Caucus, a voting bloc in Congress that often focuses on the concerns and issues that primarily affect black Americans and the need for policy initiatives, such as affirmative action, to address those concerns.

Diggs was born in Detroit on December 2, 1922. His father was the wealthy, politically connected owner of the House of Diggs, a funeral home, which at one time was described as the largest funeral home in the entire state of Michigan.

Thus when Charles Jr. decided to run for public office, he already had a political base. Educated at the University of Michigan at Ann Arbor, 1940–1942, and Fisk University in Nashville, Tennessee, he chose to leave school for the U.S. Army in 1943. He entered service as a private and left as a second lieutenant in 1945. Preparing to enter the family business, he graduated from Wayne College of Mortuary Science in Detroit. Subsequently he received his license to be a mortician and served as chairman of the House of Diggs. In 1950, he attended the Detroit College of Law.

Diggs spent the first four years of the 1950s as an elected member of the Michigan State Senate. In the 1954 congressional elections, he defeated a seven-term incumbent in the Democratic primary and then won the general election easily. He was reelected to twelve successive Congresses and served in Congress from 1955 until 1980. After arriving in Congress, he made his voice heard on the need to desegregate public schools and public transportation. He won wide acclaim for his involvement in the negotiations which led to redistricting after the 1960 U.S. census, resulting in two congressional seats in the U.S. House of Representatives. For the first time since Reconstruction, two African Americans represented one state, when Michigan sent two black representatives to the House of Representatives. Among his other great accomplishments was being a founding member and the chairman of the Congressional Black Caucus (1969–1971). Initially, this was a small but vocal group that advocated for the interests of African Americans and other minorities. Diggs was also chairman of the House District Committee, which oversees the affairs of the citizens of Washington, D.C. Under his leadership, the city received a home rule charter, which was considered to be a monumental achievement. He also worked tirelessly in the creation of the University of the District of Columbia, an open-admissions institution primarily for residents of Washington, D.C. His efforts also resulted in naming the Frederick Douglass home in the Anacostia section of Washington, D.C., a national monument. His seniority in Congress earned him a place on the former Foreign Affairs Committee and the position of chairman of the African Affairs subcommittee. He was perceived by many to be an authority on Africa, making several fact-finding and ceremonial trips to the continent. He was an ardent proponent of aid to the new countries in Africa.

In 1978, after an extensive investigation, Diggs was convicted of operating a payroll kickback scheme in his congressional office. While he maintained until the end that he was singled out for prosecution because of his race, the jury handed down guilty verdicts on twenty-nine counts. Diggs received a three-year prison sentence, but only served seven months. In spite of the scandal, conviction, and censure by Congress, his constituents reelected him to his seat in Congress; however, he resigned from Congress in 1980. His latter years were spent in the Washington, D.C., area. He received a political science degree from Howard University and during that time reentered the mortuary business in suburban Prince George's County, Maryland. He was living a life outside the national spotlight when he died of a stroke on August 24, 1998, at the age of seventy-five in a Washington, D.C., hospital.

See also Congressional Black Caucus.

FURTHER READING: Duboise, Carolyn, 1999, *The Untold Story of Charles Diggs: The Public Man*, Arlington, VA: Barton Publishing House; Lynch, Hollis, 1973, *The Black Urban Condition: A Documentary History, 1866–1971*, New York: Crowell.

BETTY NYANGONI

Disability Classifications under the Fifth and Fourteenth Amendments

The Equal Protection Clause of the Fourteenth Amendment to the U.S. Constitution and the equal protection component of the Fifth Amendment's Due Process Clause both prohibit intentional and invidious governmental discrimination and impose limitations on the affirmative action efforts of federal, state, and local governments. However, the restrictions imposed by the Fifth and Fourteenth Amendments on governmental actions that are explicitly based on the status of a group of persons as being disabled, that is, "disability classifications," are not onerous. Governments can discriminate both in favor of and against persons with disabilities without violating the U.S. Constitution far more easily than governments can discriminate in favor of or against persons because of race or gender.

Discrimination against persons with disabilities by the federal government and state and local governments is prohibited in various sectors of society by federal statutes such as the Rehabilitation Act of 1973 and the Americans with Disabilities Act. These statutes are similar in many respects to statutes prohibiting discrimination on the basis of race and sex. However, race and gender antidiscrimination statutes not only protect the original objects of the law (racial minorities and women), but also whites and men. Affirmative action programs that use racial or gender preferences may be subject to reverse-discrimination lawsuits under these statutes. Federal statutes prohibiting disability discrimination only protect persons defined as disabled under the statute. These statutes generally do not protect nondisabled persons from discrimination. There can be no reverse-discrimination lawsuits under these statutes. However, governmental affirmative action programs that grant preferences to disabled persons might be challenged by nondisabled persons as unconstitutional, arguing that they violate the equal protection guarantees of the Fifth and Fourteenth Amendments.

The equal protection guarantees of the Fifth Amendment (which applies to federal government action) and the Fourteenth Amendment (which applies to state and local government action) require the federal government and state and local governments to treat similarly situated persons equally under the law. The strictness of the limitation imposed by these guarantees depends on the level of scrutiny applied to the governmental action by courts. The level of scrutiny applicable depends on what factor (often personal immutable characteristics) the government action is based upon. Generally speaking, there are three levels of judicial scrutiny by which governmental actions are judged under the Fourteenth and Fifth Amendments (although the distinctions among these standards are often not clear as applied in specific cases): strict scrutiny, intermediate scrutiny, and rational basis scrutiny. The higher levels of scrutiny (strict and intermediate) are generally applied when the governmental action, policy, or practice is based on "suspect or quasi-suspect classifications." Suspect and quasi-suspect classifications are generally those policies that are based on a group status that has been the subject of invidious discrimination in the past. The reasoning is that courts should pay special attention to such measures to ensure that they are not invidiously discriminatory because such classifications are rarely legitimately relevant to governmental decision making.

If a governmental action is subject to strict constitutional scrutiny, the action must be narrowly tailored to meet a compelling governmental interest. This standard has sometimes been described as "strict in theory, but fatal in fact" because of how few actions have ever been held to have survived such review. The U.S. Supreme Court has held that governmental actions, plans, or policies that are explicitly based on race (racial classifications), whether they are intended and designed to injure persons because of their race or to benefit persons because of their minority racial status, such as affirmative action programs, are subject to strict scrutiny constitutional review. Under this standard, many governmental actions that invidiously discriminated against racial minorities were declared unconstitutional, but so were affirmative action plans that used racial criteria to benefit minorities.

If a governmental action is subject to intermediate constitutional scrutiny, the action must be substantially related to important governmental interests. This standard is still difficult, but has not been virtually impossible to meet. The U.S. Supreme Court has traditionally held that governmental actions, plans, or policies that are explicitly based on sex or gender, whether they benefit women or injure women, are subject to intermediate scrutiny constitutional review.

If a governmental action is subject to rational basis scrutiny, it must be rationally related to a legitimate governmental interest. This has traditionally been a very easy standard to meet. Measures are rarely declared unconstitutional under this standard. Rational basis review has been applied to governmental actions based on age and veteran status.

The U.S. Supreme Court has ostensibly held that governmental actions explicitly based on disability or "disability classifications" are subject only to rational basis scrutiny. In the case of *City of Cleburne v. Cleburne Living Center*, 473 U.S. 432 (1985), the Supreme Court addressed a local zoning ordinance that excluded group homes for the mentally retarded but allowed other group homes. The U.S. Court of Appeals for the Fifth Circuit held that the ordinance violated the Fourteenth Amendment because it did not substantially advance an important governmental interest. The court of appeals applied a heightened standard of review (intermediate) because it found that persons with disabilities have historically experienced discriminatory treatment and lacked the political power to protect themselves. The Supreme Court held that the court of appeals wrongly applied a heightened review standard but, nevertheless, struck down the ordinance as unconstitutional. The Supreme Court held that the rational basis standard was appropriate for government action based on disability status. The Court explained that governmental action based on race is subject to strict scrutiny review because race is rarely relevant to any legitimate governmental decision and race-based actions are presumed to be based on prejudicial motives. Gender may be relevant to governmental action slightly more often. Therefore, gender-based actions are held to intermediate scrutiny review. The Court explained that disability status, on the other hand, is relevant to many legitimate governmental actions and that, historically, legislation based on disability has reflected an intention to assist rather than burden persons with disabilities (citing the Rehabilitation Act of 1973). Therefore, governmental action based on disabilities should not be presumed illegitimate. Such measures should be upheld as constitutional if they are "rationally related to a legitimate governmental purpose."

Though the Court applied a rational basis standard, under which measures are rarely struck down as unconstitutional, it held that the Cleburne ordinance was unconstitutional. The Court reasoned that the city did not have any good reason for prohibiting group homes for mentally retarded persons while allowing other types of group homes. The Court concluded that the ordinance was based on "an irrational prejudice against the mentally retarded."

Justice Thurgood Marshall filed an opinion dissenting in part that was joined by Justices William Brennan and Harry Blackmun. He argued that the Court did not apply rational basis scrutiny as traditionally defined; if it had, it would have upheld the ordinance. Justice Marshall argued that the Court was actually applying a heightened level of review. Because of the history of discrimination against mentally retarded persons, these justices argued that intermediate scrutiny review should apply to governmental action based on disability status.

The *Cleburne* opinion concerned a governmental action that burdened persons with disabilities. As noted earlier, Supreme Court equal protection jurisprudence suggests that rational basis review is also applicable to governmental action that benefits persons with disabilities, such as affirmative action programs. The Supreme Court has held in two chief cases that race-based governmental action is reviewed under the strict scrutiny standard when it is challenged as a violation of the Fifth or Fourteenth Amendment equal protection guarantees whether the action is intended to benefit minorities or to burden minorities: *Adarand Constructors, Inc. v. Peña*, 515 U.S. 200 (1995), and *City of Richmond v. J.A. Croson Co.*, 488 U.S. 469 (1989). The Court explained in *Adarand* this principle of "consistency" by emphasizing that the constitutional equal protection guarantees protect all individuals and not just certain groups. A dissenting justice in the *Adarand* case, Justice John Paul Stevens, noted that this principle of "consistency" leads to an "anomalous result." Intermediate scrutiny would be applied to benign gender classifications because intermediate scrutiny has been applied to invidious gender classifications. This means that it would be easier for governments to utilize gender preferences to remedy past discrimination than preferences for African Americans under the equal protection guarantees even though these guarantees were originally meant to end discrimination against African Americans. Justice Stevens's observation can arguably be extended to the disability context: Because rational basis scrutiny applies to governmental measures that discriminate against persons with disabilities, rational basis scrutiny would also be applied to disability classifications that are used to benefit persons with disabilities. This would mean that it would be easier for governments to utilize disability preferences to remedy past discrimination than preferences for African Americans under the equal protection guarantees.

See also Adarand Constructors, Inc. v. Peña; Blackmun, Harry Andrew; Brennan, William Joseph; *City of Richmond v. J.A. Croson Co.*; Compelling Governmental Interest; Equal Employment Opportunity Commission's Affirmative Employment Management Directives; Equal Protection Clause; Fifth Amendment; Fourteenth

Amendment; Gender-Based Affirmative Action; Intermediate Scrutiny Review; Invidious Discrimination; Marshall, Thurgood; Narrowly Tailored Affirmative Action Plans; Persons with Disabilities and Affirmative Action; Race-Based Affirmative Action; Rehabilitation Act of 1973; Stevens, John Paul; Strict Scrutiny; Suspect Classification.

FURTHER READING: Silvers, Anita, 2002, "Disability, Equal Protection, and the Supreme Court: Standing at the Crossroads of Progressive and Retrogressive Logic in Constitutional Classification," *University of Michigan Journal of Reform Law* 35:81–136.

MARIA D. BECKMAN

Disadvantaged Business Enterprises

Federal, state, and local governments establish programs that grant certified disadvantaged business enterprises (DBEs), which are businesses owned by individuals from socially or economically disadvantaged groups, preferential treatment on both the supply and demand sides of the marketplace to increase the involvement of self-employed minorities in government contracting. Preferential treatments for DBEs are often challenged by non-DBE businesses. State and local policies must meet strict criteria to be considered constitutional by the U.S. Supreme Court.

DBE programs began as federal minority business enterprise (MBE) programs in the late 1960s. The proportion of self-employed persons who are minorities historically has been dramatically lower than their proportion of the U.S. population as a whole. Of those who have been self-employed, most have experienced comparatively poor economic outcomes, including dramatically lower sales and earnings on average than self-employed nonminorities. This finding remains true even when education, marital status, and other factors are controlled for and suggests that social discrimination is the cause of the disparate outcomes. Under pressure from minority groups to reduce these differences, the federal government has created MBE programs to increase minority-owned businesses' participation in government contracting. State and local governments have followed the lead of the federal government by establishing their own programs, which have often benefited women's business enterprises (WBEs) and non-minority-owned businesses able to prove that they are economically disadvantaged due to some type of social disadvantage. The inclusion of non-minority- and non-women-owned businesses in these programs has changed MBE or WBE programs into DBE programs.

The federal 8(a) Business Development Program administered by the Small Business Administration (SBA) is a prime example of how DBE affirmative action programs operate. To become a certified participant in the program, a business must be at least 51 percent owned by a person who is economically disadvantaged because of a social disadvantage. Members of minority groups, including African Americans, Asian Americans, Hispanic Americans, and Native Americans, rebuttably are presumed to be socially disadvantaged, while nonminorities must prove that they have an objective distinctive feature not common to non–socially disadvantaged society and that they have been socially disadvantaged within the United States because of that feature. Then a business owner must prove that his or her social disadvantage has made him or her economically disadvantaged by restricting his or her access to capital or credit resources. Once a business is certified by the 8(a) program, it receives technical and financial assistance to improve its ability to supply services to government. Contract set-asides, good-faith-effort subcontractor goals, bid preferences, and subcontractor compensation clauses are included in contract bid packages to increase the demand for DBE services.

Federal, state, and local MBE, WBE, and DBE programs, especially those that set aside public contracts for DBEs, have been continually challenged by individual businesses and industry groups since their inception. Challenges to federal programs had largely not been successful because the Supreme Court had historically deferred to acts of Congress in this regard. However, in the 1995 Supreme Court decision in *Adarand Constructors, Inc. v. Peña*, 515 U.S. 200 (1995), the Court held that such programs, if they included race-based classifications, should also be subject to strict scrutiny review. Challenges to state and local government programs have occasionally been successful, requiring implementing governments to show a "compelling interest" for apportioning economic resources on the basis of race. In the landmark decision in *City of Richmond v. J.A. Croson Co.*, 488 U.S. 469 (1989), the U.S. Supreme Court applied the strict scrutiny standard to rule that the city of Richmond's program, which set aside 30 percent of all city construction contract dollars for MBEs, was "reverse discrimination" and unconstitutional because it did not present clear and convincing statistical evidence documenting racial discrimination against MBE contractors in Richmond.

See also *Adarand Constructors, Inc. v. Peña*; *City of Richmond v. J.A. Croson Co.*; Color-Blind Constitution; Lending Practices and Affirmative Action; Licensing and Affirmative Action; Reverse Discrimination; Strict Scrutiny; Supreme Court and Affirmative Action.

FURTHER READING: Code of Federal Regulations, 2001, *Business Credit and Assistance: Small Business Administration: 8(a) Business Development/Small Disadvantaged Business Status Determinations, Title 13, Chapter 1, Part 124 (Revised as of January 1, 2001)*, Washington, DC: U.S. Government Printing Office; McDonald, Laughlin, and John A. Powell, 1993, *The Rights of Racial Minorities: The Basic ACLU Guide to Racial Minority Rights*, Carbondale: Southern Illinois University Press; Turner, Ronald, 1990, *The Past and Future of Affirmative Action*, New York: Quorum Books; Wainwright, Jon S., 2000, *Racial Discrimination and Minority Business Enterprise: Evidence from the 1990 Census*, New York: Garland Publishing.

MARK J. SENEDIAK

Discrete and Insular Minority

The term "discrete and insular minority" refers to certain groups that are in some sense separate from the political majority and are powerless to protect themselves from being exploited. Thus judicial protection for these groups is justified. The Supreme Court has included groups under this nomenclature that have been "saddled with such disabilities, or subjected to such a history of purposeful unequal treatment, or relegated to such a position of political powerlessness as to command extraordinary protection from the majoritarian political process." A group that is a discrete and insular minority generally is considered a "suspect class," and government action based on the group's suspect characteristics warrants a heightened level of judicial scrutiny under equal protection law. Certain racial and ethnic minorities have been considered suspect classes, and women have been treated as "semi-suspect" or "quasi-suspect."

The term "discrete and insular minority" was first articulated in footnote 4 of *United States v. Carolene Products Co.*, 304 U.S. 144 (1938). Justice Harlan Fiske Stone wrote that "prejudice against discrete and insular minorities may be a special condition, which tends seriously to curtail the operation of those political processes ordinarily to be relied upon to protect minorities, and [so] may call for a correspondingly more searching judicial inquiry." Thus Justice Stone indicated that the Court would subject a statute directed at discrete and insular minorities to a higher level of scrutiny than a statute directed at economic regulation. In later formulations, the term "discrete and insular minority" became nearly equivalent to the term "suspect class." If a group was deemed to be a suspect class, any law that imposed special burdens on that group immediately triggered extreme suspicion, and the law was subjected to strict scrutiny.

However, after *Regents of the University of California v. Bakke*, 438 U.S. 265 (1978), and *Adarand Constructors, Inc. v. Peña*, 515 U.S. 200 (1995), the Supreme Court no longer treats the disadvantaging of a suspect class as the trigger for strict scrutiny. Instead, the use of a suspect "classification" is the trigger. A classification based on race is subject to strict scrutiny without regard to whether the group disadvantaged by the classification has historically been subject to discrimination. Furthermore, according to Justice Lewis Powell in *Bakke*, "The 'rights created by the . . . Fourteenth Amendment are, by its terms, guaranteed to the individual. The rights established are personal rights. . . . ' The guarantee of Equal Protection cannot mean one thing when applied to one individual and something else when applied to a person of another color." The Supreme Court, by focusing on suspect classification rather than suspect class, has created an additional hurdle for affirmative action programs based on race, which now must be subjected to a higher level of scrutiny.

See also Adarand Constructors, Inc. v. Peña; Equal Protection Clause; Fourteenth Amendment; Powell, Lewis Franklin, Jr.; *Regents of the University of California v. Bakke*; Stone, Harlan Fiske; Strict Scrutiny; Suspect Classification.

FURTHER READING: Ackerman, Bruce A., 1985, "Beyond Carolene Products," *Harvard Law Review* 98:713–746; Roy, Jeffrey A., 2002, "Carolene Products: A Game-Theoretic Approach," *Brigham Young University Law Review* 2002:53–109; *United States v. Carolene Products Co.*, 304 U.S. 144, 152–153 n. 4 (1938).

PAMELA C. CORLEY

Discrimination

Discrimination in an egalitarian society is the resurgence of what was differently and more directly and naturally expressed in a hierarchical society. That is, in the past, societies had a hierarchy of status, which brought with it privileges and disabilities for various groups within that society. In the antebellum United States, the institution of slavery ensured that minority classes would be treated in a subservient way in relation to the whites in society. However, once the hierarchical institution of slavery was abolished, white society turned to discrimination as a means of perpetuating the values white society gained by keeping minority classes in a subservient status. Thus the conflict between those who discriminate and those who are discriminated against is not simply an argument about abstract rights or ethnic or racial bigotry. Rather, in the final analysis, it is an argument between those who insist upon the substance of a long-postponed break with the traditions and those groups that insist upon maintaining the valuable privileges and benefits they now enjoy as a consequence of that dismal history.

Affirmative action is a program designed to eliminate the vestiges of discrimination in society. That is, the passage of antidiscrimination laws does not end discrimination fully. In fact, some argue that while antidiscrimination laws clearly accomplish good, they may also have adverse side effects. For example, some argue that the elimination of traditional patterns of discrimination in the United States required by the Civil Rights Act of 1964 adversely affected the expectations of whites, since it compelled competition with black workers and other minority-group members where none previously existed. Though much of the myth of discrimination rests in institutional arrangement, another large part resides in patterns of thinking and ideological orientation of individuals and groups in society. Laws restricting discrimination may be effective to some degree, and groups may be frightened enough by the price they may pay for discriminating. Yet hierarchical mind-sets enshrined in the deeply held myths in a society may survive in a population for a long time. Thus the goal of affirmative action programs is, in essence, to act like a solvent in increasing the deterioration of these discriminatory myths.

There are two major types of discrimination in society, individual discrimination and institutional discrimination. Individual discrimination involves person-to-person discrimination in private affairs and dealings. Institutional discrimination, however, is more serious than individual discrimination. In the latter, organizational networks linked to rules, procedures, and guidelines make it difficult for members of one group to affiliate and integrate institutionally. In this case, it is not so much the individual who discriminates, though individuals may do so in their own individual positions, as institutional rules and procedures that have been established on the basis of the qualifications and standards of the group in power and serve to keep all other groups out. Although this may not have been the intent of the original rules and procedures, the rules and procedures operate in such a fashion as to exclude minority groups.

See also Benign Discrimination; Civil Rights Act of 1964; Institutional Discrimination; Racial Discrimination; Reverse Discrimination; Sex Discrimination.

FURTHER READING: Danziger, Sheldon H., 1993, *Uneven Tides: Rising Inequality in America*, New York: Russell Sage Foundation; Myrdal, Gunnar, 1963, *Challenge to Affluence*, New York: Pantheon Books.

MIRZA ASMER BEG

Disparate Treatment and Disparate Impact

Disparate treatment and disparate impact are the principal legal theories underlying the vast majority of employment discrimination cases. The key differences between the two are that allegations of disparate treatment usually involve only one claimant, whereas disparate impact generally involves a group or class of claimants; and disparate treatment requires proof of intent to unlawfully discriminate, whereas disparate impact does not require such proof. The concepts of disparate treatment and disparate impact as theories of discrimination were developed in the employment discrimination context, but may also be useful in other discrimination contexts, such as providing proof for affirmative action programs implemented to remedy previous incidents of racial discrimination.

Disparate treatment allegations are the most often encountered claims of unlawful employment discrimination. Such claims allege that the plaintiff received less favorable treatment than others who are similarly situated but not in the same protected category as the plaintiff. Proof of discriminatory motivation is critical to establishing a disparate treatment case. Discriminatory motivation may be proved by either direct or indirect evidence. Direct evidence of discriminatory motivation, such as a policy that is discriminatory on its face, is rare. Therefore, most disparate treatment cases are based on circumstantial evidence. A three-step analysis is used for disparate treatment claims based on circumstantial evidence. The first step requires the plaintiff to prove a "prima facie case" (i.e., to prove that the plaintiff is in a protected class; the plaintiff suffered an adverse employment action by the defendant; and the adverse action was based on the protected characteristic, as where similarly situated persons not in the plaintiff's protected class were not subjected to the same adverse actions), whereupon the burden shifts to the defendant. The second step requires the defendant to articulate a legitimate business reason for its conduct toward the plaintiff. The defendant is not required to prove the business wisdom of the reason(s), nor must the defendant demonstrate the legitimacy of its action(s) to prove that it did not unlawfully discriminate against the plaintiff. Once the defendant proffers a nondiscriminatory reason for its actions, the burden then shifts back to the plaintiff. The third and final step requires the plaintiff to prove by a preponderance of the evidence ("more likely than not") that the reason(s) offered by the defendant are mere pretext(s) to mask unlawful discrimination and that the defendant intended to unlawfully discriminate against the plaintiff.

A less often encountered form of disparate treatment is the "pattern and practice" case. Such cases allege that a defendant has a pattern and/or practice of engaging in disparate treatment. A prima facie case of a discriminatory pattern or practice is generally established by statistical evidence of disparity buttressed by proof of individual examples of the discriminatory pattern and practice in operation.

Disparate impact cases allege that statistically a facially neutral employment practice has a disproportionate adverse impact on a protected group. This theory of discrimination was first established by the U.S. Supreme Court in *Griggs v. Duke Power Co.*, 401 U.S. 424 (1971), and was codified into Title VII of the Civil Rights Act of 1964 by the Civil Rights Act of 1991. A three-step analysis is used for disparate impact claims. The first step requires the plaintiff to identify the particular employment practice(s) challenged and demonstrate significant statistical disparity. The burden then shifts to the defendant to prove "business necessity" for the challenged practice(s). "Business necessity" is narrowly construed and difficult to prove; therefore, most effort in litigation focuses on the first step of the analysis. Nevertheless, if the defendant can prove business necessity, the burden shifts back to the plaintiff. In the third and final step, the burden is on the plaintiff to prove that there are other methods to adequately address the defendant's business needs that are not likely to result in statistical disparity, and the defendant refuses to adopt the alternative. Unlike disparate treatment cases, the plaintiff in a disparate impact case is not required to prove an unlawful intent to discriminate on the part of the defendant. As a general rule of thumb, the Equal Employment Opportunity Commission has developed the "four-fifths rule" as an indicator of disparate impact. Under the four-fifths rule, a disparate impact is indicated when the success rate of participants from the protected group is less than 80 percent of the success rate of the nonprotected group with the highest success rate as applied to a particular employment action (hiring, promotion, and so on).

See also Civil Rights Act of 1964; Civil Rights Act of 1991; Equal Employment Opportunity Commission; Equal Employment Opportunity Commission's Affirmative Employment Management Directives; *Griggs v. Duke Power Co.*; Manifest Imbalance Standard; Statistical Proof of Discrimination; Title VII of the Civil Rights Act of 1964; *Wards Cove Packing Co. v. Atonio.*

FURTHER READING: Baldus, David C., and James W.L. Cole, 1980, *Statistical Proof of Discrimination*, Colorado Springs, CO: Shepard's; Scanlan, James P., 1988, "Illusions of Job Segregation," *Public Interest*, fall, 54–70; Scanlan, James P., 1991, "The Perils of Provocative Statistics," *Public Interest*, winter, 3–15; Scanlan, James P., 1993, "Getting It Straight When Statistics Can Lie," *Legal Times*, June 28, 40–43; Scanlan, James P., 1995, "Multimillion-Dollar Settlements May Cause Employers to Avoid Hiring Women and Minorities for Less Desirable Jobs to Improve the Statistical Picture," *National Law Journal*, March 27, 35.

RICHARD J. BENNETT

Diversity

Affirmative action not only ensures that African Americans, Latinos, and other historically underrepresented groups are provided opportunities and access to positions and institutions that were not readily accessible to them for many years, but it arguably benefits all of society as well. These benefits include impacts on needs in this society that are both economically and morally sound and that can promote a better America, in general. The belief that affirmative action programs benefit society at large, is argued by focusing on the need in society for diverse institutions and organizations. The argument follows that affirmative action is also good for the institution or organization's sake, and not just for the individual who might receive selection or advancement because of affirmative preferences. Finally, it is argued, again beyond being concerned with individual cases, that supporting affirmative action promotes society's notion of fairness and equality and improves the overall moral fabric of society.

The precise meaning of the term "diversity" can be elusive. In general, diversity is a state in which individuals with widely varying characteristics and experiences are represented in significant proportions. Diversity in higher education, in public contracting, and in public and governmental employment with respect to immutable characteristics such as race, ethnicity, national origin, sex, and disability status and experiences that may result from having these characteristics is often the goal of affirmative action programs. However, affirmative action programs that consider these immutable characteristics along with other characteristics in the diversity analysis are faring better against legal challenges.

Opponents of diversity-based affirmative action programs argue that considering minority racial status as a positive factor in order to achieve some amorphous and unexamined precept that achieving racial diversity in society is positive and necessary is too burdensome on the rights of the majority and actually unlawfully discriminates against the majority. These opponents are having some success in challenging diversity-based affirmative action programs in reverse-discrimination lawsuits.

The U.S. Supreme Court first recognized the need for achieving racial diversity as an argument for using racial preferences in affirmative action programs in the case of *Regents of University of California v. Bakke*, 438 U.S. 265 (1978). The Court ultimately decided that the affirmative action admission program of a medical school that reserved a small percentage of openings for minority students was unconstitutional. However, Justice Lewis Powell stated: "[The attainment of a diverse student body] clearly is a constitutionally permissible goal for an institution of higher education." However, he then qualified this general statement explaining:

> It is not an interest in simple ethnic diversity, in which a specified percentage of the student body is in effect guaranteed to be members of selected ethnic groups, with the remaining percentage an undifferentiated aggregation of students [which justifies consideration of race]. The diversity that furthers a compelling state interest encompasses a far broader array of qualifications and characteristics of which racial or ethnic origin is but a single though important element. Petitioners' special admissions program, focused solely on ethnic diversity, would hinder rather than further attainment of genuine diversity.

Powell ultimately decided that the medical school's plan was invalid because reserving some vacancies for minority applicants was not necessary to any valid interest in diversity.

Since the *Bakke* decision, corporations, educational institutions, and governments have attempted to develop affirmative action programs to increase diversity that would withstand legal review. In the case of *Metro Broadcasting v. FCC*, 497 U.S. 547 (1990), the U.S. Supreme Court found that the FCC's policy of giving preferences in granting licenses for minority-owned or minority-managed television and radio stations in order to promote programming diversity was constitutional not because it benefited the minority radio stations, but because programming diversity benefited the public. The Court stated: "widest possible dissemination of information from diverse and antagonistic sources is essential to the public welfare." However, Justice Sandra Day O'Connor, in a dissenting opinion, cautioned: "Social Scientists may debate how peoples' thoughts and behavior reflect their background, but the Constitution provides that the government may not allocate benefits or burdens among individuals based on the assumption that race or ethnicity determined how they think or act." This indicates that at least one justice may not accept the premise that considering racial diversity is necessary to achieve diverse viewpoints.

These Supreme Court decisions suggest that whether using preferences to achieve diversity will overcome reverse discrimination challenges will depend on the importance of the interest allegedly served by diversity and on the sufficiency of the proof that increasing diversity serves the interest identified. Therefore, it is useful to closely examine the arguments for increasing diversity.

First, affirmative action benefits institutions and organizations as a whole. One of the needs of society includes the creation and the promotion of diverse institutions. These institutions include companies, governmental agencies, and colleges and universities that should represent American society and its many groups. Diversity that is found in institutions that embrace affirmative action creates an environment that is able to target many different clients and consumer groups. This type of promotion essentially benefits the company or institution in innumerable ways, including a more creative workplace that represents diverse opinions and ways of promoting and marketing its product. Diversity also creates a more economically sound company or institution that will be able to hire more people because of its stability. It also promotes a morally sound representation of what this society should embrace in terms of securing the "general welfare" of those who may have otherwise been kept out of positions, regardless of qualifications, because of ethnicity, race, gender, or other differences. In other words, it ensures fair treatment for historically underrepresented individuals in this society and generally promotes economic fluidity. Ultimately, it ensures that the institution or organization will break away from a myopic view of society (or its client or service base) based upon notions of ethnocentrism.

A. Barry Rand states that "workers with different backgrounds and perspectives help create . . . a place where innovative solutions can flourish" (Curry 1996, 74). Curry also reiterates that "a diverse company has the edge when it comes to competing for the evolving markets of a global economy . . . a company that embraces diversity will better understand this diverse world" (Curry 1996, 75). Thus hiring, promoting, and retaining diverse groups of people are important in securing the welfare and overall capacity of the company. In short, diversity is a smart move in terms of keeping the company thriving, alive, and afloat for all involved, including society in general, which relies on economic stability of companies and institutions to keep itself economically strong.

In terms of educational organizations, particularly in regard to colleges and universities, an educational institution's commitment to hire and retain diverse faculty and staff fulfills some of the same needs that companies have in terms of economic benefits for that particular educational institution. For instance, a university that hires faculty who are members of a historically underrepresented group can use these faculty members to assist in the recruitment process of pursuing top students from the same historically underrepresented groups. These same faculty members can also assist in the retention of these diverse students and/or serve as role models for these students. A diverse faculty and staff in universities, as in businesses and companies, promote diverse ideas that bring about more creative and innovative universities. A study of a diversity and retention program established by professors, administrators, and staff at Ohio State University documented that students of color are, more often than not, supported and inspired by the presence and work of diverse faculty and staff on college campuses who are representatives and role models from their communities. In noting the benefits of affirming diversity on college and university campuses, college admissions for students must also be taken into consideration. Members of historically underrepresented groups of students on college and university campuses not only promote diversity needed for socialization purposes, but also give many historically underrepresented groups of students opportunities to increase their capacity and qualifications to be hired by companies and institutions within society to promote a sounder economic future for America. As well, students who are given knowledge and new information will be able to create and promote their own businesses and institutions that may benefit their own representative communities.

Also, colleges and universities that use race and economic background as some criteria for entrance into college programs (besides grades and standardized test scores) morally acknowledge that some students from these targeted groups have not had the same benefits as other students. For instance, mainstream and more economically affluent groups of students have access to many more resources (such as technology and test and college preparation courses and workshops) that historically underrepresented groups of individuals many times lack because of racial and economic injustices in this society. Until educational institutions on the prekindergarten through twelfth-grade level can ensure that equal access is given to all children in a democratic society, compensatory programs should be used in college admissions. In 2003, the U.S. Supreme Court, in *Grutter v. Bollinger*, 123 S. Ct. 2325, 2003 U.S. LEXIS 4800 (2003), affirmed the importance of diversity in higher education, holding that a law school had a compelling governmental interest in enrolling a racially diverse student body in light of the educational benefits that are created by a diverse student body. However, the Court also warned that affirmative action (as a means to achieve diversity in higher education) "must have a logical end point" and that "25 years from now [the date of the *Grutter* decision], the use of racial preferences will no longer be necessary to further the interest" of diversity in higher education.

Last, pressuring institutions to embrace programs like affirmative action creates and promotes a common good for society. Embracing programs like affirmative action develops a moral fiber within America and sets a moral example for young privileged people in society to recognize that not all people are always given a fair chance to pursue the so-called American dream. In that light, the benefits and reasons for affirmative action must also be explained fairly and thoroughly to privileged groups, as in this entry, by responsible individuals who understand the numerous benefits of compensatory programs. This is important so that resentment will not grow against historically underrepresented groups. In sum, the beneficial impacts of affirmative action reach far beyond economic and creative diversity arguments. These types of programs can also promote and inspire the creation of a more humane and moral society if embraced by its leaders. The debate over whether these arguments are sufficient to overcome legal and other objections to diversity-based affirmative action programs will likely occupy much of the legal and social agenda as the twenty-first century begins.

See also Affirmative Action, Arguments for; Affirmative Action, Criticisms of; African Americans; Ethnocentrism; Gender-Based Affirmative Action; *Gratz v. Bollinger/Grutter v. Bollinger*; Hispanic Americans; Majority-Group Resentment; Role Model Theory; Scapegoating/Displaced-Aggression Theories.

FURTHER READING: Aguire, Adalberto, Jr., 2003, "The Diversity Rationale in Higher Education: An Overview of the Contemporary Legal Context;" *Social Justice* 30:138–152; Curry,

George E., ed., 1996, *The Affirmative Action Debate*, Reading, MA: Perseus Books; Edley, Christopher, Jr., 1996, *Not All Black and White: Affirmative Action, Race, and American Values*, New York: Hill and Wang; Ezorsky, Gertrude, 1991, *Racism and Justice: The Case for Affirmative Action*, Ithaca, NY: Cornell University Press; Gray, W. Robert, 2001, *The Four Faces of Affirmative Action: Fundamental Answers and Actions*, Westport, CT: Greenwood Press; Hanson, Thomas E., Jr., "Rising above the Past: Affirmative Action as a Necessary Means of Raising the Black Standard of Living as Well as Self-Esteem," *Boston College Third World Law Journal* 16 (winter): 107–138; Kahlenberg, Richard D., 1996, *The Remedy: Class, Race, and Affirmative Action*, New York: Basic Books.

NICOLE M. STEPHENS

Diversity Management

Diversity management is a managerial process or program by which individuals, groups, institutions, organizations, and even governments develop the required competencies to deal with the highly complex and sometimes emotionally charged issues pertaining to race and gender. Diversity management is often a part of antidiscrimination and affirmative action programs and is necessary in institutions that are increasingly diverse in their social, cultural, economic, political, race, and gender makeup. Diversity management is hinged on the belief that unity, strength, and progress result from "multiculturalism" or "pluralism." Issues of diversity include race, ethnicity, religion, age, gender, sexual preference, politics, economy, business, and different ways of thinking and seeing the world. Sociologists view diversity management as a process of assimilation of people from wildly varied backgrounds into a common culture. The goal is the effective integration of decentralized varied interests to ensure the participation of every outsider in the decision-making process. Thus diversity management focuses on resolving those features that make each of us different and downplays the emphasis on those superficial differences that divide people.

Diversity management has the potential of permeability and ability to create links across racial and gender divisions. It seeks to build a corporate system that is supportive of the different ways of thinking and seeing the world irrespective of the superficial differences obvious in the manifestations of color, gender, age, religion, and so on. Over the past decade, diversity management has become a growing program in the United States. In fact, traditionally, the focus on the need for diversity in the workforce or within the government has been conceived as a uniquely American invention or construct. Since the emergence of the civil rights movement in America in the 1960s, a reevaluation of particular groups of people hitherto considered outsiders and minorities, such as blacks, women, immigrants, sexual minorities, and others, has occurred, causing such groups to be emboldened to fight for recognition by arguing that their outsider heritage possesses a value that must be expressed and preserved to help society thrive. Recent developments suggest that the roadmap for the global future has changed in the positive direction of diversity management. This is manifested and entrenched in the workings of globalization. Even the redefinition of the European Union to accommodate common interests in the economic front through the adoption of a common currency in the beginning of the twenty-first century is a clear indication of management of diversity. Leaders of governments, communities, and organizations realize the applicability of diversity management as a sustainable governance and business issue in their various social systems of operation.

The challenges of diversity management are met by the creativeness and dynamism attributed to heterogeneity. It operates under the normative idea of pluralism, that there should be mutual respect and freedom between different cultural systems, individuals, races, and groups to ensure peaceful coexistence and progress in the social system. Diversity management creates the environment of equality of opportunity for all to participate on issues of common interests, despite superficial or natural biological differences, as a prime focus for the progress of society. Technocrats in organizations and multicultural entities use the techniques of diversity management for discovering areas of convergence of ideas to ensure social order and the maintenance of tolerant social systems by allaying the fears of minority interests over relations of superordination and subordination that give rise to marginalization, exploitation, and oppression.

See also Affirmative Action, Arguments for; Assimilation Theory; Integration; Multiculturalism; Pluralism.

FURTHER READING: Beckford, James A., 1999, "The Management of Religious Diversity in England and Wales with Reference to Prison Chaplaincy," *Journal on Multicultural Societies* 1, no. 2, www.unesco.org/most/vl1n2bec.htm; Graham, Lawrence O., 1997, *Proversity*, New York: John Wiley and Sons; Helgesen, Sally, 1995, *The Web of Inclusion*, New York: Doubleday; Selingo, Jeffrey, 2003, "New Study Questions Educational Benefits of Diversity," *Chronicle of Higher Education*, March 28, A23; Trevor, Wilson, 2000, "The Future of Diversity," *Diversity Journal*, spring, 5–6; Weng, Garner K., 1998, "Look at the Pretty Colors! Rethinking Promises of Diversity as Legally Binding," *La Raza Law Journal* 10 (fall): 753–822.

KINGSLEY UFUOMA OMOYIBO

Diversity Rationale

See Regents of the University of California v. Bakke.

Double Consciousness

The concept of double consciousness is associated with the work of W.E.B. Du Bois and appears often in articles addressing the merits (or lack thereof) of affirmative action programs. Du Bois first coined the term in his famous book entitled *The Souls of Black Folk* (1903). Du Bois developed the concept of double consciousness to show the juxtaposition between a dominant mainstream (white) and outsider (black) perspective of the world. Du Bois's concept of double consciousness refers to the perception held by outsiders (e.g., people of color) that their everyday life is often void of value in the eyes of the dominant mainstream majority (e.g., white society). Du Bois's double consciousness also connotes the notion of a dual black identity that is simultaneously African and American, where both aspects of the dualistic identity are valuable. Phrased another way, according to Du Bois, double consciousness allows people of color to see society from two perspectives: first, the perspective of the mainstream (white) society, and second, the perspective reflecting their own unique values and cultures. Hence programs like affirmative action that arguably promote diversity and do not place a premium on assimilation are important in promoting both aspects of the double consciousness of minorities. That is, according to Du Bois, to fully achieve an egalitarian and nonracist society, one should support preserving the minority aspect of the identity and oppose requiring all people of color to surrender and assimilate their cultures and beliefs into white societal values and norms. The promotion of diversity through affirmative action is one way in which to promote both aspects of the double consciousness of minorities.

Du Bois described the notion of double consciousness as follows:

> After the Egyptian and Indian, the Greek and Roman, the Teuton and Mongolian, the Negro is a sort of seventh son, born with a veil, and gifted with second-sight in this American world,—a world which yields him no true self-consciousness, but only lets him see himself through the revelation of the other world. It is a peculiar sensation, this double-consciousness, this sense of always looking at one's self through the eyes of others, of measuring one's soul by the tape of a world that looks on in amused contempt and pity. One ever feels his twoness,—an American, a Negro; two souls, two thoughts, two unreconciled strivings; two warring ideals in one dark body, whose dogged strength alone keeps it from being torn asunder. (Du Bois 1903, 3)

Thus, according to Du Bois, the concept of double consciousness brought with it both negative and positive ramifications. The negative ramification was that people of color were always reminded of the differences between white standards and culture and the standards and culture of their own unique heritage. However, today, many authors cite this notion of double consciousness positively, in that it allows for people of color to be able to integrate and function in society, yet all the while uphold their own values and cultures.

Critical race theorists use Du Bois's notion of double consciousness in their construction of multiple consciousness as necessary for understanding the perceptions and feelings of persons who have been marginalized in U.S. society. Critical race theorists integrate the experiential knowledge of oppressed persons into critical race theory narratives to show how oppressive social structures intersect with race, ethnicity, gender, and class in U.S. society. Multiple consciousnesses recognize all forms of oppression and do not give precedence to one form of oppression over another. Multiple consciousness is nested in the assumption that individuals have multiple components in their identity, but some components are suppressed by a society that prizes objectivity, monolithic thought, and preservation of a status quo that promotes inequality.

Establishing voice for people of color in U.S. society requires the use of narrative in critical race theory writings to document the nature of oppression, social cruelty, and human exploitation. Giving voice to people of color affirms the legitimacy of their existence and shows dominant mainstream (white) society how it robs people of color of dignity and self-worth. Through voice, people of color actualize their otherness and document the privileged position of white persons in U.S. society. Narratives of and by people of color interface with the contextual and subjective nature of reality to engage a multiple consciousness that deconstructs the notion that reality is objective to challenge oppressive and dehumanizing social structures. As a result, the establishment of voice through narrative provides the foundation for a multiple consciousness.

See also Amalgamation; Assimilation Theory; Critical Race Theory; Du Bois, William Edward Burghardt; E Pluribus Unum; Integration; Multiculturalism; Pluralism.

FURTHER READING: Barnes, Robin, 1990, "Race Consciousness: The Thematic Content of Racial Distinctiveness in Critical Race Scholarship," *Harvard Law Review* 103:1864–1871; Du Bois, W.E.B., 1903, *The Souls of Black Folk*, Chicago: A.C. McClurg and Co.; Matsuda, Mari, 1989, "When the First Quail Calls: Multiple Consciousness as Jurisprudential Method," *Women's Rights Law Reporter* 11:7–10; Nan, Carolos J., 1994, "Adding Salt to the Wound: Affirmative Action and Critical Race Theory," *Law and Inequality: A Journal of Theory and Practice* 12:553–572.

ADABERTO AGUIRRE JR.

Douglass, Frederick (1818–1895)

A compelling orator, newspaper publisher, supporter of the women's rights movement, advisor to President Abraham Lincoln, and a U.S. marshal and diplomat, Frederick Douglass was a man of remarkable accomplishments and a great leader. While his life predates modern affirmative action programs, his name and views are invoked by both supporters and critics of affirmative action to justify their respective positions. Arguments that Frederick Douglass would or would not have supported affirmative action today are somewhat speculative, but Douglass's legacy and beliefs appear in affirmative action debates nonetheless. Like Martin Luther King Jr., Frederick Douglass's stature and significance in American history are such that both supporters and critics find it helpful to claim that their position is in accordance with the views of Frederick Douglass.

For example, in an article published in 2002, Thomas Sowell, a prolific writer and critic of affirmative action, quotes several statements made by Douglass and implicitly suggests that Douglass therefore would not have supported affirmative action.

> Douglass also said: "Everybody has asked the question . . . what shall we do with the Negro? I have had but one answer from the beginning. Do nothing with us! Your doing with us has already played the mischief with us. Do nothing with us." Frederick Douglass had achieved a deeper understanding in the 19th century than any of the black leaders of today. Those whites who feel a need to do something with blacks and for blacks have been some of the most dangerous "friends" of blacks. (Sowell 2002)

In the same article, Sowell also quotes a famous "self-help" statement that Douglass once made, "If the Negro cannot stand on his own legs, let him fall." Similarly, Justice Clarence Thomas, in his dissenting opinion in the landmark affirmative action case *Grutter v. Bollinger*, 123 S. Ct. 2325, 2003 U.S. LEXIS 4800 (2003), began his dissenting opinion by quoting the same Frederick Douglass speech and stating, "Like Douglass, I believe blacks can achieve in every avenue of American life without the meddling of university administrators."

However, some supporters of affirmative action argue that Douglass would have supported affirmative action based upon his speeches and statements. Those who believe that Douglass was supportive of affirmative action also point to his clear position on (and in support of) the Civil War (Reconstruction) Amendments, the Civil Rights Acts enacted during Reconstruction, the Freedmen's Bureau, equal education, and equal employment opportunities for blacks. Furthermore, in an 1870 speech, Frederick Douglass clearly and unequivocally advocated the preferential hiring of black employees over white employees as a means to remedy past discrimination and achieve equality. Douglass's comments in 1870 could easily supplement modern arguments in favor of affirmative action in the employment context:

> While I am for making no distinction, I am one of those who believe that whenever, and wherever, there is an office to be had, and a white applicant equally eligible, and equally available to obtain it; that while I am in favor of no distinctions on account of color, remembering the stripes, remembering the 250 years of bondage in this land, through which the colored man has been dragged, remembering that 250 years he has not had the right to learn the name of the God that made him, and that every man in the land has been at the liberty to kick him, and to disregard his rights . . . I say, whenever the black man and the white man, equally eligible, equally available, equally qualified for office, present themselves for that office, the black man, at this juncture of our affairs, should be preferred. That is my conviction. (Moses 1996)

One modern organization, the Coalition to Defend Affirmative Action and Fight for Equality by Any Means Necessary, is sufficiently convinced that Frederick Douglass (as well as Martin Luther King Jr.) would have supported modern affirmative action programs that it has listed Frederick Douglass and Martin Luther King Jr. in its principles and bylaws. Specifically, paragraph 15 of the organization's principles specifies that the group "looks especially to the towering figure of Frederick Douglass ('If there is no struggle there is no progress') and, as representative leaders of the 1960s, Martin Luther King . . . and Malcolm X." Thus even though Douglass died many years before the advent of the modern civil rights movement or the use of modern affirmative action programs, his views and positions still impact the debate.

Born into slavery as Frederick Augustus Washington Bailey on or about February 1, 1818, in Talbot County, Maryland, Douglass learned the unpleasant realities of slavery very early. He witnessed extreme cruelty by the slave owner Aaron Anthony. But the slave owner's daughter sent him on a mission that changed his life. When she sent Frederick Douglass to Baltimore, Maryland, to live with her brother-in-law Hugh Auld, his life as a slave field hand seemed to end. His duties with his new family were to care for the Aulds' young son and run errands. Sophia Auld, the wife of Hugh, was a regular Bible reader. Frederick Douglass was intrigued with her reading. He asked Sophia Auld to teach him to read. She readily agreed. As his skills improved and he progressed, she excitedly shared the news with her husband. Hugh Auld became very upset, for he knew that his wife had committed a crime, as it was unlawful to teach a slave to read. Also, he knew that a slave who could read and write might not remain a slave for long. He demanded an end to the reading lessons.

Undeterred, the young Frederick Douglass practiced reading when he could. He gradually mastered basic literacy by bartering bread with white children he met while running errands in exchange for reading lessons. He bought a copy of *The Columbian Orator,* a collection of speeches and essays on liberty, democracy, and courage. He continued to read other material available to him, such as the

Portrait of Frederick Douglass. Courtesy of Library of Congress.

local newspaper. Not even a teenager yet, Frederick Douglass began a long journey that would place him at the pinnacle of society. He was still a slave, though, and was sent back to the plantation near Easton, Maryland. This took him away from Baltimore, where he had enjoyed some degree of success and growth. There he had even begun to teach other black children to read. Back on the owner's new farm in St. Michaels, he was again subjected to unbearable indignities as a slave. In 1836, his attempt to escape slavery failed, and consequently he was imprisoned. In 1838, he succeeded in escaping and moved to New York. He sent for a woman he had met earlier, Anna Murray. They were married. In his new home in the North, Frederick Douglass met and became friendly with the abolitionists. Because of his spellbinding speeches, he was asked to speak at an American Anti-Slavery Society meeting. This group engaged him to undertake a lecture tour in the United States and abroad. His speeches were so eloquent and so powerful that some detractors in the South claimed that Douglass could not have been a former slave.

In 1845, his first of three autobiographies, *The Narrative of the Life of Frederick Douglass,* was published. This made him an even more popular and credible spokesperson for the abolitionist cause. While he was treated well when he was living in England, he knew that it was time to return home to America. But as an escapee from slavery, a price hung over his head. Douglass was aware that there were those who captured runaway slaves in the North and returned them to their owners and believed that this could happen to him. With the help of English friends, he purchased his own freedom, sending the required $710.96 to Hugh Auld, the slave master. On December 5, 1846, twenty-eight-year-old Frederick Douglass was a free man. He was recognized as a noted author, lecturer, and abolitionist on an international scale. In England, Douglass was considered to be an abolitionist in the William Lloyd Garrison camp. That changed upon his return to the United States.

In 1847, Douglass began another phase of an illustrious career. This former slave who had taught himself to read well and articulate eloquently began his own four-page weekly newspaper, the *North Star.* By this time, he and his family had moved to Rochester, New York. At first they were not exactly welcomed with open arms; however, in time, Rochester became more hospitable. After all, Rochester enjoyed a reputation of being antislavery. Some of the women involved in the antislavery movement were also active in the struggle for women's rights. Douglass befriended several of these activists, such as Susan B. Anthony, Elizabeth Cady Stanton, and Lucretia Mott.

The *North Star* was renamed *Frederick Douglass Paper.* It championed the cause of blacks and provided a showcase for black writers. Douglass continued publishing and lecturing for the rights of African Americans to be free. He took on the additional advocacy of the rights of women. He was one of thirty-two men who joined with sixty-eight women in signing the Declaration of Sentiments, the first women's rights convention, held in Seneca Falls, New York, in 1848. As Douglass became more famous in his work, interestingly, his wife Anna remained illiterate.

Frederick Douglass interpreted the Constitution as antislavery, while some other abolitionists interpreted the Constitution as proslavery. Eventually, this and other fundamental differences led Douglass to split from the Garrison faction of the antislavery movement. His efforts to end segregation in the schools of Rochester were fueled by the discrimination his daughter encountered while attending schools in the city. In 1858, Douglass saw the fruits of his labor when schools were desegregated in Rochester. Frederick Douglass was a leader in the Underground Railroad. He and his wife took hundreds of runaway slaves into their home. He vigorously advocated against the fugitive slave laws that were being used to return escaped slaves to slave masters.

In 1859, Frederick Douglass was linked to John Brown's raid at Harpers Ferry, Virginia (now West Virginia). Brown and Douglass were close friends, and Brown had even stayed in Douglass's house in Rochester for several weeks drafting his "Provisional Constitution of the United States" that Brown desired to implement once he had caused a massive slave rebellion in the South. In August 1859, two months prior to the actual raid, which occurred in October 1859, Brown told Douglass his plans to raid the federal arsenal and foment slave rebellion in the South. While Douglass was friends with Brown and knew of Brown's plans ahead of time, he refused to participate in the raid and advised Brown against his planned treason. Douglass argued to Brown that an attack upon federal property would "array the whole country" against the abolitionist cause. Douglass also believed that Brown's plan could not work and that Brown was "going into a perfect steel-trap, and that once in he would never get out alive." However, Douglass's assistant, a twenty-three-year-old escaped slave named Shields Green, did join in Brown's raid. Green was caught (along with the other surviving raiders) and executed by the state of Virginia. The whole Harpers Ferry incident made Douglass think that it was in his best interest to flee to Canada, as Douglass's home was only a short distance from the Canadian border. Many of Brown's other well-known financial supporters (e.g., Gerrit Smith) did the same.

Frederick Douglass wrote honestly about his close relationship with Brown, his involvement in the Harpers Ferry raid, and his respect from John Brown in his 1881 book *The Life and Times of Frederick Douglass.* He stated that John Brown did more for ending slavery than most men in America. Douglass commented, "His [John Brown's] zeal in the cause of freedom was infinitely superior to mine. Mine was as the taper light; his was as the burning sun. I could live for the slave; John Brown could die for him." In the same year (1881), Douglass gave a speech in Harpers Ferry, West Virginia, the site of John Brown's raid, on the occasion of the fourteenth anniversary of Storer College, an African American school located in the town, founded in 1867 as the first school for African Americans in West Virginia following the Civil War. In this speech, Douglass commented that "if John Brown did not end the war that ended slavery, he did at least begin the war that ended slavery. . . . John Brown began the war that ended slavery and made this a Free Republic."

During the Civil War years, Douglass initially supported Gerrit Smith from the Constitution Union Party, but later he rallied around Abraham Lincoln. Using the power of his oratory, his high-profile name recognition, and his newspaper articles, Douglass relentlessly talked about the imperative for the Civil War, namely, freeing the slaves and allowing blacks to fight in the war. On December 31, 1862, President Lincoln formally issued the Emancipation Proclamation that freed slaves the following day in those areas that were "in rebellion." Douglass persisted in his next goal of enlisting blacks into the ranks of the Union army. Three of his sons enlisted in the army. To his great disappointment, he discovered that black soldiers were subject to horrible inequities. They were paid approximately half of the white soldiers' salaries, were issued inferior weapons, were provided inadequate training, and were not allowed to rise to the officer ranks. Upon learning of these conditions, Douglass immediately appealed to President Lincoln. All told, more than 200,000 blacks enlisted in the Union army during the Civil War, making up about 10 percent of the troops. With this extra military force, the war began to shift to the side of the North. President Lincoln elicited Douglass's recommendations on some facets of the war. As was his customary practice, Douglass obliged.

After the war, Douglass declined President Andrew Johnson's offer to head the Freedmen's Bureau, which can be aptly described as the federal government's first attempt at affirmative action for black citizens. While Douglass declined to serve as the head of the Freedmen's Bureau, he did become president of the Freedmen's Savings and Trust. In the immediate years after the war, Douglass also fought for the adoption of the Civil War (Reconstruction) Amendments (the Thirteenth, Fourteenth, and Fifteenth Amendments). Douglass also lobbied for civil rights legislation to improve the lot of newly freed slaves in the South. Douglass believed that affirmative means were necessary to achieve equality. In this regard, Douglass once remarked that

> it is our lot to live among a people whose laws, traditions, and prejudices have been against us for centuries, and from these they are not yet free. To assume that they are free from these evils simply because they have changed their laws is to assume what is utterly unreasonable and contrary to facts. Large bodies move slowly. Individuals may be converted on the instant and change their whole course of life. Nations never. Time and events are required for the conversion of nations. (Douglass 1886, 8)

In 1877, he became a U.S. marshal and recorder of deeds in Washington, D.C. He had assumed residency in the Nation's capital. In 1882, his wife Anna died, and he married Helen Pitts of Rochester. He represented the United States as American consul general to Haiti and chargé d'affaires to Santo Domingo. The last five years of his life were spent in Washington, D.C. After his death on February 20, 1895, Cedar Hill, the home that he occupied in Washington, became a museum maintained by the U.S. Park Service. He has been featured on a postage stamp commemorating his contributions to the United States.

See also Abolitionists; American Civil War; Anthony, Susan Brownell; Civil War (Reconstruction) Amendments and Civil Rights Acts; Coalition to Defend Affirmative Action and Fight for Equality by Any Means Necessary; Freedmen's Bureau; King, Martin Luther, Jr.; Mott, Lucretia Coffin; Stanton, Elizabeth Cady; Sowell, Thomas.

FURTHER READING: Douglass, Frederick, 1962, *Life and Times of Frederick Douglass*, New York: Collier Books; Douglass, Frederick, 1886, *Three Addresses on the Relations Subsisting between the White and Colored People of the United States*, Washington, DC: Gibson Brothers; McFeely, William, Sr., 1991, *Frederick Douglass*, New York: W.W. Norton; Moses, Greg, 1996, "A Neglected Republican Heritage: Frederick Douglass on Immigration and Affirmative Action," paper presented at the 2d National Conference of the Radical Philosophy Association (Purdue University), November 17, author's web site: http://pages.prodigy.net/gmoses/moweb/prepub.htm; Quarles, Benjamin, 1948, *Frederick Douglass*, Washington, DC: Associated Publishing; Sowell, Thomas, 2002, " 'Friends' of Blacks," *Capitalism Magazine*, September 26, http://capmag.com/article.asp?ID=1896.

BETTY NYANGONI

Dred Scott v. Sandford, 19 How. 393 (1857)

The Supreme Court's infamous decision in *Dred Scott v. Sandford*, decided on March 6, 1857, is essential to an understanding of the legal and political atmosphere leading to the American Civil War. The case is also essential to an understanding of the history of race relations in the United States and early constitutional law doctrine on race. In the case, Chief Justice Roger B. Taney, writing for the majority, declared in part that Congress lacked any constitutional power to regulate slavery and that blacks "had no rights under the Constitution that a white man was bound to respect." The decision split the nation when it was handed down and was a factor in the election of Abraham Lincoln in 1860 and in the upcoming Civil War. Additionally, the Thirteenth, Fourteenth, and Fifteenth Amendments to the Constitution (on which civil rights legislation and affirmative action are based) were in part promulgated to specifically reverse the *Dred Scott* decision by ending slavery, providing for full citizenship and equal protection for African Americans, and enfranchising African Americans.

The facts in the underlying case involved more than eleven years of litigation in the Missouri and federal court systems. Dred Scott, a slave, was the property of Dr. John Emerson, a physician and captain in the army of the United States. He had served several tours of duty in portions of the Northwest Territories of Illinois and Wisconsin and in territories within the Louisiana Purchase. The Northwest Ordinance territories, according to the Missouri Compromise of 1820, were free. However, Louisiana was not considered a part of the Louisiana Purchase according to Roger B. Taney, chief justice of the U.S. Supreme Court.

The Scott family had traveled with the Emersons throughout the regions just mentioned. In 1842, the Scotts returned to St. Louis. After Dr. Emerson's death, the Scotts became the property of his wife. She contracted Scott's labors out to the offices of attorney Russell L. Field. The attorney believed that Scott should be emancipated according to Missouri state law and eventually carried the case from the state courts to the U.S. Supreme Court. In the prosecution of Scott's rights, his original slaveholders, the Blow family, helped finance his struggle for emancipation. Scott was fortunate that his employer, Field, also encouraged him legally.

Field first attempted to secure Dred Scott's freedom by applying Missouri state law through its antislavery concept, "once free, always free." The Missouri courts applied the Missouri Compromise of 1820 to state law. Scott's case was tried in the Missouri courts in 1847 and because of a procedural error was retried in 1850.

FRANK LESLIE'S ILLUSTRATED NEWSPAPER

IV.] NEW YORK, SATURDAY, JUNE 27, 1857. [PRICE 6 CENTS. No. 82.—VOL

...TRAVELLERS.

TO TOURISTS AN...

...of land or sea, including adventures and incidents, from every person who pleases to correspond with our paper.

We take this opportunity of returning our thanks to our numerous artistic correspondents through... the country, for the many sketches we are constantly receiving from them of the news of the day. We trust they will spare no pains to furnish us with drawings of events as they may occur. We would also remind them that it is necessary to send all sketches, if possible, by the earliest conveyance.

VISIT TO DRED SCOTT—HIS FAMILY—INCIDENTS OF HIS LIFE—DECISION OF THE SUPREME COURT.

WHILE standing in the Fair grounds at St. Louis, and engaged in conversation with a prominent citizen of that enterprising city, he suddenly asked us if we would not like to be introduced to Dred Scott. Upon expressing a desire to be thus honored, the gentleman called to an old negro who was standing near by, and our wish was gratified. Dred made a rude obeisance to our recognition, and seemed to enjoy the notice we expended upon him. We found him on examination to be a pure-blooded African, perhaps fifty years of age, with a shrewd, intelligent, good-natured face, of rather light frame, being not more than five feet six inches high. After some general remarks we expressed a wish to get his portrait (we had made efforts before, through correspondents, and failed), and asked him if he would not go to Fitzgibbon's gallery and have it taken. The gentleman present...

...should have his likeness in the "great illustrated paper of the country," overruled his many objections, which seemed to grow out of a superstitious feeling, and he promised to be at the gallery the next day. This appointment Dred did not keep. Determined not to be foiled, we sought an interview with Mr. Crane, Dred's lawyer, who promptly gave us a letter of introduction, explaining to Dred that it was to his advantage to have his picture taken to be engraved for our paper, and also directions where we could find his domicile. We found the place with difficulty, the streets in Dred's neighborhood being more clearly defined in the plan of the city than on the mother earth; we finally reached a wooden house, however, protected by a balcony that answered the description. Approaching the door, we saw a smart, tidy-looking negress, perhaps thirty years of age, who, with two female assistants, was busy ironing. To our question, "Is this where Dred Scott lives?" we received, rather hesitatingly, the answer, "Yes." Upon our asking if he was home, she said,

"What white man arter dat nigger for?—why don't white man 'tend to his own business, and let dat nigger 'lone? Some of dese days dey'll steal dat nigger—dat are a fact."

ELIZA AND LIZZIE, CHILDREN OF DRED SCOTT.

DRED SCOTT. PHOTOGRAPHED BY FITZGIBBON, OF ST. LOUIS.

HIS WIFE, HARRIET. PHOTOGRAPHED BY FITZGIBBON, OF ST. LOUIS.

Front page of *Frank Leslie's Illustrated*, dated June 27, 1857, in which Dred Scott is depicted along with his wife, Harriet, and his children, Eliza and Lizzie. This particular newspaper issue contained an array of articles relating to the infamous Supreme Court decision, along with information on Dred Scott's family and life. Courtesy of Library of Congress.

The state court, cognizant of Scott's time in the Northwest, applied the law under which Dred Scott and his family would be emancipated. The state supreme court overruled the decision of the lower state court, and Mrs. Emerson's property rights to Dred Scott were secured for the moment. After a jury verdict in the lower court in favor of John Sanford, Mrs. Emerson's brother and the person who handled her financial interests, a writ of error was filed and the case was appealed to the Supreme Court. At this point Sanford's attorney, possibly to protect his client's property, changed his legal arguments; he now stated that the Missouri law freeing slaves was unconstitutional. Aware of the vicissitudes of the law, Scott and his antislavery allies decided to pursue the matter, not having been satisfied that their freedom was subject to the whims of a state court.

However, since John Sanford lived in New York State, the constitutional requirements concerning diversity of citizenship came into operation, and the case was transferred to the federal system in New York City. The Missouri court had opened the door for Scott to appeal to the federal system when it ruled that a person owning property in a state was qualified to institute proceedings through the concept of diversity of citizenship, as guaranteed by the U.S. Constitution. The lower state court had declared that Scott's status was dependent upon state law, which defined residence, not citizenship. However, since Scott was viewed as only chattel, he could not form the necessary intent, so addressing this issue was moot. The only rights available were derivative under the law through the master, Mrs. Emerson.

The citizenship issue was not ignored by the high court. The appellants in the *Dred Scott* case confronted a Court under the tutelage of Chief Justice Roger B. Taney, a strict constructionist and no stranger to conflict and unpopular decisions. In interpreting Taney, it is relevant to note that he was a resident of Maryland, a slave state, and that he had manumitted his slaves before the *Dred Scott* case appeared on the Supreme Court's docket. In 1839, he had ruled strictly in favor of the law and had authorized the return to Africa of Africans being transported to Cuba on the slave ship *Amistad.* He was fully aware that this decision could anger many of his neighbors, but chose adherence to the law as the appropriate measure of conduct. John Quincy Adams, sixth president of the United States and an avowed abolitionist, defended the Africans and assisted their return to Africa.

Chief justice Taney understood his mandate. Given that the judiciary branch was a creature of the Constitutional Convention, which had established courts in Article III of the U.S. Constitution, he understood that his juridical authority did not extend to legislating. Having been appointed to a position on the high court, he had to deny any injection of emotion into his rulings. The granting of an appeal in the *Dred Scott* case was not meant to be a trial *de novo*; it was only to be a review of the trial evidence, and the parties could not introduce new evidence. The Supreme Court had to make a determination on whether the evidence had been interpreted within the four corners of the law, and to interpret the law within the bounds of Congress's legislative intent. The U.S. Supreme Court ruled that the issue of standing plagued Scott's case. Matters became worse. Sanford's attorney now claimed that since Scott was a slave and accordingly not a citizen, he had no legal standing to pursue a cause of action under the Constitution.

Taney wrote for the majority Court. To support his arguments, the chief justice had to analyze the issue of citizenship. He had prepared a lengthy opinion referring to American colonial history and the relationship between the colonists and the slaves. Taney could find no historic evidence or legal precedent that the framers intended the slaves to be citizens. Without the legal rationalization, Taney wandered into the realm of *obiter dictum* (i.e., comments made in a judicial decision that are not central to the holding and are not to be afforded deference as precedent) and justified his interpretation; he spoke about the Africans through the use of negative pejoratives similar to the remarks made by many antebellum clerics throughout the South to justify slavery. However, he could have avoided many legal complexities by suggesting that the legislative branch amend the Constitution to grant descendants of African slaves American citizenship. Ever mindful of the separation-of-powers doctrine, he could thus have placed the political burden on the people's representatives, the legislative branch. He could have argued that since the legislative branch had the responsibility of reflecting the mood of the sovereign, the people, it created legislation, while Taney's Court interpreted the law.

To support his interpretation of constitutional intent in reference to slavery, Taney cited the compromise at the Constitutional Convention that permitted the continued importation of slaves up to 1808. This agreement had been opposed by South Carolina and Georgia, both of whom relented to "form a more perfect union." Taney also referred to the Fugitive Slave Act that required the authorities throughout the nation to assist, in whatever way, the return of fugitive slaves should one flee one state for another, no matter the origins of the flight. This law made the federal government a party to the maintenance of slavery. A most onerous part of Taney's statement was his analysis of the social and legal positions of the slave. By extending his logic, Taney could argue that since a slave was not considered human, he did not possess the necessary requisites for citizenship.

Taney's unnecessary history lesson went further. Some supporters have expressed the opinion that his intent was to legally conclude the national debate on the question of slavery. He decreed the antislavery provisions of the Northwest Ordinance defunct; now, the states within the Northwest Ordinance were open to slavery. He continued his lesson by declaring the Missouri Compromise of 1820 unconstitutional. He was offended because the law did not provide sufficient protection for the common-law concept of the sanctity of contract, or property. Fully cognizant of the significance of the Fugitive Slave Law for the establishment of the United States, Taney, as part of his *obiter dictum*, concluded that the Missouri Compromise of 1820 was unconstitutional since it denied an individual the due process right to protect his property under the Fifth Amendment. The legal atmosphere surrounding the Kansas-Nebraska Act and the doctrine of popular sovereignty further pummeled the abolitionists; their moral, legal, and practical safety valves were instantaneously atrophied. Southern slaveholders, on the other hand, now found federal support for the "peculiar institution." The chief justice broadened his juridical reach with a further journey into the world of the *obiter dictum*. He opined that the slavery issue was a matter reserved exclusively to the states' determination under the provisions of the federal Constitution. He referred to Article III and the Privileges and Immunities Clause of Article IV.

The dissenting justices also referred to the same documents to buttress their position. When the decision was published, it was evident that Justices John McLean (from Ohio) and Benjamin Curtis (from Massachusetts) objected to the majority view that Scott lacked standing because he was not a citizen. They printed separate opinions that were published with the majority views of the Court. It has been alleged that geography accounted for the minority views: the two dissenters were from states opposing slavery. Justice McLean referred to Americans who opposed slavery, including some of the Founders: Alexander Hamilton, John Jay, and James Madison. He continued his lecture on American slavery by reminding the reader that several northern states had emancipated their slaves. Unfortunately, McLean did not address the fears of the southern states engendered by the Kansas-Nebraska Act and its consequences. McLean went beyond his purview by admonishing the southern states for being concerned with their self-interest. He attacked Taney's interpretation of the Ordinance of 1787 and the Missouri Compromise, wherein Taney alleged that the federal statutes were unconstitutional because the Constitution allegedly opened the territories to slavery. Justice Curtis joined Justice McLean in his dissent. Curtis also opposed Chief Justice Taney's decision on citizenship. Curtis said that anyone born in the United States was a citizen of the United States by virtue of the Federal Constitution. Curtis also refuted Taney's assertion that blacks had no political rights in the United States. Specifically, Curtis showed the blacks were citizens in a number of states in 1787.

Despite McLean and Curtis's interpretation of the Constitution, or the fact that Taney upheld the institution of slavery, the significance of the *Dred Scott* decision was telling. Southern reactions based on the growing fears of the slave states led some to foretell the rupture of the Union. Their sense of encirclement and their diminishing power in Congress occurred in tandem with the growing power of the Republican Party and its antislavery plank. The detractors of the decision believed that it attacked the political base of the Democratic Party and the doctrine of popular sovereignty. They were cognizant of their diminishing congressional power as the influence and power of the free states increased and believed that they were denied equal protection under the federal Constitution. Now, southerners, slave owners, and those opposed to a strong central government saw little hope for the protection of their values, and civil war was on the horizon.

See also African Americans; American Civil War; Civil War (Reconstruction) Amendments and Civil Rights Acts; Fifteenth Amendment; Fifth Amendment; Fourteenth Amendment; Slavery; Slavery and the Founding Fathers; Thirteenth Amendment.

FURTHER READING: Finkelman, Paul, 1997, *Dred Scott v. Sandford: A Brief History with Documents,* Boston: Bedford Books; Irons, Peter, 1999, *A People's History of the Supreme Court,* New York: Viking Press; Miller, Loren, 1966, *The Petitioners: The Story of the Supreme Court of the United States and the Negro,* New York: Pantheon Books.

ARTHUR K. STEINBERG

Drug Abuse Education Act of 1970

The Drug Abuse Education Act, originally passed in 1970, is an illustration of Congress utilizing the role model theory (of affirmative action) in social legislation. The act theorized that drug counselors are more effective if they racially and socially match the addicts they are trying to help. Thus the act encouraged the "use of adequate personnel from similar social, cultural, age, ethnic and racial backgrounds as those of the individuals served." The act is a prime example of the role model theory of affirmative action and the argument that affirmative action programs are needed, if for no other reason than to ensure that adequate numbers of role models exist (in different fields) throughout society to inspire, counsel, teach, and assist other younger individuals of the same social, cultural, ethnic, or racial backgrounds.

The act later became part of what is commonly referred to as the Department of Education Organization Act, which transferred functions from the Department of Health, Education, and Welfare to the Department of Education. This act also dealt with the role education is to play in reducing drug abuse in America. From the standpoint of affirmative action, the act also attempted to identify where drug abuse is most prevalent and focus particular affirmative attention in the public schools in those areas on prevention as a tool to reduce drug-abuse rates.

It was a surprise to few that the region where drug abuse was identified as the most pressing problem was the low-income areas of major cities in the United States. Since low-income areas are populated heavily by minority members, much of the impact of this law was upon African Americans and Latinos. Much of the literature in the field suggests that trying to identify where drugs are being used is very difficult because members of the middle and upper classes are not likely to use and buy drugs in the open, thus making it appear that their rates of drug use are quite low. More recent studies done on a representative sample of schools all across the United States illustrate that the drug problem is one that impacts all races and genders, not only minority members. Thus this law tended to focus upon those who had little opportunity to hide their drug use, fostering the impression that drug use was primarily a "minority problem."

See also Department of Education; Role Model Theory.

FURTHER READING: The Alcohol and Drug Abuse Education Act, referred to in subsec. (a)(2)(Q), Dec. 3, 1970, P.L. 91-527, 84 Stat. 1385, which appeared generally as 21 U.S.C.S. § 1001.

SUSAN F. BRINKLEY

D'Souza, Dinesh (1961–)

As a frequent critic of traditional affirmative action programs and a prolific author, Dinesh D'Souza has consistently argued that race-based affirmative action is a misguided social program that is incorrectly applied as a solution to existing problems in minority communities—problems not originally caused by racial discrimination. D'Souza maintains a staunch platform of abolition of affirmative action—at least race- or gender-based affirmative action—and adheres to a philosophy that merit alone (i.e., meritocracy) should dictate advancement in education or employment. D'Souza has, however, supported in theory the concept of affirmative action based not on race but on socioeconomic status.

Dinesh D'Souza was born on April 25, 1961, in Bombay, India. His father was an executive at Johnson and Johnson Pharmaceuticals, and his mother worked in the home. D'Souza was educated at private Jesuit schools that emphasized a heavily Western, primarily British curriculum. He arrived in the United States in 1978. After graduating from high school in Patagonia, Arizona, he began to attend Dartmouth College in 1979. D'Souza began his public career as the editor for the *Dartmouth Review.* The *Dartmouth Review* was not affiliated with the college and was well known to be an extremely conservative publication that was also notorious for its sometimes-outrageous editorials, which took positions against the role of affirmative action in placing nonqualified individuals at Ivy League institutions. D'Souza graduated with a bachelor of arts degree from Dartmouth in 1983 and then moved to Princeton.

In Princeton, D'Souza became the editor of *Prospect,* a magazine published by Princeton alumni. In 1984, D'Souza published his first book, *Falwell: Before the Millennium.* Jerry Falwell, an evangelist and founder of a group called the Moral Majority, is a political activist who began a conservative movement whose goal is to persuade morally conservative voters to support like-minded candidates. D'Souza's book was criticized by both sides of the political spectrum for not presenting Falwell in a balanced light. This criticism did not stop D'Souza from publishing two more books in the following two years. His next book, *The Catholic Classics* (1986), is a series of interpretive essays that analyze writings and thoughts of historically prominent Catholic thinkers. In 1987, D'Souza published *My Dear Alex: Letters from the KGB. My Dear Alex* used the style of Catholic theologian C.S. Lewis's *Screwtape Letters* as a platform for the purpose of commenting on the politics of the day.

Also in 1987, D'Souza accepted a position in the Reagan administration as an assistant to domestic policy chief Gary Bauer. In this position, he was responsible for presenting Reagan's domestic policy to congressional members and the media. In 1991, D'Souza published his fourth book, *Illiberal Education: The Politics of Race and Sex on Campus. Illiberal Education* was D'Souza's breakthrough work. It put him into the class of intellectuals who were making rounds in the media discussing issues such as political correctness, the university's role in society, and the hot topic of the inner workings of "multicultural" societies. In *Illiberal Education*, D'Souza contends that educational institutions should maintain a curriculum centered on Western tradition to maximize the learning curve of the students.

D'Souza holds many strong views on the most controversial issues, but none of his opinions have drawn as much attention as his outlook on affirmative action. Dinesh D'Souza is one of the first non-Caucasian conservatives to speak out against affirmative action programs. At a lecture at Colby College on May 2, 2001, D'Souza said, "Affirmative action has been used to try to correct problems of merit that appear to be problems of race." D'Souza believes that stereotypes and racial profiling are warranted behavior in certain cases because actions of large groups of people that are predictable deserve to be studied. He uses an example of New York taxi drivers and their choice in late-night fares. New York taxi drivers, D'Souza claims, are less likely to pick up a young black man late at night than anyone else. He then asks several leading questions, such as, "Why, then, do they often refuse to pick up young, Black men at night? Is it because White racism has so infiltrated their minds that they are blinded? Is it because the rate of crime for Blacks in New York is 11 times that of Whites? Are they being racist? Maybe. Are they acting in self-interest? Definitely" (johngaltpress.org).

D'Souza once again presented his ideas to the public in his book *Letters to a Young Conservative* (2002). In *Letters to a Young Conservative*, D'Souza continues to fuel the debate on affirmative action, political correctness, multiculturalism, government, the rich, feminism, the media, and other assorted hot topics. In his section in the book on affirmative action, he addresses the issues of affirmative action in a "letter" format. In the chapter titled "How Affirmative Action Hurts Blacks," D'Souza answers questions from a "young conservative" such as, "What is affirmative action?" "Don't women also benefit from affirmative action?" and "Can't you support any form of affirmative action?" D'Souza answers these questions and others in a way that maintains his staunch platform of abolition of affirmative action. He states, "In my previous work I have written in favor of affirmative action based not on race but on socioeconomic status. If a student who comes from a disadvantaged background and goes to a lousy school nevertheless scores in the 90th percentile on the SAT, he or she may have more college potential than another student who comes from a privileged background and scores in the 95th percentile. So colleges can and should take socioeconomic circumstances into account. Remember too, that more blacks and Hispanics would be eligible for socioeconomic affirmative action, since blacks and Hispanics disproportionately come from the ranks of the poor" (D'Souza 2004). It is clear through this statement and most others within the new book that D'Souza supports the position that ranking, admission, and the acquisition of employment should be based on merit rather than race, while still taking into consideration the individual's "socioeconomic situation."

See also Economically Disadvantaged; Gender-Based Affirmative Action; Meritocracy; Multiculturalism; Preferences; Race-Based Affirmative Action; Racial Profiling; Standardized Testing; Stereotyping and Minority Classes.

FURTHER READING: Dargon, Dan, 2001, "Dinesh D'Souza: Affirmative Action Won't Do the Trick," http://www.johngaltpress.org/2001-05/dsouza.html; D'Souza, Dinesh, 2002, *Letters to a Young Conservative*, New York: Basic Books; D'Souza, Dinesh, 2004, web site: www.

dineshdsouza.com; Jeffrey, Robert C., 2001, "Our New Political Order: The Eros of Enterprise," *Perspectives on Political Science,* 30, no. 4 (fall): 197–201; Matthews, Frank, 1995, "Dinesh D'Souza's Disquieting Views on Race, Racism and Culture," *Black Issues in Higher Education,* 12, no. 16 (October 5): 38–40.

ARTHUR M. HOLST

Du Bois, William Edward Burghardt (1868–1963)

William Edward Burghardt Du Bois, known more popularly as W.E.B. Du Bois (pronounced "due boyss"), established himself as one of the most prolific, intellectual African Americans of the twentieth century. Du Bois advocated changes in civil rights and race relations in the United States through agitation and challenging the status quo. He famously predicted that "the problem of the Twentieth Century is the problem of the color line." His work paved the way for the Pan-African, civil rights, and Black Power movements in the United States. Du Bois also believed that one of the chief ways for blacks to achieve equality was through higher education and professional training. Du Bois believed that "a Talented Tenth" was the best way to achieve equality, that is, that exceptional individuals of color (the Talented Tenth) should rise up and serve as role models and leaders. Du Bois's notions of how to achieve racial equality in the United States can be contrasted with those of another great African American leader of the same period, Booker T. Washington. Washington did not openly encourage challenging the status quo. In fact, Washington was labeled "the Great Accommodator" for his views that blacks should not openly contest Jim Crow laws, but should silently work on improving themselves, and that through such improvement, "friction between the races will pass away." Washington believed in the vocational training of blacks; Du Bois believed in higher education as a means to achieve equality. Du Bois and Washington's historic and well-documented disputes as to how best to achieve racial equality are relevant today to affirmative action and are cited in affirmative action debates and literature. Certain aspects of the affirmative action debate today are merely continuations of the century-old debates between Du Bois and Washington.

Du Bois was the product of the small New England town of Great Barrington, Massachusetts, and was born in 1868 during the administration of President Andrew Johnson. His parents separated after his birth. Even though he was reared by his mother, there is little evidence that he experienced poverty and unusual upheavals during his early years. He displayed a high degree of intellectual promise during his early life. He was valedictorian of his high-school class, albeit a class of twelve. A problematic mispronunciation of his name would follow him for much of his life, much to his constant dismay. Du Bois was adamant that his name be pronounced correctly and would remark repeatedly, "The pronunciation of my name is Due Boyss, with the accent on the last syllable." From high school, Du Bois went on to attend Fisk University in Nashville, Tennessee, on scholarship, where in 1888 he received a bachelor's degree. While attending Fisk, he traveled through rural areas of the South and read profusely about the plight of African

Americans in their quest for equality. He became increasingly aware of race issues and wanted to help improve conditions for all blacks.

Portrait of W.E.B. Du Bois. Courtesy of Library of Congress.

While he was accepted to pursue a master's degree at Harvard, he was required by Harvard to complete a second bachelor's degree. Harvard did not deem the Fisk degree one that provided an adequate foundation for the pursuit of advanced studies at Harvard. Thus Du Bois went on to attend the University of Berlin, where he gained both a different international perspective and a second bachelor's degree in 1890. Du Bois then earned a master's degree in 1891 and subsequently a doctorate of philosophy (Ph.D.) in 1897, both from Harvard. Du Bois was the first African American to earn a Ph.D. degree from Harvard. His doctoral dissertation, *Suppression of the African Slave Trade to the United States of America, 1638–1870*, published in 1896, was one of numerous publications that Du Bois would have throughout his life.

In 1896, Du Bois was asked to conduct sociological research on behalf of the University of Pennsylvania on the issue of blacks living in Philadelphia. During this research, Du Bois lived in a one-room apartment in the heart of Philadelphia's ghetto district. His research was published under the title *The Philadelphia Negro* and became a landmark sociological work on the black community in Philadelphia. In 1897, Du Bois moved to Atlanta, accepting a position as professor of history and economics at Atlanta University.

During his time at Atlanta University, Du Bois began work on what would be one of his most enduring works, *The Souls of Black Folk*, published in 1903. The book, a compilation of fourteen essays, stressed the need to advance civil rights for blacks and protect voting rights. In *The Souls of Black Folk*, Du Bois criticized Booker T. Washington for opposing higher education for blacks. Washington had previously called for a more practical vocational education for blacks, as opposed to a college education in the classical liberal tradition. In the work, Du Bois put forward his "Talented Tenth" theory, which was that an exceptional group of highly educated African Americans would lead to advancements for black society, and it was up to these members to educate and uplift the other members of the race. Interestingly, the "Talented Tenth" theory is related to one of the modern justifications of affirmative action programs, the role model theory. Several months after the release of *The Souls of Black Folk*, Du Bois contributed an essay for the second chapter of a work entitled *The Negro Problem* (1903), which contained a collection of articles by African Americans.

In 1905, Du Bois and several other African American leaders met in Niagara Falls, Canada, since they were refused hotel accommodations in Niagara Falls on the New York side. The Niagara Group discussed segregation and strategy for the advancement of black political rights. From this meeting emerged a list of demands that included equality of economic and educational opportunity for blacks and an end to segregation and discrimination in courts, public facilities, and trade unions. From this first meeting emerged the Niagara Movement, the predecessor organization to the National Association for the Advancement of Colored People (NAACP), one of the best-known civil rights organizations today. The NAACP was founded in 1909. Du Bois also created the *Crisis*, which became the official publication of the NAACP, and served as its editor for the next twenty-four years. Under his editorship, the *Crisis* became one of the most important national voices for the advancement of black issues and civil rights.

During the period from 1905 to 1952, Du Bois became more and more involved in what was described as the Pan-African movement, which called for an end to European colonialism and influence in Africa. He is known as the father of Pan-Africanism for his dogged pursuit of the unification of Africa. His book on African unification, titled *The World and Africa*, was published during this period. Du Bois also began to become more politically radical, associating with socialist and Communist elements. In part because of his radicalism, Du Bois and the NAACP leadership were divided, causing Du Bois to leave the organization in 1934. Du Bois returned to the sociology department at Atlanta University. He returned to the NAACP ten years later as a research director.

In 1945, Du Bois served as an associate consultant to the delegation of the United States at the United Nations Conference in San Francisco. He was not altogether pleased with the proceedings, charging that the proposed United Nations would be run by imperialist nations, with little regard for colonized countries. Du Bois became increasingly alienated from his own country and its racial practices. He organized Pan-African conferences abroad and continued to write and lecture on the inequities of society. Du Bois joined the American Labor Party and became a darling of Communist countries, being awarded the Lenin Peace Prize in 1950 and having a national holiday named in his honor in China.

For speaking out on the need to outlaw atomic weapons and promoting world peace through socialism, the U.S. government ordered that Du Bois register as a foreign agent. When he refused, he was indicted by the U.S. government under the Foreign Agents Registration Act. However, conservative federal district court judge James McGuire dismissed the government's charges against Du Bois for lack of evidence. After the dismissal of charges, the government revoked Du Bois's passport, and he did not have a U.S. passport from 1951 to 1958. Certainly in part because of his harassment by the government, as well as his continued dismay over the lack of progress in race relations in the United States, Du Bois converted to communism and officially joined the Communist Party in 1961. He moved to Ghana with his wife Shirley Graham Du Bois. His last scholarly undertaking was to have been a Ghana state-sponsored work, *Encyclopedia Africana*. This was not completed because Du Bois died on August 27, 1963, in Accra, Ghana, one day before the civil rights march on the capital in Washington, D.C. Du Bois had become legendary. Author John Killens recalls that on the morning of the Washington march, in a hotel in Washington, D.C., several participants of the day's events to come were congregating in the lobby when someone announced, " 'the Old Man died.' Just that. And not one of us asked, 'What old man?' " (Lewis, 4).

See also National Association for the Advancement of Colored People; Role Model Theory; Talented Tenth; Washington, Booker T.

FURTHER READING: Du Bois, Shirley Graham, 1971, *His Day Is Marching On: A Memoir of W.E.B. Du Bois,* Philadelphia: Lippincott; Lewis, David Levering, 1993, *W.E.B. Du Bois: A Biography of a Race,* New York: Henry Holt; Logan, Rayford N., 1971, *W.E.B. Du Bois: A Profile,* New York: Hill and Wang; Sundquist, Eric J., ed., 1996, *W.E.B. Du Bois: The Oxford Reader,* New York: Oxford University Press.

BETTY NYANGONI

Due Process Clause Guarantee of the Fifth Amendment

See Fifth Amendment.

E

E Pluribus Unum

"Out of many, one" is the English translation of the Latin phrase "E Pluribus Unum," the unofficial slogan of the United States adopted by the Continental Congress's Great Seal Committee in 1776. The phrase, represented on the Great Seal by the shield on the eagle's breast, provides a context for the expression of unity the members of the Congress wished to promote as they faced the herculean task of uniting the original thirteen colonies and the unique characteristics of each colony. Today, both critics and supporters of affirmative action claim that their respective visions for affirmative action, or lack thereof, are consistent with the "E Pluribus Unum" slogan. Supporters of affirmative action argue that society is best able to achieve singular success through the promotion of diversity. Critics of affirmative action argue that society should not place a premium on separateness or diversity, but rather stress the importance of integration, minority assimilation into mainstream American society, and a common vision for a color-blind society.

Visually, the image of "E Pluribus Unum" was incorporated into the design by artist Pierre Du Simitière using "thirteen vertical stripes that represent the several states all joined in one solid, compact entire, supporting a Chief, which unites the whole and represents Congress." Du Simitière also illustrated the unity concept of "E Pluribus Unum" by the use of thirteen stars forming a single constellation, said to be a sign of the colonies' position among the sovereign powers of nations, and thirteen arrows, suggested to symbolize "great military strength."

Unity became a dominant theme for the thirteen colonies as a structure for the newly formed federal government, with its three branches, legislative, executive, and judicial. Government officials chose to promote the unity theme to the masses using currency. Such symbols of identification were used for centuries by families as heraldry—coats of arms and other graphical items that identified individual members joined within the family context to represent strength in times of strife and battle. The new nation used unity and the slogan "E Pluribus Unum" liberally on early currency. For example, a gold candlestick with thirteen candles was on one bill. Another bill used a harp with thirteen strings, further promoting the theme "the whole is the sum of its parts."

See also Assimilation Theory; Diversity; Integration; Multiculturalism; Segregation.

FURTHER READING: Burnett, Edmund Cody, 1975, *The Continental Congress*, Westport, CT: Greenwood Press; MacArthur, John D., 2001, "The Great Seal of the United States of America," http://www.greatseal.com; Newman, Eric P., 1990, *The Early Paper Money of America: An Illustrated, Historical, and Descriptive Compilation of Data Relating to American Paper Currency from Its Inception in 1686 to the Year 1800*, Iola, WI: Krause Pub.; Parker, Nancy Winslow, 1995, *Money, Money, Money: The Meaning of the Art and Symbols on United States Paper Currency*, New York: HarperCollins.

THOMAS A. ADAMICH

Economic Development Administration

The Economic Development Administration (EDA) was created under the Public Works and Economic Development Act of 1965 (42 U.S.C. § 3121) for the purpose of generating jobs while keeping existing jobs, and stimulating growth in economically distressed areas of the United States. The EDA assists both rural and urban areas of the nation that are experiencing high unemployment, low income, or other factors that contribute to severe economic distress. The EDA can be classified as a type of affirmative action that is based upon socioeconomic factors.

The EDA works by the basic principle that communities in trouble must be given the opportunity to develop and put into place economic strategies of their own. To succeed with such specific local agendas, the EDA works in partnership with state and local governments, regional economic development districts, public and private nonprofit organizations, and Indian tribes. One tool that the EDA uses to empower communities that are experiencing economic distress was given to the administration in 1980 by the Supreme Court case *Fullilove v. Klutznick*, 448 U.S. 448 (1980). In *Fullilove v. Klutznick*, the Supreme Court ruled that the provision in the Public Works Act of 1977 that requires that, absent administrative waiver, at least 10 percent of federal funds granted for local public works projects must be used by the state or local grantee to procure services or supplies from businesses owned by minority-group members is not unconstitutional. The Supreme Court then resolved that the EDA would enforce this decision through the administration's locally driven economic development initiatives.

The EDA provides federal leadership in local economic development in four ways. First, the EDA provides the tools necessary for local governments to establish their own economic strategies for the purpose of revitalizing their communities. Second, the EDA targets specific areas of the local economy so as to stimulate the economy in the most efficient way. Third, the EDA shares its information with other federal agencies, such as the Departments of Defense, Labor, Energy, Agriculture, and Housing and Urban Development, the Environmental Protection Agency, the U.S. Army Corps of Engineers, the Appalachian Regional Commission, and the Federal Emergency Management Agency, to optimize local economic development. Finally, the EDA investments assist communities faced with declining natural resources to broaden local economies into alternative yet sustainable development projects.

The EDA takes action in the communities that will stimulate private capital. Since 1965, the EDA has invested more than $16 billion in grants across all programs, including local public works and initiatives such as responding to natural disasters and defense conversion. Through these investments, the EDA has stimulated more than $36 billion in private investment. Disadvantaged business enterprises (DBEs) benefit greatly from the EDA's public works investments because 10 percent of all federal funds must be used to obtain supplies or services from the DBEs. Since the EDA's public works investments generate $10.8 million in private-sector investment and $10.13 million in local tax base for every $1.0 million of EDA funds, this creates an environment that contributes greatly to the minority business community and also shows that the EDA programs pay for themselves by helping create employment opportunities while generating tax revenues in participating communities. Economic development professionals located in the EDA's regional and field offices review, recommend, and approve projects identified as state, local, and regional economic opportunities.

The EDA has several program tools to serve the nation's most distressed communities, such as public works, planning, university centers, trade adjustment, defense economic adjustment, post-disaster economic recovery, revolving loan funds, local technical assistance, national technical assistance research and evaluation, and the Economic Development Information Clearinghouse (EDIC). These program tools enable the EDA to receive information regarding economic areas of the nation in distress, evaluate and analyze the most efficient strategy for stimulating multiple economic factors in those areas, and then apply a soundly formulated strategy for economic growth.

An example of the EDA's policies and actions at work in Philadelphia, Pennsylvania, is the creation of the West Philadelphia Enterprise Center (WPEC). The WPEC is located at 4548 Market Street in Philadelphia. The purpose of the WPEC project is to incubate local, mostly minority-owed businesses. The WPEC project has already created as many as 3,500 jobs in the Philadelphia Empowerment Zone in West Philadelphia. The project is mostly funded by Prudential Foundation, with a contribution of $5,000,000. The EPA is partially funding the project with a grant of $1,100,000. The WPEC facilities are an area in the local community where neighborhood youth are able to obtain significant knowledge of computers, technology, entrepreneurial talents, and general business practices.

Practices and projects such as the WPEC exemplify what the EDA does throughout the nation concerning impoverished communities. Small business owners, especially minority-owned businesses, benefit from the EDA's constant funding and project management. Another of the EDA's self-proclaimed success stories is the project undertaken with the American Institute of Learning (AIL). The AIL works with at-risk youth, many of whom are minority, low-income, high-school dropouts who have been unsuccessful in traditional learning systems. Many live in East Austin, Texas. Seventy-six percent of the youths AIL works with are low income, 15 percent are on probation or parole, and 13 percent are parenting teens. The EDA granted $500,000 toward the building of AIL's new facility. As with the WPEC project, the construction received additional funding from private interests. The EDA classifies the AIL project as a success because in 2002 alone, 715 individuals took part in AIL's programs, and 65 percent of its graduates are either employed, in a training program, or enrolled in higher education.

The EDA serves the function of stimulating job growth and economic prosperity within impoverished communities. Using the many tools at its disposal, the EDA is able to contribute funds to worthwhile projects throughout the nation, which will have the potential not only to benefit the nation, but to turn around communities that have no obvious hope for improved conditions.

See also Disadvantaged Business Enterprises; Economically Disadvantaged; *Fullilove v. Klutznick*; Public Works Employment Act of 1977.

FURTHER READING: Economic Development Administration, www.doc.gov/eda/; Evans, Donald L., and David Sampson, 2000, *Economic Development Administration: Annual Report 2000,* http://www.osec.doc/gov/eda/pdf/Annual_RptFY2000_rev.pdf.

ARTHUR M. HOLST

Economically Disadvantaged

Proponents of affirmative action recognize past discrimination against women and ethnic minorities. Consequently, affirmative action is an attempt to formally increase the opportunities for these groups. However, several social commentators from across the political spectrum, for example, Clint Bolick, Cornel West, Alan Dershowitz, and Richard Herrnstein, have from time to time advocated an affirmative action program based upon class or economic needs. Yet generally, the phrases "economically disadvantaged" and "socially disadvantaged," when used in relation to affirmative action, are used in the context of awarding public contracts. Consideration has also recently been given to social and economic disadvantage in the context of affirmative action in higher-education admissions policies.

In the public contracts context, allocation of contracts based upon social or economic status can be seen in public contracts agencies, federal agencies, or municipalities. For example, on the federal level, the Small Business Administration (SBA) is charged with conducting programs that increase opportunities for small businesses owned by women and ethnic minorities. Its declared policy is that small businesses that are owned and controlled by socially and economically disadvantaged individuals will have the "maximum practicable opportunity to participate in the performance of contracts let by any federal agency" (15 U.S.C. § 637[d][1]). A socially disadvantaged individual is defined as someone "who has been subjected to racial or ethnic prejudice or cultural bias because of his or her identity as a member of a group without regard to their individual qualities" (15 U.S.C. § 637[a][5]). An economically disadvantaged individual is one who is socially disadvantaged and whose ability to compete in the free-enterprise system has been impaired due to diminished capital and credit opportunities as compared to others in the free-enterprise system in the same business area but who are not socially disadvantaged (15 U.S.C. § 37[a][6][A]). A socially or economically disadvantaged individual must own at least 51 percent of any small business to qualify for a federal contract pursuant to this plan. The goal is for at least 5 percent of federal contracts to go to socially and economically disadvantaged individuals. Each federal agency is required to set specific goals for participation by socially and economically disadvantaged individuals. One controversial aspect of these set-asides is that some groups are presumed to be socially and economically disadvantaged. These groups include African Americans, Hispanic Americans, Native Americans, and Asian Pacific Americans.

In 1995, the Supreme Court, in *Adarand Constructors, Inc. v. Peña*, 515 U.S. 200 (1995), addressed the question of what level of judicial scrutiny was appropriate for racial classifications used by the federal government. The company (Adarand Constructors) argued that the federal contracting law granted racial preferences. The Court in *Adarand* determined that the test to determine the constitutionality of any federal law that required government contracts to be awarded on the basis of race was strict scrutiny, which was the judicial level of scrutiny previously used to adjudicate cases involving invidious discrimination. Thus, after *Adarand*, any federal law that makes determinations upon race (even if it involves "benign discrimination") is presumed to be suspect. Once a federal law or other federal government action is suspect, it must then be viewed with strict scrutiny by a court. A law can only pass the strict scrutiny test if the governmental action is justified by a compelling governmental interest and if the governmental action is narrowly tailored to accomplish the compelling governmental interest. In only one case has the government action at issue survived the "strict scrutiny" analysis of the Court. That one case, *Korematsu v. United States*, 323 U.S. 214 (1944), involved the national security of the United States during World War II. Hence it is no wonder that Justice Thurgood Marshall once referred to the "strict scrutiny" standard as "strict theory but fatal in fact" in his concurring opinion in *Fullilove v. Klutznick*, 448 U.S. 448 (1980).

Additionally, the courts generally find several factors relevant in determining whether a federal law or action is sufficiently "narrowly tailored": first, the law or action must not be mere racial balancing; second, it must also be based on an appropriate quantification of the number of qualified minorities in an area who are capable of performing the work being awarded; third, the law or action must not erroneously overinclude undeserving candidates; fourth, it must include race-neutral alternatives; and fifth, the government action/plan may not employ quotas. Although the Supreme Court expressed concern that the law's provision that certain racial/ethnic groups are presumptively socially and economically disadvantaged might constitute a racial classification in *Adarand*, it did not decide the issue but remanded it to the lower federal court.

After *Adarand*, the government changed the way it awarded contracts so as to pass the strict scrutiny test. Not surprisingly, the parameters were much more restrictive. Among the changes was that the government now had to create benchmarks. The benchmarks are designed to be based on estimates of what the level of participation would be for the socially and economically disadvantaged groups were it not for discrimination. Then the actual participation is compared to these benchmarks. If the benchmarks are not met, then the government is entitled to use credits and incentives to raise the level of participation by socially and economically disadvantaged individuals. These incentives can include monetary incentives, credit to nonminority prime contractors for creating partnerships with socially and economically disadvantaged individuals, and a price credit of up to 10 percent on bids for government contracts. If the benchmarks are exceeded, then the credits and incentives are lowered or eliminated. If for some reason the price credits and incentives fail to achieve the benchmarks over an extended period of time, then, and only then, are specific set-asides allowed.

Whether an individual is in fact socially and economically disadvantaged must be proven under the SBA program, although there is still a rebuttable presumption that certain racial/ethnic groups are socially and economically disadvantaged. However, this presumption may be challenged, even by third parties. That is, nonminority contractors who feel that they will lose out on contracts may challenge whether or not the purported socially and economically disadvantaged individual truly meets the criteria. In addition, nonminorities must be given the opportunity to prove that they are in fact socially and/or economically disadvantaged. The burden-of-proof standard for proving social and economic disadvantage is a preponderance of the evidence. A preponderance of the evidence is evidence that shows that the fact to be proved is more likely true than false. In other words, a conclusion is supported by the preponderance of the evidence when it is supported by at least 51 percent of the evidence. This is a change from the prior requirement that proof of social and economic disadvantage for individuals not entitled to the rebuttable presumption was to be shown by "clear and convincing" evidence, a more demanding burden of proof.

The concept of socially and economically disadvantaged has recently been added in the context of affirmative action in higher-education admissions policies. In higher-education admissions, in lieu of a race-conscious policy, many universities are tailoring their admissions policies to examine an applicant's background. This examination is designed to unearth an applicant's life challenges, which could include coming from a socially or economically disadvantaged background. An institution of higher education may see some advantage to admitting such applicants to foster diversity of thought. In addition, this criterion is race neutral—applicants of all races and ethnicities are potentially socially and economically disadvantaged. This approach has the advantage of putting an applicant's other characteristics into the proper context. For example, if an applicant has been able to overcome a socially or economically disadvantaged background, then perhaps that applicant will successfully meet the challenges of higher education. The University of Texas also created several new criteria to examine each applicant's social and economic background. This could include information on household income, parents' level of education, whether the applicant is the first in his or her family to attend college, whether the applicant's household speaks primarily English, and a description of the applicant's household or other responsibilities while attending high school. Finally, reliance on one's social or economic status, instead of on race, avoids constitutional problems of violating the Equal Protection Clause of the Fourteenth Amendment.

See also Adarand Constructors, Inc. v. Peña; African Americans; Asian Americans; Bolick, Clint; Compelling Governmental Interest; Contracting and Affirmative Action; Equal Protection Clause; Fourteenth Amendment; Hispanic Americans; *Korematsu v. United States*; Narrowly Tailored Affirmative Action Plans; Native Americans; Strict Scrutiny; West, Cornel.

FURTHER READING: Mayor, Bruce, 1996, "The Court's Adarand Decision and Federal Managers," *Public Manager* 25, no. 3 (fall): 35–38; "New Affirmative Action Guidelines Proposed," 1996, *Black Issues in Higher Education* 13, no. 9 (June 27): 8–9; Oltersdorf, Cora, 1998, "Reaching Out," *Texas Alcalde*, September/October, 20–25; Seale, Abrel, 1998, "Texas Tithe," *Texas Alcalde*, July/August, 14–19.

MICHAEL K. LEE

Edley, Christopher F. (1953–)

Christopher Edley, a law professor at Harvard Law School since 1981, is a nationally recognized advocate of affirmative action. In 1995, Edley served as special counsel to President Bill Clinton and served in the capacity of director of the Clinton White House's review of affirmative action. In this capacity, Edley assisted Clinton with his formulations on the issue of affirmative action and participated in the development of Clinton's famous "Mend It, Don't End It" speech on affirmative action in July 1995. Edley is also the author of *Not All Black and White: Affirmative Action, Race, and American Values* (1996), a book that grew out of his experiences as special counsel and director for the Clinton administration in 1995.

Edley is a 1973 graduate (bachelor of arts) of Swarthmore College and a 1978 graduate of Harvard Law School (juris doctorate) and Harvard's John F. Kennedy School of Government (master of public policy). During law school, Edley served as an editor of the *Harvard Law Review.* Following his graduation from Harvard, Edley served as assistant director of the White House Domestic Policy Staff in the Carter administration. In 1981, Edley left Washington, D.C., and accepted a tenure-track assistant professor of law position at Harvard Law School. From time to time, Edley also served in the government. Most notably, in 1992, Edley served as a senior advisor on economic policy for the Clinton-Gore transition team, as well as serving for the first two years in the Clinton administration as a senior economic advisor. During these years, he also served as associate director for economics and government in the White House Office of Management and Budget. In 1995, Edley served as the point person and senior advisor for the Clinton White House on affirmative action.

After the White House review of affirmative action was completed in 1995, Edley returned to his teaching duties at Harvard. In addition to his teaching duties, Edley is a codirector and cofounder of the Civil Rights Project and is also serving a six-year term as a member of the U.S. Commission on Civil Rights. In his remaining time, Edley is working on a second book on the topic of affirmative action, race, and civil rights.

See also Carter, James "Jimmy" Earl, Jr.; Clinton, William Jefferson; U.S. Commission on Civil Rights.

FURTHER READING: Edley, Christopher, 1996, *Not All Black and White: Affirmative Action, Race, and American Values,* New York: Hill and Wang.

JAMES A. BECKMAN

Education and Affirmative Action

Affirmative action has been a controversial public policy in the United States since its modern-day inception in the 1960s. Broadly conceived, affirmative action is a term that refers to measures or practices that seek to terminate discriminatory practices by permitting the consideration of race, ethnicity, sex, or national origin in the availability of opportunity for a class of qualified individuals who have been the victims of historical, actual, or recurring discrimination. Perhaps no area of the affirmative action debate is as heated and controversial as the area of higher education. Proponents of affirmative action often argue that there is no arena more important than education for satisfying the goals of affirmative action. According to proponents, instilling values of equality and diversity through the socialization theory works best in the educational arena. Also, according to proponents, utilizing affirmative action satisfies many of the desired goals, such as increasing minorities and women in the professional ranks, increasing the availability of minority and female role models, and so on. Critics of affirmative action in higher education largely argue that such programs are unfair, engage in reverse discrimination, and ultimately cause more harm than good.

The seminal U.S. Supreme Court case dealing with affirmative action in higher education is *Regents of the University of California v. Bakke*, 438 U.S. 265 (1978). The *Bakke* decision is generally regarded as the focus point for discussions of diversity and affirmative action in higher education. Opponents of diversity and affirmative action measures in higher education have used *Bakke* to challenge the use of race, ethnicity, sex, or national origin in student admissions, financial aid, and staff and faculty employment. In the 1990s, conservative political forces used *Bakke* as a symbolic tool for promoting statewide referenda, such as California's Proposition 209 and Washington's Initiative 2000, to reverse the civil rights gains of the 1960s and 1970s. Proponents of affirmative action justify such plans as being ultimately consistent with the *Bakke* decision, which did allow for the possibility of utilizing race or gender as a factor to be considered in the admissions process.

The U.S. Supreme Court significantly shaped the contemporary legal context for affirmative action in higher education in deciding *Regents of the University of California v. Bakke.* After having twice been denied admission, Allan Bakke, a white male, alleged the invalidity of a special admissions program at the University of California at Davis School of Medicine. The medical school filled 16 of its 100 slots in its entering class through a special admissions program open only to minority applicants who were compared among themselves and not with other applicants for admissions—in essence, a quota system. Allan Bakke had a college grade point average and Medical College Admission Test (MCAT) score that were higher than those of most of the minority applicants. In deciding *Bakke*, the U.S. Supreme Court affirmed the California Supreme Court's decision that the special admissions quota program had violated the Equal Protection Clause of the Fourteenth Amendment, reversed the judgment prohibiting the defendant from considering race in its future admissions, and directed that the plaintiff be admitted to the School of Medicine.

For supporters of affirmative action initiatives in higher education, Justice Lewis Powell's opinion in *Bakke* identified the context for promoting what has been called a "diversity rationale" in higher education. Justice Powell wrote in his opinion that ethnic diversity could be considered as one factor in a range of factors for attaining heterogeneity in higher education. However, Justice Powell warned against the use of ethnic diversity to establish quotas that would harm the interests of "genuine" diversity. Justice Powell's opinion has posed a dilemma for institutions of higher education that have developed admissions policies that take race into consideration but do not formulate quotas based on race. Institutions of higher education interpret *Bakke* as identifying a diversity rationale that allows them to use race as a selective factor in admissions as long as racial quotas are not promoted. Interestingly, the diversity rationale adopted by institutions of higher education from *Bakke* is a central issue in challenges to diversity and affirmative action initiatives in higher education. From 1978 (the date of the *Bakke* decision) until 2003, the U.S. Supreme Court remained silent on the issue of affirmative action and higher education and left it to the lower courts to apply the conflicting guidance contained in the *Bakke* decision. During this time period, the most significant lower court post-*Bakke* challenges to affirmative action in higher education came almost a decade and a half after the *Bakke* decision in *Hopwood v. Texas*, 78 F.3d 932 (5th Cir. 1996), *Smith v. University of Washington Law School*, 233 F.3d 1188 (9th Cir. 2000), *Johnson v. Board of Regents of the University of Georgia*, 263 F.3d 1234 (11th Cir. 2001), and *Grutter* (and *Gratz*) *v. Bollinger*, 288 F.3d 732 (6th Cir. 2002). These post-*Bakke* challenges framed the affirmative action debate from 1978 to 2003 as it relates to diversity and affirmative action initiatives in higher education. In 2003, the Supreme Court granted a review in *Grutter v. Bollinger*, 123 S. Ct. 2325, 2003 U.S. LEXIS 4800 (2003), and *Gratz v. Bollinger*, 123 S. Ct. 2411, 2003 U.S. LEXIS 4801 (2003).

The first significant lower court decision after *Bakke* dealing with affirmative action in higher education came with the *Hopwood* case. In 1992, Cheryl J. Hopwood and three other white plaintiffs filed suit against the University of Texas Law School alleging that they were denied admission as a result of procedures granting preferences to black and Mexican American applicants. The law school utilized an admissions process that separated black and Mexican American applicants from other applicants. *Hopwood* alleged that the separate admissions process violated the Equal Protection Clause of the Fourteenth Amendment because it favored black and Mexican American applicants over nonminority applicants with comparable records. The district court ruled that a separate admissions process for minority applicants was unconstitutional because it was not narrowly tailored to the state's compelling interest in diversity and in overcoming past discrimination. In an interesting twist, the district court found that minority status could merit special consideration but expressed concern that it could result in a separate standard for minorities and nonminorities.

On appeal, the U.S. Court of Appeals for the Fifth Circuit ruled that the law school's use of racial preferences served no compelling state interest under the Fourteenth Amendment and directed the law school not to use race as a factor in admissions. The Fifth Circuit Court also ruled that while racial preferences could serve to remedy past discrimination as a compelling state interest, they could only do so if they addressed discrimination at the law school and not in the university (or the state) as a whole. Finally, the court ordered the law school to demonstrate that the plaintiffs would not have been admitted under a race-neutral admissions process.

The U.S. Supreme Court declined to hear appeals of the circuit court's decision, noting that the 1992 admissions program had been discontinued and would not be reinstated. On remand, the district court found that none of the plaintiffs would have been admitted under a race-neutral admissions process and ordered the law school not to take racial preferences into consideration in the admissions process. The university's request for en banc review by the entire Fifth Circuit Court was denied. Following the *Hopwood* case, the state's public universities stopped using racial preferences. Texas soon thereafter adopted a percentage plan, in lieu of affirmative action. The permissibility of utilizing affirmative action in higher education was also called into serious doubt in the remaining states that compose the Fifth Circuit, Louisiana and Mississippi. Indeed, many colleges and universities around the country (and outside the Fifth Circuit) decided to voluntarily drop their affirmative action plans because they viewed the *Hopwood* decision as the law to come in their jurisdictions as well.

Several years after the *Hopwood* decision, a split in the federal circuits developed on the constitutional permissibility of using affirmative action in higher education by virtue of the *Smith v. University of Washington Law School* decision. In 1997, Katuria Smith, Angela Rock, and Michael Pyle (collectively, Smith) filed a class-action suit against the University of Washington Law School alleging that they and other white applicants had been denied admission on the basis of racially discriminatory admissions policies. In this case, the U.S. Court of Appeals for the Ninth Circuit followed the majority opinion rendered in *Bakke* and held that the law school's admissions program could consider race as a factor in the promotion of educational diversity as a compelling governmental interest and that it met the demands of strict scrutiny of race-conscious measures.

In 2001, the Supreme Court declined to hear the appeal despite the contradiction between this ruling and that in *Hopwood.* The Court held that the issue was moot since the University of Washington had discontinued using race, ethnicity, and national origin as factors in the admissions process following passage of Washington Initiative 200. Initiative 200, the Washington State Civil Rights Initiative, was approved by voters in 1998. Modeled after California's Proposition 209, Initiative 200 prohibited the state from granting preferential treatment on the basis of race, sex, or national origin in the areas of public education, public contracting, and public employment. Thus the nine states that comprise the Ninth Circuit were permitted to continue utilizing affirmative action plans. However, as just pointed out, two of the nine states abolished the use of affirmative action by state referenda, California by Proposition 209 and Washington by Initiative 200.

As if the conflict between two federal circuits were not causing sufficient confusion for administrators and admissions officers at colleges and universities, the U.S. Court of Appeals for the Eleventh Circuit weighed in on the debate soon thereafter in *Johnson v. Board of Regents of the University of Georgia.* In 1999, Jennifer Johnson filed suit against the University of Georgia after she was denied admission to the freshman class for fall 1999. Her complaint was later consolidated with the complaints of Aimee Bogrow and Molly Ann Beckenhauer, who were also denied admission in 1999. Johnson was offered admission to the University of Georgia after she had filed her lawsuit, but she declined to enroll at that time. The plaintiffs alleged that they were denied admission on the basis of race (Title VI) and gender (Title IX). The University of Georgia gave automatic preference in admissions to male applicants. Also, the University of Georgia employed a formula, called a "total student index," whereby the university selected 85 percent of each entering freshman class based on academic qualifications alone, but then considered race as part of a formula to choose the remaining 15 percent. The U.S. District Court for the Southern District of Georgia ruled in favor of the plaintiffs, holding in essence that diversity on campus was not a compelling governmental interest. Thus, according to the district court, the university's admissions policy was unconstitutional under the Fourteenth Amendment. The court further argued that Justice Powell's opinion in *Bakke* was not binding precedent, and that the court was not required to assume that the university's desire to promote a diverse student body was a compelling state interest.

The district court's decision was appealed to the U.S. Court of Appeals for the Eleventh Circuit, and in August 2001, the district court decision was ultimately upheld. In upholding the district court's ruling, the Eleventh Circuit struck down the University of Georgia's admissions policy as not narrowly tailored to promote diversity. Thus affirmative action plans were invalidated and/or called into serious questions in the three states that compose the Eleventh Circuit (Florida, Georgia, and Alabama). Florida had by this time eliminated affirmative action in higher education and instituted a percentage plan in its place. With the Eleventh Circuit decision, the Eleventh and Fifth Circuits had held affirmative action plans to be unconstitutional, while the Ninth Circuit had held affirmative action plans in higher education to be permissible. Georgia ultimately did not appeal the case to the U.S. Supreme Court, concluding that better and more favorable cases to argue the merits of affirmative action in higher education was percolating through the federal courts in Michigan, the cases *Grutter* and *Gratz.*

The *Gratz* and *Grutter* cases (ultimately consolidated for U.S. Supreme Court review in 2003) involved two separate challenges to the public university system of Michigan. *Gratz v. Bollinger* dealt with the permissibility of utilizing affirmative action at the undergraduate level. *Grutter v. Bollinger* dealt with the permissibility of utilizing race at the professional law school level. In 1997, Jennifer Gratz and Patrick Hamacher filed a class-action suit on behalf of themselves and all others similarly situated against the University of Michigan alleging that the university's College of Literature, Science, and the Arts had violated Title VI of the Civil Rights Act and the Equal Protection Clause of the Fourteenth Amendment by using race as a factor in admissions decisions. Specifically, two race-conscious admissions practices were at issue. First, one plan, used from 1995 to 1998, was based primarily upon test scores and grade point averages and in essence required Asian and white applicants to meet higher minimum requirements for admissions. Second, a plan used from 1999 through 2003 rated applicants on a 150-point scale. African Americans, Hispanic Americans, and Native Americans automatically received a 20-point bonus on this scale, the equivalent of an advantage a high-school student with a 4.0 grade point average would enjoy over a high-school student with a 3.0 grade point average.

At the same time, in 1997, Barbara Grutter filed suit against the University of Michigan Law School after having been denied admission in June of that year. Grutter alleged that she was discriminated against on the basis of her race (Caucasian, "a disfavored racial group") and that the law school violated the Fourteenth Amendment and Title VI of the Civil Rights Act of 1964, which prohibits recipients of federal funds from discriminating on the basis of race. At issue on the law school level was the practice of trying to enroll a "critical mass" of underrepresented minority students under the category of an applicant's life experiences and ability to contribute to diversity.

As far as the undergraduate (*Gratz*) case was concerned, the district court largely upheld the university's present policies. The district court did declare the admissions program in existence from 1995 through 1998 to be unconstitutional on the basis that the plan was not narrowly tailored to meet the interest of diversity under the standard of strict scrutiny. However, the court noted that this affirmative action plan had been discontinued and found that the second admissions program in existence since 1999 was constitutional. Attorneys for the plaintiffs relied on the U.S. District Court for the Southern District of Georgia's decision in *Johnson v. Board of Regents of the University of Georgia* (discussed earlier) to argue that diversity is not a compelling governmental interest that can justify the use of race-conscious classification in the admissions process. The district court, however, disagreed. Moreover, it not only reasoned that admissions programs that consider race for other than remedial purposes are permitted by the Fourteenth Amendment but went on to assert that diversity in higher education, by its very nature, is a permanent and ongoing interest. The plaintiffs appealed this ruling to the U.S. Court of Appeals for the Sixth Circuit, which never ruled on the case, as the U.S. Supreme Court decided to review the *Gratz* case as part of its review of the *Grutter* case.

As far as the law school (*Grutter*) case was concerned, the district court found in favor of the plaintiff and against the law school. The court declared that the law school's use of race in its admissions decisions violated the Equal Protection Clause of the Fourteenth Amendment and Title VI of the Civil Rights Act of 1964, and it prohibited the law school from using race as a factor in its admissions decisions. The University of Michigan requested a stay of injunction and was denied by the district court. In both cases, *Gratz* and *Grutter*, the U.S. Court of Appeals for the Sixth Circuit permitted intervention by proposed defendant-intervenors—such parties as the NAACP Legal Defense and Educational Fund, the Mexican American Legal Defense and Educational Fund, the American Civil Liberties Union Foundation, the Center for Individual Rights, and several other entities.

The reasoning by the court in *Grutter v. Bollinger* was that despite the use of other factors considered in the admissions decisions, the law school placed significant emphasis on an applicant's race in deciding whether to accept or reject. It also found that the law school sought to admit an entering class comprised of from 10 percent to 17 percent of African Americans, Native Americans, and Hispanics. The court based its reasoning on the average representation of ethnic minorities in the law school's entering classes and on a statement by a faculty member who attempted to define "critical mass" in terms of percentages. That is, the district court found that the law school had an unwritten practice of trying to enroll a "critical mass" of underrepresented minority students—typically, 10 to 17 percent of each entering class. In turning to the constitutionality of using race as a factor in achieving racial diversity, the court disagreed with Justice Powell's opinion in *Bakke* and noted that *Bakke* did not support the proposition that a university's desire to have a diverse student body is a compelling state interest. The court went on to suggest that diversity could have an important educational benefit, but made a distinction between diversity of viewpoint and racial diversity. The court then concluded that the law school sought "diversity of views."

On May 14, 2002, a sharply divided Sixth Circuit Court of Appeals voted 5–4 to overturn the lower court's ruling that the admissions policy used by the University of Michigan Law School *Grutter v. Bollinger* illegally discriminated against white applicants. The majority opinion for the court noted that the law school's admissions policy set appropriate limits on the use of race and ethnicity. The court's opinion also noted that the law school intended to consider race and ethnicity in achieving a diverse and robust student body only until it became possible to enroll a "critical mass" of underrepresented minority students through race-neutral admissions process. In contrast, the minority opinion noted that the case involved a straightforward instance of racial discrimination by a state institution, and that the university's plan did not seek diversity for education's sake. Rather, the minority noted that the university sought diversity for the sake of the comfort that those abstract numbers might bring and at the expense of the real rights of real people to fair consideration. The Sixth Circuit Court of Appeals stated without explanation that it would rule in *Gratz v. Bollinger* at a later date.

With the Sixth Circuit ruling in May 2002, a significant split in the federal court rulings had developed. In essence, the Fifth and Eleventh Circuits had invalidated affirmative action plans, while the Ninth and Sixth Circuits had validated affirmative action plans. In part because of the significant conflict in federal court rulings on the subject of affirmative action in higher education, the Supreme Court announced in December 2002 that it had agreed to hear both the *Gratz* and *Grutter* cases, combined as a single case for purposes of Supreme Court review. This set the stage for the Supreme Court's decision of the "Michigan cases" in June 2003. In these two landmark cases, the Court was faced with the issue of whether a concern for diversity in higher education was a sufficient justification to engage in benign discrimination through the implementation of an affirmative action program. In the end, the Court reaffirmed the diversity rationale that Justice Powell had enunciated twenty-five years earlier in the *Bakke* case. In reaffirming diversity in higher education as a compelling governmental interest, the Supreme Court upheld the University of Michigan Law School's affirmative action plan (*Grutter* case) and endorsed affirmative action plans that utilize race as one factor or ingredient (among many) in the overall evaluation of candidates. Thus, according to the Court in *Grutter*, race could be considered as a "plus" factor, just as other factors such as one's athletic ability or musical talent or letters of recommendation might be considered. In ruling in this fashion, the Court reaffirmed the diversity that Justice Powell had put forth twenty-five years earlier in the *Bakke* case. However, the Court also warned in the *Gratz* decision that fixed racial quotas and mechanized formulas (which have the effect of operating as a quota) would not be tolerated. In the *Gratz* decision, the Court struck down the University of Michigan undergraduate admissions affirmative action plan that gave extra points for race alone. This, the Court held, was akin to racial quotas, which violate the Fourteenth Amendment.

The Supreme Court's resolution of the Michigan cases (and harmonizing the prior conflicting decisions of *Smith v. Washington, Hopwood v. Texas,* and *Johnson v. Georgia*) has aptly earned the Michigan cases the title of the most significant Supreme Court decision on affirmative action in the last quarter century and since the *Bakke* decision. Thus in order to consider the present state of affirmative action in higher education, one must turn to the Supreme Court's June 2003 decision in the Michigan cases. However, to understand the use of affirmative action in higher education during the last quarter century in America, one must turn to the foundational cases of *Bakke, Smith v. Washington, Hopwood v. Texas,* and *Johnson v. Georgia.*

See also African Americans; American Civil Liberties Union; Center for Individual Rights; Civil Rights Act of 1964; Compelling Governmental Interest; Equal Protection Clause; Fourteenth Amendment; *Gratz v. Bollinger/Grutter v. Bollinger*; Harvard Model; Hispanic Americans; *Hopwood v. Texas*; *Johnson v. Board of Regents of the University of Georgia*; Minority Professionals and Affirmative Action; Narrowly Tailored Affirmative Action Plans; National Association for the Advancement of Colored People; Native Americans; One Florida Initiative; Percentage Plans; Powell, Lewis Franklin, Jr.; Proposition 209; Quotas; *Regents of the University of California v. Bakke*; Reverse Discrimination; Role Model Theory; *Smith v. University of Washington Law School*; Socialization Theory of Equality; Strict Scrutiny; Title VI of the Civil Rights Act of 1964; Title IX of the Education Amendments of 1972; Washington Initiative 200.

FURTHER READING: Bell, Derrick, 2000, *Race, Racism, and American Law*, 4th ed., New York: Aspen; Bloom, Lackland, Jr., 1998, "*Hopwood, Bakke*, and the Future of the Diversity Justification," *Texas Tech Law Review* 29:1–72; Einat, Philip, 2002, "Diversity in the Halls of Academia: Bye-bye *Bakke*," *Journal of Law and Education* 31:149–166; Perea, Juan F., Richard Delgado, Angela P. Harris, and Stephanie M. Wildman, 2000, *Race and Races: Cases and Resources for a Diverse America*, St. Paul, MN: West Group.

ADALBERTO AGUIRRE JR.

Eisenhower, Dwight David (1890–1969)

Prior to entering politics and becoming the thirty-fourth president of the United States, Dwight D. Eisenhower had spent most of his adult life as a soldier, not as a professional politician. Eisenhower is perhaps best known today in the affirmative action context not for what he did, but rather for whom he appointed. During his administration, Eisenhower appointed three individuals who would significantly impact affirmative action, Chief Justice Earl Warren, Associate Justice William Brennan, and, to a lesser extent, Attorney General Herbert Brownell. Eisenhower is also well remembered in the civil rights context for presiding over the country during the particularly tumultuous years immediately following the Supreme Court's decision in *Brown v. Board of Education (Brown I)*, 347 U.S. 483 (1954), and during the forced integration of several southern schools (e.g., Little Rock Central High School). Finally, during Eisenhower's administration, the Civil Rights Acts of 1957 and 1960 were passed in an effort to improve voting rights and protections for minorities in the South. As part of this legislation, the Civil Rights Division of the U.S. Department of Justice was created.

Eisenhower was born in Texas and raised in Abilene, Kansas. He received a free education at the U.S. Military Academy and while there might have become an all-American football player had he not severely injured his knee while tackling the legendary athlete Jim Thorpe. He graduated from West Point in 1915 ("the class the stars fell on") and commenced his military career, working for a time under General Douglas MacArthur. Eisenhower reached the pinnacle of his military career during World War II as the supreme commander of Allied forces. His superb leadership directed the Allies to victory in Europe over Germany. He briefly retired from the service from 1949 to 1950 to serve as the president of Columbia University, but was soon recalled by President Harry Truman to lead the forces of the recently approved North Atlantic Treaty Organization. After retiring again in 1952, he was elected president on the Republican ticket. By and large, his foreign and domestic policies placed a heavy emphasis on consensus and avoidance of controversy. Eisenhower appears to have generally tried to help the African American population advance. Early in his tenure, J. Ernest Wilkins became the first black to officially sit at the president's cabinet table, and both navy military depots in the South and public places of the District of Columbia were desegregated.

In his term of office, Eisenhower nominated three critical individuals who were to mold his administration's civil rights policies, Earl Warren as chief justice of the U.S. Supreme Court (nominated in 1953), William Brennan as associate justice (nominated in 1956), and Herbert Brownell as attorney general (nominated in 1953). Ironically, Eisenhower later remarked that nominating Brennan and Warren to the Supreme Court were two of his worst mistakes as president. While Eisenhower had many differences of opinion with them and usually disagreed privately with their political proclivities, he seems to have usually supported their actions publicly.

Eisenhower's private disagreement but public support of Warren was best illustrated when Warren announced the Supreme Court's unanimous controversial ruling in *Brown v. Board of Education* on May 17, 1954. This landmark civil rights case reversed the antiquated 1896 Court ruling in *Plessy v. Ferguson*, 163 U.S. 537 (1896), which sanctioned "separate but equal" in public facilities, thereby promoting racial segregation. In the *Brown* case, the Court declared that "the public education doctrine of 'separate but equal' has no place. Separate educational facilities are inherently unequal." The Court cited the Fourteenth Amendment of the Constitution, which guaranteed all citizens "equal protection of the laws." Eisenhower personally disagreed with the Court, commenting that "I don't believe you can change the hearts of men with law," which was ironically a view shared by the Supreme Court in its antiquated 1896 *Plessy* decision. However, as a constitutionalist, Eisenhower firmly believed in the separation of powers and the legitimate role of the federal judiciary in American society. On May 18, 1954, he publicly told reporters, "The Supreme Court has spoken, and I am sworn to uphold the constitutional processes in this country; and I will obey." He shortly followed this up by ordering the desegregation of schools in Washington, D.C. Despite this model for the rest of the country, the Court had not set timelines for compliance, merely stating in *Brown v. Board of Education (II)*, 349 U.S. 294 (1955), that local school boards should move "with all deliberate speed."

Not surprisingly, there was resistance to the *Brown* ruling. More than 100 U.S. congressmen representing states below the Mason-Dixon line signed a "Southern Manifesto" pledging to fight the Court's decision whenever possible. In the fall of 1957, events reached an impasse when nine African American students were not allowed to enter Central High School in Little Rock, Arkansas. In overt defiance of the *Brown* decision, the state governor, Orval Faubus, placed the Arkansas National Guard in and around the school to prevent the new students from entering. After several unsuccessful conciliatory attempts to quietly resolve this issue, Eisenhower acted as the commander in chief of the military by deploying 1,100 soldiers from the 101st Airborne to Little Rock and federalizing the Arkansas National

Armed troops escort African American students from Central High School in Little Rock, Arkansas, in 1957. Eisenhower deployed over 1,000 federal troops to Little Rock, as well as federalizing the Arkansas National Guard in order to enforce the desegregation of Central High School. Courtesy of Library of Congress.

Guard. This resulted in the admission of the African American students, and the Supreme Court's decision was upheld.

Despite nagging health problems in 1955 and 1956, Eisenhower sought and gained reelection. During this time, Attorney General Brownell set forth his administration's first civil rights legislation, which sought to secure African American voting rights. Despite the Fifteenth Amendment to the Constitution's guarantee that citizens shall not be deprived of the right to vote on account of race or previous condition of servitude, many states had created means (such as poll "head" taxes or literacy tests) to deprive minorities of the right to vote based upon another means that was facially valid but discriminatory in practice, based upon race. In 1948, these oppressive southern tactics resulted in fewer than one in four blacks being registered to vote in the South. Unfortunately, Brownell's bill was not approved by the Democratic majority in Congress, and Eisenhower did not fully endorse it. The next year, after gaining Eisenhower's support and several congressional revisions, the bill became law. The Civil Rights Act of 1957 created the U.S. Commission on Civil Rights, a Civil Rights Division in the Justice Department, and power for the attorney general to seek an injunction against voting rights infringements. While a critical section of the bill did not pass that would have provided the attorney general the power to go into federal court to get an injunction against anyone trying to deprive a citizen of his civil rights, it was the first approved civil rights legislation since Reconstruction more than eighty years earlier. This cornerstone act created precedent for all future civil rights legislation and was actively implemented. During the remainder of the Eisenhower administration, the Civil Rights Division brought into court more than 100 cases and investigated more than 4,000 complaints of civil rights violations.

In 1956, Eisenhower appointed another crucial individual to the Supreme Court as it relates to affirmative action, William Brennan. William Joseph Brennan Jr., who served as U.S. Supreme Court justice from 1956 to 1990, is best known in the affirmative action context today for his unwavering support of affirmative action during his longtime tenure on the Court. Brennan, along with Justices Thurgood Marshall and Harry Blackmun, comprised a three-justice bloc that always voted to uphold affirmative action plans when the constitutionality of such plans was called into question. Brennan voted to affirm affirmative action plans at issue in eight major affirmative action cases that come to the Court during his more than three decades on the Court.

In 1960, at the end of the Eisenhower administration, the Civil Rights Act of 1960 was passed. This act primarily attempted to deal with the inadequacies of the Civil Rights Act of 1957, especially with regard to protecting African Americans exercising their right to vote. Like the 1957 bill, yet again a key provision that would have provided for federal officials to register African Americans was defeated by southern opposition. This act did require that voting and registration records be preserved, extended the life of the Civil Rights Commission, and set new criminal penalties against violence used to obstruct a federal court's order.

While President Eisenhower will not be remembered as a key proponent of civil rights like his successor John F. Kennedy, his administration did lay the groundwork for others to make the necessary radical changes that have shaped our current nation. Eisenhower has received much criticism for his apparent lackluster leadership in civil rights. However, he should be acknowledged as the president who gained prominent federal government recognition of a critical national problem. This point was best summarized by Brownell years after Eisenhower retired. Referencing the historical squeaker Hayes-Tilden presidential election of 1876 when Hayes won by making a deal with southern senators and emasculating the civil rights acts of Reconstruction, he stated, "Eisenhower could have done the same thing. But he didn't."

See also All Deliberate Speed; Blackmun, Harry Andrew; Brennan, William Joseph; *Brown v. Board of Education*; Civil Rights Act of 1957; Civil Rights Act of 1960; Department of Justice; Equal Protection Clause; Fifteenth Amendment; Fourteenth Amendment; Kennedy, John Fitzgerald; Marshall, Thurgood; *Plessy v. Ferguson*; Segregation; Truman, Harry; U.S. Commission on Civil Rights; Warren Court and Affirmative Action.

FURTHER READING: Eisenhower, Dwight D., 1965, *Waging Peace*, Garden City, NY: Doubleday; Ewald, William B., Jr., 1981, *Eisenhower the President: Crucial Days, 1951–1960*, Englewood Cliffs, NJ: Prentice-Hall; Miller, Merle, 1987, *Ike the Soldier: As They Knew Him*, New York: Perigee Books.

PETER L. PLATTEBORZE

Emancipation Proclamation

See Thirteenth Amendment.

Employment (Private) and Affirmative Action

The concept of affirmative action has been developed in large part within the employment context. Title VII of the Civil Rights Act of 1964 prohibits discrimination in employment (both public and private) on the basis of race, color, religion, sex, or national origin. Title VII prohibits both practices that are intentionally discriminatory and practices that are facially neutral but have an adverse impact on a group because of their race, color, religion, sex, or national origin. In 1965, under Executive Order 11246, President Lyndon Johnson gave the U.S. Department of Labor authority to enforce integration of the workforce. This order was carried out initially in the form of an analysis of the workforce. If the Department of Labor found that areas were underrepresented, it was empowered to take affirmative action to remedy that situation. In 1969, the administration of President Richard Nixon promulgated the Philadelphia Plan. The Philadelphia Plan required those employers who worked on federally funded projects to set specific minority hiring goals. Although the Philadelphia Plan was challenged in the courts, the plan's constitutionality was upheld. Finally, the U.S. Supreme Court has subsequently held that private employers are empowered to take voluntary affirmative action to eliminate current discriminatory practices or effects of prior practices that were intentionally discriminatory or that had a discriminatory adverse impact on employment opportunities even if this action involves giving preferences to some employees on the basis of race, color, religion, sex, or national origin, which would otherwise violate Title VII.

Affirmative action programs are permissible in certain circumstances in employment situations. In general, they are allowed to correct previously existing discriminatory practices. The Supreme Court upheld a voluntary training program that gave a preference to minorities in *United Steelworkers of America v. Weber*, 443 U.S. 193 (1979). The Court's reasoning was that the program was limited so that it did not unnecessarily discriminate against white employees. In addition, the program was put in place to remedy past discrimination against minorities. In *Johnson v. Transportation Agency, Santa Clara County*, 480 U.S. 616 (1987), the U.S. Supreme Court held that an employer's action of taking an employee's sex into account when promoting her over a male employee did not violate Title VII because the action was taken pursuant to an affirmative action plan that was instituted to remedy substantial underrepresentation in traditionally segregated job categories and did not unnecessarily trammel the rights of male employees.

Before deciding whether to create such an affirmative action plan, a private employer must determine whether such a plan is necessary. A private employer can do this by comparing the demographics of the employee pool with those of the persons in the general workforce that are qualified for the positions in question and available for work. If the employer finds a substantial difference between these two employee pools (generally referred to as "underrepresentation"), then there may be a basis for an affirmative action plan. This conclusion is generally based on the notion that absent discrimination, employers should naturally be employing persons in racial and gender groups roughly in proportion to their representation in the qualified and available labor pool. The employer must be careful in conducting this study, as an affirmative action plan based upon a faulty study would be grounds for claims of reverse discrimination and could be held to be a violation of Title VII. It is sometimes difficult to identify the appropriate comparison pool with which to compare the demographics of the employer's own workplace. Many concerns arise during the analysis, such as whether minorities and women are underrepresented due to past discrimination in the comparison labor pool itself so that a comparison of the employer's workforce with the comparison labor pool would not accurately identify the effects of past discrimination.

Any voluntary affirmative action plan by a private employer must include three general criteria. First, the employer must make a "reasonable self-analysis." The importance of the reasonable self-analysis is that it is the investigation upon which the plan is purportedly based. Therefore, the legitimacy flows from the objectivity of the reasonable self-analysis. There are no specific or mandatory steps to be taken in conducting the self-analysis. The only issue is whether the employer discerns that it has employment practices that tend to exclude groups of employees who have been discriminated against in the past. Alternatively, an affirmative action plan might be appropriate if the self-analysis reveals that the employer has current employment practices that leave uncorrected the effects of past discrimination. If either of these findings are revealed in the study, the employer may consider adopting an affirmative action plan. The second criterion is having a reasonable basis for the plan. This element requires the employer to review the results of the self-analysis. If the employer finds, for example, that its employment practices tend to have an adverse effect on opportunities for groups of employees who have been previously excluded or those employees have had their promotional opportunities artificially limited, there is a reasonable basis for adopting an affirmative action plan. Other indicia of a reasonable basis could be that employment practices leave uncorrected the effects of prior discrimination on the excluded group of employees or that the prior employment practice has resulted in disparate treatment of a group of excluded employees. The final criterion is whether or not the action taken by the private employer is a reasonable action. This would be a test of whether or not the affirmative action plan or program is designed merely to cure the prior discrimination and will not overcompensate and create new victims. Such a plan may take into account race, gender, or national origin of applicants and employees. The plan should also include goals and timetables to measure whether it is effective after it is implemented. The timetables should be both long term and short term. The goals must take into account the availability of qualified applicants in the job pool. The plan may also include recruitment programs, job-training programs, and alterations of selection instruments.

An affirmative action plan may even allow the employer to reorganize jobs in a way that provides greater opportunities for less skilled laborers so that these laborers may be able to obtain a position and, with additional training, progress into a higher career field. The employer is also allowed to put measures into place to make certain that those applicants who are members of a group that has suffered discrimination are included in the pool of applicants from which the decision maker will choose. It may be considered not enough simply to hire applicants. The employer may also decide to make efforts to put into place mechanisms for further training with an eye toward career advancement so that once a person is hired, there is an opportunity for promotion. Finally, the employer should take steps to create a system to monitor the success of the affirmative action plan. This serves two purposes. First, it tells the employer whether it is "on the right track" with regard to its plan. If not, then the employer can implement changes in an effort to make it more effective. Second, it acts as a preventative measure against future lawsuits. If the employer is in fact implementing practices that prevent and remedy employment discrimination, it will be, at the very least, in a better position to defend against charges of employment discrimination. At most, it will in fact have a workplace free of employment discrimination.

The Equal Employment Opportunity Commission (EEOC) has issued regulations containing standards for determining whether or not the affirmative action plan is reasonable that elaborate on these criteria. Among them is whether the plan is tailored to solve problems that are identified and supported by the self-analysis. If so, then the factors that take into account race, gender, and national origin may be maintained only as long as they are necessary to address the problems that were identified in the self-analysis. In addition, these timetables must logically address the effects of the past discrimination. If the employer reduces the plan to writing, it may submit the plan to the EEOC, and if approved, the plan will constitute a safe harbor for the private employer in the event that there are claims of discrimination by any employee. The plan need not have a written statement that admits to any violation, any discriminatory employment practices, or violations of the law.

If a private employer has an affirmative action plan pursuant to a court order, this too may provide a safe haven against any claims of discrimination by other employees. The safe haven, however, has limits. First, it does not fully resolve the issue of whether the plan in and of itself is sufficient. In addition, the plan may only provide the safe haven during the time that it is current. Whether it is current is determined by the progress it makes in meeting goals of the self-analysis.

The need for affirmative action in private employment, it is argued by supporters of affirmative action, may be seen in the continued disparity in incomes per capita between African Americans and whites. At the end of 2000, one study indicated that African American income was only 59 percent that of white Americans per capita. There is also other evidence that discrimination in the workforce contributes to this disparity. One review of statistical research claimed that current discrimination in the labor market is the cause of African American men earning 12 to 15 percent less than white men. In addition, some studies have even drawn correlations between discrimination perpetrated as much as 100 years ago and the occupational status of the descendants of those who may have suffered discrimination. In addition, some argue that the effect of private employment on the transfer of wealth can hardly be overestimated as a factor in the continuing earnings gap between African Americans and whites. The argument is that because the majority of wealth in this country is still inherited, the effects of discrimination in opportunities for private employment can be felt for generations afterward. It is argued that this can be initially observed in the differences in household wealth in the United States among different racial groups. For example, a 1996 article published in the *American Economic Review* found that the median household income of whites was more than $10,000 more than that of African American households. This household wealth also manifests itself in things like homeownership, access to higher education, and health care, all of which circle back to the disparity in inheritances.

The University of Michigan conducted a study of graduates of its law school from 1970 to 1996. Its findings are evidence for the effect of affirmative action in private employment on hiring patterns. For example, 31 percent of minorities who graduated in the 1970s took their first job in private practice, while 72 percent of minority graduates who graduated in the 1980s took their first job in private practice. Conversely, in the 1970s, 30 percent of minority law school graduates took their first job in government. This number shrank to a mere 13 percent of students who graduated in the 1980s. These numbers are especially impressive since there were many more graduates in the 1980s than in the 1970s. The other significant statistic is the comparison between minority and white students and their ability to land jobs in the private sector. For example, in the 1970s, 69 percent of white students were employed in the private sector, as opposed to 31 percent of minorities. In the 1980s, 72 percent of minorities obtained jobs in the private sector, while 85 percent of white students did so. This is a change from a disparity of 38 percentage points to only 13. Further, the percentage of minority students going into private practice more than doubled. This not only shows the positive effect of a greater commitment to diversity in private employment, but also shows how it builds upon itself. The study at the University of Michigan also showed that one of the factors in attracting minorities to a firm was the existence of other minorities at that firm. Thus the success of past diversity efforts helps enhance recruitment of minorities in the future.

See also Affirmative Action Plan/Program; Civil Rights Act of 1964; Civil Rights Act of 1991; Contracting and Affirmative Action; Department of Labor; Disparate Treatment and Disparate Impact; Equal Employment Opportunity Commission; Executive Order 11246; Johnson, Lyndon Baines; *Johnson v. Transportation Agency, Santa Clara County*; Manifest Imbalance Standard; Nixon, Richard Milhous; Statistical Proof of Discrimination; Title VII of the Civil Rights Act of 1964; *United Steelworkers of America v. Weber.*

FURTHER READING: Beckwith, Francis J., and Todd E. Jones, eds., 1997, *Affirmative Action: Social Justice or Reverse Discrimination?* Amherst, NY: Prometheus Books; Chambers, David L., Richard O. Lempert, and Terry K. Adams, 1999, "Doing Well and Doing Good: The Careers of Minority and White Graduates of the University of Michigan Law School, 1970–1997," *Law Quandrangle Notes*, summer; Crosby, Faye J., and Cheryl VanDeVeer, eds., 2000, *Sex, Race, and Merit: Debating Affirmative Action in Education and Employment*, Ann Arbor: University of Michigan Press; Darity, William, Jr., 2000, "Give Affirmative Action Time to Act," *Chronicle of Higher Education*, December 1, B18; Reskin, Barbara F., 1998, *The Realities of Affirmative Action in Employment*, Washington, DC: American Sociological Association.

MICHAEL K. LEE

Employment (Public) and Affirmative Action

Affirmative action in public employment (employment by federal, state, and local governments) is important not only because governments employ a large percentage of the workforce in the United States, but also because the employment policies governmental employers use, to some degree, make a statement as to how firmly the government involved is committed to equal employment opportunity. Affirmative efforts to ensure equal employment opportunity in the federal government are both required by and limited by statute, regulation, and executive order. In addition to those restrictions imposed by statute and regulation, the U.S. Constitution also imposes restrictions on federal governmental affirmative action programs. These constitutional restrictions had historically been considered moderate. However, in 1995, the U.S. Supreme Court, in its opinion in *Adarand Constructors, Inc. v. Peña,* 515 U.S. 200, held that the constitutional restrictions on those federal affirmative action plans that employed racial classifications were, on the contrary, quite significant. This ruling led many federal employers to revamp and water down their affirmative employment programs. Federal law does not directly require state and local governmental employers to implement affirmative action programs. However, the limitations imposed by statute and by the U.S. Constitution on federal affirmative employment plans also apply to state and local government plans.

When Title VII of the Civil Rights Act of 1964 (which prohibits discrimination in employment on the basis of race, color, religion, gender, or national origin) was first enacted, it applied to state and local governmental employers. Although Title VII originally expressed a policy of equal employment opportunity (EEO) in the federal government, its prohibition against employment discrimination did not apply to the federal government. Congress planned that the president, via executive order, would implement this EEO policy. Executive Order 11246 reiterated the EEO policy, mandated that each executive department and agency maintain "a positive program of equal employment opportunity" for its employees and applicants, and empowered the U.S. Civil Service Commission to provide guidance to agencies in developing these "positive programs" and to establish a discrimination complaint procedure for federal employees.

In 1969, Executive Order 11478 was promulgated. This order, which superseded Executive Order 11246 in part, prohibits discrimination on the basis of race, color, religion, sex, or national origin (and was later amended to prohibit discrimination on the basis of handicap, age, sexual orientation, or status as a parent) and requires that each executive agency and department "establish and maintain an affirmative program of equal employment opportunity for all civilian employees and applicants for employment."

In 1972, Congress conducted a study of federal employment and found that serious employment discrimination existed across the federal government, resulting in significant underrepresentation of women and minority groups, particularly in higher levels of employment. Partially in response to these findings, with the Equal Employment Opportunity Act of 1972, Congress added section 717 to the Civil Rights Act that extended Title VII to prohibit discrimination in the federal government. But Congress also went a step further. Because it believed that the federal government should be a model employer for minorities and women, Congress required most federal government employers to maintain "affirmative program[s] of equal employment opportunity." Title VII assigned first to the Civil Service Commission and then to the Equal Employment Opportunity Commission (EEOC) the responsibility of reviewing and approving the affirmative employment plans of federal agencies and requires the EEOC to make an annual report to Congress on the state of equal employment opportunity in the federal government.

The EEOC has promulgated management directives to guide federal employers in establishing affirmative employment programs and plans. Management Directive 715 is the current version of these guidelines concerning affirmative employment plans for minorities and women. This management directive, which became effective on October 1, 2003, replacing a previous management directive, requires agencies to make annual self-assessments of their efforts to ensure equal employment opportunity and to make detailed plans to address any barriers to equal employment opportunity identifies in the self-assessments. Agencies are required to submit an annual report to the EEOC describing their affirmative employment activities. The management directive also requires agency heads to take steps to ensure that EEO becomes part of the agency culture and requires agencies to ensure that its EEO staff is adequately supported and centrally involved in agency operations.

The Civil Service Reform Act of 1978 also requires affirmative action in federal employment. The act indicates that one of its purposes is to "provide . . . a Federal work force reflective of the Nation's diversity." That act states that it is the policy of the United States to ensure equal employment opportunity in the federal government without regard to race, color, religion, sex, or national origin. To further this policy, it requires federal government employers to take affirmative action to ensure equal employment opportunity, with a special emphasis on recruitment. Section 310 of the act requires that each executive agency

> conduct a continuing program for the recruitment of members of minorities for positions in the agency to carry out [the government's EEO] policy in a manner designed to eliminate underrepresentation of minorities in the various categories of civil service employment . . . with special efforts directed at recruiting in minority communities, in educational institutions, and from other sources from which minorities can be recruited.

The act gives the Office of Personnel Management (OPM) the responsibility to assist federal agencies in developing and implementing minority recruitment plans and to oversee and evaluate the agencies success in reducing minority underrepresentation through the recruitment program.

OPM has issued regulations providing instructions and guidance for agency equal employment opportunity recruitment programs and program plans. The regulations prescribe specific action when agencies find that their recruitment efforts have not resulted in an applicant pool adequate to allow members of underrepresented groups to be considered. The guidelines state that in such circumstances agencies must do at least one of the following: (1) take new recruitment action to increase members of the underrepresented group in the applicant pool, (2) utilize other applicant pools with sufficient numbers of persons from underrepresented groups, (3) reopen the application process to allow expanded recruitment efforts to result in greater numbers of underrepresented group members to be considered, or (4) "take other action consistent with law which will contribute to the elimination of underrepresentation in the category of employment involved." The regulations also require that agency minority recruitment plans include underrepresentation determinations and "quantifiable indices by which progress toward eliminating underrepresentation can be measured." The regulations define "underrepresentation" as the state of an agency having a lower percentage of a minority group or of women in a particular job category than exists in the appropriate civilian labor force. The regulations also require agencies to include in their recruitment program plans very specific information detailing opportunities the agency is expecting for vacancies and its plans for recruiting minorities and women for those positions in which they are significantly underrepresented.

If a federal employer decides to employ racial or gender preferences in its affirmative employment programs, it must ensure that the use of such preferences complies with the restrictions imposed by Title VII and the Fifth Amendment to the U.S. Constitution. Title VII, which ordinarily prohibits employment actions based on race, color, religion, sex, or national origin, permits employers, including the federal government and state and local governments, to consider race and gender as factors in making employment decisions to benefit minorities and women, but only if (1) the purpose for the race or gender preferences mirrors the purposes of Title VII, (2) the use of the preferences does not unnecessarily trammel the interests of nonminorities, and (3) the race- or gender-conscious aspects of the plan are limited in time. The EEOC has stated in its regulation titled "Affirmative Action Appropriate under Title VII of the Civil Rights Act of 1964, as Amended" that the purpose of Title VII is to "improve the economic and social conditions of minorities and women by providing equality of opportunity in the work place." However, to ensure that the purpose of the preferences mirrors Title VII's purpose, the employer must have a sufficient factual predicate—evidence that effects of race or gender discrimination appear to be present in its own workforce. The U.S. Supreme Court determined in *Johnson v. Transportation Agency, Santa Clara County* that a sufficient factual predicate for the use of race or gender preferences to increase representation of minorities and women in a particular job category is evidence that there is a manifest imbalance of minorities or women in the job category within the employer's workforce and that the job category has traditionally been segregated. Even where there is a sufficient factual predicate for the use of racial or gender preferences, and the purpose of the preferences is to ensure equal employment opportunity for minorities and women, the preferences may be found to violate Title VII if they unnecessarily trammel the interests of nonminorities. Strict numerical quotas and set-asides, rather than using race or gender as only one of several factors, may be too burdensome on nonminorities. Using racial or gender preferences in determining which employees will be laid off as opposed to which employees will be hired or promoted may also be too burdensome on nonminorities. Finally, using preferences to maintain rather than to attain a racially or gender-balanced workforce is not legally permissible because such preferences would no longer be temporary.

In its regulations mentioned earlier (published at 29 C.F.R. part 1608), the EEOC explained in greater detail what affirmative action measures are appropriate under Title VII. These regulations both set out the circumstances under which affirmative action (defined as "those actions appropriate to overcome the effects of past or present practices, policies or other barriers to equal employment opportunity") is appropriate and give instructions concerning how to establish an affirmative action plan. The guidance in the regulations is applicable to all affirmative action plans, whether they are implemented by the federal government, state or local governments, or private employers. The regulations provide that affirmative action is appropriate in three circumstances. First, affirmative action is appropriate when an analysis reveals that employment policies or practices instituted or contemplated have resulted in or have the potential to result in an adverse impact on women or minorities. Second, affirmative action is appropriate to correct the effects of past discriminatory practices that may be identified by a comparison between the demographics of the workforce and the appropriately qualified labor pool. Finally, when there is evidence that the qualified labor pool itself has been artificially limited by discrimination, affirmative action may be appropriate to overcome such past discrimination by, for example, instituting training programs for women and minorities and engaging in recruiting efforts to locate qualified minority and female candidates.

When the correct circumstances exist, the EEOC's regulations provide that a lawful affirmative action plan must have the following three elements: "a reasonable self analysis; a reasonable basis for concluding action is appropriate; and reasonable action." The aim of the reasonable self-analysis must be to determine whether employment policies or practices do result in the disparate treatment of or in an adverse impact upon groups because of their minority racial status or gender and/or whether the effects of such prior policies or practices are still present in the workforce. If discriminatory practices or the effects thereof are found, a reasonable basis for affirmative action exists. Finally, the action authorized by the affirmative action plan must be a reasonable response to the findings of the self-analysis. The commission specifically approves the use of numerical goals and other measures "which recognize the race, sex, or national origin of applicants or employees" but also states that "the race, sex, and national origin conscious provisions of the plan or program should be maintained only so long as is necessary" to achieve equal employment opportunity. The regulations state that opportunities may be provided to minorities and women who are members of groups that had been subject to discrimination even if the particular persons directly benefited by such measures were not themselves subject to the discrimination. Finally, the regulations provide that the affirmative action plan should avoid "unnecessary restrictions on the opportunities of the workforce as a whole."

Section 713 of Title VII provides a defense to challenges to action taken pursuant to an affirmative action plan when that plan has been developed "in good faith, in conformity with, and in reliance on any written interpretation or opinion of the [EEOC]." The EEOC's regulations state that an affirmative action plan that is adopted in good faith, in conformity with and in reliance upon them, will be entitled to the section 713 defense.

Title VII is not the only source of restrictions on affirmative employment plans implemented by the federal government. The Due Process Clause of the Fifth Amendment to the U.S. Constitution guarantees that no person shall be denied the equal protection of the laws by the federal government. In essence, this means that similarly situated persons must not be treated differently because of a factor not relevant to the governmental action at issue. Historically, federal actions have been challenged as a violation of this equal protection guarantee when it has been alleged that they have treated groups of persons less favorably because of personal characteristics such as race or gender. For example, the practice of racial segregation in District of Columbia schools was challenged and overturned as a violation of the Fifth Amendment in the case *Bolling v. Sharpe*, 347 U.S. 497 (1954). The Supreme Court has held that when the government treats groups differently because of race and gender, the governmental action must meet strict standards to be constitutional. Because race has historically been used to subjugate racial minority groups and is rarely relevant to governmental action, any governmental action based on race is "suspect" and presumptively invalid. To pass constitutional muster, the race-based governmental action must be "narrowly tailored" to meet a "compelling governmental interest." This standard, the so-called strict scrutiny standard, has been described as "strict in theory, but fatal in fact" because most governmental actions reviewed under this standard are held to be unconstitutional. Governmental gender classifications are constitutionally valid only if they satisfy the requirements of "intermediate scrutiny review." This standard, still onerous but easier to meet than strict scrutiny review, requires that a governmental gender classification be "substantially related to important governmental interests."

Affirmative action measures of federal employers are sometimes challenged as violative of the Fifth Amendment equal protection guarantee because, it is argued, via these plans, the federal government has treated some groups (minorities and women) more preferentially than others because of their race or sex. Before 1995, these plans, even those that utilized explicit racial or gender preferences, were believed to be subject to no greater than intermediate scrutiny because they were intended to benefit groups historically subject to discrimination rather than to disadvantage these groups. Intermediate scrutiny, it was believed, gave the federal government more latitude in deciding when and how to use race or gender preferences in its affirmative action programs. However, in 1995, the U.S. Supreme Court issued an opinion in the case *Adarand Constructors, Inc. v. Peña* that required a significant change in this view. Although the *Adarand* case involved racial preferences in federal contracting, not in federal employment, the holding was much broader. The Court held that all racial classifications of the federal government, whether intended and designed to benefit or injure persons because of their race, must be subject to strict scrutiny review. Although the opinion itself does not specifically define the term "racial classifications," the U.S. Department of Justice (DOJ) stated in a 1996 memorandum interpreting the *Adarand* opinion (memorandum from John R. Schmidt titled "Post-*Adarand* Guidance on Affirmative Action in Federal Employment") that a federal employer's affirmative employment plan that uses race or ethnicity as a preferential factor in decision making is subject to strict scrutiny review. The DOJ memorandum also emphasizes that federal affirmative employment measures that are race neutral, such as efforts to expand the applicant pool to include minorities, are not racial classifications subject to strict scrutiny review. Such measures would be subject only to the most lenient standard of equal protection review: they must be rationally related to legitimate governmental interests. Because the *Adarand* opinion did not address gender classifications, it is still generally believed that federal affirmative employment programs that use gender as the basis for decision making are subject only to intermediate scrutiny review.

Again, to survive strict scrutiny review, the racial classification in a federal affirmative employment plan must be narrowly tailored to further a compelling governmental interest. The U.S. Supreme Court has considered remedying past discrimination against a racial group caused or perpetuated by the federal employer to be a compelling governmental interest that may justify that employer's use of a racial preference. However, as is required under Title VII, a sufficient factual predicate must exist. That is, there must be sufficient evidence of race discrimination or the continuing effects of race discrimination in the federal employer's workforce to justify a race-based measure as a remedy. There is debate as to the quantum of proof necessary to satisfy this requirement, and there is some support in U.S. Supreme Court decisions for the view that the evidentiary burden is greater when a race-based affirmative action measure is challenged under the Fifth Amendment than under Title VII. However, evidence that would support a prima facie case that the employment practices of the federal employer discriminated against the minority group benefited by the remedial racial classification in the affirmative action plan would be sufficient. For example, statistical evidence showing that a particular racial group is very significantly underrepresented in a particular job category of an employer's workforce when compared with the civilian labor pool qualified for the job in question and anecdotal evidence of discrimination would probably be sufficient to establish the necessary factual predicate for a remedial race-based preference for selections to that job category.

Even if a racial preference is designed to fulfill a compelling governmental interest, the preference must also be narrowly tailored to achieve that interest. According to the DOJ memorandum, factors to consider in determining whether a race-based employment action is narrowly tailored are

> (1) whether the government considered race-neutral alternatives before using the racial or ethnic criteria, (2) the manner in which race or ethnicity is used in making [the] decisions—e.g., is it one of many factors to be considered, or is it the sole or dominant factor. (3) the comparison of any numerical target to the number of qualified minorities in the labor pool. (4) the scope of the program. (5) the duration of the program, and (6) the impact of the program on nonminorities.

A federal employer's affirmative action program that uses racial or ethnic criteria only as a last resort to eradicate severe underrepresentation that has not been reduced by other attempted race-neutral measures and only as one of many criteria in making the employment decision at issue is more likely to be considered narrowly tailored than one using rigid numerical set-asides. A temporary race-based affirmative action measure is more likely to be narrowly tailored than one that is in place indefinitely. A racial preference that is utilized in a hiring program is more likely to be narrowly tailored than one that uses a racial preference in determining which employees will be terminated in a federal employer's reduction in force.

Just as Title VII requires the federal government to be a model employer of minorities and women, the Rehabilitation Act of 1973 requires the federal government to be a model employer of persons with disabilities. Section 501(b) of the act requires all executive departments, agencies, and instrumentalities to create "an affirmative action program plan for the hiring, placement, and advancement of individuals with disabilities" and requires such plans to be updated annually. The act requires the plans to be submitted to and approved by the U.S. Equal Employment Opportunity Commission. The EEOC has issued management directives providing instructions and guidance for these affirmative action plans. Management Directive 715 is the version of these directives currently in effect. The EEOC is required to make an annual report to Congress concerning the effectiveness of the federal government's affirmative action programs.

Management Directive 715 requires federal employers to establish comprehensive affirmative action programs addressing the hiring, placement, and advancement of persons with disabilities in the federal employer's workforce and to maintain documentation concerning the program and its effectiveness. These programs are required to emphasize the employment of persons with certain "targeted disabilities." The targeted disabilities are deafness, blindness, missing extremities, partial or complete paralysis, convulsive disorders, mental retardation, mental illness, and distortion of limbs and/or of the spine. Agencies with 1,001 or more employees are required to set numerical goals for the employment of persons with targeted disabilities and are authorized to consider disability as a positive factor in making selection decisions to achieve these goals. Management Directive 715 also requires all agencies to develop special recruitment programs targeted to persons with disabilities.

Management Directive 715 also requires federal employers to review their personnel and employment policies and practices to ensure that they do not unnecessarily impose barriers to the employment or advancement of persons with disabilities. If such barriers are found, agencies must consider alternatives to the practices or policies.

There are far fewer restrictions on disability preferences in federal affirmative action plans than for race or gender preferences. "Reverse-discrimination" claims are not recognized under the Rehabilitation Act. Moreover, disability classifications are not subject to strict scrutiny review under the Fifth Amendment. Generally, disability classifications are subject to rational basis scrutiny. Therefore, a federal employer's preference for persons with disabilities is constitutional if it is rationally related to a legitimate governmental interest.

Finally, federal law requires federal employers to give employment preferences to "veterans" as defined by regulation of the U.S. Office of Personnel Management (5 C.F.R. part 211). Although veterans' preferences are not traditionally thought of as affirmative action programs, they do provide special treatment and a competitive advantage to a group of persons in society. Constitutional limitations on veterans' preferences are not onerous because veterans' classifications are subject to rational basis scrutiny.

Federal law does not require state and local government employers to implement affirmative action programs for minorities, women, or persons with disabilities as it does federal employers. Most affirmative action measures implemented by state and local government employers—except those imposed by a court after a finding of discrimination and those that are required by state or local law (which are outside the scope of this work)—are voluntary. However, the restrictions discussed earlier that Title VII imposes on race- and gender-conscious affirmative action measures of federal government employers are equally applicable to state and local government employers. Moreover, the restrictions imposed by the Fifth Amendment's equal protection guarantee are applicable to race- and gender-conscious affirmative action measures of state and local governments through the Fourteenth Amendment's Equal Protection Clause. In fact, most of the Fifth Amendment law discussed earlier was based on case law interpreting the Fourteenth Amendment's restrictions on race- and gender-based state action. Finally, the EEOC's regulations concerning what affirmative action is appropriate under Title VII are applicable to the affirmative action plans of state and local governments.

See also Adarand Constructors, Inc. v. Peña; Benign Discrimination; *Bolling v. Sharpe*; Civil Rights Act of 1964; Civil Service Commission; Civil Service Reform Act of 1978; Compelling Governmental Interest; Department of Justice; Disability

Classifications under the Fifth and Fourteenth Amendments; Discrimination; Disparate Treatment and Disparate Impact; Equal Employment Opportunity Act of 1972; Equal Employment Opportunity Commission; Equal Employment Opportunity Commission's Affirmative Employment Management Directives; Executive Order 11246; Executive Order 11478; Fifth Amendment; Intermediate Scrutiny Review; *Johnson v. Transportation Agency, Santa Clara County*; Manifest Imbalance Standard; Narrowly Tailored Affirmative Action Plans; Persons with Disabilities and Affirmative Action; Preferences; Quotas; Racial Discrimination; Rehabilitation Act of 1973; Reverse Discrimination; Statistical Proof of Discrimination; Suspect Classification; Title VII of the Civil Rights Act of 1964; *United Steelworkers of America v. Weber.*

FURTHER READING: Day, John Cocchi, 2001, "Retelling the Story of Affirmative Action: Reflections on a Decade of Federal Jurisprudence in the Public Workplace," *California Law Review* 89 (January): 59–127; Iheukwumere, Emmanuel O., and Philip C. Aka, 2001, "Title VII, Affirmative Action, and the March toward Color-Blind Jurisprudence," *Temple Political and Civil Rights Law Review* 11 (fall): 1–61; Jayne, Andrew C., 2002, "Constitutional Law: Affirmative Action in the Public Sector: The Admissibility of Post-Enactment Evidence of Discrimination to Provide a Compelling Governmental Interest," *Oklahoma Law Review* 55 (spring): 121–151; Lindemann, Barbara, and Paul Grossman, 1996, *Employment Discrimination Law,* 3d ed., vol. 1–2, Washington, DC: Bureau of National Affairs; Whiteside, Janice C., 1998, "Title VII and Reverse Discrimination: The Prima Facie Case," *Indiana Law Review* 31: 413–443.

MARIA D. BECKMAN

Environmental Racism

Environmental racism is a form of what has come to be known as "environmental injustice." The notion of environmental injustice refers to human degradation of the natural environment broadly and globally speaking, or to human degradation of the specific local natural environments in which people live. The former is a central idea of environmental ethics, a field of academic inquiry and social activism since at least the 1960s. Writers within the field of environmental ethics often assume that the natural environment has a kind of moral standing sufficient to generate moral, and possibly even legal, entitlements of its own, thus obligating people to "nature" itself as a subject worthy of respect. By contrast, the idea of environmental injustice in its application to human-caused degradation of the environments in which people live raises questions about what constitutes environmental degradation and who causes it, as well as about who endures its negative effects and how these effects amount to an injustice. It is this view of environmental injustice that informs the concept of "environmental racism," the idea that people of color are disproportionately victimized by human-caused environmental degradation. Though environmental injustice has no formal relation to affirmative action, there is clearly a link between environmental injustice and other forms of discrimination, and the two share common historical roots. The forms of exploitation endured by people of color in the United States have included near genocide (American Indians), slavery (African Americans), and racial and ethnic discrimination in employment, housing, education, entertainment, and nearly all other aspects of life. Today, people of color and other minorities in the United States suffer the ongoing legacy effects of such pervasive discrimination, and it has been well established that some of these same groups suffer a disproportionate burden of environmental corruption.

Environmental racism has been defined as racial discrimination in environmental policy making and the enforcement of environmental laws and regulations. It has also been defined to include the deliberate targeting of communities of people of color for siting toxic and hazardous waste facilities. Some definitions of environmental racism go further still, claiming that the history of excluding people of color from the leadership of the environmental movement is itself an instance of such racism. Although much social scientific research shows a strong correlation between some forms of environmental injustice and the residential location of specific minority groups such as African Americans and Latinos, in fact, environmental degradation correlates significantly with such various socioeconomic factors as income, industrial land use, manufacturing employment, political participation, and population density. This suggests that the more inclusive notion of "environmental injustice," with its emphasis on the fact that people of color and/or those who are economically disadvantaged are disproportionately victimized by environmental degradation, may be the more plausible rubric under which to subsume discrimination in environmental policy and practice.

Environmental injustice thus understood is sometimes alleged to be intentional discrimination, and surely some environmental injustice has been the result of deliberate policies of targeting the environments of the poor and of people of color. Yet a broader notion of governmental policy making or industry-initiated action that causes a detrimental environmental impact that falls disproportionately on the poor or on people of color better captures the idea that objectionable discrimination may be an unintended consequence of corporate and governmental policy and behavior. Such "objective" notions of discrimination, like those used by the Equal Employment Opportunity Commission (EEOC) in determining discrimination in employment, call attention to the continuing deleterious effects of prior discrimination. Examples of deliberate and unintentional environmental injustice include the legal or illegal dumping and processing of hazardous wastes in minority or lower-class neighborhoods, targeting land on Indian reservations for waste disposal sites, and the exportation by first-world nations of hazardous waste to so-called developing nations.

The environmental racism/injustice movement is relatively recent, with some crediting the birth of the movement to the 1991 First National People of Color Environmental Leadership Summit held in Washington, D.C. However, challenges to the legitimacy of siting toxic waste landfills in predominantly minority communities date back at least to 1982.

As stated earlier, while there is no formal connection of environmental injustice to affirmative action, there is clearly a link between environmental injustice and other forms of discrimination. The 1994 Presidential Executive Order on Environmental Justice made explicit the U.S. government's previously unofficial awareness of the realities of environmental discrimination. Moreover, the Environmental Protection Agency (EPA) sponsors both an informational "Environmental Justice Homepage" and an Office of Enforcement and Compliance Assurance (EPA OECA) whose job it is to monitor environmental justice activities at the EPA and at other federal agencies. In a 1994 action against the Japanese corporation Shintech, the Tulane University Law Clinic filed a Title VI complaint under the Civil Rights Act of 1964. Shintech planned to locate a processing plant in Convent, Lousiana, that would generate more than 600,000 pounds of toxic air pollution each year in the production of polyvinyl chloride (PVC). The clinic used Title VI of the Civil Rights Act, which prohibits entities that practice racial discrimination from receiving federal funds, in its argument that granting a plant permit to Shintech would be racially discriminatory under Title VI. Thus has environmental injustice been brought into explicit relation with civil rights legislation, in which affirmative action policies play a key role. In September 1998, after intense pressure from local, state, and national groups, Shintech decided not to build its plant in Convent, Louisiana.

Critics of the notion of environmental racism often charge that since it cannot be proven that the crafting of environmental laws and policies, their application, and corporate and governmental behavior within those guidelines intentionally discriminate against racial or ethnic minorities, there is no such discrimination. In the service of this objection, such critics sometimes challenge the social scientific data in support of the reality of environmental racism/injustice on the grounds that the studies are ill prepared, make critical errors, or are based on statistically insignificant findings.

As noted earlier, however, various factors correlate with the effects of environmental degradation being disproportionately experienced by people of color and the poor. Research has also shown that even the unintentional negative environmental consequences of governmental and business policies and practices are related to, and extend the effects of, past racial and class discrimination. Today, of growing concern to those in the environmental justice movement is the impact of economic globalization on human and nonhuman environments around the world. Unless checked by stringent and enforceable international policies and agreements, these forces are seen by some as harbingers of ever greater environmental discrimination against the world's most vulnerable populations, and ever-increasing degradation of "nature" itself.

See also African Americans; Civil Rights Act of 1964; Discrimination; Equal Employment Opportunity Commission; Hispanic Americans; Invidious Discrimination; Native Americans; Racial Discrimination; Racism; Title VI of the Civil Rights Act of 1964; Zoning and Affirmative Action.

FURTHER READING: Ambler, Marjane, 1991, "On the Reservations: No Haste, No Waste," *Planning* 57, no. 11:26–29; Arrandal, T., 1992, "Environmentalism and Racism," *Governing* 5, no. 5 (February): 5–63; Boer, J. Tom, Manuel Pastor, James L. Sadd, and Lori D. Snyder, 1997, "Is There Environmental Racism? The Demographics of Hazardous Waste in Los Angeles County," *Social Science Quarterly* 78, no. 4 (December): 793–810; Bryant, B., and P. Mohai, 1992, "Environmental Injustice: Weighing Race and Class as Factors in the Distribution of Environmental Hazards," *University of Colorado Law Review* 63:921–932; Bullard, Robert D., 1990, *Dumping in Dixie: Race, Class, and Environmental Quality*, Boulder, CO: Westview Press; Bullard, Robert D., ed., 1993, *Confronting Environmental Racism: Voices from the Grassroots*, Boston: South End Press; Duncan, P., 1993, "Environmental Racism, Recognition, Litigation, and Alleviation," *Tulane Environmental Law Journal* 6, no. 2:317–368; Environmental Justice Resource Center, 2003, www.ejrc.eau.edu, accessed March 2003; Louisiana

Environmental Action Network and Greenpeace USA, 1999, "Shintech Environmental Racism," September 1, 1–5; Meyer, E.L., 1992, "Why Is It Always Dumped in Our Backyard?" *Audubon* 94, no. 2 (January/February): 30–32; National Council of Churches Racial Justice Working Group, 2000, "What Is Environmental Justice and Environmental Racism?" www.ejnet.org; Robinson, Deborah M., 2001, "Environmental Racism: Old Wine in a New Bottle," *Women in Action*, no. 2:1–9; Weiskel, Tim, 2002, "Environmental Racism: An Interpretation," www.africana.com; Wigley, Daniel and Kristin Shrader-Frechette, 2002, "Environmental Racism and Biased Methods of Risk Assessment," www.fplc.edu.

PAUL M. HUGHES

Equal Employment Opportunity Act of 1972

The Equal Employment Opportunity Act of 1972 amended and strengthened Title VII of the Civil Rights Act of 1964, which had made it illegal for employers to discriminate against any individual because of race, color, religion, sex, or national origin. The 1972 act expanded the groups covered by Title VII and gave the Equal Employment Opportunity Commission (EEOC) new enforcement powers. Prior to the 1972 act, Title VII applied only to employers or unions with twenty-five or more employees; with it, the triggering number was reduced to fifteen employees. Under the original act, state and local government employees were exempt from coverage, but the 1972 act extended coverage to most of these employees. A previous exemption for educational institutions was also ended, bringing approximately six million teachers under Title VII protection. Most crucial, though, were changes in enforcement. Until 1972, the EEOC could investigate charges of discrimination and attempt to address problems through conciliation agreements; if those efforts failed, however, it was left to the aggrieved party to file suit. Under the new law, if conciliation efforts failed, the EEOC could bring a civil suit in federal court seeking an injunction to stop the practices and find remedies for the affected workers. If the case involved government employees, the attorney general was authorized to take action. Although this new power was hailed by civil rights advocates as an important tool in ending workplace discrimination, some critics have argued that at least in its early years, the EEOC did a poor job of investigating and pursuing cases.

During the long and contentious debate on the Civil Rights Act of 1964, a compromise was reached that established the EEOC, but limited its enforcement powers. Almost immediately, civil rights advocates and key congressional leaders began efforts to strengthen the EEOC so that businesses would feel that they actually had something to lose if they were investigated for discrimination. One leading idea, included in several failed legislative efforts, was to give the EEOC the authority to issue cease-and-desist orders. This policy was opposed by those who felt that it would centralize too much authority in one agency as investigator, judge, and jury. By 1972, evidence was mounting that a weak EEOC was not leading to significant reductions in discrimination cases and that in cases with reasonable cause for action, conciliation was unsuccessful well over half of the time. New legislation was therefore submitted in both houses of Congress. During a five-week Senate debate with numerous close votes, a compromise emerged whereby the EEOC would not be given cease-and-desist powers, but would be given the authority to bring civil actions against employers. With this compromise, the bill passed in the Senate 62–10, was agreed to by the House 303–110, and was signed into law by President Richard Nixon on March 24, 1972.

Under the new procedures, charges of discrimination can be made by the aggrieved party or by a member of the EEOC. The commission then has 120 days to investigate and determine whether there is reasonable cause. If there is reasonable cause, conciliation efforts begin. If, after 30 days, these efforts do not yield an acceptable agreement, the commission can bring civil action. The courts can order that the discriminatory practices be stopped and that remedies such as being rehired and receiving back pay be granted. If the aggrieved party is not satisfied with a conciliation agreement, he or she retains the right to sue individually. Overall, the hope was that the threat of civil action and its potential costs would encourage businesses to settle during the conciliation phase.

Before the 1972 changes, a major problem for the EEOC was that a lack of both resources and established procedures led to a mounting backlog of cases. The new focus on developing civil cases only exacerbated these problems, since it raised the standards of evidence collection, required hiring new lawyers and personnel, and required new coordination of the conciliation and legal efforts. By 1975, the backlog of cases had reached more than 100,000. Critics argued that this backlog had major implications for how the EEOC handled cases and for how discriminatory practices were maintained. With the pressure to handle a high volume of cases expeditiously, EEOC investigations often were not of the highest quality. Second, the backlog put pressure on the EEOC to settle cases as quickly as possible and therefore may have biased it to pursuing conciliation rather than civil action, or to accepting less dramatic business change in conciliation agreements. Third, the backlog slowed down the process of ending discrimination, since court action by either the EEOC or the individual could not occur until reconciliation efforts had failed, so the aggrieved party might have to wait years before the discriminatory actions were addressed.

Until 1972, the EEOC's major problem had been that it lacked the threat of legal action, so it had little influence. It was thus seen as imperative that the EEOC begin bringing a substantial number of cases to trial as soon as possible. This goal, however, was held back by the need to hire new workers and by the need to reorganize the office so that compliance and litigation functions were coordinated. In the first two years after being given litigation authority, the EEOC brought only four cases to trial. Trying to maximize the impact of its limited litigation, the EEOC divided cases into four tracks based on their litigation potential, with the key variable being the size of the respondent. Cases involving large companies or national unions fell into tracks one or two and received the most careful and complete investigations from the most experienced personnel, using more than half of the total commission resources in a relatively few cases. With the backlog of cases, few litigations, and lack of attention paid to smaller firms, the EEOC remained a paper tiger in the eyes of some, despite the attempts to broaden its power.

See also Civil Rights Act of 1964; Equal Employment Opportunity Commission; Nixon, Richard Milhous; Title VII of the Civil Rights Act of 1964.

FURTHER READING: Adams, Avril, 1973, "Evaluating the Success of the EEOC Compliance Process," *Monthly Labor Review* 96:26–29; Bureau of National Affairs, 1973, *The Equal Em-*

ployment Opportunity Act of 1972: Editorial Analysis, Discussion of Court Decisions under the 1964 Act, Text of the Amended Act, Congressional Reports, Legislative History, Washington, DC: Bureau of National Affairs; Spurlock, Delbert L., Jr., 1975, "EEOC's Compliance Process: The Problems of Selective Enforcement," *Labor Law Journal* 26:396–408.

JOHN W. DIETRICH

Equal Employment Opportunity Commission

The Equal Employment Opportunity Commission (EEOC) was created by the Civil Rights Act of 1964 to help "promote a more abiding commitment to freedom, a more constant pursuit of justice, and a deeper respect for human dignity," the official aims of the act. More specifically, the EEOC was created to enforce Title VII of that act, the focus of which was employment discrimination, whereas other sections of the act governed housing and education. The mandate of the EEOC was and still is to enforce equal opportunity in employment. Originally, the focus of the EEOC's concern was employment discrimination against black Americans. In its short history, the EEOC has witnessed a shift in two key aspects of its mission. The first change in the original EEOC mandate was the expansion of its focus on remedying employment discrimination against blacks to a more general concern for workplace discrimination based on race, sex, age, disability, religion, or national origin. A second change was its shift from the original rather narrow interpretation of its mandate to simply eliminate discrimination in employment to a more encompassing progressive understanding of its mission as combating ongoing negative legacy effects of past societal discrimination on employment opportunities. Its mission thus evolved to include advocating racial and minority hiring "goals and timetables" (e.g., the 1969 Philadelphia Plan that set a target for minority hiring in construction trades), training programs, and other mechanisms for leveling the employment playing field.

Although early on, the EEOC focused its Title VII enforcement efforts on eliminating and correcting only workplace discrimination that could be proven to be intentional, it later broadened its enforcement focus. In the late 1960s, the EEOC began to rely on statistical evidence to establish patterns of discrimination, signaling a greater reliance on objective grounds for ascribing discrimination and a correspondingly weaker concern that workplace discrimination be proven to have been intentional. This evidentiary change reflects the aforementioned evolution from an essentially reactive stance toward combating employment discrimination to proactive policies, such as minority recruitment plans, aimed at ameliorating and ultimately eradicating the continuing deleterious consequences of past discrimination. Ruth Bader Ginsburg, later to become a Supreme Court justice, noted these disparate orientations in the context of remarking on the relationship between equal opportunity and affirmative action. Ginsburg claimed that "equal opportunity policy implies action of two kinds. The first is an effort to stop discriminatory practices and is, thus, essentially reactive. The second, related in obvious ways to affirmative action, is an effort to create positive measures aimed at correcting the accumulated or ongoing results of previous discrimination, and is essentially proactive" (Blackstone and Heslep 1977, 137–138).

The EEOC has played a prominent role in the civil rights struggle and is, as Ginsburg recognized, closely linked to affirmative action. The EEOC has clearly been a means to the achievement of affirmative action. Affirmative action as the attempt to use special efforts in employment decisions, college admissions, and other areas of public behavior to benefit previously disadvantaged groups in society is clearly a compensatory response to past discrimination. In the context of imposing and enforcing remedial policies in employment practices, the EEOC has thus been a key enforcement agency for affirmative action. The EEOC during the past thirty years has initiated litigation against numerous corporations, large and small, on behalf of individuals and groups who have suffered workplace discrimination. The EEOC has also issued regulations providing guidance for voluntary affirmative action plans. The EEOC plays a larger role in the affirmative action plans of federal agencies. It has issued multiple management directive in recent years that provides guidelines to federal agencies, and it reviews the affirmative action plans of federal agencies on an annual basis.

The EEOC's commitment to address vestiges of past discrimination in current employment practices and its more inclusive focus on age and gender discrimination, workplace bias against the disabled, and employment discrimination against other racial and ethnic groups have led some critics to charge it with abusing its authority. For example, although racial quotas are unlawful under the 1964 act, EEOC officials have found some private companies guilty of violating or impeding equal opportunity for their failure to use "race-norm" test scoring to make the scores of less qualified "protected groups" more competitive with, or even superior to, other test takers, prompting some to argue that the EEOC promotes racial quotas. EEOC officials have also viewed the refusal of some private companies to hire unqualified but "trainable" job applicants as actionable discrimination. Thus some critics of EEOC practices decry what they see as the political manipulation of an ambiguous concept of equal opportunity to enforce an illegitimate redistribution of economic opportunity.

But the EEOC, like other civil rights initiatives and policies, is a creature of its social time and context and, like affirmative action itself, reflects changing conceptions of equality and justice. During the past thirty-five years, it has added to its enforcement roster the Age Discrimination in Employment Act of 1967, the Rehabilitation Act of 1973, the Americans with Disabilities Act of 1990, and the Civil Rights Act of 1991. Debates over whether hiring goals are objectionable "quotas" or whether "disparate impact" is or is not evidence of discrimination and thus a violation of Title VII are ongoing social debates about the very nature of social justice, not objections unique to the EEOC.

On its official web site, the EEOC reiterates its mission to remove all vestigial discrimination in employment, and it lists recent new programs and legal accomplishments as means to that end. Sponsoring talks with small businesses on employing the disabled, settling a recent racial harassment suit, and contributing to a federal alternative dispute resolution program are but a few of the activities it views as conducive to realizing its ultimate aim of genuine equality of opportunity in the workplace.

See also Civil Rights Act of 1964; Civil Rights Act of 1991; Disparate Treatment and Disparate Impact; Education and Affirmative Action; Employment (Private) and Affirmative Action; Employment (Public) and Affirmative Action; Equal Employment Opportunity Commission's Affirmative Employment Management Directives; Ginsburg, Ruth Bader; Housing; Quotas; Rehabilitation Act of 1973; Statistical Proof of Discrimination; Title VII of the Civil Rights Act of 1964.

FURTHER READING: Benokraitus, Nijole V., and Joe R. Feagin, 1978, *Affirmative Action and Equal Opportunity: Action, Inaction, Reaction*, Boulder, CO: Westview Press; Better Regulation Task Force, 1999, "Review of Anti-discrimination Legislation," 1–37, http://www.cabinet-office.gov; Blackstone, William T., and Robert D. Heslep, eds., 1977, *Social Justice and Preferential Treatment*, Athens University of Georgia Press; Bullock, Charles S., III, and Charles M. Lamb, 1984, *Implementation of Civil Rights Policy*, Monterey, CA: Brooks/Cole; Burstein, Paul, 1998, *Discrimination, Jobs, and Politics: The Struggle for Equal Employment Opportunity in the United States since the New Deal*, Chicago: University of Chicago Press; Canady, Charles T., 1998, "America's Struggle for Racial Equality," *Policy Review* 87:42–47; Eastland, Terry, 1996, *Ending Affirmative Action*, New York: Basic Books; Government Guide, http://www.eeoc.gov/; Lee, R.A., 1999, "The Evolution of Affirmative Action," *Public Personnel Management* 28:393–408; Papper, Bob, 2000, "Minority Hiring May Be Facing Retrenchment," *USA Today*, 128, no. 2658 (March): 66–67; Smelser, Neil J., William Wilson, and Faith Mitchell, 2001, "America Becoming: Racial Trends and Their Consequences," www.oclc.org.

PAUL M. HUGHES

Equal Employment Opportunity Commission's Affirmative Employment Management Directives

Most federal employers are required by federal statute to maintain affirmative programs of equal employment opportunity regardless of race, color, religion, sex, and national origin and affirmative action programs for persons with disabilities. The central policy underlying this requirement is that the federal government should be a model employer in insuring equal employment opportunity (EEO) and, as such, should take affirmative measures to detect and remove barriers to equal employment opportunity rather than just taking reactive measures in response to discrimination complaints. The U.S. Equal Employment Opportunity Commission (EEOC) has issued several management directives that provide standards for the development and administration of these programs. Three of these management directives, Management Directive 712, 713 and 714, were in effect until October 1, 2003. On August 26, 2003, the EEOC announced that these management directives would be superseded by Management Directive 715, effective October 1, 2003. This management directive applies to "all executive agencies and military departments (except uniform members) . . . the United States Postal Service, the Postal Rate Commission, the Tennessee Valley Authority, the Smithsonian Institution, and those units of the judicial branch of the federal government having positions in the competitive service." The new management directive was necessary, in part, to address changes in affirmative action jurisprudence since the earlier management directives had been issued.

Section 717 of the Civil Rights Act of 1964, as amended, 42 U.S.C. §2000e-16, requires federal departments and agencies to maintain affirmative programs of equal employment opportunity in order to eliminate discrimination based on race, color, sex, religion, and national origin in the federal government. This provision also requires the EEOC to review and approve annual affirmative employment program plans of federal agencies. Affirmative employment plans are also required by Executive Order 11478, as amended. Although Title VII and Executive Order 11478 use the term "affirmative employment" to describe the required plans, the term is basically synonymous with "affirmative action."

Management Directive 714, issued by U.S. Supreme Court Justice Clarence Thomas in 1987 while he was chairman of the EEOC, set out detailed requirements and instructions for affirmative employment programs that benefit racial minority groups and women. The management directive required each agency with at least 500 employees and major components within the agency to submit to the EEOC a multi-year affirmative employment plan and annual accomplishment reports and updates to the multi-year plan. Management Directive 714 established three steps for developing the multi-year plan. They were: Comprehensive Analysis (primarily a statistical analysis of the composition of the agency's workforce by race, national origin, and sex), Problem and Barrier Identification, and Report of Objective and Action Items. The management directive also allowed, but did not require, federal employers to set numerical goals for minority groups and women as a fourth part of its affirmative employment plans where there was either a "manifest imbalance" or "conspicuous absence" of EEO groups in that job category as compared to the appropriate civilian labor force. The terms "manifest imbalance" and "conspicuous absence" were defined by the management directive. Management Directive 714 placed restrictions on establishment of numeric goals. For instance, the goals must be reasonable in relation to the extent of the underrepresentation of EEO groups in specific job categories, the number of vacancies, and the availability of candidates. The management directive also explicitly stated that numerical goals "do not require or mandate the selection of unqualified persons or preferential treatment based on race, national origin or sex." In order to emphasize that these goals should not be a permanent feature of agency plans, the management directive stated that the purpose of these goals should be to "attain" and not to "maintain" a balanced workforce.

In addition to the multi-year plans, Management Directive 714 required federal employers to submit annual plans that include an updated statistical analysis of the demographics of the organization's workforce and an analysis of the updated data including identification of trends and changes in the demographics of the workforce from the previous year. The annual plans had to provide a report on the organization's agencies accomplishments toward achieving the established objectives and completing the specific action items planned for those objectives and a report of noteworthy EEO initiatives. Management Directive 714 also provided guidance concerning how the EEOC will evaluate their affirmative employment program. The directive stated that, with good faith EEO efforts, levels of minorities and women should increase in the workforce of the agency. Therefore, the EEOC would examine whether there was a positive change in the levels of minorities and women in its workforce. Other criteria included whether the organization successfully identified barriers and developed objectives and action items and whether it successfully completed the planned action items.

Federal employers are also required to have affirmative action plans for the employment of persons with disabilities. Section 501 of the Rehabilitation Act of 1973, 29 U.S.C. §791, requires the Federal Government to be a model employer for persons with disabilities. Section 501(b) of the act requires all executive departments, agencies, and instrumentalities to create "an affirmative action program plan for the hiring, placement, and advancement of individuals with disabilities" and requires such plans to be updated annually. The Rehabilitation Act requires the plans to be submitted to and approved by the EEOC.

Management Directive 712, entitled "Comprehensive Affirmative Action Programs for Hiring, Placement, and Advancement of Individuals with Handicaps," was issued in 1983. Management Directive 713, entitled "Affirmative Action for Hiring, Placement and Advancement of Individuals with Handicaps," was issued in 1987. These management directives were also issued by Justice Clarence Thomas during his tenure as chairman of the EEOC. They set out detailed requirements and guidance for agency affirmative action programs for persons with disabilities in federal agencies and departments.

Management Directive 712 required federal employers to establish a comprehensive program addressing the hiring, placement, and advancement of persons with disabilities in the agency's workforce and to maintain documentation concerning the program and its effectiveness. This comprehensive plan was required to include elements similar to those required by Management Directive 714, such as specific actions to assure adequate personnel and financial resources are allocated for the program, action to ensure that accountability for progress made by officials responsible for the program is measured, implementation of effective program evaluation systems, accurate information reporting concerning the representation of employees with disabilities in the workplace, and provision of training opportunities for all management staff on issues concerning the employment of persons with disabilities.

Management Directive 713 provided more specific requirements and guidelines for annual affirmative action plans and other submissions. The directive required agencies with 1,001 or more employees to submit affirmative action plans for persons with disabilities each year and annual reports of accomplishments in their affirmative action program. Management Directive 713 required that agencies emphasize the employment of persons with certain "targeted disabilities." The targeted disabilities are: deafness, blindness, missing extremities, partial or complete paralysis, convulsive disorders, mental retardation, mental illness, and distortion of limbs and/or of the spine. Agencies with 1,001 or more employees were required (not just permitted as under Management Directive 714) to set numerical goals for the employment of persons with targeted disabilities. The management directive provided that agency accomplishments would be judged, in part, on whether there is an actual increase in the representation of persons with disabilities in the work force. Agencies with less than 1,001 employees were required to submit a written assurance of nondiscrimination and an annual workforce profile indicating the representation of persons with disabilities in the workforce instead of annual affirmative action plans and accomplishment reports. These small agencies were not required by Management Directive 713 to establish numerical goals. However, the EEOC could require such goals if the federal employer failed to show an increase in the number of persons with targeted disabilities and the EEOC determined that the organization had opportunities to improve.

Management Directive 713 emphasized that even where a federal employer (whether large or small) is expecting to reduce its workforce, special efforts should be made by all federal employers to ensure that the reduction in force does not eliminate any gains made and to attempt, where possible, to avoid terminating employees who would have a particularly difficult time finding new employment because of their disability. Where agencies do not have hiring opportunities, the management directive counseled concentrating efforts on promotion and career development of employees with targeted disabilities.

The management directive required all federal employers to review their personnel and employment policies and practices to ensure that they do not unnecessarily impose barriers to the employment or advancement of persons with disabilities and to develop special recruitment programs targeted to persons with targeted disabilities. Management Directive 713 also reminded federal employers that there are special hiring authorities that permit hiring persons with disabilities more easily than others who must be hired through a more onerous competitive process and suggested that these authorities can be tools for improving the representation of persons with disabilities in the workforce. Management Directive 713 also required federal employers, regardless of size, to survey its facilities to ensure that there are no unnecessary physical barriers to the employment of persons with disabilities.

Management Directive 715 superseded Management Directive 712, 713 and 714. Management Directive 715 promulgates general policy statements and standards for affirmative action plans required by both Title VII and the Rehabilitation Act and also sets reporting requirements. It does not provide as detailed instructions and guidance for affirmative action plans as had the earlier management directives. The EEOC announced in Management Directive 715 that it would provide additional instruction and guidance concerning several elements of an agency affirmative action program.

Management Directive 715 establishes six "essential elements" of agency programs: (1) demonstrated commitment from agency leadership, (2) integration of EEO into the agency's strategic mission, (3) management and program accountability, (4) proactive prevention of unlawful discrimination, (5) efficiency, and (6) responsiveness and legal compliance.

The first element, demonstrated commitment from agency leadership, calls for agency heads to issue a written policy statement expressing a commitment to providing equal employment opportunity at the beginning of their tenure and on an annual basis thereafter. Agency heads must ensure that equal employment opportunity becomes a central element in the organizational structure of the agency and part of the agency culture.

The second element, integration of EEO into the agency's strategic mission, focuses on ensuring that the EEO staff has a direct line of communication to the agency head, has sufficient resources, and is centrally involved in human resource strategy.

The third element, management and program accountability, requires agencies to regularly evaluate the effectiveness of its programs, to ensure managers are implementing these programs by requiring that managers be evaluated on their individual efforts to ensure equal employment opportunity and by considering whether to discipline agency employees involved in a case which resulted in a finding of discrimination, and to ensure that orders of adjudicative bodies and settlements that resolve EEO complaints are complied with.

The fourth element, proactive prevention of unlawful discrimination, requires agencies to assess, on an annual basis, whether barriers to EEO exist. This assessment is to be made, in part, by conducting a statistical analysis of the demographics of the agency's workforce by race, national origin, sex, and disability. Agencies are also required to examine rates of promotions, training, awards, and separations by race, national origin, sex, and disability. Management Directive 715 requires agencies to collect data on race, national origin, and sex from applicants. Agencies are promised additional guidance on gathering data and conducting statistical analysis. However, Management Directive 715 warns that agencies should not only examine statistical analyses alone to identify barriers to EEO. Instead, the statistical result must be considered in the context of all relevant circumstances. This warning signals a significant change from the previous management directives. The earlier directives appeared to rely to a much greater degree on statistical analyses to identify barriers. Like the previous management directives, Management Directive 715 also requires agencies to create and implement detailed plans to address any barriers identified. However, Management Directive 715 again makes a significant departure from one of the earlier management directives in terms of appropriate methods to address EEO barriers. Management Directive 714 explicitly allowed agencies to set numerical goals for the employment of minority groups and for women where the agency's statistical analysis showed significant underrepresentation of these groups. While Management Directive 715 gives specific examples of steps agencies can take to eliminate barriers to EEO, it does not mention numerical goals. This silence is even more conspicuous when it is noted that Management Directive 715 does require agencies to set numerical goals for the employment of persons with disabilities. The deemphasis of Management Directive 715 on statistical analyses and numerical goals likely reflects the increasing scrutiny federal affirmative action programs have received since the 1995 landmark U.S. Supreme Court opinion of *Adarand Constructors, Inc. v. Peña. Adarand* held that the standard for reviewing federal affirmative action programs that use racial preferences under the U.S. Constitution was more onerous than had been previously believed. Since *Adarand,* courts have more closely examined whether numerical targets actually operate as quotas providing a racial preference by allowing or requiring race to be considered as a preferential factor in making employment decisions and whether the federal government had sufficient evidence of the need for racial preferences used.

In addition to conducting an annual assessment and developing plans to address identified EEO barriers, proactive prevention of disability discrimination requires agencies to establish procedures for requesting reasonable accommodations and to maintain a special recruitment program. Agencies are required to examine every policy or practice that impacts the employment of persons with disabilities. Not only are agencies required to establish numerical goals for the hiring and advancement of persons with disabilities, agencies are expressly authorized to consider an applicant's disability as a positive factor when the applicant is otherwise qualified to meet these goals. The U.S. Supreme Court has determined that governmental preferences for persons with disabilities are not as constitutionally problematic as are racial preferences. (Compare *City of Cleburne v. Cleburne Living Center,* 473 U.S. 432 (1985) with *Adarand.*) Like Management Directive 713, Management Directive 715 requires agency efforts to focus on persons with targeted disabilities.

The fifth element, efficiency, calls on agencies to ensure that actions critical to ensuring equal employment opportunity, such as processing EEO complaints and promptly acting on requests for reasonable accommodations, are made in an efficient and expeditious manner.

The sixth element requires agencies to comply with EEO law and EEOC requirements.

Finally, Management Directive 715 requires agencies to submit annual reports to EEOC describing their program activities and plans to eliminate barriers. The EEOC plans to provide further instruction for these submissions in the future.

EEOC's Office of Program Operations, Federal Sector Programs is responsible for providing advice concerning these directives.

See also Adarand Constructors, Inc. v. Peña, Disability Classifications Under the Fifth and Fourteenth Amendments, Employment (Public and Affirmative Action), Executive Order 11478, Rehabilitation Act of 1973, Title VII of the Civil Rights Act of 1964, U.S. Equal Employment Opportunity Commission.

FURTHER READING: Management Directives 712, 713, 714, and 715, published by the United State Equal Opportunity Commission; "MD-715 Checklist Can Help You Build a Model EEO Program," 2004, *Federal Human Resources Week,* April 19; "MD-715 Draws Criticism from EEO Community," 2004, *Federal EEO Advisor,* March 12; "Some Answers to Questions about the MD-715," 2004, *Federal EEO Advisor,* April 23.

MARIA D. BECKMAN

Equal Opportunity Act of 1995

Ultimately a failed piece of federal legislation, the Equal Opportunity Act of 1995 was a bill introduced in the Senate by Robert Dole in response to President Clinton's 1995 "Mend It, Don't End It" campaign on affirmative action. The bill was the most significant modern sweeping legislative attempt to end affirmative action on the federal level. The bill, as proposed by Dole, would have ended the use of any type of affirmative action based upon race, color, gender, or national origin by the federal government in allocating or awarding contracts on jobs or in connection with any other federal program or activity. The bill specifically prohibited "the Federal government from discriminating against, or granting any preference to, any person based in whole or in part on race or sex in connection with federal employment, federal contracting and subcontracting, and other federally conducted programs and activities." The proposed bill also would have prohibited the federal government from requiring contractors engaged in business with the United States to utilize and employ affirmative action, a requirement that is currently imposed on contractors by the federal government. While the bill caused much controversy in 1995 and became one of the major issues in the presidential campaign between Dole and Clinton in 1996, the proposed legislation was defeated within a year of its introduction.

See also Clinton, William Jefferson; Contracting and Affirmative Action; Employment (Public) and Affirmative Action.

FURTHER READING: Holmes, Steven, 1995, "G.O.P. Lawmakers Offer a Ban on Federal Affirmative Action," *New York Times,* July 28, A17.

JAMES A. BECKMAN

Equal Pay Act of 1963

An amendment to the Fair Labor Standards Act (FLSA) of 1938, the Equal Pay Act made it illegal for employers to discriminate in the payment of wages on the basis of sex. In 1938, Congress passed the Fair Labor Standards Act, which stated that employers had to pay a minimum wage and overtime to their employees. As more and more women entered the workforce, the gap in wage earnings between men and women grew. By 1962, women's earnings averaged 60 to 70 percent of those of men for full-time work. In 1963, Congress amended section 6 of the FLSA and called it the Equal Pay Act (EPA). Congress believed that the Equal Pay Act could correct the inequity in pay. The EPA (1963) states,

> No employer shall discriminate between employees on the basis of sex by paying wages to employees at a rate less than the rate at which he pays wages to employees of the opposite sex for equal work on the jobs the performance of which requires equal skill, effort, and responsibility, and which are performed under similar working conditions.
>
> Hence the EPA has been described as an early modern affirmative action effort, attempting to remove, by law, the discriminatory artificial barriers that work to the detriment of women in the workforce.

The Equal Pay Act (1963) established four exceptions, three specific ones and one catchall: "(i) seniority system; (ii) a merit system; (iii) a system which measures earnings by quantity or quality of production; (iv) a differential based on any factor other than sex." In other words, if employees are doing a job that requires similar or equal skill, effort, and responsibility and is performed under the same conditions, they should receive the same pay. If the pay difference is due to seniority, a merit system, incentive pay, or other factor, then such resulting pay disparity is not considered gender discrimination or a violation of the Equal Pay Act of 1963.

The history of the act suggests that once the secretary of labor has determined that the employer is discriminating in paying workers of one sex more than workers of the opposite sex for the same or equal jobs, then the burden of proof is upon the employer to show that the wage differential is justified based upon one of the four exceptions. However, employers have found loopholes in the law to get around paying "equal pay for equal work." Managers believe that they are justified in paying different wages due to difference in skills, responsibilities, and efforts. Many employers changed job descriptions and content to include tasks that women normally did not perform.

The first significant case heard under the EPA concerning physical differences between men and women was *Schultz v. Wheaton Glass Co.*, 421 F.2d 259 (3rd Cir.), *certiorari denied*, 398 U.S. 905 (1970). This case involved the $.21 per hour pay difference between male and female selector packers. Both sexes performed basically the same task, inspection, except that male inspectors did material handling approximately 18 percent of the time. Female inspectors did not perform this task because they were restricted from lifting more than thirty-five pounds. In an astounding decision, the federal Court of Appeals for the Third Circuit established a legal principle, the equal work standard, when declaring the Wheaton Glass Company in violation of the EPA. This principle has served as a guideline for other cases under the EPA. The equal work standard does not require that jobs be identical, only similar. The burden of proof is on the employer to show that the wage differential between men and women doing basically the same job is not based on sex. The court also said that there was no justification for giving all men the same pay just because a few of them performed extra duties, and that women should be offered the same opportunity to perform extra duties as men.

In many instances, employers justified a pay differential between males and females under the claim that the working conditions of males were more hazardous than those of females. In *Corning Glass Works v. Brennan,* 417 U.S. 188 (1974), the Supreme Court held that working conditions under the EPA do not refer to the time of day when work is performed. In this particular case, all the women worked day shift and the men worked night shift. The men received a higher pay, according to the employer, because of working conditions. One of Corning's own representatives testified at the trial that working conditions included two subfactors: "surroundings" and "hazards." "Surroundings" included such elements as toxic chemicals and fumes, their intensity, and their frequency. "Hazards" included physical hazards, their frequency, and the severity of injury they could cause. This case also ruled that equal pay violations could be remedied only by raising the women's wages, not lowering the men's.

Under the EPA, skills, such as education, training, and experience, are justifications for differences in pay. However, individuals must use the skills on the job, not just possess them, as was set forth in *Fowler v. Land Management Group, Inc.*, 978 F.2d 158 (4th Cir. 1992). Further, the Tenth Circuit, in *Marshall v. Security Bank & Trust,* 572 F.2d 276 (10th Cir. 1978), held that to justify pay differential in a bona fide training program, the program must be open to both sexes, employees must be notified of such a program, and there must be a defined beginning and end, a definite course of study, and advancement opportunities when the program was completed. Also, the issue of a pay differential based on responsibility normally involved professional, administrative, and executive employees. Prior to 1972, they did not fall under the purview of the Equal Pay Act. In *Hodgson v. Fairmont Supply Co.*, 454 F.2d 490 (4th Cir. 1972), the court held that the pay differential was not justified even though men made more decisions than women because the men's decisions were subject to review by higher authority.

A bona fide merit system justifies differences in pay between males and females if the pay increase is directly related to job performance. It has been found that some employers claim that pay increases are due to merit when other factors were taken into consideration. Further, salary and wage plans based on seniority are not a violation of the Equal Pay Act if there is a bona fide seniority pay plan in effect. Pay includes the area of fringe benefits. Employers claimed that women were required to pay more for their benefits than men because women lived longer. The Supreme Court held that actuarial distinctions based entirely on sex could not qualify as an exception to the Equal Pay Act (*City of Los Angeles v. Manhart,* 435 U.S. 702 [1978]). Factors other than gender include (1) temporary or permanent assignments made to a lower-rated job, but retaining the rate of the old job; (2) a bona fide training program; and (3) part-time work.

In 1986, the Equal Employment Opportunity Commission issued new regulations interpreting the EPA (29 C.F.R. part 1620; 51 C.F.R. 24716). For the most part, the EEOC adopted the regulations of the Department of Labor. The EEOC's definition of the term "establishment" was expanded to include two or more distinct physical portions of a business as "one establishment" if they are located in the same physical place. Also, the cost of fringe benefits must be the same for both males and females. The largest change was that in the definition of "equal work." Violations include paying new male employees higher wages than former or current female employees. The regulation also disallowed paying males more than females or vice versa.

The EPA did not correct the pay differences that existed between the sexes. Discrimination in pay still exists today. Among college graduates aged twenty-five to thirty-four, women earn eighty cents for every dollar earned by men. Controlling for all measures of productivity, overall, wage discrimination is somewhere between 89 and 98 percent. The gap widens with increases in age. Starting salaries for jobs that are considered traditionally female are normally lower. If males receive higher wages than females for the same work, employers claim that the jobs are different. Under EPA, wage discrimination is allowed as long as employers can demonstrate that the wage differential is based on something other than sex.

See also Department of Labor; Equal Employment Opportunity Commission; Gender Norms; Gender Segregation in Employment; Gender Stratification; Glass Ceilings; Women and the Workplace.

FURTHER READING: Harrison, Maureen, and Steve Gilbert, 1995, "Equal Pay Act," in *Landmark Decisions of the United States Supreme Court V*, Carlsbad, CA: Excellent Books; Pace, Joseph Michael, and Zachary Smith, 1995, "Understanding Affirmative Action: From the Practitioner's Perspective," *Public Personnel Management* 24, no. 2 (summer): 139–147; Sovereign, Kenneth L., 1994, *Personnel Law*, 3d ed., Englewood Cliffs, NJ: Prentice Hall.

NAOMI ROBERTSON

Equal Protection Clause

The Equal Protection Clause of the Fourteenth Amendment specifies that no state shall "deny to any person within its jurisdiction the equal protection of the laws." The Equal Protection Clause is by far one of the most central provisions of the Constitution dealing with racial and gender equality in the United States and is the crucial clause of the Constitution to consider in dealing with the constitutionality of affirmative action plans or programs. The language of the Equal Protection Clause appears in Section 1 of the Fourteenth Amendment and is only one of the many different provisions that comprise the Fourteenth Amendment. In fact, the Fourteenth Amendment spans approximately 435 words, while the Equal Protection Clause comprises only 16 of those words (less than 1 percent of the text of the Fourteenth Amendment). From these 16 words, a whole field of equal protection law and jurisprudence has developed over the course of the last century. Additionally, the protections of the Fifth Amendment have also been interpreted by the Supreme Court as implicitly including "equal protection" guarantees, even though the words "equal protection" never appear in the text of that amendment.

In modern times, the Equal Protection Clause has been central to the desegregation of public facilities and schools in America, the struggle for equality of all races and of women, and the constitutionality of affirmative action programs. Supporters of affirmative action argue that affirmative action is needed to ensure true equality of all citizens under the Equal Protection Clause. Opponents of affirmative action often argue that affirmative action programs discriminate against majority-group members (usually white males) on account of race and gender, and this discrimination, even if benign, is prohibited by the Equal Protection Clause. In essence, opponents adopt Justice John Marshall Harlan's famous 1896 statement in his dissent in *Plessy v. Ferguson* that "our constitution is color-blind, and neither knows nor tolerates classes among citizens," and that in regard to civil rights "all citizens are equal before the law."

The Equal Protection Clause is a limitation on state governments and not the federal government, although the equal protection guarantee has been imported into the Fifth Amendment as a limit on federal government action. The framers of the Fourteenth Amendment's Equal Protection Clause wished to ensure that the newly freed slaves of the South would be treated equally to other citizens of their respective states. The Equal Protection Clause language of the Fourteenth Amendment first appeared in the Civil Rights Act of 1866, a federal statute that mandated that states provide all of their citizens the equal benefits and protections of the law. However, because this guarantee of "equal protection" was only in a federal statute and could be repealed by a subsequent Congress or held to be invalid by the Supreme Court, it was thought best to include this equality guarantee in the text of the Constitution (making it more impervious to change), and it thus was made part of the Fourteenth Amendment. The Fourteenth Amendment was ratified in 1868, and states in the South were not given full statehood rights in the Union after the Civil War until they ratified the Fourteenth Amendment.

Ironically, in the immediate years after ratification of the Fourteenth Amendment, the Equal Protection Clause was not often utilized by the Supreme Court in overturning state legislation. There were only two noteworthy cases in the nineteenth century in which the Supreme Court utilized the Equal Protection Clause to invalidate governmental action: *Strauder v. West Virginia*, 100 U.S. 303 (1879) (state laws that precluded blacks from serving on juries violated the Equal Protection Clause) and *Yick Wo v. Hopkins*, 118 U.S. 356 (1886) (applying state laws only to the detriment of minorities violated the Equal Protection Clause). Furthermore, in 1896, the Supreme Court eviscerated the Equal Protection Clause when it announced its pernicious "separate-but-equal" doctrine in *Plessy v. Ferguson*, 163 U.S. 537 (1896). In essence, the Supreme Court in *Plessy* ratified and legally sanctioned the Jim Crow laws and black codes that had proliferated throughout the South and ensured that such substandard treatment of minorities (particularly, black Americans) was not a violation of the Equal Protection Clause of the Fourteenth Amendment.

It was not until the 1940s that the Supreme Court interpreted the Equal Protection Clause in a way that served as a protection for minority classes. First, in *United States v. Carolene Products Co.*, 304 U.S. 144 (1938), in its famous footnote 4, the Court indicated that "discrete and insular minorities" (a predecessor to the term "suspect classifications" that the Court employs today) should receive heightened protections under the Constitution. Second, in *Korematsu v. United States*, 323 U.S. 214 (1944), one of the two Supreme Court cases dealing with the constitutionality of the Japanese American internment camps during World War II, the Court held that racial classifications should be subject to the most exacting judicial scrutiny ("strict scrutiny") under the Fourteenth Amendment.

In the school desegregation context, the National Association for the Advancement of Colored People chipped away at the *Plessy* separate-but-equal doctrine in a series of cases throughout the South, including *Missouri ex rel. Gaines v. Canada*, 305 U.S. 337 (1938), *Sipuel v. Regents of the University of Oklahoma*, 332 U.S. 631 (1948), *Sweatt v. Painter*, 339 U.S. 629 (1950), and *McLaurin v. Oklahoma State Board of Regents*, 339 U.S. 637 (1950). The strategy in the school desegregation cases was to slowly undermine the separate-but-equal doctrine by showing that the separate public facilities provided by states for minorities were not equal and were in fact substandard and/or underfunded. The strategy involved eroding reliance on the doctrine in the courts and making the doctrine too costly to continue. If courts required states to provide actually equal separate facilities, the states would not have the resources to provide dual facilities in all the facets of public life (e.g., dual and equal public schools, hospitals, and parks) and would eventually agree to desegregate their public facilities, if for no other reason than for lack of adequate resources and funding.

Finally, in 1954, the Equal Protection Clause of the Fourteenth Amendment began to take on its modern form. In *Brown v. Board of Education*, 347 U.S. 483 (1954), the Supreme Court rejected its separate-but-equal doctrine and instead held that separate facilities in the context of public education are "inherently unequal" under the Fourteenth Amendment, no matter how equal the physical facilities might appear to the outside observer. Thus, as Yale law professor Alexander Bickel once remarked, *Brown* does not represent the end of the constitutional interpretative journey of the Equal Protection Clause, but rather signifies "the beginning" of how the Supreme Court will require states to treat their citizens.

In the modern era, the Supreme Court has generally adopted a three-tiered approach to the Fourteenth Amendment Equal Protection Clause with differing levels of judicial scrutiny, depending on which class of individuals is allegedly being discriminated against by the government action, although the distinctions between these tiers are sometimes blurred. The three tiers of review of a governmental action under the Equal Protection Clause today can be described as follows: first, the strict scrutiny tier; second, the intermediate level of scrutiny; and third, the rational basis tier. If a government statute references race and discriminates on the basis of race in the language of the statute, the constitutionality of this statute is subject to "strict scrutiny" by the courts. The classification by race is said to involve "suspect classifications." This means that for the statute to survive a constitutional challenge under the Equal Protection Clause of the Fourteenth Amendment, the government must put forth a compelling governmental interest as to why the government action is necessary. That is, the government must be trying to achieve a goal of extreme and paramount importance to society. Additionally, even if the government has a compelling governmental interest for promulgating the law, the law must be "narrowly tailored" and drafted to achieve the goals without unnecessarily impacting others.

The Supreme Court held in *City of Richmond v. J.A. Croson Co.*, 488 U.S. 469 (1989), that even benign discrimination pursuant to a federal affirmative action program is subject to strict scrutiny by the courts. The strict scrutiny analysis is a very exacting standard to meet, which prompted Justice Thurgood Marshall once to aptly remark in another case that strict scrutiny is strict in theory, but fatal in fact. Additionally, even if the statute at issue does not directly mention race on its face, the government action may still be subject to strict scrutiny review by the courts if the effect of the statute has a disparate impact on minorities, and the legislative history of the statute indicates an intent on the part of the lawmakers to discriminate on account of race. An example of a statute that satisfied the Court's strict scrutiny analysis was the one challenged in *Korematsu v. United States.* In *Korematsu,* the Court held that the racial classification (all Japanese Americans in California were to report to internment camps) was allegedly passed pursuant to national security and wartime interests, which the Court held to be a compelling governmental interest.

The second lower-level tier under modern equal protection law is that of "intermediate scrutiny." While the application of this level of scrutiny has fluctuated over time, this second tier typically involves classifications involving gender, alienage, or illegitimate children. If a statute or governmental action discriminates on the basis of one of these categories, the courts will subject the governmental action to an intermediate level of scrutiny. Under this level of scrutiny, the courts will look skeptically at the government discrimination, but will not require a compelling governmental interest for the government measure to survive constitutional challenge under the Equal Protection Clause. Rather, courts will ask whether the gender or alien classification is necessary to achieve important (but not compelling) governmental goals.

For example, in *Mississippi University for Women v. Hogan,* 458 U.S. 718 (1982), the Court invalidated a single-sex (female) state nursing program on the grounds that preserving a single-sex school (which excluded males) was not "narrowly tailored" to fulfill important governmental goals. In *Mississippi University for Women,* the Court held that women had ample educational opportunities throughout the state, were not excluded from other institutions, and were not underrepresented in the nursing profession. The Court also concluded that the presence of men would not impact the teaching patterns of instructors, would not adversely affect the performance of female students, and would not result in men dominating the classroom experience. In fact, according to the Court, the maintenance of separate-sex nursing schools continued to propagate gender myths. The Court held that the gender-based classification was not necessary to promote important societal goals. The Court came to the same conclusions again a decade later in *United States v. Virginia,* 518 U.S. 515 (1996).

The last of the three categories of review under the Equal Protection Clause is the rational basis tier. If the government statute or action does not involve a "suspect classification" (strict scrutiny) or discriminate on the basis of gender (intermediate scrutiny), the government statute that discriminates and classifies individuals will be held to the rational basis standard. The rational basis test is a very low-threshold test and is not a very judicially exacting standard. Under the rational basis test, courts defer to the government and ask only whether the government had any legitimate (rational) reason related to a societal concern for passing the legislation. Statutes are rarely overturned as unconstitutional under the Equal Protection Clause of the Fourteenth Amendment when the court is utilizing the rational basis test.

For example, legislation that provides benefits to veterans of the U.S. armed forces, such as a Veterans Administration Home Loan or the GI Bill, would be a classification that would be subject to the rational basis test. While the legislation discriminates against different classes of individuals (veterans versus nonveterans), such legislation discriminating against nonveterans has been upheld under the

Equal Protection Clause because the federal government clearly has a societal interest in passing the legislation (protecting and compensating veterans), and laws such as the GI Bill are a legitimate and rational way of promoting these interests. Thus an affirmative action program for veterans would pass a constitutional challenge under the Equal Protection Clause while a race-based affirmative action program might not survive constitutional challenge because of the different levels of judicial scrutiny applied to each case (rational basis for veterans; strict scrutiny for racial classifications/preferences). Rational basis scrutiny has also been applied to classifications based upon disabilities and age.

See also Adarand Constructors, Inc. v. Peña; Brown v. Board of Education; City of Richmond v. J.A. Croson Co.; Civil Rights Act of 1866; Civil War (Reconstruction) Amendments and Civil Rights Acts; Color-Blind Constitution; Compelling Governmental Interest; Constitution, Civil Rights, and Equality; Disability Classifications under the Fifth and Fourteenth Amendments; Discrete and Insular Minority; Fourteenth Amendment; GI Bill; Japanese Internment and World War II; Jim Crow Laws; *Korematsu v. United States; Mississippi University for Women v. Hogan*; Narrowly Tailored Affirmative Action Plans; O'Connor, Sandra Day; Persons with Disabilities and Affirmative Action; *Plessy v. Ferguson*; Race-Based Affirmative Action; Rational Basis Scrutiny; Reverse Discrimination; *Sipuel v. Regents of the University of Oklahoma; Strauder v. West Virginia*; Strict Scrutiny; Suspect Classification; *Sweatt v. Painter*; Veterans' Preferences; *Yick Wo v. Hopkins.*

FURTHER READING: Baer, Judith A., 1983, *Equality under the Constitution: Reclaiming the Fourteenth Amendment*, Ithaca, NY: Cornell University Press; Berger, Raoul, 1989, *The Fourteenth Amendment and the Bill of Rights*, Norman: University of Oklahoma Press; Curtis, Michael Kent, 1986, *No State Shall Abridge: The Fourteenth Amendment and the Bill of Rights*, Durham, NC: Duke University Press; Gunther, Gerald, 1972, "Foreword: In Search of Evolving Doctrine on a Changing Court: A Model for a Newer Equal Protection," *Harvard Law Review* 86:1–48.

JAMES A. BECKMAN

Equal Rights Amendment

The Equal Rights Amendment (ERA), a proposed amendment to the U.S. Constitution, is critical to the dialogue on affirmative action in its commitment to eradicating sex discrimination and securing equality under the law. Yet the ERA has never been ratified. The amendment was first drafted in 1923 by Alice Paul, a suffragist leader and founder of the National Woman's Party (NWP). The proposed amendment, introduced as the "Lucretia Mott Amendment," read, "Men and women shall have equal rights throughout the United States and every place subject to its jurisdiction." Paul and the organizers of the NWP believed that the proposed ERA would complement the aims of the Nineteenth Amendment, ratified in 1920, which granted long-awaited suffrage rights to women. The ERA, however, failed to pass, and Paul continued to press for its introduction in each session of Congress after its inception in 1923. Now, however, the American labor movement, orchestrating the passage of protective labor laws to treat women differently, and the rising tide of social conservatism again defeated the promises of the ERA.

By the late 1960s and early 1970s, however, the impetus for the ERA once again prompted political institutions to place women's rights, along with civil rights, on the national agenda. The ERA, which now read, "Equality of rights under the law shall not be denied or abridged by the United States or any State on account of sex," passed the House of Representatives by a vote of 354–24 in 1971 and was approved by the Senate by a vote of 84–8 on March 22, 1972. Congress stipulated that the amendment would have seven years to achieve ratification by three-fourths or thirty-eight of the state legislatures. Initially, support for the ratification of the ERA by the states was enthusiastic, as twenty-two states ratified it within the first year. But as partisan politics entered the ERA debate, the process of ratification slowed dramatically. There were only eight ratifications in 1973, three in 1974, one in 1975, and none in 1976.

The ERA had clearly been knocked off track. People wondered what had happened to the zealous support for extending equal rights to all citizens. The answer is perhaps best understood by examining interest-group or pluralist participation in American politics. An anti-ERA movement began to gain momentum as individuals such as Phyllis Schlafly, right-wing leader of the Eagle Forum and STOP ERA, insisted that the Equal Rights Amendment would prove detrimental to women's rights. The opponents insisted that women would be drafted and sent into combat; they would no longer receive alimony in the event of divorce; rape laws would be nullified; and finally, abortion rights, homosexual marriages, and unisex bathrooms would become the norm. Although these arguments were specious at best, they were powerful enough to galvanize the opponents of the ERA and hinder the ratification process. There were also other opponents from more conventional places: states' rights supporters who believed that the ERA was an encroachment on state authority and fundamentalist religious communities who were fearful of change in traditional family values.

As these anti-ERA forces kicked into gear, so did the pro-ERA supporters. The pro-ERA advocates were led by the National Organization for Women (NOW) and numerous other women's group supporters. In 1977, Indiana became the thirty-fifth state to ratify the amendment, and that same year saw the death of Alice Paul, who had worked tirelessly to support equality of rights for women under the Constitution. Soon after, however, the ratification process hit more serious procedural obstacles. Some states, like Illinois, altered their rules for ratification, requiring more votes to ratify, and still other states began to rescind or take back their affirmative votes for ratification, even though rescission bills were questioned as lacking legal precedent. One state, Missouri, filed antitrust litigation, claiming that the pro-ERA forces were urging groups to boycott those states that had not ratified the ERA. A federal judge later ruled that these actions were protected as free speech.

As the 1979 deadline for ratification approached, pro-ERA supporters now advocated for an indefinite extension that would allow more time to rebut the growing number of opponents and ensure final ratification. To help coordinate the effort for ratification, NOW supporters brought 100,000 demonstrators to Washington, D.C., in July 1978. The rally proved successful in promoting political support for the ERA, as the House of Representatives voted 233–189 and the Senate voted 60–36 to grant the extension for ratification until June 30, 1982. However, the struggle for equal rights suffered another setback when that deadline expired

Demonstrators opposed to the ERA protest in front of the White House in 1977. Courtesy of Library of Congress.

with the ERA three votes short of the necessary thirty-eight. Even hunger strikes, White House demonstrating, and other acts of civil disobedience could not counter the powerful lobbying efforts to defeat the amendment. The ERA was reintroduced in Congress on July 14, 1982, and has been before every session of Congress since that time. In the 107th Congress (2001–2002), it was introduced by Senator Edward Kennedy and Representative Carolyn Maloney. Even today, some supporters of the ERA insist that Congress should continue to acknowledge the already existing thirty-five ratifications that were passed before 1982 and work to ensure the three remaining votes necessary for final ratification.

Why is the Equal Rights Amendment necessary and what would it have accomplished had it been ratified? The amendment would seek to invalidate any state law that automatically discriminates on the basis of sex. This would protect both men and women from discrimination. Many supporters of the ERA believe that the Equal Protection Clause of the Fourteenth Amendment, which already prohibits discrimination, is not sufficient to guarantee equal rights on the basis of sex. Currently, the Supreme Court only gives intermediate scrutiny to sex discrimination cases, not the strict scrutiny that it guarantees to those classifications based on race or ethnicity. Thus supporters of the ERA insist that the ERA is necessary to compensate for what the Fourteenth Amendment Equal Protection Clause does not do. The ERA would systematize the protection of gender discrimination, eliminate the haphazard way in which the Supreme Court now interprets sex discrimination cases, and ultimately achieve the goals of Alice Paul and others who worked tirelessly for equality of rights. However, it should be noted that in the affirmative action area, it is likely that the ERA would disallow programs that preferentially favor one gender over another, as gender preferences or benign discrimination on account of gender would be prohibited under the very terms of the proposed amendment.

See also Anthony, Susan Brownell; Fourteenth Amendment; Mott, Lucretia Coffin; National Organization for Women; Nineteenth Amendment; Stanton, Elizabeth Cady; Stone, Lucy; Strict Scrutiny.

FURTHER READING: Denning, Brannon P., and John R. Vile, 2000, "Necromancing the Equal Rights Amendment," *Constitutional Commentary* 17, no. 3 (winter): 593–602; Francis,

Roberta W., "The History Behind the Equal Rights Amendment," web site: http://www.equalrightsamendment.org/era.htm; Wallsten, Peter, 2003, "Florida Senate's 'Retro' Action Revives Equal Rights Amendment," *Miami Herald*, April 2, 1.

JANIS JUDSON

Ethnic Groups

Both ethnic and racial groups may be targeted by affirmative action programs. Ethnic groups are groups of people who share a common ancestry and cultural heritage and are socially defined in some way that distinguishes them from others. Ethnic groups are social and political constructs that emphasize certain characteristics and traits as socially meaningful and significant, rather than other traits. Ethnic groups may be self-identified or defined by others. Historically, ethnic groups have been identified by others as a justification for persecution. For example, at its inception in the late fifteenth century, the term was used to identify certain communities as "heathens," and in the early twentieth century the term was increasingly used to refer to groups of immigrants to the United States from southern and eastern Europe, who were identified as less desirable than northern Europeans.

Definitions of ethnic groups vary. Narrower definitions focus on cultural characteristics such as language, religion, and national origin and see ethnic groups as distinct from racial groups. Broader definitions incorporate physical and racial characteristics as well. In recent years, there has been some debate over usage of the terms "ethnic group" and "racial group," with political implications. For example, some sociologists argue that the narrower definition of an ethnic group is more accurate because it distinguishes the experiences of ethnic groups, such as Irish Americans or Italian Americans, from the very different experiences of racial groups, such as African Americans. While minority ethnic groups faced discrimination upon immigration to the United States, they became identified as part of the dominant racial group and were afforded opportunities and benefits denied to African Americans and other racial minorities, such as the benefits of the GI Bill following World War II. When these disparate groups are all lumped together under the broader definition, the very different experiences of these groups may be overlooked. Ethnic identity is also more flexible than racial identity: white ethnic-group members may choose if, when, and where to emphasize their ethnic identity, unlike members of disadvantaged racial groups, who are usually classified by others on the basis of their physical characteristics. Affirmative action programs have historically targeted disadvantaged racial groups for that reason. Because ethnic and racial groups are social and political constructs, their definitions are subject to change, as well as much debate. For example, while many people view Hispanics as a racial group, the U.S. census has classified Hispanics as an ethnic group.

See also African Americans; Bureau of the Census; Census Classifications, Ethnic and Racial; GI Bill; Hispanic Americans; Native Americans; One-Drop Rule; Racial Privacy Initiative; Truman, Harry.

FURTHER READING: Feagin, Joe R., and Clairece Booher Feagin, 1996, *Racial and Ethnic Relations*, Upper Saddle River, NJ: Prentice Hall; Ferrante, Joan, and Prince Brown, Jr., 2001,

The Social Construction of Race and Ethnicity in the United States, 2nd ed., Upper Saddle River, NJ: Prentice Hall.

ABBY L. FERBER

Ethnocentrism

People see the world through the prism of the culture in which they are raised. Cultures have their own traditions, customs, beliefs, rules, norms, values, and the like. These tend to be passed from generation to generation. Consequently, cultures tend to share a certain view of the world. When people of different cultures interact, their cultural differences can be a source of uncertainty and, at times, conflict because people often judge others according to their own cultural circumstances. This phenomenon has been referred to as ethnocentrism. Due in part to some of the negative aspects of this phenomenon, various equal opportunity and affirmative action programs have been instituted over the years.

Broadly speaking, "ethnocentrism" represents the notion that one's culture (e.g., values, way of life, and the like) is superior to that of other cultures. Because one of the functions of culture is cultural transmission, most people are ethnocentric. In fact, arguably, ethnocentric thinking cannot be avoided. It is a common attribute of a culture that breeds similar cultural attitudes among people of the same culture. One could argue that ethnocentric attitudes are not necessarily manifested in negative ways. Pride in one's cultural values is a positive aspect of ethnocentrism. It provides a sense of group and cultural identity around which people can come to share a worldview.

However, ethnocentrism often is manifested in negative ways. The belief that one's culture is superior to cultures of other groups can foster erroneous assumptions about others based on one's own limited experience with and understanding of others' cultural values. Stereotypes, for example, reflect ethnocentric thinking. Stereotypes are attitudes shared by members of one cultural group about members (or objects) of other groups. They are learned from norms and cultural systems that perpetuate them rather than from direct experience with a specific individual who is the target of the stereotype. Prejudice is the use of these stereotypes to prejudge others. There also are negative behavioral manifestations of ethnocentrism. These include actions such as violence, discrimination, and, in extreme cases, segregation and "ethnic cleansing" by powerful groups in a society who are in a position to exercise active denigration of rather than sensitivity to cultural diversity.

Employers, landlords, agencies, educators, and others may rely on stereotypes rather than the characteristics of the person with whom they are dealing when making employment, housing, or other decisions. Thus stereotyping has impacted minority groups in the United States. Stereotypes and prejudice, which arguably reflect attitudinal and behavioral manifestations of ethnocentrism, have adversely impacted economic opportunities for such groups by hindering access to goods, services, and higher social status. Therefore, over the years, various antidiscrimination, equal opportunity, and affirmative action legislation/policies have been instituted to offset such negative perceptual and behavioral manifestations of ethnocentrism. At an organizational level, corporations and other institutions sometimes establish diversity or sensitivity training or culture-specific training programs to sensitize people to cultural differences and minimize negative manifestations of ethnocentrism.

Some scholars have juxtaposed ethnocentrism with the concept of cultural relativity. Whereas the former generally is used to reflect negative attitudes and behaviors toward people of other cultures, the latter often is used to describe greater cultural sensitivity to others' unique cultural traditions, rather than judging others based on one's own cultural standards.

See also Afrocentrism; Eurocentrism; Pluralism; Prejudice; Stereotyping and Minority Classes; Xenophobia.

FURTHER READING: Cashdan, Elizabeth, 2001, "Ethnocentrism and Xenophobia: A Cross-cultural Study," *Current Anthropology* 42, no. 5:760–765; Cox, Taylor, Jr., 1993, *Cultural Diversity in Organizations*, San Francisco: Berrett-Koehler; Infante, Dominic, Andrew S. Rancer, and Deanna F. Womack, 1997, *Building Communication Theory*, 3d ed., Prospect Heights, IL: Waveland Press; Pahnos, Markella, and Karen Butt, 1992, "Ethnocentrism—A Universal Pride in One's Ethnic Background: Its Impact on Teaching and Learning," *Education* 113, no. 1:118–125.

PAUL M. HARIDAKIS

Eugenics

"Eugenics" refers to the production of human beings. More specifically, the root term "eugenic" comes from the Greek *eugenes*, which means "well born" or "pertaining to or adapted to the production of fine offspring, especially in the human race." A *eugenist* (or *eugenicist*) is thus one who is, as the *Oxford English Dictionary* puts it, "a student or advocate of eugenics." Ultimately, historically and currently, there have been segments in society that have based their beliefs on racial superiority and/or inferiority upon the concept of eugenics. As will be discussed later, the link between eugenics and racism is an especially close one, as is attested by the historical prominence of racially based theories of superiority/inferiority that have grounded discriminatory social policies (e.g., legal segregation, antimiscegenation laws) aimed at maintaining racial or ethnic purity. Affirmative action policies and programs, along with traditional civil rights laws and legislation, are part of the legal effort to dismantle the institutional articulations of such injustice as well as its ongoing deleterious consequences.

The term "eugenics" was coined by Francis Galton in 1883 and also denotes the scientific approach to the production of human beings. This latter sense is expressed in Galton's description of his work on the genetic basis of human faculties as "the investigation of human eugenics, that is, of the conditions under which men of a high type are produced." In his work, Galton applied Darwinian evolutionary theory to the study of human hereditary traits. There have been many students and advocates of eugenics throughout the history of Western civilization, including the philosopher Plato, who premised his vision of the ideal society on a view of human beings as "naturally" suited to specific social classes. The social critic and novelist Aldous Huxley envisioned a genetically stratified society in his dystopic *Brave New World*, and ideologues such as Adolf Hitler used theories of genetic and racial superiority as a basis for campaigns of racial purification. *The Encyclopedia of Bioethics* notes that "eugenics" has had different meanings in different eras, including that of mitigating or eliminating human defects by manipulating human genetic composition.

Most writers on eugenics have distinguished between "positive" and "negative" eugenics. "Positive" eugenics emphasizes the need to reproduce the best traits of populations or subsets of populations thought to be genetically superior, while "negative" eugenics endorses restrictions (e.g., abortion, sterilization, marriage prohibitions) on the reproduction of populations thought to possess an abundance of undesirable characteristics. Both positive and negative eugenics seek to understand the genetic constitution of human beings and its evolution and to use that knowledge to intervene in and influence (always ostensibly for the better) the production of future human generations. As noted, eugenics has also provided a foundation for ideologies of racial and ethnic superiority. When yoked to supremacist political agendas, eugenics has thus been used to justify such policies as mandatory abortion, forced sterilization, ethnic cleansing, and genocide. The use of both positive and negative eugenics to inform social policies intended to improve the human condition gives concrete meaning to the notions of "social Darwinism" and "survival of the fittest" as applied to human societies.

The relation between eugenics and race/ethnicity is an intimate one because race and ethnicity were (and often still are) thought to be biological facts rather than social constructs and thus to be fundamental determinants of human character traits and social behavior. On the basis of this assumption, eugenics societies proliferated around the world by the close of the nineteenth century. These associations were influential in popularizing genetic science, including the related idea that some human groups were biologically superior to others. Post–World War I social policies in the United States and elsewhere reflected this notion. For example, the U.S. Immigration Restriction Act of 1924 favored immigration from northern Europe and greatly restricted it from countries whose populations were thought to be genetically inferior. In the period 1907–1937, a majority of states in the United States required the sterilization of the mentally ill and handicapped and those convicted of alcohol- and drug-related crimes, among other supposedly "unfit" members of society. Some thinkers have gone further and claimed that such characteristics as intelligence (IQ) and demeanor are race or ethnicity specific, thus encouraging the view that these and other biological differences between people justify theories of racial and ethnic superiority/inferiority and social policies based on these theories. Such applications of eugenics have caused a great deal of fear that knowledge of human genetics will continue to be invoked as the foundation for ethically insensitive and even unjust social practices.

Recent developments in reproductive technologies and human genetics research (e.g., the Human Genome Project), the development of genetic therapies, and the reality of cloning have renewed age-old concerns about the ethical, legal, and social implications of research in eugenics. Fears about the misuse of eugenics focus on what in contemporary parlance is referred to as "genetic engineering." Genetic engineering involves directly changing the genetic structure of an organism to provide that organism with desirable or useful traits, or to eliminate negative traits such as hereditary disorders. The genetic engineering of plants and nonhuman animals dates from the 1970s. Although concerns have been raised about genetically modified plants, animals, and, most recently, food for human consumption, much of the controversy about genetic engineering continues to focus on its direct application to human beings. Specifically, serious reservations have been expressed over using the kind of genetic engineering that has been used to modify plants and nonhuman animals on human beings. "Germ-line gene therapy," a form of genetic engineering that may enable the correction of severe hereditary disorders such as cystic fibrosis, is viewed by some as a perfectly reasonable use of genetic technology, and gene therapy grounds the hope of eliminating such hitherto incorrigible genetic maladies as Huntington's disease. Critics of such research, however, worry that this is a form of "negative eugenics," and that gene therapy is but a prelude to efforts to enhance human beings themselves, which is "positive" eugenics. In sum, the fear is that the line between "negative" and "positive" eugenics is easily blurred, and the temptation to use genetic research to enhance human beings rather than simply eliminate genetic disorders will be too great to resist.

There is no formal link between contemporary affirmative action policies and initiatives, on the one hand, and theories of racial superiority and inferiority grounded in eugenics, on the other. There is little doubt, though, that the notions of genetic determinism and the "natural" supremacy of specific racial and ethnic groups over others have influenced attitudes of racial and ethnic intolerance. Moreover, there can be no gainsaying the historical significance of the role of white supremacist ideologies in the history of racial discrimination and racial segregation within the United States and elsewhere around the world. Given these realities, affirmative action policies and programs can be seen as a deliberate attempt to blunt the social and political misapplication and even abuse of knowledge of human genetics as it has been applied to race and ethnicity.

See also Darwinism; Immigration Act of 1965; Racial Discrimination; Scientific Racism; Segregation.

FURTHER READING: Barkan, Elazar, 1992, *The Retreat of Scientific Racism: Changing Concepts of Race in Britain and the United States between the World Wars*, Cambridge: Cambridge University Press; Galton, Francis, 1907, *Inquiries into Human Faculty and Its Development*, London: J.M. Dent and Co.; Garver, Kenneth L., and Bettylee Garver, 1994, "The Human Genome Project and Eugenic Concerns," *American Journal of Human Genetics* 54, no. 1 (January): 148–158; Gerwitz, Daniel S., 1994, "Toward a Quality Population: China's Eugenic Sterilization of the Mentally Retarded," *New York Law School Journal of International Comparative Law* 15, no. 1:139–162; Hamilton, William D., 1964, "The Genetical Evolution of Social Behavior I and II," *Journal of Theoretical Biology* 7:1–51; Harris, John, 1993, "Is Gene Therapy a Form of Eugenics?" *Bioethics* 7, nos. 2/3:178–187, April 1993; Herrnstein, Richard J., and Charles Murray, 1994, *The Bell Curve*, New York: Free Press; Hunt, John, 1999, "Perfecting Humankind: A Comparison of Progressive and Nazi Views on Eugenics, Sterilization, and Abortion," *Linacre Quarterly* 66, no. 1 (February): 129–141; Kuhl, Stefan, 1994, *The Nazi Connection: Eugenics, American Racism, and German National Socialism*, New York: Oxford University Press; Lappe, Marc, 1995, "Eugenics: Ethical Issues," in *The Encyclopedia of Bioethics*, rev. ed., edited by Warren T. Reich, 770–777, New York: Macmillan; "The New Genetics," 1999, *Journal of Medical Ethics* (special issue) 25, no. 2 (April): 75–214; Pearson, Veronica, 1995, "Population Policy and Eugenics in China," *British Journal of Psychiatry* 167, no. 1:1–4; Reich, Warren T., ed., 1995, *The Encyclopedia of Bioethics*, rev. ed., 5 vols., New York: Macmillan; Roper, A.G., 1992, "Ancient Eugenics," *Mankind Quarterly* 32, no. 4 (summer): 383–419; Tucker,

William H., 1994, *The Science and Politics of Racial Research,* Urbana: University of Illinois Press.

PAUL M. HUGHES

Eurocentrism

Eurocentrism is a worldview or philosophy that elevates the culture, values, history, art, religion, and traditions of Western Europe above those of other cultures, including African, Arab, and Asian societies. Eurocentrism continues to dominate American culture and society, and many Americans have internalized its assumptions in a way that leads to racial, ethnic, and gender inequalities in the United States.

In addition to traits such as preferences for European art, literature, mythology, and social conventions, Eurocentrism involves various assumptions about community and politics that run counter to the traditions of many other races and ethnic groups. For instance, tenets of Eurocentrism include the belief in humanity's mastery over the environment and a high degree of faith in scientific discovery and technology (in spite of potential human or environmental costs). Eurocentrism also spawned cultural Darwinism, the belief that civilizations with more military or economic power had the right to dominate other groups.

The roots of Eurocentrism in the United States lie in the period of colonization by European settlers, including the English, Dutch, Spanish, and French. Because of technological superiority, the European settlers discounted the indigenous cultures of the native peoples. Later, Eurocentrism was used to justify slavery and other forms of exploitation of native peoples, including land confiscation. In contemporary times, Eurocentrism is often marked by the preference for European Americans in the workforce and in government—a preference that reinforces the arguments for affirmative action and other racial equity programs.

See also Afrocentrism; Darwinism; Ethnocentrism; Xenophobia.

FURTHER READING: Asante, Molefi Kete, 1999, *The Painful Demise of Eurocentrism: An Afrocentric Response to Critics,* Trenton, NJ: Africa World Press; Blaut, J.M., 2000, *Eight Eurocentric Historians,* New York: Guilford Press; Frankenberg, Ruth, 1997, *Displacing Whiteness: Essays in Social and Cultural Criticism,* Durham, NC: Duke University Press.

TOM LANSFORD

European Court of Human Rights

The European Court of Human Rights was one of three institutions created by the 1950 European Human Rights Convention. The court came into being in 1959 and has jurisdiction in those nations that are signatories of the convention. Since 1980, the court has seen a dramatic increase in the number of cases it hears as people and groups have endeavored to use the convention as a means to bypass or overturn existing national laws that are discriminatory or that violate basic human rights.

One of the most important successes of the court has been the advancement of common rights and freedoms among European citizens. For instance, the court has made important strides in guaranteeing religious freedom throughout Western Europe and in protecting freedom of expression and freedom of the press. The court has served as the main mechanism for enforcement of the European Human Rights Convention and has facilitated the growth of the idea of European citizenship as opposed to national citizenship.

Many of the nations of Europe have legal systems that do not allow class-action lawsuits. However, under the terms of the convention, the Human Rights Court can hear cases brought by groups. Hence many minority and disadvantaged groups have used the court to advance affirmative action policies. For example, representatives of the Roma or European Gypsies filed a variety of cases against European nations under its jurisdiction to end discrimination in employment and public accommodations. Partially as a result of these cases, Romania has instituted affirmative action programs in fields such as health care and social work to improve living conditions for this minority group. Concurrently, Hungary has adopted affirmative action programs for the Roma in areas such as higher education.

Under the terms of the European Human Rights Convention, the court hears cases brought by individuals, groups, or nations that involve suspected violations of human rights or basic freedoms. Initially the court had jurisdiction over fifteen nations, but the number of signatories of the convention has now increased to forty-one, including all of the current members of the European Union and those nations in the process of admission to the regional body. The most recent signatories to the convention include Russia, Ukraine, and Georgia. This gives the court jurisdiction over approximately 800 million people. The court hears cases only after there have been documented efforts at mediation or arbitration, and the decisions of the court are final with no right of appeal. Since the Human Rights Convention is recognized under international law, the authority of the court supersedes that of national courts. The court is located in Strasbourg, France, and its official languages are French and English, although cases may be heard in the language of the countries involved with prior permission of the court.

As new countries acceded to the Human Rights Convention, the caseload of the institutions of the convention increased dramatically. For instance, the number of cases before the court increased from 7 in 1981 to 52 by 1993 and 119 in 1997. Meanwhile, cases before the other institutions increased from 404 in 1981 to 2,037 in 1993. The number of cases more than doubled to 4,750 by 1997. The institutions were unable to keep pace with the expansion of cases, and a variety of reform efforts were initiated. In 1998, Protocol 11 to the convention was ratified. The measure concentrated all of the judicial functions related to the convention in the hands of a reformed court and abolished the Commission of Human Rights.

The new court commenced operations on November 1, 1998. Under the reforms, the number of justices was tied to the total number of countries who were signatories to the convention (hence with forty-one nations, there are forty-one justices). The justices are elected for six-year terms by the Parliamentary Assembly of the Council of Europe. There are no restrictions or quotas on the number of justices from individual countries. The elections are staged so that every three years, half of the justices stand for election. There is mandatory retirement at age seventy.

Justices are not supposed to represent their respective countries and may not hold official office outside of the court. Members of the court elect a president, two vice presidents, and two presidents for each section of the court. The court is divided into four sections based on geography and balanced in terms of gender. Justices are placed in sections for three-year terms. Within each section, there are committees that are made up of three justices chosen for one-year terms. The committees fulfill the functions that were formerly undertaken by the now-abolished commission and are given broad discretionary powers to decide which cases are appropriate for the court. Within each section, there are chambers of seven judges who actually hear individual cases. A section president presides over each case, and a representative judge from the nation involved sits as an ex officio member of the court. Decisions of the court are made on a majority basis, and judges may dismiss a case through a unanimous vote.

The court is overseen by a panel known as the Grand Chamber that is comprised of seventeen justices elected for three-year terms. The Grand Chamber includes the presidents and vice presidents of the sections. Additional judges are formed into two groups, based on geography, that rotate every nine months to ensure that the different legal traditions of Europe are equally represented. The Grand Chamber has a variety of powers. For instance, it can decide whether hearings are public or closed. In addition, the sections may ask the Grand Chamber to take over cases that exceed their capability or authority. The Grand Chamber also functions as a constitutional court for the Human Rights Convention and hears cases that concern the interpretation of the convention.

See also European Human Rights Convention; European Union and Affirmative Action; Great Britain and Affirmative Action.

FURTHER READING: Clements, L.J., 1994, *European Human Rights: Taking a Case under the Convention*, London: Sweet and Maxwell; Forsythe, David P., ed., 1994, *Human Rights in the New Europe: Problems and Progress*, Lincoln: University of Nebraska Press; Merrills, J.G., 1988, *The Development of International Law by the European Court of Human Rights*, New York: St. Martin's Press.

TOM LANSFORD

European Human Rights Convention

The European Human Rights Convention, formally known as European Convention for the Protection of Human Rights and Fundamental Freedoms, is designed to ensure a variety of individual, fundamental human rights for European citizens. It was signed on November 4, 1950, by fifteen nations in the aftermath of World War II and represents a commitment on the part of Western Europe's democracies to promote and ensure civil liberties. The convention allows Europeans to bring violations of rights before the various judicial bodies of the European Union. The agreement also forms the basis for efforts to guarantee equal pay and working conditions. Many of the more significant efforts to establish affirmative action programs within the European Union have been based on the Human Rights Convention.

The European Human Rights Convention was developed to assure that the democratic nations of Western Europe had policies in place that matched those basic rights called for by the 1948 United Nations Universal Declaration of Human

Rights. The Council of Europe was the driving force behind the creation of the convention. The agreement came into force on September 3, 1953. The adoption of the convention was one of a number of steps by the Western European states that culminated in the formation of the European Community (now known as the European Union).

Several nations that adopted the convention had to undertake reforms to their legal codes to ensure compliance between their domestic laws and the guaranteed freedoms of the convention. This has ensured a degree of equality throughout the individual nations of Western Europe that was very important as national borders became less important and citizens were granted greater freedom of movement throughout the region. Ascension to the convention is now seen as a first step toward joining the European Union. The agreement has now been signed by forty-one nations.

To oversee the implementation of the convention and to respond to complaints about violations, three structures were created. The first was the European Commission of Human Rights, which was established in 1954 and tasked to deal with broad investigations. Its membership consisted of representatives from nations that have signed the convention, and the commission had jurisdiction to investigate charges within the domestic borders of countries that have acceded to the convention. However, the commission was abolished in 1998. The second body was the European Court of Human Rights, which was created in 1959. The court is the judicial body that responds to complaints and violations of the agreement. Under the terms of the convention, individuals, groups, or states may bring complaints of violations before the court. The court that hears a case is made up of seven members, plus an ex officio justice from the nation involved in the case. The court has a broader array of cases since the abolishment of the commission in 1998. Finally, the Committee of Ministers of the Council of Europe was developed to address policy and implementation issues. The committee is composed of government representatives from the states that have signed the convention.

The original document had a preamble and sixty-six articles that covered a range of areas including individual liberties and the mechanisms for redress in case of violation of the convention's articles. The preamble affirms the signatory nations' "profound belief in those Fundamental Freedoms which are the foundation of justice and peace in the world" and declares that the convention represents the "first steps" in a broader effort to enforce the provisions of the United Nations Universal Declaration of Human Rights.

The convention itself contains a number of specific rights. Among the basic rights contained in the convention are broad assurances such as the right to life, to liberty and security, to marry, to a fair and just trial, and to privacy. Sweeping freedoms are also guaranteed, including the freedom of expression, of association and assembly, and of religion. There are also specific prohibitions against torture, slavery and forced labor, discrimination, and punishment without due process of law. Cases may be brought before the court only after mediation or arbitration fails. In addition, the convention also declares that decisions of the Human Rights Court are final.

The convention has been supplemented through the years by a succession of agreements known as protocols. Eleven such protocols have been adopted since the original ratification, and these have greatly expanded the scope of the basic rights. For instance, the first protocol added protections for private property, education, and the right to free elections using secret ballots. Other important protocols included Protocol 4, which granted people freedom of movement throughout the region, and Protocol 6, which abolished the death penalty. In addition, Protocol 7 called for equality between spouses, and Protocol 9 gave individuals the right to bring cases before the Human Rights Court.

Many of the more significant efforts to establish affirmative action programs within the European Union have been based on the Human Rights Convention. The agreement has the weight of international law and is perceived as being an effective means of spreading fundamental freedoms and rights. Its prohibitions against discrimination and its provision for the equality of spouses have been utilized by Europeans to challenge overtly prejudiced policies. However, the broad nature of most of the freedoms has also inspired many Europeans to call for more detailed protections through the development of a new human rights document.

The European Human Rights Convention faced increased criticism during the 1990s and the early 2000s. This criticism centered on the fact that the European Union itself was not a signatory to the convention (even though all of its individual members were members). As the European Union expanded, there was increasing pressure to develop its own human rights convention that would be more specific and cover more areas than the 1950 convention. Among the specific criticisms against the original convention are that it is outdated and that it lacks specific guarantees that would foster the development of affirmative action programs based on race and gender. This leaves individual nations free to develop their own programs, often with very mixed or limited results. While many European leaders called for simply amending the convention, the European Union decided in June 1999 to draft a new Charter on Human Rights that would supplement and enhance, rather than replace, the existing convention. As of January 2004, this new charter was still being debated within the European Union.

See also European Court of Human Rights; European Union and Affirmative Action; Great Britain and Affirmative Action.

FURTHER READING: Gomien, Donna, 1991, *Short Guide to the European Convention on Human Rights*, Strasbourg: Council of Europe; Jacobs, Francis G., and Robin C.A. White, 1996, *The European Convention on Human Rights*, New York: Oxford University Press; Merrills, J.G., 1988, *The Development of International Law by the European Court of Human Rights*, New York: St. Martin's Press; Robertson, A.H., and J.G. Merrills, 1993, *Human Rights in Europe: A Study of the European Convention on Human Rights*, New York: St. Martin's Press.

TOM LANSFORD

European Union and Affirmative Action

After many years of debate, the European Union (EU) began to actively promote affirmative action programs in the late 1990s. Within the EU, the practice of affirmative action is known as "positive action" or "positive discrimination." In implementing affirmative action within the EU, individual nations have considerable latitude to develop and implement their own social programs, but as the supranational organization has gained political power, there has been a corresponding effort to promote uniformity among the social programs of the member states. As some of the member states within the EU have passed domestic "positive action" legislation giving one group a preference over another, the European Court of Justice has gotten involved as well. The European Court of Justice has analyzed the legality of affirmative action programs within the EU context in two landmark cases, *Kalanke v. Freie Hansestadt Bremen*, 1995 E.C.R. I-3051 (1995), and *Marschall v. Land Nordrhein-Westfalen*, 1 C.M.L.R. 547 (1997). Unlike the United States, the primary focus of affirmative action programs in the European Union until the 2000s has been on improving women's economic opportunities and lifestyles rather than assisting ethnic or racial minorities, the latter of which is the primary focus of affirmative action programs in the United States.

The EU is a supranational entity that currently consists of fifteen nation-states in Western Europe (Austria, Belgium, Denmark, Finland, France, Germany, Greece, Ireland, Italy, Luxembourg, the Netherlands, Portugal, Spain, Sweden, and the United Kingdom). As a result of the recent Treaty of Nice, EU membership will expand from the current fifteen members to twenty-five members in May 2004. The new member states joining in 2004 will include Poland, Hungary, the Czech Republic, Cyprus, Lithuania, Slovenia, Estonia, Latvia, Slovakia, and Malta, while Romania and Bulgaria are expected to join later in the decade. Under the legal doctrine of *acquis communautaire*, all new members of the EU are said to automatically accept all of the preexisting case law and legislation of the EU that predated that country's membership in the EU. Hence EU laws or cases dealing with affirmative action, or "positive discrimination," are binding on these new members of the EU, just as they are on the older members of the EU.

The EU had its genesis shortly after World War II when Winston Churchill, in his famous Zurich speech of 1946, called for a "United States of Europe." The original composition of the EU can be traced back to 1951 (the Treaty of Paris) and the European Coal and Steel Community. However, the EU gained much of its present structure in 1957 when the European Economic Community was created by the Treaty of Rome. Since 1957, several landmark treaties have further refined the structure and institutions of the EU, namely, the Single European Act of 1987, the Treaty on European Union (Maastricht Treaty) of 1993, the Treaty of Amsterdam in 1997, and the Treaty of Nice in 2002. The Treaty of Maastricht enhanced the powers of the organization and changed its name to the European Union. The EU is a supranational organization with broad powers and is based upon the principle of three pillars. The first pillar is comprised of economic and political issues, while the second deals with all matters related to security and foreign affairs. Finally, the third pillar encompasses the fields of social justice and home affairs. Only the first pillar is subject to binding legislation by the EU and oversight from the EU's judicial bodies. The second and third pillars are based upon intergovernmental cooperation between the member states, and nations have the ability to opt out of decisions and programs in these areas.

The Council of Ministers serves as the executive of the EU and is comprised of an equal number of representatives from each member. The council is led by a presidency that rotates from nation to nation every six months. The European Commission is the main legislative body in the EU. It consists of twenty members who initiate and oversee legislation affecting the EU and supervise the organization's bureaucracy. Meanwhile, the 626-member European Parliament, despite its name, serves essentially as an advisory body for the commission and the council.

Legal matters and interpretation of the main texts and treaties of the EU are the responsibility of the European Court of Justice. The main bodies within the EU were structured so that individual nations retain significant sovereignty over both foreign and domestic policy. As a result, efforts to develop affirmative action programs in individual nations and at the level of the EU have only attained success since the late 1990s.

Affirmative action programs within the European Union exist at two levels. Many nations have adopted legislation and enacted individual programs to aid specific groups. Concurrently, the EU has slowly developed a framework for affirmative action at the supranational level. The EU's affirmative action programs have evolved from two significant treaties that form the core of the EU's social policy. The first is the European Human Rights Convention, signed in 1950. All member states of the EU are signatories to the convention, which requires states to prohibit discrimination and ensure basic human rights. The convention also established the European Court of Human Rights to oversee its implementation and adherence. The second major treaty is the Rome Treaty of 1957, which established the European Economic Community, the forerunner of the EU. While the European Convention on Human Rights contained broad protections for citizens, the Rome Treaty contained specific prohibitions against discrimination. For instance, Article 119 of the treaty mandates equal pay for equal work for men and women in the same occupation. In an effort to implement Article 119 of the Treaty of Rome at the nation-state level, the EU Council promulgated a directive in 1976 (Council Directive No. 76/207, 1976 O.J. [L 39] 0). This 1976 directive reaffirmed that countries shall not discriminate on the basis of gender; however, Article 2 of the directive further noted that the directive "shall be without prejudice to measures to promote equal opportunity for men and women."

Antidiscrimination measures seemed to be strengthened through subsequent treaties and agreements within the EU. The European Social Charter (1961) and the European Community Charter of the Fundamental Social Rights of Workers (1989) called for broad expansion of protections against discrimination toward women and ethnic and religious minorities, but both agreements only established general principles for the EU and were not legally binding on individual nation-states. In addition, for most of the history of the EU, the Council of Ministers and the commission were reluctant to enact broad affirmative action programs on their own and preferred to leave the issue to member states, as the Council did with its 1976 directive mentioned earlier.

Furthermore, until 1997, the European Court of Justice routinely struck down national initiatives that gave preferential treatment to women or ethnic groups in areas such as hiring and promotion. For example, in 1995, in *Kalanke v. Freie Hansestadt Bremen*, the European Court of Justice invalidated a local German law (in Bremen) that gave a preference to women to help them obtain governmental appointments and promotions. The local Bremen law at issue attempted to give a gender preference in two contexts: first, if a male and female candidate were tied for certain positions, gender would be the tie-breaking factor (in favor of women); and second, if a given salary bracket was composed of fewer females than one-half of the total employees in the bracket, then if a position came open (through a new hire or promotion) in that given salary bracket, the position should be awarded to the female. A male employee contested this law in the

German court system, in essence claiming that it unfairly reversely discriminated against him on account of his gender. The plaintiff claimed that such reverse discrimination was a violation of the EU laws guaranteeing equal treatment and prohibiting discrimination on account of gender. The German court, as national courts are required to do when faced with a challenge to EU laws, referred the question to the European Court of Justice for interpreting whether the local law conflicted with the EU laws on this topic. The European Court of Justice held the local law to be a violation of EU discrimination laws, stating that the local Bremen law impermissibly went "beyond promoting equal opportunities" and tried to create actual "equal representation" in certain positions, rather than just trying to achieve "equality of opportunity" (which would have been permissible under EU law).

In November 1997, in another case from Germany, *Marschall v. Land Nordrhein-Westfalen*, the European Court of Justice again analyzed the legality of local "affirmative action" laws in the context of EU law. The local German law being challenged in the *Marschall* case was similar to that challenged two years earlier in the *Kalanke* case. The local law at issue in the *Marschall* case employed a gender tie-breaking preference for certain civil service jobs in the event male and female candidates were "tied" for the position. However, the court ultimately upheld the law because the law (unlike the law at issue in the *Kalanke* case) contained a clause saying that the gender preference was not absolute, and that a male applicant could still win the position if other factors "tilted the balance in his favor." According to the European Court of Justice, as the law in essence allowed the local decision-making authorities to use gender as a factor to be considered, but not a conclusive factor, the local law was valid under EU antidiscrimination laws.

Thus the European Court of Justice overturned decades of precedent and ruled that national governments could give preference to the recruitment and promotion of women over men in government services, so long as there was not a concrete quota or preference, but rather, gender was a factor to be considered. This ruling has been compared to the famous *Regents of the University of California v. Bakke*, 438 U.S. 265 (1978), opinion of Justice Lewis Powell, in which he stated that race could be considered as one factor among many. Justice Ruth Bader Ginsburg, in a law review article she authored with law professor Deborah Jones Merritt, has commented on this comparison as follows:

> The judgment in the *Marschall* case bears more than a little kinship to Justice Powell's controlling opinion in the *Bakke* case. Both opinions stress the need for individualized decision making and the infirmity of automatic preferences. Under *Bakke* and *Marschall*, race and sex may constitute plus factors favoring employment, promotion, or admission to an educational institution, but the preference may not be absolute and unyielding. (Ginsburg and Merritt 1999, 279)

Thus while gender may be used as a "plus factor" under EU law (according to the *Marschall* court), the court also declared that using gender quotas in employment remained illegal.

The court's decision reflected growing sentiment and political precedent within the EU that affirmative action was a legitimate tool to encourage diversity and ensure equality. Indeed, this sentiment is based upon actual gender inequities in employment. For example, within the EU in 2000, average unemployment among males was 9.3 percent, but it was 12.6 among females. In addition, women earned only approximately 79 percent of the salary of men in comparable occupations, despite long-standing laws on gender income equity. Article 13 of the Maastricht Treaty reinforced the ability of the EU to enact programs and initiatives to combat racism and genderism. The treaty specifically gave the EU the ability to "take appropriate action to combat discrimination based on sex, racial or ethnic origin, religion or belief, disability, age or sexual orientation." Furthermore, the original equal pay provision of the Treaty of Rome (Article 119) in 1957 was amended by the Treaty of Amsterdam in 1997 to reflect that "the principle of equal treatment shall not prevent any member state from maintaining or adopting measures providing for specific advantages to make it easier for the under-represented sex to pursue a vocational activity or to prevent or compensate for disadvantages in professional careers." Last, the EU designated 1995 as the European Year against Racism and undertook a variety of conferences and public programs both to highlight the presence of racism within the EU and to develop the means to combat it.

One of the features of the Rome Treaty was that it allowed for the free movement of labor within the area of the organization. As a result, citizens of one nation have the right to move anywhere within the EU. This has led to substantial internal immigration and has increased the number of racial, ethnic, and religious minorities within the EU. For instance, once an immigrant gains permission to enter any nation within the EU, he or she then can move freely within the member states. This system was complicated by the legacy of colonialism that caused large numbers of minorities to relocate to their former colonial powers following independence. Hence countries such as Belgium, France, the Netherlands, and the United Kingdom have large immigrant populations (in some cases as much as 10 percent of the general population). In many instances, these groups face a variety of forms of discrimination and have unemployment and poverty rates that are twice the national average. Poverty and the lack of economic opportunity are particularly prevalent among minority groups in France and Germany. The circumstances of these minority groups are complicated by citizenship laws. Most European nations, prominently including Germany, base citizenship upon ethnic background. Ethnic Germans gain automatic citizenship; however, foreign workers, even those who have been in the country for generations, are unable to become German citizens.

In 1998, the EU European Commission sought to expand affirmative action programs to include more minority groups and called for each member state to draw up a plan of action for increasing minority and immigrant economic opportunities, including the development of affirmative action programs. These plans were included in a revised European Employment Strategy that used monies from the EU's Social Fund to support affirmative action and other programs to aid women and minority groups. Countries are required to monitor companies' efforts to improve diversity and to report to the commission every two years on their progress. To oversee compliance, the EU established the European Monitoring Center on Racism and Xenophobia, headquartered in Vienna, in 1997.

On a philosophical level, the EU has embraced a concept of affirmative or "positive" action that is designed around rewards for compliance rather than severe punishments for noncompliance. Among the types of programs that the EU encourages are governmental procurement policies that reward companies that initiate affirmative action or diversity management procedures. Similarly, companies that lack such programs may lose government contracts to their competitors with more highly developed policies to promote gender or minority equality. As a result, states such as the United Kingdom developed a variety of "positive" action initiatives. In the case of the United Kingdom, initiatives included directives to increase the hiring and promotion of Catholics in Northern Ireland or immigrant populations from South Asia in other areas of Great Britain. Another example of positive action programs is special vocational or advanced job training for women and minority groups.

Within the EU, there is a widespread perception that by emphasizing the "carrot" rather than the "stick" in regard to affirmative action, much of the backlash that has occurred in the United States can be avoided. The EU is also reluctant to develop substantial affirmative action programs at the supranational level out of concern that national governments would resist these policies or simply negotiate an "opt-out." The need for consensus in the decision-making procedures further underscores such sentiments. Nonetheless, the EU recognized the need for avenues for individuals or groups to file grievances against specific employers and specific national governments. Therefore, outside organizations and individuals are allowed to file suit before the European Court of Justice and the European Court of Human Rights on behalf of parties. In addition, under the terms of the EU's Race Directive, the burden of proof in discrimination cases rests with the employer, who must prove that acts or actions were not undertaken for discriminatory reasons.

In areas related to education, the EU has also embraced the use of incentives rather than mandatory quotas as a means to improve equality of opportunity. For example, many nations provide additional tutoring or special classes (including bilingual education) to bolster the skills of minority or immigrant students. Furthermore, a variety of institutions of higher learning have also adopted gender and minority admissions set-asides so that a guaranteed number of new enrollments come from disadvantaged groups. Educational opportunities are particularly limited for minority groups in the top universities and colleges in the EU. On average, racial and ethnic minorities comprise only about 3 percent of the students at the premier institutions within the EU.

Affirmative action programs in the EU have met with far greater success in political areas. The use of such initiatives to expand the role of women in politics has been particularly productive. Individual nations within the EU have used quotas to dramatically increase the number of women in political office. These quotas exist at two levels. First, several nations have enacted legislation that guarantees that a certain number of legislative seats are reserved for women. As a result, countries such as Belgium and Finland increased their number of female legislators by 50 percent. Concurrently, in Denmark in 1985, an act was passed that required all public committees and government agencies to be gender balanced. Second, within most EU states, political parties have adopted internal regulations that establish specific quota targets for female candidates. Hence the German Social Democratic Party requires that at least 33 percent of its candidates and 40 percent of party officials be female, while Sweden's four largest political parties require that 50 percent of their candidates be female (a figure matched by various parties in other EU states, including Austria and the United Kingdom).

See also Affirmative Action Plan/Program; European Court of Human Rights; European Human Rights Convention; Ginsburg, Ruth Bader; Great Britain and Affirmative Action; Powell, Lewis Franklin, Jr.; Quotas.

FURTHER READING: Bellamy, Richard, and Alex Warleigh, eds., 2001, *Citizenship and Governance in the European Union,* New York: Continuum; Bright, Christopher, 1995, *The EU: Understanding the Brussels Process,* New York: John Wiley; Forsythe, David P., ed., 1994, *Human Rights in the New Europe: Problems and Progress,* Lincoln: University of Nebraska Press; Ginsburg, Ruth Bader, and Deborah Jones Merritt, 1999, "Affirmative Action: An International Human Rights Dialogue," *Cardozo Law Review* 21 (October): 253–282; Hervey, Tamara, and David O'Keeffe, eds., 1996, *Sex Equality Law in the European Union,* Chichester: John Wiley; Papademetriou, Demetrios G., 1996, *Coming Together or Pulling Apart? The European Union's Struggle with Immigration and Asylum,* Washington, DC: Carnegie Endowment for International Peace; Rossilli, Mariagrazia, ed., 2000, *Gender Policies in the European Union,* New York: Peter Lang.

TOM LANSFORD

Executive Order 8802

Executive Order 8802 was issued by President Franklin D. Roosevelt on June 25, 1941, to expand the economy of World War II to African American workers. It was through the efforts of A. Philip Randolph, organizer and head of the Brotherhood of Sleeping Car Porters, and his colleagues that President Roosevelt issued Executive Order 8802. Executive Order 8802 is formally titled "Reaffirming Policy of Full Participation in the Defense Program by All Persons, Regardless of Race, Creed, or National Origin, and Directing Certain Action in Furtherance of Said Policy." It declared "that there shall be no discrimination in the employment of workers in defense industries or government because of race, creed, color, or national origin . . . to provide for the full and equitable participation of all workers in defense industries, without discrimination because of race, creed, color, or national origin." The order also established a Committee on Fair Employment Practices, whose purpose was to "receive and investigate complaints of discrimination" in violation of it.

Before the United States entered World War II, blacks were discriminated against in both the armed services and the defense industry. Blacks were considered inferior to whites and had to serve under white officers. When African Americans attempted to get jobs through the various defense industries, they were often turned away at the door. During a 1940 convention of the Brotherhood of Sleeping Car Porters, the members drew up a resolution to call upon the president, Congress, and other governmental departments to cease discrimination in the armed services. Eleanor Roosevelt, who was also attending the convention, urged her husband, the president, to meet with Randolph, Walter White, head of the National Association for the Advancement of Colored People (NAACP), T. Arnold Hill of the Urban League, and service secretaries to discuss the rights of blacks. During the meeting, Randolph, White, and Hill presented a memo to the president "calling for the immediate end to segregation in the armed services and in defense industries."

No action was taken on the memo. Instead, the White House issued a statement that the "policy [in the armed services] is not to intermingle colored and white enlisted personnel in the same regimental organization." The statement implied that Randolph, White, and Hill supported this policy. The three demanded a clarification statement that was late in coming. Randolph became upset over the matter. On a speaking tour throughout Georgia and Florida, Randolph stated that he was going to organize a march on Washington, composed of 10,000 people. Many people were enthusiastic about the march and supported Randolph. The numbers for the march grew. It was estimated that about 100,000 black people would participate in the march on Washington, scheduled for July 1, 1941. Roosevelt was growing nervous over the proposed march and even asked Eleanor to talk to Randolph on his behalf.

At the urging of his advisors, Roosevelt called another meeting, which was attended by Randolph and White. Randolph complained that blacks were still being turned away at the gates of the defense industries and urged Roosevelt to do something about this. Roosevelt said that he would let the heads of the industries know to hire blacks. Randolph disagreed and asked Roosevelt to issue an executive order making it mandatory to hire blacks. Roosevelt replied, "You call off this march of yours." Randolph refused. After consulting with his advisors, Roosevelt decided to issue the order that became the predecessor of state and federal antidiscrimination laws. Randolph canceled the march.

Six months later, America entered World War II. Many blacks became involved in the war effort. More than 1 million were drafted. By the end of the war, approximately 12 percent of federal workers were black. The order did not end discrimination, but discrimination in government jobs and specifically in the defense industry was greatly reduced.

See also African Americans; Brotherhood of Sleeping Car Porters; National Association for the Advancement of Colored People; Randolph, Asa Philip; Roosevelt, Eleanor; Roosevelt, Franklin Delano.

FURTHER READING: Hollaway, Kevin, 1997, "WW II and Executive Order 8802," Civil Rights Status Report, website: www.ghgcorp.com/hollaway/civil/civil27.htm; Davis, Kenneth S., 2000, *FDR: The War President, 1940–1943: A History*, New York: Random House; Equal Employment Opportunity Commission, web site: www.eeoc.gov ("Executive Order 8802").

NAOMI ROBERTSON

Executive Order 10925

Executive Order 10925, issued by President John F. Kennedy on March 6, 1961, included the first official modern use of the term "affirmative action." The order forbade any contractors with the federal government to discriminate against their employees and mandated that "the contractor will take affirmative action to ensure that applicants are employed, and that employees are treated during employment, without regard to their race, creed, color, or national origin."

In the preamble to Executive Order 10925, President Kennedy outlined six main justifications for the issuance of the order: First, discrimination because of race, creed, color, or national origin is contrary to the constitutional principles and policies of the United States. Second, it is the plain and positive obligation of the government to promote and ensure equal opportunity for all qualified persons seeking employment with the federal government and on government contracts. Third, it is the policy of the executive branch to encourage by positive measures equal opportunity for all qualified persons within the government. Fourth, it is in the general interest and welfare of the United States to promote its economy, security, and national defense through the most efficient and effective utilizing of all available manpower. Fifth, a review and analysis of existing executive orders, practices, and government agency procedures reveal an urgent need for expansion and strengthening of efforts to promote full equality of employment opportunity. Finally, a single governmental committee should be charged with responsibility for accomplishing all these objectives.

The order was the first to monitor compliance and outline penalties for non-compliance. The order also established the President's Committee on Equal Employment Opportunity, chaired by the vice president, to monitor and report on whether federal contracts were meeting the decree of the order and to "consider and recommend additional affirmative steps which should be taken by executive departments and agencies to realize more fully the national policy of nondiscrimination." All executive departments and agencies were directed to initiate studies of current contractor employment practices. Each contractor was required to place a statement of nondiscrimination in all employment solicitations and advertisements and "permit access to his books, records, and accounts by the contracting agency and the Committee for the purpose of investigation to ascertain compliance." Further, "in the event of the contractor's non-compliance with the nondiscrimination clause," the contractor might be "declared ineligible for further government contracts," with sanctions and remedies imposed as deemed appropriate by the committee. Criminal charges would be imposed by the Department of Justice against any contractor providing false information. The order was eventually superseded by Executive Order 11246, issued in 1965 by President Lyndon B. Johnson, which further outlined procedures for federal contractors to meet requirements to ensure employment equality without regard to race, religion, or national origin.

See also Department of Justice; Executive Order 11246; Johnson, Lyndon Baines; Kennedy, John Fitzgerald; President's Committee on Equal Employment Opportunity.

FURTHER READING: Drake, W. Avon, and Robert D. Holsworth, 1996, *Affirmative Action and the Stalled Quest for Black Progress*, Urbana: University of Illinois Press; EEOC, "Executive Order 10925," web page: http://www.eeoc.gov; Weiss, Robert J., 1997, *We Want Jobs: A History of Affirmative Action*, New York: Garland Publishing.

GLENN L. STARKS

Executive Order 11246

Executive Order 11246 (E.O. 11246) is the fountainhead from which all modern affirmative action requirements flow. Issued by President Lyndon Johnson on September 24, 1965, E.O. 11246 prohibits employment discrimination based on race, color, religion, or national origin by executive branch agencies and federal contractors and subcontractors. This executive order, which superseded President

John F. Kennedy's Executive Order 10925, remains in the center of the debate regarding affirmative action and the use of preferences in hiring decisions. President Johnson's E.O. 11246 basically reiterated much of Kennedy's E.O. 10925, but expanded its coverage and added more stringent enforcement and reporting mechanisms for violations of the order. President Johnson subsequently amended E.O. 11246 on October 13, 1967, to prohibit discrimination on the basis of sex. E.O. 11246 has also been amended to call for affirmative action programs for the handicapped, the disabled, and Vietnam-era veterans.

E.O. 11246 requires federal contractors and subcontractors to "take affirmative action to ensure that applicants are employed, and that employees are treated during employment, without regard to their race, color, religion, sex or national origin." This requirement has been broadly interpreted to mean that contractors must increase qualified minority and female employment in jobs where their numbers fall below what the labor-market statistics indicate are available, even where no unlawful discrimination may have occurred. The order also prohibits discriminating against any employee or applicant for employment on account of race, color, religion, sex, or national origin.

The order is divided into four parts. Part I requires nondiscrimination in government employment. Part II addresses nondiscrimination in employment by government contractors and subcontractors. Part III requires nondiscrimination provisions in federally assisted construction contracts. Part IV addresses miscellaneous matters.

Part II contains the most extensive provisions regarding affirmative action, itself being divided into five subparts. Subpart A delegates administration of the order to the secretary of labor. Subpart B specifies the nondiscrimination provisions that must be contained in all government contracts (section 202); specifies the requirements for and contents of compliance reports to be provided by contractors/subcontractors to the secretary of labor (section 203); and allows the secretary of labor to exempt a contracting agency from complying with all or part(s) of section 202 under certain circumstances (section 204). Subpart C sets forth the powers and duties of the secretary of labor and contracting agencies, including the requirement that each contracting agency cooperate with the secretary of labor and appoint a compliance officer (section 205); the power of the secretary of labor to initiate investigations of a contractor or subcontractor's employment practices and to receive and investigate complaints by employees or prospective employees of a contractor or subcontractor who allege discrimination contrary to the contractual provisions of section 202 (section 206); the power of the secretary of labor to encourage labor unions overseeing apprenticeship or training programs to comply with the purposes of the order and to report any potential violations of Title VII of the Civil Rights Act of 1964 to the appropriate enforcement agency (section 207); and the power of the secretary of labor to hold hearings for compliance, enforcement, and educational purposes and the requirement of a hearing before a contractor may be debarred. Subpart D sets forth the sanctions and penalties available to the secretary of labor to enforce the order, including, in part, suspension or cancellation of existing contracts and/or debarment from participating in future government contracts. Subpart E addresses the issuance, suspension, and revocation of certificates of merit.

See also Civil Rights Act of 1964; Contracting and Affirmative Action; Department of Labor; Executive Order 10925; Johnson, Lyndon Baines; Kennedy, John Fitzgerald; Title VII of the Civil Rights Act of 1964.

FURTHER READING: Crosby, Faye J., and Cheryl VanDeVeer, eds., 2000, *Sex, Race, and Merit*, Ann Arbor: University of Michigan Press; EEOC, "Executive Order 11246," web site: www.eeoc.gov; Executive Order 11246, September 28, 1965, 30 *Federal Register* 12315.

RICHARD J. BENNETT

Executive Order 11375

Executive Order 11375, issued on October 13, 1967, amended President Lyndon Johnson's Executive Order 11246, which had promoted the notion of affirmative action in federal employment. Executive Order 11246, in turn, was an expansion of President John F. Kennedy's famous Executive Order 10925, ordering that federal agencies take "affirmative action" in ensuring that minorities are recruited and hired by federal contractors. Johnson's Executive Order 11375 amended Executive Order 11246 to ensure that the equal employment opportunity (EEO) programs expressly prevent discrimination on the basis of gender, in addition to the bases of race, color, creed, and national origin.

Executive Order 11375 incorporates the following provisions as enshrined in Executive Order 11246 and expands them to gender as well: first, there shall be no discrimination in federal employment because of race, creed, color, gender, or national origin; second, the federal government shall promote the full realization of equal employment opportunity through a positive, continuing program in each executive department and agency; third, the head of each executive department and agency shall establish and maintain a positive program of equal employment opportunity for all civilian employees and applicants for employment; fourth, the Civil Service Commission shall supervise and provide leadership and guidance in the conduct of equal employment opportunity programs for the civilian employees of and applicants for employment within the executive departments and agencies and shall review agency program accomplishments periodically; fifth, the Civil Service Commission shall provide for the prompt, fair, and impartial consideration of all complaints of discrimination in federal employment on the basis of race, creed, color, gender, or national origin; sixth, the Civil Service Commission shall issue such regulations, orders, and instructions as it deems necessary and appropriate to carry out its responsibilities under Executive Order 11375.

Furthermore, both Executive Order 11375 and Executive Order 11246 before it mandated that federal contractors not discriminate against any employee or applicant for employment because of race, creed, color, gender, or national origin. The executive orders famously commanded that

> the contractor will take affirmative action to ensure that applicants are employed and that employees are treated during employment, without regard to their race, creed, color, gender, or national origin. Such action shall include, but not be limited to the following: employment, upgrading, demotion, or transfer; recruitment or recruitment advertising; layoff or termination; rates of pay or other forms of compensation and selection for training, including apprenticeship. The contractor agrees to post in conspicuous places, available to employees and applicants for employment, notices to

> be provided by the contracting officer setting forth the provision of this discrimination clause.

In the charged atmosphere of the 1960s, with civil rights issues occupying prime attention for the Johnson administration, Executive Order 11375 was heralded as another triumph in the war against inequality and discrimination and as an extension of civil rights legislation of the era. A direct result of Executive Order 11375 was the formation of Federally Employed Women (FEW), a private organization, to make sure that Executive Order 11375 was being implemented in its entirety at all levels—national, regional, and local. As part of the coalitional strategy, FEW activists also tapped into the resources of other distinct minorities such as blacks, Asian-Pacific Americans, American Indians, Alaskan Natives, or persons with disabilities to promote the employment, development, and advancement of all the underrepresented groups in American society.

See also Equal Employment Opportunity Commission; Executive Order 11246; Johnson, Lyndon Baines; Kennedy, John Fitzgerald.

FURTHER READING: Clark, Kenneth B., 1967, *Dark Ghetto: Dilemmas of Social Power*, New York: Harper; Dickerson, Debra J., 2000, *An American Story*, New York: Pantheon; D'Souza, Dinesh, 1991, *Illiberal Education: The Politics of Race and Sex on Campus*, New York: Free Press.

MOHAMMED B. ALAM

Executive Order 11478

Executive Order 11478 was established on August 8, 1969, under the Nixon administration. The order mandated equal employment opportunities in the federal government and originally prohibited "discrimination in employment because of race, color, religion, sex, national origin, handicap, or age." The order was later amended to expand protection to cover discrimination based on sexual orientation or status as a parent. Each executive department agency was ordered to "establish and maintain an affirmative program of equal employment opportunity for all civilian employees and applicants," provide supporting resources, utilize and enhance the skills of all employees, provide managers and employees training on the order, and ensure participation in cooperative efforts internal and external to the agency. The executive order also covered "those portions of the legislative and judicial branches of the Federal Government and of the Government of the District of Columbia having positions in the competitive service" and the U.S. Postal Service and Postal Rate Commission.

The Equal Employment Opportunity Commission was given the responsibility for directing and furthering the implementation of this policy, and the authority to issue "rules, regulations, orders, and instructions and request such information from the affected departments and agencies as it deems necessary and appropriate to carry out its responsibilities under this Order." The Office of Personnel Management was further authorized by the Clinton administration in May 2000 to "develop guidance on the provisions of this order prohibiting discrimination on the basis of an individual's sexual orientation or status as a parent" (Equal Opportunity Directive 2000–17, June 2000). The amendments to the original order were mandated by Executive Order 11590, April 23, 1971, which expanded coverage to the U.S. Postal Service and to the Postal Rate Commission; Executive

Order 12106, December 28, 1978, which amended "or national origin" to "national origin, handicap, or age"; Executive Order 13087, May 28, 1998, which expanded coverage to include sexual orientation; and Executive Order 13152, May 2, 2000, which defined seven categories constituting "parent."

See also Employment (Public) and Affirmative Action; Equal Employment Opportunity Commission; Nixon, Richard Milhous.

FURTHER READING: U.S. National Archives and Records Administration, Office of the Federal Register, web site: http://www.archives.gov/federal_register/index.html.

GLENN L. STARKS

Executive Order 11598

See Vietnam Era Veterans' Readjustment Assistance Act of 1974.

Executive Order 12900

On February 22, 1994, at the White House, President William Jefferson Clinton signed Presidential Executive Order 12900. The order was subtitled "Educational Excellence for Hispanic Americans." The stated goal of this order was "to advance the development of human potential, to strengthen the Nation's capacity to provide high-quality education, and to increase opportunities for Hispanic Americans to participate in and benefit from Federal education programs." Executive Order 12900 illustrates the Clinton administration's dedication to the notion of affirmative action and assisting minority groups in excelling in higher education.

Executive Order 12900 established the President's Advisory Commission on Educational Excellence for Hispanic Americans in the Department of Education. The commission reported to the secretary of education. The commission was to consist of "representatives who: (a) have a history of involvement with the Hispanic community; (b) are from the education, civil rights, and business communities; or (c) are from civic associations representing the diversity within the Hispanic community" and was to provide advice to the president and the secretary on the following: (*a*) the progress of Hispanic Americans toward achievement of the National Education Goals and other standards of educational accomplishment; (*b*) the development, monitoring, and coordination of federal efforts to promote high-quality education for Hispanic Americans; (*c*) ways to increase state, private-sector, and community involvement in improving education; and (*d*) ways to expand and complement federal education initiatives.

This order also established the White House Initiative on Educational Excellence for Hispanic Americans in the Department of Education. The initiative was an interagency working group coordinated by the Department of Education to provide staff, resources, and assistance for the commission. The secretary, in consultation with the commission, submitted to the president an Annual Federal Plan to Promote Hispanic American Educational Excellence. The plan was designed to help Hispanic Americans attain the educational improvement targets set forth in the National Education Goals and any standards established by the National Education Standards and Improvement Council. The plan also included data on eligibility for, and participation by, Hispanic Americans in federal education programs, and such other aspects of the educational status of Hispanic Americans as the secretary considered appropriate. The Annual Federal Plan prepared a plan for and documented each executive department agency's effort to increase Hispanic American participation in federal education programs where Hispanic Americans currently are underserved and the agency's effort to improve educational outcomes for Hispanic Americans participating in federal education programs. This plan also addressed, among other relevant issues, (*a*) the elimination of unintended regulatory barriers to Hispanic American participation in federal programs; (*b*) the adequacy of announcements of program opportunities of interest to Hispanic-serving school districts, institutions of higher education, and agencies; and (*c*) ways of eliminating educational inequalities and disadvantages faced by Hispanic Americans. It also emphasized the facilitation of technical, planning, and development advice to Hispanic-serving school districts and institutions of higher education.

The agency's plan was to provide appropriate measurable objectives for proposed actions aimed at increasing Hispanic American participation in federal education programs where Hispanic Americans currently are underserved. After the first years, each executive department and agency's plan also assessed that agency's performance on the goals set in the previous year's annual plan. These plans were to be submitted by a date and time established by the secretary. The commission and the initiative were funded from the Department of Education. This order revoked Executive Order 12729, a more broadly worded executive order that stated that "agencies shall be actively involved in helping advance educational opportunities for Hispanic Americans." Executive Order 12900 was itself revoked in the early days of President George W. Bush's administration by Executive Order 13230. Executive Order 13230, effective October 12, 2001, rescinded the Clinton administration executive order and created a new body, the President's Advisory Commission on Educational Excellence for Hispanic Americans, which is to study and provide guidance to the administration on how best to accomplish academic achievement.

See also Bush, George W.; Clinton, William Jefferson; Department of Education; Hispanic Americans.

FURTHER READING: Executive Order 12900, http://www.haa.omhrc.gov/HAA2pg/executive.htm.

SEAN RICHEY

Executive Order 13005

Executive Order 13005, signed on May 21, 1996, by President Bill Clinton, called for empowerment contracting by mandating the development of "policies and procedures to ensure that agencies, to the extent permitted by law, grant qualified large businesses and qualified small businesses appropriate incentives to encourage business activity in areas of general economic distress, including a price or an evaluation credit, when assessing offers for government contracts in unrestricted competitions, where the incentives would promote the policy set forth in this order." The goal of the order was to promote economy and efficiency in federal procurement by securing broad-based competition for federal contracts. The order stated, "A great and largely untapped opportunity for expanding the pool of such contractors can be found in this Nation's economically distressed communities." This executive order represents efforts by the government to affirmatively encourage businesses in economically distressed areas.

The order's Empowerment Contracting Program called for the cooperative consultation of the secretaries of the Departments of Housing and Urban Development, Labor, and Defense, the administrator of the General Services Administration, the administrator of the National Aeronautics and Space Administration, the administrator of the Small Business Administration, and the administrator for federal procurement policy, the secretary of the Department of Commerce. The secretary of commerce was responsible for monitoring the implementation of the order, evaluating its effectiveness, and reporting its status to the president by December 1 of each year.

The order defined areas of general economic distress "for all urban and rural communities, as any census tract that has a poverty rate of at least 20 percent or any designated Federal Empowerment Zone, Supplemental Empowerment Zone, Enhanced Enterprise Community, or Enterprise Community." The secretary was given the authority to expand this definition to any rural or Indian reservation area based on its unemployment rate, degree of poverty, extent of out-migration, or rate of business formation and rate of business growth.

See also Clinton, William Jefferson; Contracting and Affirmative Action; Disadvantaged Business Enterprises; Economically Disadvantaged.

FURTHER READING: U.S. National Archives and Records Administration, Office of the Federal Register, 1996, web site: http://www.archives.gov/federal_register/index.html (61 F.R. 26069, May 24, 1996).

GLENN L. STARKS

Executive Order 13021

Executive Order 13021, which was issued by President William Jefferson Clinton on October 19, 1996, reaffirmed the unique relationship the U.S. government has with American Indians and natives of Alaska. The executive order was issued with six distinct educational purposes in mind, ranging from ensuring that tribal institutions have access to the same opportunities as other educational institutions to promoting the preservation of the languages and traditions of American Indians and Alaskan Natives. A presidential advisory committee was established within the Department of Education to advise on the steps taken in fulfillment of the objectives outlined in this executive order.

The advisory committee was named the President's Board of Advisors on Tribal Colleges and Universities. The board members, who were to total no more than fifteen, consisted primarily of representatives of various tribal colleges and universities. However, membership was not limited to these individuals. The board could encompass various members of the educational community at large, as well as individuals from businesses, financial institutions, and other private foundations. The board was to meet annually, providing advice to the chief executive and the secretary of education on how the tribal colleges and universities can strengthen institutional viability, improve financial management, develop institutional capacity, enhance infrastructure, and achieve the National Education Goals found in 20 U.S.C. § 5812.

By operation of this executive order, the president also provided for the creation of a White House Initiative on Tribal Colleges and Universities. The initiative, also part of the Department of Education, was given authorization to provide administrative support to the board. The initiative was to be the vehicle through which the board could utilize the resources of other federal, state, local, or tribal agencies to accomplish its goals.

In section 5 of this order, the president mandated the development of a five-year plan for each executive department and agency that participated in the program described in this executive order. The agencies and departments were required to collaborate with the tribal colleges and universities on how best to develop a plan for the most effective implementation of this order. The plans were to contain agency objectives and performance indicators. It was the intent of the president that these plans address the barriers that might impede a tribal college or university from accessing federal funding opportunities. Suggestions for elimination of these barriers were also to be included in the plan. According to the order, each agency should also discuss what technical assistance and program information the agency intended to make available to the tribal colleges or universities. Finally, each agency was required to outline its annual goal for the amount of funding that it would award to the tribally controlled universities.

The order gave the White House Initiative Office the duty of monitoring the degree of success each agency had in adhering to the goals contained within the five-year plans. It was to do so by analyzing the annual performance reports that each agency was required to submit to the Initiative Office. After initial analysis was done by the Initiative Office, it was required to generate one complete report and submit it to the secretary of education.

The order went on to instruct the White House Initiative Office to encourage assistance from various institutions in the private sector. The suggested means of assistance included fund matching, increasing training resources, and further development of finance management skills, information systems, and facilities. As time passed, Executive Order 13021 was amended several times. On July 3, 2002, President George W. Bush revoked Executive Order 13021 by operation of Executive Order 13270, a similar order dealing with tribal colleges and universities. Executive Order 13270, like Executive Order 13021, established a White House Initiative on Tribal Colleges and Universities and the President's Board of Advisors on Tribal Colleges and Universities. Executive Order 13270 also mandates that federal executive agencies work in concert with Alaska Native Communities to implement Bush's No Child Left Behind Act of 2001 (Public Law 107–110).

See also Alaskan Natives; Bush, George W.; Clinton, William Jefferson; Native Americans.

ADDITIONAL READING: Evergreen State College, 2002, Tribal Government Sources, Federal Agencies: Department of Education, July, http://www.evergreen.edu/library/govdocs/tribalgov/federal/education.html; Executive Order 13021, 1996, *Federal Register* 61, no. 206 (October 23): 54929–54932; Executive Order 13104, 1999, http://nodis3.gsfc.nasa.gov/library/eo_list.cfm?year=1998; Executive Order 13138, 1999, http://nodis3.gsfc.nasa.gov/library/eo_list.cfm?year=1999; Executive Order 13225, 2001, http://nodis3.gsfc.nasa.gov/library/eo_list.cfm?year=2001; Executive Order 13270, 2002, *Federal Register* 67, no. 130 (July 28): 45288–45291.

SCOTT S. BRENNEMAN

Executive Order 13145

Executive Order 13145, signed on February 8, 2000, by President Bill Clinton, prohibited discrimination in federal employment based on genetic information. Specifically, the order mandated that the "Equal Employment Opportunity Commission shall be responsible for coordinating the policy of the Government of the United States to prohibit discrimination against employees in Federal employment based on protected genetic information, or information about a request for or the receipt of genetic services." The order forbade genetic monitoring ("the periodic examination of employees to evaluate acquired modifications to their genetic material"), genetic services ("health services, including genetic tests, provided to obtain, assess, or interpret genetic information for diagnostic or therapeutic purposes, or for genetic education or counseling"), and genetic testing ("the analysis of human DNA, RNA, chromosomes, proteins, or certain metabolites to detect disease-related genotypes or mutations"). Both employees and their family members were protected.

Departments were prohibited from discharging, failing or refusing to hire, or refusing compensation, terms, conditions, or privileges of employment to employees; limiting, segregating, or classifying employees; requesting, requiring, collecting, or purchasing protected genetic information; and disclosing protected genetic information. Any acquired information "shall be treated as confidential medical records and kept separate from personnel files." Exceptions to this order include circumstances where the request is consistent with the Rehabilitation Act and other applicable law; the information is to be used exclusively to assess whether further medical evaluation is needed to diagnose a current disease or medical condition or disorder; such current disease or medical condition or disorder could prevent the applicant or employee from performing the essential functions of the position held or desired; the information will not be disclosed to persons other than medical personnel involved in or responsible for assessing whether further medical evaluation is needed to diagnose a current disease or medical condition or disorder; and the employee has provided prior, knowing, voluntary, and written authorization.

See also Clinton, William Jefferson; Equal Employment Opportunity Commission; Persons with Disabilities and Affirmative Action; Rehabilitation Act of 1973; Scientific Racism.

FURTHER READING: U.S. National Archives and Records Administration, Office of the Federal Register, http://www.archives.gov/federal_register/index.html.

GLENN L. STARKS

Executive Order 13163

Executive Order 13163, signed on July 26, 2000, by President Bill Clinton, was adopted to increase opportunities for individuals with disabilities in federal government employment, provide a "more level playing field," and support the goals articulated in section 501 of the Rehabilitation Act of 1973 (which prohibits employment discrimination against individuals with disabilities in the federal sector). Due to "qualified persons with disabilities being refused employment despite their availability and qualifications" and not being made aware of available employment opportunities, agencies were ordered to expand outreach programs to locate qualified disabled workers and to increase their efforts to accommodate individuals with disabilities. Further, "As a model employer, the Federal Government will take the lead in educating the public about employment opportunities available for individuals with disabilities."

Each federal agency was ordered to "prepare a plan to increase the opportunities for individuals with disabilities to be employed in the agency" and submit this plan to the Office of Personnel Management. The Office of Personnel Management was given the responsibility of developing "guidance on the provisions of this order to increase the opportunities for individuals with disabilities employed in the Federal Government."

See also Clinton, William Jefferson; Employment (Public) and Affirmative Action; Level Playing Field; Persons with Disabilities and Affirmative Action; Rehabilitation Act of 1973.

FURTHER READING: U.S. National Archives and Records Administration, Office of the Federal Register, http://www.archives.gov/federal_register/index.html (65 F.R. 46565, July 28, 2000), accessed January 2002.

GLENN L. STARKS

F

Fair Housing Amendments Act of 1988

The Fair Housing Amendments Act of 1988 (FaHAA) modifies and strengthens Title VIII of the Civil Rights Act of 1968, commonly known as the Fair Housing Act. The 1968 act outlaws discrimination in the sale or rental of housing on the basis of race, color, religion, or country of origin (on the basis of sex was added in 1974). The FaHAA added two new protected groups: disabled citizens and families with children under eighteen. It also created two new and tougher forms of enforcement by giving aggrieved parties and respondents the choice of having their case heard either by administrative law judges (ALJs) or by federal courts. The FaHAA also greatly expanded the potential penalties imposed on violators by removing the 1968 limit of $1,000 in punitive damages, allowing ALJs to impose compensatory damages, attorneys' fees, and civil penalties, and permitting federal courts to award punitive damages. These and other changes shifted the burden of enforcement away from victims of discrimination to the Department of Housing and Urban Development (HUD) and, by increasing the costs of discrimination, were designed to encourage respondents to settle quickly and correct discriminatory policies.

The 1968 act was extremely detailed in outlawing a number of discriminatory practices, such as bias in the provision of information, in decisions to sell or rent, or in mortgage loan applications or mortgage terms. Plaintiffs only needed to show that the actions had discriminatory effects, not the tougher burden of proving discriminatory intent. To pass the bill through the Senate, however, several compromises were required. Single-family homes and apartments in owner-occupied, small units were exempted. Punitive damages were limited to $1,000. The statute of limitations for complaints was set at only 180 days. Most crucially, the role of the federal government in enforcement was greatly curtailed. HUD could investigate charges and try to reach conciliation agreements, but legal action could only be brought through "pattern and practice suits" when there was systematic discrimination. Thus the burden of enforcement fell largely on the states, which often were not interested in aggressive enforcement, or on individuals who could bring federal suits.

In time, civil rights supporters and government officials concluded that the 1968 act's enforcement mechanisms were not strong enough to end discrimination or bring major federal action. These views were reinforced by several statistical studies in the 1980s that showed ongoing discrimination and by the Reagan administration's lack of interest in pursuing pattern and practice suits. In 1987, new legislation began the congressional process. At the committee level, members agreed to postpone debate on enforcement mechanisms, so most of the discussion centered on the idea of expanding coverage to the disabled and families with children. Some feared that adding new groups would take time and resources away from racial complaints. Others feared that including the disabled would require expensive building modifications and that adding family protection would jeopardize senior-citizen housing. These concerns led to several amendments. Before consideration on the floor, intense negotiations were held among congressmen, their staffs, representatives from HUD, civil rights lawyers, and the National Association of Realtors. The groups worked out a compromise amendment on enforcement that set up the ALJs, but also allowed the option of moving the case to federal court to avoid the problem of denying defendants the right to a jury trial. The amendment was accepted unanimously by the House, and after further debate on the coverage of new groups, the underlying bill passed easily in both houses of Congress. FaHAA was signed into law on September 13, 1988.

Under the FaHAA procedures, an aggrieved party must first go to state agencies, if the state has a law substantially equivalent to federal law. If state remedies are exhausted or not available, the case can be brought to HUD. Investigators determine whether there is "probable cause" to believe that discrimination occurred. If cause is found, HUD tries to reach an agreement with the respondent. If none is reached, the case is sent to an ALJ who hears the case under the Federal Rules of Evidence. The ALJ can order the discriminatory actions stopped and award damages of up to $50,000 for a repeat offender. Decisions by the ALJs are reviewed by the HUD administrator and can be appealed to the federal court of appeals. Before the ALJ begins, however, either the complainant or the respondent can elect to have the case sent to the Justice Department for prosecution in federal court. Electing to go to court assures a jury trial and opens the possibility of punitive damages, but can delay action due to the backlog of cases in the court system.

In addition to expanding those protected and changing the enforcement procedures, the FaHAA made several other changes. The statute of limitations was lengthened to two years for private suits and one year for complaints to HUD. The $1,000 limit on damages was repealed. The role of the HUD administrator in overseeing cases was expanded. HUD was also given the power to initiate complaints if evidence from audits or other types of investigation showed discriminatory patterns.

In the late 1990s, several scholars from the Center for Real Estate and Urban Policy at New York University School of Law were given extensive access to HUD files and computer records so that they could assess implementation of FaHAA. These scholars found that on average, HUD receives about 10,000 complaints per year. In every year between 1989 and 1997, the top three categories of complaints dealt with race, disability, and family status, with race being the most common category. Many assumed that states would continue to receive most of the complaints, but HUD, in fact, received the majority. This trend has shifted over time as more states have adopted laws patterned on federal law. Interestingly, between 1989 and 1997, less than 3 percent of cases were found to have cause. This number hides the fact that 37 percent of cases were settled with agreements at this stage, but the rest were either found to lack cause or were rejected on various technical grounds. In 65 percent of the 1,408 cases with cause, one or more parties, usually the respondent, elected to have their case heard in federal court. During proceedings of either the ALJs or the courts, HUD continued to pursue agreements, and almost 80 percent of the cases were settled before a ruling. Altogether, that meant that ALJs ruled on only ninety-two cases and the federal courts on twenty-nine cases in a decade. Complainants won a majority of both kinds of cases, but their winning percentage was much higher in cases decided by ALJs. On the other hand, complainants on average won larger monetary rewards in either settlements or judgments when the case moved to the court system. The new procedures do seem to have encouraged respondents to settle, which greatly speeds the process and reduces court costs, but the law's effect in limiting housing discrimination is harder to measure.

See also Civil Rights Act of 1968; Department of Housing and Urban Development; Department of Justice; Housing; Housing and Urban Development Act of 1968; Lending Practices and Affirmative Action; Reagan, Ronald.

FURTHER READING: Kushner, James A. 1989, "The Fair Housing Amendments Act of 1988: The Second Generation of Fair Housing," *Vanderbilt Law Review* 42:1049–1120; Schill, Michael H., and Samantha Friedman, 1999, "The Fair Housing Amendments Act of 1988: The First Decade," *Cityscape: A Journal of Policy Development and Research* 4:57–78; Yinger, John, 1995, *Closed Doors, Opportunities Lost: The Continuing Cost of Housing Discrimination*, New York: Russell Sage Foundation.

JOHN W. DIETRICH

Fair-Race Metaphor

See Level Playing Field.

Farmer, James (1920–1999)

James Farmer was a notable civil rights activist and a founder of the Congress of Racial Equality. Later in his career, Farmer joined the Nixon administration, serving as assistant secretary of health, education, and welfare (which is now the Department of Education and the Department of Health and Human Services). Farmer described Nixon as "the strongest president on affirmative action—up to that point" in time. As one of Nixon's liberal advisors, Farmer helped to frame Nixon's position on civil rights.

James Farmer was born on January 12, 1920, in Marshall, Texas. Farmer, a brilliant student, graduated from Wiley College (1938) and Howard University (1941). Equipped with a college education, Farmer was now ready to participate actively in the struggle for racial equality. Accordingly, Farmer and several Chris-

James Farmer, national director of the Congress of Racial Equality (CORE), leads a demonstration at the New York World's Fair in 1964. Courtesy of Library of Congress.

tian pacifists founded the Congress on Racial Equality (CORE) in 1942. The aim of the organization was to apply nonviolent direct challenges to American racism in line with Mahatma Gandhi's tactics against British colonial rule in India. Farmer's dislike for violence, which in itself was informed by his religious beliefs, made him refuse to enlist in the U.S. Army during World War II. His first activity in civil rights protests came in 1947 when he participated in CORE's campaign of sit-ins to end Chicago restaurants' discriminatory practices against blacks. By his forty-first birthday, and as director of CORE, Farmer brought his charisma to work when he led a group of thirteen freedom riders (eleven men and two women), black and white, in 1961. They left Washington, D.C., planning to challenge segregation practices along the way to New Orleans, Louisiana. In Rock Hill, South Carolina, the freedom riders were attacked by whites. Throughout the Deep South, thousands of civil rights supporters were jailed, including James Farmer.

In 1966, Farmer resigned his position as CORE's national director to direct a national adult literacy project. He ran for Congress in 1968, but failed. In recognition of his contribution to the struggle for equality as well as his support for the Republican Party, however, Farmer was appointed assistant secretary of health, education, and welfare by President Richard Nixon. After leaving this post in 1971, he worked for the Council on Minority Planning and Strategy, an African American think tank. Farmer taught at Mary Washington College in Virginia for some time and wrote his autobiography, titled *Lay Bare the Heart* (1985). In 1998, Farmer was awarded the Congressional Medal of Freedom. The civil rights activist died on July 9, 1999.

See also Civil Rights Movement; Congress of Racial Equality; Freedom Riders; Nixon, Richard Milhous.

FURTHER READING: Franklin, John Hope, and Isidore Starr, 1967, *The Negro in Twentieth Century America: A Reader on the Struggle for Civil Rights*, New York: Vintage Books; Gordon, Irving L., 1980, *American Studies: A Conceptual Approach*, New York: Amsco School Publications; Spartacus, 2001, "James Farmer," http://www.spartacus.schoolnet.co.uk/USAfarmerJ.htm.

PAUL OBIYO MBANASO NJEMANZE

Farrakhan, Louis (1933–)

A controversial figure, Louis Farrakhan has been labeled by his critics as a racist and demagogue and by his supporters as a civil rights leader. Farrakhan is the current leader of the Nation of Islam, a religious movement comprised primarily of African Americans based on the tenets of Islam and the doctrines of the late Elijah Muhammad, who was the founder of the Nation of Islam. Farrakhan is on record as opposing affirmative action plans. In a series of speeches in 1995, Farrakhan remarked that "we must stop depending on others to do for us what we could, what we should, and what we must do for ourselves." In addition to being opposed to affirmative action, Farrakhan is also opposed to the integration of blacks in society and preaches separation for blacks.

Often described as a spellbinding speaker and charismatic figure, Louis Farrakhan is not without critics. Throughout his leadership of the Nation of Islam, he has been accused of hating Jewish and white people, largely as a result of his own incendiary comments. He has called Judaism "a gutter religion," Adolf Hitler "a great man," and nonblack merchants who operate in black neighborhoods "bloodsuckers." On the other hand, some in the African American community view him as a role model. His neat, clean-cut appearance, eloquent speeches, advocacy of a drug-free society, belief in moral fidelity, and urging blacks to support blacks resonate strongly among many followers and nonfollowers of the Nation of Islam. In 1995, Farrakhan organized the Million Man March, which brought nearly 1 million black men to Washington, D.C., on October 16, 1995, to rededicate themselves to their families and the community. This was an impressive, peaceful affair that attracted international attention and acclaim.

The Nation of Islam under Louis Farrakhan recruits actively in jails, prisons, and other correctional institutions. Inmates are recruited while incarcerated, and when they leave, a support system is already there for them through the Nation of Islam. It urges blacks to establish black-owned and operated businesses and not depend on government subsidies. The group owns thousands of acres of land and property. It also operates numerous restaurants, bakeries, clothing stores, bookstores, hair-care shops, and other enterprises. Its bean pies are known far and wide. It has also been very successful in providing building security at apartments and housing projects. The federal government, through the Department of Housing and Urban Development, has given more than $20 million to the Nation of Islam to provide this service in such cities as Washington, D.C., Baltimore, and Philadelphia.

Farrakhan was born on May 11, 1933, and was given the name Louis Eugene

Walcott. He grew up with his mother, a native of St. Kitts, and a brother, Alvin, in Roxbury, Massachusetts. Artistic talent was discovered in Louis before his sixth birthday. By his fourteenth birthday, he had played his violin in the Boston College Orchestra and the Boston Civic Symphony and had won the competition on the *Ted Mack Amateur Hour*, a national television show. Even today, he is an accomplished string musician.

Farrakhan completed high school by the time he was sixteen years old. After high school, he headed south to attend Winston-Salem State University (then called Winston-Salem Teachers College) in Winston-Salem, North Carolina, on a track scholarship. In 1953, before graduating, he married his childhood sweetheart and left college. Back in Boston, he began to perform as a calypso singer. He was known variously as "the charmer" or "Calypso Gene." His career appeared to be promising. However, his friend Malcolm X asked him to attend a Muslim convention in Chicago, where the Honorable Elijah Muhammad was speaking. Shortly afterwards, he joined the Nation of Islam. First, he changed his name to Louis X, then to Abdul Haleem Farrakhan, and eventually to the name he currently bears, Louis Farrakhan. His speaking, organizational, and singing talents helped him progress through the ranks of the Nation of Islam. He had to give up his public performing and devote himself to the Nation of Islam. After entering the Nation of Islam as a member of the New York Mosque, he displayed discipline and dedication. Soon he was sent to Boston, where he built up the temple there to one of the strongest in the nation. He was considered by many inside the organization to be a rising star in the movement.

While Farrakhan and Malcolm X had been friends, when Malcolm broke away from Elijah Muhammad, the friendship ended. In fact, there are persistent allegations that Farrakhan was responsible for Malcolm's murder. Although it is undisputed that Farrakhan was not in the ballroom when Malcolm X was murdered, rumors persist that Farrakhan was involved in the planning of the murder. Later, Farrakhan admitted to helping create the atmosphere that led to the assassination of Malcolm X. In 1978, Farrakhan split with the World Community of Islam, which Elijah Muhammad's son Wallace renamed the religious group after his father's death. Farrakhan named his group the Nation of Islam. In 1993, Farrakhan broke with a tradition of refusing to participate in electoral politics. He registered to vote and campaigned for the Reverend Jesse Jackson in the U.S. presidential race. Additionally, after the Million Man March in 1995, Farrakhan embarked on three worldwide friendship tours that included visits to many predominantly Muslim nations. He, like Malcolm X before him, was welcomed by leaders of the faith in places he visited.

Millions have attended his lectures, and his organization continues to grow. Farrakhan has established mosques and study groups in more than eighty cities in America and Great Britain and a mission in Ghana. Farrakhan, the father of nine, grandfather of twenty-three, and great-grandfather of four, continues to exert vigorous leadership of the Nation of Islam. Together they continue to recruit youth gang members, prison inmates, college-educated youth, and some from the African American middle class.

See also Department of Housing and Urban Development; Integration; Malcolm X; Racial Discrimination; Segregation.

FURTHER READING: Farrakhan, Louis, 1972, *Seven Speeches by Louis Farrakhan*, Chicago: WKU and the Final Call; Farrakhan, Louis, 1993, *A Torchlight for America*, Chicago: FCN Publishing Co.; Lincoln, C. Eric, 1994, *The Black Muslims in America*, 3d ed., Grand Rapids, MI: William B. Eerdmans; Megida, Arthur J., 1996, *Prophet of Rage: A Life of Farrakhan and His Nation*, New York: Basic Books.

BETTY NYANGONI

Federal Communications Commission

The Federal Communications Commission (FCC) is a federal agency that reports to Congress. It was established pursuant to the Communications Act of 1934, which is the principal law governing broadcasting in the United States. According to the U.S. Code, the FCC is responsible for regulating interstate and international communications by radio, television, wire, satellite, and cable and ensuring that broadcasting serves the "public convenience, interest, or necessity." Through its broadcast licensing authority, the FCC has implemented affirmative action policies designed to promote diversity in programming and reflect the viewpoints of minorities and women.

The FCC is directed by five commissioners appointed by the president and confirmed by the Senate. Commissioners serve five-year terms, except when filling an unexpired term. Only three commissioners may be members of the same political party, and none can have a financial interest in any commission-related business. The FCC has six operating bureaus and ten offices that provide support services. Together, the bureaus develop and implement regulations, process applications, analyze complaints, conduct investigations, take part in hearings, and the like.

The Communications Act establishes the parameters of the FCC's authority and responsibility. Therefore, the FCC's authority is limited to areas in which the act specifically empowers it to act. The act does give the FCC the authority to implement and enforce rules and regulations for administering the act. Challenges to FCC decisions must follow an internal administrative process. If the dispute is not resolved after the administrative process is exhausted, the challenging party may appeal the matter to a federal circuit court of appeals.

As a federal agency, the FCC took steps to further the government's opposition to employment discrimination by establishing formal equal employment opportunity (EEO) regulations in the late 1960s. In the case of broadcast stations, the FCC evaluates compliance with its EEO regulations, as amended over the years, when making license renewal decisions during the license renewal process. With the Communications Policy Act of 1984, Congress amended the Communications Act of 1934 and granted the FCC authority to oversee affirmative action efforts of cable companies as well. Over the years the FCC has modified its EEO and affirmative action position and has implemented policies designed to promote diversity in programming and reflect the viewpoints of minorities and women. At times, the propriety and constitutionality of such policies have been challenged.

For example, two minority preference programs specifically designed to increase ownership of broadcast and other spectra by minorities and women were challenged, but were upheld by the Supreme Court in *Metro Broadcasting, Inc. v. FCC*, 497 U.S. 547 (1990). The Court used an intermediate level of scrutiny to find the policies constitutional. Specifically, the Court found that the policies served "the important governmental objective of broadcast diversity" and were "substantially related to the achievement of that objective." However, in *Adarand Constructors, Inc. v. Peña*, 515 U.S. 200 (1995), the Supreme Court ruled that government affirmative action programs must be assessed using a strict scrutiny analysis. This test requires that federal and state affirmative action programs, to be constitutional, must serve a compelling governmental interest and use narrowly tailored means to serve that interest. Although this case did not deal with an FCC affirmative action policy, the Court specifically overruled the intermediate standard of review it had applied in the *Metro Broadcasting* case five years earlier.

This important issue was raised again when the FCC's EEO program regulations pertaining to hiring at broadcast stations were challenged. In *Lutheran Church–Missouri Synod v. FCC*, 154 F.3d 487 (D.C. Cir. 1998), the Court of Appeals for the District of Columbia determined that the government's asserted goal of "diversity of programming" was not a compelling interest sufficient to withstand strict scrutiny. The court, therefore, ruled that the FCC's EEO rules at issue in *Lutheran Church* were unconstitutional. A more recent EEO rule adopted by the FCC for broadcast and cable subsequent to the *Lutheran Church* case also was found to be unconstitutional by the District of Columbia Court of Appeals (*DC/MD/DE Broadcasters Association v. FCC*, 253 F.3d 732 [D.C. Cir. 2001]), which held that a portion of the outreach requirements of the broadcast EEO rule adopted in 2000 did not survive strict scrutiny. In light of the *Lutheran Church* and *Broadcasters Association* decisions, the propriety of the FCC's affirmative action and EEO policies is unclear. The FCC recently drafted new EEO rules in an effort to find a legitimate basis to support its EEO and affirmative action rules within the scope of its authority.

See also Adarand Constructors, Inc. v. Peña; First Amendment; Licensing and Affirmative Action; *Lutheran Church–Missouri Synod v. FCC*; Media and Affirmative Action; *Metro Broadcasting, Inc. v. FCC*; *Red Lion Broadcasting Co. v. FCC.*

FURTHER READING: Federal Communications Commission, web site: http://www.fcc.gov; Tedford, Thomas L., and Dale A. Herbeck, 2001, *Freedom of Speech in the United States*, 4th ed., State College, PA: Strata Publishing; Zuckman, Harvey L., Martin J. Gaynes, T. Barton Carter, and Juliet Lushbough Dee, 2000, *Mass Communications Law in a Nutshell*, 5th ed., St. Paul: West Publishing Co.

PAUL M. HARIDAKIS

Federalism

Federalism is the constitutional division of power between a central government and its subnational governments and deals with the proper balance of powers in the American federal system. In the United States, the central government is known as the federal or national government, and the subnational governments are called states. Both derive their powers from a common source, the Constitution. The term "federal" also refers to the system of government that consists of the states and the national government. As a consequence of federalism, affirmative action–type legislation might exist at both the state and federal levels. Under the concept of federalism, the federal government is able to pass laws and programs relating to the states so long as the legislation relates to one of the federal government's enumerated constitutional powers. For example, the Civil Rights Act of 1964, which was passed pursuant to Congress's enumerated power to regulate interstate commerce among the states, prohibits discrimination in places of public accommodation. Likewise, in the area of affirmative action and civil rights, the last provision in each of the three Civil War (Reconstruction) Amendments (the Thirteenth, Fourteenth, and Fifteenth Amendments) has an authorization/enforcement clause that specifies that Congress shall have authority to pass implementing legislation under each of the three amendments. Federal lawmaking powers in the areas of social programs and law enforcement often are controversial and a source of friction to adherents of the states' rights doctrine (that states under the Tenth Amendment should have the power to legislate for the general welfare and to exercise their police power, and the federal government should be limited to its expressly enumerated powers).

Nowhere in the Constitution is the word "*federal*" mentioned. During the Constitutional Convention, the Federalists and Anti-Federalists argued over the form of government that should exist, whether the power should rest with the states or with the national government. As a compromise, federalism was created. The division of powers is the key element of federalism. The national government exercises enumerated or delegated powers, implied powers that are "necessary and proper" to carry out the enumerated powers, and inherent powers. All other powers are "reserved" to the states under the Tenth Amendment, except concurrent powers that are shared by both the national and state governments. Additionally, certain prohibited powers are denied both to the states and the national government.

The alternatives to federalism are a unitary system and a confederation. In a unitary system, the constitution vests all of its powers in the central government. The subnational governments have only those powers granted to them by the national or central government. In other words, the national government grants the subnational governments powers and can also take them away. Great Britain is an example of a unitary system. A confederation is basically a league of friendship in which the national government possesses only those powers that have been granted to it by the subnational governments. There has been a confederation in this country on two occasions, under the Articles of Confederation from 1781 to 1789 and when the Southern states seceded from the Union to form a new government, thus precipitating the American Civil War.

In the United States, there are 87,000 different governmental units, consisting of the states, counties, municipalities, special districts, and school districts. Most of these have their own taxing authority and the authority to represent a certain public entity. Many of these governmental entities have overlapping jurisdictions that cause conflict and confusion. Local governments are not mentioned in the Constitution, but are "creatures of the states." Their autonomy is limited, and their authority is clearly and strictly interpreted. The term "intergovernmental relations" is often used to refer to the relationships that exist between the thousands of governmental entities in the United States.

The Supremacy Clause of the Constitution (Article VI, Clause 2) states that the "Constitution and the Law of the United States" shall be the "supreme Law of the Land." In other words, the U.S. Constitution and federal laws supersede those of the states. Consequently, legitimate national action supersedes conflicting state action. The supremacy of the national government was validated in the case of *McCulloch v. Maryland*, 17 U.S. (4 Wheat.) 316 (1819). Based on the Supremacy Clause, national legislation preempts conflicting state or local laws in areas in which they exercise concurrent powers.

The relationship between the states and the national government has been largely adversarial. Federalism has gone through various periods or eras. The early period of federalism was known as dual federalism, in which the federal and state governments exercised powers in distinct policy areas. The national government primarily exercised its powers in the areas of national defense and foreign affairs. The state governments exercised power for the general welfare and security of individuals within the state. Cooperative federalism began in the 1930s with the implementation of President Franklin D. Roosevelt's New Deal program, which needed the cooperation of the several governments to pull the country out of the depression. This period also marked the real beginning of national supremacy. President Lyndon B. Johnson's Great Society legislation and War on Poverty marked a period of creative federalism. This involved providing grants not only to states and local governments for Johnson's antipoverty programs, but also to community and citizen groups.

Beginning with the New Deal era, the size of the federal government expanded. Many Americans thought that the federal government had grown too large and was getting involved in policy areas that should be left up to the states. During the 1970s and 1980s, the Nixon and Reagan administrations attempted to turn more power back to the states. This period of new federalism gave the states more power over how they could spend federal government funds. The idea of returning more power to the states is known as the devolution revolution.

The provision of federal grants to states and local governments is another way in which the federal government exercises control over state and local governments today. Categorical grants are favored most by the federal government as a means of controlling state action through fiscal assistance. Because of the stringent requirements of categorical grants, state governments prefer block grants because they give the states and local governments more autonomy over spending in a particular policy area. One of the most controversial issues between the states and the federal government is that of federal mandates, especially unfunded mandates. Those who oppose federal preemption argue that whosoever proposes a policy should also implement and pay for it. Those who favor preemption believe that the states should pay their fair share, thus creating a level playing field among the states.

See also Articles of Confederation; Bill of Rights; Civil Rights Act of 1964; Constitution, Civil Rights, and Equality; Johnson, Lyndon Baines; Nixon, Richard Milhous; Roosevelt, Franklin Delano.

FURTHER READING: Anton, Thomas J., 1989, *American Federalism and Public Policy: How the System Works*, New York: Random House; Peterson, Paul E., 1995, *The Price of Federalism*, Washington, DC: Brookings Institution; Walker, David, 1995, *The Rebirth of Federalism*, Chatham, NJ: Chatham House; Wright, Deil S., 1988, *Understanding Intergovernmental Relations*, Monterey, CA: Brooks/Cole.

NAOMI ROBERTSON

The Feminine Mystique

The book *The Feminine Mystique*, written by Betty Friedan and published in 1963, is regarded as the catalyst that sparked the second wave of the women's movement in America. The first wave, which was focused on suffrage issues during the nineteenth and early twentieth centuries, ended for all intents and purposes with the passage of the Nineteenth Amendment in 1920. The second wave began in the United States with the publication of this landmark text. While earlier work was being accomplished on issues of women's equality and women's liberation (for example, in France, Simone de Beauvoir was writing extensively on the plight of women in modern societies and publishing her classic text, *The Second Sex*), nothing significant or widely popular had stirred within the United States.

The genesis of *The Feminine Mystique* was Betty Friedan's dissatisfaction at her home life. Betty Goldstein married Carl Friedan, with whom she had three children. (They divorced in 1969.) Friedan, a graduate of Smith College in 1942, found herself at home with three small children. When she experienced great disparity between the life she lived and the current image of the American woman as portrayed by the media, she began to wonder if other women were experiencing the same feelings of dissatisfaction and contradictions that were present in her life. To answer this question, Friedan administered an intensive questionnaire to her college classmates in 1957, fifteen years after their graduation.

Friedan coined the term "the feminine mystique," which embodied the image of the American woman as portrayed in society since World War II. In addition to her questionnaires, Friedan, to further research this mystique, conducted in-depth interviews with editors of women's magazines, advertising motivational researchers, and theoretical experts on women in such disciplines as psychology, psychoanalysis, anthropology, sociology, and family life education. She also conducted a life-course analysis of eighty women, with participants in three major life-phase categories that she described as follows:

> high school and college girls facing or evading the question of who they were; young housewives and mothers for whom, if the mystique were right, there should be no such question and who thus had no name for the problem troubling them; and women who faced a jumping-off point at forty. These women, some tortured, some serene, gave me the final clues, and the most damning indictment of the feminine mystique. (Friedan 1963, 8)

As her first chapter in *The Feminine Mystique* is titled, Friedan began her book by discussing "The Problem That Has No Name." In it, she noted that while current societal messages praised most highly the woman who delighted in her femininity, housewives isolated in the gender roles of suburbia were asking themselves, "Is this all?" Yet they were unable to name or relate to others their hidden discontents. Friedan noted that by the 1950s, the average marriage age for women had dropped to twenty, with 14 million girls engaged by age seventeen. At the time of Friedan's writing, the proportion of women attending college had also dropped, from 47 percent in 1920 to 35 percent in 1958. She stated,

> A century earlier, women had fought for higher education; now girls went to college to get a husband. By the mid-fifties, 60 percent dropped out of college to marry, or

> because they were afraid too much education would be a marriage bar. (Friedan 1963, 12)

For the first time, Friedan explored the question of why American women who had achieved the "full feminine ideal" were dreadfully unhappy in their roles. She labeled and examined the expectations that women were to find both their identity and their happiness through the lives of their husbands and children, rather than through their own personal growth and development. Friedan's writings hit a nerve among women throughout the nation in the early 1960s, and *The Feminine Mystique* flew off the shelves at the paperback cost of seventy-five cents a book. Its publisher, W.W. Norton, had limited its first printing to 2,000 copies. The demand was totally unexpected, and it soon reached best-seller status. Within ten years, the book had sold 3 million hard-cover copies and many more in paperback.

In her book, Friedan covered topics of housework, gender roles, female identity crisis, sexuality, discrimination, confinement, institutional sexism, women helping women break barriers, the "forfeited self," and plans for a new image of women. Her writings, which accurately depicted the American woman, also provided an inspirational glimmer of hope for a more equitable world:

> And when women do not need to live through their husbands and children, men will not fear the love and strength of women, nor need another's weakness to prove their own masculinity. They can finally see each other as they are. And this may be the next step in human evolution. . . . But the time is at hand when the voices of the feminine mystique can no longer drown out the inner voice that is driving women on to become complete. (Friedan 1963, 363–364)

The women's liberation movement of the twentieth century was ignited by this book. Friedan went on to cocreate the National Organization for Women (NOW) in 1966 and was a founding member of the National Women's Political Caucus in 1971. She is the author of other books, including *The Second Stage* (1981), which examined the status of the women's movement, *It Changed My Life: Writings on the Women's Movement* (1991), *The Fountain of Age* (1993), a breakthrough text for feminist gerontology, *Beyond Gender: The New Politics of Work and Family* (1997), and her memoir, *Life So Far* (2000). She has traveled and lectured around the world and has been a visiting distinguished professor at the University of Southern California, New York University, and George Mason University. She is currently an adjunct scholar at the Wilson International Center for Scholars at the Smithsonian and Distinguished Professor of Social Evolution at Mount Vernon College.

See also Gender Norms; Gender Segregation in Employment; National Organization for Women; Nineteenth Amendment; Sex Discrimination; Stereotypes, Gender; Suffrage Movement.

FURTHER READING: Friedan, Betty, 1963, *The Feminine Mystique*, New York: W.W. Norton; Hymowitz, Carol, and Michaele Weissman, 1978, *A History of Women in America*, New York: Bantam Books; Lunardini, Christine, 1994, *What Every American Should Know about Women's History*, Holbrook, MA: Bob Adams.

SHEILA BLUHM

Feminist Majority and Feminist Majority Foundation

The Feminist Majority and the Feminist Majority Foundation are organizations dedicated to advancing general equality and are supportive of affirmative action programs as a means of promoting gender and racial equality. Peg Yorkin, Eleanor Smeal, Katherine Spillar, Toni Carabillo, and Judith Meuli founded the Feminist Majority Foundation in 1987. The organization got its name as the result of a *Newsweek*/Gallup Public Opinion Poll that reported that "the majority (56 percent) of women in the United States self identified as feminists."

The mission of the Feminist Majority Foundation is to "develop bold, new strategies and programs to advance women's equality, non-violence, and economic development and most importantly, empower women and girls in all sectors of society." There is a strong focus on cultivating leadership skills of young feminists and addressing issues surrounding reproductive rights. As an active advocacy organization for women's rights, the group engages in research and public policy development, public education programs, grassroots organizing projects, and leadership-training and development programs, as well as participating in organizing forums on a wide range of women's issues.

Formally known as the Fund for the Feminist Majority, the Feminist Majority is the sister organization to the Feminist Majority Foundation. It engages in lobbying and other direct political action. It is deeply involved in promoting gender balance in elective and appointive offices. It is located in the Washington, D.C., suburb of Arlington, Virginia, with an office in Los Angeles, California. As articulated in the founding documents of the organization, the principles of the Feminist Majority and the Feminist Majority Foundation clearly support the concept of equality, equal access, and affirmative action. Three of the principles that illustrate these commitments are as follows: first, the Feminist Majority Foundation promotes equality between women and men and girls and boys and supports constitutional and statutory measures to gain full equality locally, statewide, nationally, and globally; second, the Feminist Majority Foundation is dedicated to achieving affirmative action programs for women and people of color; and third, the Feminist Majority Foundation does not permit discrimination on the basis of sex, race, sexual orientation, socioeconomic status, religion, ethnicity, age, marital status, national origin, or disability.

In 2002, *Ms. Magazine*, which was cofounded in 1972 by feminist activist Gloria Steinem, was transferred to the Feminist Majority Foundation. This and a number of other regular publications, such as reports, occasional papers, newsletters, and press releases, assure a high-profile status for the organization and those issues that it supports. Some of the most publicized projects and involvements of the Feminist Majority since it was founded are as follows: the Campaign for RU-486 (now known as mifepristone) and Contraceptive Research, which would make this contraceptive available to American women; the Campaign to Stop Gender Apartheid in Afghanistan, which addressed human rights for women in that country; the campaign to "Get Out the Vote," which is an initiative tasked with registering and mobilizing voters; the Campaign to Stop Violence against Women, which was launched to bring awareness about and to prevent violence against women and girls; and finally, the National Clinic Defense Project, which was launched to protect abortion clinics from violence and assaults. In 1991, the Feminist Majority Foundation was the recipient of the largest financial donation for women's rights. Peg Yorkin, chair and cofounder of the organization, announced the $10-million donation.

See also Gender-Based Affirmative Action; National Organization for Women; Suffrage Movement.

FURTHER READING: Farmer, Rebecca, 2003, "Feminist Majority Foundation, Ms. Magazine Join Forces," http://www.now.org/nnt/special-2001/msmagazine.html; Feminist. Org, 2003, web site: http://www.feminist.org; Nevergoback.Org, 2003, web site: http://www.nevergoback.org.

BETTY NYANGONI

Fifteenth Amendment

The Fifteenth Amendment established an affirmative right to vote that also eventually would lay the foundation for affirmative action for African Americans and other minority classes through voting rights and enfranchisement. The Fifteenth Amendment was enacted by the Fortieth U.S. Congress in December 1868 and was ratified in February 1870. The Fifteenth Amendment states, "The right of citizens of the United States to vote shall not be denied or abridged by the United States or by any State on account of race, color, or previous condition of servitude." The amendment also provides that Congress shall have power to enforce the amendment by appropriate legislation.

The Fifteenth Amendment was the result of the commitment of Radical Republicans to the full acquisition of citizenship by African Americans. The issue of African American male suffrage was a central component of Reconstruction. The Radical Republicans suggested that as citizens, African Americans were entitled to the right to vote. Hence the right to vote as guaranteed by the Fifteenth Amendment provided a mechanism whereby African American males could protect their civil rights. This amendment was the last of the three Civil War (Reconstruction) Amendments (the Thirteenth and Fourteenth Amendments are the other two). The adoption of the Fifteenth Amendment's grant of suffrage to African American males was viewed as a grant of equal citizenship. The Fifteenth Amendment was a watershed landmark in the history of the right to vote and democracy in the United States. The right to vote as granted by the Fifteenth Amendment was essential if African Americans were to have the ability to participate in governmental processes and thereby become a viable part of the decision-making process. The guarantees of the Fifteenth Amendment carried an expectation by its drafters that it would provide African Americans with a means of protecting themselves from violence by participating in the political process.

The legislative objective of the Fifteenth Amendment was to safeguard the rights of African Americans against the adherents of white supremacy. Therefore, the wording of the amendment provides that the guarantee of the right to vote cannot be abridged by the United States or any state on account of race or previous condition of servitude. The Fifteenth Amendment also became a political safeguard for Republicans, who benefited from the votes of newly freed slaves. Adoption or ratification of the Fourteenth and Fifteenth Amendments also became prerequisites for the readmission of those states that had previously withdrawn from the Union. Republican support for the amendment was a political maneuver to regain control of the South.

However, in part to ensure adoption, the amendment allowed the states to determine their own voting criteria. The Fifteenth Amendment simply provided that states could not deny citizens the right to vote based on race, color, or previous condition of servitude. Thus the Fifteenth Amendment had the effect of opening polls for northern African Americans, but it provided only a brief period of protection for southern African Americans. The broad wording of the Fifteenth Amendment permitted states to utilize means other than race or previous condition of servitude to limit the right to vote, including the adoption of literacy tests, poll taxes, and property requirements for voting. The wording of the Fifteenth Amendment also allowed southern Democrats the opportunity to implement procedures to negate the effectiveness of the amendment with such practices as the use of white primaries (excluding all but white candidates in primary elections). These tactics were also supported by the violent actions of the Ku Klux Klan, Night Riders, and other white supremacy groups. Due to the broad wording of the Fifteenth Amendment, a significant number of African Americans were disenfranchised by southern states, especially through the usage of the literacy test and the poll tax.

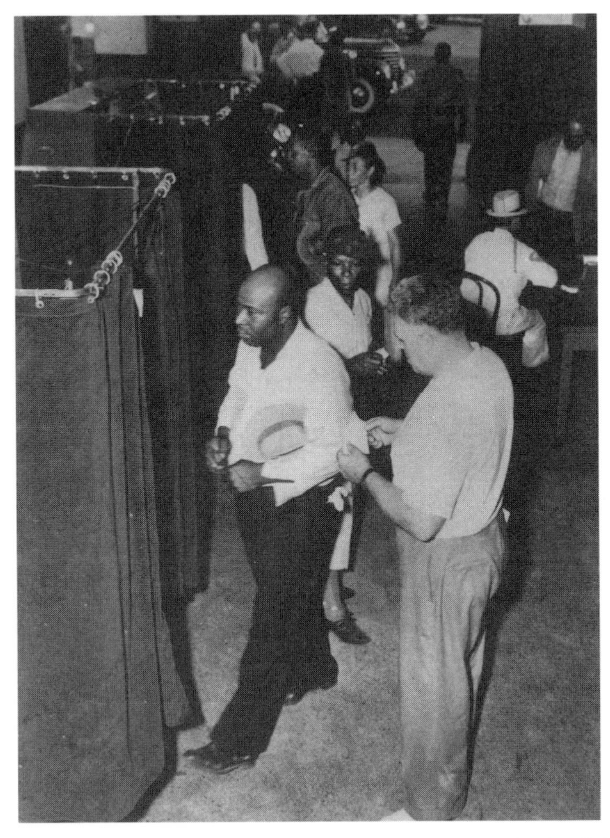

Voters exercise the right to vote, which may not be constitutionally deprived from citizens on account of race since the ratification of the Fifteenth Amendment in 1870. Courtesy of Library of Congress.

Several practices were adopted to circumvent the legal requirements of the Fifteenth Amendment and to disenfranchise African Americans. For example, the "grandfather clause" gave the right to vote to those who had the right before a certain date and gave their descendants the right to register permanently before a certain time had elapsed without complying with the educational requirements for all other voters. This meant that illiterate whites could qualify to vote simply because their ancestors had had the right to vote, while newly freed black citizens (often illiterate) would not be able to vote because they could not pass an unfair literacy test and, as their ancestors had not previously been entitled to vote, they could not qualify to vote under the "grandfather clause." The date affixed to the grandfather clauses was 1866, thereby establishing a date fixed at the time when African Americans were not permitted to vote. This practice allowed illiterate whites to vote while disenfranchising illiterate African Americans, thus circumventing the Fifteenth Amendment.

The white primary was another practice implemented to prevent African Americans from effectively exercising their right to vote. The white primary was an ingenious device that took advantage of the one-party politics that prevailed in the South and effectively frustrated the desire of African Americans to vote by excluding them from voting in private primary elections. Winning the primary election was tantamount to winning the general election since only one party, the Democrats, dominated southern politics. The consequence of this practice was to negate the right to vote, as the general election (where blacks could vote) was often a facade election. The election that mattered was the primary election, an election from which blacks were excluded.

Another means that states employed to circumvent the guarantee of the Fifteenth Amendment was usage of poll taxes. Poll taxes served more as a financial deterrent to prospective African American voters than as a grant of administrative discretion to register African Americans. State governments used the device in a myriad of ways, all designed to bar the ballot to African Americans. The rationale was that many African Americans at the time could ill afford to pay prohibitively high "taxes" to vote, especially when the money could be used to meet basic expenses of living. Another deterrent used to prevent African Americans from enjoying the right to vote was the literacy test, a test that one had to pass to become eligible to register to vote. The test was created by local white registrars and was graded by them as well. In many southern states, the literacy tests were composed of reading and of interpreting either the U.S. Constitution or a state constitution. Finally, sometimes ad hoc and sometimes organized campaigns of threats, intimidation, economic sanctions, and violence were also used to discourage African Americans from either registering to vote or exercising the right to vote.

Ironically, rather than reduce the amount of violence exhibited toward African Americans, the Fifteenth Amendment intensified it, particularly in the South. Much of the violence came as a result of southern attempts to circumvent the true meaning and spirit of the Fifteenth Amendment. Also, the withdrawal of federal troops from the South and the end of Reconstruction following the presidential election of 1876 signaled national acceptance of (or at least acquiescence in) violent behavior against African Americans attempting to exercise the right to vote.

Eventually, the federal courts restored the right to vote that had been circumvented by southern political tactics. The practice of the grandfather clause was successfully challenged by the National Association for the Advancement of Colored People (NAACP) in the case of *Guinn v. United States*, 238 U.S. 347 (1915). The practice challenged by the NAACP regarded a provision that gave all those who had the right to vote before a certain date and their descendants the right to register permanently before a certain time had elapsed without complying with the educational qualifications required of all other voters. In *Guinn v. United States*, the Supreme Court for the first time used the Fifteenth Amendment to invalidate a discriminatory voting practice, thereby declaring the utilization of the grandfather clause unconstitutional.

Additionally, in *Smith v. Allwright*, 321 U.S. 649 (1944), the Court reopened the question of whether discrimination effected by a state convention that denied African Americans the right to participate in primaries was a private or state action when, in conducting the primary, the private political party was fulfilling duties delegated to it by a statutory election scheme. The Court ruled that the statutory system for the selection of party nominees for inclusion on the general election ballot made the party that was required to follow these legislative directions an agency of the state insofar as it determined the participation in a primary election, thereby declaring the white primary practice to be unconstitutional under the Fifteenth Amendment because the white primary was held to involve governmental action under the "state action" doctrine. The Court explained that the constitutional right to be free from racial discrimination in voting was not to be nullified by a state through casting its election process in a form that permitted a private organization to practice racial discrimination in the election. However, the Supreme Court did not declare the practice of paying a poll tax unconstitutional until 1966. In the case of *Harper v. Virginia Board of Elections*, 383 U.S. 663 (1966), the Court finally declared the payment of a state poll tax unconstitutional. In combination with the Supreme Court's ruling in 1966, the issue of a poll tax requirement was ultimately resolved with the ratification of the Twenty-Fourth Amendment in 1964, which constitutionally prohibits the practice of assessing poll taxes as a condition to voting in any federal election (i.e., elect of president, U.S. senator, congressman, etc.).

The Fifteenth Amendment has continued to have an impact on election procedures throughout the United States, even though it has been circumvented by various state practices over the years. However, not until the Voting Rights Act of 1965 did discrimination in voting truly begin to come to an end in South, owing in part to vigorous enforcement of voting rights by the Department of Justice and the federal courts in the 1960s. The Voting Rights Act of 1965 was designed to enhance the rights guaranteed under the Fifteenth Amendment. Finally, an additional legacy of the Fifteenth Amendment is that it raised the potential of extending to women the right to vote as well. However, the right to vote for women would not be achieved until ratification of the Nineteenth Amendment in 1920.

See also Civil War (Reconstruction) Amendments and Civil Rights Acts; Fourteenth Amendment; Ku Klux Klan; National Association for the Advancement of Colored People; Nineteenth Amendment; State Action Doctrine; Thirteenth Amendment; Voting Rights Act of 1965; White Primary; White Supremacy.

FURTHER READING: Bell, Derrick, 1992, *Race, Racism, and American Law*, Boston: Little, Brown and Company; Keyssar, Alexander, 2000, *The Right to Vote: The Contested History of Democracy in the United States*, New York: Basic Books; Kyvig, David E., ed., 2000, *Unintended Consequences of Constitutional Amendment*, Athens: University of Georgia Press; Thernstrom, Abigail M., 1987, *Whose Votes Count? Affirmative Action and Minority Voting Rights*, Cambridge, MA: Twentieth Century Fund Study.

RONNIE B. TUCKER SR.

Fifth Amendment

The Fifth Amendment to the U.S. Constitution provides Americans with a plethora of individual liberties. The text of the Fifth Amendment contains several important and often-litigated clauses. They include the Grand Jury Clause, the Double Jeopardy Clause, the Self-incrimination Clause, the Just Compensation Clause, and the Due Process Clause. A clause that is not found patently within the text of the amendment, but that has spawned many legal battles in the affirmative action context, finds its roots in the Fifth Amendment's Due Process Clause. The U.S. Supreme Court has interpreted the Fifth Amendment Due Process Clause to include an equal protection component, which applies to affirmative action programs or actions taken by the federal government. This hidden equal protection clause has helped establish a legitimate basis for individuals who wish to bring suit against the federal government if they believe that a federal government entity has acted in contravention of their equal protection rights.

When the U.S. Constitution was ratified, it did not contain a Bill of Rights. Certain states made such a list of rights a condition for their ratification of the document. In 1791, the first ten amendments to the U.S. Constitution were ratified. This Bill of Rights, as it has been named, contains a list of some of the most valued and cherished individual liberties in the United States. The rights to speak freely, to practice one's own chosen religion, and to be free from unwarranted government searches and seizures are just a few of the rights enumerated in the first ten amendments. As evidenced by the text of the Fifth Amendment, the framers intended that life, liberty, and property be given special protection. However, according to the Supreme Court in the famous case *Barron v. Baltimore*, 32 U.S. 243 (1833), the Bill of Rights was initially only applicable to the federal government, not the state governments. It was not until the twentieth century that many of the provisions of the Bill of Rights began to become applicable to the states through the Supreme Court's selective incorporation of those rights via the Due Process Clause of the Fourteenth Amendment.

After the Civil War ended, the nation saw a need to provide special protections, in addition to those already found in the Bill of Rights, for certain less fortunate members of society. Furthermore, since the Bill of Rights was not originally applicable to state governments, there was a need for some basic constitutional protections for newly freed slaves, protections that the states would be bound to obey. One of these protections presented itself in the form of the Fourteenth Amendment. Among other things, the Fourteenth Amendment prohibited the states from denying equal protection of the laws to those within their jurisdiction. As time passed, a need surfaced for an equal protection requirement that applied not just to actions taken by individual states, but to those taken by the federal government. Therefore, the U.S. Supreme Court expanded its interpretation of the Fifth Amendment Due Process Clause to include an equal protection component, even though the exact words "equal protection" appear nowhere in the express language of the Fifth Amendment. In *Bolling v. Sharpe*, 347 U.S. 497 (1954), the Supreme Court indicated that under the Fifth Amendment Due Process Clause, the federal government has a duty to respect an individual's right to equal protection of the laws.

When addressing an alleged violation of an individual's civil rights under the Fifth Amendment, the Court must determine which level of constitutional scrutiny to apply. The three levels of constitutional scrutiny are the rational basis test, the middle-tier balancing test (intermediate scrutiny), and the strict scrutiny test. The rational basis test is used for questions involving age, sexuality, and other social or economic rights. The middle-tier balancing test is used when a case implicates gender and legitimacy issues. Finally, the strict scrutiny test is used when state action negatively impacts an individual's rights due to his or her race, ethnicity, national origin, or alienage. This test is also used when the state is alleged to have violated other fundamental rights. As with most fundamental rights, when addressing violations of one's equal protection rights, the Supreme Court will apply the highest level of scrutiny. To pass constitutional muster, a government regulation that infringes upon an individual's Fifth Amendment equal protection rights must advance a compelling governmental interest and must be narrowly tailored to meet that interest.

When individuals, generally nonminority persons, believe that their civil rights have been negatively impacted by federal affirmative action programs, they have the ability to file suit in federal court. Specifically, their petitions assert that the federal government, by way of its affirmative action program, is violating their equal protection rights. Such petitioners further assert that the federal affirmative action program is actually state-sponsored discrimination and, therefore, a violation of the equal protection component of the Fifth Amendment. For example, in 1980, the U.S. Supreme Court decided the case of *Fullilove v. Klutznick*, 448 U.S. 448 (1980), utilizing the Fifth Amendment Due Process Clause framework. The case centered on a federal public works program, the Public Works Employment Act, which required a 10 percent set-aside of federal monies for what the program called minority business enterprises. If African Americans, Hispanics, Asians, or American Indians held more than half of the business's shares, then that business was considered a minority business enterprise under the program. Nonminority business enterprises claimed that the set-aside portion of the program infringed upon their rights by placing a financial burden upon them. In spite of a Fifth Amendment equal protection argument, the Supreme Court upheld the program based upon the government's intent to remedy the present effects of past discrimination and to promote the general welfare of the country. For the next nine years, the Supreme Court appeared to be deciding its cases in favor of various affirmative action programs. However, in 1989, the Court decided the case *City of Richmond v. J.A. Croson Co.*, 488 U.S. 469 (1989). The case involved a set-aside plan similar to the one contested in *Fullilove*, but that was used by a municipal government. However, in this case, after applying the strict scrutiny test, the Court found that this state-sponsored plan did violate the Fourteenth Amendment Equal Protection Clause.

The tide seemed to shift once again in 1990 when *Metro Broadcasting, Inc. v. FCC*, 497 U.S. 547 (1990), was decided. In *Metro Broadcasting*, the Supreme Court, applying the middle-tier balancing test, upheld two federal affirmative action policies that had as their goal the increase of minority participation in broadcasting. One program allowed the FCC to use an applicant's minority status as a "plus factor" when deciding whether to grant a radio or television operator license. The other program provided added benefits to current operators who chose to sell their station to a minority buyer. The Supreme Court ruled that increasing minority participation in broadcasting through application of these programs is substantially related to the important governmental interest of increasing diversity in broadcasting. The Court found no equal protection violation. In reconciling *Metro Broadcasting* and *Fullilove* with the decision made in *Croson*, it appears that the Court was indicating that federal affirmative action programs are "entitled to a greater presumption of validity" than similar state programs (Stephens and Scheb 2003, 734).

In 1995, Justice Sandra Day O'Conner authored the decision in *Adarand Constructors, Inc. v. Peña*, 515 U.S. 200 (1995). Under the Subcontracting Compensation Clause program at issue in *Adarand*, the federal government gave financial incentives to general contractors if they employed subcontractors whose businesses were controlled by socially and economically disadvantaged individuals. Adarand Constructors submitted the lowest bid for guardrail work and should have received the contract. The general contractor, however, did not award the job to Adarand Constructors. Due to the added incentives offered by the federal government, the general contractor awarded the job to Gonzales Construction Company, a business that was controlled by socially and economically disadvantaged individuals. The plaintiff argued that this practice and the practice of using race-based presumptions in identifying the disadvantaged persons violated the equal protection component of the Fifth Amendment.

Once again, the Court was faced with the task of choosing which level of scrutiny to apply to this affirmative action program. In no uncertain terms, the Court held that all racial classifications, whether made by state or federal governmental entities, must be analyzed using the strict scrutiny test. It went on to state that as long as race-based governmental action is taken to advance a compelling governmental interest and the action utilizes the least restrictive means, the action would not be found to violate either Fifth or Fourteenth Amendment equal protection rights. The Supreme Court vacated the court of appeals ruling that the equal protection component of the Fifth Amendment had not been violated. The case was remanded to the lower court for further proceedings in accordance with the decision of the Supreme Court.

It is apparent from the *Adarand* decision that at least five of the nine justices currently sitting on the U.S. Supreme Court believe that racial classifications deserve the most detailed examination by the judiciary. As a result of this decision, cases arising out of the equal protection component of the Fifth Amendment Due Process Clause are ensured the application of the strictest constitutional standard.

See also Adarand Constructors, Inc. v. Peña; African Americans; Asian Americans; Bill of Rights; *Bolling v. Sharpe; City of Richmond v. J.A. Croson Co.*; Compelling Governmental Interest; Disadvantaged Business Enterprises; Equal Protection Clause; Fourteenth Amendment; *Fullilove v. Klutznick*; Hispanic Americans; Intermediate Scrutiny Review; *Metro Broadcasting, Inc. v. FCC*; Native Americans; O'Connor, Sandra Day; Quotas; Rational Basis Scrutiny; Strict Scrutiny.

FURTHER READING: Brody, Carl E., Jr., 1996, "A Historical Review of Affirmative Action and the Interpretation of Its Legislative Intent by the Supreme Court," 29 *Akron Law Review* 29 (winter): 291–334; Gentile, Leslie, 1996, "Giving Effect to Equal Protection: *Adarand Constructors, Inc. v. Peña*," *Akron Law Review* 29 (winter): 397–421; Green, Robert P., 2000, *Equal Protection and the African American Constitutional Experience: A Documentary History*, Westport, CT: Greenwood Press; Kairys, David, 1996, "Unexplainable on Grounds Other Than Race," *American University Law Review* 45 (February): 729–749; Stephens, Otis H., Jr., and John M. Scheb II, 2003, *American Constitutional Law*, 3d ed., Belmont, CA: Wadsworth/Thomson Learning.

SCOTT S. BRENNEMAN

Firefighters Local Union No. 1784 v. Stotts, 467 U.S. 561 (1984)

Firefighters Local Union No. 1784 v. Stotts (1984) presented the Supreme Court with the issue of deciding the legality of bona fide seniority systems in conjunction with affirmative action programs during periods of employee layoffs. One of the key issues in the case dealt with whether minorities hired under affirmative action plans should be laid off before white employees with more seniority on the job. This case was important in the area of affirmative action because the Court held that because the individual minority employees could not prove that they were themselves the victims of past discrimination by the city of Memphis, the seniority system in place was legitimate and took precedence over affirmative action plans. Under this decision, the Court held that white employees with more seniority on the job could not be laid off in lieu of newer minority employees on the job, regardless of the existence of affirmative action plans. That is, a bona fide seniority system was a legitimate and protected practice under Title VII of the 1964 Civil Rights Act.

The legality of layoff plans and seniority systems was the focal point of the *Stotts* case. The issue in this case centered on a consent decree enacted by the Memphis, Tennessee, Fire Department, which was passed by the city in an effort to remedy past incidents of discrimination. The purpose of the consent decree was "to remedy the hiring and promotional practices" of the fire department regarding the employment of African Americans. The city of Memphis had agreed to promote thirteen named individuals and provide back pay to eighty-one employees of the fire department. The consent decree included provisions that established the interim hiring goal of filling on an annual basis 50 percent of the departmental vacancies with qualified African American applicants. The decree also provided for the awarding of 20 percent of the promotions in each category to African Americans. The decree did not mention how its remedial purpose might affect a layoff.

Based upon a projected budgetary deficit, the city of Memphis announced the reduction of nonessential personnel throughout city government. The announced layoffs were based on the "last hired, first fired" rule that was the basis for the citywide seniority system. In 1977, a recently hired minority employee named Carl Stotts filed a complaint charging the Memphis Fire Department and certain city officials with engaging in a pattern or practice of implementing hiring and promotion decisions based on race in violation of Title VII of the Civil Rights Act of 1964. The case was also confirmed as a class-action suit and consolidated with an action filed by another employee claiming denial of promotion based on race.

The federal District Court for the Western District of Tennessee issued an injunction forbidding the layoff of any African American employees. While the district court ruled that the city's seniority-based layoff policy was in compliance with the city's seniority system and "was not adopted with intent to discriminate," the court nevertheless ordered that the city of Memphis not implement the seniority-based layoff policy because it allegedly resulted in a reduction of African Americans employed in such positions as lieutenants, drivers, and inspectors. As a result, an approved modified layoff plan designed to protect African American employees was submitted. The revised layoff plan resulted in white employees with greater seniority than African American employees either receiving layoffs or demotions in rank.

On appeal, the Court of Appeals for the Sixth Circuit ruled that the seniority system for the city of Memphis was not a permissible plan. The court of appeals further held that the district court acted properly in preventing African Americans from being adversely affected by unanticipated layoffs. The court of appeals reasoned that the district court had authority to "modify the consent decree because the new and unforeseen events created a hardship on one of the parties to the consent decree." The court of appeals also ruled that the decree modifications were not in violation of Title VII of the 1964 Civil Rights Act. Finally, the decision suggested that the claims set forth were moot, based on the fact that all of the white employees laid off had been restored to their old positions only one month after the layoffs and demotions.

In a 6–3 decision, the U.S. Supreme Court reversed the findings and decisions of the lower courts. The Court first dealt with the issue of mootness. It was the decision of the lower courts in the case that since "all white employees laid off as a result of the injunction had been restored, the injunction was no longer in effect and the case was now moot." However, the Supreme Court disagreed with this assessment and made note that the injunction was still in force and would therefore affect future layoffs (unless the injunction was terminated to avoid this). Thus the issue was not whether the injunction was still in effect, but "whether the mandated modifications of the consent decree continues to have an impact on the parties such that the case remains alive." Hence the Supreme Court stated that even though the white employees who had been laid off or demoted had received restoration, "the employees had not been made whole again, and thus, the case was not moot because there was a concrete interest in the outcome of the litigation."

According to Justice Byron White, writing for the majority of the Court, another key issue was whether the federal district court had exceeded its powers with the implementation of an injunction requiring the layoff of white employees with more seniority. The Court's majority ruled that the court of appeals had erred. While the city of Memphis had a general obligation to increase the proportion of African Americans in the fire department and the purpose of the consent decree was to remedy specific past hiring and promotion practices, the Court importantly held that the consent decree was not a permissible means of displacing white employees with seniority under seniority systems in the workplace. The Court ruled that Title VII of the 1964 Civil Rights Act "protected bona fide seniority systems and that it was inappropriate to deny an innocent employee the benefits of seniority to provide remedial relief."

See also Affirmative Action Plan/Program; African Americans; Civil Rights Act of 1964; Employment (Private) and Affirmative Action; Supreme Court and Affirmative Action; Title VII of the Civil Rights Act of 1964; White, Byron Raymond.

FURTHER READING: Barker, Lucius J., and Mack H. Jones, 1994, *African Americans and the American Political System,* Englewood Cliffs, NJ: Prentice Hall; Perry, Huey L., and Wayne Parent, eds., 1995, *Blacks and the American Political System,* Gainesville: University Press of Florida; Spann, Girardeau A., 2000, *The Law of Affirmative Action: Twenty-five Years of Supreme Court Decisions on Race and Remedies,* New York: New York University Press; Tucker, Ronnie B., 2000, *Affirmative Action, the Supreme Court, and Political Power in the Old Confederacy,* Lanham, MD: University Press of America.

RONNIE B. TUCKER SR.

First Amendment

The First Amendment is most often recognized for its delineation of civil liberties, freedoms, and protections. The First Amendment prohibits the establishment of a state-supported church and requires the separation of church and state. It guarantees freedom of worship, freedom of speech and the press, and the rights of peaceable assembly, association, and petition. Freedom of expression consists of the rights to freedom of speech, press, and assembly and to petition the government for a redress of grievances, and the implied rights of association and belief. Interpretation of the extent of protection provided by the First Amendment rests with the Supreme Court. The Court has interpreted the First Amendment as applying to the entire federal government although it is only expressly applicable to Congress. Similarly, the Court has interpreted the Due Process Clause of the Fourteenth Amendment as protecting the rights in the First Amendment from interference by state governments. The First Amendment is part of the overall Bill of Rights, which consists of the first ten amendments, contains procedural and substantive guarantees and protection of individual liberties, and sets limits upon government control and intervention. The Bill of Rights to the U.S. Constitution was ratified on December 15, 1791.

In the affirmative action context, the First Amendment is relevant in several key respects. First, there have been authors who have encouraged the use of affirmative action in allocating speech rights (or denying them), particularly in the hate-speech context, in essence (in the words of author Alice Ma) "pitting the First Amendment against the Fourteenth." Second, affirmative action has been used by the Federal Communications Commission (FCC) in allocating broadcast licenses to minority broadcasters under the First and Fourteenth Amendments to ensure diversity of information being broadcast over the airwaves. This practice was upheld by the Supreme Court as constitutional in *Metro Broadcasting, Inc. v. FCC*, 497 U.S. 547 (1990). Third, violating an employee's freedom of religion (under the First Amendment) often also involves violations of Title VII of the Civil Rights Act of 1964 and applicable affirmative action plans as well. Fourth and finally, the First Amendment is relevant in ensuring that all voices are heard on controversial debates such as affirmative action, and one voice or opinion (even if such opinion is the unpopular opinion) is at least entitled not to be quashed due to First Amendment protections.

The most basic component of freedom of expression is the right to freedom of speech. The right to freedom of speech allows individuals to express themselves without interference or constraint by the government. The Supreme Court requires the government to provide substantial justification for interference with the right of free speech when it attempts to regulate the content of the speech. A less stringent test is applied for content-neutral legislation. The Supreme Court has also recognized that the government may prohibit some speech that may cause a breach of the peace or cause immediate violence. The right to free speech includes other mediums of expression that communicate a message. Similarly, despite popular misunderstanding, the right to freedom of the press guaranteed by the First Amendment is not very different from the right to freedom of speech. It allows an individual to express himself or herself through publication and dissemination. It is part of the constitutional protection of freedom of expression. It does not afford members of the media any special rights or privileges not afforded to citizens in general.

In the context of freedom of speech, several authors have argued that an affirmative action approach should be used in the hate-speech context. That is, proponents of this theory argue that purveyors of hate lack a legitimate message; the message is hurtful to society and the individual and should be barred under a liberal interpretation of the Fourteenth Amendment's Equal Protection Clause. Just as the goal of traditional affirmative action programs is to remedy past racial discrimination, silencing hate speech would be remedying racial discrimination as well, in essence giving minorities equal speech rights. Critical race theorists like Richard Delgado and Mari Matsuda argue that hate speech is just as insidious and damaging as actual discrimination and has the effect of silencing minorities (thereby depriving the minorities of their right of free speech). Thus, like traditional affirmative action in the fields of education, employment, contracting, and so on, affirmative action should be used in the speech arena as well. One author has even argued that only white hate speech be curtailed:

> Because whites have not been systematically silenced by racist speech, protecting them from such speech is not logically justified under affirmative action law. Hence, whites would be prohibited from using hate speech against minorities, but minorities would not be prohibited from using such speech against whites. (Ma 1995, 714)

The other side to this debate argues that even hate speech should be protected under the First Amendment, and any governmental censorship is dangerous and should not be contemplated. The courts have thus far not expanded affirmative action programs to combat problems like hate speech.

As noted earlier, the Federal Communications Commission's use of affirmative action in the allocating of broadcast licenses to minority broadcasters under the First and Fourteenth Amendments was upheld by the Supreme Court as constitutional in *Metro Broadcasting, Inc. v. FCC.* In *Metro Broadcasting,* there was a challenge, based on the Equal Protection Clause, to the FCC's minority preference policies. The Court's decision in *Metro Broadcasting* held that the FCC's minority preference policies did not violate the Equal Protection Clause because they provided appropriate remedies for the victims of discrimination and were consistent with legitimate congressional objectives of program diversity.

The next protection contained in the First Amendment guarantees to the people the right to assemble, which allows people to gather for peaceful and lawful purposes. Implicit within this right is the right to association and belief. The Supreme Court has expressly recognized that a right to freedom of association and belief is implicit in the First, Fifth, and Fourteenth Amendments. This implicit right is limited to the right to associate for First Amendment purposes. It does not include a right of social association. The government may prohibit people from knowingly associating in groups that engage in and promote illegal activities. The right to associate also prohibits the government from requiring a group to register or disclose its members or from denying government benefits on the basis of an individual's current or past membership in a particular group. There are exceptions to this rule where the Court finds that governmental interests in disclosure/registration outweigh interference with First Amendment rights. Generally, the government may also not compel individuals to express themselves, hold certain beliefs, or belong to particular associations or groups. Additionally, the right to petition the government for a redress of grievances guarantees people the right to ask the government to provide relief for a wrong through the courts (litigation) or other governmental action. This right works with the right of assembly by allowing people to join together and seek change from the government.

The next major protection found in the First Amendment deals with religious protections. Although two clauses in the First Amendment guarantee freedom of religion, the Establishment Clause prohibits the government from passing legislation to establish an official religion or preferring one religion over another. The First Amendment enforces the "separation of church and state." Some governmental activity related to religion has been declared constitutional by the Supreme Court. For example, providing bus transportation for parochial school students and the enforcement of "blue laws" are not prohibited. The Free Exercise Clause prohibits the government, in most instances, from interfering with a person's practice of his or her religion.

The Free Exercise Clause has often been the subject of employment disputes. Federal courts have held religious harassment to be unlawful under Title VII of the Civil Rights Act of 1964, as well as under applicable affirmative action/diversity management plans that may be in place. These cases involve one of two fact patterns: first, where a plaintiff claims that he or she has been harassed because of his or her religious beliefs and he or she is entitled to be protected in his or her own religious beliefs per the First Amendment; second, where a plaintiff claims that he or she is being harassed by an employer's religious statements and proselytizing (the employee claims a Title VII violation; the employer claims that his/her speech and religion should be protected under the First Amendment). In the first scenario, courts will look at the workplace effect of the employee's practices and, if such practices are disruptive or inappropriate, rule in favor of the employer under Title VII. In the second scenario, in essence, the First Amendment is being pitted against Title VII protections. Generally, courts have ruled in favor of the employee under Title VII, but not in every case.

While some Supreme Court justices have declared that First Amendment freedoms are absolute or occupy a preferred position, the Court has routinely held that they may be limited to protect the rights of others (e.g., libel, privacy) or to guard against subversion of the government and the spreading of dissension in wartime. Thus the Court's majority has remained firm—the First Amendment rights are not absolute. Only two Supreme Court justices, Justice Hugo Black and Justice William O. Douglas, insisted that First Amendment rights are absolute, and their dissenting opinions fell to the wayside. Most court cases concerning the First Amendment involve weighing two concerns: public versus private. Also, the Supreme Court has often defined certain speech, also known as "at-risk speech," as being unprotected by the First Amendment. For example, burning draft cards to protest the draft is prohibited because of superior governmental interest. Words likely to incite imminent violence, termed "fighting words," and words immediately jeopardizing national security are not protected, and newspaper publishing of false and defamatory material is considered libel.

Freedom of speech and expression is not a luxury of democracy, but should be recognized as a necessity. For a democratic form of government to function and continue to exist, it must have free expression and educated criticism. Most of the development of the free society of the United States has come about because of public debate and disclosure, in both spoken and written form. The First Amendment has endured more than 200 years without significant changes and reversals. This limited history of change should stand as a testament of the First Amendment's importance and role in U.S. democracy. In U.S. history, there have been few instances where the First Amendment has been set aside. The most notable periods of government censorship, which are few, involve sedition acts and wartime censorship.

The first significant governmental violation of the First Amendment came within seven years of the ratification of the amendment. The Sedition Act of 1798, signed by President John Adams, gave federal authorities the right to prosecute any individual suspected of plotting against the federal government. This act also included a provision that made it a criminal act to speak or write maliciously of the president or of Congress, which was defined as "with the intent to defame" or to bring either "into contempt or disrepute." The Sedition Act of 1798 effectively stifled legitimate political discussion, and for this reason the American public was very critical of it. Critics of the government either bowed to the pressure of this act or were punished. In 1800, the act expired and was not renewed. Congress had voted that reparations to its victims be instituted, based on the opinion that if they were adhering to the beliefs of the Founding Fathers, such an act was inconsistent with the First Amendment.

During the period of slavery in the United States, many slave states ignored the First Amendment and censored abolitionists' pamphlets, writings, and speeches. The states' defense of ignoring the protections of the First Amendment was derived from the Supreme Court case *Barron v. Baltimore*, 32 U.S. 243 (1833), which held that the Bill of Rights was applicable only to the federal government, not to the various state governments. It was not until well into the twentieth century that the Supreme Court held the state governments to be accountable under the First Amendment. In *Gitlow v. New York*, 268 U.S. 652 (1925), the Court finally reversed its previous ruling in *Barron* and held that the First Amendment prohibitions were now binding on the various state governments as well as the federal government. The Court concluded that the Fourteenth Amendment's Due Process Clause provided a means to extend the freedom-of-speech protections of the First Amendment to include state governments. Within fifteen years of the *Gitlow* case, in the famous "Scottsboro Boys" cases, the Court used the Fourteenth Amendment to extend other aspects of the Bill of Rights, such as the Sixth Amendment right to representation in capital cases. Today, the First Amendment has been entirely incorporated by the Supreme Court and made applicable to the states under the Due Process Clause of the Fourteenth Amendment (the doctrine of selective incorporation).

As was arguably the case with the Alien and Sedition Acts of 1798, wartime censorship has been used to protect national security interests. The phrase "clear and present danger" serves as the gauge by which censorship rights of government as opposed to the free-speech rights of individuals are measured in such times of crisis. President Abraham Lincoln first used this type of censorship during the Civil War. First Amendment freedoms and protections were secondary, according to Lincoln, to the preservation of the nation. Lincoln believed in the argument "the ends justified the means" in preserving all the laws. The Civil War alterations to the protections guaranteed under the First Amendment consisted of opening mail and censoring anti-Union newspapers.

Wartime censorship was also employed during World War I. Another Sedition Act, passed in 1918, considered speaking "disloyal or abusive language" about the flag, Constitution, and government a criminal act. Passage of the Espionage Act of 1917 hindered First Amendment protections. The Espionage Act made it a crime to write or say anything that might encourage disloyalty or interfere with drafting of servicemen. Subversive books were removed from the shelves in stores and libraries. A Federal Censorship Board was assigned to regulate such activities. Again, the argument of protecting national security interests was maintained. Similar activities took place during World War II. It was considered an illegal activity to advocate violent overthrow of the government at any level or to say, do, or write anything that might encourage insubordination among the military or encourage disloyalty. After World War II, censorship became a hot issue during what is commonly referred to as the "McCarthy era" and "the Red Scare." The target was communism. Writings, speeches, and activities were scrutinized for Communist propaganda and leftist advocacy. Eventually, such censoring activities were eliminated, and the First Amendment was restored to its original legislative intent.

During the 1930s, the Federal Communications Commission established a policy of requiring broadcast station owners that engage in airing editorial opinions on a controversial issue to offer time on the air to any opposing opinion. The FCC argued that it was not violating First Amendment rights of broadcasters because the airwaves were a limited resource and belonged to the public. Thus the right of public access to the airwaves must be protected. The FCC had long imposed the requirement that radio and television broadcasters must devote a reasonable period of time to the reporting and discussion of public issues, as well as assuring fair and balanced coverage to each side in the debate. This FCC requirement, known as the "fairness doctrine," was justified by the federal government in light of the scarcity of broadcast frequencies, the government's responsibility in allocating those resources, and that not all individuals and/or entities will have equal standing in gaining access to and utilizing those frequencies.

The FCC's "fairness doctrine" was challenged in the courts but ultimately upheld by the Supreme Court in *Red Lion Broadcasting v. FCC,* 395 U.S. 397 (1969). Interestingly, state attempts at imposing a "fairness doctrine" on traditional print media was met with universal disapproval by the Supreme Court. In *Miami Herald Pub. Co. v. Tornillo,* 418 U.S. 241 (1974), a unanimous Court struck down a Florida "right to reply" statute, which required newspapers to print, on demand and free of cost, rebuttals of candidates responding to attacks of a personal nature or relating to the candidates official record. Thus, the Court sanctioned the use of the "fairness doctrine" for the broadcast media, but disapproved of the doctrine as it relates to the traditional print media. Ultimately, however, the FCC decided to scrap the "fairness doctrine" in 1987, "pointing in particular to the marked increase in the information services marketplace since *Red Lion* and the effects of the doctrine in application" (Shiffrin and Choper 1996, 492).

Today, the First Amendment freedoms include various areas tangentially related to speaking, such as the right of freedom of information, government access, and citizens' right to know and right to privacy. James Russell Wiggins, former editor of the *Washington Post,* noted that the public's "right to know" consists of five separate parts: freedom from prior restraint; freedom from punitive censorship; the right to collect information; the right to have access to the media and materials necessary for collecting that information; and the right to distribute information and to make it directly available to all members of the public without interference from the government under law or from private groups acting outside the law.

See also Bill of Rights; Civil Rights Act of 1964; Critical Race Theory; Equal Protection Clause; Federal Communications Commission; Fifth Amendment; Fourteenth Amendment; Hate Crimes; Licensing and Affirmative Action; *Metro Broadcasting, Inc. v. FCC*; Scottsboro Boys; Title VII of the Civil Rights Act of 1964.

FURTHER READING: Alderman, Ellen, and Caroline Kennedy, 1995, *The Right to Privacy*, New York: Vintage Books; Allen, David S., and Robert Jensen, eds., 1995, *Freeing the First Amendment: Critical Perspectives on Freedom of Expression*, New York: New York University Press; Borjesson, Kristina, ed., 2002, *Into the Buzzsaw: Leading Journalists Expose the Myth of a Free Press*, New York: Prometheus Books; Bosmajian, Haig A., 1987, *Freedom of Expression*, New York: Neal-Schuman; Chafee, Zechariah, Jr., 1954, *Free Speech in the United States*, Cambridge, MA: Harvard University Press; Goring, Darlene C., 1999, "Affirmative Action and the First Amendment: The Attainment of a Diverse Student Body Is a Permissible Exercise of Institutional Autonomy," *University of Kansas Law Review*, April, 591–654; Ma, Alice K., 1995, "Campus Hate Speech Codes: Affirmative Action in the Allocation of Speech Rights," *California Law Review* 83 (March): 693–732; Shiffrin, Steven H., and Jesse H. Choper, 1996, *The First Amendment*, 2nd ed., St. Paul: West Pub. Co.

PAULETTE PATTERSON DILWORTH

Fletcher, Arthur

See Nixon, Richard Milhous.

Footnote 4

See Discrete and Insular Minority; Stone, Harlan Fiske.

Ford, Gerald Rudolph (1913–)

Gerald Rudolph Ford, the thirty-eighth president of the United States and longtime Republican member of the House of Representatives, is best remembered in the affirmative action context as supporting President Richard Nixon's affirmative action programs as the minority leader in the House of Representatives and continuing the programs when Ford himself succeeded Nixon as president. As a congressman and minority leader, Ford supported Nixon's revitalized Philadelphia Plan, an affirmative action plan in the area of federal governmental contracts, and helped shepherd it through the House of Representatives. As president, Ford opposed forced integration via busing. Also, in 1975, Ford signed into law the rules implementing Title IX of the 1972 Education Amendments to the Civil Rights Act of 1964, rules meant to ensure that colleges fund male and female sports in proportion to their respective enrollments or demonstrate a continuing history of expanding sporting activities for women. Ford's wife, Betty, also served as a spokeswoman for the Equal Rights Amendment. In August 1999, Ford wrote a rare editorial in the *New York Times* defending the use of affirmative action and race-conscious criteria in admissions for institutions of higher learning, and specifically at the University of Michigan.

Gerald Ford was born on July 14, 1913, in Omaha, Nebraska. His original name was Leslie Lynch King Jr., but his name was subsequently changed when his mother was married to Gerald Ford Sr. Ford's adolescent years were spent in Grand Rapids, Michigan, where he attended high school and graduated in 1931. Upon graduation from high school, Ford attended the University of Michigan, majoring in economics and political science. He also played on two collegiate national championship football teams as the center. His football career at Michigan later served as fodder for pundits of his politics. For example, Lyndon Johnson once remarked that "the trouble with Jerry Ford is that he used to play football without a helmet." Ford graduated from the University of Michigan in 1935, went on to graduate from Yale Law School in 1941, and was admitted to the Michigan bar in 1941. During World War II, Ford served in the navy as an aviation officer. In October 1948, he married Elizabeth "Betty" Bloomer Warren, and the couple had four children, Michael, John, Steven, and Susan.

Ford's political career began in 1948 when he ran for Congress. He defeated Republican Bartel J. Jonkman in the primary and won the general election. After taking his seat in 1949, Ford became a Republican Party loyalist, slowly rising through the ranks. In 1963, he was elected chairman of the House Republican Conference. In 1965, he was elected minority leader in the House, winning by a vote of 73–67. As minority leader, Ford was a constant critic of Lyndon Johnson's policies in regard to the Vietnam War and a constant supporter of President Richard Nixon. He held the minority leader position until he was selected by Nixon to be vice president in 1973, following the resignation of Vice President Spiro T. Agnew.

As a congressman, Gerald Ford was viewed as moderately conservative. Ford was a staunch fiscal conservative and a strong supporter of foreign policy containment. Ford's voting pattern in the House of Representatives has also been characterized as conservative. During his twenty-five years of service in the House, it can be seen through his voting that he held a fierce loyalty to the Republican Party and to Presidents Dwight Eisenhower and Richard Nixon. He was an opponent of big government and an expanded role of the national government. He opposed federal aid for education and voted to decrease federal funding for higher education. Ford also supported Nixon's revitalized Philadelphia Plan and defended it during its debate in Congress. Finally, Ford had a lukewarm record on civil rights. He sought to limit the government's role in protecting civil rights; however, he did vote for the passage of the Civil Rights Act of 1964 and the Voting Rights Act of 1965.

Upon the resignation of Spiro T. Agnew in October 1973, Richard Milhous Nixon nominated Ford for vice president under the terms of the Twenty-Fifth Amendment. When Nixon resigned the presidency due to his involvement in Watergate, Ford became president on August 9, 1974. Ford named his vice president (Nelson Rockefeller), thus providing the only unelected vice president and president combination in U.S. history. Ironically, while Gerald Ford had no significant national following or presidential aspirations, he has the distinction of being the only person in American history to serve as both an unelected vice president and president of the United States.

As president, he sought to restore prestige and honor to the office of the presidency after the infamous Watergate scandal. He served as president of the United States for only 895 days. During his tenure, his most controversial action was granting a pardon to Richard Nixon for his role in the Watergate scandal. This action angered many Americans and was probably a major factor in his loss in the 1976 presidential election to governor of Georgia, Democratic candidate, and eventual winner Jimmy Carter. Ford appeared before the U.S. House Judiciary Committee to provide a rationale for Nixon's pardon. Ford explained that he hoped that the pardon would help end the nation's fixation with the Watergate scandal and help Nixon regain his health and move on with his life.

In the aftermath of Watergate, Ford inherited a plethora of domestic and foreign affairs problems. Domestically, Ford inherited a crippled economy with high inflation and high unemployment. Unemployment was above 9 percent, new housing starts were quite low, and new car sales were down. Ford acted quickly to curb the trend toward government intervention and spending as a means of solving the problems of American society and the economy. He insisted that Congress cut individual and corporate taxes by $16 billion and reduce the nation's reliance on foreign oil importation. He called for reductions in spending and insisted that the federal budget be held as low as possible. During his tenure as president, Ford vetoed more than fifty pieces of legislation that he believed increased spending, and Congress was able to override only a few of these vetoes.

During his presidency, Ford also opposed forced racial integration via busing, but he maintained an "open-door policy" with leaders of the African American community to discuss major civil rights issues and even appeared on television to urge that Americans support the United Negro College Fund. Ford also signed into law the rules implementing Title IX, designed to ensure some semblance of gender equality in collegiate sporting activities.

In the Republican primaries of 1976, Ford faced a hotly contested battle against Ronald Reagan, the former governor of California. Reagan attacked Ford's negotiations over a new Panama Canal Treaty. However, there were no major differences in Reagan and Ford's conservative views and politics, which ultimately caused a split in the party along regional lines. When the nomination came to a vote at the Republican Convention, Ford narrowly beat Reagan. In November 1976, Ford lost to Jimmy Carter of Georgia in the general election. The margin of victory was 1.7 million votes, with a smaller margin in the electoral college. Since leaving the presidency, Ford has spent his years in retirement and sitting on the boards of several prominent institutions. In August 1999, he authored an editorial in the *New York Times* strongly arguing in favor of the use of race-conscious admissions practices in higher education.

See also Busing; Carter, James "Jimmy" Earl, Jr.; Civil Rights Act of 1964; Equal Rights Amendment; Nixon, Richard Milhous; Reagan, Ronald; Title IX of the Education Amendments of 1972; Voting Rights Act of 1965.

FURTHER READING: Ford, Gerald, 1973, *Gerald Ford: Selected Speeches*, Arlington, VA: R.W. Beatty; Ford, Gerald, 1977, *A Discussion with Gerald R. Ford: The American Presidency*, Washington, DC: American Enterprise Institute for Public Policy Research; Kotlowski, Dean J.,

2001, *Nixon's Civil Rights: Politics, Principle, and Policy,* Cambridge, MA: Harvard University Press; Shouse, Aimee, 2002, *Presidents from Nixon through Carter, 1969–1981: Debating the Issues in Pro and Con Primary Documents,* Westport, CT: Greenwood Press; Urofsky, Melvin, ed., 2000, *The American Presidents,* New York: Garland Publishing; White, Jack E., 1999, "Affirmative Action's Alamo: Gerald Ford Returns to Fight Once More for Michigan," *Time* 154, no. 8 (August 23): 48.

F. ERIK BROOKS

Fourteenth Amendment

The Fourteenth Amendment is one of the most important features of the American Constitution in ensuring racial, ethnic, and gender equality. Passed in the aftermath of the Civil War, the amendment was initially designed to ensure that newly freed slaves were made full citizens of the United States and were provided equal treatment under the law. Although early Supreme Court decisions limited the impact of the Fourteenth Amendment, the twentieth century witnessed the gradual expansion of the measure, and the Courts have utilized aspects of the amendment to apply elements of the Bill of Rights to state governments. Today, the Equal Protection Clause of the Fourteenth Amendment is the key constitutional provision in analyzing the legality of discrimination and affirmative action laws.

The Fourteenth Amendment was one of three constitutional amendments passed following the end of the Civil War. The Thirteenth Amendment abolished slavery, and the Fifteenth Amendment forbade discrimination in voting based on race. After the ratification of the Thirteenth Amendment in 1865, southern states began enacting black codes that were designed to politically and economically disenfranchise African Americans. In response, Republicans in Congress developed the Fourteenth Amendment in an effort to ensure equality of all citizens, especially in regard to their ability to vote. One goal of the amendment was to expand the franchise to include African Americans and undercut the control of the Democratic Party in the southern states. However, by 1866, twelve states had rejected the amendment. In response, Congress enacted the Reconstruction Acts (1867), which stipulated that in order for the former Confederate states to rejoin the Union, they had to accept the amendment. The acts also divided the South into five military districts and imposed martial law as a means to prompt ratification and restoration of state sovereignty. The amendment was formally ratified on July 9, 1868.

The amendment itself is divided into five sections. The most significant portion of the amendment was the first section, which itself was divided into four parts. The first clause guarantees citizenship to all Americans born or naturalized in the United States. The clause overturned the Supreme Court decision in *Dred Scott v. Sandford,* 60 U.S. (19 How.) 393 (1857), which decreed that slaves had no rights. The second clause, known as the Privileges and Immunities Clause, expressly forbade legislation designed to infringe upon the rights of citizens or to discriminate. However, in the *Slaughterhouse Cases,* 83 U.S. (16 Wall.) 36 (1873), the Supreme Court held that the clause's protections applied to the privileges and immunities of national citizens of the federal government. As a result, states were free to pass discriminatory legislation that resulted in the system of segregation. State-sponsored segregation was upheld by the U.S. Supreme Court in *Plessy v. Ferguson*, 163 U.S. 537 (1896). In 1927, Chief Justice William Howard Taft, in the unanimous opinion in *Lum v. Rice*, 275 U.S. 78 (1927), wrote that segregation is "within the discretion of the State in regulating its public schools and does not conflict with the 14th Amendment." The third clause of the first section is the Due Process Clause, which mandates that states cannot deprive citizens of "life, liberty or property" without legal processes. The fourth and final part is the Equal Protection Clause, which was designed to prevent state governments from discrimination based on race.

The second section of the amendment dealt with congressional apportionment and mandated that if states attempted to deny the right to vote to the newly freed slaves, their congressional representation would be lowered in proportion to the percentage of the population that was disenfranchised (it overturned the Three-Fifths Compromise in the Constitution whereby slaves counted as three-fifths of a person for purposes of determining congressional representation). The provisions of the second section were never enforced because of the ratification of the Fifteenth Amendment. The third section forbade former Confederates from holding state or federal office and limited the president's power of pardon in cases related to the Civil War. In 1898, Congress, as was permitted by the section, removed this restriction. The fourth section mandated that neither the federal government nor state governments could assume debts incurred by the Confederate governments. The final section gave Congress the power to pass legislation to enforce the other sections of the amendment.

The Fourteenth Amendment differentiates between citizens and persons. Under the amendment, citizens have the full range of political rights, including voting and running for or holding elected office, as well as established privileges and immunities such as the right to work, own property, and travel. All persons, whether they hold citizenship or not, also have the right to due process and to enjoy the protection of the law.

The key points of the amendment, those that would later be used to extend broader protections to minority groups, are the notions of equal protection and due process. While other provisions of the Constitution deal with both individual and group rights, the Fourteenth Amendment is the only provision of the document that specifically takes up the concept of equality of persons. Using the Equal Protection Clause, the Supreme Court has developed standards to ensure the fair treatment of persons within the United States. The Fourteenth Amendment generally only applies to state action; however, the U.S. Supreme Court found in *Bolling v. Sharpe*, 347 U.S. 497 (1954), that these equal protection guarantees were incorporated and applied to the actions of the federal government through the Fifth Amendment's Due Process Clause. For instance, the Court has ruled that most group classifications are reasonable if they have a logical relationship to a legitimate government purpose. This places the burden on those challenging the classification to prove that it is arbitrary. An example of the difference between a reasonable and an unreasonable classification by a state would be setting the driving age at sixteen (a reasonable distinction) versus only allowing people with blonde hair to drive (a distinction that would be arbitrary and therefore unreasonable and invalid).

However, the Court has ruled that all racial and ethnic classifications are inherently suspect classifications. Hence a government may use them only if the government's actions are narrowly tailored to achieve a compelling governmental interest. When dealing with inherently suspect classifications, such as those based on race, the Court has held that the state governments have the burden to prove that such classifications are necessary. For example, the federal and state governments may use categories involving race and ethnicity as a means to remedy past discrimination (the main legal justification for affirmative action).

Gender classifications have been designated in an intermediate category (neither always constitutional nor always unconstitutional), which means that the government must have a substantial and important goal in order to justify their use. For instance, in *Michael M. v. Superior Court of Sonoma County*, 450 U.S. 464 (1981), the Supreme Court held that states could enact laws that punish males for statutory rape, but not females. The acceptable use of gender classification in the case comes from the government's compelling interest in preventing teenage pregnancy. However, in *Dothard v. Rawlinson*, 433 U.S. 321 (1977), the Court ruled that police and fire departments could not use equal height or weight requirements for both men and women since the practical result of these restrictions was de facto segregation and discrimination against female applicants and workers. While the Equal Protection Clause does not mandate that all citizens must be treated exactly the same or that states must specifically develop methods to promote equality among citizens, the amendment became the foundation for later constitutional and legal efforts to accomplish these goals. The method for the expansion of these rights was the incorporation doctrine.

Initially, the Supreme Court upheld only a narrow version of the scope of the Fourteenth Amendment. In the *Slaughterhouse Cases*, 83 U.S. (16 Wall.) 36 (1873), the Court significantly diluted the federal control over state actions, especially in regard to broad police powers. Furthermore, in *Strauder v. West Virginia*, 100 U.S. 303 (1879), the high court struck down a West Virginia law that barred African Americans from jury service on the basis of the Fourteenth Amendment; however, the Court also refused to extend the coverage of the amendment to include other, less overt forms of racial discrimination. This reflected long-standing Court doctrine that the Bill of Rights applied only to the national government following the principle set forth in the 1833 Supreme Court case *Barron v. Baltimore*, 32 U.S. 243 (1833).

In *Gitlow v. New York*, 268 U.S. 652 (1925), the Court reversed its previous stance and held that the Fourteenth Amendment provided a means to extend the freedom-of-speech protections of the First Amendment to include state governments. The case began a process of dramatically limiting the powers of state governments. Within fifteen years of *Gitlow v. New York*, the Court used the Fourteenth Amendment to extend other aspects of the Bill of Rights, including freedom of the press, the right to representation in capital cases, freedom of assembly and petition, and freedom of religion. Throughout the twentieth century, the incorporation doctrine was used to continue to expand individual rights.

In the 1954 Supreme Court case *Brown v. Board of Education*, 347 U.S. 483 (1954), the justices held that the Fourteenth Amendment's guarantee of equal protection was violated by state-sponsored segregation. The Court decreed that separation of the races was inherently unequal and ordered states to desegregate public educational systems, a decision that was reinforced by later court action and federal law.

The Fourteenth Amendment was seen as the primary justification for the development of affirmative action programs. One of the main areas that the Fourteenth Amendment did not address was economic equality. As a result, in 1964, Congress passed the Civil Rights Act in order to end discrimination in either public or private institutions because of race, ethnicity, gender, color, or national origin. The Fourteenth Amendment was seen as the main constitutional and legal basis for both affirmative action programs and federal legislation, including the 1964 and 1991 Civil Rights Acts, the Equal Pay Act of 1963, Title IX of the 1972 Education Amendments, the 1991 Americans with Disabilities Act, and the Civil Rights Restoration Act of 1988. Successive presidents also utilized the Fourteenth Amendment in justifying executive orders that either developed or expanded policies related to federal workers or federal contracts.

Besides affirmative action programs in employment and government contracts, the Fourteenth Amendment has played a role in the establishment of affirmative action policies in college admissions. For instance, in 2000, the Ninth Circuit Court of Appeals in *Smith v. University of Washington Law School,* 233 F.3d 1188 (9th Cir. 2000), argued that the Fourteenth Amendment allows the use of "admissions programs which consider race." More significantly, the Ninth Circuit asserted that consideration of race in higher-education admissions was justified not only on the basis of past discrimination, but also because the government had a compelling interest in promoting "educational diversity." However, the Fourteenth Amendment has also been utilized by opponents of affirmative action who argue that the Equal Protection Clause is violated by programs that give preferential treatment to one race or ethnicity over others. In the case *Hopwood v. Texas,* 78 F.3d 932 (5th Cir. 1996), the Fifth Circuit Court of Appeals ruled that race-based admissions policies violated the Fourteenth Amendment's Equal Protection Clause. This led the state of Texas to eliminate race-based admissions programs in higher education. The Supreme Court refused to review the case. In addition, the proponents of Proposition 209 in California, a ballot initiative that ended the use of racial preferences in college admissions, also used the Fourteenth Amendment as the basis of their arguments.

In 2002, in *Grutter v. Bollinger,* 288 F.3d 732 (6th Cir. 2002), the Sixth Circuit Court of Appeals held that a law school's consideration of race in admissions was valid under the Fourteenth Amendment because it was necessary to achieve a compelling governmental interest in admissions, namely, student diversity. This opinion was subsequently affirmed by the Supreme Court in 2003 in *Grutter v. Bollinger,* 123 S. Ct. 2325, 2003 U.S. LEXIS 4800 (2003), and *Gratz v. Bollinger,* 123 S. Ct. 2411, 2003 U.S. LEXIS 4801 (2003), wherein the Supreme Court held that narrowly tailored race-conscious affirmative action plans may be promulgated to achieve diversity in higher education, so long as fixed racial quotas or rigid mechanized formulas (akin to quotas) are not utilized.

See also Affirmative Action Plan/Program; African Americans; Bill of Rights; *Brown v. Board of Education*; Civil Rights Act of 1964; Civil Rights Act of 1991; Civil Rights Restoration Act of 1988; Civil War (Reconstruction) Amendments and Civil Rights Acts; Color-Blind Constitution; De Facto and De Jure Segregation; *Dred Scott v. Sandford*; Education and Affirmative Action; Employment (Private) and Affirmative Action; Employment (Public) and Affirmative Action; Equal Pay Act of 1963; Equal Protection Clause; Fifteenth Amendment; Fifth Amendment; First Amendment; *Gratz v. Bollinger/Grutter v. Bollinger*; *Hopwood v. Texas*; *Johnson v. Board of Regents of the University of Georgia*; Ku Klux Klan; Persons with Disabilities and Affirmative Action; Proposition 209; *Plessy v. Ferguson*; Racial Discrimination; *Regents of the University of California v. Bakke*; Segregation; *Smith v. University of Washington Law School*; *Strauder v. West Virginia*; Suspect Classification; Thirteenth Amendment; Three-Fifths Compromise; Title IX of the Education Amendments of 1972.

FURTHER READING: Baer, Judith A., 1983, *Equality under the Constitution: Reclaiming the Fourteenth Amendment*, Ithaca, NY: Cornell University Press; Berger, Raoul, 1989, *The Fourteenth Amendment and the Bill of Rights*, Norman: University of Oklahoma Press; Curtis, Michael Kent, 1986, *No State Shall Abridge: The Fourteenth Amendment and the Bill of Rights*, Durham, NC: Duke University Press; Meyer, Howard N., 2000, *The Amendment That Refused to Die: Equality and Justice Deferred: The History of the Fourteenth Amendment*, Lanham, MD: Madison Books; Nelson, William E., 1988, *The Fourteenth Amendment: From Political Principle to Judicial Doctrine*, Cambridge, MA: Harvard University Press; Schnapper, Eric, 1985, "Affirmative Action and the Legislative History of the Fourteenth Amendment," *Virginia Law Review* 71 (June): 753–798; West, Robin, 1994, *Progressive Constitutionalism: Reconstructing the Fourteenth Amendment*, Durham, NC: Duke University Press.

TOM LANSFORD

Franks v. Bowman, 424 U.S. 747 (1976)

Franks v. Bowman is the U.S. Supreme Court case that held that an award of retroactive seniority relief ("slotting the victim in that position in the seniority system that would have been his had he been hired at the time of his application") should be available under section 706(g) of Title VII of the Civil Rights Act of 1964 for victims of unlawful employment discrimination. Furthermore, this remedy should only be denied if there are "unusual facts and circumstances," and the court must carefully articulate these circumstances. This type of remedy is one form of affirmative action. The Supreme Court reasoned that retroactive seniority relief is necessary to make persons whole for injuries suffered. Although the Court held that federal courts have broad equitable discretion to "order such affirmative action as may be appropriate," scholars have argued that the Court actually narrowed the discretion of the lower courts in fashioning appropriate relief for proven violations in employment discrimination cases.

In *Franks v. Bowman*, a class-action suit was brought by blacks who were not hired by a trucking firm because of their race. Although the district court permanently enjoined the trucking firm from continuing its discriminatory hiring practices, the court did not grant the members of the class any of the specific relief they sought, which included an award of back pay and retroactive seniority status. Although the court of appeals vacated the district court's judgment as to the back pay, it affirmed the district court's denial of any form of seniority relief.

The Supreme Court opined in *Franks* that one of the central purposes of Title VII is "to make persons whole for injuries suffered on account of unlawful employment discrimination." To attain this objective, section 706(g) gives federal courts broad equitable discretion to "order such affirmative action as may be appropriate." The Court reasoned that seniority systems affect an individual employee's economic security, and, in this case, seniority determined the order of layoff and recall of employees, pension benefits, and the length of an employee's vacation. Thus merely requiring the employer to hire the victim of discrimination does not make the victim whole. An employee who is not awarded seniority credit "will never obtain his rightful place. . . . He will perpetually remain subordinate to persons who, but for the illegal discrimination, would have been in respect to entitlement to these benefits his inferiors." The *Franks* Court held that there is a "presumption in favor of rightful-place seniority relief" that can only be denied "on the basis of unusual facts and circumstances."

Although the employer argued that a court must balance the interests of the employment expectancies of the innocent employees who obtained a seniority advantage over some of the plaintiffs because of the discriminatory hiring practices of the employer, the Court rejected this argument. The Court opined that denying seniority relief merely because that relief adversely affects other innocent employees would frustrate the "make-whole" objective of Title VII. The Court stated that "sharing the burden of past discrimination is presumptively necessary."

Justice Lewis Powell dissented, arguing that the majority failed to differentiate between benefit-type seniority, which is used to determine an employee's "fringe benefits," and competitive-type seniority, which determines job-related "rights" such as the worker's right to keep his job while someone else is laid off. According to Powell, the primary objective of Title VII is to eradicate discrimination. However, a retroactive grant of competitive-type seniority does not even affect the employer at all, and, consequently, the employer is not deterred from discriminating. Furthermore, Powell argued that the Court, by requiring district courts to give full retroactive seniority to discrimination victims without taking into account innocent employees, stripped the district courts of their equity powers.

See also Civil Rights Act of 1964; Employment (Private) and Affirmative Action; Powell, Lewis Franklin, Jr.; Racial Discrimination; Reverse Discrimination; Supreme Court and Affirmative Action; Title VII of the Civil Rights Act of 1964.

FURTHER READING: Belton, Robert, 1983, "Harnessing Discretionary Justice in the Employment Discrimination Cases: The *Moody* and *Franks* Standards," *Ohio State Law Journal* 44:571–610; *Franks v. Bowman,* 424 U.S. 747 (1976).

PAMELA C. CORLEY

Freedmen's Bureau

Perhaps the earliest example of a federal affirmative action program for blacks in the United States, the Freedmen's Bureau, more completely titled the Bureau of Refugees, Freedmen, and Abandoned Lands, was a temporary federal agency set up in 1865 in the aftermath of the Civil War to aid millions of newly freed slaves throughout the country. Specifically, the Freedmen's Bureau was charged with assisting approximately 4 million newly freed slaves in their transition from slavery to independence. The Freedmen's Bureau assisted African Americans in a plethora of different areas, including providing land, housing, employment, education, and schools, the dispensing of relief aid and medicine, and the creation

A man representing the Freedmen's Bureau stands between armed groups of white and black Americans. The illustration originally appeared in *Harper's Weekly* on July 25, 1868. Courtesy of Library of Congress.

of special bureau courts. The Freedmen's Bureau has been described as "one of the most idealistic and far-reaching programs ever attempted by the federal government" (Altman 1997, 92) and has clear parallels to modern affirmative action programs.

Supreme Court justice Thurgood Marshall, in his opinion in *Regents of the University of California v. Bakke*, 438 U.S. 265 (1978), pointed out that the Freedmen's Bureau and other Reconstruction legislation constituted, in his opinion, the first affirmative action programs in the United States. Supporters of the bureau argued that simply unshackling the chains of slavery was not sufficient to have true equality of opportunity; rather, newly freed individuals needed preferential treatment and programs to live successful lives in postbellum America. Critics of the Freedmen's Bureau (like some critics of affirmative action today) argued that the bureau was not needed once blacks were free and (in the terminology of one Supreme Court justice of the time) asked "why African Americans should be singled out as the 'special favorites of the law.' " These are arguments one hears today in the affirmative action debate. Furthermore, the relationship between the Freedmen's Bureau and modern affirmative action is relevant today to the debate of whether or not the Fourteenth Amendment's Equal Protection Clause was really meant to be color blind in application. That is, critics of affirmative action programs today often insist that the Fourteenth Amendment is color blind and, in the words of Justice John Marshall Harlan, "neither knows nor tolerates classes among citizens." Critics of affirmative action argue that even benign discrimination based upon race (such as affirmative action programs) is impermissible under the Equal Protection Clause of the Fourteenth Amendment.

However, in rebutting this argument of a completely and strictly color-blind

Fourteenth Amendment, supporters of affirmative action argue that the framers of the Fourteenth Amendment intended the amendment to correct past discrimination against African Americans, protect African Americans against further racial discrimination, and support legislative programs to advance the political and economic equality of African Americans, even if such programs benignly discriminated based upon race. Supporters of this position point to two main pieces of evidence that arguably support the notion that the Fourteenth Amendment allows for race-conscious legislation designed to promote the equality of African Americans. First, there is an enforcement clause at the end of the Fourteenth Amendment that specifies that "Congress shall have power to enforce, by appropriate legislation, the provisions" of the Fourteenth Amendment. According to supporters of affirmative action, this recognized that Congress would pass subsequent legislation ensuring equality for blacks.

Second, supporters of race-conscious affirmative action argue that such programs certainly cannot be contrary to the Fourteenth Amendment, as many of the same individuals who were responsible for drafting the Fourteenth Amendment (and its predecessor statute, the Civil Rights Act of 1866, on which the Equal Protection Clause was based) were also responsible for constructing race-conscious programs such as the Freedmen's Bureau. The Freedmen's Bureau was not color blind. While other Reconstruction legislation (e.g., the Homestead Act and the Morrill Act) offered assistance to any "loyal refugees" (not just African Americans), the Freedmen's Bureau was a preferential race-conscious program designed to improve the lot of African Americans. Thurgood Marshall pointed out in his *Bakke* opinion that the Freedmen's Bureau benefits were provided almost exclusively to newly freed African Americans. Marshall remarked as follows:

> It is plain that the Fourteenth Amendment was not intended to prohibit measures designed to remedy the effects of the Nation's past treatment of Negroes. The Congress that passed the Fourteenth Amendment is the same Congress that passed the 1866 Freedmen's Bureau Act, an Act that provided many of its benefits only to Negroes. . . . After the Civil War our Government started several "affirmative action programs."

The fact that the Freedmen's Bureau and its programs were not color blind is also illustrated by the remarks of critics of the legislation. One critic commented that the legislation was "solely and entirely for the freedmen, and to the exclusion of all other persons." Another comment, alleging in essence reverse discrimination, came from a minority (dissenting) House report that acidly quipped:

> A proposition to establish a bureau of Irishmen's affairs, a bureau of Dutchman's affairs, or . . . those of Caucasian descent generally . . . would be looked upon as the vagary of a diseased brain. . . . Why the freedmen of African descent should become these marked objects of special legislation, to the detriment of the unfortunate whites, your committee fail to understand. (Rubio 2000, 46)

Clearly, the same political leaders who drafted the Civil Rights Act of 1866, the Equal Protection Clause of the Fourteenth Amendment, and the race-conscious Freedmen's Bureau were aware of the arguments that the Freedmen's Bureau "reversely discriminated" and passed the legislation despite this objection.

The genesis of the Freedmen's Bureau dates to earlier in the Civil War. Abolitionists, who considered the notion of a Freedmen's Bureau a key component of reconstructing the South after the Civil War, lobbied Congress to make the bureau a reality. The Confiscation Acts of 1861 and 1862 (allowing seized land to be turned over to freed slaves) and the Freedmen's Department of the U.S. Army were precursors to the Freedmen's Bureau. Proposed legislation creating the Freedmen's Bureau was debated in Congress in 1864–1865. The phrase "forty acres and a mule" was heard often in the legislative debates. The Freedmen's Bureau legislation was passed by Congress on March 3, 1865, and was quickly signed into law by President Abraham Lincoln. The law provided for a Freedmen's Bureau to last "during the present War of Rebellion, and for one year thereafter."

Upon creation of the bureau in 1865, Lincoln nominated Union general Oliver O. Howard to serve as its commissioner. By most accounts, Howard was an able administrator and accomplished many feats given limited resources. W.E.B. Du Bois described Howard and his efforts as follows: "He was sympathetic and humane, and tried with endless application and desperate sacrifice to do a hard, thankless duty" (Du Bois 1970, 223). However, the bureau was a temporary agency. Its original authorization terminated one year after the conclusion of the Civil War. In 1866, Congress passed a bill extending the bureau's life and powers; however, this bill was originally vetoed by President Andrew Johnson. Johnson's reasons for vetoing the legislation (similar to arguments raised by some critics of affirmative action today) were that it was unfair to whites and that it would make the recipients dependent on social welfare. Johnson believed that the Freedmen's Bureau courts would be unjustly adverse to white litigants and that compensating blacks would have a crippling effect. Johnson's veto was overridden by a two-thirds vote in Congress, and the Freedmen's Bureau received a breath of new life in 1866.

From 1865 to 1869, the bureau did much to improve the lot of African Americans and to assist the new citizens in their long and arduous struggle to "level the playing fields" of equality. The bureau issued rations, aid, and medicine to blacks. In a four-year period, the bureau issued 21 million rations to blacks and expended $3,168,325 for clothing and food. The bureau also created hospitals for the care of the sick and elderly and hired staff doctors. By 1867, there were forty-six hospitals with 5,292 beds, and approximately 1 million people were treated. According to W.E.B. Du Bois in his comprehensive work *Black Reconstruction in America, 1860–1880*, as a result of the Freedmen's Bureau, "The death rate among freedmen was reduced from 30% to 13% in 1865, and to 2.03% in 1869" (Du Bois 1970, 226).

In the area of legal affairs and courts, the bureau devised fair-labor contracts for African American workers to ensure that they would not be cheated by unscrupulous white employers in regard to the agreed-upon wages or terms of employment. Du Bois estimated that in a single state of the South, "not less than 50,000 such contracts were drawn in duplicate and filled up with the names of all of the parties" (Du Bois 1970, 225). The bureau also set up special bureau courts, which were utilized for African Americans who did not trust the local state court system and wished to defend their rights to hold property or enforce a contract. These courts were successful. However, many of the courts were abolished by 1867 in the tragically mistaken belief that state courts in the South could treat freed blacks equally with white litigants.

Perhaps the biggest impact of the Freedmen's Bureau was in the area of education. Nearly all of the historically black colleges and universities in the United States today were founded or significantly aided by the Freedmen's Bureau. For example, Storer College, in Harpers Ferry, West Virginia, the first free school in what was part of Virginia before the Civil War, was founded in 1867 by a group of northern church workers with aid from the Freedmen's Bureau. The Freedmen's Bureau also assisted the founders of Storer College by transferring ownership of several abandoned government buildings to the college for its new campus. The impact of the bureau on education was so great that one author reports that in five years, the bureau spent "$5,000,000 building 4,329 schools and hiring 10,000 teachers," and "over 247,333 African Americans were able to take advantage of these educational opportunities" (Altman 1997, 92).

How the Freedmen's Bureau's aid and support (even if indirect) could change the life of an individual can be illustrated in one typical case study. In Harpers Ferry, site of John Brown's raid on the federal arsenal in 1859, an African American named George Weaver resided. In addition to its goal of education, Storer College aided African Americans in their efforts to gain adequate housing. In 1867, George Weaver was able to buy an existing middle-class home in Harpers Ferry with the assistance of Storer College. In the succeeding several decades, all of George Weaver's children and grandchildren were able to take classes at Storer College and to learn a trade. By 1892 (long before the Voting Rights Act of 1965), George Weaver was a registered voter in Jefferson County, West Virginia. When he passed away in 1918, in the same house he had had assistance purchasing fifty-one years earlier in 1867, his obituary in the local paper described him as a respected citizen of the town. His house still stands in Harpers Ferry today as a tribute to both George Weaver and the institutions that assisted him in his struggle for equality.

In 1869, with the exception of some educational programs, the Freedmen's Bureau was dismantled, in large part due to the mistaken notion that African Americans had now been made "whole" and could provide for themselves throughout the South. This premature termination of the bureau prompted W.E.B. Du Bois to write that "the Freedmen's Bureau did an extraordinary piece of work but it was but a small and imperfect part of what it might have done if it had been made a permanent institution, given ample funds for operating schools and purchasing land, and if it had been gradually manned by trained civilian administrators" (Du Bois 1970, 230). Yet in the end, from 1865 to 1869, the Freedmen's Bureau expended the not insubstantial amount of $13,000,000 in supplies and another $5,000,000 to $6,000,000 in army payroll salaries, all in its effort to improve the lot of newly freed Americans. One contemporary writer remarked that "notwithstanding abuses and extravagances, the bureau did a great, an indispensable work of mercy and relief, at a time when no other organization or body was in a position to do that work" (Du Bois 1970, 227). A comment from the official report in 1874 ending the Freedmen's Bureau perhaps summarized the bureau's life and legacy best when it said, "No thirteen millions of dollars were ever more wisely spent . . . with God on its side, the Freedmen's Bureau has triumphed; civilization has received a new impulse, and the friends of humanity may well rejoice."

See also Abolitionists; African Americans; American Civil War; Civil Rights Act of 1866; Color-Blind Constitution; Du Bois, William Edward Burghardt; Equal Protection Clause; Fourteenth Amendment; Historically Black Colleges and Universities; Marshall, Thurgood; *Regents of the University of California v. Bakke*; Reverse Discrimination.

FURTHER READING: Altman, Susan, 1997, *The Encyclopedia of African-American Heritage*, New York: Facts on File; Du Bois, W.E.B., 1970 (reprint of 1935 work), *Black Reconstruction in America, 1860–1880*, New York: Atheneum; Rubio, Philip F., 2001, *A History of Affirmative Action, 1619–2000*, Jackson: University Press of Mississippi; Schnapper, Eric, 1985, "Affirmative Action and the Legislative History of the Fourteenth Amendment," *Virginia Law Review* 71 (June): 753.

JAMES A. BECKMAN

Freedom Riders

The Freedom Ride was an event organized to test the Supreme Court's order to integrate interstate transportation and transportation facilities. Several federal court rulings and the Interstate Commerce Commission (ICC) had outlawed segregation in public transportation, but the segregation continued, especially in the Deep South. Organized by the Congress of Racial Equality (CORE), the Freedom Ride called for black and white passengers to sit in seats reserved exclusively for the opposite race and travel through the South. Each rider agreed that, if arrested, he or she would remain in jail rather than pay a fine or post bail. The goal was to force the federal government to enforce the Supreme Court's decision.

On May 4, 1961, the buses left Washington, D.C., for New Orleans, Louisiana. Traveling through the upper South, the buses met little resistance. However, when the first bus crossed into the state of Alabama, the trouble began. In Anniston, Alabama, the bus was met by an angry mob that threw stones and slashed its tires. The driver managed to evade the mob, but six miles outside of town the bus was firebombed. The second bus traveled without incident until it reached the Birmingham bus terminal. Although notified of its arrival, the police were not on hand. A mob armed with baseball bats and bicycle chains was waiting as the bus pulled into the terminal. Nine passengers were seriously injured. After this second attack, the bus company refused to continue the trip. Two days of negotiation proved unsuccessful, and the remaining passengers flew to New Orleans.

The Student Nonviolent Coordinating Committee (SNCC) sent replacement riders to Birmingham so the trip could continue. Attorney General Robert Kennedy pressured Greyhound officials to provide drivers, and the state highway patrol agreed to escort the bus to its next stop, Montgomery, Alabama. The police followed the bus to Montgomery, but disappeared at the city limits. At the Montgomery bus terminal, the passengers were met by more angry people and no police. Twenty riders, news reporters, and bystanders were injured. In response, the Department of Justice flew 600 U.S. marshals to Montgomery to escort the bus to its next stop, Jackson, Mississippi. The bus was met at the Mississippi line by the state police and escorted to the bus terminal. The riders were moved quickly through the terminal and transported to the local police station, where they were arrested for violating the segregation code. At their trial, the judge turned his back while the defense attorney spoke and, without deliberation, sentenced the riders to sixty days in jail.

Members of the "Washington Freedom Riders Committee," en route from New York City to Washington, D.C., in 1961, hang signs from the bus windows to protest segregation. Courtesy of Library of Congress.

The riders never reached New Orleans, but they did achieve their goal. Across the South, hundreds of protesters organized similar rides. By the end of the summer, more than 300 riders had been arrested in Jackson alone. Under pressure from the White House, the ICC moved quickly to enforce the Supreme Court's decision. A year and a half later, CORE conceded that Jim Crow laws in public transportation were dead.

See also Congress of Racial Equality; De Facto and De Jure Segregation; Department of Justice; Jim Crow Laws; Segregation.

FURTHER READING: Barnes, Catherine A., 1980, *Journey from Jim Crow: The Desegregation of Southern Transit*, New York: Columbia University Press; Carson, Clayborne, 1981, *In Struggle: SNCC and the Black Awakening of the 1960s*, Cambridge, MA: Harvard University Press; Meier, August, and Elliott Rudwick, 1975, *CORE: A Study in the Civil Rights Movement, 1942–1968*, Urbana: University of Illinois Press; Schlesinger, Arthur M., Jr., 1978, *Robert Kennedy and His Times*, Boston: Houghton Mifflin.

AIMÉE HOBBY RHODES

Frontiero v. Richardson, 411 U.S. 677 (1973)

In *Frontiero v. Richardson*, the U.S. Supreme Court held that federal statutes requiring that differential treatment be accorded to male and female members of the armed services seeking increased quarters allowances and medical and dental benefits for spouses violated the Due Process Clause of the Fifth Amendment. The federal statutory scheme permitted male service members to receive benefits for a spouse regardless of whether the spouse actually depended upon the serviceman for support, yet denied female service members benefits for a spouse absent proof of the spouse's dependence upon the servicewoman for support. The statutory distinction apparently rested upon the presumption that husbands are typically the family breadwinner, and wives are financially dependent upon their husbands. It is this type of societal presumption, and its discriminatory impact, that affirmative action seeks to redress.

In an effort to promote reenlistment of military personnel, Congress authorized in 37 U.S.C. § 403 an increase in basic allowance for quarters for service members with dependents and authorized comprehensive medical and dental care for the dependents of service members under 10 U.S.C. § 1076. A "dependent" for purposes of an increase in the basic allowance for quarters included the spouse of a service member, but specifically provided that a person was not a dependent of a female member unless he was in fact dependent upon her for more than one-half of his support. A "dependent" for purposes of medical and dental care included the wife of a service member and the husband of a service member. However, though no limitation existed for the wife of a service member, a husband of a service member would only be considered a dependent if he were "in fact dependent on the member . . . for over one-half of his support."

Sharron Frontiero, a female officer in the U.S. Air Force, applied for an increase in basic allowance for quarters, as well as comprehensive medical and dental care for her spouse, claiming her husband as a dependent under the provisions of 37 U.S.C. § 401, 403 and 10 U.S.C. § 1072, 1076. Although a serviceman was entitled to claim his wife as a dependent without regard to whether the wife in fact depended upon him for any part of her support, Frontiero could not claim her husband as a dependent unless her husband was shown to actually depend upon her for more than one-half of his support. The application filed by Frontiero and her husband, Joseph Frontiero, demonstrated that Joseph Frontiero, a full-time college student, had monthly expenses of approximately $354 while receiving $205 per month in veteran's benefits. As Frontiero could not establish that her husband depended upon her for more than one-half of his support, the application for benefits was denied. Frontiero filed suit contending that by making a distinction in the application of benefits to male and female service members, the statutes discriminated on the basis of sex in violation of the Due Process Clause of the Fifth Amendment.

Frontiero argued that the statutes defining the term "dependent" in a manner so as to exclude only the spouse of a female service member without proof of dependency had a twofold discriminatory impact. First, the process for seeking benefits discriminated against female service members by requiring a female service member seeking benefits to file an application and document her spouse's dependence, while no such filing was required for male service members. Additionally, a female service member would be denied benefits as a result of failure to actually provide more than one-half of her husband's support, while a male service member would receive benefits despite failure to provide more than one-half of his wife's support.

Noting that the United States has had a long and unfortunate history of sex discrimination, and that sex, like race and national origin, is an immutable characteristic that frequently bears no relation to the ability to perform or contribute in society, the Court held that classifications based upon sex are inherently suspect and must be subject to strict judicial scrutiny, a standard which would change approximately a decade later in *Mississippi University for Women v. Hogan*, 458 U.S. 718 (1982). In so holding, the Court found that awarding benefits to a male service member who provides less than one-half of the support of his wife while denying such benefits to a female service member who provides less than one-half of her husband's support results in dissimilar treatment for men and women who are similarly situated, thereby violating the Due Process Clause of the Fifth Amendment.

The government argued that as an empirical matter, wives in U.S. society frequently are dependent upon their husbands, while husbands are rarely dependent upon their wives, and that Congress, in enacting the statutory provisions, may have concluded that it would be cheaper and easier to conclusively presume that wives of male service members are financially dependent upon their husbands while requiring female service members to establish dependency in fact. The Court, however, stated that when entering the realm of "strict judicial scrutiny," there can be no doubt that "administrative convenience" is the kind of arbitrary legislative choice forbidden by the Constitution. The Court noted that under the demands of strict judicial scrutiny, the government, for example, would have to demonstrate that it was actually cheaper to grant benefits with respect to all male service members than to determine which male service members were actually entitled to benefits as a result of having a wife who was in fact dependent upon her husband for more than one-half of her support. The Court stated that the government offered no evidence tending to support its proposition that treating male and female service members differently in fact saved the government money, and it questioned whether, if required to do so, the government could make such a demonstration, noting that substantial evidence existed that many of the wives of male service members would fail to qualify for benefits under the standard applied to the husbands of female service members. In addition, the Court questioned the purported cost savings to the government of its current program, as determinations of dependency were made upon the filing of an affidavit as opposed to a more costly hearing process. Therefore, the statutory scheme was determined to be constitutionally invalid.

In a concurring opinion, Justice Lewis Powell, joined by Chief Justice Warren Burger and Justice Harry Blackmun, objected to extending the classifications considered inherently suspect to include sex. Justice Powell found such an extension of the limited group of suspect classifications unnecessary, noting that the Court's prior opinion in *Reed v. Reed*, 404 U.S. 71 (1971), supported the Court's finding that the statutes at issue violated the Due Process Clause without a need to rule on whether classifications based on sex are inherently suspect and subject to strict judicial scrutiny. Justice Powell also opined that by deciding a sensitive issue of broad social and political importance with the Equal Rights Amendment having been approved by Congress to resolve issues of sex-based discrimination, the decision by the Court failed to respect the legislative process.

See also Blackmun, Harry Andrew; Equal Rights Amendment; Fifth Amendment; Gender Norms; Gender-Based Affirmative Action; Intermediate Scrutiny Review; *Mississippi University for Women v. Hogan*; Powell, Lewis Franklin, Jr.; Stereotypes, Gender; Strict Scrutiny.

FURTHER READING: Crosby, Faye J., and Cheryl VanDeVeer, eds., 2000, *Sex, Race, and Merit: Debating Affirmative Action in Education and Employment*, Ann Arbor: University of Michigan Press.

EILEEN HUSSELBAUGH

Fullilove v. Klutznick, 448 U.S. 448 (1980)

In *Fullilove v. Klutznick*, the Supreme Court upheld the constitutionality of an affirmative action set-aside program enacted by Congress in order to ensure that the effects of past racial discrimination in public contracting would not be perpetuated but would be remedied. The *Fullilove* decision was significant in that the Court acknowledged the permissibility of congressional race-conscious affirmative action plans to remedy previous incidents of discrimination. The Court ruled that the set-aside was permissible to remedy prior discrimination so long as the prior discrimination was documented and the set-aside was reasonable and not unnecessarily broad. Despite the importance of the *Fullilove* decision to the issue of affirmative action and employment, the holding in the case was limited by the Supreme Court nine years later when it decided *City of Richmond v. J.A. Croson Co.*, 488 U.S. 469 (1989), and again in 1995, when it decided *Adarand Constructors, Inc. v. Peña*, 515 U.S. 200 (1995), both cases also involving the issue of minority set-asides in the contracting context.

The facts of the *Fullilove* case were as follows: In an effort to assist minority-owned businesses and contractors who had been previously impacted by discrimination, Congress enacted the Public Works Employment Act of 1977. As part of this legislation, state and local recipients of federal funds for local public works projects were required to spend not less than 10 percent of the allocated federal funds on goods and services provided by minority-owned businesses (previously referred to as minority business enterprises and presently referred to as disadvantaged business enterprises). Under the plan, the 10 percent set-aside could be waived if no minority-owned businesses were available.

The plan was challenged by non-minority-owned businesses who claimed that the Due Process Clause of the Fifth Amendment and the Equal Protection Clause of the Fourteenth Amendment prohibited Congress and states from acting in a race-conscious manner, that Congress lacked the authority to pass legislation requiring contractors to set aside funds, and that the plan was too broad. However, the Supreme Court upheld the set-aside program as constitutional, holding that so long as Congress was acting to remedy prior discrimination, it was not required to act in a color-blind manner. Congress had the clear authority to pass such a contracting scheme under its Commerce Clause power, its spending power, and its power under the Enabling Clause (Section 5) of the Fourteenth Amendment, which authorizes Congress to enforce the provisions of the Fourteenth Amendment, including its requirement that states not deprive any person of the equal protection of the laws. Finally, the Court held that the legislation was not "overbroad" because it allowed for waivers if minority contractors were not able to provide the required goods and services, and also the set-aside amount was limited and reasonable (i.e., a 10 percent set-aside was not onerous or unreasonable). This last factor is one of the chief distinguishing features between the set-aside plan upheld in *Fullilove* (10 percent set-aside) and the set-aside plan rejected in the *Croson* case (30 percent set-aside). The other key difference was that the set-aside plan was established by Congress in *Fullilove* and created by a state in *Croson*. The Court emphasized in its *Fullilove* decision that Congress was exercising authorized power when it established the set-aside program and was therefore entitled to deference. Finally, according to the Court, the set-aside in *Fullilove* was implemented by Congress after specifically finding and documenting previous discrimination, while in *Croson*, the plan at issue had no such concrete findings of previous discrimination prior to implementation. This factor was of crucial importance to Justice Lewis Powell, who wrote a concurring opinion in *Fullilove* stressing the need for concrete findings of prior discrimination before affirmative action plans are implemented.

Although the majority of justices agreed that the congressional set-aside should be upheld, they reached this result through different analyses. Justices Warren Burger, Lewis Powell, and Byron White concluded, in an opinion written by Chief Justice Warren Burger, that the set-aside was constitutional because (1) its objective was within the power of Congress and (2) Congress's use of racial and ethnic criteria in determining which firms were entitled to the preference was a constitutionally permissible means for implementing the objective because it was limited and narrowly tailored to achieve the objective. This opinion did not explicitly classify its standard of review as "strict" or "intermediate." It stated that racial or ethnic criteria, even when used in the remedial context, were subject to "close examination," but also noted that Congress was entitled to deference. However, one of these justices, Justice Lewis Powell, writing separately, stated that this was basically the strict scrutiny test. That is, the measure was unconstitutional unless it was narrowly tailored to fulfill a compelling governmental interest. Justices Thurgood Marshall, William Brennan Jr., and Harry Blackmun agreed that the set-aside was constitutional, but concluded that the appropriate review standard was whether the set-asides "serve important governmental interests and are substantially related to achievement of those objectives"—intermediate scrutiny. These justices applied the lower level of scrutiny because the set-aside was remedial and designed to benefit minorities instead of to disadvantage minorities.

In 1995, the U.S. Supreme Court decided *Adarand Constructors, Inc. v. Peña*, 515 U.S. 200 (1995). In this case, the Court examined a contracting set-aside program for "socially and economically disadvantaged" businesses where minority-owned businesses were entitled to a rebuttable presumption of social and economic disadvantage. The Court held that all federal racial preferences, including the set-aside at issue, were subject to strict scrutiny constitutional review. To the extent that *Fullilove* was inconsistent with this holding, it was overruled. It is unclear whether the Court would have approved the set-aside program in *Fullilove* if all of the justices who voted to uphold the program had to apply the strict scrutiny review standard.

See also *Adarand Constructors, Inc. v. Peña*; Affirmative Action Plan/Program; Burger Court and Affirmative Action; *City of Richmond v. J.A. Croson Co.*; Contracting and Affirmative Action; Disadvantaged Business Enterprises; Fourteenth Amendment; Public Works Employment Act of 1977; Quotas; Supreme Court and Affirmative Action.

FURTHER READING: Spann, Girardeau A., 2000, *The Law of Affirmative Action: Twenty-five Years of Supreme Court Decisions on Race and Remedies*, New York: New York University Press.

MARIA D. BECKMAN

G

Garvey, Marcus (1887–1940)

Marcus Garvey was a Jamaican-born Black Nationalist leader who is remembered today chiefly for creating the first Black Nationalist movement in the United States. Although Garvey's Black Nationalism movement was a failure, he had a tremendous impact on the civil rights leadership and movement during the 1920s and 1930s. He was able to attract blacks whom the National Association for the Advancement of Colored People (NAACP) had failed to reach. Interestingly, Garvey's position has relevancy and is analogous to the separatism movement (and its relation to affirmative action) today. Garvey's solution for many of the racial woes in the United States was a "back-to-Africa" movement. Garvey believed that blacks could never rely on whites for justice, and waiting for white social charity (if it came at all) as a means of achieving equality was useless. Thus Garvey's approach for improving civil rights can be contrasted with those of two great African American leaders of the time, Booker T. Washington and W.E.B. Du Bois. Booker T. Washington advocated peaceful assimilation, accommodation, and achieving equality not by directly challenging racist laws, but by working within the system and developing one's own economic worth, causing "friction between the races" to "pass away" as black individuals gained economic worth and power. W.E.B. Du Bois advocated challenging the status quo by a "Talented Tenth" in an effort to cast off the racist Jim Crow laws and believed that only through changing racist laws (in conjunction with higher education of black individuals) could true equality in society be achieved. These historical positions of Garvey, Du Bois, and Washington are relevant to the affirmative action debate, as individuals today still advocate each of these approaches when debating the efficacy of modern affirmative action programs.

Born on August 17, 1887, in the little town of St. Ann's Bay, Jamaica, Garvey was one of eleven children. Due to financial difficulties, Garvey left school at fourteen to become a printer's apprentice. At seventeen, he moved to Kingston to work at his new trade. There he acquired an interest in public speaking and politics. In 1907, Garvey was fired for taking a leadership role in the first Printers'

Union strike. Garvey later worked at a variety of jobs and became keenly interested in reform activities. He traveled to several countries throughout the Caribbean and South and Central America. Wherever he traveled, Garvey found fellow Jamaicans and other people of color subjected to discrimination and abuse. Distressed, Garvey returned to Jamaica to seek the aid of the colonial government. Failing to obtain any assistance from the British consulate, Garvey concluded that blacks could never rely on whites for justice and equal treatment.

Garvey then began to lay the groundwork for his Universal Negro Improvement Association and the African Communities League. In 1912, he traveled to London to seek financial backing for his organizations. There he found that blacks in London were also discriminated against. He met many native Africans and personally saw the horrible conditions for blacks in Africa and other parts of the British Empire. He also met Duse Mohammed Ali, a scholarly Egyptian nationalist who raised Garvey's interest in the cause of African freedom. Garvey also became interested in the conditions of blacks in the United States when he read Booker T. Washington's *Up from Slavery*.

Garvey returned to Jamaica in 1914 in hopes of uplifting Jamaican blacks and uniting blacks of the world. He established the Universal Negro Improvement and Conservation Association (UNIA) and the African Communities League on August 1, 1914. Garvey had hopes of gaining support for his organizations in the United States from Booker T. Washington, but before Garvey could complete travel arrangements, Washington died in 1915. When Garvey arrived in New York in the spring of 1916, many black Americans were going through extreme social changes and disillusionment with white America and were ready for a black Moses. During 1916 and 1917, Garvey toured the United States talking about race redemption and trying to raise money for his organizations. In 1918, Garvey began publication of the *Negro World*, which became one of the most popular black weeklies, with a readership of about 50,000 people.

Early in 1919, Garvey began talking about a fleet of black-owned and operated steamships that would link the black races of the world. He established the Black Star Steamship Line and sold stock to African Americans for five dollars a share. In August 1920, the UNIA held a monthlong convention in Harlem. Thousands of blacks from all over the world attended. Composed mostly of working-class blacks, the UNIA was the largest organization ever to exist among blacks in America and the West Indies. During the convention, the delegates voted to establish a free African Republic with Garvey as president. The UNIA delegation went to Liberia to develop Liberia's rubber and other resources. However, it was later expelled due to pressure from the French and the British. The concessions that Garvey claimed in Liberia were later given to the Firestone Rubber Company.

The UNIA was an almost immediate success in the United States, but failed within five years. With the failure of the Black Star Line, Garvey was convicted of mail fraud and sent to federal prison in Atlanta in 1924. Some believed that Garvey was sent to prison because the American government wanted to break up the UNIA and take the focus off the deal made with Firestone. In 1927, Garvey's sentence was commuted by President Calvin Coolidge, and Garvey was deported to Jamaica. He later moved to London, where he died in 1940.

See also Black Nationalism; Du Bois, William Edward Bunghardt; Jim Crow Laws;

National Association for the Advancement of Colored People; Talented Tenth; Washington, Booker T.

FURTHER READING: Cronin, E. David, ed., 1973, *Great Lives Observed: Marcus Garvey*, Englewood Cliffs, NJ: Prentice-Hall; Cruse, Harold, 1987, *Plural but Equal*, New York: William Morrow; Garvey, Amy Jacques, ed., 1926, *Philosophy and Opinions of Marcus Garvey*, vol. 2, New York: Universal Publishing House.

NAOMI ROBERTSON

Gates, Henry Louis, Jr. (1950–)

Henry Louis Gates Jr. is considered one of the most prominent academics in the United States, and in 1997 he was voted one of *Time* magazine's "25 Most Influential Americans." Since the early 1990s, he has headed the Afro-American studies program at Harvard University. His work has resulted in a greater acceptance of African American studies and has given it more recognition and respectability as a serious field of study. He has discovered and restored thousands of works by African American writers, including Harriet E. Wilson's *Our Nig* (1859) and, most recently, Hannah Craft's *The Bondwoman's Narrative* (circa 1855–1859, published in 2002), believed to be the first novel known to have been written by a black woman in America and the only one written by a fugitive slave. In addition, Gates has authored on coauthored numerous books and is general editor of *The Norton Anthology of African American Literature.*

Gates is a nationally known supporter of affirmative action. Along with Cornel West, Derrick Bell, and Toni Morrison, Gates took out a national advertisement in 1996 advocating the continuation of affirmative action in the United States. In December 2001, Gates threatened to resign from Harvard University because Harvard did not adequately support affirmative action. However, some have claimed that Gates's threat had more to do with the treatment of Cornel West than with affirmative action. This threat followed shortly after Gates's colleague Cornel West left Harvard after being, in the words of West, "dishonored" by Harvard. West had allegedly been rebuked by Harvard president Lawrence Summers for spending time recording a rap CD, leading an exploratory presidential committee for the Reverend Al Sharpton, and allowing grade inflation in his courses. When West left, he also accused Summers of being unsupportive of affirmative action. However, in December 2002, Gates announced that he had turned down an offer from Princeton University (where West had gone after leaving Harvard) and promised to remain at Harvard.

Henry Louis Gates Jr. was born on September 16, 1950, in Keyser, West Virginia. His father, Henry Louis Sr., worked at a mill during the day and worked nights as a janitor at the local telephone company. His mother, Pauline, cleaned houses and became the first African American to serve on the nearby Piedmont PTA. Gates Jr. graduated summa cum laude with a degree in history from Yale in 1973. He earned his master's and doctorate in English literature from Clare College at the University of Cambridge, becoming the first African American to receive a doctorate from Cambridge. He taught English literature and Afro-American studies at Yale and Cornell before joining Harvard in 1991, where he is currently the director of the W.E.B. Du Bois Institute for Afro-American Research. In 1988, at Cornell, Gates was the first African American male to hold an endowed chair in the history of the university. He is the author or editor of more than fifteen books and is also the winner of the 1998 National Humanities Medal.

See also Bell, Derrick A., Jr.; Morrison, Toni; West, Cornel.

FURTHER READING: Fogg, Piper, and Kate Galbraith, 2002, "Gates to Remain at Harvard; Yale's Provost Will Be First Woman to Lead U. of Cambridge Full Time," *Chronicle of Higher Education,* December 13, A7; "Princeton May Snare 2nd Black Harvard Scholar," 2002, *Record,* February 4, A6; Wilson, Robin, and Scott Smallwood, "Battle of Wills at Harvard," *Chronicle of Higher Education,* January 18, A8.

PAULINA X. RUF

Gates Millennium Scholars Program

The Gates Millennium Scholars (GMS) program was established in 1999 by a grant from the Bill and Melinda Gates Foundation in the initial amount of $1 billion with the purpose of providing outstanding African American, American Indian/Alaska Native, Asian Pacific Islander American, and Hispanic American students with "an opportunity to complete an undergraduate college education, in all discipline areas and a graduate education for those students pursuing studies in mathematics, science, engineering, education, or library science." Opponents of affirmative action have criticized the GMS because it is limited to students of particular racial and ethnic backgrounds. For example, Roger Clegg, general counsel for the Center for Equal Opportunity, has commented that "I have some sympathy for the argument that Mr. Gates should be able to spend his money any way he wants, but that does not mean what he's doing is morally right. There is no reason to limit this scholarship to particular races and ethnicities." In turn, proponents of the GMS argue that the scholarships broaden the achievement opportunities for students who are not likely to fit the profiles of Ivy League schools and who would likely not complete their academic degrees because of lack of funds.

The Gates Foundation established the GMS to encourage and support students to complete their college education and pursue graduate degrees in fields where ethnic and racial groups are underrepresented. The United Negro College Fund is the administrator of the GMS. It has subcontracted with the American Indian Graduate Center Scholars, the Hispanic Scholarship Fund, and the Organization of Chinese Americans to assist in the implementation of the scholarship program. The Gates Millennium Scholars program is the largest scholarship fund in the history of higher education. In the first years of the program, low-income minority students at all levels of higher education have been permitted to apply. It is expected that in the future, only high-school seniors will be eligible.

See also African Americans; Asian Americans; Center for Equal Opportunity; Hispanic Americans; Native Americans.

FURTHER READING: Hoover, Eric, 2001, "The First Class of Gates Scholars," *Chronicle of Higher Education,* July 13, A34; Pulley, John L., 2000, "A $1-Billion Experiment Seeks a New Way to Identify Talented Minority Students," *Chronicle of Higher Education,* June 23, A41; Rivers, Elaine, 1999, "Bill Gives Big," *Time,* September 27, 48; Schubert, Ruth, 2001, "Freedom to Chase Their Dreams: Gates Scholarship Offers Help, Hope to Minority Students," *Seattle Post-Intelligencer* (final ed.), May 30, A1.

PAULINA X. RUF

Gender Attitudes on Affirmative Action

The study of gender-based affirmative action has been focused mainly on the psychological and behavioral effects of affirmative action on women, including measures of motivation and task interest, choice, and self-evaluations of ability and performance. With respect to the relationships between measures of motivation and task interest, the question that researchers have addressed is whether gender-based selection procedures decrease women's motivation. Results of research are inconsistent.

Some studies indicate that gender-based selection procedures decrease women's motivation on the job. Thomas Chacko (1982), for example, found that women who believed that they had been hired on the basis of their gender reported lower job commitment and satisfaction and greater role ambiguity and conflict than women who did not believe that gender had played an important role in their hiring. However, other studies did not find this result. Heilman and colleagues (1987) did not find negative effects of gender-based affirmative action on measures of task motivation or interest. A similar finding was reached by Turner and Pratkanis (1994).

Women's task and job choice seem to be more consistently affected by gender-based affirmative action. Females are more likely to choose easier versus harder tasks when gender is used as the unique basis for selection. For example, Heilman, Rivero, and Brett (1991) reported that women selected on the basis of gender chose less demanding tasks than did women selected on the basis of merit. In a second study with similar characteristics, Heilman found that only females selected on the basis of gender and who were given no information about their qualifications chose the less demanding task. Females who were selected on the basis of gender and given positive information about their qualifications were more likely to choose the more demanding task. It seems that the effect on women's task choice is determined by the nature of the implementation strategy. When the implementation strategy provides explicit information about qualifications, gender-based affirmative action affects task choice to a lesser extent.

Other sets of studies of gender-based affirmative action examine the effects of affirmative action on women's self-evaluations of ability and performance. Research suggests that gender-based preferential selection could have negative effects on women's self-perceptions. Heilman and her colleagues (1998) studied whether these negative effects were dependent on the type of affirmative action policy and found that women who had been selected by a preferential selection process reported lower job satisfaction and greater evaluation apprehension and role stress than women selected on a merit basis. Furthermore, they devalued their leadership capability and task performance and selected less demanding work tasks. Results supported these ideas by demonstrating that preferential selection as opposed to merit-based selection has more negative effects on women's self-evaluations. However, the method of selection had little effect on men (Heilman, 1993). The study by Heilman and colleagues (1993) showed the negative consequences of hard preferential selection policies for women beneficiaries, but when it was clear that merit played a central role in the preferential selection decision, women's performance evaluations and assessments of their leadership ability did not differ from those of women selected on a merit basis.

Research suggests that the nature of the implementation strategy could determine the negative effects on females' self-evaluations. Information about qualifications must be unambiguous in its confirmation of the woman's competence. Information about the woman's qualifications should be explicit. Strategies that provide only subtle indications of competencies produce poorer evaluations than merit-based selection strategies. Finally, the evidence should be focused. Feedback must be related to the recipient's performance on specific components of the task.

Turner and Pratkanis (1993) developed a model in which affirmative action was perceived as a form of help that could be applied to beneficiaries by affirmative action. Turner and Pratkanis (1994) suggested that affirmative action has positive outcomes when it is self-supportive for the recipient. When affirmative action provides positive self-relevant messages (provides explicit, unambiguous, and focused evidence of qualifications), conforms to societal norms (it follows a fair procedure and rewards excellence), and provides instrumental benefits (it provides information about future success and removes barriers to success), it is likely to produce positive immediate and long-term outcomes such as positive evaluations of ability and performance, positive affect, low motivation to alter the situation, and low degree of self-protective defensive behavior.

Few studies have experimentally examined the effects of gender-based selection on task performance, and they revealed a complex relationship between gender-based selection procedures and task performance. The effects of selection procedure on performance seem to be moderated by variables such as self-efficacy and task characteristics. Another aspect related to gender-based affirmative action is the evaluations of women hired under affirmative action programs. Several studies indicate that majority members view women selected through affirmative action programs as less competent than those selected without affirmative action (Heilman, McCullough, and Gilbert 1996). This perception is more evident when affirmative action is operationalized as strong preferential selection than when affirmative action is simply mentioned. Several works report that people present more positive attitudes toward affirmative action programs for women than toward those for other minority groups. Fletcher and Chalmers (1991) found that attitudes were more negative toward affirmative action programs targeted at French Canadians than toward affirmative action programs targeted at women. Similarly, programs directed at blacks are viewed less positively by whites than programs directed at women. Reasons for this difference are unclear. Eberhardt and Fiske (1994) considered that these differences are related to differences in racial and gender stereotypes. This may be because gender based affirmative action is perceived as being implemented on a much smaller scale in society, and that not all women benefit from affirmative action. This can be contrasted with the majority belief that all African American (or other minorities) are beneficiaries of affirmative action.

See also Gender Norms; Gender Segregation in Employment; Gender Stratification; Gender-Based Affirmative Action.

FURTHER READING: Chacko, Thomas I., 1982, "Women and Equal Employment Opportunity: Some Unintended Effects," *Journal of Applied Psychology* 67:119–123; Eberhardt, Jennifer L., and Susan T. Fiske, 1994, "Affirmative Action in Theory and Practice: Issues of Power, Ambiguity, and Gender versus Race," *Basic and Applied Social Psychology* 15, nos. 1 and 2:201–220; Fletcher, Kenneth, and Garth Chalmers, 1991, "Attitudes of Canadians toward Affirmative Action: Opposition, Value Pluralism, and Non-attitudes," *Political Behavior* 13, no. 1:67–95; Heilman, Madeleine E., 1994, "Affirmative Action: Some Unintended Consequences for Working Women," *Research in Organizational Behavior* 16:125–169; Heilman, Madeleine E., William S. Battle, Chris E. Keller, and Andrew L. Lee, 1998, "Type of Affirmative Action Policy: A Determinant of Reactions to Sex-Based Preferential Selection," *Journal of Applied Psychology* 83, no. 2:190–205; Heilman, Madeleine E., Stella R. Kaplow, Mary Anne Amato, and Peter Stathatos, 1993, "When Similarity is a Liability: Effects of Sex-Based Preferences," *Journal of Applied Psychology* 78, no. 6:917–928; Heilman, Madeleine E., Winston F. McCullough, and David Gilbert, 1996, "The Other Side of Affirmative Action: Reactions of Non-beneficiaries to Sex-Based Preferential Selection," *Journal of Applied Psychology* 81: 346–357; Heilman, Madeleine, Juan Carlos Rivero, and Joan F. Brett, 1991, "Skirting the Competence Issue: Effects of Sex-Based Preferential Selection on Task Choices of Women and Men," *Journal of Applied Psychology* 76:99–105; Heilman, Madeleine E., Michael C. Simon, and David P. Repper, 1987, "Intentionally Favored Unintentionally Harmed," *Journal of Applied Psychology* 72, no. 1:62–69; Turner, Marlene E., and Anthony R. Pratkanis, 1993, "Effects of Preferential and Meritorious Selection on Performance: An Examination of Intuitive and Self-Handicapping Perspectives," *Personality and Social Psychology Bulletin* 19:47–58; Turner, Marlene E., and Anthony R. Pratkanis, 1994, "Affirmative Action as Help: A Review of Recipient Reactions to Preferential Selection and Affirmative Action," *Basic and Applied Social Psychology* 15, nos. 1 and 2:43–69.

MARIA JOSE SOTELO

Gender Norms

Affirmative action programs can help undermine the traditional gender norms that foster discrimination in the workplace. Traditional gender norms pervade the workplace and reinforce an inequitable division of labor in the home. According to traditional gender norms, women are passive, dependent, vulnerable, emotional, nurturing, caring, empathetic, and in need of protection; men are the opposite: aggressive, independent, in control, and invulnerable. Traditional gender norms define women as natural caregivers and men as breadwinners and the head of the family. Women's first responsibility is to the family and home; men's first responsibility is to work. This assumption of inherent gender difference has justified gender inequality as a mere reflection of nature. However, sociologists, anthropologists, and biologists have demonstrated that these "traditional gender norms" are social, rather than biological, and that ideas about gender difference are in fact a product of inequality. Gender norms vary tremendously from one culture to another, as well as within one culture over time.

What most individuals assume to be the "traditional" division of labor is in fact a relatively recent invention. Prior to the industrial revolution, there was far less differentiation between men's and women's spheres. Both worked in and around the home to provide for the family. Industrialization in the mid-nineteenth century separated work from the home, and the ideology of separate spheres was created. The public sphere became associated with men, and women were assigned to the private sphere. Work was defined as work for pay performed outside of the home, rendering "women's work" invisible. Many historians argue that this new division of labor and accompanying ideology represented a decline in women's status. This new separation of spheres was largely confined to the white middle class, but it was held up as the norm for all families. It was not until the 1950s that the model of the breadwinner father and stay-at-home mother was embraced as the ideal family in response to the return of men from World War II and the need for women to return to the home to free up jobs for these returning men. Less than 10 percent of households now fit the "traditional" family form, yet this mythical ideal reinforces gender inequality and the myth of gender differences.

Traditional gender norms reinforce inequities in the workplace. Some employers assume that women will make less serious employees who will get married, have kids, and quit or not be as committed to their jobs if they stay. According to traditional gender norms, men need a "family wage" to support their families, whereas women work for "pin money." Traditional gender norms create stereotypes that limit opportunities for both men and women. These stereotypes define women and men in oppositional terms. An individual learns what his or her culture considers appropriate gendered behavior from a very early age, beginning in the family and continuing in schools where girls have been discouraged from advanced math, science, and technology courses. These stereotypes reinforce segregation in the labor market by defining certain occupations as "natural" for men or women. This is not the case, however, because there is tremendous cultural and historical variation in job segregation. For example, in Europe, most dentists are women; in the United States, the field is dominated by men. There is nothing about the job itself that makes it more appropriate for men or women. While jobs are gender typed differently from one society to the next, they consistently pay less when they are performed by women. One also finds historical variation. For example, in the United States, clerical work was once a male-dominated profession; however, by the middle of the twentieth century, it became female dominated. At the same time, clerical work became devalued and seen as less demanding of skill, and the wages dropped.

Traditional gender norms put women in a double bind in the workplace. Workplaces are constructed around the needs of male workers and assume that employees require masculine qualities to get the job done. Women are frequently punished for not being womanly enough, yet these womanly characteristics are also seen as making women unable to compete in the male domain. Further, few workplaces offer either flexible working schedules or other family-friendly policies; most assume that workers have wives at home to care for the children and home.

Traditional gender norms shape the division of labor in the home as well. Women who are married and employed full-time outside of the home still perform 70 percent of the housework and child care for their families, and domestic labor remains largely unrecognized and devalued in our culture. Consequently, women must perform a double shift each day, making it difficult for women to balance work and family responsibilities. Thus traditional gender norms restrict both women and men by delimiting a narrow definition of appropriate gendered behavior that individuals are expected to adhere to. Both women and men face consequences when they step outside of these narrowly defined roles.

See also Gender Attitudes on Affirmative Action; Gender Segregation in Employment; Gender Stratification; Gender-Based Affirmative Action; Glass Ceilings; Sex and Gender; Stereotypes, Gender.

FURTHER READING: Burke, Phyllis, 1996, *Gender Shock: Exploding the Myths of Male and Female,* New York: Anchor Books; Crittenden, Ann, 2001, *The Price of Motherhood: Why the Most Important Job in the World Is Still the Least Valued,* New York: Metropolitan Books; Hubbard, Ruth, 1990, *The Politics of Women's Biology,* New Brunswick, NJ: Rutgers University Press; Kimmel, Michael S., 2000, *The Gendered Society,* New York: Oxford University Press.

ABBY L. FERBER

Gender Segregation in Employment

While affirmative action policies have enabled many women to enter traditionally male occupations, sex segregation in the workplace is still widespread. Job segregation is the most pervasive form of inequality in the workplace. Women and men are largely concentrated in different occupations, industries, jobs, and levels. For example, as of 2002, women made up only 2 percent of employees in the construction trades, 8 percent of engineers, and 13 percent of dentists, while they represented 93 percent of nurses, 99 percent of secretaries, and 99 percent of dental hygienists. Furthermore, even in fields where women have apparently made significant progress, men and women are segregated into different specializations. For example, women doctors are disproportionately gynecologists or pediatricians, while female educators are disproportionately preschool and elementary-school teachers. Men who do specialize in primary education are more likely to become principals and superintendents. Segregation is so pervasive that less than 10 percent of American workers have a coworker of the opposite sex who does the same job, at the same employer, on the same shift. In fact, women are overwhelmingly concentrated in only five occupations. This segregation is one of the most significant factors in contributing to the wage gap. Research by sociologists, historians, and economists reveals that the gender composition of an occupation is a much better predictor of wages than the skills or training required or any other features of the job itself.

Gender segregation is tied to stereotypical definitions of gender roles. Women are seen as nurturing, emotional, supportive, and dependent; men as the opposite: independent, aggressive, unemotional, invulnerable, in control, and the primary breadwinner. People learn what their culture considers appropriate gendered behavior from a very early age. This segregation begins in the family and continues in schools. Different occupations may be seen as masculine or feminine terrain, and both men and women face consequences, ranging from ridicule to harassment, for stepping outside of these stereotypical roles and occupations.

These stereotypes act to reinforce segregation between the sexes by defining certain work roles as "natural" for men or women. However, these stereotypes do not hold true across the globe. There is tremendous cultural and historical variation in job segregation from country to country. For example, in Europe, the dentistry profession is dominated by women; in the United States, the field is dominated by men. There is nothing the profession of dentistry itself that makes it more appropriate for men or women. This example also reveals the way in which segregation is tied to wages: in the United States, dentists are near the top of the income hierarchy, yet in Europe, where women predominate in the field, incomes only fall in the middle. Researchers have documented this phenomenon in many fields: jobs are gender stereotyped differently from one society to the next, but they consistently pay less when they are performed by women. There is also historical variation. For example, in the United States, clerical work was once a male-dominated profession and was relatively well paying. In the early 1900s, more women began to enter clerical jobs, males left the field, and by the middle of the twentieth century it became female dominated. At the same time, clerical work became devalued and seen as less demanding of skill, and the wages dropped. Sociologists have contended that the decrease in pay was not a cause of this gender shift, but instead a consequence. There are numerous occupations where this has occurred.

An opposite pattern has occurred in other occupations, for example, in computer programming. In the 1940s, women worked as key-punch operators, the occupational predecessor to computer programming. However, once the high skill levels demanded of the job were recognized, men were increasingly hired, and the wages rose significantly. While the gendered division of labor varies from one time and place to another, most societies do have a gendered division of labor, and the tasks assigned to women are generally devalued and lower paying.

Comparable-worth policies have been proposed and developed to remedy the wage gap due to gender segregation of jobs. To provide similar wages for roughly comparable jobs, these programs systematically review jobs and devise pay levels based on established criteria such as education, complexity, and skills so that jobs can be compared and wages not tied to gender. While gender segregation plays a significant role in perpetuating the wage gap, it is not the only factor. Women make less money at the exact same jobs as men, even when they are working for the same employers. Within the vast majority of jobs, women earn less. For example, not only do women doctors earn less than men, but women dermatologists, gynecologists, anesthesiologists, radiologists, and other specialists earn less than males. This holds true in most occupational fields.

See also Gender Attitudes on Affirmative Action; Gender Norms; Gender Stratification; Gender-Based Affirmative Action; Glass Ceilings; Sex and Gender; Stereotypes, Gender.

FURTHER READING: Kimmel, Michael, 2000, *The Gendered Society*, New York: Oxford University Press; Reskin, Barbara, ed., 1984, *Sex Segregation in the Workplace: Trends, Explanations, Remedies*, Washington, DC: National Academy Press; Reskin, Barbara, and Patricia Roos, eds., 1990, *Job Queues, Gender Queues: Explaining Women's Inroads into Male Occupations*, Philadelphia: Temple University Press; Stromberg, Ann Helton, and Shirley Harkess, 1988, *Women Working: Theories and Facts in Perspective*, Mountain View, CA: Mayfield Publishing Company.

ABBY L. FERBER

Gender Stratification

Gender stratification is produced at almost all levels. At the societal level, men are placed in higher economic and political positions than women. In the organizational arena, men generally have more power than women. Men occupy positions with more pay and stature in the organization, exercise more control over the economic resources of the organization, and supervise more people. At an interpersonal level, gender stratification exists as power differences between men and women. For example, in marital relationships, men generally spend more time on leisure activities than women. Gender-specific affirmative action plans are said to ameliorate the deleterious effects of gender stratification.

Different theories have examined the causes of gender stratification. One theory is the social role theory. According to sociologist Alice Eagly, the division of labor, in which men are more likely to be in paid occupational positions and women are more likely to be in the homemaker role, affects beliefs and behaviors about men and women. In this line, others have suggested that beliefs about gender could cause men and women to make different career choices and lead others to pressure males and females into different social roles. Observing the distribution of men and women in different occupational roles, it is argued, can contribute to the formation of gender stereotypes.

Another approach/theory to the study of gender stratification is the expectation state theory. According to author Cecilia Ridgeway, "Gender is an institutionalized system of social practices for constituting males and females as different in socially significant ways and organizing inequality in terms of those differences" (Ridgeway 2001, 637). The gender system is related to social stratification because gender stereotypes contain status beliefs (shared cultural schemas about the status position in society of groups based on gender and other categories) that associate greater status competence with men than with women and elicit differential performance expectations. Men are expected to perform better than women, and because others hold this expectation, they have more opportunities to participate, to act, and to have more influence.

The structure of group relations legitimizes ideologies, that is, systems of belief that justify the relative positions and relationships of social groups. Research has confirmed that status differences foster beliefs in the relative superiority of high-status groups, even among members of low-status groups, especially in traits related to competence. Thus male dominance results in stereotypes of male superiority in competence and the belief that women are relatively inferior. Another dimension of structural group relations is whether perceived relations are cooperative or competitive. Male-female group relations are cooperative due to the interdependence between the sexes. In cooperative relationships, both dominants and subordinates have an interest in adopting ideologies that characterize the subordinate group as superior on a social warmth dimension. Because men depend on the interaction with women, they have an incentive to reward women for exhibiting warm traits.

See also Gender Attitudes on Affirmative Action; Gender Norms; Gender Segregation in Employment; Gender-Based Affirmative Action; Glass Ceilings; Sex and Gender; Stereotypes, Gender.

FURTHER READING: Eagly, Alice, 1987, *Sex Differences in Social Behavior: A Social-Role Interpretation*, Hillsdale, NJ: Erlbaum; Eccles, Jacqueline S., 1987, "Gender Roles and Women's Achievement-Related Decisions," *Psychology of Women Quarterly* 11:135–172; Jackman, Mary R., 1994, *The Velvet Glove: Paternalism and Conflict in Gender, Class, and Race Relations*, Berkeley:

University of California Press; Jost, John T., and Mahzarin Banaji, 1994, "The Role of Stereotyping in System-Justification and the Production of False Consciousness," *British Journal of Social Psychology* 33:1–27; Ridgeway, Cecilia L., 2001, "Gender, Status, and Leadership," in "Gender, Hierarchy, and Leadership," edited by Linda L. Carli and Alice H. Eagly, *Journal of Social Issues* 57, no. 4:637–655; Sidanius, Jim, Felicia Pratto, and Lawrence Bobo, 1994, "Social Dominance Orientation and the Political Psychology of Gender: A Case of Invariance?" *Journal of Personality and Social Psychology* 67:998–1011.

MARIA JOSE SOTELO

Gender-Based Affirmative Action

Gender-based affirmative action programs refer to affirmative action plans that focus on achieving equality of opportunity in employment, education, contracting, and other areas for women. Such plans often utilize gender-based preferences. Gender-based affirmative action plans are subject to some of the same legal standards as are race-based affirmative action plans. For example, Title VII of the Civil Rights Act of 1964 permits employers to voluntarily adopt affirmative action programs benefiting racial minorities and women. However, gender preferences and racial preferences are permissible as part of these affirmative action plans only if their purpose mirrors the purpose of Title VII, they do not unnecessarily trammel the interests of nonminorities and males, and they have a rational end point. On the other hand, governmental gender preferences in affirmative action programs can be distinguished from racial preferences in governmental affirmative action programs because of the differing levels of judicial scrutiny to which each is subject when challenged as unconstitutional. According to the U.S. Supreme Court, governmental race-based programs are subject to strict scrutiny analysis by the Court under the Fifth or Fourteenth Amendment; however, gender-based plans have traditionally been subject to a lesser judicial scrutiny, intermediate scrutiny.

The constitutionality of a gender-based affirmative action program was reviewed for the first time in *Mississippi University for Women v. Hogan*, 458 U.S. 718 (1982). The *Mississippi University for Women* case involved a Fourteenth Amendment Equal Protection Clause challenge to a state statute prohibiting males from being enrolled in a public nursing school in the state. The state argued that the statute was justified to compensate for past discrimination against women. In an opinion authored by Justice Sandra Day O'Connor, the Court held that in order to use gender as a basis for a governmental decision, the gender classification must be substantially related to the achievement of important governmental objectives—the traditional formulation of the intermediate scrutiny standard. While this standard requires a rigorous review, it is not as rigorous as the strict scrutiny standard. In order to satisfy strict scrutiny review, a challenged governmental action must be narrowly tailored to fulfill a compelling governmental interest. However, the Court also stated that the government must have an "exceedingly persuasive justification" for its gender classifications. Some commentators have viewed this as elevating the review standard applicable to gender classifications to a rigor between traditional intermediate scrutiny and strict scrutiny. Others have treated this phrase as merely an additional description of the traditional intermediate scrutiny standard.

Ultimately striking down the admissions policy, Justice O'Connor found that the state of Mississippi did not have an "exceedingly persuasive justification" for admitting only women. The Court held that not only was there not an underrepresentation of females in the nursing professions, but also the male nursing school exclusion "tends to perpetuate the stereotyped view of nursing as an exclusively women's job."

In 1996, the Supreme Court reaffirmed its intermediate scrutiny approach to gender classifications in *United States v. Virginia,* 518 U.S. 515 (1996), a case dealing with whether or not females could be excluded from the Virginia Military Institute (a traditionally male-only institution). The Court decided that Virginia did not have an "exceedingly persuasive justification" for the male-only admission policy. *United States v. Virginia* did not involve an affirmative action program. However, its determination that intermediate scrutiny is appropriate for gender classifications that burden women is important because the Supreme Court decided in *Adarand Constructors, Inc. v. Peña,* 515 U.S. 200 (1995), that the level of scrutiny for race-based government action is the same (the highest level of scrutiny, strict scrutiny) regardless of whether the race-based action is meant to benefit or to burden racial minorities. By analogy, then, if gender classifications that burden women are subject to intermediate scrutiny review, gender classifications in affirmative action plans that benefit women would also be subject to intermediate scrutiny review. Some U.S. courts of appeal have adopted this reasoning. Others, however, have held that strict scrutiny review should apply to gender preferences in affirmative action programs—a significantly more difficult standard to meet.

See also Employment (Public) and Affirmative Action; Equal Employment Opportunity Commission's Affirmative Employment Management Directives; Fifth Amendment; Fourteenth Amendment; Ginsburg, Ruth Bader; Intermediate Scrutiny Review; *Mississippi University for Women v. Hogan*; O'Connor, Sandra Day; Race-Based Affirmative Action; Rational Basis Scrutiny; Strict Scrutiny; Suspect Classification; Title VII of the Civil Rights Act of 1964; Title IX of the Education Amendments of 1972.

FURTHER READING: O'Melveny, Mary K., 1996, "The Sesquicentennial of the 1848 Seneca Falls Women's Rights Convention: American Women's Unfinished Quest for Legal, Economic, Political, and Social Equality: Playing the Gender Card: Affirmative Action and Working Women,"*Kentucky Law Journal* 84 (summer): 863–901; Skaggs, Jason M., 1998, "Justifying Gender-Based Affirmative Action under *United States v. Virginia*'s 'Exceedingly Persuasive Justification' Standard," *California Law Review* 86 (October): 1169–1210; Spann, Girardeau A., 2000, *The Law of Affirmative Action: Twenty-five Years of Supreme Court Decisions on Race and Remedies,* New York: New York University Press.

JAMES A. BECKMAN

Gendered Racism

Gendered racism can be described as the discrimination that black women suffer on the grounds of their sex as well as their color and culture. While considerable literature exists on the broad category of racial discrimination, little or no attention has been directed to the kinds of discrimination that women in certain racial categories have endured. For example, little or no research has been carried out with respect to women of other minority groups such as Asians, Latin Americans, American Indians, Muslims, and Hindus. Indeed, where women were included in the racial discourses, they were stereotyped as wives, mothers, or daughters. While it was true that much of the literature on race and ethnicity, in the case of American society, tended to focus on the African American minority group, there was a concern to examine racial and ethnic issues as they related to the economy, employment, policing, and public law. Thus what actually occurred was that in examining the broad relationship between race and policy, questions of gender were largely ignored.

In most known societies, women by virtue of their sex had to occupy subordinate roles on the grounds of their alleged physical abilities and biological makeup. What occurred, consequently, was a role specialization in which the dominant and preferred roles were occupied by men. Political and other kinds of changes, however, over the years have been eroding the justification for gender-based role specialization, while liberal democratic programs, such as affirmative action, have increasingly eroded the structures on which traditional society rested. When "feminism" emerged during the 1960s, however, it did not focus on those women who were the most victimized or who were beaten down mentally, physically, or spiritually. Rather, Betty Friedan's 1963 book *The Feminine Mystique*, which was heralded as paving the way for the contemporary feminist movement, was written as if these women did not exist. She, according to Hooks (2001), actually referred to a select group—college-educated, middle- and upper-class, married, white housewives—and thus, like a number of feminist writers who followed in her footsteps, ignored the larger questions of class and racial difference. Indeed, it appeared that the argument of most feminist writers was that "all women were oppressed." This assertion implied that women shared a common lot, and factors like race, religion, and sexual preference played a minimal role. It should be noted, however, that two main factors were largely responsible for the promotion of this broad-based ideology of feminism. First, it has been suggested that the feminist struggle was launched to serve the interests of the conservative and liberal feminists. In other words, feminism in the United States was essentially a bourgeois ideology. Second, black women did not organize themselves collectively around the "issues of feminism" or access the machinery or power that would allow them to share their analyses or theories about gender with the American public.

Yet race had a critical impact on black women in terms of their experiences of and treatment in areas such as education, the health services, and the labor market. Black women were subject to all the restrictions against blacks and those against women. They were part of a group that has traditionally been treated as inferior by American society, yet because they were women, their experiences were largely ignored. It should be recalled that as part of the institution of slavery, black women had been sexually exploited by white men through rape or enforced sexual services. These sexual mores that were characteristic of the relationship of colonizers to the women of the conquered group functioned not only symbolically but actually served to fasten the badge of inferiority onto the enslaved group. The black man was degraded by being deprived of the power and the right to protect his women from white men. The black woman was directly degraded by the sexual attack and more profoundly by being deprived of a strong black man on whom she could rely on for protection. The role of the black woman was thus an ambiguous one in relation to white society. Because they were women, white society considered them more docile, less of a threat than black men. It rewarded them by forcing them into service with the white family. As Lerner (2001) pointed out, black women ever since slavery have nursed and raised white children, attended white people in sickness, and kept white homes running smoothly. Their intimate contact with white people has made them interpreters and intermediaries of white culture in the black home. At the same time, they have struggled in partnership with their men to keep the black family together and to allow the black community to survive (Lerner 2001, 48). It has been suggested that this dual role has resulted in the remarkable resilience of the black woman.

Yet it was a resilience that faltered in the years after slavery. Black women were usually accorded lower-paying jobs than their white counterparts and were usually seen as a form of "cheap labor." For example, in Britain, 200,000 to 400,000 women are employed as "home workers" employed in the manufacturing industry. Of this number, 30 to 50 percent are black women (Lewis 2001, 310). According to Lewis (2001), these workers were employed on low wages and were engaged in "home working" largely because of their geographical immobility. Yet after the 1980s, even low-paying employment became difficult to obtain. The decline in the world economy during the 1980s, along with technological changes that had a significant impact on a number of lower-paying clerical and office jobs, has served to limit the employment opportunities of black working-class women, who are generally confined to the inner cities. However, the present situation is one in which a number of trends are occurring. While many existing areas of employment for black women are closing altogether or experiencing major decline, others are opening up (fast food, office work). Lewis (2001) suggests, however, that the extent to which these potential opportunities can be turned into real jobs will depend on the success of black women's autonomous organizations both on the shop floor and outside. Others have argued, however, that it will depend on the kind of affirmative action policies that are introduced by the various governments.

See also The Feminine Mystique; Gender Norms; Gender Segregation in Employment; Gender Stratification; Sex Discrimination.

FURTHER READING: Friedan, Betty, 1963, *The Feminine Mystique*, New York: W.W. Norton; Hooks, Bell, 2001, "Black Women: Shaping Feminist Theory," in *Feminism and Race*, edited by Kum-Kum Bhavnani, Oxford: Oxford University Press; Lerner, Gerda, 2001, "Black Women in White America," in *Feminism and Race*, edited by Kum-Kum Bhavnani, Oxford: Oxford University Press; Lewis, Gail, 2001, "Black Women's Employment and the British Economy," in *Feminism and Race*, edited by Kum-Kum Bhavnani, Oxford: Oxford University Press; Young, Lola, 2001, "Race, Identity, and Cultural Criticism," in *Feminism and Race*, edited by Kum-Kum Bhavnani, Oxford: Oxford University Press.

ANN MARIE BISSESSAR

General Accounting Office

The General Accounting Office (GAO) was founded in 1921 as the investigative arm of Congress. Today, the GAO has eleven offices around the United States and is involved in numerous activities designed to act as a watchdog over the spending of public monies. This nonpartisan group is technically independent of Congress, and this allows the organization to evaluate federal programs without the interference of elected officials. The GAO has many tasks included within these evaluations and offers analysis and recommendations on policy and funding decisions. Since part of any evaluation is to examine the practices used by programs under study, affirmative action along with hiring/promotion policies are often included within its charge. The GAO has authored many reports about affirmative action, and archived GAO reports can be searched and viewed at the official GAO web site.

In addition to governmental evaluations, the GAO advises Congress and the heads of government agencies on how to make their role more responsive to the citizens. Sometimes this advice leads to investigations and legal opinions on findings that can then become the law of the land. In other words, the GAO is designed to get action from those in government who may otherwise not be responsive to individual citizens. Thus the GAO reports to Congress on the actions and accountability of the executive branch as required by the Constitution and makes sure that government is accountable to the people it serves. Currently the GAO is involved in terrorism detection, homeland security, legal decisions about bid protests (including affirmative action in the governmental bidding process and governmental hiring policies), and reports of fraud allegations and mismanagement of federal funds, in addition to all of the tasks identified earlier.

See also Contracting and Affirmative Action; Employment (Public) and Affirmative Action.

FURTHER READING: General Accounting Office, web site: http://www.gao.gov.

SUSAN F. BRINKLEY

Gentrification

Gentrification is a process in which there is an inflow of capital and the middle-upper class to the inner city while poorer residents and the under-lower class are forced out of their neighborhood, but often not without a fight. Gentrification is a concept that relates to the issue of housing and race, particularly the use of affirmative action in housing as a means of continuing to afford ample housing opportunities despite the gentrification phenomena in many large cities. Gentrification is also closely related to issues of lending and race and the use of affirmative action to ensure that traditionally minority applicants qualify for home loans in areas subject to gentrification. Finally, gentrification also relates to the issue of environmental racism because the poorer residents and the lower classes are forced into areas where environmental degradation often occurs. Urbanization, a process related to gentrification, is one in which large numbers of people are attracted to cities because of jobs and other opportunities that one finds in urban areas. Urbanization serves as the forerunner to gentrification.

Poor white immigrants were attracted to medium and large cities in the northern and eastern parts of the United States when they arrived and settled in America. Huge immigration waves of white ethnic immigrants from southern, eastern, and western Europe occurred from the 1880s to the 1930s. In particular, large waves of Italian, Polish, Jewish, Irish, and German immigrants settled in urban areas of the country seeking better economic opportunities and greater freedom than in their native countries. Political machines and economic opportunities went hand in glove, and political machines became a major force in politics in cities.

Because these immigrants were given the opportunity to work, they eventually were able to gain an economic foothold. By the late 1940s, the federal government was offering 3 percent interest loans to buy a home coupled with building major freeways leading into and out of the cities. This provided second- and third-generation immigrants who had begun to amass assets and money with new opportunities further away from crowded cities that, after World War II, began to be inhabited by poor and working-class blacks. These blacks were part of "push and pull" migration. Racism and lack of economic opportunity were factors pushing them out of the South, while greater job opportunities coupled with less overt racism were pulling them to the North. The "push and pull" migration often is described as the Great Migration as well. This migration of African Americans to northern cities caused a subsequent movement of whites into the surrounding suburbs of cities that became known as "white flight."

However, by the 1970s, living in the suburbs and working in the city became a nightmare for many suburbanites, who had to commute for up to two hours going to and coming from work because of the rush hour and traffic congestion. Living in the suburbs became an incubus for many who had to endure so much time commuting to and from work. The process of gentrification began to take root, and living back in the inner city became attractive. For others of affluence coming to the city, certain areas of the inner city were also attractive. The inner city has a number of benefits, including easy accessibility to jobs, a transit system close to home and job, an abundance of historical structures, and a vigorous cultural milieu. Speculation on the part of the wealthy and professional classes coupled with easy loans from banks provides the climate for the "landed gentry" to buy land and/or houses or apartments or condominiums. Concurrently, landlords and property owners make a concerted effort to force the poor out of their homes using a number of tactics that include failure to maintain the existing structure, continually raising rents, and eviction. Once this occurs, they begin to remodel and refurbish housing structures and dramatically raise the rents or costs of ownership for another class of people. As members of the gentry move into these newly created structures and neighborhoods that have a new facelift, the process of gentrification is complete.

See also Busing; Department of Housing and Urban Development; Environmental Racism; Fair Housing Amendments Act of 1988; Housing; Housing and Urban Development Act of 1968; Lending Practices and Affirmative Action; Zoning and Affirmative Action.

FURTHER READING: Foley, Donald L., 1980, "The Sociology of Housing," *Annual Review of Sociology* 6:457–478; McKelvey, Blake, 1973, *American Urbanization: A Comparative History*, Glenview, IL: Scott, Foresman and Company; Wetzel, Tom, 2002, "What Is Gentrification?" http://www.uncanny.net/~wetzel/gentry.htm; Zukin, Sharon, 1987, "Gentrification: Culture and Capital in the Urban Core," *Annual Review of Sociology* 13:129–147.

MFANYA D. TRYMAN

Gerrymandering

See Baker v. Carr.

GI Bill

The Servicemen's Readjustment Act of 1944, usually referred to as the GI Bill of Rights, constituted what is possibly the most generous and largest social welfare program in U.S. history. Renowned historian Stephen Ambrose felt that the "G.I. Bill was the best piece of legislation ever passed by the U.S. Congress and it made modern America" (MacNeil/Lehrer NewsHour, July 4, 2000). It was designed to provide extensive opportunities to the returning World War II veterans and can be described as an affirmative action program for veterans. Provisions included up to a year of readjustment (i.e., unemployment) benefits; education and training allowances, with college aid sufficient to cover tuition, fees, and room and board; guaranteed home, farm, or business loans; medical and dental care; special advantages in competition for civil service jobs; pensions and compensation; low-cost life insurance; and vocational rehabilitation. Initially the GI Bill was administered by the Veterans Administration, but it is currently administered largely by the Department of Veterans Affairs.

The bill was passed in June 1944 and signed into law by President Franklin Delano Roosevelt during the D-day invasion. The American Legion is largely credited with designing its main features and driving it through Congress despite intense debate. This was not the first bill of its nature; traditionally, America has compensated its veterans for their services. These benefits date back to the Pilgrims and, interestingly, Revolutionary War veterans receiving land bonuses.

While the GI Bill offered a diverse range of options, its greatest impact was on the national education system. Millions who would have flooded the domestic labor market during the post–World War II demobilization period instead opted for education, which significantly reduced joblessness. Of a total veteran population of 15,440,000 in 1947, some 7.8 million received training. This included 2,230,000 in college, 3,480,000 in other schools, 1,400,000 in on-the-job training, and 690,000 in farm training. When these GIs entered the labor market, most were better prepared to contribute to the support of their families and society. Approximately 450,000 became engineers, 240,000 accountants, 238,000 teachers, 67,000 doctors, and 22,000 dentists, and there were thousands more in other professional careers.

The bill spurred the American economy by democratizing higher education, which prior to World War II had been confined largely to the upper class. To meet the increasing demands of the larger student body, there was tremendous growth in the university system. In 1947, veterans accounted for 49 percent of college enrollment, and three years later American colleges had doubled the number of graduates. These individuals then went out into the world and applied what they had learned, resulting in the beginning of modern America. In effect, the GI Bill transformed the American higher-education establishment into the envy of the world.

Education was not the only GI Bill benefit used by a massive number of recipients. Veterans were also eligible for government-subsidized home loans. Veterans used the bill's guaranteed mortgages and low interest rates to buy new homes in the suburbs, kicking off a development boom. Before the war, two-thirds of all

Americans had rented their homes. After the war, two-thirds of Americans owned their homes.

The unprecedented national support for the education of World War II veterans provided by the GI Bill was notably race neutral in its statutory terms. It held special promise for the more than 1 million black men who had served in the military (6.9 percent of the veterans) during the war, most of whom needed financial assistance to enroll in college. Many hoped that it would significantly reduce racial gaps in educational opportunity and long-run economic outcome. Studies revealed that whites were far more likely than blacks to obtain college aid, while blacks were more likely to obtain training and vocational rehabilitation services. However, by 1960, some 350,000 black men and women were attending college via government funding. Most historians conclude that the availability of benefits to black veterans had a substantial and positive impact on their educational attainment, excluding those who resided in the South. For these latter individuals who had a much smaller number of collegiate choices and suffered through extensive Jim Crow laws, the bill actually expanded rather than narrowed social differences between the races.

The GI Bill's benefits have been adjusted over the years to fit the needs of a changing America. The current bill is known as the Montgomery GI Bill and has proven to be extremely popular among young enlistees. Almost 95 percent of those who enlisted in the armed services in fiscal year 1996 enrolled in the program, and there has been a 75 percent enrollment of all enlistees since the inception of the program.

Many feel that the GI Bill was the most massive affirmative action program in U.S. history. It was a milestone in federal funding for higher education and helped to remove economic and social barriers so that unprecedented numbers of Americans could attend college. Since its inception, more than 20 million veterans have participated in education and training programs. A 1988 report by a congressional subcommittee on education and health estimated that 40 percent of those who attended college under the GI Bill would not otherwise have had the opportunity. The report also found that for every dollar invested educating the GIs, there was a $6.90 return in national output due to extra education and increased federal tax revenues from the extra income the beneficiaries earned. We are still constantly seeing testimony to the benefits of the bill in U.S. society. Examples include the inventor of the pacemaker, others who helped establish the space program, Martin Perl, the winner of the 1995 Nobel Prize in physics, and Andrew Brimmer, a sharecropper's son, who became the first African American appointed to the Federal Reserve Board.

See also Jim Crow Laws; Roosevelt, Franklin Delano; Veterans' Preferences; Vietnam Era Veterans' Readjustment Assistance Act of 1974.

FURTHER READING: Jones, Russell L., 1996, "Affirmative Action: Should We or Shouldn't We?" *Southern University Law Review* 23 (winter): 133–143; Patterson, Orlando, 1999, "The Nexus between Race and Policy," *Georgetown Public Policy Review* 4 (spring): 107–114; Williams, Gerald A., 1999, "A Primer on Veterans' Benefits for Legal Assistance Attorneys," *Air Force Law Review* 47:163–187.

PETER L. PLATTEBORZE

Ginsburg, Ruth Bader (1933–)

Ruth Bader Ginsburg, only the second female to become a Supreme Court justice, was appointed to the U.S. Supreme Court in 1993 by President Bill Clinton. Since her appointment to the Court, Ginsburg has been part of the liberal bloc on the Court on the issue of affirmative action. Justice Ginsburg and Justices John Paul Stevens, David Souter, and Stephen Breyer comprise a four-justice bloc that always has voted to uphold affirmative action plans when the constitutionality of such plans has been called into question. According to Georgetown University law professor Girardeau Spann, "In addition to Justice Stevens, the other three justices who make up the present Court's liberal bloc on affirmative action—Justices Souter, Ginsburg, and Breyer—have voted to uphold each affirmative action program that they considered in a constitutional case" (Spann 2000, 161). In light of her previous dedication and work in the area of women's rights, she was described by President Clinton as the Thurgood Marshall of the women's rights movement. In addition to her work on the Supreme Court, in 1999, she coauthored a frequently cited law review article titled "Affirmative Action: An International Human Rights Dialogue," in which she argued that affirmative action constitutes an international law obligation.

Ginsburg, born on March 15, 1933, in Brooklyn, New York, began her federal career as a law clerk in the U.S. District Court for the Southern District of New York. In the years following, Ginsburg served as a law professor in the United States and at law schools in Europe before coming back to the federal bench in 1980, being appointed to the U.S. Court of Appeals for the District of Columbia by President Jimmy Carter. This varied background, coupled with her degrees from Harvard and Columbia law schools and her experience on the law review from both institutions, can be seen in many of her decisions in some very significant cases.

As a champion of women's rights, Ginsburg argued six sex discrimination cases (winning five) before the U.S. Supreme Court. She has not only been a supporter of women's rights but has also been involved in cases on a wide range of topics of public interest. For example, she favored upholding the warnings to suspects first articulated in *Miranda v. Arizona*, 384 U.S. 436 (1966), when *Miranda* was rereviewed by the Court in 2000. She also favored denying the use of the death penalty without consideration of mitigating evidence, no roadblocks with drug-sniffing dogs, allowing rape victims to sue attackers as a gender-bias crime, and supporting a limit of six months on the detention of illegal immigrants. In her role on the U.S. Supreme Court with relation to affirmative action cases dealing with voting rights, she has always voted to uphold affirmative action plans in each instance. Sometimes finding herself part of the majority, but often among the dissenters, she has never swayed from her support of affirmative action and plans to ensure equality under the law.

Shortly after joining the Supreme Court, Ginsburg aligned herself as a proponent of minority and women's voting rights in several key voting rights cases. First, in 1994 in *Holder v. Hall*, 512 U.S. 874 (1994), she sided with the dissenters who supported the black voters of Bleckley County, Georgia, in their action against the single-commissioner form of government even though that was not the scheme authorized by the state. Further, she offered her own dissent in this case, arguing that it was the role of the judiciary to decipher and act upon the dual objectives of the prevention of vote dilution and the avoidance of proportional representation of minority voters. Later in 1994, a second voting rights case, *Johnson v. DeGrady*, 512 U.S. 997 (1994), was before the Court. In this case, black and Latino voters in Florida challenged the reapportionment plan for the state, arguing that the plan destroyed the districts where minorities had strength in numbers. In this case, Ginsburg found herself in the majority (7–2) in holding that the plan being challenged had not destroyed the minority votes in question because both minorities had numbers in the districts in question that corresponded to the proportion they represented in the county.

In *Shaw v. Reno*, 509 U.S. 630 (1993), the Court was to review the remand for strict scrutiny application. Ginsburg sided with the dissenters by opposing the application of strict scrutiny as the standard for cases dealing with race-conscious voting rights remedies. Further, Ginsburg stated that states must consider race as a factor when drawing the boundaries of voting districts as a matter of law. In 1995, in the major affirmative action case *Adarand Constructors, Inc. v. Peña*, 515 U.S. 200 (1995), the Court was called on to address the validity of the federally sponsored affirmative action plan of the Small Business Act and the Surface Transportation Act that held that financial considerations would be given to businesses in the awarding of contracts to disadvantaged subcontractors. Of special significance in the case was the issue of which minorities were considered "disadvantaged" under the provision. The case dealt with bids for a construction project where the lowest bidder was denied the contract in favor of the second-lowest bidder, a minority company. The result of this case was the invalidation of the government's program because of the use of strict scrutiny as the standard employed. It is important to note that Ginsburg supported the dissenters' position that if there is general societal discrimination and that discrimination can be demonstrated, then that is enough to warrant that an affirmative action program be implemented. Furthermore, Ginsburg was opposed to the utilizing of strict scrutiny as the judicial standard in evaluating "benign" instances of discrimination in governmental affirmative action programs. She also aligned herself as being firmly in favor of affirmative action in the landmark cases *Grutter v. Bollinger*, 123 S. Ct. 2325, 2003 U.S. LEXIS 4800 (2003), and *Gratz v. Bollinger*, 123 S. Ct. 2411, 2003 U.S. LEXIS 4801 (2003).

With few exceptions, Justice Ginsburg has attempted to make decisions in an environment of judicial restraint and to let the law evolve in time with social attitudes. For example, she is often quoted as being critical of the famous abortion case *Roe v. Wade*, 410 U.S. 113 (1973), in that she felt that it went too far in specifying the trimester scheme when it should have merely addressed the issue of the antiabortion restriction at issue in the case. It is said that Ginsburg gives careful thought to the written word, and her opinions are often focused upon the narrow issue at hand as opposed to sweeping fundamental changes. As such, she is the caretaker of many of the social issues facing America today, with women's rights and voting rights leading the way.

See also Adarand Constructors, Inc. v. Peña; Benign Discrimination; Breyer, Stephen Gerald; Clinton, William Jefferson; *Gratz v. Bollinger/Grutter v. Bollinger*; Marshall, Thurgood; *Shaw v. Reno*; Souter, David Hackett; Stevens, John Paul; Strict Scrutiny; Voting Rights Act of 1965.

FURTHER READING: Ginsburg, Ruth Bader, and Deborah Jones Merritt, 1999, "Affirmative Action: An International Human Rights Dialogue," *Cardozo Law Review* 21 (October): 253–282; Rosen, Jeffrey, 1997, "The New Look of Liberalism on the Court," *New York Times*, October 5, 6:60, column 1; Spann, Girardeau A. 2000, *The Law of Affirmative Action: Twenty-five Years of Supreme Court Decisions on Race and Remedies*, New York: New York University Press.

SUSAN F. BRINKLEY

Glass Ceiling Commission

The federal Glass Ceiling Commission, once a part of the U.S. Department of Labor, was created with the passage of the Civil Rights Act of 1991 and went out of existence when it completed its statutorily assigned mandate in January 1996. The Glass Ceiling Commission was charged with studying and reporting on the extent to which women and minorities were able to fully integrate into the employment/workplace environment. The commission was to study and report on the extent of both barriers and opportunities for women and minorities in the employment context. The commission focused on three areas in particular: integration of senior management positions; training opportunities; and the compensation and reward system in place for women and minorities.

Composed of twenty-one members appointed by the president and Congress and chaired by the secretary of labor, the Glass Ceiling Commission produced a landmark 1995 report in which it confirmed the existence of "glass ceilings" in employment for minorities and women, barriers that effectively excluded advancement in corporate America. The commission found that as of 1995 and despite modern improvements in employment opportunities for women and minorities, white males still constituted 95 to 97 percent of the upper senior management positions in businesses and corporations in the United States.

See also Civil Rights Act of 1991; Department of Labor; Employment (Private) and Affirmative Action; Gender Segregation in Employment; Glass Ceilings.

FURTHER READING: U.S. Department of Labor, OFCCP, Glass Ceiling Commission, 1995, *Good for Business: Making Full Use of the Nation's Human Capital/The Environmental Scar*, Washington, DC: U.S. Government Printing Office; U.S. Government Reports, Glass Ceiling Commission (Archived Glass Ceiling Commission Reports and Documents), 1991–1996, http://www.ilr.cornell.edu/library/e_archive/gov_reports/GlassCeiling/.

JAMES A. BECKMAN

Glass Ceilings

From a representational point of view, the presence of a "glass ceiling" is a prominent issue not only in the American organizational culture but in many countries of the world as well. The term "glass ceiling" is defined as the "actual or perceived barrier or cap beyond which few women (or other previously excluded minorities) in public and private organizational structures are able to move" (Bullard and Wright 1993, 189). In other words, glass ceilings, an invisible barrier to advancement of women beyond a certain point, are said to exist at every level in an organization and can be found both in the public and the private sectors. It has been held, though, that affirmative action programs have helped create significant new opportunities for women, allowing some of them to circumvent or break through the glass ceiling.

A number of surveys and research projects have been conducted to probe whether glass ceilings in fact exist. Many writers agreed that part of the problem with respect to the erection of this invisible barrier (the glass ceiling) had to do with the distinction between power and culturally legitimated authority and between the ability to gain compliance and to gain recognition. Yet, they argued, one could not really understand the existence of a glass ceiling without first going back to the basic ordering of traditional societies. They thus turned to the discipline of anthropology to provide the explanation. Renowned anthropologists such as Margaret Mead have suggested that the root cause of inequality between the sexes had to do with early socialization and the way both sexes were segregated. She pointed out that although there were some groups in the world where men wore skirts and women wore pants or trousers, yet it was found that there were characteristic tasks, manners, and responsibilities primarily associated with women or men. She argued that what was most striking and surprising about all these groups was the fact that male as opposed to female activities were always recognized as predominantly important and that the cultural systems accorded authority and value to the roles and activities of men. She contended that whatever the arrangements were in regard to descent or ownership of property, the activities of men were always considered more valuable than those of women.

Another issue was that in many societies, particularly traditional societies, a major part of a woman's adult life was spent giving birth to and raising children, which led to a differentiation of domestic and public spheres of activity. Anthropologists argued that as societies became increasingly developed, this differentiation continued and to a large extent was responsible for a number of relevant aspects of human social structure and psychology. They suggested that because women were consigned to the role of wife and mother, their economic and political activities were constrained. Thus while men were free to form unions and engage in political discussion, women were confined to home matters. This early socialization eventually led to the development of sex-role behavior, different levels of integration in the society, self-imaging and identification, and the acceptance of male authority systems. In other words, early socialization widened the gap between the sexes and provided the barrier to male-female interaction.

Many writers have not only supported the anthropological perspective but have reinforced the view that early socialization was responsible for the cultural barriers that prevented women from achieving the same opportunities as their male counterparts. They also argued that institutions such as the church, the school, the structure and ordering of the society, and the public services were major obstacles to women's entry at the higher levels. In an international study of women's upward mobility conducted during the period 1984–1987, the sociocultural, economic, political, educational, legal, and organizational factors related to the level of participation of women in administrative policy-making positions and the policies and practices that constrained or advanced women's opportunities were explored. In all nineteen nations where the research was conducted, it was found that the upward mobility of women was constrained by international and legal restrictions. For example, the results of the study revealed that while the civil service in Thailand was predominantly female (54 percent), Thai women were clustered at the lower levels and were legally denied entry to a key position, deputy district officer. The research data further revealed that Brazilian women were concentrated in ministries such as social service, education, health, and social security that were considered typically "soft ministries" (Cole, Meksawan, and Sopchokchai 2001, 923). In another study that was carried out in Trinidad and Tobago, West Indies, it was found that the barriers to upward mobility were not confined to legal or international restrictions. Rather, although women made significant strides in the public services at the middle level, the hierarchical structures of the civil services that had been introduced by the departing colonials prevented them from attaining higher-level positions. Women, it should recalled, were late entrants into the public services, and because promotional policies were based primarily on seniority, the hierarchical arrangement and policies in place prohibited late entrants from gaining top-level posts. Women, particularly during the 1960s and early 1970s, therefore, had little or no access to top-level positions.

It was evident, therefore, that while increasingly women were gaining access to lower- and middle-level positions, entry to the higher-level positions was dependent on a number of factors, including socialization, education, culture, and the institutional arrangements in place. Other writers have suggested that in some countries upward mobility was dependent on the economic and political development and in some cases the urban development of the country. On the other hand, it was found that economic decline and unemployment adversely affected the career advancement of women.

In the case of the United States, however, certain remedies appear necessary to bridge the gender gap and circumvent the glass ceiling. Two major policies that allowed for greater equality among the sexes were the introduction of affirmative action policies and the emergence of a stronger business culture. Certain initiatives introduced by agencies like the Small Business Development Center (SBDC), such as the Women's Business Owners Roundtable, the listing of a Directory of Women Business Owners, and networking, along with centers for women, create a business climate that is especially suited for women. Other remedies that have benefited minority groups, including females, include governmental funding for educational upgrading, job training, the use of quota systems, and subsidized housing. Others have argued, though, that although the sociocultural barriers can be overcome, what is necessary is that both males and females accept the legitimacy of women in power positions. It should be recognized also that continued global activities have provided platforms for raising issues of "women's rights" and to a large extent have led to the promotion of various nongovernmental organizations that are concerned with organizing women into social, economic, and political interest groups.

See also Gender Norms; Gender Segregation in Employment; Gendered Racism; Stereotypes, Gender.

FURTHER READING: Albeda, Randy, and Chris Tilly, 1997, *Glass Ceilings and Bottomless Pits: Women's Work and Poverty,* Boston: South End Press; Bissessar, Ann Marie, 1999, "Determinants of Gender Mobility in the Public Service of Trinidad and Tobago," *Public Personnel Management* 28, no. 3:409–422; Bullard, Angela M. and Deil S. Wright, 1993, "Circumventing the Glass Ceiling: Women Executives in America," *Public Administration Review,* 53, no. 3

(May/June): 189–203; Cole, Jeanne-Marie, Dhipavadee Meksawan, and Orapin Sopchokchai, 2001, "Women in Bureaucracies: Equity, Advancement, and Public Policy Strategies," in *Handbook of Comparative and Development Public Administration*, edited by Ali Farazmand, 2d ed., New York: Marcel Dekker; MacDonald, Sandra, and Irene Hardill, 1999, "Targeted Small Firms Policies: The Case of Affirmative Action in the US," *Regional Studies* 33, no. 6 (August): 576–581; Reynolds, Andrew, 1999, "Women in the Legislatures and Executives of the World: Knocking at the Highest Glass Ceiling," *World Politics*, July, 547–573.

ANN MARIE BISSESSAR

Glazer, Nathan (1923–)

Nathan Glazer is a Columbia University–trained sociologist who has studied a wide range of topics within the discipline but has been especially noted for his study of race and ethnicity. His body of work on ethnicity has examined a range of topics, including immigration, assimilation, and multiculturalism, as well as affirmative action. Glazer has been a prominent critic of affirmative action for nearly four decades and continues to write and speak on the subject. In 1963, Glazer entered the national scene on race relations studies when he authored (with Daniel Patrick Moynihan) the book *Beyond the Melting Pot*, a classic work on race and urban development. *Beyond the Melting Pot* has been required reading on college campuses for decades and is also regarded as one of the quintessential statements from the assimilationist school of thought, which held that incorporation into mainstream American culture was not only an ideal but a possibility for all racial and ethnic groups. Glazer and Moynihan argued that while each group tries to get ahead utilizing its own strategies and many groups retain their racial/ethnic identities, achieving the goal of assimilation is still possible.

The most complete statement of Glazer's views on affirmative action is contained in *Affirmative Discrimination* (1975), which is an attack on affirmative action as a workable program to improve race relations and equality. In this work, he examines affirmative action programs in three public policy arenas: employment, education, and housing. Overall, he suggests that affirmative action policies have failed to bring about greater equality of the races and have in some cases inflamed racial tensions. Additionally, Glazer argues in the book that affirmative action is largely un-American, and "it would undermine the values that had made America's unique experiment with pluralism possible." One policy that Glazer suggests has been particularly damaging is busing, which led many white Americans to abandon public schools and has required the spending of funds that might have been better spent improving the quality of schools regardless of their racial composition.

The root of Glazer's opposition to affirmative action derived from his view that such programs had come to depend on a quota system that was in direct opposition to the color-blind ideal that liberals and civil rights activists aspired to in the 1960s. However, he felt that since such programs had become an institutionalized part of the American system, they should be maintained if they had proven successful in accomplishing desegregation and/or had led to improvements in the material condition of African Americans. He gave an example of the sort of affirmative action program he thought should be maintained in his discussion of the Starett City public housing program in Brooklyn. Authorities set aside a limited number of public housing units for African Americans. While increasing the racial heterogeneity of the community, the number was low enough to forestall white flight. However, Glazer found that the majority of programs were not as effective, in which case he argued that race neutrality and strong prohibitions against racial discrimination are preferable policy directives because they are consistent with the Constitution and have greater public support. Interestingly, Glazer had worked as a sociologist on several government programs as part of the Kennedy administration's War on Poverty, and it has been alleged that the many governmental "social welfare" failures caused Glazer to conclude that the problem of inequality and racism could not be eradicated based upon governmental programs, but required changes on the individual and family levels. He codified this view of his in another influential book titled *The Limits of Social Policy*.

In *Affirmative Discrimination*, Glazer suggested that the discriminatory treatment of African Americans was effectively dealt with through passage of the Civil Rights Act of 1964. He argued that because the average African American continued to be less well off materially than the average white American after the passage and enforcement of the Civil Rights Act, civil rights activists and American politicians turned to racial quota systems as a way of creating racial equality. However, he contended that this outlook ignored research that showed that much of the decrease in the black/white economic gap was accomplished in the period between passage of the Civil Rights Act and the expansion of affirmative action programs. Glazer has appeared to maintain this position in the years since writing *Affirmative Discrimination*. In an article he wrote on affirmative action in 1998, Glazer remarked, "Although affirmative action has probably contributed something, one can hardly doubt that a good part of the movement of blacks into public jobs of all sorts would have occurred independently, as discrimination declined and as blacks became dominant, demographically and then politically, in so many cities" (Glazer 1998, 28).

In addition, like many critics of affirmative action, Glazer disagreed with the notion that statistical inequality is evidence of discrimination. In fact, building on his work in *Beyond the Melting Pot*, Glazer held that history presents a pattern whereby ethnic groups tend to achieve economic success through concentration in particular occupations or economic sectors (e.g., Irish police officers and Jewish small business owners), which is in part facilitated by segregation into ethnic enclaves. Therefore, Glazer argued that government intrusions into the assimilation process through programs that attempt to achieve strict proportional representation are misguided.

Glazer seems to have reevaluated some of his beliefs regarding racial policies in the ten years between the release of the second edition of *Affirmative Discrimination* (1987) and the publication of a more recent book, *We Are All Multiculturalists Now* (1997), particularly his beliefs on assimilation and multiculturalism. In the latter book, Glazer suggests that despite the removal of legal barriers to assimilation, African Americans, especially the poor, remain marginalized within the larger American society. He views multiculturalism (at least its more moderate forms), with its critiques of dominant culture and attempts to refocus attention on the role that marginalized groups have played and continue to play in the creation of society, as a response to the unfulfilled aspirations for full inclusion. Thus in this book, Glazer appears to have given up his long-held belief that full assimilation is possible and to suggest that multiculturalism might play a legitimate role in struggles for equality. However, Glazer has not substantially changed his critical views on affirmative action, holding that affirmative action reversely discriminates. In a 1998 *New York Times* interview, Glazer stated that "a lot of the arguments for affirmative action are weak and illusory." More telling, in March 1998, Glazer authored an article in which he clearly called for the end of affirmative action:

> I would like colleges and universities, and employers and public contractors, to be freed to do what they feel impelled to do, on the basis of their ideology and their sentiments, as affected by political and market forces that shape them. That would be for the best, and much better than either a universal standard that says there must be preferences—we have lived under something like this for 25 years—or a universal standard that says there must not be preferences. With the free and voluntary action of autonomous institutions, I think we can move ahead, slowly, in dealing with our race problem. (Glazer 1998, 32)

Finally, in recent years, Glazer has written about the need to remove racial classifications as part of the federal census, as a way to get beyond race.

Glazer has held a number of impressive appointments and received a number of awards during his long and illustrious career. He is an emeritus professor of sociology and education at Harvard University. He has also written and edited for a general reading audience in his positions as contributing editor for the *New Republic* and coeditor of the *Public Interest.*

See also Criticisms of; Affirmative Action, African Americans; Assimilation Theory; Census Classifications, Ethnic and Racial; Civil Rights Act of 1964; Immigration Act of 1965; Kennedy, John Fitzgerald; Moynihan, Daniel Patrick; Multiculturalism; Racial Privacy Initiative.

FURTHER READING: Glazer, Nathan, 1987, *Affirmative Discrimination: Ethnic Inequality and Public Policy*, Cambridge, MA: Harvard University Press; Glazer, Nathan, and Daniel Patrick Moynihan, 1970, *Beyond the Melting Pot: The Negroes, Puerto Ricans, Jews, Italians, and Irish of New York City*, 2nd ed. (reprint of 1963 ed.), Cambridge, MA: MIT Press; Traub, James, 1998, "Nathan Glazer Changes His Mind, Again," *New York Times*, June 28, 6:23. Glazer, Nathan, 1997, *We Are All Multiculturalists Now*, Cambridge, MA: Harvard University Press; Glazer, Nathan, 1998, "Nathan Glazer (Is Affirmative Action on the Way Out? Should It Be? A Symposium)," *Commentary* 105, no. 13 (March): 18–40; Glazer, Nathan, 2002, "Do We Need the Census Race Question?" *Public Interest*, fall, 21–33.

KYRA R. GREENE

Global Implementation of Affirmative Action Programs

Writers generally claim that affirmative action involves treating a subclass or group differently to improve its members' chances of obtaining a particular good or to ensure that they obtain a portion of a certain good (Faundez 1994, 3), or sometimes define it as "the proactive policy of making special efforts in employment decisions, college entrance, and other areas of public behavior as a way of compensating for past discrimination" (Lee 1999, 25). In other words, affirmative actions are policies whose goals are to ensure that all groups in a society, particularly those who are considered to be "disadvantaged," are afforded equal opportunities. Affirmative action policies may therefore be introduced in a wide variety of areas. They are, however, more generally applied in areas such as education, housing, and public employment.

In the case of public employment, it has been found that different countries have adopted varying approaches in designing and implementing affirmative action programs. Some countries, for example, have some form of affirmative action in the public sector, while others have programs both in the public and private sectors. In countries such as Fiji, India, Malaysia, and Namibia, affirmative action clauses are included in the constitution, and policies of affirmative action are implemented by the central and local administrations with a minimum amount of external monitoring. In countries such as the United States, however, although the Constitution does not contain affirmative action clauses, a variety of programs have been developed through legislation, executive regulation, and judicial intervention. For example, in the United States, the most comprehensive affirmative action program, contract compliance, is embodied in a series of executive orders. In Canada, one institution, the Canadian Human Rights Commission, has the power to investigate and redress complaints of discrimination, including discriminatory practices in employment matters.

The beneficiaries of affirmative action policies vary from country to country. The most common categories, however, are ethnic, national, or racial minorities, aboriginal peoples, women, and people with disabilities or war veterans. However, while generally these policies are directed toward minorities, in certain countries where the minority group holds or formerly held the reins of power, such as South Africa or Malaysia, affirmative action is often directed toward the majority group. Other exceptions include India, where residents of a particular locality as well as a particular caste are beneficiaries of some programs, the Australian public service, where affirmative action programs are directed toward people of non-English-speaking background, or the public services of Ontario, where francophones are viewed as a "designated group."

Faundez (1994, 34) observes that while the criteria for the beneficiaries may vary from case to case, the objective of these programs of affirmative action is essentially the same, the achievement of equality in one form or another. In most cases, groups are selected because in the past they have suffered severe social, economic, political, or educational disadvantages. The policies of affirmative action that are introduced thus serve two major purposes: to compensate these groups for past wrongs that were perpetrated, or to eliminate existing patterns of discrimination. In other cases, groups that have not been the victims of past discrimination are selected to accelerate their integration into a society and thus avoid the risk of future discrimination.

In the quest for greater equality in employment practices, a number of mechanisms have been employed, including the establishment of institutions such as the Equal Employment Opportunity Commission, the Civil Service Commission, the Office of Federal Contract Compliance Programs, and the U.S. Commission on Civil Rights in the case of the United States, and the Canadian Human Rights Commission in the case of Canada. Another mechanism that is commonly applied is the use of a quota system to allow for a more representative bureaucracy.

A number of criticisms have been directed against policies that promote affirmative action. Nathan Glazer (1987), a notable affirmative action critic in the United States, not only contends that affirmative action policies are another form of discrimination but argues that because businesses are under pressure from government to hire minorities, this results in a reduction in the quantity and quality of the final product. Frederick Lynch (1989) has also argued that the introduction of affirmative action policies involves significant administrative, social, and labor costs, while Glenn Loury (1989), another notable critic of affirmative action in the United States, suggests that affirmative action may act as a self-fulfilling prophecy by discouraging black workers from investing in skills improvement. Other writers have also observed that if affirmative action operates on the basis of a preference or quota, it is "non-merit-based," or it is likely to result in reverse discrimination since it selects less qualified workers. Still other writers like S. Harding (1993) suggest that in cases where only marginal groups are given aid, these groups are more easily denigrated and isolated by their opponents.

In the United States, legal challenges to affirmative action have arisen mainly in two contexts: the constitutional context, in which it is claimed that affirmative action programs are inconsistent with equal protection guarantees in the Constitution, or the civil rights context, in which it is claimed that affirmative action programs are inconsistent with the provisions of Title VII of the Civil Rights Act of 1964. In a number of instances, the issue of the legality of affirmative action programs has been heard by the courts; some of the better-known cases have been *Regents of the University of California v. Bakke*, 438 U.S. 265 (1978), *Fullilove v. Klutznick*, 448 U.S. 448 (1980), *United States v. Paradise*, 480 U.S. 149 (1987), and *City of Richmond v. J.A. Croson Co.*, 488 U.S. 469 (1989).

In the case of the Commonwealth Caribbean, there has always been a concern with the protection of merit, and in the 1960s, executive public service commissions were introduced in all the Commonwealth countries. Yet in plural societies such as Guyana and Trinidad and Tobago, charges were leveled against these agencies since it was alleged that Africans were dominating the public services, the armed forces, and the police services. To a large extent, these charges were supported by research: in the case of Guyana in *The Report of the International Commission of Jurists* (1965), in the case of Trinidad and Tobago in *Ethnicity and Employment Practices in Trinidad and Tobago* (1994). Yet in Guyana, there has been no attempt to address these imbalances. In the case of Trinidad and Tobago, however, by Act 29 of 1999, the then government attempted to set up joint select committees to investigate the administrative procedures and practices within the ministries. However, because each ministry was under the control of a different minister, no coordinated effort between the ministries was effectuated, thereby causing this piece of legislation to be largely ineffective. In another effort to address charges of discrimination, the government embarked on legislation to establish an Equal Opportunity Commission. Unfortunately, with the change in governmental administration in 2001, it is highly unlikely that this commission will be set up.

See also Brazil and Affirmative Action; Canada and Affirmative Action; China and Affirmative Action; *City of Richmond v. J.A. Croson Co.*; Civil Rights Act of 1964; Civil Service Commission; Equal Employment Opportunity Commission; Equal Protection Clause; European Union and Affirmative Action; *Fullilove v. Klutznick*; Glazer, Nathan; Great Britain and Affirmative Action; India and Affirmative Action; Japan and Affirmative Action; Loury, Glenn C. Merit Selections; Office of Federal Contract Compliance Programs; Performance-Based Selections; Preferences; Quotas; *Regents of the University of California v. Bakke*; Reverse Discrimination; South Africa and Affirmative Action; Title VII of the Civil Rights Act of 1964; U.S. Commission on Civil Rights; *United States v. Paradise.*

FURTHER READING: Coleman, Major G., 1999, "Merit, Cost, and the Affirmative Action Policy Debate," *Review of Black Political Economy* 27, no. 1 (summer): 99–113; Faundez, J., 1994, *Affirmative Action: International Perspectives*, Geneva: International Labor Organization; Glazer, Nathan, 1987, *Affirmative Discrimination: Ethnic Inequality and Public Policy*, Cambridge, MA: Harvard University Press; Harding, S., ed., 1993, *The Racial Economy of Science*, Bloomington: Indiana University Press; Lee, R.A., 1999, "The Evolution of Affirmative Action," *Public Personnel Management* 28, no. 3 (fall): 393–409; Long, Robert E., ed., 1996, *Affirmative Action*, Reference Shelf 68, no. 3, New York: H.W. Wilson Company; Loury, Glenn, 1989, "Why Should We Care about Group Inequality?" in *The Question of Discrimination: Racial Inequality in the U.S. Labor Market*, edited by S. Shulman and W. Darity Jr., Middletown, CT: Wesleyan University Press; Lynch, Frederick R., 1991, *Invisible Victims: White Males and the Crisis of Affirmative Action*, New York: Praeger; Sowell, Thomas, 2003, "International Affirmative Action," *Jewish World Review*, June 5, www.jewishworldreview.com.

ANN MARIE BISSESSAR

Goals

See Quotas.

Good-Old-Boy Factor

A primary goal of affirmative action policy is to combat the negative effects on minorities and women of the good-old-boy factor, which is a labor-rationing device informally used by employers and labor unions seeking efficiency and social control through hiring and promoting others similar to themselves. Since white men have often dominated corporate hierarchies and unions, the negative affects of this discrimination have disproportionately and illogically affected women's and minorities' employment opportunities.

This employment factor has formally and informally affected hiring, promotional, and firing activities and opportunity within the workplace. Informally, those in charge of making decisions about an individual's employment opportunities have inadvertently or purposefully favored those whom they consider part of their "in-group" (i.e., similar background, values, and the like), providing them with an edge over anyone considered a part of their "out-group." Race, gender, or other factors that are predetermined to be indicative of out-group status force those in a different group than the decision maker to prove that they are part of the in-group even before their relevant individual qualifications can be considered. The traditional business rationale applied by employers for this practice has been that by ensuring likeness among employee work teams, the actions of those teams will be homogeneous and efficient, creating more profit, which is the primary mission of the business. Both business and organized labor groups have supported and even negotiated formal good-old-boy–influenced hiring and promotional rationing into collective-bargaining contracts. Historically, labor's support has been based on the belief that utilizing this factor removes out-group employees from the competitive labor market, which provides labor organizations the ability to artificially maintain their own price of labor, including wages and benefits, especially if there is a split labor market.

See also Employment (Private) and Affirmative Action; Ethnocentrism; National Labor Relations Act of 1935 (Wagner Act); National Labor Relations Board; Split-Labor-Market Theory.

FURTHER READING: Arvey, Richard D., 1979, *Fairness in Selecting Employees,* Reading, MA: Addison-Wesley; Bonacich, Edna, 1972, "A Theory of Ethnic Antagonism: The Split Labor Market," *American Sociological Review* 37, no. 5 (October): 547–559; Dennen, Johan M.G. van der, 1986, "Ethnocentrism and In-Group/Out-Group Differentiation: A Review and Interpretation of the Literature," in *The Sociobiology of Ethnocentrism: Evolutionary Dimensions of Xenophobia, Discrimination, Racism, and Nationalism,* edited by Vernon Reynolds, Vincent Falger, and Ian Vine, Athens: University of Georgia Press; Gregory, Charles O., and Harold A. Katz, 1979, *Labor and the Law,* New York: W.W. Norton; Noland, William E., and E. Wright Bakke, 1949, *Workers Wanted: A Study of Employers' Hiring Policies, Preferences, and Practices in New Haven and Charlotte,* New York: Harper and Brothers; Pelling, Henry, 1960, *American Labor,* Chicago: University of Chicago Press; Powell, Reed M., 1969, *Race, Religion, and the Promotion of the American Executive,* Columbus: College of Administrative Science, Ohio State University; Wellman, Barry, and S.D. Berkowitz, 1997, *Social Structures: A Network Approach,* Greenwich, CT: JAI Press.

MARK J. SENEDIAK

Gratz v. Bollinger, 123 S. Ct. 2411, 2003 U.S. LEXIS 4801 (2003), and *Grutter v. Bollinger,* 123 S. Ct. 2325, 2003 U.S. LEXIS 4800 (2003)

On June 23, 2003, the U.S. Supreme Court released its much-anticipated rulings in the cases *Gratz v. Bollinger* and *Grutter v. Bollinger.* In these opinions, the Court addressed whether the University of Michigan's undergraduate and law schools' race-conscious admissions programs were unconstitutional. While a majority of the Court with a 6–3 split found the University of Michigan's undergraduate admissions program unconstitutional in *Gratz,* the Court upheld the University of Michigan Law School's admissions program by a 5–4 majority vote in *Grutter,* stating that the "Equal Protection Clause does not prohibit the Law School's narrowly tailored use of race in admissions decisions to further a compelling interest in obtaining the educational benefits that flow from a diverse student body." Ultimately, both rulings permit undergraduate, graduate, and professional school programs to take into consideration the factor of race, along with other factors. However, an admissions policy that takes race into account must be carefully designed to comply with the law. Guidelines for compliance are delineated in the *Grutter* majority opinion. However, the Court also indicated that affirmative action "must have a logical end point," and "25 years from now, the use of racial preferences will no longer be necessary to further the interest approved today."

The background of the *Gratz* and *Grutter* cases extends back several years. In the fall of 1997, two lawsuits were filed against the University of Michigan. The *Gratz* case contested the use of race in admissions decisions at the undergraduate level, and the *Grutter* case contested the same issue at the professional law school level. In both cases, as in others across the country, the plaintiffs challenged the University of Michigan's admissions procedures and rationale for using race in its respective admissions policies. With these lawsuits, the University of Michigan was added to a pipeline of selective public institutions sued by the Center for Individual Rights (CIR), a conservative public interest law firm that challenged the use of race in admissions and notions of access in higher education.

In the undergraduate lawsuit, two plaintiffs, Jennifer Gratz and Patrick Hamacher, legally challenged the University of Michigan, claiming that because they were white, they were treated less favorably in the admissions process. Essentially, the two plaintiffs argued that the University of Michigan "did not merely use race as a 'plus' factor or as one of many factors to attain a diverse student body. Rather, race was one of the predominate factors . . . used for determining admissions."

Gratz was a state resident who applied to the College of Literature, Science, and the Arts in 1994 for the 1995–1996 academic year. She was placed on the "wait list" and was later rejected. She subsequently attended the University of Michigan at Dearborn. Hamacher was also a state resident who applied for admission to the College of Literature, Science, and the Arts as an undergraduate in 1996. He was placed on the "wait list" and later received a rejection letter in the spring of 1997. He attended Michigan State University but stated that he would have transferred to the University of Michigan if offered the opportunity. Defendants named in the undergraduate lawsuit were former president James Duderstadt, former president Lee Bollinger, and the University of Michigan's College of Literature, Science, and the Arts.

Similarly to the undergraduate plaintiffs, Barbara Grutter, who filed a lawsuit against the University of Michigan Law School, argued that the institution did not admit her because of her race. Grutter was a resident of Michigan and applied for admission to the University of Michigan Law School in the academic year 1997–1998. After being placed on the "wait list," she was later rejected. She did not attend any other law school. Defendants named in the law school case were former dean Lee Bollinger, former dean Jeffrey Lehman, former dean of admissions at the law school Dennis Shields, and the Regents of the University of Michigan. Both lawsuits argued that race was weighted heavily in the admissions process in order to grant preferences to minority students. Both legal challenges centered on the constitutionality of using race as a factor in admissions. Each case was granted class-action status approximately one year after each petition was filed.

The University of Michigan's stance for both lawsuits was argued from the same vantage point: emphasizing the need for a diverse student body to benefit the education of all students. This became known as the diversity rationale, which had legal precedent in an earlier case heard by the U.S. Supreme Court. In 1999, the University of Michigan outlined its legal defense in an expert-witness report titled "The Compelling Need for Diversity in Higher Education." Michigan's defense stated that "the last Supreme Court decision addressing the use of race in admissions to institutions of higher education, *Regents of the University of California v. Bakke*, 438 U.S. 265 (1978), affirmed that the role of diversity in colleges and universities is both essential and compelling" (University of Michigan 1999, 1). Drawing on the expertise of various scholars and researchers from a variety of disciplines, the University of Michigan launched a sophisticated research effort to prove the hypothesis that Justice Lewis Powell assumed to be true in his *Bakke* ruling: a diverse student body enhances the educational experience of all students. In essence, the interpretation of Justice Powell's diversity rationale was on trial, and the University of Michigan brought forth testimonies from expert witnesses who provided evidence to support the link between diversity and educational enhancement or excellence. Furthermore, expert witness Patricia Gurin showed that patterns of racial segregation and separation, which are historically rooted in U.S. national life, can be broken if diversity experiences are facilitated in higher education. Hence the University of Michigan's defense asserted that if racial diversity benefits both individuals and society, then racial diversity is certainly a compelling societal interest that merits a positive judgment for the continued use of race as a factor in college admissions.

About two years into the litigation, third parties were granted defendant-intervenor status. In *Gratz*, the undergraduate case, individually named minority high-school students and the Citizens for Affirmative Action's Preservation (CAAP) were permitted to become third parties to the litigation as defendant-intervenors. In *Grutter*, the law school case, individually named law school students, undergraduate students from across the country, high-school students from Michigan, and organizations, including the Coalition to Defend Affirmative Action, Integration, and Fight for Equality by Any Means Necessary (BAMN), Law Students for Affirmative Action (LSAA), and United for Equality and Affirmative Action (UEAA), were also granted defendant-intervenor status. With the concerted efforts of newly formed defendant-intervenor groups—CAAP, BAMN, LSAA, and UEAA—students and citizens had a rare opportunity to voice their arguments and perspectives in the courtroom.

Overall, the intervening parties for both cases argued that the University of Michigan would not and could not best argue on behalf of the educational interests of underrepresented minority students. Essentially, the defendant-intervenors argued that the University of Michigan could not adequately represent the intervenors' interests due to pressures from various constituencies; furthermore, it was assumed that the institution would not address questions regarding past or present discriminatory practices if they were raised. The intervenors argued that inadequate representation of minority students in higher education and limited access for minority applicants to higher education justified the university's affirmative action programs. With respect to educational access, the defendant-intervenors argued that opportunities for African American and Latino students would be limited and the educational environment would suffer due to its lack of diversity. Both intervening groups also sought to have their own research conducted through written expert-witness testimonies in order to document the past and current practices of discrimination at the University of Michigan.

On December 13, 2000, after summary judgment proceedings were held, Judge Patrick Duggan, who presided over the undergraduate lawsuit, issued a decision that favored the University of Michigan's current admissions policy. Duggan stated that diversity was a compelling governmental interest and that the university's current undergraduate admissions program met the standards set by the U.S. Supreme Court in *Bakke*. However, he also ruled that the admissions programs in effect from 1995 to 1998 were unconstitutional because the institution engaged in a "practice of 'protecting' or 'reserving' seats for underrepresented minority students," which the judge concluded was the "functional equivalent of a quota."

In contrast, on March 27, 2001, Judge Bernard Friedman issued his opinion in the law school case and ruled in favor of the plaintiffs. He did not agree with the *Bakke* ruling. Friedman found that even if the law allowed race-conscious admissions, the law school admissions policy used the factor of race too heavily. In both cases, the defendant-intervenors' claims that race should be used to remedy the present effects of past discrimination were dismissed. In neither case did the intervening parties prove to the court that there was evidence of past or present racial discrimination with respect to the University of Michigan's admissions practices. Both cases were appealed, and the full court of the Sixth Circuit Court of Appeals heard arguments by all parties on December 6, 2001.

About five months later, on May 14, 2002, the U.S. Court of Appeals for the Sixth Circuit rendered a decision that upheld the University of Michigan Law School's admissions policy. With a 5–4 split, the majority agreed with the rationale that racial diversity was indeed a compelling interest. The same 5–4 split also exposed how politicized the judicial system can become when a controversial public policy issue is the focal point: as all but one Democratic appointee decided in favor of the university's policy, and all Republican appointees decided against the institution's use of race. In light of the district and circuit court decisions, the diversity rationale proved to be a convincing and powerful argument for the University of Michigan. However, the issue of narrow tailoring or how race is weighted in admissions decisions continues to be the central point of judicial contention.

Before the Sixth Circuit could rule on the undergraduate case, on August 9, 2002, the Center for Individual Rights filed a petition requesting that the U.S. Supreme Court review the University of Michigan Law School decision upholding its admissions program. In response, the University of Michigan filed a petition arguing that the Sixth Circuit Court ruling should stand. Unlike the university, the intervening parties for the law school case wanted the Supreme Court to accept the petition. According to their brief, embedded in the institution's admissions policies was an inherent bias that discriminated against minority applicants; therefore, affirmative action was the only means by which qualified minorities could fairly be considered for admission. Even though the intervenors agreed that the Sixth Circuit's decision should stand, they hoped that the Supreme Court would address their concerns by concluding that the race-conscious admissions program was justified not only to increase student-body diversity but also to remedy discrimination.

On December 2, 2002, the U.S. Supreme Court announced that it would hear both of the affirmative action cases from the University of Michigan. With the cases slated for hearings in April before the highest court in the land, there was an explosion of media coverage in the national press, radio, and television. This explosion allowed the voices of both supporters and opponents to be heard across the country. Numerous long-standing and relatively new supporters and opponents weighed into the debate. Their legal arguments also weighed into the courtroom through friend-of-the-court briefs. Given the importance of these cases, an unprecedented number of amicus briefs were filed on behalf of the University of Michigan.

Approximately four months after announcing that it would review the case, on April 1, 2003, the U.S. Supreme Court heard oral arguments for both cases under much national attention and scrutiny. Although the plaintiffs and defendants,

Affirmative action supporters protesting University of California regent Ward Connerly as he took his campaign against racial preferences to the University of Michigan campus in Ann Arbor, Michigan, on July 8, 2003. Several weeks after the Supreme Court rendered its opinion in the *Gratz* and *Grutter* cases (in June 2003), Connerly announced a campaign to persuade Michigan voters to support a state initiative measure that would strike down the usage of affirmative action in higher education. © AP/ Wide World Photos.

along with the U.S. solicitor general, had an opportunity to state their positions on the matter of the use of race in admissions, none of the intervening parties had an opportunity to do so. Nevertheless, their presence and position did not go unnoticed on that day. The Coalition to Defend Affirmative Action, Integration, and Fight for Equality by Any Means Necessary (BAMN), in collaboration with many other student organizations, citizens' groups, politicians, and advocacy organizations across the country, sponsored a march and rally in Washington, D.C. Estimates of the number of people at this historic event ranged from 3,000 to as high as 50,000. Continuing in the tradition of the civil rights movement, many wished to show their support for the University of Michigan and affirmative action, but more importantly to show support for the democratic ideal that racial diversity is critical to advance the nation toward racial integration in education and other aspects of American life.

On June 23, 2003, the Court handed down its opinions. The Court first had to determine what standard to use in judging whether the challenged programs were constitutional. The Court determined in both cases that the appropriate standard was strict scrutiny review. This meant that in order to be upheld, the university's use of race in its admissions processes had to be narrowly tailored to serve a compelling governmental interest. The Court concluded that the law school's admissions program met this test, but that the undergraduate admissions program did not.

Justice Sandra Day O'Connor wrote the Court's majority opinion in the *Grutter* case. Justices Stephen G. Breyer, Ruth Bader Ginsburg, David H. Souter, and John

Paul Stevens joined the majority opinion. The majority opinion adopted the rationale of Justice Powell's opinion in the *Bakke* case and agreed with the University of Michigan's argument that devising a student body that is diverse in terms of race and ethnicity but also in other ways for the purpose of achieving educational benefits is a compelling governmental interest. In so holding, the Court granted the institution a degree of deference with respect to the law school's claim that student diversity yields educational benefits because of the importance of academic freedom to First Amendment guarantees. Numerous expert reports and studies were submitted to substantiate the law school's diversity rationale, including social science research, as well as amicus curiae (friend-of-the-court) briefs from prominent American corporations and high-ranking retired officers of the U.S. military.

The Court found that "the Law School's admissions program bears the hallmarks of a narrowly tailored plan." The opinion held that in order to be constitutional, a university's use of race in its admissions program must not interfere with giving applicants individualized consideration so that each can compete and be considered on one's own merits, taking into account all pertinent factors. Within the context of individualized consideration, an institution may consider race as a modest "plus" factor for an individual applicant, but not to the extent that this consideration becomes a predominant factor and insulates the applicant from competition for admissions because he or she is a member of a particular racial or ethnic group. The Court held that the law school did not maintain quotas for certain racial or ethnic groups and did not attribute a fixed score to race or ethnicity, as was done in the undergraduate review process. Since the review process was flexible enough to weigh each factor with respect to the individual applicant's academic credentials, background characteristics, talents, skills, and educational goals, all factors that contribute to a broadly diverse class were considered in a nonformulaic manner and rendered for the institution prospective students who would contribute to the law school in a plethora of ways. The Court also noted that the race-conscious program was not unduly burdensome to nonminorities and was limited in time.

Chief Justice William H. Rehnquist wrote a dissenting opinion that was joined by Justices Anthony M. Kennedy, Antonin Scalia, and Clarence Thomas. This opinion concluded that the law school was engaging in racial balancing in its aim to maintain a critical mass of minority students and that racial balancing was unconstitutional. However, according to the majority ruling, the goal of establishing a critical mass was not for racial balancing but for deriving educational benefits that resulted from a racially diverse student population.

Justice Thomas also wrote a separate opinion in which he passionately argued against the use of race-conscious affirmative action in higher-education admissions programs. Justice Thomas agreed with the majority that the law school's race-conscious program must be subject to strict scrutiny review, but held that the program failed that test. Justice Thomas argued that governmental racial preferences are not only unconstitutional, but are harmful to members of the minority races such measures are intended to benefit. Both Justice Thomas and Chief Justice Rehnquist argued that the majority did not really apply the strict scrutiny test to the admissions program because of the deference it gave to the university's justification.

Chief Justice William H. Rehnquist wrote the majority ruling for the *Gratz* case. Justices Kennedy, O'Connor, Scalia, and Thomas joined this opinion, which held that the University of Michigan's undergraduate admissions policy that automatically awarded twenty points to every underrepresented minority applicant—African American, Hispanic American, and Native American—"solely because of their race, is not narrowly tailored to achieve the interest in educational diversity" that the institution claimed justified its admissions program. The majority held that the mechanical use of awarding twenty points to every minority applicant had the effect of making race/ethnicity a defining and decisive factor of the applicant without further individualized consideration and restricted flexibility to consider other factors that could also contribute to educational diversity, such as traveling abroad, employment experience, and community service. Such a mechanized formula, according to the Court, would be akin to a fixed racial quota, which violates the Equal Protection Clause of the Fourteenth Amendment and Title VI of the Civil Rights Act of 1964, which bans racial discrimination by any private or public educational institution that is the recipient of federal funding.

Justices Ginsburg, Souter, and Stevens dissented. In an opinion written by Justice Ginsburg and joined by Justice Souter and in part by Justice Breyer, the three justices acknowledged that consistent treatment of all individuals regardless of race would be suitable if it were not for the past system of racial discrimination imposed by law in this nation and the present effects of that legacy. The justices noted that the present effects are manifested in vast racial disparities in employment, poverty, health care, and education. Hence the dissenting justices concluded that there was a justifiable reason for the University of Michigan to institute a policy of inclusion that utilized a race-conscious measure to address vestiges of racial discrimination.

See also African Americans; Breyer, Stephen Gerald; Center for Individual Rights; Coalition to Defend Affirmative Action, Integration, and Fight for Equality by Any Means Necessary; Compelling Governmental Interest; Democratic Party and Affirmative Action; Diversity; Diversity Management; Education and Affirmative Action; Employment (Private) and Affirmative Action; Employment (Public) and Affirmative Action; Equal Protection Clause; Fourteenth Amendment; Ginsburg, Ruth Bader; Harvard Model; Hispanic Americans; *Hopwood v. Texas; Johnson v. Board of Regents of the University of Georgia*; Kennedy, Anthony McLeod; Minority Professionals and Affirmative Action; Narrowly Tailored Affirmative Action Plans; Native Americans; O'Connor, Sandra Day; Powell, Lewis Franklin, Jr.; Quotas; Race-Based Affirmative Action; Racial Discrimination; *Regents of the University of California v. Bakke*; Rehnquist, William Hobbs; Republican Party and Affirmative Action; Scalia, Antonin; Segregation; *Smith v. University of Washington Law School*; Souter, David Hackett; Stevens, John Paul; Supreme Court and Affirmative Action; Thomas, Clarence.

FURTHER READING: "The Michigan Decisions," 2003, *Chronicle of Higher Education*, July 4, B10; Schmidt, Peter, 2002, "Next Stop, Supreme Court? Appeals Court Upholds Affirmative Action at University of Michigan Law School," *Chronicle of Higher Education*, May 24, A24; Schmidt, Peter, 2002, "U.S. Supreme Court Agrees to Hear 2 Key Affirmative-Action Cases from Michigan," *Chronicle of Higher Education*, Today's News, December 2; Schmidt, Peter, 2003, "Friends and Foes of Affirmative Action Claim Victory in Rulings on Michigan

Cases," *Chronicle of Higher Education*, June 24, A1; Schmidt, Peter, 2003, "Affirmative Action Survives, and So Does the Debate: The Supreme Court Upholds Race-Conscious Admissions in Principle, but Not Always as Practiced," *Chronicle of Higher Education*, July 4, S1; Selingo, Jeffrey, 2003, "Decisions May Prompt Return of Race-Conscious Admissions at Some Colleges," *Chronicle of Higher Education*, July 4, S5; University of Michigan Expert Witness Reports, "The Compelling Need for Diversity in Higher Education," *Gratz & Hamacher v. Bollinger, et al.*, No. 97-75231, and *Grutter v. Bollinger, et al.*, No. 97-75928 (E.D. Mich. filed January 1999); Wilgoren, Debbi, and Manny Fernandez, 2003, "A Defense Team of Thousands: Diverse Crowd Urges High Court to Protect Affirmative Action," *Washington Post*, April 2, B01; Young, Jeffrey, "Student Activists Prepare for New Battles in Wake of Decision," *Chronicle of Higher Education*, July 4, S7.

DENISE O'NEIL GREEN

Great Britain and Affirmative Action

Like many of the former colonial powers, Great Britain has had to adjust to the influx of a large number of racial and ethnic minority groups. The increase in diverse groups within a nation that was traditionally relatively homogeneous in terms of race, language, and religion resulted in tension and societal pressures that successive governments have endeavored to overcome. In many ways, the depth and breadth of affirmative action programs and racial equality in the United Kingdom have been dependent upon the political party in power.

Although the percentage of ethnic and racial minorities in Great Britain is small (in 2001, these groups comprised 7.1 percent of the population, or 4 million people), there is great diversity among the minority population. The largest groups are Indians with 1 million people, followed by Pakistanis with 600,000 and Caribbean blacks with 500,000. In addition, there are significant numbers of African blacks, Bangladeshis, and Chinese Asians. All of these groups face varying degrees of discrimination in employment and everyday life, especially in matters related to hiring and promotion in employment. Another group now given minority status is the Irish, who comprise about 1.5 percent of the population and who also face similar various forms of discrimination.

A number of demographic factors tend to separate racial, ethnic, and religious minorities in Great Britain. First, minority groups live predominantly in urban areas. In 2001, some 47.6 percent of all minorities lived in the greater London metropolitan area. Other major population concentrations are in the industrial areas of northern England. Only 1.9 percent of minorities live in Scotland, and only 1.2 percent live in Wales. Racial and ethnic minorities often are of other religions than the mainstream Protestant churches, with Hindus, Sikhs, and Muslims being the main religious groups. The minority groups tend to be younger, with 45 percent of their population under the age of twenty-four, while 30 percent of the white population is under the same age. This is partially the result of higher birthrates among minority groups. Furthermore, unemployment among some groups is double the national average, as are poverty rates. High unemployment and poverty are not true of all groups, as the Indians and Chinese tend to have income levels and employment rates similar to those of the white population. Nonetheless, the general demographic factors among racial and ethnic groups reinforce negative stereotypes about minorities.

Great Britain was a generally homogeneous society until the end of World War II and the onset of the period of decolonization. As the empire disbanded, many former citizens of the colonies immigrated to Great Britain to avoid political and economic oppression. There were large waves of new minority groups until the 1970s, when immigration laws were significantly tightened.

In an effort to end discrimination in employment and social policies, Parliament passed the Race Relations Act in 1976. This law forbade discrimination based on "color, race, nationality or ethnic or national origins." The law was interpreted to cover the Irish born in the Republic of Ireland, and in 1997, the Race Relations (Northern Ireland) Order extended protections to those from Northern Ireland. As a result of the act, a variety of affirmative action programs were developed in Great Britain. However, the Conservative governments of the 1980s and 1990s undertook several initiatives to eliminate or reduce such programs. For instance, under Prime Minister Margaret Thatcher, the government ended preferences in official contracts and procurement programs for companies with substantial affirmative action programs. However, the 1997 election of a liberal Labour government under Prime Minister Tony Blair reversed this trend. For example, the 2000 Race Relations Act, which amended the original legislation, restored affirmative action preferences in government contracts and imposed a duty on all public agencies, including the police and health services, to implement policies to promote equality and end practices that might indirectly result in discrimination.

Issues related to discrimination or to racial inequality are under the purview of the Commission for Racial Equality (CRE). The CRE is tasked with developing codes of conduct and implementing affirmative action programs in both government and the private sector. It also serves as an advisory body for public agencies on matters of race and ethnicity. In general, British equality policies differ from those of the United States in that they tend to be based on rewards or incentives rather than punishments. Such "positive" action programs include special training for racial and ethnic minorities in economic fields where they are underrepresented and the development of hiring statements specifically encouraging minority applicants. Companies are also encouraged through incentives to offer sensitivity training for employees on issues of race and religion. Such measures extend beyond employment practices and include education where specialized language and cultural courses are offered to racial and ethnic minorities in a broad effort to promote equality of opportunity.

Although it is a signatory to the European Human Rights Convention and a member of the European Union (EU), unlike many of its European neighbors, Great Britain has opted out of many of the social policies of the EU and has not incorporated many aspects of the convention into national law. Instead, the British continue to assert national sovereignty on many issues related to human rights. In addition, under the doctrine of devolution, the Blair government has ceded significant political power to regional governments. Hence Scotland, Wales, and Northern Ireland all now have legislative assemblies with varying degrees of power. These parliaments have adopted different approaches to racial and ethnic inequality. In addition, unlike most democracies, Great Britain does not have a specific written bill of rights to protect individuals. This means that future Parliaments or governments could revoke current legal protections for disadvantaged groups.

See also European Court of Human Rights; European Human Rights Convention; European Union and Affirmative Action.

FURTHER READING: Alleyne, Brian W., 2002, *Radicals against Race: Black Activism and Cultural Politics*, New York: Berg; Goulbourne, Harry, 1998, *Race Relations in Britain since 1945*, New York: St. Martin's Press; Solomos, John, 1989, *Race and Racism in Contemporary Britain*, Houndmills, Basingstoke, Hampshire: Macmillan Education; Sowell, Thomas, 2003, "International Affirmative Action," *Jewish World Review*, June 5, www.jewishworldreview.com; Thomas, Huw, 2000, *Race and Planning: The UK Experience*, New York: UCL Press.

TOM LANSFORD

Great Society

See Johnson, Lyndon Baines.

Griggs v. Duke Power Co., 401 U.S. 424 (1971)

Title VII of the Civil Rights Act of 1964 prohibits discrimination in employment against persons based on their race, color, religion, sex, or national origin. It applies to employers, labor organizations, including unions, and employment agencies. The U.S. Supreme Court case *Griggs v. Duke Power Co.* is a seminal case in Title VII jurisprudence and presented the issue of whether an employment practice that appeared to be neutral on its face, but had a disparate impact on members of racial minority groups, violated Title VII. Ultimately, the Court importantly held that the Civil Rights Act of 1964 "proscribes not only overt discrimination but also practices that are fair in form but discriminatory in practice."

African American employees of Duke Power Company's Dan River plant brought a class-action lawsuit in U.S. district court. Prior to July 2, 1965, the effective date of the Civil Rights Act of 1964, the company had openly discriminated against African American employees in the hiring process and in determining their job assignments. The Dan River plant had been organized into five operating departments: (1) Labor, (2) Coal Handling, (3) Operations, (4) Maintenance, and (5) Laboratory and Test. African Americans were employed only in the Labor Department, where the highest-paying jobs paid less than the lowest-paying jobs in the other four departments, which employed only whites.

In 1965, the company added a requirement for new employees. To qualify for placement in any position other than the Labor Department, an employee was required to obtain satisfactory scores on two professionally prepared aptitude tests and to have a high-school education. Neither test was directed or intended to measure the ability to learn or to perform a particular job or category of jobs. The U.S. district court upheld the new requirement because it found that the company's discriminatory conduct had ceased. In addition, it held that Title VII was intended to be prospective only, and consequently, the impact of prior discrimination was beyond the reach of the law's corrective action.

The U.S. court of appeals concluded that there was no showing of a discriminatory purpose in the adoption of the high-school diploma and intelligence test requirements. It therefore held that there was no violation of Title VII because section 703 (h) of the statute had authorized the use of a professionally developed ability test, provided that it was not designed, intended, or used to discriminate. The court of appeals rejected the claim that because these requirements had not been shown to be job related and had a disproportionate impact on African Americans, they violated Title VII.

On certiorari to the U.S. Supreme Court, Chief Justice Warren Burger, writing for a unanimous Court, held that Title VII prohibited an employer from requiring a high-school education or passing of a standardized general intelligence test as a condition of employment or transfer to a preferred job when (1) neither measure was shown to be significantly related to successful job performance; (2) both requirements operated to disqualify African Americans at a substantially higher rate than white applicants because 58 percent of whites passed the test, as compared with only 6 percent of the African Americans; and (3) the jobs in question formerly had been filled only by white employees as part of a long-standing practice of giving preference to whites. Burger stated that under Title VII, "practices, procedures, or tests neutral on their face, and even neutral in terms of intent, cannot be maintained if they operate to 'freeze' the status quo of prior discriminatory employment practices." Moreover, Title VII required "the removal of artificial, arbitrary, and unnecessary barriers to employment when the barriers operate invidiously to discriminate on the basis of racial or other impermissible classification." Further, the high-school diploma standard and the general intelligence tests operated as "built-in headwinds" for minority groups that were unrelated to measuring job capability and therefore violated Title VII.

It is important to note that *Griggs* interpreted Title VII to prohibit not only intentional employment discrimination based on race, color, religion, sex, or national origin, termed "disparate treatment," but also employment practices that appear to be neutral, but have the effect of excluding groups of persons from job opportunities. Such practices, which have a "disparate impact" on the members of protected groups, are illegal under Title VII as well.

The *Griggs* decision did not say, however, that all job testing is prohibited by Title VII. Rather, the employer seeking to use a particular testing device or standard that has a disparate impact on the members of protected groups must meet "the burden of showing that any given requirement [has] . . . a manifest relationship to the employment in question." The Supreme Court later shifted the burden of proof in disparate impact cases to plaintiffs in *Wards Cove Packing Co. v. Atonio*, 490 U.S. 642 (1989). That decision was overturned by the Civil Rights Act of 1991, which placed the burden of justifying a practice that caused a disparate impact in these cases squarely on employers.

The Supreme Court outlined the process that a plaintiff must use to prove that an employer's test exerts a disparate impact on a protected group in *Albemarle Paper Co. v. Moody*, 422 U.S. 405 (1975). First, the plaintiff must show that the challenged tests "select applicants for hire or promotion in a racial pattern significantly different from that of the pool of applicants." Next, if the employer is able to demonstrate that the test is "job related," the complaining party may then "show that other tests or selection devices, without a similarly undesirable racial effect, would also serve the employer's legitimate interest in 'efficient and trustworthy workmanship.' " This showing "would be evidence that the employer was using its tests merely as a 'pretext' for discrimination."

In practice, the types of employment criteria that will pass muster under Title

VII and Equal Employment Opportunity Commission guidelines are those that are related directly to job performance. In *Dothard v. Rawlinson*, 433 U.S. 321 (1977), the U.S. Supreme Court invalidated an Alabama law that specified minimum height and weight requirements of five feet, two inches, and 120 pounds for employment as a state prison guard because it discriminated against women. The Court observed that the height and weight restrictions violated Title VII because Alabama's law served to disqualify approximately 41 percent of the female population while excluding less than 1 percent of all males. In addition, the state had made no effort to develop countervailing evidence that its height and weight restrictions should be upheld.

The case was not over, however. The state of Alabama had argued as well that its regulation prohibiting the hiring of women as prison guards was a "bona fide occupational qualification" (BFOQ) permitted by Title VII because it was reasonably necessary to the normal operation of its prisons. The Supreme Court held that in the circumstances of this case "the use of women as guards in 'contact' positions under the existing conditions in Alabama maximum-security male penitentiaries would pose a substantial security problem, directly linked to the sex of the prison guard." These conditions included the use of dormitory housing for aggressive inmates and an inmate population that included a substantial number of sex offenders.

International Union, U.A.W. v. Johnson Controls, Inc., 499 U.S. 187 (1991), presented a similar issue involving an employer's contention that a woman's gender should disqualify her from a particular job. Johnson Controls manufactured automobile batteries. A primary ingredient in the company's manufacturing process was lead. Even a slight amount of exposure to lead causes health risks, including the potential for serious harm to any fetus carried by a pregnant female employee. After eight of its employees became pregnant while maintaining blood lead levels exceeding those recommended by the Occupational Safety and Health Administration (OSHA), the company adopted a policy barring all women except those who could document their infertility from jobs involving exposure to lead. Several of the company's female employees challenged the policy as a violation of Title VII in federal court. The U.S. district court granted the company's motion for a summary judgment, and the U.S. court of appeals affirmed.

The U.S. Supreme Court held that the company's policy violated Title VII. Citing *Dothard v. Rawlinson*, Justice Harry Blackmun asserted that "discrimination on the basis of sex because of safety concerns is allowed only in narrow circumstances . . . [and] is limited to instances in which sex or pregnancy actually interferes with the employee's ability to perform the job." The Court concluded: "[W]omen as capable of doing their jobs as their male counterparts may not be forced to choose between having a child and having a job."

Since *Dothard* and *International Union*, the Supreme Court has provided only limited guidance about the scope of Title VII's protections. Lower federal courts, however, have provided considerable direction in these areas. For example, police officers and firefighters may be required to demonstrate that they are capable physically of performing their jobs. Therefore, basic physical fitness tests, which include running, strength, and lung capacity measures, would be permissible under Title VII. Likewise, employers may require teachers, lawyers, physicians, engineers, accountants, and other professionals to possess academic degrees in their chosen fields.

See also Albemarle Paper Co. v. Moody; Blackmun, Harry Andrew; Civil Rights Act of 1964; Civil Rights Act of 1991; Disparate Treatment and Disparate Impact; Equal Employment Opportunity Commission; Manifest Imbalance Standard; Title VII of the Civil Rights Act of 1964; *Wards Cove Packing Co. v. Atonio*; Warren Court and Affirmative Action.

FURTHER READING: Player, M.A., 1992, *Federal Law of Employment Discrimination*, St. Paul, MN: West Pub. Co.; Rothstein, M.A., 1994, *Cases and Materials on Employment Law*, 3d ed., Westbury, NY: Foundation Press.

THOMAS J. HICKEY

Grove City College v. Bell, 465 U.S. 555 (1984)

In *Grove City College v. Bell*, the U.S. Supreme Court held that a private liberal arts college receiving no funds or financial assistance directly from the federal government was nevertheless a recipient of federal financial assistance under Title IX of the Education Amendments of 1972 through the enrollment of students receiving Basic Educational Opportunity Grants. As a result of the ruling, educational institutions that sought to avoid government imposition of affirmative action programs by declining to accept direct financial assistance were held to be accountable to the federal government in prohibiting sex discrimination through the indirect receipt of federal funds obtained by their students. The Court additionally held that only the specific program or activity at the institution that received federal funds was required to comply with Title IX, and not the institution as a whole (if no federal funds were received beyond those for the specific program). Congress was so adamantly in disagreement with this point that it passed, over President Ronald Reagan's veto, the Civil Rights Restoration Act of 1988, which required that the entire institution must comply with Title IX, and not just specific programs, as the Court had held in its *Grove City* decision.

Grove City College, a private, coeducational, liberal arts college, sought to preserve its institutional autonomy by refusing to apply for direct state and federal financial assistance. The college also declined to participate in federally sponsored student assistance programs under which the college was required to assess a student's eligibility and determine the amounts of loans, work-study funds, or grants the student should receive. The college did, however, enroll a large number of students receiving Basic Educational Opportunity Grants from the Department of Education under the Alternative Disbursement System.

Basic Educational Opportunity Grants (BEOGs) issued by the Department of Education were administered under one of two procedures. The Regular Disbursement System involved the Department of Education estimating the grant funds needed by an institution, with such funds being advanced directly to the institution. The institution would then determine student eligibility under the program, calculate awards, and distribute the funds to the student. Under the Alternative Disbursement System, award calculations and disbursements of funds were made directly to eligible students by the Department of Education, thereby limiting an institution's involvement in the administration of the BEOG program.

Grove City College declined to participate in the Regular Disbursement System, but did enroll students who had received BEOG funds through the Alternative Disbursement System.

The Department of Education determined that Grove City College was a recipient of federal financial assistance as a result of the receipt of federal funds under the BEOG program by students enrolled at the college. Consequently, the Department of Education required Grove City College to execute an assurance of compliance, including an agreement not to discriminate on the basis of sex in any educational program or activity for which federal financial assistance was received. Grove City College refused to execute the assurance of compliance, arguing that neither the college nor any of its education programs or activities received federal financial assistance as a result of the use of BEOG funds by students enrolled at the college to pay for their education. Because Grove City College refused to execute an assurance of compliance, the Department of Education initiated proceedings to declare Grove City College and its students ineligible to receive funds under the BEOG program.

The Court found that the language of section 901(a) of Title IX contained "no hint that Congress perceived a substantive difference between direct institutional assistance and aid received by a school through its students." In addition, the Court noted that congressional intent and a long-standing administrative construction of the term "receiving Federal financial assistance" supported its conclusion that Title IX coverage is not foreclosed because federal funds are provided to college students and not directly to a college's educational program. In fact, the department's sex discrimination regulations specifically provided that federal financial assistance included scholarships, loans, and grants extended directly to students for payment to an institution. The Court suggested that Congress would not elevate "form over substance" by making nondiscrimination at an institution dependent upon whether BEOG funds were received through the Regular Disbursement System or the Alternative Disbursement System. Therefore, Grove City College was found to be a recipient of federal financial assistance under Title IX through its students' use of BEOG funds for payment of educational expenses.

However, the Court refused to find Title IX applicable to the entire institution simply because BEOG funds eventually reached the college's general operating budget. Noting that Title IX applies to the "education program or activity" of the college "receiving" federal financial assistance, the Court rejected Grove City College's contention that treating BEOG funds, which were not tied to any specific "education program or activity," as federal financial assistance would subject the college itself to compliance with Title IX in contradiction of Title IX's program-specific language. Instead, the Court found BEOGs to constitute federal financial assistance to the college's own financial aid program, thereby making the financial aid program the "education program or activity" subject to the provisions of Title IX and its requirement for an assurance of compliance.

Justice Lewis Powell, in a concurring opinion joined by Chief Justice Warren Burger and Justice Sandra Day O'Connor, reluctantly agreed that the language, legislative history, and Department of Education regulations made Title IX applicable to Grove City College's financial aid office. In what Justice Powell characterized as "an unedifying example of overzealousness on the part of the Federal

Government," the Department of Education was criticized for taking a small independent college through six years of litigation to execute an agreement to operate its programs and activities in a nondiscriminatory manner although, admittedly, Grove City College had engaged in no discrimination whatsoever. Noting that the department's termination of student grants and loans would most directly affect the students themselves, many of whom would have to abandon their college education or choose another school, Justice Powell asserted, "I cannot believe that the Department will rejoice in its victory."

Justice John Paul Stevens, concurring in the result, asserted that the issue before the Court was whether the Department of Education could terminate federal financial assistance to Grove City College as a result of its receipt of federal financial assistance and refusal to execute an assurance of compliance. Justice Stevens found the Court's holding that Grove City College was required to refrain from sex discrimination only in its financial aid program to be unnecessary and merely advisory. In addition, Justice Stevens considered the record insufficient to make any determination as to the college's programs and activities that could be said to receive, or benefit from, the federal financial assistance the BEOG program provides, with the result that the Court's advice was "predicated on speculation rather than evidence."

Justice William Brennan, joined by Justice Thurgood Marshall, concurring in part and dissenting in part, argued that Title IX coverage for an institution of higher education is appropriate if federal monies are received by or benefit the entire institution. Noting that the Court correctly decided that Grove City College "receives Federal financial assistance" through student BEOGs, and that the purpose of such programs is to benefit colleges and universities as a whole, Justice Brennan suggested that it "necessarily follows" that the antidiscrimination provisions of Title IX apply to the entire undergraduate institution operated by Grove City College. According to Brennan, the practical effect of the Court's decision demonstrated its "absurdity." For example, the ruling would prohibit Grove City College from discriminating in the area of financial assistance, but allow discrimination in admissions, athletics, or academic departments. Such a result, argued Brennan, Congress clearly could not have intended.

See also Brennan, William Joseph; Civil Rights Restoration Act of 1988; Department of Education; Marshall, Thurgood; O'Connor, Sandra Day; Powell, Lewis Franklin, Jr.; Sex Discrimination; Stevens, John Paul; Title IX of the Education Amendments of 1972.

FURTHER READING: Bryjak, George J., 2000, "The Ongoing Controversy over Title IX," *USA Today Magazine*, July, 4; Czapanskiy, Karen, 1984, "*Grove City College v. Bell*: Touchdown or Touchback?" *University of Maryland Law Review* 43 (winter): 379–412; Friedman, Leon, 2001, "Overruling the Court," *American Prospect* 12, no. 15 (August 27): 12–15; Marcus, Ruth, 1988, "Veto Override Turned Reagan's Court Victory into Major Loss," *Washington Post*, March 24, A4; Marks, Brian A. 1989, "A Model of Judicial Influence on Congressional Policymaking: *Grove City College v. Bell* (1984)," Ph.D. thesis, Washington University; Schultz, Jon S., 1989, *Legislative History and Analysis of the Civil Rights Restoration Act*, Littleton, CO: F. B. Rothman.

EILEEN HUSSELBAUGH

Grutter v. Bollinger

See Gratz v. Bollinger/Grutter v. Bollinger.

Guinier, Lani (1950–)

Lani Guinier is a prominent civil rights lawyer, legal theorist, writer, professor of law, and frequent advocate of race-conscious reforms in the democratic voting process. She lectures extensively on social justice, civil rights, race, and gender. She is also the author of *The Tyranny of the Majority* and *Lift Every Voice* and coauthor of *Becoming Gentlemen* and *Who's Qualified?* Guinier gained national name recognition when she was nominated in 1993 by President Bill Clinton to serve as assistant attorney general for civil rights. Clinton withdrew her nomination when conservative critics labeled her the "quota queen" and attacked her previous legal writings on race and democracy.

Guinier, a longtime professor of law at the University of Pennsylvania, now serves as a professor of law at Harvard. She graduated in 1971 from Radcliffe College and in 1974 from Yale Law School. For years, Guinier had wanted to be a civil rights lawyer and spent most of her career working in that area. Her primary focus was voting rights because she believed that in any voting system there were permanent locked-in winners and losers, and race was often the dividing factor. Guinier served as a civil rights lawyer with the National Association for the Advancement of Colored People (NAACP) Legal Defense and Educational Fund and the U.S. Department of Justice prior to her teaching career.

When President Clinton nominated her for the assistant attorney general position in 1993, she was attacked by members of Congress and the press and accused of advocating a "racial spoils system" or "segregating black voters in black-majority districts." She was even called a "quota queen" by Clint Bolick, a Reagan-era Justice Department official. Before Guinier had the opportunity to defend her position and writings before the Judiciary Committee and the full Senate, Clinton withdrew her nomination. A friend of Bill and Hillary Clinton since law school, Guinier felt betrayed.

In part to respond to those who attacked her record, Guinier authored the book *The Tyranny of the Majority: Fundamental Fairness in Representative Democracy* (1994), which contains a collection of the law journal articles she wrote prior to her nomination. She believes that the concepts of "majority rule" and "winner takes all" are unfair. In her book, she states:

> "It is no fair" if a fixed, tyrannical majority excludes or alienates the minority. It is no fair if a fixed, tyrannical majority monopolizes all the power all the time. It is no fair if we engage in the periodic ritual of election, but only the permanent majority gets to choose who is elected. Where we have tyranny by The Majority, we do not have genuine democracy. (Guinier 1994, 6)

In essence, Guinier was trying to find a middle ground where everyone would be treated fairly and equitably in a democratic society. She wanted to give minorities an opportunity to influence legislative outcomes in a more concentrated fashion. To improve the current voting rights strategy, Guinier proposed "interest representation," a strategy in which voters of the same interest would join together and vote for the candidates of their choice instead of voting along jurisdictional lines. Guinier has espoused plurality voting and representation approach, rather than a simple majority winner-take-all approach. Guinier also criticized the Reagan administration and the Department of Justice for allegedly working against women and minorities and protecting the white majority, especially males. She accused them of enforcing the Voting Rights Act to protect the white majority. Guinier is the founder of Commonplace, a nonprofit organization whose purpose is to promote open communications across all barriers, language, racial, and cultural, in the decision-making and problem-solving process.

See also Baker v. Carr; Bolick, Clint; Clinton, William Jefferson; Department of Justice; National Association for the Advancement of Colored People; Reagan, Ronald; *Shaw v. Reno*; Voting Rights Act of 1965.

FURTHER READING: Guinier, Lani, 1994, *The Tyranny of the Majority: Fundamental Fairness in Representative Democracy*, New York: Free Press; Guinier, Lani, and Susan Sturm, 2001, *Who's Qualified?* Boston: Beacon Press; Richie, Rob, and Jim Naureckas, 1993, "Lani Guinier: 'Quota Queen' or Misquoted Queen?" *Extra!*, July/August: 6.

NAOMI ROBERTSON

H

Harvard Model

Associate Justice Lewis F. Powell's lead opinion in *Regents of the University of California v. Bakke*, 438 U.S. 265 (1978), and the vote reflected in that opinion were critical both to striking down the University of California at Davis Medical School's race-conscious admissions program that set aside sixteen slots for disadvantaged minorities and to establishing the precedent that more flexible plans could survive scrutiny under the Equal Protection Clause of the Fourteenth Amendment. In reaching the conclusion that the plan at issue was unlawful while more flexible plans would not be, Justice Powell contrasted the university's plan with Harvard College's plan for taking race into account in admitting students to the first-year class (which plan Justice Powell attached as an appendix to his opinion). Quoting from the Harvard Plan's description of how race could be used as a factor to distinguish among "the large middle group of applicants who are 'admissible' "—as distinguished from the clear admits and clear rejects—Justice Powell opined that such use of race as a "plus" in the selection process would conform to his vision of constitutionally permissible race-conscious action to increase diversity among university students. Hence under the Harvard model, each applicant's file is read and a wide variety of factors are considered when making admissions decisions. Twenty-five years later, in *Gratz v. Bollinger*, 123 S. Ct. 2411, 2003 U.S. LEXIS 4801 (2003), and *Grutter v. Bollinger*, 123 S. Ct. 2325, 2003 U.S. LEXIS 4800 (2003), the Supreme Court affirmed Powell's position as the opinion of the Court.

The notion that using race as a "plus," or one of numerous factors, to alter the outcome yielded by race-neutral consideration of the other factors significantly differs from reserving a portion of openings for a particular racial group has been extremely resilient. It was a recurring theme in Justice William J. Brennan's majority opinion upholding a gender-conscious preferential selection in *Johnson v. Transportation Agency, Santa Clara County*, 480 U.S. 616 (1987), as well as in Justice Sandra Day O'Connor's concurrence in that case. It later figured significantly in Justice Brennan's majority opinion upholding congressionally mandated race-conscious preferences in the distribution of broadcast licenses in *Metro Broadcasting, Inc. v. FCC*, 497 U.S. 547 (1990), the last decision in which the U.S. Supreme Court upheld race-conscious affirmative action until the *Grutter* decision in 2003. It has also underlain numerous decisions by the lower federal courts and state courts upholding race- or gender-conscious affirmative action plans in a variety of contexts.

Whether a constitutionally relevant distinction exists between a plan that sets aside a certain number or proportion of selections for a certain group and one that allows group membership to be given specified or unspecified weight in attempting to increase the number of selections from the group is something that many will debate, particularly when the plus factor is employed in a consistently successful effort to cause the group to comprise a certain number or proportion of selections. It warrants note that at Harvard itself, the plan had been implemented in a manner to cause African Americans to comprise 7 percent of admitted freshmen for each year from 1973 to 1979. Only time will tell whether the Supreme Court ultimately will credit a distinction between plans that set aside a certain portion of positions for a group and plans that achieve the same result by treating race or gender as a plus factor. However, in the 2003 landmark *Gratz* and *Grutter* cases, the Court reaffirmed Justice Powell's diversity rationale. In reaffirming diversity in higher education as a compelling governmental interest, the Supreme Court upheld the University of Michigan Law School's affirmative action plan (*Grutter* case) and endorsed affirmative action plans that utilize race as one factor or ingredient (among many) in the overall evaluation of candidates. The concept of a "plus" factor that the Court ultimately sanctioned in *Grutter* can be traced back to the *Bakke* decision and, more specifically, to information about the Harvard Model, which was attacked as an appendix to the *Bakke* opinions. Consistent with the Harvard Model, the Court in *Grutter* held that race could be considered as a "plus" factor, just as other factors such as athletic ability or musical talent or letters of recommendation might be considered. However, the Court warned in the *Gratz* decision that deviation from a flexible plan (like the Harvard Model) would not be tolerated and that fixed racial quotas and mechanized formulas (which have the effect of operating as quotas) would be struck down as unlawful.

See also African Americans; Education and Affirmative Action; Equal Protection Clause; Fourteenth Amendment; *Gratz v. Bollinger/Grutter v. Bollinger; Johnson v. Transportation Agency, Santa Clara County*; *Metro Broadcasting, Inc. v. FCC*; O'Connor, Sandra Day; Powell, Lewis Franklin, Jr.; *Regents of the University of California v. Bakke.*

FURTHER READING: *Grutter v. Bollinger*, 288 F.3d 732 (6th Cir. 2002); Law, Sylvia, "White Privilege and Affirmative Action," *Akron Law Review* 32: 603–627; *Regents of the University of California v. Bakke*, 438 U.S. 265 (1978); Schmidt, Peter, 2003, "Affirmative Action Survives, and So Does the Debate: The Supreme Court Upholds Race-Conscious Admissions in Principle, but Not Always as Practiced," *Chronicle of Higher Education*, July 4, S1.

JAMES P. SCANLAN

Hate Crimes

Hate-crime legislation, like affirmative action, attempts to counteract ongoing discrimination and bias by increasing penalties for crimes in which the victim was chosen because of race, religion, national origin, or some other identified status. Hate crimes are distinguished from other crimes in that they target and affect not only the individual victim, but the victim's entire group. Hate crimes serve to intimidate and threaten an entire group of people by signaling that the victim was not selected because of any individual characteristics, but because of his or group membership. Hate crimes are thus symbolic acts aimed at a community.

Nearly every state has instituted increased penalties for hate crimes. However, states vary in the definition of protected classes. Some states include crimes aimed at victims based on sex, age, disability, national origin, color, or creed. Race, religion, and ethnicity are the categories most frequently cited. Over time, state statutes have become more inclusive; however, only about half of the states include gender, sexual orientation, and disability. Hate-crime legislation includes only those statuses that are rooted in history, as well as systems of oppression that civil rights movements have identified and organized around. The categories most frequently included are those associated with the first wave of the civil rights movement.

Some argue that these laws are more properly understood as targeting "bias crimes" because it is not the hateful views, but the act of bias itself that defines the offense as a hate crime. Over time, these laws have become broader, encompassing a wider array of statuses and crimes. Hate crimes are notoriously underreported due to a variety of factors, including distrust of law enforcement and fear of retaliation. As in other forms of law enforcement, enforcement of hate-crime law varies tremendously.

The Federal Hate Crime Statistics Act was signed by President George Bush in 1990, requiring the Attorney General's Office to collect data on crimes motivated by prejudice based on race, ethnicity, religion, or sexual orientation. In 1994, disability was added, and in 1996, hate-crime data collection was made a permanent feature of the FBI's Uniform Crime Report (UCR). The legal definition of a hate crime is limited to the commission of a criminal offense. Additionally, the UCR only counts hate crimes based upon eight criminal offenses, excluding other criminal acts and perhaps equally injurious noncriminal acts. The federal government keeps track of hate crimes committed based only on the five categories of group membership. However, numerous organizations (e.g., the Anti-Defamation League, the Southern Poverty Law Center, and the National Gay and Lesbian Task Force) track hate crimes targeting other groups. While much crime against women is indistinguishable from the definition of hate crime, crimes targeting women are frequently excluded, making accurate estimates of crime against women difficult to tabulate.

Both workplace discrimination and hate crimes are motivated by belief systems, as well as social and political factors. Hate crimes target groups already marginalized or stigmatized in society and consequently serve to reify inequality. Sociologists and criminologists argue that our culture encourages hate crime; it is simply an extreme manifestation of the biases entrenched in our culture and institutions. There is some debate whether hate-crime perpetrators are expressing frustration over their powerlessness or are attempting to maintain their power over subordinate groups. The definition of hate crime is socially and historically constructed.

While hate crimes have occurred throughout history, they have only very recently been identified as a specific class of crime. Hate-crime statutes represent an attempt to utilize the law to combat injurious attitudes and behaviors with long, historic roots. In the 1970s through the 1990s, a variety of social movements, including the civil rights movement, the victim's rights movement, the women's movement, and the gay and lesbian movements attempted to highlight the problems of discriminatory violence. Thus there has been an increase in visibility of and concern with this social problem.

Contrary to popular myth, most hate crimes are not associated with members of white supremacist hate groups, but instead are committed by average, young (sixteen to twenty-five), white, frequently working-class males, indistinguishable from their nonoffending counterparts. Hate crimes are most often unplanned, random acts, with the perpetrators usually outnumbering the victims. The language utilized by the attackers frequently reveals bias as a motive. Hate crimes are more likely to consist of crimes aimed at persons rather than property and usually involve violence or the threat of violence. Approximately two-thirds of hate-crime victims are targeted because of their race, and African Americans are the group most often targeted because of their race (usually in the form of assault or intimidation). Jews are the group next most frequently victimized by hate crimes (these usually take the form of property crimes), followed by gays and lesbians.

See also African Americans; Anti-Defamation League; Bush, George Herbert Walker; Civil Rights Movement; Criminal Justice System and Affirmative Action; Department of Justice; First Amendment; Women and the Workplace.

FURTHER READING: Ferber, Abby L., Ryken Grattet, and Valerie Jenness, 1999, *Hate Crime in America: What Do We Know?* Washington, DC: American Sociological Association; Jenness, Valerie, and Kendal Broad, 1997, *Hate Crimes: New Social Movements and the Politics of Violence*, Hawthorne, NY: Aldine de Gruyter; Jenness, Valerie, and Ryken Grattet, 2001, *Building the Hate Crime Policy Domain: From Social Movement Concept to Law Enforcement Practice*, New York: Russell Sage Foundation; Perry, Barbara, 2001, *In the Name of Hate: Understanding Hate Crimes*, New York: Routledge.

ABBY L. FERBER

Hawaiian Natives

See Native Hawaiians.

Head Start

Head Start is a child development program established to advance the school readiness of children in low-income households. The Head Start program is viewed by some as an alternative social program to affirmative action programs that are traditionally based upon racial or gender categories. Head Start can be described as a social program designed to give children born into different economic circumstances equality in learning and, hopefully, equal opportunity in other areas later in life. Founded in 1965, Head Start is a program administered by the Department of Health and Human Services (DHHS). The program includes a variety of services in three primary areas: education and early childhood development, child health and development, and family and community partnerships.

Group of children drawing in a classroom. © Fotosearch.

The Head Start program was originally designed as an eight-week summer program to develop the skills of young children before they enrolled in elementary school. Today, it is a year-round program serving pregnant women and children from birth to age five. Services differ from program to program. Educational programs are customized, taking into consideration the child's interests, learning style, temperament, and current level of development. Qualification for Head Start programs is not based upon racial characteristics or racial/gender-group membership, but rather upon an individual's economic resources. Many programs provide health services that include medical, dental, and mental health care. Head Start programs also strive to establish a network of local organizations and agencies that parents can rely on during and after the program. Critics of affirmative action, such as Stephen Carter, have advocated that perhaps more governmental spending should be devoted to social projects such as Head Start, instead of utilizing the funding for affirmative action programs based upon race.

There are currently more than 1,400 programs throughout the United States. Although the Head Start program receives 80 percent of its funding from DHHS, the programs are operated by community-based organizations, which include school districts, universities, community health centers, tribal governments, and other profit and nonprofit agencies. The remaining funding comes from local sources, which allows the program to reflect the flavor of the community. Head Start children consistently show progress in both their reading and math skills during the first four years of elementary school. In addition, parents and teachers report that children who have participated in the program adjust positively to the school environment. Between 1965 and 2002, the program served a total of 19,397,000 children.

See also Bolick, Clint; Carter, Stephen L.; Department of Health and Human Services; Economically Disadvantaged.

FURTHER READING: Ellsworth, Jeanna, and Lynda J. Ames, 1998, *Critical Perspectives on Project Head Start: Revisioning the Hope and Challenge*, Albany: State University of New York Press; Head Start, web site: http://www2.acf.dhhs.gov/programs/hsb; Ramey, Sharon L., Craig T. Ramey, Martha M. Phillips, Robin G. Lanzi, Carl Brezausek, Charles R. Katholi, Scott Snyder, and Frank Lawrence, 2000, *Head Start Children's Entry into Public School: A Report on the National Head Start/Public School Early Childhood Transition Demonstration Study*, Birmingham: Civitan International Research Center, University of Alabama at Birmingham; Zigler, Edward, and Susan Muenchow, 1992, *Head Start: The Inside Story of America's Most Successful Educational Experiment*, New York: Basic Books; Zigler, Edward, and Sally J. Styfco,

1993, *Head Start and Beyond: A National Plan for Extended Childhood Intervention,* New Haven, CT: Yale University Press.

AIMÉE HOBBY RHODES

Health Care and Affirmative Action

See Department of Health and Human Services.

Herrnstein, Richard

See The Bell Curve.

Hispanic Americans

The term "Hispanic" refers to native language and to cultural background rather than to a specific race. It includes people of diverse ethnic origins such as blacks and American Indians as well as individuals with European backgrounds whose families migrated to the Americas generations ago. Hispanics include individuals who were incorporated into the United States as a result of the Mexican War as well as others who classify themselves in one of the specific Spanish, Hispanic, or Latino categories (i.e., Mexican, Mexican American, Chicano, Puerto Rican, Cuban, or Other Spanish/Hispanic/Latino). Individuals classified as Hispanic Americans are typically a type of minority group provided for in affirmative action programs and plans.

According to the 2000 U.S. census, the Hispanic population in the United States had more than doubled during the 1990s. This is attributed to the high birth and immigration rates experienced by this population. Among the Hispanic population in the United States, 66.1 percent were of Mexican origin, 14.5 percent were Central and South American, 9.0 percent were Puerto Rican, 4.0 percent were Cuban, and 6.4 percent were of other Hispanic origins. One of the significant reasons for the jump in Hispanics in the latter half of the twentieth century is changing U.S. immigration policies, and specifically the passage of the Immigration Act of 1965. Prior to 1965, the leading source of immigrants was Europe. However, since 1965, Mexico has been the leading country of origin of immigrants coming into the United States. Today, Hispanics account for 13 percent of the U.S. population and now constitute the largest minority group in the United States.

See also Affirmative Action Plan/Program; Census Classifications, Ethnic and Racial; Immigration Act of 1965; Native Americans.

FURTHER READING: Fernandez-Shaw, Carlos M., 1991, *The Hispanic Presence in North America from 1492 to Today,* New York: Facts on File; Gonzalez, Juan, 2000, *Harvest of Empire: A History of Latinos in America,* New York: Viking; Ochoa, George, 2001, *Atlas of Hispanic-American History,* New York: Facts on File; Olson, James S., 2003, *Equality Deferred: Race, Ethnicity, and Immigration in America since 1945,* Belmont, CA: Wadsworth; Rodriguez, Richard, 2002, *Brown: The Last Discovery of America,* New York: Viking.

PAULINA X. RUF

Historically Black Colleges and Universities

Within American higher education, there are currently 105 colleges and universities that have a history of serving the African American population of the country. These colleges, both public and private institutions, are collectively referred to as historically black colleges and universities and among themselves and within other circles in higher education are often recognized merely by the acronym HBCUs. Since the end of segregation, and even more since the beginning of affirmative action, questions have abounded about the continued existence of historically black colleges and universities: their nature, their relevance, their value, and their viability.

The total number of 105 HBCUs includes 40 four-year public institutions, 49 private four-year and graduate professional institutions, and 16 two-year institutions (11 public, 5 private). Three are single-sex institutions: for women, Bennett College, in Greensboro, North Carolina, and Spelman College, in Atlanta, Georgia; for men, Morehouse College, in Atlanta, Georgia. Although the total number of historically black colleges and universities represents a small percentage of American higher education—much less than 5 percent of all such institutions—HBCUs award approximately 30 percent of all black bachelor's degrees, and a large percentage of blacks who obtain doctoral degrees first receive undergraduate degrees from HBCUs.

The impact of HBCUs on African American higher education has been enormous, but for the general American public, awareness of these institutions is minimal. Representations of these institutions have entered the media through the film *School Daze*, directed by Spike Lee in 1988, and the television series *A Different World* (1987–1993), a spin-off of the enormously popular *Cosby Show*. Besides these fictional treatments, public awareness is often limited to the few institutions, such as Fisk University and Howard University, that have achieved national recognition and to such national fundraising activities as the United Negro College Fund and whatever local news and fundraising activities may be evident in the communities in which these institutions exist.

Since the original founding of the majority of these institutions, the United States has gone through profound change, and the historically black colleges have been impacted by these changes. Although most HBCUs still serve a predominantly black student population, white enrollment at some is on the rise. At a dozen HBCUs, white enrollment runs between 19 percent and 49 percent, and blacks have become the minority at three institutions: Bluefield State College in West Virginia, Lincoln University in Missouri, and West Virginia State College. Several other institutions, such as Storer College (located in Harpers Ferry, West Virginia, near the site of John Brown's raid to free slaves in 1859 and which boasted Frederick Douglass as one of the original Board of Trustees members), closed their doors in the immediate aftermath of *Brown v. Board of Education*, 347 U.S. 483 (1954).

Before the Civil War, a college education for blacks was extremely rare in the North and nonexistent in the South. Many states in the antebellum South criminalized the education of blacks. Cheyney University, in Cheyney, Pennsylvania, is the oldest institution of higher education founded for black students. It was originally established as the Institute for Colored Youth in 1837 from the estate of

Quaker Richard Humphreys. Only it and two other HBCUs—Wilberforce University (originally Ohio African University) in Ohio and Lincoln University (originally Ashmun Institute) in Pennsylvania—were established before the Civil War. However, there were several integrated schools in the North, such as Oberlin College in Ohio, that still are in existence today.

Following the Civil War, the years of Reconstruction (1865–1877) saw the founding of even more such institutions by the Freedmen's Bureau, the freedmen's societies, and northern white churches and the boards of black denominations, with support from industrial philanthropic groups and individuals, and the majority of the historically black colleges and universities were established by the end of the nineteenth century. For example, Storer College, in Harpers Ferry, West Virginia, the first free school in what was part of Virginia before the Civil War, was founded in 1867 by a group of Northern church workers in conjunction with the Freedmen's Bureau. North Carolina Central University, in Durham, North Carolina, founded in 1910, was the first fully state-supported liberal arts college for blacks. Many of these schools, though, like Storer College, were colleges and universities in name only and offered elementary and high-school instruction to a population formerly excluded from all education. Even as the academic quality of the students and the institutions developed, the institutional missions were often divided, caught in conflicting conceptions of the proper education—for example, liberal arts education or industrial education—for African Americans in a still largely segregated, unequal society. These differing theories of education at the HBCUs are best illustrated by the divide that was developing between the two leading civil rights leaders of this era and their conflicting visions for the integration of blacks into white society, Booker T. Washington and W.E.B. Du Bois.

The implications of affirmative action for historically black colleges and universities are complex and ironic, as are the implications of HBCUs for affirmative action. From their founding, HBCUs were a beacon of hope for a disadvantaged, underserved (or totally neglected) population. This was especially true of the private, mostly church-founded institutions, but even the state colleges founded as nominally separate-but-equal institutions to provide education without integration offered a way out of ignorance and poverty and an avenue toward opportunity and a hope of equality to those who otherwise would have had none. Even though the students in the early age of HBCUs may have been unprepared for college, they were "the best and the brightest," for whom the limited opportunities of the HBCUs were reserved.

But since the demise of segregation and especially since the initiatives created under affirmative action, black students have been actively recruited by formerly segregated institutions, often spawning charges of "reverse discrimination" when they have been admitted under special set-aside programs or when they have been admitted with lower grade point averages and SAT scores than white students who have been rejected. Regardless of the merits of accusations of reverse discrimination, the effect upon HBCUs has been to limit the pool of African American college students who will choose to attend HBCUs. This has resulted in limited enrollment for many HBCUs. Tragically, it has also resulted in institutions (like Storer College) closing their doors altogether.

In their enormous study of affirmative action at highly selective colleges and universities, *The Shape of the River* (1998), William Bowen and Derek Bok pay scant attention to the HBCUs except in noting a few striking statistics about African American higher education prior to affirmative action:

> By the mid-1960's, amid a rising concern over civil rights, a number of schools began to recruit black students. Nevertheless, the numbers actually enrolled remained small, with blacks making up only 1 percent of the enrollments of selective New England colleges in 1965. . . . Similarly, few blacks were enrolled in the nation's professional schools. In 1965, barely 1 percent of all law students in American were black, and over one-third of them were enrolled in all-black schools. Barely 2 percent of all medical students were African American, and more than three-fourths of them attended two all-black institutions, Howard University and Meharry Medical College. (Bowen and Bok 1998, 5)

However, the results of that study have enormous ramifications for the future of historically black institutions. Although *The Shape of the River* strongly supports affirmative action in higher education, it also questions the legitimacy of over-simplified concepts of "merit" and emphasizes the positive outcomes for matriculants who would have been rejected by race-neutral admissions policies. Bowen and Bok further acknowledge the continuing standardized testing (SAT and other such tests) gap between white and black applicants and the reduction in black matriculants that would result from race-neutral policies. Having been generally successful at the highly selective colleges studied, these matriculants, Bowen and Bok claim, would have done well at any institution and would presumably have been admitted to a lower-ranked school. The implication is that the elimination of affirmative action plans in college admissions would significantly shift the demographics of college populations, with many black students who might attend the highest-ranked, most competitive schools being shifted "down" to lower-ranked, less competitive schools. Presumably, this "downward" shift would ripple through higher education as it removed the affirmative action advantage from minority students and granted them admission only to schools for which they met the same admission standards as white students.

While it would be unfair to say that current students at HBCUs attend these schools only because they cannot gain admittance elsewhere, even with the preferences of affirmative action, the loss of affirmative action preferences would make historically black colleges the beneficiaries of students who, as Bowen and Bok demonstrate, while lacking the highest academic credentials, are able to succeed in college work and to go on to build upon their college successes to have rewarding lives that contribute to society. However, while this would be a boost to many of the struggling HBCUs that have suffered declining enrollment, it would also appear to resurrect a segregated system in American higher education. The mention of this possibility should not provoke panicked responses, for while race-neutral admissions would significantly diminish the levels of integration and diversity in the "upper" reaches of American higher education, they would not wipe out them out. "There is a strong tendency to frantically reject this prospect as 'resegregation,' " John McWhorter comments in *Losing the Race*, "but this hyperbole sells minority students short" (McWhorter, 2000, 242). Minority students would still be represented even at the most competitive levels in higher education, though in smaller numbers, and while there remains a black-white gap in SAT score averages, it is not so large that minority students in large numbers might not successfully rise to the challenge of competing for admissions on a race-neutral basis. In that case, the much-lamented loss of diversity resulting from the absence of affirmative action might be much less than feared, and might be temporary at that.

History class at Booker T. Washington's Tuskegee Institute in Tuskegee, Alabama. Courtesy of Library of Congress.

The possibility that the abolition of affirmative action could lead to even partial "resegregation" in higher education and could benefit some of the HBCUs highlights the ambivalent status of these largely segregated institutions within an integrated society, for while there is extraordinary popular support for the preservation of these institutions and honor for their contributions to the educational and social uplifting of the African American population, few would want to see these institutions again become the only avenue to higher education open to African Americans. The implications of affirmative action for historically black colleges and universities are not restricted to student populations, but also concern the quality of education received, the nature of the faculty bodies of these institutions, and the relations between faculty and administrators.

Understandably, the HBCUs have been especially responsive to students' desires for the same kinds of changes in the college curriculum that have swept through American higher education in the last decades of the twentieth century, with greater emphasis on multicultural studies, especially African American literature and African American history courses. However, historically black colleges have been a special breeding ground for an alternative worldview called "Afrocentrism," which teaches that the philosophy of ancient Greece was a culture "stolen" from ancient Egypt, whose population was black, and that much of the traditional college curriculum, especially in the humanities and social sciences, is a racist "Eurocentric" program that deprives Africans (including, by Afrocentric definition, Egyptians) of credit for their contribution to Western civilization. Although the roots of these Afrocentric theories stretch much further back in African American culture, in the 1980s and 1990s they gained greater general public exposure, and Afrocentric curricula were adopted in a number of public schools across the country and established footholds in HBCUs as well. In light of the appeal of this alternative worldview for students at HBCUs, it comes as no surprise that George G.M. James, the author of *Stolen Legacy*, one of the long-popular "underground" classics of this ideology, was himself a professor at two HBCUs—first at Livingstone College, in Salisbury, North Carolina, and later at the University of Arkansas at Pine Bluff.

Even predominantly white institutions have felt the impact of the Afrocentric theories, but the HBCUs often have a built-in audience that is eager to learn these "truths" about a cultural "legacy" from Africa. In *Shameful Admissions*, Angela Browne-Miller tells the story of Christie Farnham Pope, a white professor of black studies at predominantly white Iowa State University, who "was threatened by one of her students with a 'jihad' or holy war" for "brainwashing African-American students with material that undercut the teachings of the Nation of Islam" (Browne-Miller 1996, 178). In contrast, though, at some historically black colleges, the Afrocentric perspective is not voiced merely by students who have encountered and fallen under the spell of this alternative worldview, but is actually adopted into the curriculum and promoted by the institution. For example, in his chapter "You Just Wouldn't Understand," which tells of his experiences at Bennett College, in Greensboro, North Carolina, Matthew Redinger tells of having had to reeducate himself to comply with the "institutional movement to 'Afrocentrize the curriculum' ":

> I discovered, in the midst of this process of reeducation and "un-learning," what I had previously learned that much of the philosophical thought for which we traditionally credit Socrates, Plato, and Aristotle actually had roots in the much older tradition of the Egyptian "Mysteries." (Redinger 1999, 26)

Many of the new "truths" Redinger cites are among the myths promulgated in James's notorious *Stolen Legacy*, and Redinger actually cites Martin Bernal, author of the controversial *Black Athena*, as if he and his work were not at all controversial.

In addition to the Afrocentric emphasis at some of the country's HBCUs, students at HBCUs are also especially subject to a variety of hoaxes, some of which are evident in the wider population, but particularly victimize African Americans. The increased availability of Internet access and e-mail, especially among teenagers, has created a deluge of hoaxes that proliferate like chain letters. Fake "computer virus" warnings and fake prizes for forwarding e-mail proliferate wherever e-mail is available, but at HBCUs, students are subjected to a variety of race-related hoaxes and attacks, such as the following: a plan of the U.S. Postal Service to destroy leftover Black Heritage stamps and to discontinue printing stamps in the Black Heritage series; the reputed lynching-related origin of the word "picnic"; fears that black colleges would be closing due to the hidden agenda of conservative politicians (this rumor, widely circulated during the 2000 election, mentioned fourteen specific colleges, seven of which are in Texas, and urged recipients not to vote for George W. Bush); and so on. Despite the relative triviality of these race-mongering theories of Afrocentrism and the race-baiting accusations and rumors proliferating across the Internet, they demonstrate the need for a rational balance against one-sided misinformation campaigns.

At the same time, these same nuisances provide an odd negative example regarding the "diversity" argument used in predominantly white institutions to justify the use of affirmative action. Whereas that argument is used to emphasize the positive effects on the whole student body and their education through the admission of minority ("diverse") applicants, the relative lack of "reverse" diversity at HBCUs must raise questions about the relative absence of those diverse viewpoints much lauded by proponents of affirmative action. The argument may even be pushed to question whether these institutions truly educate their students for a place in American society in a quasi-segregated environment.

While the status of affirmative action in the United States has affected, and will continue to affect, the student bodies, either by offering students one avenue to education when no other existed or when they qualified for no other, or offering them a "black" one among other options, affirmative action also has played a major role in employment situations in these institutions. Just as segregated America historically barred blacks from higher education at "white" institutions, black employment as professors at these institutions was similarly restricted. Thus just as HBCUs offered blacks education, it also offered employment. However, throughout the history of HBCUs, white teachers have always been employed as well, but their role has changed over the decades not only through the effects of affirmative action, but through the various levels of "acceptance" they meet in the students and the school administrations.

Since many of the students at the HBCUs clearly choose such a school for its black "identity" or the history of the institutions, white teachers may not be what the students envisioned. Matthew Redinger, whose experience with Afrocentrism was previously cited, tells of an incident during his first year at Bennett College:

> Near the end of a lecture on Reconstruction, one student erupted into a loud series of accusations that I was lying to the class. When I confronted her, she claimed that I was clearly "an agent of the Ku Klux Klan assigned to get a job at Bennett so [I] could misinform young African-American princesses about their own history." It simply stupefied me to face such blatant accusations that I embraced a racist agenda. . . . She was outraged that she had to pay money to go to a private college for African-American women only to have to take a course from a man—a white man. (Redinger 1999, 31)

Redinger's experience at Bennett College closely parallels that of many white professors at HBCUs, and Ann Jones's similar report in her semi-fictionalized account of her experience in *Uncle Tom's Campus* (1973), set more than twenty years before Redinger's experience, lamentably shows that while much has changed within the larger society as regards equal opportunity and race relations, little has changed at some of the HBCUs. Ann Jones, as a white female, relates that her mere presence at an HBCU was suspect, and that she was constantly viewed as having some hidden agenda to thwart the efforts of the student population in education and advancement.

Today, the truth regarding faculty integration and faculty equality is a bit different. White faculty members are represented today at HBCUs. While all but a few HBCUs still serve a predominantly black student body, and while institutional power often rests in the hands of almost exclusively black administrations, the faculty at these institutions are remarkably diverse, including not only large numbers of both black and white American professors, but often a significant representation of foreign teachers. However, the issues of faculty integration and equality at HBCUs now revolve around whether or not these white professors enjoy the same resources, autonomy, and faculty governance as the similarly situated black professors. Writing in *Academe: Bulletin of the American Association of University Professors*, Ivory Paul Phillips, a professor of social science at Jackson State University (and president of the faculty senate and of the Mississippi Coalition on Black Higher Education), itemizes ten specific areas in which HBCUs generally fall short in shared governance:

> (a) faculty representation on policy and decision-making bodies; (b) searches and hiring of academic personnel; (c) faculty grievances; (d) promotion, tenure, and post-tenure hearings and procedures; (e) evaluations of peers and administrators; (f) salary determination and other budgetary matters; (g) program development, review, and revision; (h) development and revision of faculty handbooks; (i) access to information needed for decision making; and (j) the status of the faculty senate as a decision- and policy-making unit. (Phillips 2002, 50)

The continuation of administrative abuses and mismanagement in the age of affirmative action has helped create a volatile situation at many of the HBCUs, for while affirmative action in employment has opened opportunities for African Americans at predominantly white institutions, it has also led to charges of reverse discrimination among white applicants and professors seeking advancement from within the HBCU system. These white professors, however, have had experiences in higher education (if only as students themselves) at institutions where faculty have played a larger role in academic policies and governance. Their background has often been at odds with what has come to be called the "plantation" mentality prevalent at many of the HBCUs, and "charges of discrimination and bias against white faculty have increased" (Guyden, Foster, and Miller 1999, 12).

For example, at Cheyney University of Pennsylvania, the country's oldest HBCU, two white science professors saw their careers destroyed when they opposed their administration's plans to violate the institution's hiring policies to ensure the hiring of a minority candidate. In 1991, Fred Gentner, a physics professor, and Robert Stevenson, a chemistry professor, together had taught at Cheyney for fifty-three years, but when they complained about the violation, they set in motion a series of events that eventually forced their resignations. They sued for discrimination, testifying during the trial to an administrative plan to eliminate white faculty and to replace them with African Americans. They were awarded $1 million each. Other cases of discrimination at HBCUs have occurred at St. Augustine's College, Elizabeth City State University, Delaware State University, Morris College, Grambling University, Texas Southern University, and Livingstone College, among others. These cases frequently involve termination of white faculty, violation of institutional policies, denial of promotion and tenure, and harassment.

In addition to complaints filed with the Equal Employment Opportunity Commission (EEOC) and lawsuits filed by white professors at HBCUs, in recent years the HBCUs have frequently been investigated and censured by the American Association of University Professors (AAUP) for violations of academic freedom and professional standards. As of 2002, of the fifty-three institutions of higher education censured by the AAUP, three were historically black colleges and universities: Talladega College (Alabama), Benedict College (South Carolina), and the University of the District of Columbia. Although these are the only HBCUs currently under censure by the AAUP, numerous others have been censured in the past but have remedied their situations to have censure removed—both state-supported institutions (including Morgan State University in Maryland, Tennessee State University, Jackson State University in Mississippi, and Central State University in Ohio) and private institutions (including Voorhees College and Clark College). The reasons for censure generally fall under the category of violations of "academic freedom and due process," but specific cases may involve retaliation for faculty criticism of administrations, termination of tenured faculty for alleged "financial" reasons, denial of hearings, or other violations of the professional standards of the AAUP.

It is indeed ironic that the name through which most Americans are familiar with HBCUs, *A Different World,* is actually quite appropriate, although from a different perspective. The historically black college in America is often viewed as being on the margins of American higher education, and the conditions that exist in many of the institutions make them all too often a "different world" from that known throughout the rest of American higher education.

See also Affirmative Action, Arguments for; Affirmative Action, Criticisms of; African Americans; Afrocentrism; American Association of University Professors; American Civil War; *Brown v. Board of Education*; Douglass, Frederick; Du Bois, William Edward Burghardt; Education and Affirmative Action; Equal Employment Opportunity Commission; Eurocentrism; Freedmen's Bureau; Meritocracy; Race-Neutral Criteria; Reverse Discrimination; Role Model Theory; Segregation; *The Shape of the River*; Standardized Testing; Washington, Booker T.

FURTHER READING: Bowen, William G., and Derek Bok, 1998, *The Shape of the River: Long-Term Consequences of Considering Race in College and University Admissions,* Princeton, NJ: Princeton University Press; Browne-Miller, Angela, 1996, *Shameful Admissions: The Losing Battle to Serve Everyone in Our Universities,* San Francisco: Jossey-Bass Publishers; Guyden, Janet A., Lenoar Foster, and Andrea L. Miller, 1999, "White Faculty at Historically Black Colleges and Universities: A Historical Framework," in *Affirmed Action: Essays on the Academic and Social Lives of White Faculty Members at Historically Black Colleges and Universities,* edited by Lenoar Foster, Janet A. Guyden, and Andrea L. Miller, Lanham, MD: Rowman and Littlefield; Jones, Ann, 1973, *Uncle Tom's Campus,* New York: Touchstone, 1974; Magner, Denise K., 1993, "Several Black Colleges Accused of Racism," *Chronicle of Higher Education,* October 13, A20; McWhorter, John, 2000, *Losing the Race: Self-Sabotage in Black America,* New York: Free Press; Phillips, Ivory Paul, 2002, "Shared Governance on Black College Campuses," *Academe: Bulletin of the American Association of University Professors* 18, no. 4 (July–August): 50–55; Redinger, Matthew A., 1999, "You Just Wouldn't Understand," in *Affirmed Action: Essays on the Academic and Social Lives of White Faculty Members at Historically Black Colleges and Universities,* edited by Lenoar Foster, Janet A. Guyden, and Andrea L. Miller, Lanham, MD: Rowman and Littlefield.

ROBERT A. RUSS

HOPE Scholarship Plan

See Percentage Plans.

Hopwood v. Texas, 78 F.3d 932 (5th Cir. 1996)

Hopwood v. Texas was a landmark case in the legal evolution of affirmative action policy. In *Hopwood,* the U.S. Court of Appeals for the Fifth Circuit broadly held in 1996 that the state of Texas "may not use race as a factor in law school admissions" and may not even take race into account for purposes of improving diversity. The Fifth Circuit, in so holding, struck down an affirmative action plan utilized at the University of Texas School of Law. Furthermore, the Fifth Circuit rejected Justice Lewis Powell's opinion in *Regents of the University of California v. Bakke,* 438 U.S. 265 (1978), in which Powell had recommended the use of race as a factor in achieving diversity in higher education. However, Powell's position was subsequently affirmed by the Supreme Court in 2003 in the landmark cases *Gratz v. Bollinger*, 123 S. Ct. 2411, 2003 U.S. LEXIS 4801 (2003), and *Grutter v. Bollinger*, 123 S. Ct. 2325, 2003 U.S. LEXIS 4800 (2003), casting serious doubt on the viability of the *Hopwood* decision.

To understand the significance of the *Hopwood* decision in the framework of the affirmative action discussion, a brief examination of the *Bakke* decision is necessary. In a case that examined the use of race-based admissions in the University of California at Davis Medical School and was the first major modern affirmative action case heard by the Supreme Court, the Court held that race may be considered as a factor in admissions decisions so long as "fixed quotas" are not utilized. However, while the outcome in *Bakke* was clear, the rationale for the ruling was not. Six separate opinions emerged among the nine justices. One group of justices (John Paul Stevens, Warren Burger, Potter Stewart, and William Rehnquist) believed that the case should have been handled under Title VI, as opposed to the Fourteenth Amendment, and that the affirmative action plan was illegal because Title VI prohibits the exclusion of individuals from any publicly funded program based upon race. Another group of justices (William Brennen, Thurgood Marshall, Byron White, and Harry Blackmun) wished to uphold the affirmative action plan on the grounds that racial preferences are a valid way to compensate a group for previous discrimination. Justice Lewis Powell was the swing fifth vote. He voted with the first group on the illegality of racial quotas in admissions, but voted with the second group on the permissibility of using race in some circumstances in order to compensate for prior discrimination. However, Justice Powell authored his own opinion, which evinced the view that "race-sensitive" affirmative action plans can be utilized to ensure the goals of diversity and opportunity in higher education.

Rather than definitively answering the broader question as to the constitutionality of all affirmative action plans, the Court only held that "fixed quotas" based upon race for admissions were impermissible. Additionally, the Court held that race might be utilized as one factor among many in the admissions process. As a result, since the *Bakke* decision, preferential minority programs have "proliferated in academic institutions, ranging from informal preference-granting to formally race-normed admissions lists to specifically reserved scholarships" (Fullinwider 1997, 9). For decades, the *Bakke* decision has led the way for educational institutions to begin redressing the past wrongs of racial and ethnic discrimination.

In adherence to *Bakke*, the state of Texas also began a commitment to securing the goal of minority recruitment. The University of Texas Law School, one of the nation's leading law schools, with an annual admissions pool of more than 4,000, in the early 1990s implemented a specific policy to achieve ethnic and racial diversity. "The goal of the program was to admit an entering class that contained 5 percent black and 10 percent Mexican American students" (Spann 2000, 64). In essence, as described more thoroughly later, white applicants were treated differently than black and Mexican American students, and separate procedures and admissions subcommittees were utilized depending on the applicant's race.

The law school based its admissions decisions on an applicant's Texas Index (TI) number, which was created as a composite of the undergraduate grade point average and the results of the Law School Admission Test (LSAT). The law school then devised three categories according to the respective TI scores: "presumptive admit," "presumptive deny," and a middle "discretionary zone." An applicant's TI score determined how much attention was given to his or her particular credentials. Most of the applicants who were placed in the "presumptive admit" category received offers of admission to the law school, and those placed in the "presumptive deny" category were generally denied admission unless a member of the committee deemed that an applicant's TI score inadequately reflected his or her potential to succeed in law school. In that rare case, applicants in the "presumptive deny" group might be bumped up to the higher category. However, the applicants in the "discretionary zone" garnered the greatest scrutiny in the admissions process. All students in this section except blacks and Mexican Americans were reviewed by subcommittees consisting of three members of the full admissions team.

Applications from blacks and Mexican Americans were treated differently from all other candidates, including those in the discretionary field. TI ranges for black and Mexican American applicants were adjusted in order for the law school to admit more minority students. For example, in March 1992, the presumptive TI score for resident whites and nonpreferred minorities was 199, while the presumptive TI score for blacks and Mexican Americans was 189. Additionally, the "presumptive deny" score for nonminorities was 192, while the denial score for those preferred minorities (blacks and Mexican Americans) was 179. The disparate standards for the different groups of students clearly impacted their opportunities for admission to the law school. The school insisted, however, that the stated objective of differential TI scoring was the admittance of an entering class that comprised 10 per cent Mexican Americans and 5 per cent blacks, as stated earlier—a figure comparable to those percentages of racial and ethnic identities graduating from all Texas colleges.

In 1992, four students who were denied admission to the entering class challenged the affirmative action plan set in place by the University of Texas Law School. Texas residents Cheryl Hopwood, Douglas Carvell, Kenneth Elliott, and David Rogers, who were all white, sued under the Equal Protection Clause of the Fourteenth Amendment after all were placed in the discretionary applicant pool and eventually denied admission. The plaintiffs also insisted that they were victims of statutory violations under Title VI of the Civil Rights Act of 1964, which prohibited discrimination on the basis of race, color, or national origin in programs and activities receiving federal financial assistance.

The U.S. district court ruled that although the plaintiffs had been denied their equal protection rights, the court refused to enjoin the law school from employing race as a key factor in the admissions process. The district court insisted that Texas's long history of racially discriminatory practices resulted in a serious underrepresentation of diverse populations in the student body and in a perception that the law school was actually "hostile" to minority students. The district court also determined that the law school had devised the affirmative action policy for a legitimate reason and that white plaintiffs had not met the requisite burden in showing that they would have been admitted "but for the unlawful system."

On appeal to the Fifth Circuit Court of Appeals, the court posited two important constitutional questions for review. First, did the racial classification serve a compelling governmental interest, and second, was the affirmative action plan narrowly tailored to achieve that goal? Specifically, the Fifth Circuit addressed the issue of whether the law school's consideration of race as a factor in the admissions process violated the Fourteenth Amendment guarantee of "equal protection of the laws." The federal circuit court claimed that other than Justice Powell's lone opinion in *Bakke*, the Supreme Court had not intended to make the state's interest in diversity in higher education a compelling justification needed for race-based discrimination. In fact, the Fifth Circuit opinion insisted that Powell's view in the *Bakke* case would not serve as a binding precedent for the *Hopwood* appeal.

The court emphatically agreed with the plaintiffs that any consideration of race or ethnicity for the purpose of achieving diversity was not a compelling interest according to Fourteenth Amendment equal protection law (and the Supreme Court's corresponding levels of scrutiny for Equal Protection Clause cases). As for the second question of whether the admissions process of assigning different TI indices to certain minority constituents was a narrowly tailored plan, the court also answered in the negative. The court held that past discrimination in other educational venues did not justify the use of racial preference in law school admissions. Finally, the court importantly held that the presence of race for the purpose of diversity in higher education "contradicted, rather than furthered, the aims of equal protection." On two subsequent appeals to the U.S. Supreme Court, the Court denied certiorari and declined to review the *Hopwood* decision. Justices Ruth Bader Ginsburg and David Souter issued a statement that accompanied the denial of certiorari on July 1, 1996, in which they stated that the issue of using race in admissions in higher education was a question of "great national importance." However, according to Ginsburg and Souter, review should not be granted in the *Hopwood* case because the legal issues were moot, as Texas had discontinued the affirmative action plan at issue in the case.

The *Hopwood* case was important for several reasons. It specifically ended affirmative action in higher education in the state of Texas, but in a broader sense the decision highlighted the trend of dismantling affirmative action plans as inappropriate remedies for the nation's past injustices. For opponents of affirmative action, the new solution would have to be color-blind initiatives for all educational opportunities. But a critical question for social policy that will persist is whether this race and ethnic neutrality actually succeeds in increasing the percentage of minority representation in academic institutions or decreases "diversity" at these institutions. If "diversity" decreases, additional questions emerge as to the overall effect of this decrease on the educational experience of college students and the society into which these students will emerge. These are several of the questions that the Supreme Court took up in 2003 in *Gratz v. Bollinger* and *Grutter v. Bollinger*, in which the Court explicitly affirmed Powell's diversity arguments in *Bakke* and implicitly rejected the holdings of the *Hopwood* decision.

See also Blackmun, Harry Andrew; Brennen, William Joseph; Civil Rights Act of 1964; Compelling Governmental Interest; Education and Affirmative Action; Equal Protection Clause; Fourteenth Amendment; Ginsburg, Ruth Bader; *Gratz J. Bollinger/Grutter v. Bollinger*; Harvard Model; Marshall, Thurgood; Minority Professionals and Affirmative Action; Narrowly Tailored Affirmative Action Plans; Powell, Lewis Franklin, Jr.; Preferences; Quotas; *Regents of the University of California v. Bakke*; Rehnquist, William Hobbs; Stevens, John Paul; Title VI of the Civil Rights Act of 1964; Warren Court and Affirmative Action; White, Byron Raymond.

FURTHER READING: Fullinwider, Robert K., 1997, "Civil Rights and Racial Preferences: A Legal History of Affirmative Action," *Philosophy and Public Policy* 17:9–20; Schmidt, Peter, 2003, "Affirmative Action Survives, and So Does the Debate: The Supreme Court Upholds Race-Conscious Admissions in Principle, but Not Always as Practiced," *Chronicle of Higher Education*, July 4, S1; Spann, Girardeau A., 2000, *The Law of Affirmative Action: Twenty-five Years of Supreme Court Decisions on Race and Remedies*, New York: New York University Press.

JANIS JUDSON

Housing

The history that arguably shows the necessity for affirmative action in housing can be traced back to the original patterns of housing segregation in the migration of African Americans from the South to the North in the early twentieth century. One of the ironies of the issue of housing discrimination is that in the initial migration patterns, the neighborhoods into which African Americans moved in the North were ethnically diverse. However, they were not economically diverse, as all of the ethnic groups were poor. As African Americans moved north and tried to find housing, restrictive covenants, racial zoning, and discrimination in the areas of sales, rental, and financing of housing were still acceptable and common. Remarkably, there was a significant amount of legal and economic support for segregation. For example, the *Underwriters Manual* published by the U.S. Federal Housing Administration in 1938 embraced and encouraged institutionalized segregation. Further, a realtors' code of ethics in effect at the time spoke of preventing the introduction of so-called inharmonious racial groups into white neighborhoods. These issues only exacerbated the problem of segregation.

This was true even though in the early twentieth century, in *Buchanan v. Warley*, 245 U.S. 60 (1917), the Supreme Court struck down zoning prohibitions that were based upon racial characteristics. Soon afterwards, in *Harmon v. Tyler*, 273 U.S. 668 (1927), the Supreme Court also struck down discriminatory ordinance prohibitions based upon race. Finally, in 1948, the Supreme Court outlawed the enforceability in court of racially restrictive covenants in *Shelley v. Kraemer*, 334 U.S. 1 (1948). This period also coincided with the beginning of industrial expansion in the North. The expansion attracted more migration from the South to the North in search of higher-paying jobs. Some of those migrating were African Americans. However, this did not result in coincidental integration. On the contrary, many of the new residents were confined to isolated neighborhoods, continuing the segregation pattern. Even when minorities were able to obtain housing outside the traditionally segregated neighborhoods, the end result was not integration because most of these new housing opportunities became available as a result of so-called blockbusting techniques, a method by which realtors would use the threat of a minority family moving onto a block to frighten other white homeowners into selling their homes at greatly reduced prices.

Ultimately, both the Fair Housing Administration and the Veterans Administration announced their intention not to grant mortgages on property with restrictive covenants. While this was impressive, it should be noted that it was an attempt to reverse fifty years of housing segregation. Title VI of the Civil Rights Act of 1964 requires that "no person in the United States shall, on the ground of race, color, or national origin, be excluded from participation in, be denied the

Demonstration against integrated housing with a group gathered along the street and near furniture on a truck. Courtesy of Library of Congress.

benefits of, or be subjected to discrimination under any program or activity receiving Federal financial assistance." In 1968, Congress passed the Fair Housing Act. The purpose of the Fair Housing Act was to create not just integrated housing but an integrated society through integrated housing. The U.S. Supreme Court had outlawed the concept of "separate but equal" some fourteen years before in the area of public education, and by the mid-1960s there was a general recognition that separate but equal was unworkable in all aspects of society. In response, there was a desire to create a plan that would integrate the society at large, not just the public schools. This was a much more ambitious goal even than that of the 1964 Civil Rights Act, which was designed to create employment opportunities for minorities. The Fair Housing Act had as its primary goal the integration of society.

The Fair Housing Act of 1968 was not entirely successful. One theory is that the enforcement mechanisms in the 1968 act were no match for the solidly entrenched segregation of the previous fifty years. In 1988, the Fair Housing Act was amended. The purpose of the amendments was to strengthen the enforcement mechanisms. These amendments expanded the range of transactions that were covered by the Fair Housing Act to include not just the sale or rental of housing, but actions that were related to real-estate transactions as well. This increased coverage was designed to give potential victims a greater number of weapons to fight segregation. It was also designed to combat behavior that did not rise to the level of refusing to sell or blockbusting, but coerced others to do so. Among other things, the amendments lengthened the statute of limitations for a private cause of action. The amendments also eliminated the cap on punitive damages. It should also be noted, however, that the 1988 amendments of the Fair Housing Act specifically did not authorize the use of race-conscious methods in promoting integration, nor did they authorize the use of quotas. This was not done by accident but was purposeful on the part of Congress. As strongly as Congress felt about creating an integrated society, it did not feel comfortable in utilizing quotas and set-asides in working toward the goal of an integrated society. Thus Congress chose not to add these elements to the statute. In effect, this left these issues to the courts to decide.

In *Trafficante v. Metropolitan Life Insurance Co.*, 409 U.S. 205 (1972), the U.S. Supreme Court gave guidance on the parameters of interpreting the Fair Housing Act. The Supreme Court determined that the most important elements in interpreting the act were that the law be broadly interpreted, that the goal of an integrated society remain important, that courts could use Title VII cases in interpreting the Fair Housing Act, and that courts were to give a great deal of deference to the interpretations of the Fair Housing Act by the Department of Housing and Urban Development (HUD). The deference to HUD is not surprising. In general, when there is an administrative agency that is charged with enforcing and interpreting a statute, that administrative agency's interpretation is given great weight. In fact, the Court in *Trafficante* was persuaded in part by the interpretation of HUD officials that the plaintiffs had standing to sue.

However, for the most part, HUD was not active in interpreting the act. With the exception of one publication in 1972, HUD basically abdicated its interpretive authority by not issuing any publications on the act. Finally, in 1980, HUD issued a flurry of interpretive rules. Unfortunately, this occurred at the end of the administration of President Jimmy Carter. Before these regulations became effective, President Ronald Reagan took office, and the regulations were withdrawn under the Reagan administration.

The amendments of the Fair Housing Act of 1988 made it unlawful for anyone to refuse to rent or make available a dwelling based on an individual's race, color, national origin, religion, gender, disability, or family status. Or to offer discriminatory terms or conditions or privileges of rental. This includes making, printing, or publishing statements that indicate a preference for a certain race, color, or national origin. Finally, it is unlawful to represent to a person that a dwelling is not available for rental when such a dwelling is in fact available. These amendments affect not only those actions that are based on racial discrimination, but also those actions that disproportionately affect minorities, even if they are not intended to do so. The purpose of these amendments is to make sure that people are not limited in their housing choices based on their race, color, or national origin. Congress was also determined to avoid the problem of HUD failing to exercise its interpretive powers. The 1988 amendments required HUD to issue rules within 180 days of the date that the amendments were passed into law. This time, HUD did in fact issue rules, and those rules became effective on March 12, 1989.

Moreover, there are other laws that cross-reference these rights. For example, 42 U.S.C. § 1982, which has been a federal law since the Civil Rights Act of 1866, states, "All citizens of the United States shall have the same right in every State and Territory, as is enjoyed by white citizens thereof to inherit, purchase, lease, sell, hold, and convey real and personal property." This law was designed to help enforce the newly passed Thirteenth Amendment, which outlawed slavery. In *Jones v. Alfred H. Mayer Co.*, 392 U.S. 409 (1968), the U.S. Supreme Court expanded on the breadth of section 1982. The Supreme Court declared that section 1982 "bars all racial discrimination, private as well as public, in the sale or rental of property, and that the statute, thus construed, is a valid exercise of the power of Congress to enforce the Thirteenth Amendment." Minorities have the right to bring an action whenever a landlord, developer, homeowners' group, or any other individual denies them the right to buy, rent, or even negotiate for housing. Under section 1982, this action may also include a claim against any third parties who interfere with a minority's rights under the act.

The interplay between section 1982 and the Thirteenth Amendment is unclear. Section 1 of the Thirteenth Amendment outlaws slavery, while Section 2 empowers Congress to pass legislation that gives force and effect to Section 1. In addition, since section 1982 outlaws nearly every possible permutation of housing discrimination, it is difficult for some courts to articulate a basis for acknowledging a separate cause of action under Section 1 of the Thirteenth Amendment.

In the area of housing, affirmative action can mean not only the consideration of race, but also the ordering of equitable specific performance. These powers may be exercised by a court even on behalf of private litigants. The purpose of granting courts this power is to fulfill the Fair Housing Act's purpose of changing the outward signs of past discrimination as well. By ordering equitable relief, a court can be the impetus to dismantle the barriers erected by these past discriminatory practices. A court may even order injunctive relief where it feels that the vestiges of prior discrimination remain and that these vestiges need to be eliminated.

For example, in *United States v. Starrett*, 840 F.2d 1096 (2d Cir. 1988), the defendants were trying to create an interracial housing development. They did so, however, by limiting the numbers of minorities who would be accepted to certain percentages. The defendants claimed that this was necessary because far more minorities were applying than they could accommodate. The court rejected the defendants' argument, reasoning that the plan was of indefinite duration and contained rigid racial quotas. The court also drew a distinction between "access quotas," which were designed to increase access of minorities, and "ceiling quotas," which placed outside limits on the access those minorities would receive.

While the amendments of the Fair Housing Act specifically refused to address the use of race-conscious remedies, the courts have been divided. In passing the 1988 amendments, Congress had the *Starrett* case before it. Congress certainly could have written amendments that particularized or created a mathematical formula for the basis of an acceptable integration plan. In light of the fact that it was certainly an issue, Congress's conscious decision not to articulate the extent to which race-conscious practices could be used is significant. In some instances, the courts have allowed the use of racial favoritism to avoid having segregated housing. However, most recently, courts have determined that racial distinctions may be allowed if these distinctions are temporary in nature and have a defined termination point. As a practical matter, this means that such plans will be assessed on a case-by-case basis. This gives the responsibility and the burden to the courts.

It also allows for the ability to adjust the constitutionality of affirmative action plans as changes take place in society. In light of all of the difficulty that Congress encountered trying to bring about an integrated society, there is something to be said for language that prevents anyone from being locked in to a certain formula.

All of these statutes that guarantee an opportunity to purchase are of no use unless there is also a realistic opportunity to finance housing. The Equal Credit Opportunity Act, 15 U.S.C. §§ 1691–1691f, prohibits any creditor from discriminating against someone who is applying for credit on the basis of race, color, religion, or national origin. Unfortunately, it appears that the problem is not as easily remedied as might have been hoped. For example, in a demographic study based on the 1980 census, the nation's seventeen largest metropolitan areas were only slightly less segregated than they had been in 1970.

See also African Americans; Carter, James "Jimmy" Earl, Jr.; Civil Rights Act of 1866; Civil Rights Act of 1964; Civil War (Reconstruction) Amendments and Civil Rights Acts; De Facto and De Jure Segregation; Department of Housing and Urban Development; Discrimination; Fair Housing Amendments Act of 1988; Housing and Urban Development Act of 1968; Integration; Lending Practices and Affirmative Action; Licensing and Affirmative Action; Reagan, Ronald; Segregation; Title VI of the Civil Rights Act of 1964; Title VII of the Civil Rights Act of 1964; Thirteenth Amendment; Zoning and Affirmative Action.

FURTHER READING: Bernotas, Bob, 1991, *Know Your Government: The Department of Housing and Urban Development*, New York: Chelsea House; Grier, George W., 1966, *Equality and Beyond: Housing Segregation and the Goals of the Great Society*, Chicago: Quadrangle Books; McFarland, M. Carter, 1978, *Federal Government and Urban Problems: HUD: Successes, Failures, and the Fate of Our Cities*, Boulder, CO: Westview Press.

MICHAEL K. LEE

Housing and Urban Development Act of 1968

The Housing and Urban Development Act of 1968 (HUDA 1968) expanded housing assistance to low-income home buyers and renters, created new and modified existing community redevelopment programs, created the Government National Mortgage Association (GNMA), and required under section 3 that administrators of housing projects assisted by the Department of Housing and Urban Development (HUD) take affirmative action to provide contract and employment opportunities to businesses and low-income individuals residing near the project area. Section 3 requirements were subsequently expanded to include all projects receiving financial assistance from HUD. HUDA is an example of a major governmental affirmative action program in the area of public housing.

HUDA 1968 authorized housing assistance to low-income families through Titles I, II, III, IX, and X. Title I added section 235 to the National Housing Act (NHA) authorizing HUD to pay Federal Housing Administration (FHA) lenders the portion of eligible low-income families' mortgages above 20 percent of their adjusted income after writing down the interest rate to 1 percent. It also provided interest-free loans to nonprofit housing sponsors, created organizations to study low-income housing, and added section 237 to the NHA to apply less strict credit guidelines on low- and moderate-income home buyers or anyone purchasing a home in a declining area and to pay default claims out of a special risk insurance fund. Title II added section 236 to the NHA authorizing HUD to pay the mortgagee financing a rental housing project enough to reduce the mortgagor's interest rate to 1 percent. The interest savings was passed on to low-income tenants, who would pay the greater of a low basic charge or 25 percent of their income up to the market price of the rental. It also authorized additional funds for other existing low-rent public housing programs. Title III modified FHA mortgage insurance programs to expand situational eligibility. Title IX authorized the creation of national housing partnerships to secure private investment in low- and moderate-income housing projects. Title X authorized the Department of Agriculture to provide grants and loans to low-income families for self-help housing projects and to subsidize mortgage insurance for low-income rural families to write down their interest rates to 1 percent.

HUDA 1968 authorized urban redevelopment assistance through Titles IV, V, VI, VII, and XI. Title IV enacted the New Communities Act authorizing HUD to guarantee private developer loans and to give financial grants to states and localities for land acquisition and development to create new communities within urban areas. Title V expanded and amended urban planning and renewal programs to add more resources for more projects, to allow projects to be completed in stages over several years, and to require that 20 percent of any housing portion of the development be reserved for low-income families. Title VI authorized HUD and the Department of Agriculture to provide financial and technical assistance to communities to help configure comprehensive plans. Title VII authorized additional funds for mass-transportation-project grants. Titles XI and XII enacted the Urban Property Protection and Reinsurance Act authorizing HUD to provide reinsurance to private insurers if they comply with state fair-access-to-insurance requirements, reimbursing them in the event of a riot and making property insurance available in all urban areas. Title XIII enacted the National Flood Insurance Act authorizing HUD to subsidize property insurance companies to encourage them to provide flood insurance. Title XIV enacted the Interstate Land Sales Full Disclosure Act making it illegal for a developer to sell a lot in a subdivision of fifty or more lots without registering it with HUD and providing a property report to the purchaser. Title XV authorized FHA mortgage insurance for nonprofit hospitals. Titles XVI and XVII required further research on low-income housing matters and provided additional funds for urban renewal projects, college housing, state technical assistance, and the Model Cities program, which rebuilt low-income urban areas for the benefit of their residents. Title VIII of HUDA 1968 split the Federal National Mortgage Association (FNMA), keeping special assistance functions, including mortgage guarantees, within a newly established GNMA and making FNMA a government-controlled corporation operating the secondary mortgage market.

See also Civil Rights Act of 1964; Civil Rights Act of 1968; Department of Housing and Urban Development; Disadvantaged Business Enterprises; Housing; Lending Practices and Affirmative Action; Zoning and Affirmative Action.

FURTHER READING: Bernotas, Bob, 1991, *Know Your Government: The Department of Housing and Urban Development*, New York: Chelsea House; McFarland, M. Carter, 1978, *Federal Government and Urban Problems: HUD: Successes, Failures, and the Fate of Our Cities*, Boulder, CO:

Westview Press; U.S. Department of Housing and Urban Development, 1968, *Housing and Urban Development Act of 1968: Public Law 90–448,* Washington, DC: Department of Housing and Urban Development; U.S. Department of Housing and Urban Development Library Staff, 2000, "Library Resources for Understanding the Department of Housing and Urban Development," November, HUD web site: http://www.hud.gov/about/libraryresources.cfm.

MARK J. SENEDIAK

I

Ideological Racism/Racist Ideology

Racist ideology and ideological racism both refer to the belief that some races are intellectually, culturally, and/or biologically inferior to other races. The primary function of racist ideology is to justify the domination and exploitation of one group by another by emphasizing that the group's superiority (or inferiority) is natural or innate. This ideology has been widely believed and adopted, especially in Europe and North America. For instance, white Europeans used racist ideology to justify the exploitation and colonization of the indigenous peoples of Asia, Africa, the Americans, and Oceania. Likewise, throughout U.S. history, arguments of innate inferiority were used against a variety of groups, such as the Irish, Italians, Jews, blacks, Mexicans, and Native Americans, when it served the interests of the dominant group of the time. The connection between racist ideology and affirmative action is obvious. The fundamental argument behind affirmative action is that it is the only way to address the negative effects of past and present discrimination that has largely resulted from society's adoption of racist ideology. On the other hand, proponents of the belief that affirmative action is no longer needed argue that the program itself is reinforcing the very racist ideology that made it necessary in the first place.

For some, racist ideology has risen to the status of scientific theory, which allowed for the emergence of scientific racism. The implication is that science proves that some groups are innately inferior to others, where the "others" are most frequently members of the dominant group. An example of scientific racism is Richard Herrnstein and Charles Murray's 1994 book *The Bell Curve*, which attempted to prove a genetic link between race and intelligence. Despite the popularity of racist ideology among the Nazis in Germany and Ku Klux Klan members in the United States, scientific studies do not support the claim of innate cultural, intellectual, and biological differences. Yet racist ideology has become a widely accepted part of our culture and is often used to justify the domination and exploitation of one group, usually the subordinate group, by another, usually the dominant group.

See also The Bell Curve; Ku Klux Klan; Scientific Racism.

FURTHER READING: Hauser, R.M., 1995, "Review Symposium: *The Bell Curve*," *Contemporary Sociology* 24:149–153; Montagu, A., 1963, *Race, Science, and Humanity*, Princeton, NJ: Van Nostrand; Montagu, A., 1974, *Man's Most Dangerous Myth: The Fallacy of Race*, 5th ed., New York: Oxford University Press; Taylor, H.F., 1995, "Review Symposium: *The Bell Curve*," *Contemporary Sociology* 24:153–158; Wilson, W.J., 1973, *Power, Racism, and Privilege*, New York: Free Press.

PAULINA X. RUF

Immigration Act of 1965

The Immigration Act of 1965 stands as the most significant piece of legislation regarding immigration in the United States. The history of immigration in the United States can be divided into immigration before 1965 and immigration after 1965. The Immigration Act of 1965 transformed American immigration law and the lives of countless individuals attempting to gain entrance into the United States. In the early twentieth century, before 1965, immigration into the United States was largely determined by discriminatory quotas based upon national origins, which largely favored western European countries. The pre-1965 immigration practice has been described as both discriminatory and racist, denying immigration to peoples from Africa, Asia, and Latin America while encouraging western Europeans. After 1965, the United States adopted a "family preference" approach, which allowed relatives of individuals who were already in the United States to immigrate into the United States without having to meet the country-specific quotas. Also, while numerical limitations for entrance continued to be placed on the Eastern Hemisphere (including European) countries, for the first time in American history, no numerical per country limits were placed on immigration from the Western Hemisphere countries, which arguably allowed for (and encouraged) much more immigration from the Caribbean and Central and South America.

With the signing of the Hart-Celler Immigration Bill by President Lyndon B. Johnson on October 3, 1965, the bill henceforth became the Immigration Act of 1965. The Immigration Act contained many significant provisions that transformed immigration law. First, it abolished the quota system based on national origins that had been the hallmark of the earlier immigration laws, in particular, the Immigration Act of 1924 and the Immigration and Nationality Act of 1952. The 1965 act eliminated national origin, race, or ancestry as a basis for immigration to the United States. Second, the act established allocation of immigrant visas (green cards) on a first-come, first-served basis, subject to a seven-category preference system. The preference system for visa admission detailed in the law was as follows: unmarried adult sons and daughters of U.S. citizens; spouses and children and unmarried sons and daughters of permanent resident aliens; members of the professions and scientists and artists of exceptional ability; married children of U.S. citizens; brothers and sisters of U.S. citizens over the age of twenty-one; skilled and unskilled workers in occupations for which there is insufficient labor supply; and refugees given conditional entry or adjustment, chiefly people from Communist countries and the Middle East.

Third, the act allocated 170,000 visas to countries in the Eastern Hemisphere and 120,000 to countries in the Western Hemisphere. This change in number increased the annual upper ceiling on immigrants from 150,000 to 290,000. Each country in the Eastern Hemisphere was allowed an allotment of 20,000 visas, while in the Western Hemisphere there was no per country limit. In the history of the United States, this was the first such occasion when any numerical limitation had been placed on legal immigration from the Western Hemisphere. Fourth, the act introduced a prerequisite for the issuance of an immigrant visa by way of an affirmative finding by the secretary of labor that an alien seeking entry to the United States as a worker will not replace a worker in the United States nor adversely affect the wages and working labor conditions of similarly employed individuals in the United States.

The immediate implications of the Immigration Act of 1965 were tremendous. For the first time, place of birth was not a determining factor for legal immigration to the United States. This paved the way for waves of people from Asia, Africa, and Latin America, who had hitherto been restricted due to Western bias in the immigration laws prior to 1965, to apply for U.S. immigration. Civil rights activists championed the Immigration Act of 1965 because it ended one of the most visible and overt forms of discrimination so that people who were interested in applying for legal U.S. immigration could now hope for a better and more prosperous future in the land of opportunity. It is not a coincidence that the Immigration Act of 1965 was promulgated into law at a time when the proponents of civil rights had achieved spectacular successes in other areas, including the Civil Rights Act of 1964 and the Voting Rights Act of 1965.

Foreign policy concerns were also a motivating factor resulting in the significant change in the national-origin policy in the U.S. immigration system. By 1960, most countries in Asia, Africa, and Latin America were undergoing a process of decolonization and economic reconstruction. The United States, being a leading superpower while competing with the Soviet Union at the ideological level of the Cold War period, could not afford to have a low moral ground in its striving for global dominance and expansion of its sphere of influence. With U.S. policy being respect for all people all around the world, the proactive stand and the loud message of the Immigration Act of 1965 silenced critics of the United States both at home and abroad. At the public relations level, it was a big coup for U.S. policy makers as they tried to portray the provisions related to the end of quota system in the Immigration Act of 1965 as yet another vivid example of reaching out to all people living in faraway underdeveloped regions of the world.

Persons who had been living in the United States also welcomed the 1965 Immigration Act. Scores of people had relatives who were on long immigration waiting lists because of small quota allotments for their respective countries of origin. Italy, for instance, had an annual quota of 5,666 immigrants, Poland 6,448, Greece 308, Yugoslavia 942, and so on. Abolition of this quota system was considered necessary and imperative so that applicants from a country such as Italy, which had 249,583 people waiting for lawful admission to the United States, could be processed by the representatives of the Immigration and Naturalization Service.

The refugee issue was one of paramount consideration by the Kennedy administration of 1961 and the subsequent Johnson administration. Since the end of World War II and with the creation of newly independent nations in various parts of the world, there have been refugees in significant numbers who for a variety of reasons have wished to move to the United States with the hope and expectation that they would start their lives anew both for themselves and their families. The changes brought about in the Immigration Act of 1965 provided windows of opportunity to these refugees, most of whom wished to flee from the iron curtain societies of Communist regimes or from the unstable, politically volatile nations of Asia, the Middle East, and Latin America.

By permitting members of professions, scholars, and artists of exceptional ability to immigrate, the Immigration Act of 1965 legally encouraged potential talents, mostly from Asia, Africa, and Latin America, to migrate to the United States, where they could get recognition of their talents as well as enhance their skills due to the abundance of resources available in U.S. institutions of higher learning and in its numerous research centers. For example, many foreign-born doctors in the United States today took advantage of the unique opportunity provided to skilled professionals in the 1965 Immigration Act and chose to migrate to the United States, thus helping meet the health-care needs of the American people, particularly those living in the rural and interior sections of the continental United States, such as the Deep South and the Appalachian regions.

Although most Americans supported the Immigration Act of 1965, there were some critics, particularly conservative Republicans, who voiced opposition to the new wave of immigrants to the United States from less affluent and nonwhite countries of Asia, Africa, and Latin America. They feared that the sudden influx of these classes of immigrants might dilute the existing class and racial balance in the United States to the detriment of the whites who in the pre-1965 years mostly came to the United States from various European countries. The Republican opponents of President Johnson also feared that the Democratic Party could get electoral mileage from the 1965 Immigration Act in the congressional and presidential elections by virtue of receiving overwhelming support from these newly arrived immigrants who came to the United States in the aftermath of the promulgation of this new act. Many Republican critics were of the opinion that the landslide victory of the Democratic Party in the 1966 election was due at least partly to massive support it received from the newly arrived immigrants.

Because of the change in the immigration laws in the United States, non-European countries for the first time could make their presence felt in American society in making the country truly multicultural and multiracial. After 1965, while Mexico sent the largest number of immigrants, the next four most important sending countries were the Philippines, Korea, China, (the People's Republic of China and Taiwan), and Vietnam. With these newly arrived immigrants, American society, instead of being a melting pot, slowly and surely transformed into a salad bowl.

See also Assimilation Theory; Census Classifications, Ethnic and Racial; E Pluribus Unum; Integration; Johnson, Lyndon Baines; Kennedy, John Fitzgerald; Multiculturalism; Pluralism; Quotas.

FURTHER READING: Foner, Eric, and John A. Garraty, eds., 1991, *The Reader's Companion to American History*, Boston: Houghton Mifflin; Fuchs, Lawrence H., 1990, *The American Kaleidoscope: Race, Ethnicity, and Civic Culture*, Middletown, CT: Wesleyan University Press; Glazer, Nathan, and Moynihan, Daniel P., 1970, *Beyond the Melting Pot; The Negroes, Puerto Ricans, Jews, Italians, and Irish of New York City*, 2d ed. (reprint of 1963 ed.), Cambridge, MA: MIT Press; Graham, Hugh Davis, 2002, *Collision Course: The Strange Convergence of Affirmative Action and Immigration Policy in America*, New York: Oxford University Press; Jones, Maldwyn Allen, 1974, *American Immigration*, Chicago: University of Chicago Press; Skrentny,

John David, 2001, *Color Lines: Affirmative Action, Immigration, and Civil Rights Options for America*, Chicago: University of Chicago Press; Weisberger, Bernard A., 1971, *The American Heritage: History of the American People*, New York: American Heritage Publishing Company.

MOHAMMED B. ALAM

India and Affirmative Action

India is considered to be the largest democracy in the world. It is a nation with great cultural, religious, and ethnic diversity. More than 80 percent of the population is Hindu, and around 12 percent is Muslim. Among Hindus, there is a hierarchy of castes that is theoretically based on their relative degree of purity. Taking advantage of this, the higher castes have exploited and oppressed the lower castes. Therefore, India has employed affirmative action to remove the vestiges of discrimination and eradicate the old caste system. India, like the United States, has had a long history of overt invidious discrimination against disfavored castes and groups of people. However, India's usage of affirmative action is much older than the usage of affirmative action in the United States. Additionally, India's practice of reservation, sometimes labeled "compensatory discrimination," matches the remedial theory behind affirmative action in the United States. That is, India's reservation policy is an attempt to remedy past discrimination and injustices in government service suffered by those at the lower levels of India's caste hierarchy. However, most scholars recognize that India's usage of affirmative action to remedy past discrimination is far more ambitious and comprehensive than any affirmative action program in the United States. Finally, while in recent years the U.S. Supreme Court has continued to limit affirmative action plans through its judicial decisions, the Supreme Court of India, amid riots and protests, has continued to chart a different course by affirming the practice of reservations (quotas in government positions) for groups considered disadvantaged in their ability to access equal opportunity.

In India, where traditional conceptions of hierarchy and the caste system are still very much alive, the Indian Constitution, which was drafted in 1948 and went into effect in 1950, has declared India to be in favor of equality and the employment of affirmative means to promote equality. The association between caste and occupation is breaking down as a result, and individual social mobility is becoming increasingly possible. Individual castes are no longer as homogeneous in their lifestyles as they had been in the past. Even though caste endogamy is still the general practice, the Indian Constitution has withdrawn the legal support for this system.

Most notably, the Indian Constitution employs affirmative action in the voting and representation setting, reserving seats in the legislative branch for individuals from the lowest social castes in India. Seats are reserved for scheduled castes and scheduled tribes in the lower house of parliament and state legislative assemblies. These provisions under Articles 330 and 332 of the Indian Constitution were initially enacted for a period of ten years from the commencement of the constitution, but have been extended continuously. Provisions have also been made for the proper representation of these sections of the population in institutions of local self-government. Likewise, Article 16 of the constitution permits the reservation of governmental jobs to individuals from "any backward class of citizens, which, in the opinion of the State, is not adequately represented in the services under the State." The Indian Constitution also provides in Article 335 that the claims of the members of the scheduled castes and scheduled tribes shall be taken into consideration, consistent with the maintenance of efficiency of administration, in making appointments to posts and services, as regards the affairs of the union or of a state.

In 1978, a Commission for Scheduled Castes and Scheduled Tribes was set up. The commission investigates all matters relating to constitutional safeguards and reservations in public services. It studies the implementation of the Civil Rights Act (1955), mainly in regard to the objective of removal of untouchability and the discrimination arising from this caste classification. It also monitors the socioeconomic and other relevant circumstances responsible for the commission of offenses against persons belonging to scheduled castes and tribes. The commission makes reports to the government on progress (the reports are recommendatory in nature).

Article 14 of the Constitution of India provides that "the state shall not deny to any person equality before the law or equal protection of the law within the territory of India." The words "equal protection of the law" have been interpreted to mean that every citizen shall be accorded the same treatment in similar circumstances, both in privileges conferred and obligations imposed by the law. The Supreme Court of India maintained that this concept did not deny the state the power of classifying persons for legitimate purposes, because the state had to deal with different types of persons who had or created different types of problems. That is, claims of reverse discrimination under the Indian Constitution are not generally possible.

Article 15 of the Constitution of India laid down that the state shall not discriminate against any citizen on grounds only of religion, race, caste, sex, place of birth, or any of the factors in combination, but clause 3 of the same article provided that this stipulation would not "prevent the state from making any special provision for women and children." Similarly, clause 4 of Article 15 laid down that the provision shall not prevent the state from making any special provision for the advancement of any socially and educationally backward classes or for scheduled castes and scheduled tribes, thus leaving ample room for affirmative action programs and for deflecting claims of reverse discrimination. In fact, India's reservation practice in government was made possible by this exception clause, thereby allowing political participation by underrepresented minority classes.

As discussed earlier, the right to equality has been further guaranteed by Article 16 of the constitution. Clause 1 of that article provides that there shall be equality of opportunity for all citizens in matters relating to employment or appointment to any office under the state. Furthermore, while Article 16 prohibits public employment discrimination on the grounds of "religion, race, caste, sex, descent, place of birth, or residence," Article 16(4) provides that nothing in the article "shall prevent the State from making any provision for the reservation of appointments or posts in favor of any backward class of citizens which, in the opinion of the State, is not adequately represented in the services under the State." This exception clause, like clause 4 of Article 15, allows for India's reservation practice in government.

Article 46 of India's Constitution likewise imposes a duty on the states to "promote with special care the educational and economic interests of the weaker sections of the people, and in particular, of the [disadvantaged castes]." In a series of Supreme Court cases spanning roughly four decades, the Supreme Court has upheld the constitutionality of affirmative action programs in higher education, whereby a certain number of seats are held or reserved for individuals from India's disadvantaged castes. While the Supreme Court has placed a limit on the number of seats that can be reserved to disadvantaged applicants, the limitations are very weak (i.e., no more than 50 percent of the total number of seats can be reserved for disadvantaged caste members). In the latest landmark judgment, in November 2002, the Supreme Court of India again upheld the right of colleges to use quotas based upon religion, language, and caste when admitting students.

Further provisions to guarantee equality were made by Article 17, which abolished "untouchability" (i.e., the Dalits class). That article provided that the enforcement of any disability arising out of "untouchability" shall be an offense punishable in accordance with law. Promotion of their educational and economic interests and their protection from social injustice and all forms of exploitation is mentioned in Article 46 as well. To enlarge the scope and make the penal provisions more stringent, the Untouchability (Offences) Act 1955 was comprehensively amended by the Untouchability (Offences) Amendment and Miscellaneous Provisions Act of 1976, which came into force in November 1976. With the 1976 amendment, the name of the principal act has been changed to the Protection of Civil Rights Act, 1955. The act provides penalties for preventing a person, on the ground of untouchability, from enjoying the rights accruing out of the abolition of untouchability. Enhanced penalties/punishments have also been provided for subsequent offenses. Finally, the Preamble to the Constitution of India speaks of India as a secular republic. The state shall have no religion; it may neither patronize any religion or religious group nor discriminate on this basis. It must have a stance of equidistance from all religions. This religious neutrality is important in light of how religion has historically contributed to the rigidity of the caste structure and hierarchy. Until recently, some of the most powerful sanctions for social inequality derived from religious beliefs and dogma. In India, Hinduism provided the ideological basis for inequality on the basis of the caste system.

Last, Chapter IV of the Constitution of India contains the Directive Principles of State Policy that are meant as guidelines for the government. An underlying ideology of these principles is egalitarianism. The state is required to follow these principles to bring about political, social, and economic equality. The Directive Principles, however, are not enforceable through the judiciary. The reason for this is that even though the framers of the constitution were sincere and enthusiastic about egalitarianism, they were fully conscious of the limitations of succeeding governments, particularly the limitations of meager financial resources, widespread illiteracy, and ever-increasing population. Had they made the Directive Principles enforceable by the courts, the state would have become involved in endless litigation. Devotion to the egalitarian credo was, nevertheless, affirmed time and again in the successive five-year plans that spelled out goals for development, in which the egalitarian and affirmative action ideologies were prominent. The process of modernization, along with constitutional provisions, has contributed to the loosening of the rigidity of the traditional structure and has provided greater choice to the individual in entering into interpersonal relations that cut across the boundaries of the old, established groups.

Interestingly, India's reservation policies have been subject to many of the same criticisms leveled against affirmative action in the United States. Some critics argue that the reservation practice is divisive and will only solidify discrimination between classes/castes. Others argue that equality now exists in India, and the reservation practice is no longer of value. That is, some believe that the backward or low castes have achieved significant social and economic equality, thereby negating the need for preferential treatment in government. Finally, as in the United States, there is some disagreement as to who should be the proper beneficiaries under affirmative action programs. A whole series of Supreme Court of India cases deal with who constitutes a "backward class" for purposes of the constitution (and its reservation and affirmative action provisions). Indeed, since the 1970s, more and more classes have been classified as disadvantaged for purposes of the affirmative action remedies. As discussed later, there are between 2,000 and 3,000 castes in India. Most opposition to affirmative action and reservation programs in India derives from members of the highest caste.

While every society can be said to have a "caste system," India's caste system is arguably the modern world's best example of a true caste system. The caste system has been the fundamental institution of traditional Hindu India. The caste system in India is a four-echelon hierarchy that divides society into group membership in one of the four classes on account of birth: Brahmins (the highest class, traditionally known as the priests and scholars); Kshatriyas (traditionally known as the warrior/ruler class); Vaishyas (traditionally known as the merchant and farmer class); and Sudras (traditionally known as the menial servant class). Outside of these four classes existed the Dalits, or the untouchables of society.

In India, the hierarchy of castes is based on their relative degree of purity. Purity as understood in the Hindu caste system means much more than purity and cleanliness of blood. Ritual purity can be lost in many ways and not merely through "contamination" of blood. But it is true nonetheless that the most severe rules against "pollution" applied to marriage or sexual contact between women of higher castes and men of lower castes. Even today, among all the strictures associated with caste, the ones relating to endogamy have been the least affected by change.

In India, the divisions and subdivisions within the caste system were both rigid and elaborate. At every point these divisions were reinforced by a variety of ritual sanctions. The traditional caste system can be seen as a series of groups, each separated from the other by a greater or lesser ritual distance. Brahmins and the untouchables stood at the two extremes, and social relations between them were conditioned by many ritual restrictions. Ideas of birth and descent play a significant part in maintaining the structure of caste. They give to the individual caste a basis for unity and also serve to maintain distances between different castes, which, according to the principle, derive from different stocks. The caste system is hierarchically structured in that each layer is an occupationally specialized group characterized by endogamy and unrestricted commensality.

Social honor in India's caste system is very closely tied to ritual values. Styles of life that are highly esteemed are generally associated with a large number of ritual restrictions. Another distinctive feature of the caste system as a system of status groups is the extreme proliferation or multiplicity of castes. Various estimates place the number of castes in India at between 2,000 and 3,000. Each subcaste, or *jati,* however, should not be considered as a discrete entity in any absolute sense of the term. It has been shown that a subcaste has a distinct identity only in relation to another subcaste of the same order of segmentation and merges itself within a wider group in relation to one of a higher order of segmentation. Besides, the general tendency among castes today is one of fusion, rather than of fission.

Prior to the Indian Constitution of 1950, the caste system enjoyed legal and religious sanction in traditional Indian society. Different castes were assigned different rights not only in economic matters but over a wide range of social phenomena. In traditional society, punishment differed not only according to the nature of the offense committed, but also according to the caste of the offender. Power was largely subsumed by the structure of caste.

Today, however, power is no longer the monopoly of any single caste. It has to some extent detached itself from the matrix of caste. The older balance of power between caste groups has been altered. Non-Brahmins have wrested a good deal of power from the Brahmins. Moreover, new loci of power, based on factors other than caste, have been built over the last few decades. One's caste continues to be an important basis of power and an important factor in making political decisions, although other factors are also now acquiring importance. A new economic order is emerging in towns and cities, not based upon caste in the same way in which the traditional order was based upon caste. Within the caste system, there has been a general trend toward the contraction of structural distance between proximate segments. This is largely a consequence of the two processes of secularization and westernization, along with an aggressive affirmative action program that is specifically sanctioned by the constitution. Contraction of structural distance has not, however, taken place in a uniform manner at every level. Thus the cleavage between Brahmins and non-Brahmins may in some ways be regarded as having deepened. This holds true mainly of political relations.

See also Canada and Affirmative Action; Caste System; China and Affirmative Action; European Union and Affirmative Action; Great Britain and Affirmative Action; South Africa and Affirmative Action.

FURTHER READING: Austin, Granville, 1966, *The Indian Constitution, Corner-Stone of a Nation,* Oxford: Clarendon Press; Ginsburg, Ruth Bader, and Deborah Jones Merritt, 1999, "Affirmative Action: An International Human Rights Dialogue," *Cardozo Law Review* 21 (October): 253–282; Overland, Martha Ann, 2002, "India's Supreme Court Upholds Use of Quotas by Minority Colleges, but Gives States Some Oversight Powers," *Chronicle of Higher Education,* November 5; Sowell, Thomas, 2003, "International Affirmative Action," *Jewish World Review,* June 5; Sridharan, Priya, 1999, "Representations of Disadvantage: Evolving Definitions of Disadvantage in India's Reservation Policy and the United States' Affirmative Action Policy," *Asian Law Journal* 6 (May): 99–149.

MIRZA ASMER BEG

Indian

"Indian" is the term most commonly used in American federal law to refer to the native peoples of the Northern Hemisphere. This term is somewhat controversial; many believe that "Native American" is more sensitive, is more accurate, and eliminates confusion with people from India. The term "Indian" is nonetheless still in widespread use, especially in the law, where it graces everything from Title 25 of the U.S. Code to the Bureau of Indian Affairs. The term has many different legal meanings under U.S. law, each of which carries political rights.

While being an "Indian" in common parlance refers to a culture or ethnicity, being an "Indian" under federal law means that an individual has the political status of being an Indian for the purposes of the law in question. The determination of this status is usually done through the certification of the tribal government. As sovereign entities, federally recognized tribes have the right to control their membership. Some tribes require that an individual have a certain quantum of Indian blood or a direct relationship to another member to become a member; the requirements vary from tribe to tribe. For the purposes of most federal laws, being an Indian means being an enrolled member of a federally recognized tribe. As of 2002, there were more than 500 federally recognized Indian tribes or Native Alaskan villages.

Some federal programs use different definitions of "Indian" that are specific to particular programs or laws. To qualify for hiring preferences at the Bureau of Indian Affairs, an individual must be an enrolled member of a federally recognized tribe and have at least one-quarter Indian blood. Other programs are more expansive. The Indian Health Service (IHS) hospitals typically only require that the individual seeking care state that he or she is an Indian. Widespread abuse of this policy is somewhat unlikely, given that most IHS facilities are located near Indian populations. Other nongovernment programs such as scholarships use a variety of standards.

The Indian Child Welfare Act (ICWA) has one of the most complicated definition schemes because so many different "Indian" individuals are defined under it. This law provides for added protection of the relationship between an "Indian child" and his or her tribe by authorizing a role for the tribe to participate in permanent child placement decisions and by requiring high burdens of proof before terminating parental rights. In general, an "Indian child" is a minor who is a member or who is the child of a member of a federally recognized tribe. An "Indian custodian" can be any Indian person, whether a member of the child's family or not, who has custody of an Indian child in accordance with tribal custom or law. All these different kinds of "Indians" are protected by the ICWA.

In general, the legal definitions reflect the intention of the program or policy. Because the hiring preference is intended to provide some degree of Indian control over Indian policy, the law limits its application to those individuals who are especially "Indian" through the use of the blood-quantum requirement. Similarly, tribes use blood-quantum requirements to ensure that individuals seeking enrollment are really a part of the community and not simply opportunists. The Indian Health Services, which is a social service, does not want to turn away an individual who needs medical attention for lack of correct paperwork. The Indian Child Welfare Act is designed to protect a child's relationship with his or her tribe and so uses a somewhat expanded definition to be somewhat overinclusive in protecting children, as well as in trying to allow tribes to determine proper family relations.

The term "Indian" is both confusing and controversial because it has been attached to a wide variety of historical ideas and programs that often contradicted each other. Christopher Columbus termed the inhabitants of North America "Indians" because he mistakenly believed that he had arrived in India. While that mistake was quickly corrected, the term has remained. While different terms have been suggested, such as Native Americans, indigenous peoples, First Nations, or any of the names for "the people" in the myriad of living Native American languages, the term "Indian" is likely to remain in use because of its legal significance.

See also Alaskan Natives; *Morton v. Mancari*; Native Americans; *Rice v. Cayetano.*

FURTHER READING: Indian Child Welfare Act of 1978, 25 U.S.C. §§ 1901–1963.

RACHEL BOWEN

Institute for Justice

See Bolick, Clint.

Institutional Discrimination

Institutional discrimination refers to the policies and practices of institutions that create and sustain patterns of discrimination based on gender (institutional sexism) or racial characteristics (institutional racism). Since institutional policies and practices may be legal or customary, they may not be socially disapproved but be seen as legitimate. For instance, minimum physical requirements for certain jobs tend to favor male over female applicants, yet these requirements are rarely challenged. Ideologies, such as sexism, paternalism (which sees women as less capable than men and in need of protection and guidance), and racism serve to legitimize patterns of discrimination. These ideologies reinforce the belief in differences based on sex, where women are seen as inferior to men, or on perceived inferiority because of race.

In patriarchal societies like the United States, sexism is part of the institutional structure of society. Likewise, the United States has a well-documented history of racial discrimination. The result is unequal distribution of societal resources based on gender (gender stratification) or race (racial stratification). For example, regarding institutional sexism, while about 1 billion adults around the world cannot read, the vast majority of them are women (two-thirds). In the United States, the gap between the numbers of men and women attending and completing college is closing. However, gender tracking (the fact that degrees tend to follow gender divisions) is still a significant issue. For instance, 83 percent of bachelor's degrees in engineering, which is considered a masculine field, are earned by men. On the other hand, 88 percent of bachelor's degrees in library science, considered a feminine field, are earned by women. Because women's work, including professions traditionally seen as feminine, is widely devalued, it is not surprising that library scientists on average earn far less than engineers. Affirmative action programs have allowed women and people of color the opportunity not only to pursue higher education in fields traditionally considered masculine or white monopolized, but have also assisted many women and minorities in obtaining positions in organizations and fields that would normally not have considered them for employment.

See also Discrimination; Gender Segregation in Employment; Gender Stratification; Gendered Racism; Segregation; Stereotypes, Gender.

FURTHER READING: England, Paula, 1992, *Comparable Worth: Theories and Evidence*, New York: Aldine de Gruyter; Feagin, Joe R., and Clairece Booher Feagin, 1978, *Discrimination American Style: Institutional Racism and Sexism*, Englewood Cliffs, NJ: Prentice-Hall; Ollenburger, Jane C., and Helen A. Moore, 1998, *A Sociology of Women: The Intersection of Patriarchy, Capitalism, and Colonization*, 2d ed., Upper Saddle River, NJ: Prentice Hall; "State of the World's Children 2001," 2001, *Reading Today* 18, no. 4 (February–March): 24; *Statistical Abstract of the United States*, 2000 and 2001, Washington, DC: Bureau of the Census; Zimbalist Rosaldo, Michelle, and Louise Lamphere, 1974, *Woman, Culture, and Society*, Stanford, CA: Stanford University Press.

PAULINA X. RUF

Integration

Integration in the United States refers to the process and the phenomenon of racial mixing of individuals in public settings and has been a measure utilized to combat one of the evils in society, that of racial prejudice. As a dividend of the civil rights movement, full integration has become one of the aims of affirmative action programs. America has always promoted the notion of integration, as illustrated by the use of such slogans as "E Pluribus Unum" on currency and describing America as the great melting pot.

Before the notion of integration gained currency as a catchword phrase and as a government policy aimed at the formation of a harmonious landscape and the extension of the American dream to all, the notion of assimilation was the vogue. Under the assimilation theory, minority groups were expected to cast off their minority cultural identity and assimilate socially, economically, and politically into mainstream American society. The assimilation theory connotes a process of absorption of persons or groups of differing ethnic heritage into the dominant culture of a society. Assimilation of new immigrants into the white Anglo-Saxon Protestant culture and interactive web was not an easy task. The primary problem was that not all new arrivals were equally situated. In generally ascending order, the burden of "assimilation" has been borne by the new immigrants from continental Europe (Germans, Dutch, Swiss, Swedes, Finns, French, Spanish, Italians, Portuguese, Spanish Jews, and others), Latinos, Asians, Native American Indians, and Africans.

In the same manner, when the situation in the United States changed after the civil rights movement, those who bore the greatest burden of assimilation faced the greatest difficulty in peacefully integrating into mainstream society. As the United States arguably moved toward two societies, one white and the other black, integration in America became principally a black problem. This division was determined by the legacy of slavery.

Historically, African Americans were rejected by their white counterparts and not permitted to integrate into American culture. The African American equality boat moved against the tide in slavery and in freedom. During the period of slavery, most whites refused to recognize the humanity of black slaves. The U.S. Constitution counted a slave as three-fifths of a person for taxation and representation purposes, and the U.S. Supreme Court stated in 1857 in *Dred Scott v. Sandford*, 60 U.S. (19 How.) 393 (1857), that Blacks could never be U.S. citizens, that a slave was the property of the owner, and that blacks "did not have any rights which a white man was bound to respect." With the end of slavery, the country witnessed the birth of both de facto and de jure segregation. In the Deep South, Jim Crow laws were at work to keep the blacks "in their place"—in the cabins and in the twilight zone between slavery and freedom. The Supreme Court ruling in *Plessy v. Ferguson*, 163 U.S. 537 (1896), which gave legal sanction and approval to the practice of segregation, further solidified this substandard treatment.

As the fortunes of the ex-slaves continued to dwindle in the Deep South, "Come Out from among Them" became the catchword phrase and slogan in the African American community. Thus the country witnessed the great African American migration, first from the rural South to southern cities and then to the industrial cities in the North and West. However, the North was not a haven from racism and discrimination. An interplay of white institutional racism and a black ideology of self-help led to the further repression of African Americans in ghettos. Perhaps the best known of the ghettos is Harlem in New York City. It is pertinent to note here that with the overthrow of Reconstruction, the dialogue in the black community centered on three options: migration and separation, emigration, and integration and equality. Booker T. Washington accepted the notion of separation and accommodation between the races. Marcus Garvey preached the emigration of the black race. Finally, W.E.B. Du Bois insisted on integration and political equality for the black race. Each of these theories had adherents in the larger African American community. Although many African American nineteenth- and twentieth-century leaders supported integration, some did not. For example, Stokely Carmichael described integration as "a subterfuge for the maintenance of white supremacy."

The efforts toward integration were made on many fronts, including housing, schools, and public amusement facilities. With *Brown v. Board of Education*, 347 U.S. 483 (1954), and the revocation of the notion that segregated schools were permissible under the Fourteenth Amendment, the struggle for integration started to gather momentum. The prominent associations within the civil rights movement that championed desegregation of public facilities included the National Association for the Advancement of Colored People, the National Urban League, the Southern Christian Leadership Conference, and the Student Nonviolent Coordinating Committee. Through protests and court actions, the desegregation of facilities moved slowly on various fronts. The improvements did not come without stiff opposition from the sectors who were against desegregation. On the educational front, for instance, there was substantial acceptance of desegregation in states like Delaware, Kentucky, Maryland, Missouri, Oklahoma, and West Virginia, with small black populations. Opposition to desegregation was very strong in the Deep South, where blacks were largely concentrated. A similar development took place in the employment sector. The measures adopted in these areas did not bring about total desegregation of facilities and integration of the various elements that made up the U.S. population.

It was because of the failure to achieve complete integration via the civil rights movement that affirmative action programs were instituted. Yet in spite of these new affirmative action initiatives, the United States still has not attained full racial integration, and many cities and schools are still segregated in fact. In the final analysis, the full integration of the races in the United States is still an ongoing process.

See also African Americans; Assimilation Theory; *Brown v. Board of Education*; Carmichael, Stokely; Civil Rights Movement; De Facto and De Jure Segregation; *Dred Scott v. Sandford*; Du Bois, William Edward Burghardt; E Pluribus Unum; Garvey, Marcus; Jim Crow Laws; National Association for the Advancement of Colored People; *Plessy v. Ferguson*; Slavery; Three-Fifths Compromise; Urban League; Washington, Booker T.

FURTHER READING: Brisbane, Robert H., 1972, "Booker T. Washington and the Black Militants," in *Afro-American History*, edited by Charles W. Simmons and Harry W. Morris, Columbus, OH: Charles E. Merrill Publishing Company; Broderick, Francis L., 1959, *W.E.B. Du Bois: Negro Leader in a Time of Crisis*, Stanford, CA: Stanford University Press; Cronon, E. David, 1955, *Black Moses: The Study of Marcus Garvey and the Universal Negro Improvement Association*, Madison: University of Wisconsin Press; Drimmer, Melvin, ed., 1968, *Black History: A Reappraisal*, Garden City, NY: Doubleday; Gordon, Irving L., 1980, *American Studies: A Conceptual Approach*, New York: Amsco School Publications; Groh, George W., 1972, *The Black Migration: The Journey to Urban America*, New York: Weybright and Talley; Osofsky, Gilbert, 1960, *Harlem: The Making of a Ghetto*, New York: Harper and Row; Spear, Allan, 1971, "The Origins of the Urban Ghetto, 1870–1915," in *Key Issues in the Afro-American Experience*, vol. 2, edited by Nathan I. Huggins, Martin Kilson, Daniel M. Fox, and John Merton Blum, New York: Harcourt Brace Jovanovich.

PAUL OBIYO MBANASO NJEMANZE

Intermediate Scrutiny

Intermediate scrutiny refers to a legal standard against which courts must analyze certain government action challenged under the U.S. Constitution. Government action reviewed under this standard will be held unconstitutional unless the action is substantially related to an important governmental interest. In the affirmative action context, intermediate scrutiny review has been held to apply to affirmative action involving preferences based on gender.

Affirmative action programs used or required by federal, state, or local governments are often challenged in federal court on the grounds that they violate the equal protection guarantees of the Fifth and Fourteenth Amendments by discriminating against whites and males. When a governmental action is challenged as a violation of constitutional equal protection guarantees, courts must determine what standard of judicial review applies. The court must examine both whether the purpose of the governmental action is permissible and whether the method used to achieve the purpose is acceptable. Throughout the years, the U.S. Supreme Court has generally developed a three-tiered system: strict scrutiny review, intermediate scrutiny review, and rational basis review. The more rigorous the review, the less deference that is given to the governmental actor and the more likely that the challenged measure will be held to be unconstitutional.

Strict scrutiny review is the most rigorous standard and applies to a governmental action based on a "fundamental right" or "suspect classification." A suspect classification (most relevant in the affirmative action context) is a government classification that treats an individual or group less favorably than others under law because of membership in a group (such as a racial or ethnic group) that has historically been subject to invidious discrimination and whose members are not able to protect themselves through the regular political process. Because governments have historically misused race to disadvantage racial minorities and because race is so seldom a legitimate basis for governmental decision making, racial classifications of a state, for example, in governmental affirmative action programs, are subject to strict scrutiny review. Under strict scrutiny review, the government action will be unconstitutional unless it is "narrowly tailored to meet a compelling governmental interest."

On the opposite side of the scale, the basic and least rigorous standard of review is rational basis scrutiny. Under this standard, if the government action is rationally related to a legitimate governmental interest, it will be upheld as constitutional. For example, governmental distinctions based on age or disability have been held to be subject to rational basis scrutiny. According to the federal courts, age and disability status are relevant to many governmental decisions. That the government treats groups differently depending on age or disability does not automatically raise suspicion that the action is unfairly discriminatory, and thus a heightened standard of judicial review is not necessary.

Somewhere between rational basis and strict scrutiny review lies intermediate scrutiny review. Intermediate scrutiny applies to "quasi-suspect" classifications. Quasi-suspect classifications are differences in treatment based on factors that have been the basis for discrimination, but that also are legitimately relevant to some governmental decision making. Governmental action based on gender is a quasi-suspect classification. Intermediate scrutiny requires the government to show that the classification is "substantially related" to "important governmental interests." Intermediate scrutiny review is an easier standard to meet than is strict scrutiny, but is still a substantial limit on a government's ability to rely on gender in making decisions.

Affirmative action programs that include gender preferences are subject to intermediate scrutiny review. In its opinion in *Mississippi University for Women v. Hogan*, 458 U.S. 718 (1982), the U.S. Supreme Court described the intermediate scrutiny test as applied to gender classifications as follows:

> [T]he party seeking to uphold a statute that classifies individuals on the basis of their gender must carry the burden of showing an "exceedingly persuasive justification" for the classification. The burden is met only by showing at least that the classification serves "important governmental objectives and that the discriminatory means employed" are "substantially related to the achievement of those objectives."

Justice John Paul Stevens once noted that subjecting racial preferences in affirmative action programs to strict scrutiny while subjecting gender preferences in affirmative action programs to intermediate scrutiny leads to an "anomalous result": that it would be easier for governments to utilize gender preferences for women in affirmative action programs than preferences for African Americans under the equal protection guarantees even though those guarantees were originally meant to end discrimination against African Americans.

See also African Americans; Compelling Governmental Interest; Fifth Amendment; Fourteenth Amendment; Invidious Discrimination; *Mississippi University for*

Women v. Hogan; Narrowly Tailored Affirmative Action Plans; Rational Basis Scrutiny; Stevens, John Paul; Strict Scrutiny; Suspect Classification.

FURTHER READING: Barnes, Jeffrey A., 1997, "The Supreme Court's 'Exceedingly [Un]persuasive' Application of Intermediate Scrutiny in *United States v. Virginia*," *University of Richmond Law Review* 31:523–547; Deutsch, Norman T., 2003, "*Nguyen v. INS* and the Application of Intermediate Scrutiny to Gender Classifications: Theory, Practice, and Reality," *Pepperdine Law Review* 30:185–271.

MARIA D. BECKMAN

Invidious Discrimination

Invidious discrimination is discrimination that is wholly arbitrary or capricious, unequal treatment that does not have any rational basis. The Constitution does not require that different things be treated as if they were the same. In fact, the legislature frequently makes laws that classify and discriminate. For example, progressive tax rates discriminate against the rich, yet courts have ruled that progressive tax rates are reasonable, not invidious. In the words of the Supreme Court, "[It] is only the invidious discrimination, the wholly arbitrary act, which cannot stand consistently with the Fourteenth Amendment." Thus the Constitution requires that similarly situated people be treated equally. The Supreme Court has expressed the concept of invidious discrimination in different terms, such as "discriminatory intent," "purposeful discrimination," and "invidious intent." Both intent and invidiousness are necessary to show a violation of the Equal Protection Clause.

Although the Supreme Court has failed to articulate a definition of invidiousness, the Court has expressed its meaning in certain contexts. For example, in *Yick Wo v. Hopkins*, 118 U.S. 356 (1886), the Court held that if a law is "applied and administered by public authority with an evil eye and an unequal hand, so as to make unjust and illegal discriminations between persons in similar circumstances, material to their rights, the denial of equal justice is still within the prohibition of the Constitution." Sometimes, as in *Yick Wo*, the Supreme Court requires some sort of animus or hostility to declare a statute unconstitutional; at other times, the Court focuses on the classification being arbitrary without examining the intent or motivation of the actor.

Proponents of affirmative action have argued that affirmative action programs do not involve invidious discrimination; instead, they involve "benign" discrimination. However, in *Adarand Constructors, Inc. v. Peña*, 515 U.S. 200 (1995), the Court blurred the distinction between "benign" and "invidious" discrimination by holding that strict scrutiny should be used to examine all racial classifications because "despite the surface appeal of holding 'benign' racial classifications to a lower standard . . . it may not always be clear that a so-called preference is in fact benign." Justice John Paul Stevens dissented, arguing that "[t]here is no moral or constitutional equivalence between a policy that is designed to perpetuate a caste system and one that seeks to eradicate racial subordination." Thus Stevens believed that good motives were less suspect, and a lower level of scrutiny was justified for "benign" discrimination.

See also Adarand Constructors, Inc. v. Peña; Benign Discrimination; Caste System;

Census Classifications, Ethnic and Racial; Discrimination; Equal Protection Clause; Fourteenth Amendment; Stevens, John Paul; Strict Scrutiny; Suspect Classification; *Yick Wo v. Hopkins.*

FURTHER READING: Pillai, K.G., 2001, "Shrinking Domain of Invidious Intent," *William and Mary Bill of Rights Journal* 9 (April): 525–589; Strasser, Mark, 1994, "The Invidiousness of Invidiousness: On the Supreme Court's Affirmative Action Jurisprudence," *Hastings Constitutional Law Quarterly* 21 (winter): 323–403.

PAMELA C. CORLEY

Islamic-Based Nationality and Affirmative Action

Islam, a monotheistic religion founded by Muhammad in the seventh century, is the second most followed religion in the world, with more than 1 billion adherents. Islamic-based countries can be found throughout the Middle East, North Africa, and Southeast Asia. Additionally, there are substantial minority members of the Islamic faith in many European countries, Russia, China, and India. In several countries (e.g., China), Muslims are beneficiaries under existing affirmative action programs. There is an erroneous tendency to view Islam in a monolithic fashion. While Islam stresses the need for the unity of nations (*summa*) of Islam, significant branches of the Islamic faith have developed (e.g., Shi'ite, Sunni, and Sufism).

Although Islam does not talk of affirmative action in the sense understood by Western democracies today, it does talk of giving certain special rights and privileges to the weaker and disadvantaged sections of society. It makes it obligatory for the Islamic state, which is an institution of divine trusteeship, to provide all citizens, irrespective of their race and faith, with the necessities of life and with peace and security of person, honor, and prosperity. The state is required to be sympathetically alive to the needs of the people and actively solicitous of their welfare. These rights are conferred upon mankind by God as part of the faith and, therefore, are universal and eternal. In Islam, any affirmative action is not group based, as in modern states, where all such programs and laws have considerations like race, caste, or gender as their bases. In Islam, all such action is directed at the individual and is based on his or her need. As such, Islam supports the notion of special rights and/or privileges being awarded to an individual on the basis of socioeconomic status.

Islam has recognized the rights of the weak and needy. The Holy Quran has not only conferred a right on every man who asks for assistance from the wealth of Muslims, but has also laid down that if a Muslim comes to know that a certain person is without the basic necessities of life, then, irrespective of whether he asks for assistance or not, it is his duty to give all the help he can. For this purpose, Islam does not depend on voluntary charity, but has made charity compulsory charity (i.e., *Zakat,* its third pillar, mandates charity as important and only superseded by one's obligations of faith and worship).

Every possessor of wealth in the Islamic commonwealth is required to contribute annually one-fortieth of his wealth to a common fund that is managed by the state, or by the Muslim community where there is no Muslim state. This fund is utilized by the state or community for the amelioration of the condition of the disadvantaged and poor. Therefore, the obligation of *Zakat* acts not only as a leveling influence in society, but also as a means of developing higher sentiments of man, the sentiments of love and sympathy toward fellow individuals. By this, wealth is made to circulate in the body politic of Islam, a fixed portion of the wealth of the richer members being drawn to the center, whence it is sent forth to those parts of the body politic that need it most.

The obligation of *Zakat* is implemented by the state institution (or where there is no Muslim state, by the national authority in place). The individual is not at liberty to calculate and spend his *Zakat* as he likes. It must be collected by the state on a national basis and spent by the state or community. The donor is required not to give a certain portion of his *Zakat* to deserving persons, but to contribute all of it to a fund that must be used for the uplift of the community. It was in this sense that the prophet Muhammad understood it, and when he assumed control of the government, he made *Zakat* a state institution, appointing officials to collect it and directing his governors to do the same even in distant provinces under his control. Muhammad said that the government is the guardian of everyone who has no guardian (*Al-Mawardi, Al-Ahkam-ut Sultania*). It is the duty of the state to assist and support orphans, the old, the sick, and the unemployed. It is one of the fundamental duties of an Islamic government to guarantee the livelihood of the people.

Although *Zakat* is the most important Islamic belief dealing with extending help to the disadvantaged, it is not the only institution of Islam for the benefit of the disadvantaged members of society. There are two other Islamic practices of a similar nature, both connected with the festivals of *Id*, whereby into Muslim hearts is instilled the idea that when one is in his or her best situation, he or she must never forget the distress of the poor and weak. The first of these institutions is *Sadaqat al-Fitr*, which is a charity connected with the *Id-al-Fitr*. Every Muslim on that occasion is required to give to charity a certain amount of food or its equivalent in cash. This sum must be collected by every Muslim community and distributed among those who deserve it. The second institution is related to *Id-al-Azha*, on which occasion poor members of the community are fed with the meat of sacrificed animals.

Thus the notion of affirmative action programs of the West and the doctrines of charity of Islam have close similarities, but as a legal and moral frame of reference, there are differences between the two. First, as explained earlier, charity and social benefits under Islamic tenets are distributed to those who are socioeconomically disadvantaged. Islamic belief does not dictate special programs for individuals based upon gender or race. Second, the affirmative action laws of the West are more ephemeral and constantly changing with the passing of different administrations. It becomes increasingly difficult to implement laws and policies as regards affirmative action, however strong and legally solid, if the social philosophy is not receptive to them. People can evade and avoid them in innumerable ways. Moreover, these are subject to changes according to changing political realities. In Islam, all laws and privileges are part of the faith and are therefore permanent and immutable. In no circumstances can they be subject to review or suspension.

See also Economically Disadvantaged; India and Affirmative Action.

FURTHER READING: Esposito, John L., ed., 2003, *Oxford Dictionary of Islam,* New York: Oxford University Press; Guillaume, Alfred, 1924, *Traditions of Islam,* Oxford: Clarendon Press; Krieger, Joel, ed., 1993, *The Oxford Companion to Politics of the World,* 473–475, New York: Oxford University Press; Rahman, Fazlur, 1979, *Islam,* 2d ed., Chicago: University of Chicago Press.

MIRZA ASMER BEG